THE
DEADLY
DEEP

THE
DEADLY
DEEP

THE DEFINITIVE HISTORY OF SUBMARINE WARFARE

IAIN BALLANTYNE

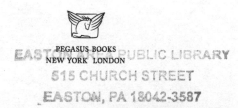

PEGASUS BOOKS
NEW YORK LONDON

THE DEADLY DEEP

Pegasus Books, Ltd.
148 West 37th Street, 13th Floor
New York, NY 10018

Copyright © 2018 by Iain Ballantyne

First Pegasus Books hardcover edition December 2018

ISBN: 978-1-68177-877-8

10 9 8 7 6 5 4 3 2 1

Printed in the United States of America
Distributed by W. W. Norton & Company, Inc.

For both the hunter and the hunted,
especially those who never came home

Contents

MAPS

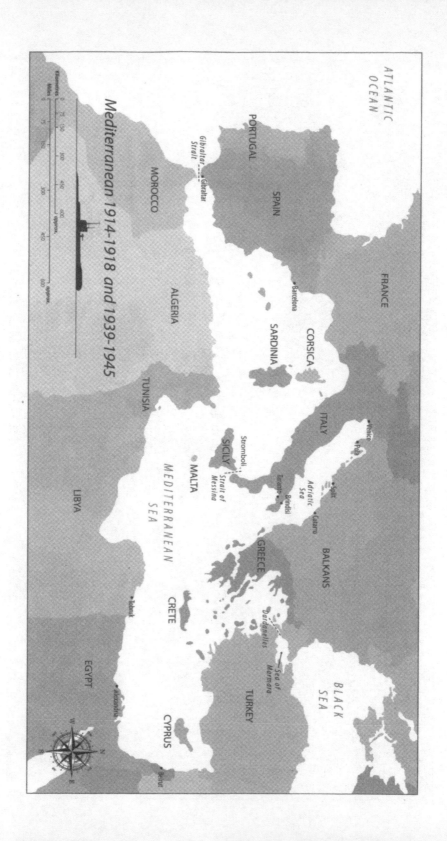

Mediterranean 1914-1918 and 1939-1945

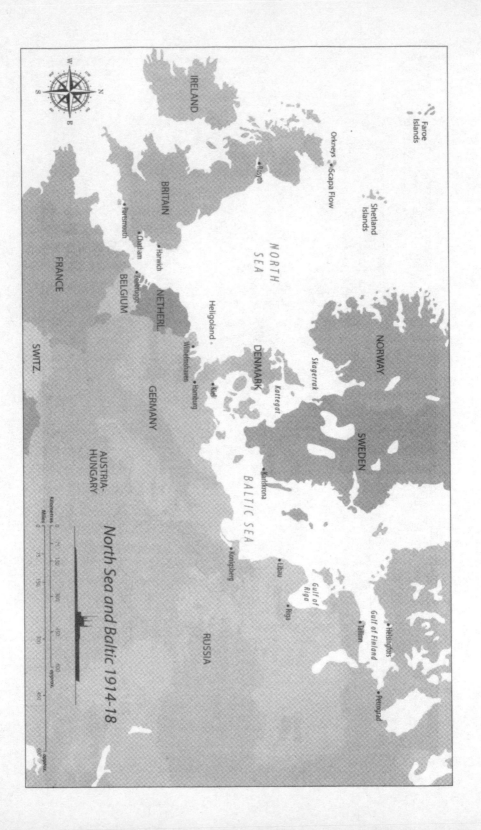

North Sea and Baltic 1914-18

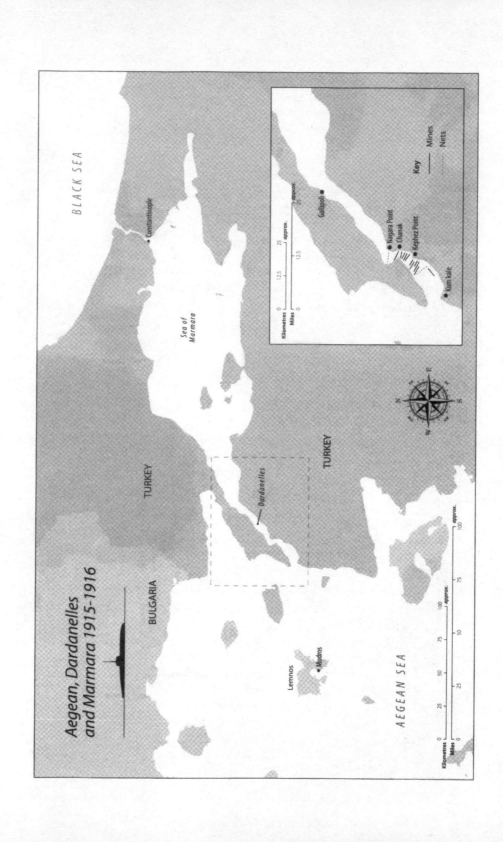

Aegean, Dardanelles and Marmara 1915–1916

BLACK SEA

Constantinople

TURKEY

Sea of Marmara

BULGARIA

Dardanelles

TURKEY

Lemnos

Mudros

AEGEAN SEA

Kilometres
0   25   50   75   100 approx.
Miles
0   25   50   75   100 approx.

Key
Mines
Nets

Gallipoli

Nagara Point

Chanak

Kephez Point

Kum Kale

Kilometres
0   12.5   25 approx.
Miles
0   12.5   25 approx.

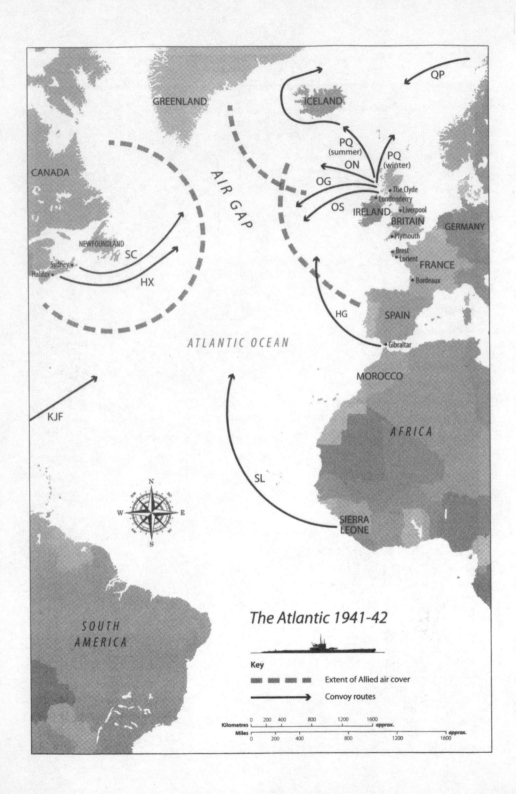

The Atlantic 1941-42

Key

▬ ▬ ▬ ▬   Extent of Allied air cover

→   Convoy routes

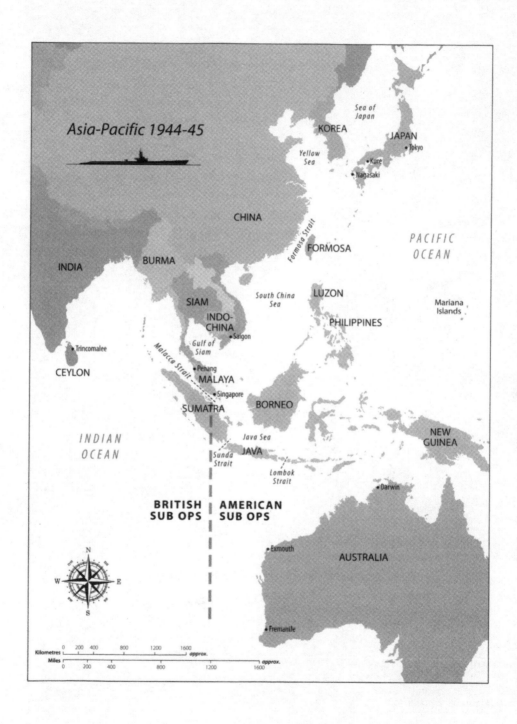

Asia-Pacific 1944-45

Sea of Japan

KOREA

JAPAN
• Tokyo
• Kure

CHINA

Yellow Sea

• Nagasaki

PACIFIC OCEAN

FORMOSA

Formosa Strait

INDIA

BURMA

South China Sea

LUZON

Mariana Islands

SIAM

INDO-CHINA
• Saigon

PHILIPPINES

Trincomalee

Gulf of Siam

Malacca Strait

• Penang

CEYLON

MALAYA

• Singapore

BORNEO

NEW GUINEA

SUMATRA

Java Sea

INDIAN OCEAN

Sunda Strait

JAVA

Lombok Strait

• Darwin

BRITISH SUB OPS

AMERICAN SUB OPS

• Exmouth

AUSTRALIA

N
W   E
S

• Fremantle

Kilometres 0 200 400   800   1200   1600
                                          approx.
Miles 0   200   400   800   1200   1600
                                                  approx.

PART ONE

GENESIS

Ancient Times to 1914

'. . . there are two ways of dying in the circumstances in which we are placed . . . The first is to be crushed; the second is to die of suffocation. I do not speak of the possibility of dying of hunger, for the supply of provisions in the Nautilus will certainly last longer than we shall. Let us then calculate our chances.'

Captain Nemo in *Twenty Thousand Leagues Under the Sea* by Jules Verne

Introduction: 'The Trade'

A century ago Rudyard Kipling penned a piece of verse in salute to what he called 'The Trade', which was plied by submariners playing what he described as 'grisly blindfold games'. The grim potential of submarines had been displayed during the First World War, with their commanders using periscopes to seek out targets and delivering Kipling's 'one-eyed Death'.

'The Trade' concludes:

Unheard they work, unseen they win.
That is the custom of 'The Trade'.

Over the years 'The Trade' has attracted as its deadly practitioners daring and courageous, glamorously unconventional and even dangerously eccentric young men. Many of them have lived fast and died young.

Sometimes gamblers and egomaniacs, among the best of them have been supremely ambitious captains with unswerving pride and confidence in their own abilities and that ultimate victory will be theirs. Some of the most effective have been of a different demeanour – quiet, even bookish, more like academics than the popular image of the macho warrior, but lethal all the same. During war certain nations have treated the young submarine captains like gods, awarding them gilded shore leave before going back to sea and finding death or more glory.

Many thousands – including others drafted not so willingly into submarines – have paid the ultimate price for a moment's miscalculation by their commanders. Undersea combat itself – whether submarine versus ship, or sub versus sub – can be a nerve-shredding blend of cold unflinching calculation and technical precision, with a dash of (potentially) insane risk-taking and terror. A single error, whether in war or peace, can mean death for a captain and an entire crew – and there are many ways to die. Apart from drowning there is suffocating, being burned alive, crushed, gassed or blown apart. Yet, despite all that, submariners and submarines exert a fatal attraction, not only among those who sign up to pursue 'The Trade'– and these days women are at sea in the boats of some nations and are even commanding flotillas of them – but in the general population.

Undersea warfare has since the Ancients been the stuff of both dreams and nightmares. Over the centuries artists and scientists, generals and kings have been fascinated by the idea of voyaging beneath the surface of the ocean. They have also feared the ruination such a powerful vessel might inflict upon the world. The dreamers have seen underwater warriors and submarines as a means to beat empires that might otherwise be invulnerable, or even as an opportunity to liberate the world's vital trade from the tyranny of surface navies. Some nations have at various times loathed submarines so much that they sought worldwide bans on the infernal machines and threatened to hang the men who operated them.

Yet for some visionaries the lure of creating a means to wage war from below the ocean – and a vessel to voyage through its dark, alluring depths – has outweighed all other concerns of morality or even danger to life.

Those men were either geniuses ahead of their time or they were nothing more than mercenary traitors, willing to create underwater weaponry for the highest bidder.

To some politicians and admirals, submarines have seemed to be the magic bullet – the equaliser for the weaker nation against the stronger power, but more than once it has proved to be a chimera.

The fate of nations has been gambled on the abilities of submariners to wreak havoc on an enemy – for primarily their objective has been to destroy the oceanic trade that is the lifeblood of the world. Submarine warfare is, in short, a direct attack on the very means by which the civilian populace is fed, clothed and has its homes heated. For that reason, more than once submarine warfare has been declared an outrage inflicted by brutish war criminals and pirates – an attempt to starve innocent men, women and children to death and force their homeland to surrender. There can be no doubt that the submarine – in its various forms over the decades – has proved decisive in conventional warfare in a fashion very few people imagined prior to the twentieth century.

Despite a ruthless, brutal aspect to the deadly trade, we remain fascinated by those who live, fight and die in submarines. We see them as otherworldly beings who pursue an unknowable existence, living for weeks, or even months, at a time beneath the waves. Yet, for all their bad reputation, submariners have also often shown great humanity to their victims (something that is perhaps overlooked) and have even been worshipped as the bravest of the brave.

The vessels themselves remain mysterious, carrying out deep, dark deeds away from our sight and in the twenty-first century nuclear-powered submarines are just about the most complex, costly ships in existence. Creating and operating them is the mark of a true front rank nation. Armed with nuclear weapons, they have the ability to destroy millions of lives.

This book necessarily has a broad canvas, telling the epic story of submarine warfare from the efforts of dreamers and inventors centuries ago through devastating global conflicts to dangerous Cold War-era confrontations – some of which turned rather hot – and touches on today's accelerating underwater arms race.

1 Many Falsehoods, Some Truths

Striving for an edge on a foe – a decisive killer advantage – has been a feature of undersea warfare for centuries.

Before there were vessels that went under the sea, there were men who took war below the surface and for them there was no finer exemplar of that ferocity in combat than the greatest warrior of ancient Greek mythology, Achilles. His lethal prowess in the water was vividly described in *The Iliad*. According to Homer, 'Olympian-born Achilles' left his spear on the banks of the river Scamander and, armed only with his sword, 'leapt in like something superhuman, with murder in his heart, and laid about him right and left'.[1]

The first real-life warriors beneath the waves had more prosaic origins, for they were utilising the same diving skills they used to harvest shellfish, pearls and sponges, or to retrieve treasure from sunken vessels. According to Thucydides, in 414 BC during the siege of Syracuse in Sicily the Athenians sent men under the sea to saw through and clear wooden piles blocking the harbour mouth. They also broke underwater chains, all with the aim of enabling galleys carrying troops to enter harbour. Cutting the anchor cables of enemy vessels – so they would be driven ashore to destruction or collide with each other – was another favourite tactic.

The earliest image of submerged men carrying weapons is a wall painting in the Nile Valley of duck hunters armed with spears stealthily approaching their prey while using reeds to suck in air. Aristotle claimed Greek combat divers used an early form of snorkel 'like the trunk of an elephant'[2] but many of the Mediterranean's underwater warriors could hold their breath for a phenomenal amount of time. They carried rocks to give themselves the ballast needed to sink to the seabed, countering pressure at depth by putting olive oil in their ears – to stop their eardrums bursting – and also holding it in their mouths to be expelled on reaching the seabed.

Yet, while tactically useful, divers could not offer *control* of the sea.

That power belonged to those who sent their men to war in surface warships. The triremes of the Greeks, Romans and Phoenicians and the galleys of the Persians reigned supreme.

When it came to men climbing inside vessels to go under the sea, it is said descending into the depths held no fear for a king who conquered much of the known world. In 332 BC, during an attempt by his army to take the port of Tyre, Alexander the Great ordered divers to carry out harbour clearance. To check on progress he allegedly submerged in a glass diving bell lowered from a galley on long chains.

Another ancient Greek connected to the story of submarining was the mathematician Archimedes. He devised many weird and wonderful weapons in his time and during another siege of Syracuse (214 BC–212 BC) helped defend it from the Romans. He used mirrors to reflect the sun, producing a heat ray that set fire to Rome's galleys. Archimedes also devised a huge mechanical claw to pick up warships and smash them on the surface of the sea. While he did not construct a submarine, Archimedes experienced a key moment of discovery while having a bath. Puzzling over how to please the ruler of Syracuse, King Hiero, by telling the exact weight of a new crown – and hence the purity of the gold used to make it – Archimedes noticed that when he climbed into his bath he displaced water equivalent to his own weight. This became the Principle of Buoyancy, which he expressed as: 'Any object, wholly or partially immersed in a fluid, is buoyed up by a force equal to the weight of the fluid displaced by the object.' Screaming 'Eureka!' ('I've found it!') Archimedes sprang from the tub, so excited that he ran down the street naked.

In years to come those attempting to voyage under the water would use Archimedes' principle to design craft capable of altering their density. By making the density of such a vessel *less* than the surrounding water, positive buoyancy would be achieved and so it would float on the surface. By making its density *more* it would attain negative buoyancy, enabling the vessel to sink below the surface. How to achieve an overall density *equal* to the surrounding water – neutral buoyancy, enabling it to hold position submerged – vexed many an inventor over the centuries. Enabling the craft to propel itself – and mount some kind of effective weapon system, all while sustaining the life of the operators who must navigate it – would present challenges of a whole different order of magnitude. Archimedes never got to explore the war-making

In this hand-coloured woodcut, c.1547, Greek mathematician and inventor Archimedes is depicted in his bath during the process of evolving his Principle of Buoyancy. Also seen are what appear to be spherical weights and crowns to test their comparative displacement in water. (*World History Archive/TopFoto*)

possibilities offered by his Principle of Buoyancy for he did not survive the siege of Syracuse. A sword-wielding Roman soldier took exception to Archimedes ignoring him in favour of solving a mathematical problem and killed him.

Waging war under the sea remained the preserve of divers for some centuries and the chosen weapon of some was 'Greek Fire', which was possibly naphtha and pitch mixed with other things to a secret formula. A predecessor of napalm, it could not be extinguished once exposed to water. During one European war an intrepid thirteenth-century French diver carried Greek Fire in sealed jars to destroy an enemy's submerged stockade on the River Seine, smashing them against the timbers.

An alternative means of achieving destructive effect under the water was to simply create a hole. On 24 June 1340, during the Battle of Sluys off the Flemish shore, English and French divers used augers[3] to drill below the waterline of enemy ships. They wore a type of protective helmet that looked like an upside-down kettle, with air sucked in via the spout. Soldiers aboard target vessels dropped rocks onto them to try to halt the drilling. Rocks were also hurled at the sections of hull where holes had been created in the hope of creating an even bigger breach.

More usually in general sea warfare the objective was to take the vessel as a prize, in order to seize the cargo, but there were also those who attempted to conjure up a means of total destruction. At the end of the fifteenth century, while working for the Doge of Venice, Leonardo da Vinci made sketches for what he called 'a ship to sink another ship'. He envisioned a submersible deterring or defeating the Turks, who it was feared intended to conquer Venice. The craft would remain invisible under the waves so it could strike with the utmost devastation. It was propelled by a hand-cranked paddle that twitched from side to side in the manner of a fish tail, though Leonardo also proposed a propeller. His undersea vessel was to have fins both on top and bottom, with small, stubby hydroplanes on either side of the hull to enable diving and ascending. For its main offensive weapon Leonardo's submarine also had an auger to drill holes in enemy vessels.

Favouring deterrence rather than conflict, Leonardo suggested the Turks should receive a warning. If they did not surrender they would be advised that within four hours they could expect to find their fleet destroyed by mysterious means. Leonardo imagined the prospect of wielding such awesome power would impress the Venetians so much they would grant him great riches. In the end, so horrified was he at the terrible possibilities offered by his 'ship to sink another ship', Leonardo kept the plans secret. He feared the mercenary merchants of Venice would sell the terrible machine to the highest bidder, possibly even to the Turks.

In the sixteenth century, among those with enquiring minds attracted to the idea of actually voyaging under water was William Bourne, an English mathematician and former naval gunner. He created designs for oar-powered submersibles and, while he never actually built one, in 1578 Bourne published proposals for just such a craft. He advocated a 'screw-operated bilge tank ballast system',[4] comprising empty tanks on each side into which water could either be permitted, in order to take the craft under, or expelled, letting air in. According to Bourne this would enable it to 'goe under water unto the bottome, and so come up againe at your pleasure'.[5] The vessel would have a tall mast hollowed out, down which fresh air would come, its top to remain above the surface at all times.

Necessity was the mother of Bourne's striving for invention. Spain was the superpower of the day, with massive monetary and military resources, so technological innovation was necessary to beat its brute force. The English needed to avoid fighting on equal terms with their principal enemy and a submersible would have been a very useful adjunct to more conventional warships.

In his *Naval Tracts*, Bourne's old Commanding Officer, William Monson, applied himself to a means of warfare complementary to the retired gunner's ideas. Monson believed underwater cannon fire would more effectively sink enemy vessels than pounding them above the waterline or using divers to bore holes below it. He proposed mounting a cannon in the hold of an attacking ship. Once an enemy craft had been secured snugly alongside with grappling irons, the weapon was to be fired. Monson suggested this was how great galleons could be sunk by small boats.

Drawing on Bourne's work, in the 1620s Cornelius Drebbel, a Dutchman living in London, staged a series of public trials with a submersible craft that looked as if one rowing boat had been fixed on top of another.

It had a wooden frame covered in planking, overlaid with greased leather. There were half a dozen watertight oars with their rowlocks likewise sealed by leather, three to each side. A team of 12 oarsmen was recruited from among the hardy watermen of the River Thames, tempted by money to take the extraordinary risk. It was the third prototype that Drebbel had constructed and could supposedly carry 16 passengers, though it took a brave soul to go aboard for a ride.

During one public demonstration the banks of the Thames were packed with thousands of onlookers, eager for the vicarious thrill of seeing the mad Hollander and his crew perish. Much to everyone's surprise, the craft dived successfully – according to contemporary accounts down to 15ft. The sweating, grunting oarsmen drove it under as Drebbel adjusted primitive hydroplanes fore and aft to angle the bows down. With the oarsmen toiling away, the inventor himself crouched between them at the fore end, urging greater effort.

Drebbel's craft allegedly voyaged from Westminster to Greenwich and back. Throughout, its stubby conning tower poked above the water, Drebbel navigating by peering through small windows. In 1623 Drebbel allegedly took King James I under the Thames. By instinct cautious, the King was nevertheless fascinated by science and mechanical things, so curiosity may have overcome his anxiety. The King subsequently gave Drebbel grants to live off and also, according to English State Papers, to rent workshops in which he created 'water engines' and 'water mines' and even 'underwater explosive machines'.[6]

Cornelius Drebbel, the Dutch inventor of a prototype submersible. He allegedly took the submerged craft down the Thames in the 1620s – with King James I along for the ride. (*TopFoto*)

The practicalities of Drebbel's diving boat supposedly included floats attached to hoses for drawing air down. Alternatively, he may have used the fumes of strong gin to make the oarsmen so light-headed they did not mind the lack of oxygen. Another explanation is that prior to each voyage Drebbel created oxygen gas by burning potassium or sodium nitrate in large bottles, which he unstopped on recognising that the air, along with his human propulsion system, was becoming exhausted.

Apart from muscle power and inclined hydroplanes adjusted by hand, Drebbel's submersible may also have dived using a system of pigs' bladders stowed under the rowers' seats. They were connected to pipes that penetrated the hull, which were unstopped to allow water in, the increased displacement settling the boat lower in the water.

To surface, the oarsmen squeezed, or carefully stamped on, their respective pigs' bladders, expelling the water, and then tied them off. The lightening of the craft caused it to rise, the hydroplanes arranged to drive it to the surface. Despite Drebbel's apparent ingenuity across all manner of disciplines in science and alchemy, according to one naval historian his submersible was probably nothing more than a 'large leather-covered barge . . . weighted until the crew was below the surface'.[7] Drebbel's craft merely had water washing over its hull rather than actually diving, the fast-flowing current of the Thames assisting the exertions of the oarsmen.

With the English naval establishment losing interest in his purported submarine vessel and explosive devices, Drebbel's fortunes declined. He ended up as the landlord of a London alehouse and died forgotten in 1634, at the age of 62. A crater on the moon has at least been named after 'Drebbel . . . Cornelius; Dutch inventor',[8] forming a lasting memorial in outer space to a man who dreamed of voyaging through inner space.

2 Into Perpetual Night

On the other side of the English Channel a pair of priests – Marin Mersenne and Georges Fournier – proposed an undersea man-o'-war with a streamlined hull and resembling a giant fish. This metal monster would be armed with cannons and fitted with wheels so it could crawl along the seabed. It would achieve lethal surprise by rising to the surface in the middle of enemy fleets. Unleashing devastating broadsides it would then disappear below the waves again. Mersenne freely admitted to being inspired by the work of Bourne and Drebbel. How to manoeuvre such a craft, its propulsion and other essential technical challenges were not addressed in any detail.

Enmity for Oliver Cromwell's Commonwealth of England, which under the dictator's guidance created a powerful and aggressive fighting navy, would be a driver for others seeking to create underwater fighting machines. The Frenchman Louis de Son built a semi-submersible craft at Rotterdam in the early 1650s, during the first of the Anglo-Dutch Naval Wars. It boasted a clockwork motor to drive an internally mounted paddle wheel, breaking new ground by suggesting a means of propulsion other than oars. Muscle power was still needed to regularly wind the spring.

De Son's craft attracted the intense interest of Dutch naval authorities, potentially offering an opportunity to gain the upper hand in a bitter struggle for control of sea trade with the English.

Referred to as 'the Rotterdam ship that would kill the English under water', able to 'run as Swift as a bird can flye'[1] it allegedly had the potential to complete a voyage to the Netherlands' rich colonies in the East Indies within six weeks (rather than months).

De Son himself promised it would destroy 100 ships in a day: 'No fire, no cannon ball or rocket, no storm or waves can hinder him unless God the Lord should intend to do so.'[2] This wooden wonder, running with its hull awash at up to 9 knots rather than actually diving, would inflict destruction by ramming. A major flaw was the lack of a spring powerful enough to stand any chance of moving the 8ft-wide, 72ft-long vessel through the water. The Dutch had to rely on their sailing men-o'-war to beat the English.

One of the problems with marking milestones of sacrifice in maritime history, especially involving submarines, is that both the vessels and the people lost have disappeared forever below the waves.

With casualties on land there is invariably something tangible – whether it is the graves of the fallen or wreckage – to visibly mark the spot where something important and tragic happened. This is not the case with unlucky submariners and the craft that take them to their doom.

Today cross-Channel ferries, fishing boats and even nuclear-powered submarines pass to and fro over the spot where naval history claimed its first recorded submariner casualty.

John Day was an illiterate ship's carpenter's labourer from Norfolk well known for his love of inventing, despite lacking formal education or a profession. In early 1774 the 24-year-old Day achieved the remarkable feat of submerging to a depth of 30ft in one of the Yarmouth Broads.

He stayed down for at least six hours before emerging in perfect health from his vessel when the tide receded. Day had realised that wooden barrels could both keep water out and air in, so why not apply that logic to a sealed box inside a boat? All he needed was stones for ballast to sink and a means of releasing them to rise again. To go one better, and enhance his fame with financial gain, Day contacted gentleman gambler Christopher Blake, proposing a scheme that could make them both rich. 'I have found out an affair by which many thousands may be won,' Day wrote to Blake,[3] who advanced him £350 for constructing a new diving boat. If it proved successful Day would receive a percentage of the bets placed with Blake.

The 50ft sloop *Maria* was adapted by a Plymouth shipwright to accommodate a watertight cabin in the hold alongside 10 tons of gravel and a further 20 tons of rock in special holders suspended from either side of the keel. The latter were connected by rods to levers within the cabin. These would be released from inside when it was time to surface. Day intended descending to 100ft where he would stay for 12 hours, using valves to let in water fore and aft to ensure *Maria* maintained balance as she slipped under. Seventy-five large, empty oak barrels strapped inside the hold for extra buoyancy would aid the subsequent ascent of *Maria*.

After a well-executed shallow plunge, Day was emboldened to go even deeper. By then a respectable sum of money had been wagered on his success or failure. *Maria* would make her next dive in 132ft of water and to pass the time while he sat on the bottom Day would repose in a hammock, the cabin illuminated by a wax taper. He had a supply of ship's biscuits and bottled water in case he felt hungry or thirsty and a clock so he could tell when the time was right to surface.[4] Day intended sending up a white indicator buoy to advise spectators 'all is well'. Should he release a red buoy it meant he had declined into 'indifferent health'. If they saw a black buoy he was 'in great danger'.[5]

On 28 June 1774 *Maria* was towed out by the 32-gun frigate HMS *Orpheus* to a spot between Drake's Island and Millbay but refused to go down until a further 20 tons of ballast was added. *Maria* took around five minutes to disappear, just astern of *Orpheus*, from whose quarterdeck specially invited guests watched. News of Day's exploit – and possible death – drew hundreds of onlookers to the shores of Plymouth Sound, who waited expectantly for the appointed hour when he would surface in *Maria*. Neither Day nor the *Maria* was ever seen again and there had been no signal buoys to indicate his status. Onlookers aboard *Orpheus* described how 'a number of very large bubbles kept rising from the bottom, and the sea became covered with white froth for some yards round'.[6] That could well have been the moment Day met his end. It is thought on reaching a depth of over 100ft the fledgling submariner discovered something he had hitherto been ignorant of. This was the ability of water pressure to crush a vessel, or at least rupture its hull enough for water to flood in. It would not have affected Drebbel in the comparatively shallow Thames, or indeed Day on his earlier Yarmouth Broads adventure, but it did pertain to the deepest part of Plymouth Sound.

The Dutch doctor Nikolai Falck suggested Day actually froze to death or was suffocated when a vacuum was created inside the water-tight cabin. Falck concluded Day had 'descended . . . into perpetual night!'[7] No matter how exactly he met his end, he became the first of many thousands who would lose their lives in a diving vessel.

While innovators in England led the way in the conceptualisation and even practical development of submersible boats, the desire to harm the British state continued to motivate others. The Continental Europeans saw the Royal Navy as the primary target, for it increasingly dominated the oceans, ensuring Britain's trade prospered at the expense of other nations.

Even so, the most serious threat from under the sea came from within the embrace of the Empire, for it was British American rebels seeking independence from the mother country who mounted the first serious seagoing attempt at a practical combat submersible.

One of those fighting to break away was David Bushnell, a pioneer in underwater explosive charges from Connecticut who had attended Yale University (graduating in 1775). He came to the conclusion that a gunpowder charge was more devastating if it exploded in the water, under a target vessel's hull, rather than expending its force into air. A submersible craft was needed to ensure the charge could be placed below the waterline in a position to cause catastrophic damage.

Bushnell aimed to deliver a decisive blow to the very foundation of British power – the fleet that guaranteed troops and supplies could be conveyed to wherever trouble broke out in the colonies.

The vessel he created was named *Turtle*, though it more resembled a gigantic walnut than a water-dwelling reptile. The sole crewman of *Turtle* would be pursuing much the same task as combat divers since ancient times – using an auger to create a hole in an enemy vessel. In this case explosives, rather than well-aimed rocks, would exploit it. A clockwork-detonated charge would be attached and shatter the target vessel's hull. A suitable time delay would ensure *Turtle* had enough time to get away without being sunk.

Putting together two large scooped-out pieces of oak six inches thick created the *Turtle's* hull. A broad iron band bound them tightly together, with the seam sealed. The craft was 7ft long with a beam of 3ft and a draught of 6ft. Propulsion was provided by a pair of hand-cranked, two-bladed propellers, with one mounted on the vessel's side for propulsion in the horizontal plane and the other on top for movement in the vertical. Steering came courtesy of a single rudder and *Turtle* was capped by a small, hinged copper conning tower with some windows so the pilot – squeezed into the space left among all the machinery – could see where he was going. He let water into a tank to submerge – increasing the density of the craft – and when surfacing used a hand pump to expel it (following Archimedes' principle of reducing density). Ballast necessary to counter the craft's innate buoyancy took the form of lead attached to the bottom. To ensure the pilot did not rapidly lose consciousness, carbon dioxide was evacuated from the *Turtle* via pipes. The sheer effort of manoeuvring while submerged would anyway use up oxygen enclosed in the *Turtle* very quickly, probably in a quarter of an hour.

The commander of the rebel American army, General George Washington, authorised funding and practical support for the *Turtle* project, with Bushnell's brother Ezra volunteering as its pilot.

On the appointed day Ezra was poorly, so the mission fell instead to Sergeant Ezra Lee, one of several other volunteers. The target was to be HMS *Eagle*, a 64-gun ship of the line, which, in September 1776, flew the flag of Vice Admiral Richard Howe, commander of the North America Station.

On the night of 6 September *Turtle* was towed out from Manhattan into the Hudson River, with *Eagle* at anchor not far from where the Statue of Liberty stands today. Casting off, Sgt Lee fixed his gaze on *Eagle* through the portholes in the small conning tower. Remarkably, if legend is to be believed, he managed to creep up to the man-o'-war without being spotted, despite *Turtle* going at no more than three miles an hour. Taking *Turtle* under the British warship, Lee was guided in the gloom by a primitive depth gauge utilising a cork float in a glass and a compass. Both the needle of the compass and the float were coated in bioluminescent Foxfire fungus. Unfortunately for the rebel cause, Lee failed to attach his charge, supposedly due to anti-parasite copper sheathing on *Eagle*'s hull. Alternatively, he may have attempted to drill into an iron plate that was part of the warship's rudder mounting.

Or maybe none of it happened. The late Richard Compton-Hall, retired submarine captain, historian and also one-time director of the Royal Navy Submarine Museum, was a leading *Turtle* debunker. He suggested sentries pacing up and down *Eagle*'s upper decks would easily have spotted *Turtle* had the craft actually managed to get near the ship. It would probably have been impossible in such a strong current for Lee to hold position and keep drilling. Compton-Hall pointed out that *Eagle* 'was not coppered until 1782',[8] so the idea that Lee was frustrated in that fashion does not match the facts.

Compton-Hall felt Sgt Lee was more likely to have just drifted on a strong tide past *Eagle* without mounting an attack.

According to Lee when *Turtle* emerged from under *Eagle*, he opened a vent to suck in some fresh air and was spotted. A small British boat gave chase but was deterred when he cast his explosive charge adrift and it exploded. As Lee didn't talk about his *Turtle* exploits for four decades, his memories of what actually occurred were probably somewhat imperfect.

Whatever really happened it was enough to persuade the British to withdraw their blockading fleet to a safer distance, giving rebel New Yorkers more of a chance to bring people and supplies in and out.

After several further attempts to attack British warships failed, the sloop acting as *Turtle*'s mother ship was caught and sunk by a Royal Navy frigate; Bushnell's submersible accompanied the sloop to a watery grave.

George Washington regarded both Ezra Lee's original attack and *Turtle*'s later attempts as heroic failures. In 1785 he remarked: 'I then thought, and still think, that it was an effort of genius.'[9]

3   Humane Torpedoes

The most ambitious of the early would-be underwater warriors was Robert Fulton, an American who did not let any of his supposed antipathy towards the British prevent him from travelling to London to seek his fortune.

When he first set foot on English soil Fulton was intent on becoming a wealthy portrait artist rather than a submarine inventor. By 1787 he was training in London with the renowned artist Benjamin West, a fellow American from Fulton's hometown who, with his famous 1770 depiction of the heroic death of General Wolfe at Quebec, had won international renown.

Born in 1765, in Lancaster, Pennsylvania, Fulton combined an artist's soul with a talent for engineering and explosives. Among other things he built while still very young was a paddle-powered craft for his friends to go fishing in and a rocket to launch in celebration of American Independence. Acquiring the arts of gunsmithing, as a teenager Fulton even made an airgun, was at one time apprenticed to a silversmith and became a skilled miniaturist.

Britain was in the late 1780s the centre for artistic, scientific and engineering innovation, so when fame and fortune as an artist proved elusive Fulton turned his attention to becoming a mechanical engineer. Fulton was especially interested in the potential for steam engines to propel commercial passenger ships. He also made himself into a well-respected expert on canals, their navigation and mechanical devices to take barges up steep inclines.

Travelling to France in the summer of 1797, Fulton intended staying only a few months before heading back to the United States to further explore canal engineering opportunities. He ended up spending seven years there, with success remaining elusive. His canal schemes frustrated, Fulton embarked on an ill-starred projects for rope-making, an important and lucrative industry during the age of sailing ships but not for the American, who failed to prosper. Still looking for his main chance he turned to devising a submersible attack craft.

The design drawings he revealed in Paris were well thought out and detailed. It has been speculated that he gained inspiration for his submersible during an art expedition to the British fleet anchorage and convoy assembly point of Torbay in Devon.[1] He may well have gazed at the warships that dominated and controlled world trade, pondering how weaker nations might deliver a devastating blow to liberate their commerce from such hegemony. A scientifically minded man like Fulton – blessed with the artistic skills to conjure up designs while also an engineering craftsman – just needed the vision and motivation to offer a solution.

He proposed a 'plunging boat' and might have received added inspiration – even technical advice – from Bushnell, for the *Turtle*'s inventor was in France at the same time. Following service as an officer in the Continental Army during the War of Independence, including at the siege of Yorktown in 1781, Bushnell had apparently vanished. There followed unsubstantiated stories about him being swept up in the French Revolution and possibly losing his life.

By the time Fulton reached France, Bushnell was making wild claims about new underwater craft, promising French authorities 'a means quite as terrible as it was invisible to force the British to lift their blockade'.[2] The French heard Bushnell vow that he would 'undertake to drive the enemy from our shores' and also 'carry the war to the shores and ports of Great Britain, hereto inviolable'.[3] For all his promises he was rebuffed. The French did not regard Bushnell's proposals as realistic, especially with no evidence of *Turtle* ever having sunk a ship. It is entirely possible he and Fulton met in Paris. On hearing of Bushnell's exploits, Fulton possibly thought he might succeed where the other man had failed.

In 1798 Fulton provided an insight into the higher purpose of his submarine project, writing that for America 'a free ocean is particularly Important'. Unfortunately, he said, its prosperity and defence was restricted 'owing to the Naval systems of Europe', which Fulton labelled 'licenced Robbery on the ocean'. He asked: 'How then is America to prevent this?' Fulton suggested the answer lay not in trying to build a fleet of warships to rival those of Europe but 'by Rendering the European fleets useless'.[4]

He aimed for nothing less than making warfare at sea redundant, ensuring peace reigned and free trade prospered, with his 'plunging boats' wresting supremacy of the sea from the British. They would deploy

'Torpedoes' – floating explosive charges named after a type of electric ray that paralyses its prey with an electric shock.

Fulton felt the plunging boat and torpedo combination would shatter even the largest warship. Yet, when the American laid out his submarine proposals, the French were surprisingly unenthusiastic. They were possibly reluctant to finance the creation of a war vessel the British could seize – just as they had many French warships – and use against them.

Even so, a commission was formed to consider Fulton's proposals. It raised severe concerns about a plunging boat's effectiveness in war conditions and also about flouting internationally accepted rules of conflict that not even Revolutionary France dared break. Fulton decided he had to prove the point to make the French change their minds. Part funding submarine construction work by the creation of a grand panorama of Paris that people paid to see, Fulton also managed to persuade a Dutch backer to provide finance.

Fulton's plunging boat was constructed at Rouen and launched on the River Seine in May 1800. With a copper skin on iron ribs, its construction drew on Fulton's metallurgical skills and of course it was not the first vessel he'd built. It was, however, somewhat more complex than a fishing boat.

Christened *Nautilus*, his craft was more than 20ft in length with a beam of 6ft, had ballast tanks for diving and surfacing and was steered by horizontal rudders aft. Propelled under the water by a hand-cranked propeller at the stern – with a bow-mounted 'horizontal propeller'[5] to maintain depth – when on the surface *Nautilus* used sails, also boasting a primitive periscope and snorkel. Fulton staged a well-received public display at Paris, with an audience of thousands lining the banks of the Seine.

Yet, for all his apparent technical success, Fulton recognised that continuing with a private enterprise – including expensive sea trials out of Le Havre and an unsuccessful attempt to attack British ships – would be ruinous and pointless if there was no desire from the French to use *Nautilus*.

After much lobbying, on Napoleon's authority 10,000 francs in credit was authorised to develop *Nautilus* and construct support vessels, though this was probably about 18,000 francs short of the actual cost.[6]

Napoleon insisted Fulton must base himself at Brest and, after sea trials, attack the British. In March 1801 Fulton transported *Nautilus* to the Breton naval dockyard and on 3 July staged a demonstration dive in the harbour. Taking it easy, he took the *Nautilus* down in stages, 5ft at a time, but declined to go deeper than 25ft. Fulton was wary of the effects of water pressure, showing he had taken heed of Day's fatal error.

Nautilus was dived for an hour, the first time without internal illumination but on subsequent descents with candles lit. They tended to burn up the air contained within the craft, so Fulton ordered a design modification – windows.

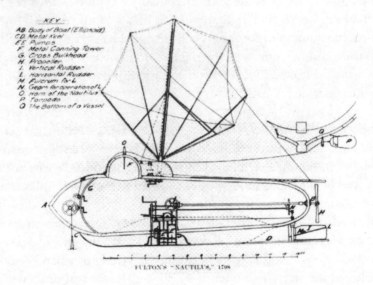

FULTON'S "NAUTILUS," 1798

A drawing of Robert Fulton's *Nautilus* plunging boat, with an inset showing how its torpedo would be attached to the bottom of the target vessel. (*Reproduced by permission of Mr John Wyckoff Mettler of New York and New Brunswick, New Jersey, owner of the original drawings now in the William Barclay Parsons Collection in the New York Public Library. Courtesy Naval History & Heritage Command.*)

Three weeks later Fulton carried out another dive, checking his ability to read a compass through the window light and also trialling the boat's manoeuvring capabilities. Before the month's end he was again at sea to observe how smoothly *Nautilus* might switch from surface cruising to plunging.

Once dived, at around 5ft, Fulton divided duties between himself and his three crewmates. Two worked the propulsion with the third on the helm, while Fulton acted as captain. It took about seven minutes for *Nautilus* to cover around 500 yards. After surfacing, Fulton took her down again. He later claimed to have successfully brought the vessel around so she headed back the way she had come. Some historians have cast doubt on this, maintaining Fulton actually discovered *Nautilus* was uncontrollable when dived.[7]

According to this view attacks would have to be carried out on the surface, with *Nautilus* under sail and the torpedo on the end of a long spar to ensure the explosive charge made contact with an enemy vessel's hull. Recognising the potential for this method to sink *Nautilus* at the same time as the target, Fulton proposed charges should be attached. This torpedo took the form of a spike with a charge on the end of it, which was to be hammered into the bottom of the enemy hull by means of a device fitted into the small conning tower. Thanks to its clockwork detonator the torpedo would only explode once *Nautilus* was at a safe distance. While *Nautilus* appeared to have sailed well, failing to actually sink a vessel undermined the case for further investment, though Fulton did manage to destroy a small craft using a torpedo shoved towards it from a rowing boat. So that he might use *Nautilus* for trial attacks on the British, the French agreed to give Fulton and his assistants legal cover through naval commissions. This ruse would prevent them being hanged as pirates. Fulton was made an admiral.

He wrote to French officials in September 1801 promising to create a flotilla of submarines that could be used to blockade the Thames and principal English naval dockyards.

Napoleon showed no urgency in commissioning plunging boats. He did send word for Fulton to stage a new demonstration but the impulsive American had already broken the vessel up. He told the First Consul *Nautilus* had sprung too many leaks and was no longer 'further useful'.[8] Fulton sold any worthwhile metal parts for their scrap value and destroyed what remained. He feared the French would seize *Nautilus* and manufacture their own version without any financial benefit to himself.

Napoleon declared Fulton a charlatan and things were not helped by the new Minister of Marine, an old school admiral, taking a dim view of submarine warfare altogether. He felt it was both impractical and of dubious legality.

The Treaty of Amiens of March 1802 temporarily brought an end to warfare between Britain and France, so the plunging boat was no longer needed. Fulton went to the Netherlands and, while he still found no interest in his submarine schemes, during a three-month stay he secretly met a British emissary. No less than the Prime Minister himself, Henry Addington, had sent 'Mr Smith' – a fellow American Fulton knew from his earlier time in England – to Amsterdam. Such a rendezvous could not easily take place in France due to Fulton being closely watched by government agents.

The British were well aware of his proposals to sink their blockading ships including mines attached to grappling hooks. They had decided they would far rather have him on their side than working for the French but Fulton declined the terms initially offered, putting forward his own proposals: £10,000 to return and £10,000 to actually construct a plunging boat.[9] Despite the risk, 'Smith' came to Paris in March 1804 for further discussions, which must have been a very dangerous undertaking as Britain and France were again at war. 'Smith' handed over several hundred pounds as an inducement along with a letter from Lord Hawkesbury, Secretary of State for Foreign Affairs. It pointed out that the British needed proof of his plunging boat's viability before they could hand over the sums Fulton requested.

Installed in lodgings at 13 Sackville Street, Piccadilly, Fulton used the cover name Robert Francis as he had good reason to be careful. The French had indicated that if they ever captured anyone using plunging boats or torpedoes against them the penalty would be death.

Even before he left France the American had proposed a new design to the British, which was 'vastly superior' to Nautilus.[10] It was 35ft long, capable of matching the surface speed of a fishing boat, with a crew of six, and would carry enough provisions to stay at sea for nearly three weeks. To refresh the air it would not need to show itself above the surface, replenishing oxygen via two tubes – one ejecting foul air, the other one pulling in fresh (a process taking no more than four minutes). Fulton suggested his vessel could remain submerged during the hours of daylight and surface under cover of darkness while, for attacking purposes, it would be able to carry '30 submarine bombs'.[11] To bring it all to fruition 'Mr Francis' needed £7,000 and the full assistance of a British naval dockyard. Fulton also required 100 Royal Navy seamen who could swim well. Many, if not most, sailors at that time couldn't swim a stroke, so that was not an easy thing to sort out. He requested an experienced sea officer, plus 40 tons of gunpowder for making torpedoes. To show how dedicated he was to proving the feasibility of his proposals, Fulton promised to lead attacks against the French invasion fleets assembling in Brest and Boulogne.

Addington's administration lost office, yielding to a government led by William Pitt, and he turned out to be more interested in torpedoes than undersea craft.

While the Admiralty felt Fulton's submarine would eventually mature into a proper vessel of war there was no time to waste, especially with Napoleon's Army of England massing on the French coast.

The Royal Navy might dominate the high seas – successfully bottling up enemy fleets – but it had failed to get in among the growing enemy invasion flotillas. Small raiding craft of a kind that could do so were used widely in the Mediterranean but deploying them in the Channel, with its more turbulent seas and stormy prevailing weather, was problematic.

Allied with new vessels constructed specifically for the job, including catamarans of Fulton's devising, torpedoes might offer a means to effect the required destruction. A secret agreement was drawn up and for the next two years Fulton worked for the Admiralty. It paid him £200 a month for the exclusive use of his inventions (and also a lump sum of £7,000). This was not the end of the incentives, for if Fulton's devices managed to sink an enemy line-of-battle ship he would be rewarded with £40,000, a substantial fortune. During a breakfast meeting with Fulton, the Prime Minister conceded the potentially transformative nature of such a weapon. Pitt felt that should it be successfully introduced into service, 'it could not fail to annihilate all military marines [navies]'.[12]

Fulton's torpedoes were used in two major attacks by the British against invasion flotillas at Boulogne and Calais, launched by his catamarans and other craft. The catamarans operated as semi-submersibles, gaining a very low profile, with the crews wearing black body suits and facemasks to further reduce visibility, but none of the raids was a success, the majority of torpedoes failing to make contact with targets, exploding in the wrong place or not detonating.

Even placing and detonating torpedoes next to a couple of small French naval vessels served only to rock them severely and shock their crews. The force of the explosions dissipated into the air, rather than shattering their hulls.

It must have enraged Fulton that had his submarine been built and deployed, the foul Channel weather would not have mattered. A submarine would have been able to escape into the relative tranquillity below the waves and more easily deliver destruction. The torpedoes could have been detonated with the whole force of a devastating explosion exerted upwards.

As it was, the threat of invasion remained suspended over Britain, so Fulton pressed on, staging a spectacular demonstration of how powerful his torpedoes could be when used properly.

On 15 October 1805 a 200-ton brig named *Dorothea* was deliberately blown up off Walmer Castle, the Kent coastal residence of William Pitt, just north of Dover. Torpedoes suspended on lines designed to catch anchor cables were taken underneath the craft's hull by the prevailing tide, with mechanical timers detonating them.

Unfortunately the Prime Minister had been called away by urgent business but senior naval officers were among those on hand to see events unfold. They included a certain Captain Kingston, who was determined to remain unimpressed. Prior to the explosion Kingston told Fulton that were he aboard *Dorothea* having dinner in his cabin, 'he should feel no concern for the consequence' of the torpedoes. With some relish Fulton later related that the explosion 'appeared to raise her [*Dorothea*] bodily about six feet; she separated in the middle, and the two ends went down in twenty seconds, nothing was to be seen of her except floating fragments'. This sight had a decisive effect, with even Kingston deeply shocked. Fulton noted drily: 'Occular demonstration is the best proof for all men.'[13]

The full force of the explosion had been transmitted into the water under the *Dorothea*, a mass of which was punched upwards to wrench her apart. To some in the British naval establishment it illustrated a cowardly and cruel form of warfare they would not entertain, but to Fulton it was an 'experiment of the most satisfactory kind'.[14]

The top man in the Royal Navy, First Lord of the Admiralty Earl St

An original engraving of a portrait of Robert Fulton as painted by Benjamin West. Engraved by W. S. Leney. In the background (left) it shows the brig *Dorothea* being split in two by the explosion of a Fulton torpedo. (*NHHC*)

Vincent, thought the Prime Minister ill-advised to pursue such methods. St Vincent told Fulton it was foolishness 'to encourage a mode of war which they who commanded the seas did not want, and which, if successful, would deprive them of it . . .'[15]

Ignoring such trenchant opposition, Fulton proposed that his torpedoes should be used to destroy the primary means by which the enemy intended to wrest control of the Channel from Britain – the Franco-Spanish Combined Fleet, then lurking at Cadiz. Should this powerful force escape the Mediterranean Fleet it might enable invasion troops to be conveyed safely to England. Despite the Army of England itself having already turned east – marching to war against a coalition led by the Austrians – until the Combined Fleet was destroyed the threat of invasion was not entirely lifted.

Fulton, using his cover name of 'Francis', wrote to Admiral Lord Nelson on 4 September 1805, while the latter was still in England prior to taking command of the Mediterranean Fleet. The American sought to persuade Britain's greatest naval hero to back his catamarans and torpedoes, describing the latter as 'submarine navigation carcasses'.

Fulton told Nelson: '. . . it is on the application of those engines I wish to see your Lordship as I am convinced you will find the explanation of them interesting. I should be extremely happy to have a few minutes conversation before you leave Town . . .'[16]

There is no evidence Nelson ever read the letter but Viscount Castlereagh, Secretary of State for War, wrote to him aboard *Victory* off Cadiz, conveying information on schemes offered by 'Francis'.[17]

Nelson confessed he had 'but little faith' in their chances of success, though he promised 'Francis' would still get 'every assistance' were he to be sent out to try his luck with the attack craft and 'carcasses'.

Deliverance for Britain's invasion arrived six days after Fulton blew up the *Dorothea*, with Nelson's ships decisively defeating the Combined Fleet during the Battle of Trafalgar. There was now no need for Fulton's torpedoes and his catamarans and certainly not for a submarine. Nelson was killed saving his nation, with those final moments depicted by Fulton's mentor, Benjamin West, in his epic *The Death of Nelson*, painted in 1806.

In the aftermath of Trafalgar, the British wanted to pay Fulton to suppress his inventions, provoking him to respond furiously: 'In fact, I will do my utmost to make it a good philosophic work and give it to the world.' He added: 'I shall hope to succeed in my first object that of annihilating all Military Marines and giving liberty to the Seas.'

Worn out and demoralised by trying in vain to convince two major global powers that plunging boats and torpedoes offered a decisive edge, Fulton departed England aboard a packet sailing out of Falmouth in October 1806.[18]

By the time Britain and America went to war with each other in 1812 – over trade disputes and the Royal Navy's habit of impressing US-born mariners into its service – Fulton was working on schemes to attack his old sponsors. In 1810 – three years after trying and failing to interest the American government in a submarine vessel – Fulton published an account of his time in England, called *Torpedo War, and Submarine Explosions*. This was in blatant contravention of an agreement with the Admiralty, which required him not to publish anything for 14 years.

Fulton took the risk because he was eager for the American government to invest in his inventions. This would prove his patriotism – his habit of changing sides did not endear him to some people – and also provide funds to pursue the long-held dream of a steam-propelled commercial passenger vessel.

Fulton proposed swarms of small boats fitted with harpoon guns. The harpoon would slam into the wooden hull of an enemy warship while a length of line attached to the other end of it would jerk a torpedo into contact, hopefully followed by an explosion. Fulton maintained the Royal Navy would have no option but to retreat in the face of the harpoon boats. In that moment, so he forecast, 'the power of the British marine is for ever lost, and with it the political influence of the nation'. Britain would find that 'her merchant vessels could be attacked, destroyed and her trade ruined . . . England, who has usurped the dominion of ocean . . . would be the most humble supplicant for the liberty of the seas.'[19]

The morality of what he was proposing troubled Fulton, with some people suggesting such warfare would be inhumane. Fulton proposed his torpedoes would be no more likely to encourage inhumane behaviour than muskets might encourage highway robbery. He felt civilised society would not allow his torpedoes to be abused but did admit 'it is barbarous to blow up a ship with all her crew'.

Fulton lamented that this should be necessary, but pointed out: 'all wars are barbarous, and particularly wars of offence.'

If torpedoes 'should prevent such acts of violence, the invention must be humane'.[20] Congress did ultimately fund research into Fulton's torpedoes while he was also working on a design for a large, 80ft-long submersible named *Mute*. Another project aimed to create a floating fortress to safeguard New York.

A Fulton prototype submarine, or something similar, was used to attack the British line-of-battle ship HMS *Ramillies* in 1812. Her presence was keeping US Navy frigates trapped in harbour, but they were not powerful enough to take her on. The 74-gunner was riding at anchor off New London when a strange craft, apparently propelled by oars, made three attempts to drill into and fasten an explosive charge to her hull.

Each time the alarm was raised and the would-be assailant was seen off. Increasingly irritated by this impudent vessel's repeated forays, the British decided to take a hundred American citizens prisoner, and place them aboard *Ramillies* as human shields.

The American government was advised that should its submarine boat destroy *Ramillies* and her crew, it would be responsible for also killing its own citizens. This ruse worked and the Americans withdrew their annoying vessel. Other craft – showing barely anything above the water, and also armed with Fulton torpedoes – were sent against the same British flotilla, making unsuccessful bids to destroy *Victorious*, *Plantagenet* and *Hogue*.

In retaliation *Ramillies* ran her big guns out and let rip with several broadsides. Cannon balls plunged onto the small town of Stonington, which was, according to one British officer, entirely justified. It was 'conspicuous in preparing and harbouring torpedoes, and giving assistance to the enemy's attempts at the destruction of His Majesty's Ships . . .'[21]

Fulton did not live long enough to see the end of the war with Britain. He was not lost in a submarine at sea or in fighting the British but caught pneumonia after saving a friend from drowning and died in February 1815 aged 49.

As for the other major submarine innovator of the same era, David Bushnell, after his frustrations in France he changed his name to Bush and settled in Georgia, becoming a teacher and a doctor. Keeping his previous life under wraps, Bushnell's past as submarine pioneer only became known on his death in 1826, at the age of 86.[22] Discovered in the home of 'Dr Bush' after his passing was a model for a new design of torpedo.[23]

4   A Bonnet Full of Secrets

Submarine development was incrementally moving forward with various people borrowing ideas and adding a few of their own. As a riposte to the Americans the British were said to have worked on some kind of submarine during the War of 1812. It allegedly bore startling resemblance to Fulton's proposed improved *Nautilus*.

Then there is the tale of a traitorous former Royal Navy officer who, on seeing Napoleon exiled to St Helena in the South Atlantic, reportedly offered his services (and a submarine) to enable the emperor's escape. Napoleon expired before the submersible could sail to the rescue.

In the 1830s a Spaniard named Cervo built a spherical vessel out of timber, which vanished on its first dive along with its creator. In the same decade a French doctor named Jean Baptiste Petit took a metal coffin-shaped craft out into the Seine estuary for its maiden voyage, dived and was embedded in the mud. Petit was trapped and suffocated.

In 1850, when the German Confederation roused itself to resist Danish aggression, a Bavarian artillery corporal named Wilhelm Bauer devised a steel boxy type of submersible called *Fire Diver*. Its purported means of attacking and destroying the enemy was by a pair of mechanical hands to attach an explosive device to a ship's hull.

The 27ft long, 39 tons displacement *Fire Diver* put to sea in the Baltic with Bauer navigating by peering through small windows in a metal snout poking above the surface. Propelled by two muscle men working a treadmill turning its screw, the strange craft's approach scared off the Danes, who decided to withdraw and mount their blockade further out.

Fire Diver subsequently got stuck in mud on the bottom of Kiel harbour with more than 50ft of water overhead. Trapped for five hours, salvation for the three occupants came when Bauer used valves to let in water – despite efforts at physical restraint and the terrified exhortations of his companions, eager to prevent such (apparent) foolishness.

Bauer knew what he was doing. The ingress compressed the air inside the craft and increased pressure until it was equal to that of the water outside the hull. This enabled Bauer to open the hatch, with *Fire Diver*'s occupants shooting to the surface in what was the first escape from a submarine.

In 1853 Bauer took his designs to England, seeking backers at a time when Russia was at war with Britain and France in the Crimea, Baltic and Arctic. He found sponsorship via an introduction to Prince Albert, a fellow German interested in the possibilities offered by submarine warfare. Albert put him in touch with renowned Scottish shipbuilder and naval engineer John Scott Russell, who was working on a kind of submarine with the engineering firm of Fox & Henderson, which was famous for having constructed the Crystal Palace.

Bauer was employed at the Millwall shipyard on the Thames, where

Russell was building a massive steam-powered paddle steamer called the *Great Eastern* in partnership with Isambard Kingdom Brunel. When not working on the *Great Eastern*, Bauer honed his own designs.

Russell's private venture prototype submarine was modelled on a diving bell that would sink to the bottom, after which its crew would walk it along the seabed. It was suggested divers could deploy from it to attach explosive charges to the sea walls of the Russian naval fortress of Kronstadt in the Baltic. During a test in the Thames the submarine-diving bell followed the familiar pattern of diving and not coming up again. Stuck in the mud, its two crewmen perished. Meanwhile, Bauer became paranoid that someone was sneaking into the Millwall drawing office late at night to plagiarise elements of his design. Angrily accusing Russell of ripping off his hard work, Bauer decamped to St Petersburg, determined to help Britain's enemies. In 1854 he unveiled *Sea Devil*, a sausage-shaped craft almost double the size of *Fire Diver*. It could accommodate a 13-strong crew, employed primarily in operating a screw using a treadmill. Ballast tanks were operated by hand pumps, a laborious and inexact process. Successfully completing more than 130 dives – straight up and down affairs but with some bottom slithering – *Sea Devil*'s most notable exploit came in September 1856. She submerged carrying a musical quartet that serenaded Tsar Alexander II from beneath the waves to celebrate his coronation.

When it came to a practical demonstration of war-fighting potential *Sea Devil* failed. Bauer was asked to attack and sink a redundant vessel in Kronstadt harbour using a large mine containing 500lb of explosives. This required a crewman to stand in the nose of the vessel and insert his arms into a pair of rubber gloves attached to the outside of the hull. Via these he was meant to unclip an explosive charge and fix it to the hull of the target. Navigating more or less blind, using only a compass, *Sea Devil* hit a mud bank. Unable to make further progress she eventually extracted herself from trouble by surfacing but then sank as water poured into an open hatch, fortunately without taking Bauer or his crewmates down too. Salvaged and restored to operation, *Sea Devil* was lost permanently in mysterious circumstances, possibly scuttled by order of senior Russian officers. They had suffered quite enough hare-brained proposals from the upstart Bavarian. Wandering around Europe looking for other backers, Bauer made a bid to interest Emperor Napoleon III of France in a submarine but this came to nothing.

He returned to Bavaria, where he died in 1875, like Drebbel before him forgotten and poverty-stricken.

When war ripped the United States apart, with brother Americans pitted against each other, there would be a sudden enthusiasm on both sides for unconventional warships.

The Civil War started in April 1861, when the army of the southern Confederate States, which had seceded from the Union that February, bombarded Fort Sumter, guardian of the gate to the South Carolina port of Charleston. Thereafter, the US Navy, also known as the Federal Navy, sought to strangle the Confederacy's maritime trade, imposing a blockade to ensure the agrarian South could not export its cotton or import crucial supplies and tools of war. In reply the South constructed blockade-running ships, some of them, much to the fury of the North, built in England.

Finding it increasingly difficult to break the blockade, the South turned to submarines. In October 1861 intelligence was received in the North from an agent in the South, revealing construction of a small four-man submersible. This alarming news had been obtained because the Director of the Federal Secret Service, Allan Pinkerton, had sent Mrs E.H. Baker to become the North's mole in Richmond, the Confederate capital. Her specific mission was to discover all she could about the South's torpedo and submersible schemes. Although she had most recently been with Pinkerton's Detective Agency in Chicago, Baker was a native of Richmond and soon rekindled old friendships.

Introduced to a Confederate officer and his wife, they got along so well that the couple offered Baker lodgings. She expressed curiosity in submersibles and, flattered by her interest, the officer invited her to tour an ironworks where a number of weapons projects were underway.

When the ironworks visit was postponed, due to the officer being required to observe trials of a submersible in the James River, it was a fortuitous turn of events. The Confederate officer invited both his wife and Mrs Baker to accompany him.

They witnessed the craft submerging about half a mile down river from a vessel playing the target, a large scow (flat-bottomed cargo vessel). Onlookers were only able to tell where the submersible was thanks to the progress of a dark green-painted float, which enclosed an air hose. This was a snorkel of the kind advocated by previous submarine innovators but now effectively put into practice.

Using binoculars Mrs Baker saw the float had stopped moving a little way from the target. What she couldn't see was that a diver had exited the submersible and attached a torpedo to the bottom of the scow. The float began moving away from the target, the submersible still connected to the torpedo by a long wire that unreeled behind it. This would enable electrical detonation at a safe distance.

After a pause there was a massive explosion, the scow lifting into the air and then sinking, provoking loud cheers from spectators. With a craft such as this to destroy blockading warships, the South's fast steamers packed with cotton would soon be sailing in safety for England.

Mrs Baker was doubly alarmed to learn she had only seen a small prototype of a larger submersible. To communicate this imminent danger to the North, on returning to her lodgings she immediately retired to her room in order to begin composing a report for Pinkerton.

After a subsequent tour of the ironworks, when she saw the other vessel, Baker also made sketches. These were carefully folded up and, along with the report, sewn into a bonnet. Claiming that being so close to the horrors of war was causing her too much distress, Baker left Richmond, telling her hosts she was returning to Chicago. She actually met Pinkerton at Fredericksburg to hand over the bonnet.

After seeing its secrets Pinkerton decided 'there was no longer any doubt that the submarine ... could be used with deadly and telling effect on the ships constituting the Federal blockading squadron'.[1] He went to see both General George McClellan, commander of the Army of the Potomac, and Secretary of the Navy Gideon Welles to brief them.

An attack by a Confederate submersible on the USS *Minnesota*, lying off Hampton Roads, in October 1861 almost succeeded but the torpedo could not be attached. The submersible withdrew but was spotted by sailors aboard *Minnesota*, who later boasted to reporters about their narrow escape. A Northern newspaper subsequently claimed that the Confederate craft had a crew of two, possessed a screw propeller, used a rudder to steer itself and had a system of water ballasting to go up and down. It used a compass to navigate and a 'velocimeter'[2] to report distance travelled. A snorkel device to pull in air was also mentioned. Such a level of detail could only have been leaked to the press by Pinkerton.

Union naval forces were instructed to watch out for green floats and use grapples to drag the James River, hopefully snagging the air hoses of Confederate submersibles. A few weeks later Pinkerton received a report claiming a blockading warship had 'caught the air-tubes and this effectually disabled the vessel from doing any harm, and no doubt drowning all who were on board of her'.[3] Newspapers claimed that the attack was foiled due to pure chance but Pinkerton observed: 'I knew much better and that the real credit of the discovery was due to a lady of my own force.'[4]

5   Troublesome *Alligator*

Finding an effective means to wage submarine warfare was, not surprisingly, also an aspiration for the North's navy. The story of how it constructed its first submersible was initially marked with indifference to, and then suspicion of, the proposed design.

On 8 March 1861 an enterprising French immigrant named Brutus de Villeroi wrote to President Abraham Lincoln proposing a submarine boat that would carry out reconnaissance of the enemy coast and 'land men, ammunition, etc., at any given point, to enter harbors'.[1]

De Villeroi claimed his craft could also accomplish intelligence-gathering and 'carry explosive bombs under the very keels of vessels'. All this would be achieved 'without being seen'.[2]

The Frenchman assured Lincoln 'a few such boats' could guarantee that 'the most formidable fleet' was 'annihilated in a short time'. These boasts were in keeping with the Frenchman's description of himself as a 'natural born genius'.[3] The President – who frequently received offers of wonder weapons and was not above inspecting some of them – failed to absorb the intellectual brilliance of de Villeroi and ignored the letter.

De Villeroi had actually been in the submarine inventing business for many years and had already taken a vessel under water. Born at Tours in 1797, he grew up to become a professor of drawing and mathematics at Nantes who allegedly taught a young scholar named Jules Verne in the early 1840s. Even if he never actually took a lesson with de Villeroi, the future visionary novelist could not help but be aware of the professor's exploits, which were eagerly reported by newspapers.

By the 1830s de Villeroi was experimenting with a fish-shaped submarine. Operated by a crew of three, this craft – a mere four feet in diameter and about ten feet long with a submerged endurance of around an hour – demonstrated its diving prowess by retrieving rocks and seashells from the seabed. It possessed a retractable conning tower, and propulsion was provided by three sets of duck's feet-shaped paddles. A sealed ball and socket arrangement enabled them to be manipulated from inside. Dubbed the *Waterbug*, it was steered by a large rudder and to provide ballast water was taken in or hand-pumped out via a lever and piston system.

Admiral Sir Sidney Smith, who had encountered Robert Fulton in the early 1800s, was hired by the French government to inspect de Villeroi's creation. As a fugitive from Britain, where he risked being gaoled for gambling debts, it was welcome paid work for Sir Sidney. After witnessing a demonstration in 1835, he chaired a commission to decide the *Waterbug*'s viability. The resulting report expressed dissatisfaction, claiming it was not a realistic means of waging war. Although interest was aroused in the Netherlands, no contracts were forthcoming. Never one to give up easily, a further attempt was made by de Villeroi to get the French Navy to use his craft during the Crimean War, but his proposal was again declined. Seeking more productive horizons, in 1856, at the age of 59, de Villeroi emigrated to the USA with his family.

Despite President Lincoln's lack of interest, de Villeroi saw the Civil War as a fantastic opportunity and in May 1861 took a new cigar-shaped craft out on an audacious trip along the Delaware River.

With its black, humped back cutting through the water and a row of deadlights peeping just above the surface, it exerted a sinister, animalistic presence. A waterborne police investigation team under the command of Lieutenant Benjamin Edgar set off to locate and apprehend the vessel and arrest its occupants. When questioned, de Villeroi explained he was merely showing the craft off to provoke interest. He claimed that naval officials were expecting it, but when consulted they denied all knowledge.

Experts were sent to make an inspection, discovering an iron-hulled, cylinder-shaped craft that could accommodate a crew of 12. There was an air lock permitting divers to exit and return while it sat under a target. When interviewed by the navy, de Villeroi proposed entering the Confederate naval base at Norfolk to destroy shipping. He should not be paid any bounty if the mission failed, though he would require funding to design and produce a vessel specifically for naval use.

In November 1861 de Villeroi got what he failed to find in his native land – a contract to construct a proper undersea combat vessel. Yet, far from realising his long-cherished dream, the French inventor was plunged into a nightmare.

The US Navy gave de Villeroi only 40 days to build his submarine and get it ready for action. He had previously suggested he could build several submarines 'promptly', but could never have imagined such a tight time frame.

The appearance of the formidable ironclad warship CSS *Virginia* was piling the pressure on. She was a reconstructed captured steam warship, the *Merrimack*, which had been abandoned at Norfolk Navy Yard, burned to the waterline by retreating Federal forces. Her machinery and propulsion had been left in working order and once rebuilt and rechristened she looked likely to be invulnerable to cannon fire. While the North was proceeding apace with its own ironclad – the future USS *Monitor* – perhaps striking *up* through *Virginia*'s vulnerable hull could destroy her? For that purpose a submersible seemed ideal, hence de Villeroi's proposal looked enticing.

His decision to recruit an entirely French crew hurt American naval pride and won him quite a few enemies. De Villeroi said he did this not because French mariners were better, but rather to be 'sure of their fidelity and obedience'.[4] He feared Americans might give submarine secrets away because of divided personal loyalties between North and South.

As the deadline for delivery came and went, de Villeroi's conduct became erratic and the US Navy grew increasingly impatient.

De Villeroi fell out with an American contractor he was relying on to help construct the submarine, complaining materials to complete the interior were not forthcoming. Even his French crew wanted rid of the autocratic inventor and the Americans feared that, actually, it was de Villeroi who would talk to other nations about his submarine.

The inventor again wrote to President Lincoln, this time demanding to be made absolute commander of the project. For the second time he received no direct response and the US Navy sacked him from the project.

In May 1862 a new, all-American crew was enlisted along with an expert in underwater demolition, possessing good knowledge of 'electrics' and 'submarine explosions',[5] who was selected as Superintendent.

Fifty-two-year-old Samuel Eakins was a former army ordnance expert who had seen action in America's Far West and was also a one-time silversmith and jeweller. He had recently spent 18 months clearing warship wrecks at Sevastopol and was well versed in how to detonate explosives by electronic means and also underwater weaponry. In 1859 Eakins had, with a colleague, patented an underwater cannon triggered by an electric battery for blasting rock. He seemed to be the perfect mix of hands-on experience and willingness to experiment with new technology.

With the craft's inventor divorced from the project and Sam Eakins in charge, the North's new submarine was launched in May 1862. At 47ft long, with a beam of around 4ft, hand-operated paddles propelled *Alligator*, though de Villeroi's earlier prototype had used a single screw at the stern.

With a submerged displacement of 350 tons the deepest *Alligator* could go was 50ft. Requiring 22 sailors – 18 of them as oarsmen, with two helmsmen and a pair of divers – the green-painted vessel departed under tow in June.

The *Alligator*'s primary target was by then gone, for the Confederates had scuttled CSS *Virginia* on being forced to withdraw from Norfolk. *Alligator* would instead try to attack enemy shipping on the James River. Following the Confederacy's own practice, *Alligator*'s divers aimed to attach torpedoes to the hulls of target vessels. A long cable was to be unreeled back to the submarine and, having recovered the divers via the airlock, *Alligator*'s commander would trigger electrical detonation.

There was another change of plan, with *Alligator*'s underwater warriors reassigned to clear obstructions in the James River and make a foray to destroy the Petersburg Bridge on the Appomattox River. This would sever a vital railway link with the Confederate capital, which would then be starved of supplies. It turned out the Appomattox was not navigable by *Alligator*, clogged as it was with all manner of wreckage. She would not be able to dive, barring any hope of deploying in stealth (her only defence). *Alligator* needed clear water more than seven feet deep to fully submerge. Should she remain on the surface Confederate forces could easily hit her with cannon and rifle fire. It was feared *Alligator* might become trapped in fishing nets, be captured and then be used to attack the North's warships, including *Monitor*. She was a liability and in early July 1862 was ordered back to Washington Navy Yard.

De Villeroi surfaced that August, full of injured Gallic pride and seeking redress. Utterly humiliated, with his prize creation taken brusquely off him, he was also out of pocket and fired an angry letter at Navy Secretary Gideon Welles, demanding payment for his services.

He was affronted by the fact that even the French crewmen he'd engaged received something for their trouble while he – *the creator of the vessel!* – got nothing. The US Navy considered de Villeroi was in breach of contract so still refused to pay him anything.

Shortly after *Alligator*'s return to Washington, Eakins departed and so did the crew, with a new batch of American sailors assigned and a fresh Commanding Officer appointed. *Alligator*'s new captain, Lieutenant Thomas Selfridge, was not impressed with the craft. Among many defects, it was especially discouraging that the air purifier was broken. The secret of how exactly it worked had been lost to the US Navy when it parted ways with de Villeroi. Instead, *Alligator* was to be fitted with an air compressor to provide oxygen for the crew and divers. Further sea trials were scheduled to prepare for an attempt to sink two Confederate ironclads, the *Chicora* and *Palmetto State*. Selfridge thought the prospects of success were zero and regarded *Alligator* as a death trap, which struggled to even dive properly or obtain neutral buoyancy. The propulsion system was ineffective and unable to overcome strong tides. Her submerged mobility consisted of nothing more than sinking to the seabed, with Selfridge praying *Alligator* would surface when required.

His anxiety was reinforced by a near disaster. Successfully diving and surfacing *Alligator*, he made course for home, but her bow suddenly dipped. The crew was gripped by panic, fearing they were about to drown. Selfridge, piloting from the conning position on the hull, shouted reassuring words down the hatch to calm the men and ordered them to climb up and out one by one. With the bow still under

water, *Alligator* drifted, her men clinging on to the hull. Fortunately a
tow back to harbour was obtained from a passing vessel. Despite this
mishap, Selfridge and his men persevered, but *Alligator* only ever had
enough air for an hour submerged. This was not enough to complete
any war task while the lock-out chamber did not work, at least not
without potentially drowning the poor soul put into it.

Selfridge was grateful to be relieved of command and eagerly departed, with Eakins brought back as Superintendent. He requested
a refit in an attempt improve *Alligator*'s capabilities. In Eakins's view
the paddles were a huge error. They were ineffective, requiring a large
number of men to operate them and in the most trying of circumstances. They were replaced with a hand-cranked screw, requiring
fewer crew and improving the vessel's speed to 4 knots.

In early 1863 *Alligator* put on a show for President Lincoln, cruising
up and down and even diving below the Anacostia River. Orders were
issued for her to attack Confederate ironclads and help subdue Fort
Sumter.

Alligator was towed south by a steam warship named USS *Sumpter*,
departing on the last day of March 1863. Three days later they were
enveloped by a savage storm off Cape Hatteras, with *Sumpter* taking in
water and her galley funnel torn away. As she was twisted by the storm,
Sumpter's engines came close to giving out, due to the sheer effort of
trying to keep the ship head-on into gigantic waves.

Alligator pitched and yawed alarmingly, and the glass in her portholes
smashed, allowing the sea to pour in. The port hawser parted and it was
clear the starboard one might not hold much longer. In the meantime
Alligator might sink and pull *Sumpter* down with her, so she was cut free
and disappeared below the heaving ocean.

Shunned by the Americans, in the spring of 1863 de Villeroi wrote to
Emperor Napoleon III offering a new, 125ft-long submarine armed
with giant saws and guns. The emperor asked for blueprints, which
were studied by his naval experts. In June 1863 a commission set up by
imperial order delivered a crushing verdict, judging de Villeroi's vessel
'completely unnavigable, the artillery could not work, and the saws
would never have any useful purpose . . . de Villeroi's project cannot
sustain the kindest scrutiny and as a consequence NO follow-up action
should be given to this submission'.[6]

The French preferred to persevere with their own boat, *Le Plongeur*. Designed by Captain Siméon Bourgeois of the French Navy, she was launched at Rochefort in May 1863. This impressive craft followed the cigar-shaped pattern and was around 126ft long, displacing 450 tons on the surface. Using a compressed air propulsion system, *Le Plongeur* was capable of 4 knots on the surface but with enough compressed air stored aboard for only two hours' cruising. The compressed air was also used to expel water from her ballast tanks and to keep her crew alive while submerged.

A nineteenth-century engraving, depicting the French submersible *Le Plongeur*. (*AJAX Vintage Picture Library*)

Le Plongeur's maximum diving depth was 30ft and a spar torpedo attached to her prow provided her armament. Very hard to handle, according to one account when dived she 'pitched wildly like a porpoise'.[7] The French Navy grew tired of trying to make her work and decided submarines were a dead end.

Meanwhile, having again been rejected by his native France, de Villeroi died in Philadelphia on 24 June 1874, aged 81, his health having been poor for some time. Attempts to find and recover the *Alligator* have continued to this day. The most recent – by the Office of Naval Research (ONR) – was staged in 2005, but *Alligator* remains lost in a stretch of the ocean known to mariners as 'The Graveyard of the Atlantic'.

6   The Murdering Machine

Before the Civil War James McClintock was the youngest riverboat captain on the Mississippi, also displaying a talent for engineering design.

It was as he witnessed the stranglehold of the North's blockade of the South growing tighter that McClintock became ever more determined to take action, proposing a new kind of submersible.

Pioneer was built at New Orleans in 1862, with 39-year-old McClintock and his partners awarded a Letter of Marque by the Confederate government. This permitted them to operate the vessel as a privateer – basically, a licensed pirate ship protected by international law in the pursuit of capturing or destroying enemy vessels, both on the open ocean and up rivers.

With a three-man crew – two of them to hand-crank a propeller, and the other operating the rudder and hydroplanes – *Pioneer* was navigated by compass, McClintock admitting she was otherwise blind while submerged.

Despite this, in the spring of 1862 *Pioneer* proved her effectiveness by successfully diving and during a practice attack used a torpedo to sink

James McClintock, who played a leading role in creating *Hunley*. (*Courtesy of US Naval Historical Foundation/NHHC*)

a barge on Lake Pontchartrain. Before *Pioneer* could be unleashed on the enemy, New Orleans fell to the Union and she was scuttled. The US Navy salvaged *Pioneer* but did not press her into service, though studies were made of the design.

Elsewhere the South constructed and deployed ultra-streamlined, steam-powered torpedo boats called Davids to take on the northern Goliath. They possessed such a low freeboard that only their funnels, a conning position and a small part of the hull were visible above water. Substantial bounties were offered to anyone brave, or foolhardy, enough to take one into action. Using a spar torpedo, they were not very successful though a David did damage the USS *New Ironsides*.

There had to be a more effective way of attacking Union blockaders and so the men behind *Pioneer* decided to try again, with Horace L. Hunley, a New Orleans lawyer and cotton trader sorely affected by the North's blockade, coming aboard again as one of the principals. By May 1862, McClintock, Hunley and Baxter Watson – another *Pioneer* partner and owner of a machinery workshop – were at Mobile, Alabama, developing a new craft named *American Diver*. Taken out for sea trials under tow, she sank, fortunately with no casualties. Undeterred by this mishap, McClintock, Watson and Hunley pressed on with another submersible, partly funded by E.C. Singer of the sewing machine family. This led to the enterprise being dubbed the Singer Submarine Corporation.

An adapted boiler tube with tapered ends, the new craft displaced eight tons dived and was 40ft long, with a beam of 3ft. She was given ballast tanks (both stern and aft) enabling her to assume the negative buoyancy necessary to enable burly crewmen working a hand-cranked screw to drive her under. Conversely, once water had been expelled from the tanks and air admitted, they were theoretically able to propel her back to the surface. There was a large rudder and she also possessed hydroplanes forward to help her dive or surface, depending on their settings.

The CSS *H. L. Hunley*, as she was christened, was not blessed with longitudinal stability. Any major shifting around inside by her crew or a sudden ingress of water into the forward ballast tank would cause her to make a dramatic dive. This tendency would eventually prove fatal. An iron drop weight secured to her bottom kept *Hunley* floating rightways up, while for navigation there were two stubby conning towers

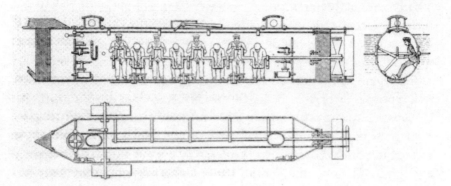

Cutaway drawings of the Confederate diving boat *Hunley*, as published in France, and based on sketches by William A. Alexander. (*NHHC*)

with glass scuttles, one forward and one aft. Not much more than hatch coamings, these were the only means of entry and exit. A crude snorkel was provided to draw in fresh air.

Man-powered propulsion was not necessarily the first choice. McClintock had pushed for an electromagnetic engine when designing *American Diver*. While it did not work out then, he hoped it would in *Hunley*. Sending an undercover agent to New York to buy the electromagnetic engine was proposed, but rejected on security grounds. Should that person be caught, details about the project would probably be given away under interrogation.

The steam engine alternative posed huge challenges – air needed to be taken in for the fuel to burn in the boiler, smoke had to be evacuated, fumes expelled and heat dissipated. Steam pressure might offer a solution. The craft was only intended to dip below a target vessel for a short period, towing a torpedo that would explode on contact after the submersible was safely on the other side. Prior to diving, the boiler fire would be extinguished and the funnel collapsed, tucked away and sealed off. The craft would be propelled while under the water using latent steam pressure.

This seemed much too complex and McClintock and his partners picked the safest, simplest option: a man-powered screw. It would prove capable of driving *Hunley* at 5 knots through the water 'without exertion to the men working her'.[1] The idea of a towed torpedo was abandoned when, after a trial run in Charleston Harbour, the cable got wrapped around *Hunley*'s screw. Ultimately a spar torpedo was to be used.

A key player in the endeavour, both on *American Diver* and *Hunley*, was English-born Lieutenant William Alexander, who had only emigrated to the USA from Britain two years earlier.

A mechanical engineer by trade, he had become an officer in the 21st Alabama Volunteers, which was blessed with a high proportion of mechanically minded troops. Alexander's men were ordered to assist in the fabrication of the new submarine, which like *Pioneer* would operate under a Letter of Marque to provide a return on the investment.

Launched in July 1863, *Hunley* was sent to Charleston by rail the following month as the best hope to break the blockade of the port.

Preparations were made for a night attack on an enemy warship – including providing *Hunley*'s crew of civilian volunteers with Confederate Army uniforms so they would not be hanged as pirates if captured.

In the meantime, with the siege of Charleston growing ever tighter and frequent bombardments of the city by enemy warships, the local military commander grew tired of waiting for *Hunley* to strike a blow.

The vessel was seized and handed over to the Confederate Navy. Lieutenant John A. Payne, an experienced officer who had served in the ironclad CSS *Chicora*, was put in command, with a volunteer crew drawn from gunboats. Misfortune struck on 29 August, after Payne had carried out a series of successful dives and ascents to determine how to handle *Hunley* safely and was heading back to a pier at Fort Johnson. In the approaches to it, or while being secured alongside, *Hunley* came to grief.

Her horizontal rudder was accidentally set to dive while her hatches were open. Lieutenant Payne immediately escaped though Charles Hasker, another Englishman and recent immigrant, was trapped when the forward hatch shut on the calf of one of his legs. Taken down 42ft to the bottom, Hasker showed extraordinary cool. He waited calmly until *Hunley* was full of water, so the pressure inside and outside the boat equalised, then lifted the hatch off his leg and swam to the surface. Two other men managed to escape through *Hunley*'s aft hatch, but five were drowned. She was raised on 14 September, after which the grim business of removing decomposing corpses began, with half a box of soap and scrubbing brushes procured for the purpose of making *Hunley* clean.

McClintock had taken *Hunley* out on several occasions and believed the fault was not with the vessel but rather her crew suffering from 'want of sufficient knowledge'.[2] Hunley himself decided to restore confidence by going out on 15 October with a new crew, to make a practice attack against a Confederate vessel. *Hunley* dived and didn't come up, having buried herself nose first in the thick sticky mud of the Cooper River. At Confederate military headquarters, the Journal of Operations noted sombrely: 'As soon as she sunk air bubbles were seen to rise to the surface of the water, and from this fact it is supposed the hole in the top of the boat by which the men entered was not properly shut. It was impossible at the time to make any effort to rescue the unfortunate men, as the water was some 9 fathoms deep.'[3]

Everybody aboard was killed and when *Hunley* was recovered the sights within were 'indescribably ghastly' according to one senior Confederate officer. The crew lay contorted 'into all kinds of horrible attitudes' and clutched candles, presumably to try and see where the hatches were (an error as it only consumed oxygen more swiftly). Their faces were blackened and 'presented the expression of their despair and agony'.[4]

Hunley was found slumped under the forward hatch, as if he had been trying to open it, a hopeless task due to exterior water pressure. Once the corpses were removed, a group of slaves was brought in with brushes, buckets of hot water, soap and also lime to once again give *Hunley*'s insides a good scrubbing.

A fresh Commanding Officer was appointed, Lieutenant George Dixon, a former steamboat captain now of the 21st Alabama Infantry. He could not have been reassured by the nicknames given to his new command, including 'The Murdering Machine' and 'The Peripatetic Coffin'.

Alexander was made second in command of *Hunley*, her two officers resolving to raise a new crew and take the craft into action as soon as possible. Visiting the floating barracks *Indian Chief*, Dixon and Alexander were obliged not to hide the grim facts of *Hunley*'s record but volunteers still stepped forward.

7   First Kill

The North's commanders were well aware of the *Hunley* threat thanks to information provided by Confederate deserters. From aboard his steam flagship USS *Philadelphia*, Rear Admiral John Dahlgren, commander of the South Atlantic Blockading Squadron, issued orders for 'defensive measures against Confederate torpedo boats'.[1] He decreed that netting should be weighted down with shot and dropped over the sides of vessels. Lookouts must be vigilant at all times, with ships' guns loaded with canister shot and ready to fire. Calcium lights were to be made available for illuminating surrounding waters. Dahlgren instructed: 'It is also advisable not to anchor in the deepest part of the channel, for by not leaving much space between the bottom of the vessel and the bottom of the channel it will be impossible for the diving torpedo [*sic*] to operate except on the sides . . .' Dahlgren added that keeping to shallower water would mean 'less difficulty in raising a vessel if sunk'.[2]

Meanwhile, on the other side Dixon and Alexander had been working hard, each afternoon setting out for a seven-mile hike along the shore heading for *Hunley*'s base at Battery Marshall. This, according to Alexander, 'exposed us to fire, but it was the best walking'.[3] After a few hours of practice with *Hunley* in safe waters, the two officers would head off to lie on the beach, using a compass to take bearings on Federal warships as they went to their night anchorages.

Taking *Hunley* out as often as possible after dark – an average of four times a week between November 1863 and late January 1864 – they tried to make attacks, but each time were defeated by the prevailing wind and sea conditions. On one occasion, when testing *Hunley*'s submerged endurance by putting her on the bottom – watched by dozens of curious Confederate soldiers lounging on the shore – the remarkable time of two hours 35 minutes was clocked up. Candles were burned as an indicator of oxygen – or lack of it – inside *Hunley*'s hull and they had gone out just 25 minutes after diving. Despite this, not one of *Hunley*'s men wanted to admit he was struggling. The rule was that the craft would not surface until all nine men aboard agreed, each in turn gasping: 'Up!'[4]

Finally, unanimity about the need to surface was achieved. After clearing seaweed clogging the ballast tank pump the boat ascended and the hatches were opened. 'Fresh air! What an experience!' exclaimed Lt Alexander, who was first onto *Hunley*'s hull. 'It was now quite dark, with one solitary soldier gazing on the spot where he had [last] seen the boat until he saw me standing on the hatch coming [*sic*], calling to him to stand by to take the line.' The soldier shouted back that *Hunley* and her crew 'had been given up for lost'.[5]

While Lt Dixon commanded *Hunley* when she finally went into action against the enemy on the night of 17 February 1864 – the wind was favourable and sea conditions much improved – Alexander was not his second in command. He had been ordered away to Mobile to build 'a breech loading repeating gun' and felt it 'a terrible blow'.

It fell to Captain Joseph Green, Commanding Officer of the steam sloop USS *Canandaigua*, off Charleston, to convey the momentous news to Navy Secretary Gideon Welles.

'SIR: I have respectfully to report that a boat belonging to the *Housatonic* reached this ship last night at about 9:20, giving me information that that [*sic*] vessel had been sunk at 8:45 p.m., by a rebel torpedo craft.'[6]

Canandaigua slipped her cable and headed for the *Housatonic*'s anchorage, arriving a quarter of an hour later. Green discovered *Housatonic* sunk on an even keel with her hammock nettings – the place just above the upper deck where sailors placed their hammocks to air – actually below water. Two of *Housatonic*'s boats had been launched and were packed with survivors. *Canandaigua* lowered her own boats, rescuing 21 officers and 129 men but four of *Housatonic*'s crew were missing and feared drowned (a junior officer and three sailors). Green found *Housatonic*'s Commanding Officer, Capt. Charles Pickering, 'very much, but not dangerously, bruised, and one [other] man is slightly bruised'.[7]

Pickering was so shocked by the manner in which his ship had been lost that he was quite unable to make a report.

It was *Housatonic*'s second in command, Lt F.J. Higginson, who drafted an account of how the sloop was sunk. '. . . the officer of the deck, Acting Master J.K. Crosby, discovered something in the water about 100 yards from and moving toward the ship,' revealed Higginson. 'It had the appearance of a plank moving in the water. It came directly toward the ship, the time from when it was first seen till it was close alongside being about two minutes.'[8] Crosby thought it looked 'like a porpoise, coming to the surface to blow . . .'⁹ The upper deck sentries discharged their weapons at the object, which appeared to be emitting a faint light.

Both Higginson and Capt. Pickering rushed on deck and fired their small arms – in the captain's case a double-barrelled shotgun loaded with buckshot. Ensign Charles Craven leaned over the side to fire his revolver at the attacker, another futile gesture.

Pickering ordered the ship to get underway, as steam pressure was always maintained to ensure *Housatonic* was ready to move at any moment. 'During this time the [anchor] chain was slipped, [steam] engine backed [taking the ship astern] and all hands called to quarters,' Lt Higginson reported. 'The torpedo struck the ship forward of the mizzenmast, on the starboard side, in a line with the magazine. Having the after pivot gun pivoted to port we were unable to bring a gun to bear upon her. About one minute after she was close alongside the explosion took place, the ship [which had managed at most four turns of the screw] sinking stern first and heeling to port as she sank. Most of the crew saved themselves by going into the rigging, while a boat was dispatched to the *Canandaigua*.'¹⁰

Prior to the explosion the attacker had stopped, presumably placing the spar torpedo against the *Housatonic*'s hull, then backed off. The spar had a hinge so that it could be tilted and poked under the target vessel, leaving the charge below the waterline. Its barbs stuck into the wood enabling it to remain in place while the boat withdrew. Once the charge detached itself from the spar and was hooked into *Housatonic*, a detonator cable most likely unspooled between it and *Hunley*.

The plan was for Dixon to set the charge off when *Hunley* was out of the blast zone. While there was 150ft of cable, it is suspected there was a problem and *Hunley* failed to get far enough away before the explosion.

Recent research has suggested the charge – containing 135lb of explosive – may not actually have detached and *Hunley* was only 20ft away from *Housatonic* when detonation occurred.¹¹

Bearing in mind the casualty rate she had previously racked up when venturing to submerge, there are those who suggest *Hunley*'s attack was made on the surface, using cover of darkness as best defence.

In the view of one historian this 'in no way robs *Hunley* of title to the first wartime sinking by a submarine',¹² for in years to come surface attack would be the favoured method of attack for submersible craft.

It has been speculated that Dixon commanded the entire mission with his head and shoulders poking out of the fore hatch, with a candle lit so he could see the compass. This may have been the light the men of *Housatonic* saw. Alternatively, *Hunley* dipped under for part of the attack. One of *Housatonic*'s men, looking over the side of his ship, had noticed only 'a tide ripple on the water'.[13] Or maybe only Dixon's viewing ports were above the water with the hatch tight shut. Capt. Pickering saw something 'shaped like a large whale boat, about two feet, more or less under the water'.[14] A definitive answer is not available as none of *Hunley*'s men survived. The loss of yet another crew brought the total number of lives claimed by 'the murdering machine' to twenty-one.

Rear Admiral Dahlgren was sorely embarrassed by the Confederate success but mightily relieved it was not worse, reporting to Gideon Welles by letter on 19 February: 'Happily the loss of life was small.'[15] In terms of casualties *Hunley*'s attack may have achieved minor impact, but as the herald of a new form of warfare it was epoch-making.

The psychological and tactical effects of *Hunley*'s successful foray against *Housatonic*, and the exploits of other Confederate submersibles, were significant if not strategically decisive. A state of fear was experienced in the South Atlantic Blockading Squadron, which found the constant vigilance wearing. Its ships were forced to withdraw out to sea at night, so opening up the possibility of Confederate vessels slipping through to, or out of, Charleston. The *Hunley* attack had achieved its aim.

What exactly happened to *Hunley* would remain unclear for 131 years.

After the war the famous showman P.T. Barnum offered $100,000 to anyone who could find *Hunley* but it wasn't until 1995 that an expedition funded and led by the novelist Clive Cussler – using the latest sonar technology – located her. *Hunley* was just beyond Charleston Harbour, covered by sand and silt. This showed that the explosion had not immediately sunk her, for the wreck was some distance from where *Housatonic* went down. It has been suggested that the torpedo explosion compromised *Hunley*'s watertight integrity and she was ultimately overwhelmed as she headed for home.

In August 2000, a Remotely Operated Vehicle (ROV) skimmed low over the wreck and *Hunley* was revealed to the world for the first time since 1864, with both hatches tight shut. She was soon recovered and is now undergoing a careful process of investigation and preservation. The crew's remains were removed in 2001.

One telling piece of evidence suggests the blast impact from the *Housatonic* attack was severe enough to have potentially buckled her hull plates and let in water. An 18-carat gold pocket watch made in Liverpool for Lt Dixon was found, which may have stopped due to shock at the same time as the explosion. There is no way of telling if its hands are permanently frozen at 8.23 in the morning or at night (in other words, whether or not it stopped prior to the attack or during it).

However death came, the remains of the crewmen were found at their action stations, rather than tumbled together underneath the hatches. This suggests they calmly met their ends rather than fighting to escape.

8 Captain Nemo's Monster

In the wake of the *Housatonic* sinking the US Navy was flooded with proposals for submarines and newspapers around the world regaled their readers with stories of strange undersea machines.

Firing the public's imagination in 1869 was the latest work by French novelist Jules Verne. The sensational *Twenty Thousand Leagues Under the Sea* told the story of messianic genius Captain Nemo and his revolutionary submarine *Nautilus*, which sought to liberate the oceans from the tyranny of surface navies.

Nemo's cigar-shaped *Nautilus* was 232ft long, with a beam of 26ft, a displacement of 1,500 tons dived, an interior pressure hull and an exterior casing, a craft very similar to nuclear-powered submarines of the twentieth century's Cold War. Possessing electric engines of massive power, Nemo's boat had pump jet propulsion and destroyed surface vessels by ramming them.

In the novel *Nautilus* completes a circumnavigation of the world under the sea, very similar to the enterprises of the 1950s and 1960s. As a result, latterly Verne has been lauded for predicting the pure submarine of the atomic age. One character tells Nemo during a discussion aboard *Nautilus*: 'It is true . . . your boat is at least a century before its time, perhaps an era.'[1] Yet, while he was startlingly futuristic, Verne was drawing on the dreams and inventions of everyone from William Bourne right down to the pioneers of the nineteenth century. '. . . moderns are not more advanced than the ancients,' Nemo admits at one point.[2]

Verne's submarine not only bears more than a passing resemblance to Fulton's craft – sharing the same name – but it also sounds similar to the creations of de Villeroi (the novelist's alleged former maths teacher and fellow citizen of Nantes).

The newspapers of the 1850s, 1860s and 1870s were full of stories about submarines and their potential for inflicting massive devastation and Verne must have kept track of developments during the American Civil War. *Hunley*'s achievement was the closest in reality to his fictional submarine's form of attack. The steam frigate sent to hunt Nemo's 'monster' is even named *Abraham Lincoln* while Verne may have based Nemo's philosophy on the more revolutionary propositions of Fulton (who made no secret of his ideas for violent action to liberate global trade).

The messianic inclinations of the real submarine inventors – outsiders whose ideas deeply alarmed the naval establishment – more often than not aroused alarm and fearful contempt. They were, after all, daring to propose a radically new vessel that threatened to undermine the whole basis of sea warfare.

The admirals might stoop to using the submarine out of desperate necessity, as both sides had tried to do during the Civil War, but it would not be their first choice of weapon.

They loathed it, for should the submarine prove reliable and lethally effective – against people other than its own operators – the magnificent surface fleets of the world might be instantly rendered dinosaurs.

Verne's Captain Nemo is a genius, but also criminally insane, a label certain naval officers possibly applied to the real-life submarine inventors. They were, above all, decidedly *not officers and gentlemen*. Like the brave pioneers of submarining, Jules Verne was big on ambition – painting fantastical propositions in print. Unlike the submarine inventors he never risked his life or fortune actually trying to build and voyage in a submarine. Nor was he left penniless, like Drebbel or Bauer. Verne earned a substantial fortune from his tale of Nemo and his submarine. He does, though, owe a great debt to real-life submarine pioneers.

The submarine torpedo, with the exception of *Hunley*'s attack on *Housatonic*, had stubbornly refused to claim victims in combat. During the American Civil War, Rear Admiral David Farragut declared the use of torpedoes 'unworthy of a chivalrous nation'.

At the Battle of Mobile Bay in August 1864, legend has it that Farragut showed his contempt by bellowing the order: 'Damn the torpedoes, full speed ahead!'[3] Whether he said that precisely is open to question, but it is a phrase that has passed into the English language.

The torpedoes Farragut was defying were still of the non-self-propelled variety. Whether floating free, screwed into an enemy vessel's hull or on the end of a spar, such explosive charges remained difficult weapons for a submarine to use effectively (or at least without risking its own destruction).

It fell to an Englishman named Robert Whitehead to create the most successful and popular solution, though he was not the only one going down the self-propelled torpedo route. His competitors included a German who served the Confederate cause during the Civil War. Victor von Scheliha's weapon attracted Russian attention but in the end he failed to find backers for his offering and was financially ruined. There was also the Irish-born Australian Louis Brennan, who sold self-propelled, wire-guided torpedoes to the Corps of Royal Engineers of the British Army. This organisation would create a chain of complex coastal installations for launching Brennan's torpedoes against anyone attempting to assault key British ports. An American naval officer, Lt Cdr J.A. Howell, also came up with a similar weapon that could be launched from warships.

In terms of engineering simplicity and reliability – combined with business acumen – nobody could beat Robert Whitehead, not even the aptly named Louis Schwartzkopff of Berlin, who acquired the Englishman's design while working as a machinist for him. Schwartzkopff's product turned out to be too expensive and not so efficient. It was Whitehead's self-propelled torpedo that became the standard that all rivals had to beat if they wanted to sell them in the same quantities to the world's navies.

Whitehead was born at Bolton in the industrialised north-west of England in January 1823. A grammar school boy, by the age of 14 he was an apprentice engineer and attended the Mechanics Institute in Manchester. After working in France during the mid-1840s, Whitehead moved to Milan in northern Italy, at the time under Austrian rule.

In the 1860s Whitehead established a works on the shores of the Adriatic, at Fiume, and carried out engineering projects for the Austro-Hungarian Navy. The basis for his success was a 'locomotive torpedo' designed by Austrian naval officer Giovanni de Luppis. To his flawed proposal Whitehead applied solid engineering and scientific skills, making it function properly. He used compressed air propulsion and (at the suggestion of an Austrian colleague) brought in an invention called the gyroscope. This, along with other tweaks, gave the new weapon the ability to keep an intended course and depth. Whitehead dubbed his new weapon an 'automobile device'.[4]

Whitehead's first torpedo possessed a warhead containing 18lb of explosives. The compressed air propulsion took it swiftly to target and the gyroscope/depth-keeping arrangement ensured it struck below the waterline. The Whitehead torpedo was aimed by pointing the launch vessel at the target. Within two years the English engineer had developed both 14-inch and 16-inch diameter weapons that could reach 7 knots and had a range of 700 yards. The British Admiralty was offered exclusive rights to this revolutionary weapon, Whitehead hoping the navy with potentially the most to lose would pay the highest price to acquire it.

The British admirals were, however, too frightened to see beyond their prejudices – the sheer impudence of the self-propelled torpedo outraged them. While their battle fleet had been developed over centuries, Whitehead's weapon meant an enemy with no comparable tradition could build a flotilla of small torpedo-carrying craft. These could, potentially, destroy a much more powerful navy (or at least inflict decisive damage).

By turning down Whitehead's offer of exclusivity, the British guaranteed he would go elsewhere and that his weapons' usage would spread. Limited rights to use the Whitehead torpedo were sold to the Austrians and they embarked on a programme of development. It was not energetic, as they didn't have much money to spare after a coffer-draining war with Prussia.

Following a further demonstration, in 1870, the Admiralty relented and decided to also invest in limited rights. A year later 16-inch torpedoes were being produced at the Royal Ordnance Factory in Woolwich, with a works established by Whitehead at Portland in Dorset.

Meanwhile, Fiume turned out self-propelled torpedoes for numerous clients and for a time they were simply known as 'Whiteheads'. There was, though, no point in having a Whitehead without the means of launching it. Cradles, which could be lowered over the side of surface craft, were devised. Once the torpedo was in the water its propulsion was started and the weapon released. Small, fast surface ships armed with self-propelled torpedoes were built and, in some cases, even carried by battleships. The torpedo cradles were awkward to use and so a launch tube was devised. The first vessel to be fitted with one was HMS *Lightning*, which was built by John Thornycroft at his Chiswick yard on the Thames and launched in 1876. *Lightning* was 84ft long, could reach 19 knots and by 1879 was capable of firing a torpedo from a bow-mounted tube. She could also drop one from a stern cradle. As a purely experimental vessel, *Lightning* never saw action and would be sent to the breakers before the end of the century.

When it came to using Whiteheads successfully in combat that distinction fell to the Russians, though the Royal Navy came close to pulling it off a little earlier. In May 1877, the ironclad frigate HMS *Shah* launched a torpedo, probably using a cradle, at a Peruvian rebel gunboat called *Huascar*. She had been taking coal from British merchant ships to feed her own boilers and this warranted a response from the RN. The *Shah*'s shot missed, but just over two years later *Huascar* herself launched a torpedo – of a type designed by the American inventor John Louis Lay, which was less reliable than Whitehead's – against a Chilean warship. This weapon swiftly reversed course and seemed likely to hit *Huascar*. It was allegedly diverted away by a brave Peruvian officer plunging into the water and shoving it.[5]

The Russians fired several Whitehead torpedoes against Turkish vessels in the late 1870s. They scored the first ever sinking using one in January 1878, claiming a Turkish steamer in Batoum harbour, drowning 23 of those aboard. Another Whitehead torpedo, captured by the Turks in a battered but functioning state, was sent to the Fiume factory with a cheeky note asking for repairs so it could be used against its original owners. The Fiume works was happy to assist whoever needed its weaponry.

More success followed in the Chilean Civil War of the 1890s when the British-built ironclad warship *Blanco Encalada* was the first ever warship sunk by a self-propelled torpedo.

By 1892 a torpedo boat race was underway between the leading powers, in parallel with a battleship construction competition. Britain had 186 torpedo boats, while Germany possessed 143. France commissioned 220 and Russia 152. While proliferating and used in anger by surface craft around the world, the self-propelled torpedo had yet to be launched by a submarine. An Englishman who possessed a genius for mechanical invention addressed that problem and others.

9 I Shall Rise Again

This was an era in which men of religion saw nothing wrong in attempting to achieve fame and fortune through the creation of war vessels.

One such was the Reverend George Garrett of Liverpool, who launched two submarines that were the product of solo endeavour.

Born in July 1852, at Lambeth in London, within sight (and smell) of the Thames, one of five sons of an Irish clergyman, he spent some of his boyhood in Cornwall and Lancashire, attending Manchester Grammar School. A very bright lad, his prodigious scientific talent began to stand out from an early age. He studied at the Kensington Museum, a renowned centre for scientific research and experimentation, and was a graduate of Trinity College, Dublin. Garrett was imbued with a particularly robust form of muscular Christianity, for he was a pugilist, giving boxing lessons in the back yards of public houses. In the 1870s, while still only in his early twenties, he was appointed headmaster of a school in trouble-torn Ireland. The threat to his students from Fenian groups was so serious the children had to be escorted to and from school under armed guard. For further protection, Garrett devised a close-quarters fighting weapon by inserting a steel plate into the mortarboards worn by his teachers. This was clearly a man with a talent for lethal invention.

Later, after settling down into the humdrum existence of a curate in his father's parish at Moss Side in Manchester, it was the exploits of a Russian naval officer that fired up young Garrett. In the summer of 1877 Lieutenant Zinovi Rozhdestvensky commanded a pair of small attack craft in action against Turkish warships on the Danube. Anti-torpedo nets, through which his craft thrust their spar torpedoes to no avail, frustrated Rozhdestvensky's bid for glory. They could not make contact with the hulls of the enemy, coming away merely with their own bows crumpled. Garrett read of this engagement in the newspapers and wondered if it might be better for maritime assailants to dodge under the nets.

Following on from earlier experimentation with diving apparatus to enable a man to carry out such a task, Garrett decided on a submarine craft carrying a torpedo. His first vessel was nicknamed *The Curate's Egg*, in reference to the shape and her creator's then occupation. It was a simple design, just 14ft long, with a displacement of four tons, and was merely a test model for Garrett's second submarine, the optimistically named *Resurgam*.[1] This was built at Birkenhead in the J.T. Cochran yard at the cost of £1,538, some of which Garrett is said to have obtained via Masonic connections.

To overcome the problem of fire in an enclosed space – especially risky in a dived craft – Garrett used a Lamm engine, which dispensed with fire in favour of superheated steam. The Lamm had been created to push streetcars up and down the hilly streets of San Francisco. It was also used successfully to propel trains of the newly established London Underground, for the Lamm utilised superheated water, which, when transferred into a boiler, created steam. Under pressure in Garrett's *Resurgam* it turned the submarine's screw. Innovative though it might have been, Garrett's creation was handicapped by a lack of war-fighting practicality. There were two major problems for any navy seeking to use such a submarine to respond in a timely fashion to hostile surface ship forays. Firstly, it took days to build up enough latent heat. Secondly, the propulsion system would run out of steam (literally) after a mere 20 miles. There again, submarines at this time were regarded – if they were entertained at all – as offering potential only for coastal defence. They wouldn't need to go very far, only requiring the range and submerged endurance to reach blockading enemy warships and scare them off. There was only so far that a vessel could get on man-powered propulsion and limited ability to replenish air while dived. Garrett was reaching beyond those limitations.

Ballasting for *Resurgam* was achieved by the familiar hand-operated plunger mechanism – pulled out to allow water into the tanks and pushed in to expel it. In *The Curate's Egg* attacking an enemy vessel would involve use of a Fulton-style torpedo, requiring it to get alongside a target. Somebody was then supposed to put their hands into leather gauntlets on the outside to affix the explosive charge to the enemy's hull. *Resurgam* was to be capable of unleashing a pair of Whitehead torpedoes carried in cradles on the exterior.

When it came to ensuring *Resurgam*'s crew did not suffocate, Garrett was able to draw on his time studying in Kensington, where he'd researched how to enable human beings to breathe in a con-fined environment, and also his more recent experiments with diving suits.

His Kensington work looked at making the dangerous occupation of mining safer, revealing obvious applications for preserving life inside a submarine. It would not be the last time parallels were drawn be-tween miners and submariners – both extremely risky occupations in enclosed spaces.

Garrett had invented a primitive carbon dioxide scrubber to purify air, which he called the Pneumatophore.[2] While he solved the idea of how to provide plentiful motive power and also enable his crew to breathe – at least for a limited period – his vessels found it difficult to stay down. *Resurgam* did not adjust buoyancy via tanks to dive or sur-face – from positive to negative and vice versa – but ran on the surface almost awash and drove herself under. Once she stopped moving she fulfilled the promise of her name due to innate buoyancy. Her hydro-planes were also inefficient and made it difficult to remain submerged even when under power.

While he was a ball of energetic innovation, Garrett sometimes lacked patience and did not always apply meticulous attention to detail, or pursue the most practical solutions. This would ultimately ruin his career as a submarine inventor, but in the short term he would become

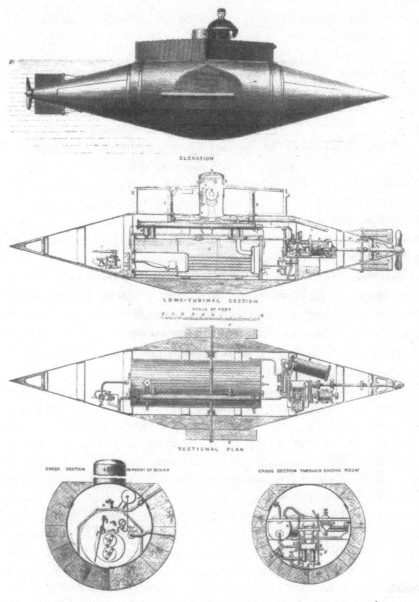

Elevations and plans of the Reverend George Garrett's *Resurgam* submarine boat c. 1879. (*Topham*)

successful on an international scale with the assistance of at least one very dubious character.

Asked to stage a demonstration for the Royal Navy at Portsmouth, in a typical display of bravado Garrett decided *Resurgam* should get there under her own power, rather than by canal or on a seagoing barge.

This was not going to be easy for the boat's interior was so filled with machinery there was barely enough room for the crew.

Another major difficulty was the heat produced, reaching a temperature of up to 37 degrees Celsius (98.6 degrees Fahrenheit). It was soon unbearable for mere human beings, so *Resurgam* usually cruised on the surface, with part of the hull and the squat conning tower showing, the hatch left open for ventilation.

Departing the Mersey on a misty night in December 1879, Garrett was *Resurgam*'s pilot, with assistance from a Master Mariner named Jackson and an engineer called George Price. *Resurgam* had to be buttoned up to prevent the craft from being swamped by water pouring down the hatch. In the dark, with visibility poor, Jackson failed to keep his bearings to get out of Liverpool Bay.

Fortunately a merchant ship was spotted, so Garrett took his craft alongside to ask for directions. The captain of this vessel was astonished to be hailed by a voice coming from somewhere very close by in the darkness. Perched on the sill of the open hatch, Garrett shouted that he was the commander of 'a submarine torpedo boat, and had been under his ship for two or three hours'.[3] Alarmed at the hazard posed by such a craft blundering about on a misty night, the captain tetchily provided a positional fix. He told Garrett that he and his crew were 'the three biggest fools he had ever met'.[4] Forced to seek refuge at Rhyl in North Wales after *Resurgam*'s propeller lost a blade, Garrett procured a steam yacht, intending to tow his craft the remainder of the way to Portsmouth.

After fitting a new propeller and making modifications to reduce the heat given off by the Lamm, Garrett and his companions departed Rhyl aboard *Resurgam* in February 1880. A storm blew up and, with the yacht already suffering her own engine trouble, things took a turn for the worse when *Resurgam*'s closed hatch began to let in water. Next, the hawser snapped and *Resurgam* disappeared below the surface of the

Irish Sea, but fortunately only after her occupants had been plucked to safety.

Garrett's boat did not rise again but she would be discovered in the mid-1990s after a trawler's nets repeatedly snagged on something not marked on any chart. A diver discovered the wreck of a strange spindle-shaped craft, lying only 54ft down. There are currently no schemes underway to raise and conserve *Resurgam*, due to the likely cost, but there is a facsimile of her at Birkenhead, close to where she was built.

Garrett's ill-fated adventures were notable enough to convince a Swedish engineer and arms trader that the former curate was onto something offering reasonable prospects for a profit. In return for putting money into, and placing his reputation behind, Garrett's submarine designs, Thorsten Nordenfelt insisted the next craft carried his name. The first Garrett-designed Nordenfelt boat emerged in 1881, under a contract to construct a submarine for the Greeks. The vessel didn't work very well, but it did provoke intense interest in their bitter foe Turkey, which decided it must match the development. Garrett became deeply involved in a project to construct Turkey's fledgling submarine force at Barrow-in-Furness and also in a shipyard at Chertsey on the Thames. These submarines were as useless as the one built for Greece.

That such vessels could be sold at all was down to the amazing ability of a master salesman – or confidence trickster, depending on your point of view – named Basil Zaharoff, who would win global notoriety as the so-called 'Merchant of Death'.

A man of arcane practices and devious double-dealing, Zaharoff was later blamed for playing a key part in the arms race that led to the First World War and also prolonging the conflict. Often depicted as a demon, a heartless, money-grubbing capitalist – even a real-life Count of Monte Cristo – Zaharoff's origins and identity shifted to suit his mercenary needs. Born around 1849, Zaharoff either entered the world at Odessa, in the deep south of Tsarist Russia, or Constantinople. As a young man in Constantinople, he allegedly worked as a tourist guide with dubious specialities, including leading clients to brothels. Fiercely intelligent, cunning and ruthless, Zaharoff entered the story of the submarine's evolution in the 1880s as a high-profile salesman for Maxim-Nordenfelt, the company that would soon be absorbed by Vickers.

A multilingual chameleon, he insinuated himself at the highest circles of commerce and society in Russia, Britain and France. He was knighted in Britain and secured a key role in the country's biggest manufacturer of arms, Vickers, Sons and Maxim (a direct result of his days selling submarines and machine guns).

Zaharoff had long been aware of the possibilities offered by hiding under the water. He had observed Constantinople pickpockets escape arrest by diving into the Bosphorus and swimming away while breathing through short pipes. Zaharoff assessed that a submarine boat could offer a stealthy means of approaching a target and striking with lethal effect before escaping.

To show off the revolutionary product he purveyed, Zaharoff had a large model submarine built, demonstrating its potential wherever he could find a conveniently located lake or pond, or even hotel swimming baths. It was Zaharoff who pioneered the system of selling the same weaponry to each side – playing one off against the other – persuading them to invest vast sums in an arms race of his own devising.

It was he who convinced the Greeks that with ownership of a Nordenfelt submarine they would gain enormous prestige and standing in the world. This was rather appealing to a nation only recently born out of a war of liberation with the Turks. Claiming to be a Greek patriot, Zaharoff suggested a submarine would allow Greece to get one up on its old foe. He even provided intelligence on the most vulnerable Ottoman ports to attack while offering the submarine at a reduced price. It was a Greek sprat to catch a Turkish mackerel, with the alarmed Ottomans placing their even bigger order. Even though it was a duffer, the Garrett-designed *Abdul Hamid* was the first ever submarine to launch a torpedo from a tube while submerged. Such was the warm glow created by this achievement that Garrett – who had travelled to Turkey to oversee the project – was made an officer in the service of the Sultan. He became Commander the Reverend George Garrett Bey, or Garrett Pasha for short, reaching the peak of his fame and fortune.

In 1887 Zaharoff pulled off another sales coup by selling a submarine to the Russians, despite their having no shortage of home-grown undersea warfare innovators. *Nordenfelt IV* was massive, at more than 120ft long, and was capable of up to 14 knots on the surface. There were claims of almost 20 knots, which meant she was theoretically able to outrun contemporary battleships. When dived this impressive-looking craft could, at best, reach 3 knots. Her propulsion again relied on super-heated water in the boiler generating steam pressure, something that, as with earlier Garrett boats, could only be managed for a short time. It took an entire day of sailing on the surface to store up enough latent energy for a submerged foray. *Nordenfelt IV* was an unlucky vessel, running aground on her delivery voyage to Kronstadt. She was so badly damaged the Russians refused to accept her.

This delivered a death blow to Garrett's submarine building career, terminating his partnership with Nordenfelt. He gave up on submarines altogether for a while, emigrating to the USA where he tried his hand at farming and failed. Attempting to revive his prospects as a submarine designer-engineer, Garrett found no takers.

After a short time as a sailor in the Customs Service, with the outbreak of the Spanish–American War in 1898 Garrett joined the US Army. Joining up as an engineer with the First New York Volunteers, he gained American citizenship but in both the Customs Service and the army was disciplined for drinking and other insubordination.

Service in tropical climes utterly debilitated him, making the tuberculosis he had contracted – and hid from army recruiters – much worse. Garrett's bronchial problems were undoubtedly exacerbated by all the fumes and heat he had suffered while voyaging in submarines. Sometimes when he fell into a restless fever Garrett would mumble about sultans and submarines. Worn out, he succumbed in February 1902 and was buried in a pauper's grave while Nordenfelt and Zaharoff became immensely rich and received honours from nations grateful for their, sometimes, flawed weaponry. Garrett would not be the last innovator to be used and abused, left to die in obscurity, struggling to make ends meet – a pawn of captains of industry and rascally arms dealers hungry for big profits.

Robert Whitehead and his son had also passed away by the early 1900s, with Vickers by then holding ownership of the Whitehead Torpedo Company. The long-derided submarine was, as the century turned, on the cusp of becoming a proper weapon system – a platform capable of launching self-propelled torpedoes into the guts of battleships. The arms trade sharks circled, sensing they could capitalise on the fear of not having a submarine then growing in navies and governments.

10 Fenian Ram

The Irishman who would become the father of the modern submarine – if anyone could lay claim to the title – would also fall victim to ruthless capitalism. In the process he would deliver the first truly effective, practical underwater vessel of war. After a long period of trial and error – and stiff competition from others – he produced a boat that became the template for a balanced, effective submarine design.

John Philip Holland was born in 1841 at Liscannor, on the unforgiving, storm-battered west coast of Ireland. It was a small settlement and Holland's father was employed as a coastguard, but following his death in 1853 the family left for a new life in nearby Limerick.

A staunch Roman Catholic, schooled by the Christian Brothers, on completing his education John Holland joined the order. With a keen interest in science and fascinated by the possibility of man taking flight, Brother Holland taught mechanics and applied mathematics, among other things. In his spare time he investigated the possibilities of voyaging below the waves.

By 1859 he had produced a submarine design, assisted by Brother James Burke, who had experimented with electrically detonated torpedoes and submarine propulsion. Their joint objective was perhaps, like so many other experimenters, to launch nefarious schemes against the British.

Chronically unable to control unruly scholars, Holland quit the Catholic Brothers and in 1873 followed his mother and brothers to the USA, settling in Boston.

Holland's first, canoe-shaped submersible was only 16ft long and pedal-powered. The sole crewman wore a diving helmet connected by hoses to onboard air tanks. Sending plans to the Navy Department in early 1875, Holland did not receive a positive reaction, a senior naval official dismissing his proposal as 'a fantastic scheme of a civilian landsman'.[1]

The local Fenians were more interested and Holland was persuaded to assist in their anti-British activities by building a diving boat to attack the Royal Navy.

Fenian development money enabled Holland to perfect his design drawings when not teaching at St John's Parochial School in Paterson, New Jersey. Constructed in a small engineering workshop, the 14ft-long, cigar-shaped vessel displaced just over two tons and was propelled by a petrol engine, something only recently invented. Even its modest output of 4hp was better than pedal power, or so Holland hoped.

Launched in May 1878, with a large crowd looking on, the craft splashed into the Passaic River and the story nearly ended there. In all the excitement someone forgot to seal the holes through which the screw shaft went. Water gushed in and all looked sure to be lost. One onlooker sneered that Holland had 'built a coffin for himself'.[2]

The Fenians still decided it was a scheme worth devoting further funds to and asked Holland to prepare a more advanced vessel. They

John Philip Holland in the conning tower of the submarine *Holland* (later USS *Holland*) c. 1898-9. (*Courtesy of the US Naval Institute, Annapolis, NHHC*)

planned to acquire a small merchant vessel that would be converted to carry the submersible. Once the mother ship was at anchor close to British warships the craft would emerge by an exit point under the waterline. The Fenians hoped one day to launch swarms of such craft against the Royal Navy. With a touch of wistful Irish subterfuge they called their project The Salt Water Enterprise.

Holland's next craft, launched in 1881, had a 17hp petrol engine that could push the 19-ton vessel at 9 mph (7.8 knots) on the surface and achieve 7 mph (6 knots) dived. Demonstrating that Holland had a care for the well-being of the proposed three-strong crew, it was even fitted with a water closet system. The submariners were to be sustained by the same compressed air supply that operated the ballast tanks and supplied the engine, with toxic fumes produced while submerged evacuated overboard through a flap valve. Air was consumed at a prodigious rate by the engine, limiting dived endurance severely and swiftly posing a threat to the crew.

For surface navigation Holland relied on scuttles in an elongated conning tower, but clear vision was only ever possible in calm conditions. Submerged, the craft proceeded blind, its pilot using intuition and guesswork. Much good fortune was needed not to wander disastrously and collide with another vessel, run onto rocks or hit mud.

To destroy the enemy Holland's boat relied on a so-called underwater cannon that used compressed air to launch a projectile. The centre-line launching tube had a breech inside the hull, via which the projectile would be loaded, and a bow cap outside the hull. Holland intended turning his ever-fertile mind to designing his own projectile but an offer of something suitable in 1883 was an appealing shortcut.

It was supplied by the Swedish-born John Ericsson, designer of the ironclad Monitor for the US Navy during the Civil War. At first relocating to England in the 1820s, Ericsson worked on many projects including steam locomotives and new designs of screw propellers. Emigrating to the USA in the 1830s, he played a key role in designing the US Navy's first screw ship and became an American citizen. During the Crimean War he scrutinised reports of sea battles between wooden warships and decided ironclads with most of their structure below the water could prove a winner.

He proposed a 'sub aquatic system of warfare'[3] and a decade later his proposal found favour with the USN, to counter the CSS Virginia.

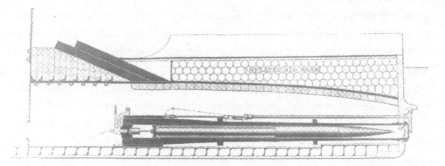

Longitudinal section of the bows of John Ericsson's *Destroyer*, showing the underwater gun and its projectile torpedo, c. 1881, and looking very much like the torpedo compartment of a submarine. (*NHHC*)

Ericsson later explored submarine warfare, constructed several more warships and even for a time conducted experiments with self-propelled torpedoes and solar power.

Keeping active until the very end of his life, the 80-year-old gladly loaned John Holland practice projectiles intended for his own new vessel, the *Destroyer*, a very fast semi-submersible craft. Ericsson's attempts at interesting the USN in *Destroyer* – which from certain angles resembled submarines developed during the First World War – had come to nothing. The futuristic Ericsson projectile – in appearance much like a present day supersonic missile – proved wayward. Successfully launched from the tube it had the unfortunate habit of breaking the surface and flying through the air. One of the projectiles achieved the remarkable altitude of 60ft before plunging back into the water and burrowing into the muddy bottom.

Holland resorted to a different type of projectile, which this time remained under the water and successfully carved a straight path at ranges up to 130ft. This was both good and bad, for while accurate, it was highly unlikely lookouts would not spot the approaching submarine boat prior to launch.

Holland recognised that details of his project would filter back to the British, who possessed a highly efficient global espionage network. This was made all the more likely by newspaper reporters constantly bothering him for details. He was, not surprisingly, reluctant to provide any, but the gentlemen of the press filled the information vacuum anyway.

A reporter for the *New York Sun*, aware of the vessel's connections to the cause of Irish Liberation, unhelpfully dubbed it *The Fenian Ram*.

Meanwhile, the Fenians, who had poured $6,000 into the first vessel and a further $15,000 into the second, were becoming impatient to unleash it. They grew tried of Holland's experimentation with *their* submarine and angry at his insistence on further exhaustive trials and tests. He urged them to be patient but some of the fiery Fenians hijacked the craft and sailed it away downriver. Although frustrated in their attempts to dive, they still caused widespread alarm among other water users.

The Fenians soon grounded the *Ram*, causing the authorities to officially declare it (and them) a menace to other maritime traffic. The *Ram* was beached permanently, with Holland deciding he'd sooner let his boat rot than give the Fenians any further assistance. Stranded with it was the likelihood of a Holland boat ever being commissioned as a proper war vessel. Or so it must have seemed at the time, even to the indefatigable John Holland.

Rather than the go-ahead United States, it was a European nation that was in submarine development pole position. Driven on by a fierce passion to beat *Les Rosbif* (the English), French inventors were also willing, like Fulton before them, to create new submarine boats on a speculative, privately funded basis in the hope of fame and fortune.

Inspired by Siméon Bourgeois with his *Le Plongeur* of the 1850s, the innovators of late nineteenth century France belonged to *La Jeune Ecole*, which did not signify their youth but rather an inclination to think in new ways. They depended on the patronage of sympathetic navy ministers and persevered despite fierce opposition from traditionalist admirals who remained loyal to battleships.

Goubet I was created by Claude Goubet and trialled by the French Navy in the late 1880s and early 1890s, proving that electrical drive could work. A battery that could hold a charge for a significant amount of time drove a propeller that swivelled to provide propulsive direction. A French physician named Gaston Planté had created the first battery that could be recharged in the late 1850s. Its utility in powering submarines was obvious – it could provide light and power without recourse to air, provided it could hold its charge long enough (and there was a means of recharging at hand).

Sold to the Brazilian Navy, *Goubet I* had paddles for the crew to use when working within hearing range of the enemy (for it was feared an electrical hum might betray its position). To enable penetration of anti-torpedo nets, *Goubet I* had a pair of net-cutting clippers on the end of a long pole.

Goubet II had a fixed propeller that pushed against a rudder whose position was altered to turn the vessel. Capable of not more than 5 knots on the surface, there was only enough battery power to sail for a mile. It was more of a toy than anything else and was sold to a Swiss entrepreneur. He used *Goubet II* to take tourists on pleasure trips both on and under Lake Geneva.

Distinguished naval architect Henri Dupuy de Lôme – who had earlier put steam propulsion in the wooden capital ship *Napoleon* and constructed the world's first ironclad battleship, *La Gloire* – by the 1880s was offering a submarine called *Gymnote*. He was also working on plans for submersible troop ships that would spew invading armies onto English shores.

Dupuy de Lôme promised an end to the supremacy of the battleship and the torpedo boat, in 1883 vowing that submarines would be capable of 'suppressing both of them'.[4] He also dabbled in airships and played a role in the creation of the Panama Canal, but died before construction of *Gymnote* got underway.

She was completed and improved under the direction of his good friend, and fellow naval architect, Gustave Zédé. Launched in 1888, the 58ft-long *Gymnote* had a dived displacement of more than 30 tonnes, and could manage over 7 knots on the surface and just over 4 knots dived.

At speeds of more than 6 knots she was very unstable, while firing projectiles from her two torpedo tubes with accuracy was somewhat problematic. *Gymnote* derived her electrical propulsion from 204 battery cells but was limited by being unable to recharge at sea and was obliged to return to port in order to do so. Despite this, French submarine designers felt there was no other small, feasible – and safe – power plant for use in the confined environs of such a craft at that time. They had rejected steam, while petrol engines posed a fire risk, produced poisonous fumes and consumed scarce air.

Initially lacking hydroplanes and relying on a rudder, *Gymnote* had a tendency to porpoise, hitting the bottom several times during the course of her career. The addition of hydroplanes amidships helped, enabling her to voyage below the surface at 6 knots in a level position, rather than with her bows angled down.

Gymnote was a stepping stone towards the larger *Gustave Zédé*, another electric boat, with a length of 159ft and a beam of 12ft. She was ordered in 1890 and originally was to be named *Silure*, but in 1891 Zédé was killed when a torpedo he was testing exploded. It seemed appropriate to rename the new craft in his honour.

Meanwhile, the *Narval* – the brainchild of Maxime Laubeuf – in 1896 won a submarine design and construction competition. *Narval* boasted ballast tanks sandwiched between a pressure hull and an outer hull. Achieving a good performance both dived and surfaced, she was commissioned into the French Navy in 1899.

With a maximum standard surface range of 100 nautical miles and ten nautical miles if dived, *Narval* was devised to sally forth from one of the French Navy's naval bases in Brittany. Going as fast as possible on the surface she would submerge when in sight of Plymouth, Portsmouth or the Thames estuary. *Narval* would then start sinking enemy merchant and naval shipping. It was claimed her dived range could be extended to 70 miles if travelling at 5 knots or 25 miles at 8 knots. Despite French misgivings she had steam propulsion for surface cruising, which was also used to top up the battery charge. *Narval* even had a periscope – a development of Fulton's model and by now an optical instrument enabling submarine captains to see where their boat was going and to both spot and attack the enemy. The earlier *Gymnote* had one too, while the Spanish had fitted periscopes to their experimental submarines in the 1880s.

By contrast, in addition to possessing no means of charging her battery at sea, *Gustave Zédé* lacked a periscope, so was forced to show her stubby conning tower to get a view of the target. *Narval* on the other hand could stay hidden at all times if need be.

Tactically, it was better to go fast on the surface at night using the cloak of darkness and then during the day stay dived and conserve battery power while searching out targets. The major problem with the combination of steam propulsion and battery was that, prior to diving, the oil-fired boiler had to be cooled down and steam dissipated. This could take as long as 21 minutes, during which time an enemy vessel might make an attack. To offset this fallibility, there were claims of 225 miles surfaced range at 12 knots without *Narval* needing to stop for coal. This was as good as any battleship of the time.

French Minister of Marine Edouard Lockroy desired up to a dozen *Narvals*, but in the end only one was built. Similarly only a single *Gustav Zédé* was constructed. While France would by 1914 have one of the world's largest submarine forces – 46 commissioned and 28 more being built – too many of them were experimental prototypes. Construction took so long that by the time they were commissioned other nations' submarines often outclassed them. There was too much focus on technical innovation and not enough on how such vessels could be used in waging war against France's enemies. There were squabbles between various factions and jealousies afflicted rival submarine inventors. As part of this multi-track, chaotic approach the French favoured externally mounted apparatuses for launching torpedoes, such as drop collars invented by Stefan Drzewiecki (a Pole who had worked for the Russians) or torpedo-launch frames.

They could not be reloaded while the vessel was deployed at sea and that, in the end, summed up the problem with French submarine development. Great strides were made in innovation but in terms of submarine warfare it was all rather too impractical.

In the 1880s and 1890s, submarine ideas had proliferated across Europe even if they did not always materialise into actual vessels.

For all the various efforts, the prospect of submarine flotillas ever being assembled in the world's navies to wage war still seemed as remote as ever. Submarines now used electric propulsion, but it didn't seem to get them very far. They had compressed air systems for ballasting – and even for moving them through the water. Some used a weight to alter the angle up or down while others had propellers on top of the hull to pull themselves up, or push themselves down, rather than hydroplanes. Others employed directional propellers rather than rudders. For armament they had the self-propelled torpedo, or some other projectile. This was sometimes fired from an internal centre line tube or mounted externally.

So far, so good, but it was all a case of *close, but no cigar . . .*[5]

It would be John Holland who came back from his Fenian troubles to ultimately achieve the remarkable feat of creating a vessel with the right balance. The ground-breaking submarines of John Holland were not technically the most innovative. They just achieved a better combination of the technology – with a higher level of operational practicality, for example – than the motley collection the French were creating.

Holland would experience more than a little trouble along the way and some stiff competition from a fellow American-based inventor inspired by *Twenty Thousand Leagues Under the Sea*.

11   Striking the Balance

Simon Lake, born at Pleasantville, New Jersey in September 1866, came from a family of inventors and entrepreneurs, responsible for, among other things, the roller blind and the establishment of Atlantic City as a holiday resort. Lake made his name inventing a canning machine and an oyster-dredge windlass, as well as other devices, but always dreamed of voyaging under the sea after reading Verne's novel.

In 1893, when the US Navy initiated its latest competition to design and construct a submarine for commissioning into its fleet, Lake seized the opportunity eagerly. Two previous competitions had been won by Holland, but due to business difficulties no prototype vessel emerged.

Lake's proposal ignored battery power in favour of steam while on the surface and compressed air propulsion after diving. It submerged while maintaining an even keel, rather than nose first. The chosen mode of transport was along the seabed on wheels.

For all the efforts of Lake and others taking part in the competition, Holland's determined ingenuity, sheer hard work and pragmatism remained a winning combination. The Irishman also had a track record in constructing submarines – and had even established the Holland Torpedo Boat Company – whereas Lake's proposal was on paper only.

Holland secured his win with a boat called the *Plunger*, but on realising it was a deeply flawed proposition – the navy had insisted on steam power and that made the boat slow to dive and like an oven inside – he substituted a better design. This was *Holland VI*, which was 54ft long, with a beam of more than 10ft, displacing 64 tons on the surface and

74 tons when submerged. She could dive safely to 100ft and was armed with a single torpedo tube and carried an 18-inch Whitehead.

Launched on 17 May 1897, this craft eventually entered service with the US Navy as USS *Holland*, becoming the basis for most submarine designs used in the opening years of the twentieth century and beyond.

Events in the Spanish–American War heightened the USN's enthusiasm for getting a submarine into service. The battleship USS *Maine* was sunk in Havana harbour on 15 February 1898, probably by a sea mine, with 250 of her 400 men losing their lives. A means of hitting back in similar fashion was thought essential after America declared war on Spain in April.

Following a series of sea trials in which *Holland VI* acquitted herself well, the Assistant Secretary of the Navy, Theodore Roosevelt, remarked: 'Sometimes she doesn't work perfectly, but often she does, and I don't think in the present emergency we can afford to let her slip.'[1] The conflict ended in December, too soon for the Holland boat to be used but she was commissioned into service on 12 October 1900.

Holland's design possessed efficient ballast tanks, together with hydroplanes for manoeuvring, a large rudder mounted behind the screw and, most crucial of all, electric propulsion that could be reliably recharged while the vessel was at sea – without resorting to cumbersome, impractical steam engines. What ultimately made the Holland boat more attractive than others – and an appealing proposition for several navies – was a combination of factors that are the basis for submarine operation to this day: a reliable means of propelling the vessel through the water, effective steering and an ability to descend and ascend at will.

Holland saw that using a large hydroplane aft would enable the vessel to dive under like a porpoise. He also introduced multiple ballast compartments so the boat's attitude and state of buoyancy could be altered to suit, ensuring the centre of gravity could remain stable.

The key to Holland's success was realising that the way to solve so many problems was to take both an internal combustion engine and battery to sea. It could be used to power the vessel while surfaced, at the same time charging the battery and providing energy for all the ancillary services, including creating more compressed air. All it needed was careful management underway. With a fully charged battery *Holland VI* could run for 30 nautical miles submerged. The use of highly inflammable petrol was a concern – a fire in such a small space while dived would be catastrophic – and poisonous fumes were a definite hazard.

Though it was Gaston Planté who created the world's first effective electric storage battery, it took John Philip Holland to prove that the combustion engine could be teamed with it to make the perfect propulsion partnership in a submarine. It would not be a Holland boat that grabbed global headlines by showing that a submerged craft could actually attack and even hit a surface vessel with self-propelled torpedoes. That honour fell to the endlessly experimental French.

It was an episode that sent a shock wave through the navies of the world, making a case for submarines that could not be ignored even by their most diehard opponents.

The modern, steam-powered, heavily armoured battleship *Jauréguiberry* was, with other capital vessels of the French fleet, processing majestically out of Ajaccio harbour in July 1901 when the jarring sound of a loud thud reverberated through her hull. A torpedo had struck the mighty castle at sea, below the waterline. Fortunately it carried a dummy warhead or the shame of being assailed by a mere submarine might have been profoundly worse, with both the ship and lives lost.

A British newspaper presciently noted of the incident: 'After every deduction has been made there is no disproving the fact that the submarine has proved its tremendous possibilities in warfare.'[2] The guilty party was the Toulon-based *Gustav Zédé*, displacing a mere 274 tonnes submerged, with a crew of less than twenty. She was armed with a single torpedo tube compared to the *Jauréguiberry*'s mighty 12,000 tonnes displacement, 600-strong complement and a dozen big guns. *Gustave Zédé* had delivered a serious jolt but still the battleship admirals and others favouring the naval status quo resisted the idea of the submarine as a serious proposition.

In Britain there had been a reluctant admission more than a year earlier by the First Lord of the Admiralty, Viscount Goschen, that the Royal Navy was weighing up submarine feasibility.

Around the same time Hugh Oakeley Arnold-Forster, the Parliamentary and Financial Secretary to the Admiralty, told MPs: 'The Power which possesses a really effective submarine boat, especially in the narrow waters of the Channel, will not be the inferior, but the superior Power . . .'[3]

Arnold-Forster later explained that the best answer to a submarine was another submarine, adding for good measure that 'this class of vessel cannot be regarded merely as the weapon of the weaker power'.[4]

With submarines in their navy, the French, who had been forced to acknowledge British mastery of the seas for almost a century, might not be so scared of the Royal Navy.

As France confirmed plans to construct a flotilla of submarines, across the Atlantic the US Navy had, in the shape of USS *Holland I*, managed to commission a boat potentially better than *Gustave Zédé*.

Meanwhile the Royal Navy had not a single submarine in commission but by April 1901 the British had ordered five Holland boats for a total cost of £175,000. Lord Selborne, who had succeeded Goschen as First Lord of the Admiralty, explained to MPs that they were an exploratory step. 'What the future value of these boats may be in naval warfare can only be a matter of conjecture, but experiments with these boats will assist the Admiralty in assessing their true value.'[5]

Vickers at Barrow-in-Furness was building the Hollands under licence while in the USA the Holland Torpedo Boat Company had entered into a partnership with the Electric Boat Company. That joint enterprise swiftly outgrew the father of the submarine and within a few years John Philip Holland would be estranged from the company. His former partners even contested ownership of Holland's designs and patents. He continued working on submarine projects and even devised a means of escaping from the craft if they sank. Holland was, though, a broken man and in 1914 caught pneumonia and died, aged 73.

HM Submarine *Holland No. 1*, an adaptation of the basic Holland design, would displace 122 tons submerged, with an overall length of 63 feet 10 inches. *No. 1* could manage a maximum of 8 knots on the surface and around 7 knots submerged; her endurance dived was limited by the volume of oxygen her hull could contain. The primitive periscope used a knuckle pivot on the outside of the hull, so it could be swung up rather than extended vertically from inside the boat. Its optics delivered a disorientating picture of the outside world – if looking astern everything was displayed upside down, on the beam vertically. Things were only the right way up if looking directly ahead. This was less than satisfactory, but some vision of the surface was better than none at all.

The first Commanding Officer of *No. 1*, or *Holland I*, was none other than the nephew of the Admiralty Secretary. Lieutenant Forster D. Arnold-Forster took up his command in August 1901, just two months before the vessel was launched. Yet the ambitious young officer did not feel much enthusiasm for submarines and it had seemed an unwise career move.

Tired of sitting around with nothing else much to do but practise his banjo, Lt Arnold-Forster had submitted an application for service in submarines. He would have much preferred life aboard a battle-ship in the Mediterranean but a command was a command and the extra money awarded to those who served in submarines was a real incentive.

The conditions of secrecy surrounding the project – even though it had been announced in Parliament – were such that Arnold-Forster was assigned to the submarine support ship HMS *Hazard* 'for Special Service'[6] rather than specifically to a new command.

On entering the yard at Barrow, he asked a few people where the submarine was being constructed. They had no idea what he was talking about. Eventually someone suggested he tried the mysterious 'Yacht Shed'. On first catching sight of *Holland I* Arnold-Forster was astonished by how small she was, 'like a very fat and stubby cigar'.[7]

The boss of the new submarine force was the enterprising, forward-thinking Captain Reginald Bacon, a torpedo expert. He had been delighted when his application to command the experimental flotilla resulted in the desired appointment but was under no illusions about the dim view of submarines (and those who sailed in them) embedded in the upper echelon of the RN.

Rear Admiral Arthur Wilson, while Controller of the Navy in the early 1900s, expressed his intention to 'announce that we intend to treat all submarines as pirate vessels in wartime and we'll hang the crews'.[8]

Such was the wish among many admirals to hold submarines at arm's length that Bacon was left to get on with things with little or no interference. Expanding and improving the submarine force would still require some powerful friends in the top tier of the navy.

Cometh the hour, cometh the man and a messiah for revolution in the Royal Navy was rising up through the ranks, exerting a decisive influence even before he took over command of naval forces in Portsmouth.

In 1903, during a speech at the Royal Academy Banquet, Admiral Sir John Fisher highlighted what he saw as the necessity for the navy to be open to any reform. He identified both 'the Submarine Boat and Wireless Telegraphy' as offering a revolution, once they were perfected. Fisher suggested: 'In their inception they were the weapons of the weak. Now they loom large as the weapons of the strong.' Yet Fisher still perceived submarines as coastal defence weapons and wondered if any fleet could survive in 'narrow waters'.[9]

12　Feelings of Humanity

There was one particular nation of growing economic and industrial importance – with an established reputation for martial might and aggression – which would soon set aside hostility towards submarines in favour of their development. This was Germany, with designs on establishing an overseas empire to rival Britain's, and so requiring naval power to match. Having established a unified navy as recently as 1871, Germany was by the early 1900s engaged in a competition to build bigger and better battleships than the Royal Navy's.

In the early 1890s Germany toyed with submarines, constructing a pair based on a Nordenfelt design but finding them unsatisfactory.

Towards the end of the same decade a submarine privately constructed at Kiel boasted electric propulsion and the by now usual multibladed propeller, together with stern hydroplanes and rudder.

Despite this the founder of the modern German fleet, Admiral Alfred von Tirpitz, was extremely worried that submarines represented a dead end. They might divert funds, raw materials and also shipyards away from the key area of effort – the construction of battleships. Such a digression would be unwelcome at a time of intense rivalry between Germany and Britain and, to a lesser extent, with France. Tirpitz gave this verdict when considering the worth (or otherwise) of submarines in 1901: 'We have no money to waste on experimental vessels.'¹ He suggested wealthier nations such as France and Britain should be left to squander their resources on submarines.

Within a few years even Tirpitz was persuaded that at least one *Unterseeboot* (Underseaboat, or U-boat) should be constructed for experimental reasons by the navy, in order to establish its potential.

Even without the distraction of submarines, the Germans were still finding it hard to keep up with the British, and new battleships and cruisers were outdated before they even entered the water. The crisis peaked in 1906, following the launch of *Dreadnought* at Portsmouth. Pre-dreadnought battleships of all nations, including Britain's, were rendered obsolete by this all-big-gun, steam turbine marvel. Everybody started from scratch, though the Royal Navy had the narrow head start of one. Was it, therefore, any accident the German Navy changed its mind about submarines in 1906? Tirpitz feared he might need a few in his back pocket to counter *Dreadnought*.

He was mindful of at least trying to keep up with developments in Britain where Admiral Fisher – the man who fathered the radical new British capital ship – drove submarine programmes along with equal energy.

By January 1910, when Fisher retired for the first time as First Sea Lord, the Royal Navy would have 61 operational boats, which were enhanced variants of the Holland type. The final craft in the A Class, *A13*, was 105 feet 6 inches long, with a beam of 12 feet 8 inches, plus a displacement of 190 tons (surfaced) and 205 tons submerged. Fitted with two 18-inch launch tubes, the A Class could carry four torpedoes. *A13* was notable for pioneering the submarine diesel engine in the Royal Navy, though petrol engines would be used for some years yet.

A recent invention, the diesel engine did not need an ignition spark to work and when cruising on the surface and expelling fumes, those produced by diesel were far less visible.

The inventor of the new engine, Rudolf Diesel, lost his life in mysterious circumstances in September 1913. On his way to discuss new arrangements to manufacture engines for submarines in Britain, the Franco-German inventor vanished from a ferry. His body was eventually located in the North Sea. Diesel, who suffered from depression and allegedly faced financial ruin, was assumed to have killed himself by jumping overboard. Claims he was murdered soon arose. The fact that the inventor's badly decomposed corpse was not actually retrieved from the sea fuelled suggestions of foul play.

The Royal Navy introduced B and C Class submarines – both with a beam of 13 feet 7 inches and 142ft long – offering a more substantial deck casing, which improved surface performance and enabled a bigger reserve of buoyancy. The C Class were the first submarines to be built with full deck casings, further increasing their surface performance but not their underwater speed, though an attempt was made to offset this with hydroplanes on the bows. Both B and C Class boats were fitted with a pair of hydroplanes on the forward edge of the conning tower to improve underwater handling. It was a first for the Royal Navy and an innovation not repeated until 50 years later, when reintroduced in American nuclear-powered attack submarines.

The 500-ton D class boats were the first British submarines intended for overseas operations. Nearly twice as large as their predecessors, they were proper ocean-going craft, could manage 15 knots top speed on the surface and proved most successful.

Aside from diesels, greater internal volume and a larger crew lightened the workload on long patrols, even if it put a further strain on the use of buckets for toilets. In that respect, since the Hollands, with their integral water closets, the Admiralty had regressed.

Using saddle tanks for the ballast increased internal space, while twin screws gave greater manoeuvrability. The Ds were also the first British submarines that could send and receive radio messages, though the extendable mast had to be rigged and taken down by hand before a boat could dive. This lengthy process risked greater exposure to the enemy.

D4 was the first submarine to be fitted with a gun. It was felt wise to have additional armament that enabled a submarine to stay within the Prize Laws, requiring merchant vessels to be warned so that passengers and crew could escape before the ship was sunk. Prize Regulations required submarine crews to fire a shot across the bows of any merchant ship they stopped. They would then have to send across a boarding party of sailors to search for contraband goods. Sinking a ship without warning – via torpedoes – was not permitted. If found to be carrying cargo for a foe, the ship's crew and any passengers were required to be taken into custody. If there were no sailors available to sail the captured vessel to a port only then would the ship be sunk.

By 1914 there would be 400 submarines in service with 16 navies.

Of Britain's 77 boats in commission, 25 possessed diesel engines and were capable of more than a coast-hugging role.

The Germans had 29 submarines ready for operations while a further 25 were being built. All had diesel engines and almost half Germany's U-boats could venture up to 5,000 miles from home, while they were capable of diving deeper than most other submarines.

The British at best only matched them, the majority of their craft being inferior to the Kaiser's. Britain's E Class boats did not have the range and endurance of the modern German submarines, although they were probably better fighting machines.

In response to suggestions from submariners, the hull of the first E Class boat (ordered in 1910) was enlarged to accommodate a pair of beam torpedo tubes, while retaining one in the bow and another in the stern. Rather than point a submarine's bows or stern at an enemy, the torpedoes would shoot out of the boat's sides. It was thought they would be more accurate at short ranges.

The French in their push for numbers and innovation had turned to Germany as the first decade of the twentieth century ended, seeking technology including MAN diesel engines, but it was suspected the Germans were deliberately tardy in delivering them. It was even claimed they omitted key features to ensure French submarines would not work as efficiently as they should.

Getting a full picture of the potential offered by the submarine was not easy when there had been no resolute demonstration of its power in war since 1864. That new moment of validation almost came during the First Balkan War of 1912–13 when the Greeks, along with their Serbian and Bulgarian neighbours, got together to kick the Ottomans out of the Balkans.

It fell to the submariners of the Hellenic Navy to wield a modern boat with determination and courage enough to sink an enemy vessel . . . almost. The French had supplied the Greeks with two submarines, with *Delfin* operating from the island of Tenedos in the approaches to the Dardanelles. On 9 December 1912, *Delfin*, under the command of Lieutenant Commander Stefanos Paparrigopoulos, spotted the Ottoman cruiser *Medjidieh* along with her escorting warships.

The 295-ton Greek submarine fired a Whitehead 18-inch torpedo when only 150ft from the target but, even with her assailant so close, the cruiser got away as the weapon malfunctioned. Instead of planting itself in the intended victim's bowels, the torpedo sank. Carried in an exterior cradle exposed to the sea it had lost buoyancy.

Meanwhile, in Britain the author of the futuristic novel *War of the Worlds* poured scorn on submarines. H.G. Wells declared them of not much use except for suffocating those unfortunate enough to voyage in them.

On the other side of the debate, another literary titan, Sir Arthur Conan Doyle, agreed with Admiral Fisher that submarines were revolutionary and that Britannia was best advised to have them in her armoury. Conan Doyle tolled the bell for greater vigilance against enemy submarines in a short story called 'Danger!', published in July 1914.

Despite the incredible growth in submarine numbers, they were still regarded as experimental by the broader naval community. That included the German naval high command, which used them as glorified picket boats, not exactly offensive, free-ranging predators of the seas. For safety's sake German submarines were meant never to operate beyond the vision and care of a mother ship and other escorts.

The idea that submarines might be used in a war on trade – to sever the vital artery of commerce that fed the beating heart of an enemy nation – was considered both beyond their capabilities and an outrage against the conventions of war. There were some, however, that suggested it was probable. Submarines armed with torpedoes could finally be used to destroy the hegemony of Britain's naval power and control of global trade. Among those who feared the advent of war against an entire nation via destruction of its vital maritime commerce was Admiral Sir Percy Scott. In the long hot summer of 1914 he wrote to *The Times* proposing that modern war required striking where an opponent was at his most vulnerable. In the case of Britain, sea trade was the obvious Achilles heel. 'Our most vulnerable point is our food and oil supply,' wrote Scott. 'The submarine has introduced a new method of attacking these supplies.' Most chillingly, he asked *Times* readers: 'Will feelings of humanity restrain our enemy from using it?'[2]

To the Admiralty such a prospect seemed unlikely and Scott's letter stirred up a storm. In any future war the Prize Regulations would bind submarines and due to their vulnerability while on the surface, and their small crews, they could not possibly perform this whole process.

Then there was the impracticality of submarines taking aboard captured merchant seamen or passengers and of escorting the prize vessel to port. The Germans at this stage agreed submarines could not be used against sea trade in an unrestricted fashion, though they might still be wielded aggressively against enemy warships. It was just such a mission that would make bloody history in waters off the British Isles.

PART TWO

BLOOD IN THE WATER

1914 to 1919

'Home is the sailor, home from the sea,
And the hunter home from the hill.'

'Requiem' by Robert Louis Stevenson

1 Jump you Devils!

Despite being blind in one eye, Aldous Huxley could not fail to notice the terrible moment on 5 September 1914 when the doors of perception crashed open on a terrifying new form of warfare. The 20-year-old future dystopian novelist was staying at Northfield House, near St Abbs on the edge of the Firth of Forth, and was out on a coastal walk. There was a terrific explosion out to sea and Huxley gazed in bemused wonder at a column of white smoke. Curious about what had happened, he went down to the shore, where he found the local lifeboat coming in with a terrible tale.

A ship had been destroyed and, according to the lifeboatmen, there was 'not a piece of wood . . . big enough to float a man – and over acres the sea was covered with fragments – human and otherwise'.[1]

A torpedo was suspected and Huxley thought a submarine or even a German trawler disguised as a British vessel might have launched it. The victim was HMS *Pathfinder*, patrolling about 15 miles off St Abb's Head. Capable of 25 knots, the 2,940-ton *Pathfinder* proceeded slowly on that fateful day; limited to 5 knots thanks to almost empty coal bunkers. The elderly cruiser was gate guard for the new purpose-built dockyard at Rosyth and her end came out of the blue. When destruction arrived, for a few seconds officers in the wardroom were mute and wide-eyed with astonishment. Tumbling crockery in the pantry shattering on the deck broke the spell.

The surest sign of the culprit was a white torpedo track dissipating on the surface of the sea. Within moments a sharp-eyed senior rating spotted a periscope about 1,300 yards away. He shouted the bearing of the incoming torpedo but at her slow speed *Pathfinder* had not enough head of steam to turn away. Desperate, contradictory orders were rung down to the engine room, asking for full astern on one prop and full ahead on the other. The seemingly nonsensical order was ignored, but it didn't matter, for within seconds there was an almighty explosion. The torpedo hit below the waterline, right under *Pathfinder*'s bridge and detonated ammunition in the forward magazine.

The force of the explosion vented across the sea was so powerful the crew of a trawler ten miles away felt it. In *Pathfinder* there was a terrific rumble below decks, the ship shuddering as bulkheads collapsed.

Such was the speed and scale of the catastrophe that the crew's limited skills at damage control were overcome. Lifeboats were smashed or jammed into their davits, rendering attempts to launch them pointless. There were very few lifejackets either, even though most Royal Navy sailors still disdained learning to swim.

In his cabin aft, having just left the bridge, the ship's Commanding Officer, 45-year-old Capt. Francis Leake, felt the cruiser's screws slowing down as the Officer of the Watch (OOW) issued his forlorn evasion order. As the ship 'gave a veritable stagger and tremble',[2] Leake leapt across the cabin and out into a passageway. Springing up a ladder, he pushed open a hatch and climbed onto the upper deck.

Leake found the forward end of the ship had been torn apart by explosions and was a mass of flame and smoke. He realised everybody in that section of the ship must be dead and *Pathfinder* was doomed. With more bulkheads crumpling, the cruiser sagged in the middle and tore in two like a wet toilet roll. The forward funnel tipped over and disappeared into a frothing sea. The front end of the cruiser stood on her bow, poised in the air at a 60-degree angle. On the aft part, with the water rushing up towards him, a rating heard an officer cry out: 'Abandon ship! Every man for himself!'

Pulling his boots off and casting aside his jacket, the rating jumped into the water. 'I think I broke all swimming records,' he recalled, 'trying to put as much space as possible between myself and the ship, being afraid of suction.'[3] Capt. Leake stayed with what remained of the ship until the very last moment. Perched on a searchlight stand, as the aft end of *Pathfinder* slid under, Leake called out to any men still aboard: 'Jump you devils, jump!'[4]

Pulling himself to the surface, Leake was astonished to find both parts of *Pathfinder* poking up out of the water, but 'she then fell over and disappeared'.[5]

There were very few of the crew in the water, for of *Pathfinder*'s 268 men 256 were lost. Just four minutes had elapsed between the explosion and her ends disappearing. On the surface of the sea was a scum of coal dust, sodden paperwork, fragments of furniture and body parts. Survivors clung to oars and other bits of woodwork while Capt. Leake clambered into a wooden meat locker. Bleeding profusely from a head wound, he lost consciousness. Leake was picked up by Torpedo Boat 26 and taken below decks, where he was stripped off so he could be revived with rum rubbed into his skin.

As *Pathfinder*'s destruction unfolded, the long, thin stalk of *U-21*'s periscope brazenly poked above the surface. Below in the conning tower 28-year-old Kapitänleutnant Otto Hersing watched intently. He was obliged by standing orders to ensure no further 'eels' (as the Germans referred to their torpedoes) were necessary. *Would the target still be an asset to the enemy and need further attention?* The answer was pretty obvious.

Hersing had discovered *Pathfinder* by default, for his submarine was actually sent to penetrate the defences of Rosyth to find much bigger quarry. British newspaper reports had given away that important units of the Royal Navy were using the Forth, so both *U-20* and *U-21* were sent to take a look. The former got as far as the Forth Bridge, but stayed on the seaward side. Had she gone further in, *U-20* would have found battlecruisers at anchor.

U-21 was just about to make a run up the Firth of Forth but caught sight of the British cruiser, so diverted to attack her instead.

In Britain it was solemnly noted that *Pathfinder* was 'the first victim of a submarine in the whole history of naval war'.[6] *Housatonic*'s loss at the hands of *Hunley* half a century earlier was not of the same order.

Over the next three years *U-21* would notch up a formidable record, sinking 40 warships and merchant vessels. But Hersing's defining contribution to the grim evolution of submarine warfare remained sinking the British cruiser. In Berlin the supreme warlord himself, Kaiser Wilhelm II, was ecstatic, declaring *Pathfinder*'s demise a 'ray of light'.[7]

In the wake of such a shocking debut, revenge would be a motivating factor in the early bloodletting by submarines of both sides. It was made particularly keen for the Germans by the deep fury they felt at Britain for going to war against them. They wanted to be respected and loved – even feared – by the British, whom they saw as a sister race. Yet Britain had come down on the side of the hated Slavs and French. It was an intervention that complicated what should have been a Continental conflict settled very quickly. It was Germany's rapid development of a navy that provoked British involvement. In the 1870s the Germans had no fleet worth worrying about but by 1914 they fielded a powerful maritime force seeking to rival the Royal Navy. Germany's ambition for overseas colonies and a greater share of world trade threatened British global security. A Germany allowed to dominate the Continent militarily could be sure to look for further expansion at sea and abroad, so Britain felt compelled to intervene.

German submariners were sent out into waters off the British Isles to exact a measure of retribution for that, but prior to *Pathfinder*'s destruction things had not gone well. One U-boat disappeared – it was thought after hitting a mine off the main Royal Navy base at Scapa Flow in the Orkney Islands. Elsewhere, *U-15* caught a trio of British battleships in her sights but missed with all her shots and on 9 August was herself sunk. Stuck on the surface, trying to resolve a defect in her machinery, despite fog she was spotted by the cruiser HMS *Birmingham* whose lookouts had already heard hammering. *U-15* tried to dive but one of *Birmingham*'s shells hit the submarine's conning tower, blowing apart an officer. Charging at ramming speed, *Birmingham* sliced through *U-15* just aft of the conning tower. For a brief moment both parts stayed afloat and then the U-boat and her entire crew went to the bottom. *U-15* was the first submarine sunk due to ramming by an enemy surface ship.

The subsequent sinking of HMS *Pathfinder* went some way to evening the score and in response the Royal Navy decided to set a thief to catch a thief. It assigned 15 C Class coastal submarines to the role of hunting and killing U-boats trespassing in British waters. As far as the head of the Submarine Service was concerned the most promising tactic was, however, not to lie in wait for the enemy but to provoke him in his home waters.

Such thinking was typical of Roger Keyes, who had replaced Stephen Hall as Inspecting Captain of Submarines in 1910, and was promoted to Commodore (Submarines) in 1912. Born in India, the 42-year-old Keyes was cast in the Edwardian gentleman adventurer mould. He joined the navy aged 13 in 1885 and took part in small boat actions against slavers on the east coast of Africa. Like other senior officers of the day he saw action ashore during the brushfire wars of Empire, not least at the turn of the century during the Boxer Rebellion in China. Keyes helped to lift the siege of the Legations at Peking. Described a little unfairly by one eminent historian as 'an officer of modest intelligence but immense dash and energy',[8] whereas his predecessors had been promoted from within the ranks of the flotilla, Keyes was an outsider with no service in submarines or technical knowledge specific to his new job. He was brought in to impose tighter integration with the surface navy. The prevailing doctrine was that submarines were an adjunct of the main battle fleet. They were meant to work with the battleships and do their bidding in both scouting and screening, rather than be a freebooting band maximising their submerged stealth as solo hunters.

Keyes was cut from the same risk-taking, non-conformist cloth as the men he commanded and was interested in improving the ability of British submarines to attack from under the sea. To the chagrin of domestic industry, he went overseas for better periscopes and diesel engines. He even bought in French and Italian submarine designs. The latter were not necessarily a success but procurement of French and German periscopes – soon copied and improved on by British firms – represented a huge step forward.

Rather than a fixed scope on the outside of the hull – elevated via a knuckle pivot, with the submarine porpoising to poke it above the waves or withdraw it – the new type could be extended and retracted mechanically from inside the submarine (which could now keep a steady depth).

When war came the best of Keyes's vessels – the D and E Class boats – were based at Harwich, north of the Thames estuary on the east coast of England. This made it easier for them to get at the Germans in the North Sea.

Less advanced British submarines were posted at various other points around the coast while Gibraltar, Malta and the China Station each had a trio of boats.

The older the boat, the less aggressive the task but the Ds and Es were defined as 'Overseas types'[9] and were expected to carry the war to the enemy in his own waters.

The B and C classes worked with surface warship flotillas in key areas off Britain, with special attention given to the Dover patrol. They aimed to shut the door on the narrowest part of the English Channel. Finally, there were elderly A Class submarines assigned to defending harbours. Supposedly under the aegis of the Grand Fleet – Britain's foremost bulwark against invasion – Keyes was meant to report directly to its commander, Admiral Sir John Jellicoe. None of this dampened Keyes's independent spirit and he was determined to boldly probe the Heligoland Bight, a stretch of water lying between the island of Heligoland – a very heavily fortified naval base from where U-boats operated – and the Jade estuary around which lay the primary German fleet bases. Keyes hoped to cause trouble and sink some valuable enemy units. When leading his boats out on a venture from Harwich, he did not command them from the cramped confines of a submarine, with restricted speed and vision, but from a racy surface warship. He had been awarded the use of two modern, high-speed destroyers, *Lurcher* and *Firedrake*, but controlling submarines at the scene of the action was a complex and tenuous business.

Due to limited wireless range other ships were used to relay communications between the Admiralty in London and Keyes aboard *Lurcher* (and vice versa). This might require *Firedrake* to sail within transmission range of the submarine depot ship at Harwich, which was in turn connected by telephone to the Admiralty in London. *Firedrake* would receive messages from the Admiralty via the depot ship then shoot off back out into the North Sea. Once within range of *Lurcher* she would pass on signals to Keyes.

In the meantime, he would be trying his best to marshal his submarines, giving instructions by wireless, semaphore flags or signal lights during those occasions when they were on the surface. For solo submarines out on the patrol lines – some not blessed with wireless – things were even more fraught with potential communication pitfalls. To send reports home they relied on messenger pigeons. If a submarine on picket duty spotted a German warship, or even a Zeppelin passing overhead, coded messages were to be carried ashore by the pigeons. Ship's mascots had been a feature of life aboard ship in the Royal Navy for centuries, and sometime the submariners looking after the pigeons loved their little feathered pals rather too much. These pampered creatures became overfed and lazy, refusing to leave the comfort of their submarine nest.

Often more than one bird would be released. If the boat was far out into the Heligoland Bight the pigeons might have to fly 140 miles, battling strong winds to reach home.

The message would be taken to the nearest Post Office and a telegram sent to the Admiralty in London, where it would be decrypted. The message would then be passed on, again in code, to the submarine force depot ship in Harwich. It would transmit it, using another code, to Keyes in *Lurcher* (possibly via *Firedrake*). He might then direct his submarines to attack the enemy (or avoid them).

Keyes and Cdre Reginald Tyrwhitt, commander of the Harwich Force – mainly composed of destroyers with a few cruisers – devised a cunning plan that would lead to the first major sea battle of the war, a confused engagement in the Heligoland Bight on 28 August 1914.

The original proposal was to blatantly place three submarines – *E6*, *E7* and *E8* – on the surface in a string close to Heligoland itself, in order to tempt the Germans out. Once the enemy had taken the bait, the Harwich Force would pounce. In seeking heavy-duty back-up – close enough to be readily available but out of sight over the horizon – Keyes and Tyrwhitt cheekily requested that the Grand Fleet make itself available.

When Keyes formally proposed the plan on 25 August he received a cool reception from the Naval Staff in the Admiralty. In a fit of anger he requested a meeting with the First Lord. As a maverick himself, Winston Churchill welcomed a bold plan forcefully put. Impressed that Keyes was determined to take the initiative, Churchill called a meeting the following day attended by Keyes, Tyrwhitt and the First Sea Lord, Admiral Louis Battenberg. The Admiralty assigned the battlecruisers HMS *New Zealand* and HMS *Invincible*, along with some elderly Bacchante Class cruisers.

The plan settled on was to trap German destroyers and cruisers north of Heligoland Island not long after daylight as they carried out the tricky manoeuvre of handing over to the next watch. While the main job of destruction was to be carried out by the British destroyers and cruisers, submarines would be arranged in two groups across the likely path of any major enemy ships coming out to assist embattled comrades.

Admiral Jellicoe subsequently offered to support the operation, for he regarded it as too risky without the entire Grand Fleet on hand.

Jellicoe assigned Admiral Sir David Beatty and three further battle-cruisers, together with a squadron of modern cruisers under Commodore William Goodenough, to provide close cover. Tyrwhitt only learned the big boys were going to provide massive cover after he had sailed, while Keyes knew nothing at all of the extra Grand Fleet support.

For the submarines misty conditions were not good news. They might have no warning of approaching German vessels until they were almost upon them. Calm seas also meant periscope wakes could be easily spotted.

Keyes in *Lurcher* mistook two of Goodenough's extra cruisers for German ships, sending a signal to *Invincible* saying he intended shadowing enemy vessels. Goodenough intercepted this and went to Keyes' assistance with his other four ships.

When Keyes saw them coming up fast he thought they were German reinforcements. Tyrwhitt, who had also been monitoring signals traffic, asked Goodenough to help Keyes assault the interlopers.

Goodenough was being asked to attack himself.

Fortunately, Keyes recognised Goodenough's flagship, *Southampton*, and sent a teeth-grinding signal that, in fact, his 'enemy' cruisers were British of 'whose presence in this area I was not informed'.[10]

Unfortunately, Keyes had no means of warning his dived submarines that unexpected British cruisers were about to cross their path, falling into the carefully prepared trap. A testy exchange of signals followed, in which Keyes admonished Goodenough for upsetting the plans. The cruiser force commander responded that he was following orders and was astonished Keyes had not been informed of his presence.

Submarine *E6*, thinking *Southampton* was German, launched a pair of torpedoes, which missed. Alarmed by the tracks and with her lookouts spotting a periscope, *Southampton* did her best to ram *E9*. The submarine only avoided destruction by going deeper, diving right under her assailant.

As more and more British and German ships piled into the subsequent scrap, the sheer weight of firepower the Royal Navy could summon up began to tell. Beatty's battlecruisers barged in, taking great chances in waters where the enemy could have laid minefields and U-boats might lie in wait.

The Germans had actually not yet sown mines off their main fleet bases for fear of catching their own capital ships and instead relied solely on the layered defence of patrolling destroyers, cruisers and U-boats.

This was something Keyes's scouting trips had discovered but the message had not been passed on to the Battle Cruiser Fleet (BCF). Beatty charged into action with *Lion*, leading the equally impressive and heavily armed *Princess Royal* and *Queen Mary*, with the Humber-based *Invincible* and *New Zealand* tacked on at the end. He did not know there were British submarines waiting that might well mistake his battlecruisers for the enemy. After assisting Goodenough's cruisers and Tyrwhitt's destroyers in laying about the Germans, Beatty's force withdrew on receiving a report of submarines in the area (which could have been British).

It might all have developed into a massive slugging match had it not unfolded at low water, when German capital ships could not get over the sandbars impeding exit from the main fleet anchorage in Jade Bay.

The Germans lost three light cruisers and a destroyer while the British suffered a damaged cruiser. More than 1,000 Germans were either killed or taken prisoner, while the Royal Navy got away comparatively lightly, with 75 casualties.

Called 'The Great Raid' by the British press, the Heligoland Bight battle had not given submarines much of a chance to show what they could do. They had tried to sink enemy destroyers and failed. Keyes was told off for recklessly leading his forces into battle aboard *Lurcher* and barred from doing it again. He complained bitterly, but to no avail, for the ban was confirmed by the First Sea Lord himself.

How exactly submarines ought to be used in combat was yet to be defined. The urge on both sides was still to tie them to whatever the surface fleet did. In the case of the Dover patrol this mindset had exposed a deep flaw in tactical thinking. Instead of being predators the British submarines were tethered goats, secured to buoys, awaiting intelligence of an approaching enemy. Other submarines patrolled around the area at slow speed accompanied by torpedo boats, hoping to catch the enemy out.

The day before the Heligoland foray a U-boat attacked the torpedo boat *Attentive* as the latter loitered in company with submarines. The torpedo missed, passing close by *Attentive*'s bows. Suitably alarmed, British submarines and surface ships headed for safe harbour but were ordered out again to hunt the enemy. Instructions were soon issued to stop the foolish practice of securing submarines to buoys in the Channel. Patrolling slowly in waters where U-boats might well be waiting was also forbidden.

For the Germans a much more serious aversion to risk took hold, but this would cause a tactical revolution. The Kaiser was appalled at the loss of three cruisers close to home during the Heligoland Bight battle, so banned sorties without his prior approval.

Tirpitz protested at 'this muzzling policy'.[11]

It would lead to a heavier reliance on U-boats, while the main battle fleet ventured out only under the most propitious conditions. Submarines now took the lead for Germany, going out to wage war against the British navy.

It fell to a remarkable British officer, operating close to German bases, to play a decisive role in the next round of submarine warfare. Lieutenant Commander Max Horton was aggressive and self-confident, something that did not always endear him to his peers. While he was willing to be daring, and was fond of gambling, the 30-year-old Horton was never reckless with his command.

Legend has it that Horton only became the first British submarine captain to sink an enemy warship due to the extreme flatulence of a man in his boat's crew. Having suffered from constipation due to poor diet, this officer took some laxative pills, but rather too many. As a result he evacuated his bowels several times, making life inside submarine E9 unbearable as she lay on the bottom to preserve battery power. Horton ordered the boat surfaced for a quick intake of fresh air and the expulsion of nasty odours. A few minutes later E9 dived, but with dawn coming Horton decided to stay at periscope depth. Shortly before 7.30 a.m. on 13 September, a cruiser – the slow, 19-year-old, 2,000-ton displacement Hela – hove into view. Two of E9's torpedoes were sent to greet her. Twenty-five seconds after the second tinfish powered out of its tube the dull sound of an explosion was heard inside E9. Rather than immediately take a look, Horton kept his boat down. He put the periscope up again 15 minutes later to find Hela mortally wounded with a severe list and destroyers gathering around to take off her crew. All but a dozen of the German ship's 200 men survived.

On the same patrol Horton also sank destroyer S116, on 6 October, in the southern North Sea. Horton and his crew would be awarded £1,050 for sinking *Hela* and £350 for *S116*, representing prize bounty 'at the rate of £5 per head of the crew on board the German vessels'.[12]

Horton gained fame for inaugurating the tradition of flying a piratical skull and crossbones flag from a boat's conning tower on returning from a mission, to indicate that an enemy ship, or ships, had been sunk.

2 Slaughter in Narrow Waters

Horton's valiant deeds provided a welcome boost for the national war effort at sea, for just over a week after he sank *Hela* a German boat inflicted terrible slaughter on the Royal Navy.

The foul deed fell upon the 7th Cruiser Squadron, composed of five Bacchante Class cruisers, which was very much a second-line force, and part of the RN's English east coast command. Around 20 years old, the Bacchantes were thoroughly obsolete and prior to the war had been consigned to reserve fleet status. Their main purpose was to work with destroyers and other patrol vessels safeguarding precious convoy routes across the Channel, particularly against minelaying vessels and torpedo boats.

The cruisers had settled into an unmolested routine, the repetition of which became a danger in itself, though a few people were alive to the complacency they represented. Roger Keyes suggested in late August that if the Germans sent out their modern cruisers the Bacchantes would be massacred. 'God help them,' he observed. Some criticised the idea of even using such elderly vessels in war, labelling the Bacchantes 'the live bait squadron'.[1]

Few anticipated that the threat would come from a submarine, at least not in waters where conditions were often very rough, supposedly making it impossible for the tiny craft to operate effectively.

In late September, bad weather saw the temporary withdrawal of the cruisers' escorting destroyers. As conditions started to improve, three of them continued patrolling off the coast of Holland at slow speed, to conserve coal, and without the precaution of zigzagging. This latter manoeuvre was meant to make the course of a surface warship unpredictable, but it consumed more fuel and in itself established a pattern that enemy submarines could use to time the firing of torpedoes.

The U-boat threat was still regarded as negligible in the English Channel but at daybreak on 22 September a torpedo slammed into *Aboukir*. Within 25 minutes she had rolled over, killing hundreds of her men and leaving the rest fighting for their lives in the cold sea. This already terrible event was made worse when *Cressy* and *Hogue* came to the rescue, making perfect targets.

U-9 had been surfaced 20 miles off the coast of Holland, using diesel engines to charge her battery while allowing fresh air in via open hatches. The boat's First Lieutenant, Johannes Spiess, saw masts coming over the horizon and called out the sighting to Kapitänleutnant Otto Weddigen, who was below having breakfast. The submarine dived and cut the distance, Weddigen putting the periscope up for a few seconds at a time so he and Spiess could take several looks. Having been deployed from her base at Heligoland to seek out supply vessels sailing between France and England, instead here were three lumbering enemy cruisers. Weddigen initially thought the British ships might be the vanguard of a large fleet so he waited a little while to make sure this was not the case.

Keeping his focus on the middle vessel of the three, Weddigen ordered the first torpedo fired, pulling the scope down as it sped away.

U-9 was very close, around 1,500ft from target and the German submariners couldn't help being anxious about the blast. There were cheers as explosions reverberated through the hull, but without any ill effects for *U-9*. The next victim was *Hogue*, stopped dead in the water to rescue survivors from *Aboukir*. Two torpedoes were fired this time. The Germans offset their guilt at preying on men picking up their comrades by loudly invoking hatred of the British. They cursed them for being instrumental in ensuring the whole of Europe – and even the Japanese! – waged war against the Fatherland.

Despite the boat's battery power being dangerously low, Weddigen chose not to withdraw, instead attacking the remaining cruiser.

Another two torpedoes saw to *Cressy*, with Spiess and Weddigen taking it in turns to watch her demise through the periscope.

Spiess felt he was witnessing a 'tragic horror'.[2] Even in their moment

Kapitänleutnant Otto Weddigen, commander of *U-9* when she sank three British cruisers early in the First World War. (*NHHC*)

of furious triumph the German submariners were stunned into silence by the enormity of what they had done. While many of their victims were veterans there were also young officer cadets among them, sent to ships in which it was hoped they could learn seafaring skills without being especially at risk. In total 1,459 British sailors and marines were killed, with 800 rescued, 300 by the Dutch trawler *Titan* alone.

There were bitter recriminations in Britain. A court of inquiry delivered criticism of senior officers, especially the War Staff of the Navy, for not issuing withdrawal orders to the cruisers.

Claims of a Dutch trawler directing multiple submarines were dismissed but greater discipline in keeping warship watertight doors shut was to be enforced, slowing down or preventing flooding. There would be higher levels of damage control training and improved internal lighting aboard warships. The practice of only having a lifebelt for one in ten men was lamented. Sir Arthur Conan Doyle added his weight by writing to the War Office and newspapers advocating inflatable rubber belts for all seagoing naval personnel. In Conan Doyle's view the scale of deaths in the three cruisers could have been much reduced had this been the case. From now on every man and boy in a British warship was to have his own lifebelt.

There was fury in some quarters that *Cressy* and *Hogue* did not exit the scene as quickly as possible to avoid also being sunk. It was decreed that, as soon as it became clear a U-boat was the guilty party, major British naval units should retreat. Speed and distance was their best defence.

A tidal wave of grief broke over the Kent dockyard town of Chatham, to whose naval division the dead belonged. The deaths of 13 teenage cadets were considered a particularly monstrous atrocity. Unaware of his attempts to have the cruisers withdrawn, some accused Churchill of ignoring an obvious danger. He was meanwhile dismayed at the U-9's captain being hailed a national hero, even receiving awards from the Kaiser.

In the German naval high command Weddigen's deed reinforced the contention of some that the Royal Navy's massive superiority could be eroded by using submarines without mercy.

Weddigen killed a further 525 British sailors and marines when he sank HMS *Hawke* on 15 October 1914 in the North Sea.

Never before had it been possible for a Commanding Officer of such comparatively junior rank to claim so many lives in such a short space of time. Just one small submarine had used a handful of torpedoes to sink four cruisers; the enemy had paid a high price for Germany's modest expenditure on submarines and their weapons. It appeared to make the vast investment of money, industrial effort and crew training poured into battleships and cruisers ludicrous and beyond sense. Submarines might yet prove the great equaliser, or rather the leveller, of mighty fleets.

The shock for the British people was profound, so used were they to Britannia ruling the waves. It seemed hearts of oak were not good enough against the cold and merciless mechanical submarine boat. Fulminating in retirement, Admiral Fisher stormed: 'It was pure murder sending those big armoured ships in [sic] the North Sea.'[3]

There was also evidence of the foe targeting an even greater pressure point, one that some in Germany regarded as a means to take the British out of the contest entirely: war on sea trade.

On 20 October Oberleutnant Johannes Feldkirchner stopped a British merchant ship off the Norwegian coast. Running on the surface, *U-17* used her 2-inch gun to put shots across the bows of the British-flagged *Glitra*, which was loaded with coal and oil and heading for Stavanger. She showed no sign of stopping until Feldkirchner warned by signal lamp that he intended firing his torpedoes. Complying with the Prize Regulations, a boarding party composed of two officers and a pair of ratings, all armed with revolvers, was sent across to interrogate the merchant vessel's master. They decided the cargo was contraband.

Glitra's crew were given ten minutes to abandon ship while the boarding party set about scuttling her by opening sea cocks. To accelerate the process *U-17* spent the next couple of hours pouring shells into *Glitra*.

It was the first time in history that a submarine had sunk a merchant ship. Again observing Prize Rules, which required the passengers and crew of merchant vessels to be treated with humanity, *U-17* towed *Glitra*'s lifeboats towards Norwegian territorial waters where they were more likely to be picked up.

On both sides of the North Sea, navies were afflicted with a psychosis dubbed 'periscopeitis'. Provoked by the now proven menace of the stalking submarine, there were numerous sightings of phantom periscopes.

Whales and porpoises were wrongly declared submarines and attacked. Wakes of destroyers escorting bigger vessels were sometimes mistaken for periscope disturbance and fired at by nervous battleships or cruisers. In reality, no submarine could hope to catch and sink a warship capable of at least 15 knots, so the best means of defence was fleeing.

When the fleets came to rest, in supposedly safe harbours, there was no respite from periscopeitis and, for the British, Scapa Flow was a far from reassuring place to be. At the time the three old cruisers were sunk it lacked any serious protection against U-boats and sea mines, some of the latter already laid by German surface vessels in Orkney waters.

Little thought or investment had been devoted to protecting the world's largest, most powerful and expensive fleet from undersea attack. This was perhaps a result of the pre-war tendency for traditionalists to stick their heads in the sand, rather than admit the unpalatable truth about new threats.

During one incident, warships at anchor firing on phantom periscopes hit houses ashore. Nobody was killed, though a baby suffered minor injuries. Farcical it may have been, but it was no laughing matter and a gamekeeper who started a U-boat scare at Scapa for a joke was arrested. Imaginary periscopes or not, Admiral Jellicoe decided that, until things were made better, it would be wiser to shelter at Lough Swilly in northern Ireland and places on the west coast of Scotland.

The Germans were handed a major tactical win, for now the Grand Fleet was not so well placed to dominate the North Sea and approaches to the Baltic with its blockade. Fortunately for the British the enemy remained ignorant of this remarkable achievement.

Never mind in harbour, at sea the harsh reality was that against fresh threats – both the submarine and mine – the navies of 1914 were unprepared tactically and technologically. They possessed no effective countermeasure, other than avoidance of mines – or shooting at them to cause detonation.

In Britain, less than helpful proposals for neutralising the undersea menace included painting over periscope lenses. Alternatively, perhaps periscopes could be snared and explosives attached to them?

Some bright spark proposed unleashing specially trained seabirds to perch on periscopes, blinding them with their droppings.

Pairs of Royal Navy sailors were trained to neutralise a submarine's ability to find targets or navigate. On spotting a periscope from their patrolling craft, they were meant to leap into the water and either smash its glass with a hammer or put a hood over it. It was also suggested, quite reasonably, that U-boats might be spotted from the air. A less practical idea was the employment of mystics to reveal where the craft lurked.

There were some useful, even practical, countermeasures but these were generally passive, not proactive. They included carefully laid and charted defensive minefields to preclude submarines from entering certain waters, closing avenues of approach to key naval bases and ports. There were anti-torpedo nets arrayed around vessels and also attached to booms at harbour mouths. The use of blockships – redundant vessels deliberately sunk to block deep channels – could help close the door to submerged intrusions.

Hydrophones for ships to listen out for the giveaway propeller noises of submerged submarines were being developed, but would remain ineffective until at least 1916. It would take until 1917 for there to be a truly effective depth charge (high explosive in barrels set to detonate at certain depths via a hydrostatic fuse). Destroyers and other patrol vessels relentlessly roved areas where submarines might loiter, hoping to catch a submarine on the surface or shortly after diving. They would endeavour to use their guns to sink the enemy with plunging shellfire. This was possible when a submarine was dived at periscope depth, around a dozen feet, or less, below the surface.

The British again demonstrated ramming to be effective before the end of 1914. *U-18* was sunk in late November, thanks to the efforts of both the destroyer *Garry* and a naval patrol trawler with the unlikely name of *Dorothy Grey*, during an incident within Scapa Flow. *Dorothy Grey* rammed *U-18* twice as she tried to escape the anchorage. A dived submarine trapped in such enclosed waters with patrol vessels over-head was doomed, especially in daylight. The need for frequent use of the periscope for navigation was a giveaway and that was how *U-18*'s penetration of Scapa was rumbled. A surface attack at night in Scapa might have been a better proposition but it would be left to another generation of U-boatmen to prove that point.

To do something proactive and target harbours in occupied Belgium, where some of the enemy submarines now lurked, battleships were more than once in late 1914 sent to bombard Zeebrugge, Ostend and Bruges. All they achieved was the destruction of a hotel, a railway station and a water tower. This did not put the Admiralty off trying again. At 2.20 a.m. on 2 January 1915 – after conducting gunnery and tactical manoeuvring exercises in Start Bay ahead of a repeat perfor-mance – pre-dreadnoughts of the Channel Fleet strayed into the vision of Kapitänleutnant Rudolf Schneider in *U-24*.

The conditions – a bright moon, though the swell was increasing – were favourable for an attack and the battleships were, most obligingly, sailing in line ahead at only 8 knots. As they paraded past, disdaining to even zigzag, *U-24* could not fail to hit something. It was, though, the very first ever submerged night attack by a submarine, so the challenge was not to be taken lightly. To make extra sure, Schneider brought his boat very close. A single torpedo fired at HMS *Queen* missed but one of two aimed at HMS *Formidable* hit, giving a rude awakening to 500 officers and men slumbering in her mess decks and cabins. Striking the battleship under the forward funnel, it just missed an ammunition magazine but managed to knock out the electricity supply. This plunged *Formidable* into darkness and prevented her from sending a U-boat warning signal by wireless. At 4.40 a.m., after receiving another torpedo hit, *Formidable* disappeared, taking 547 of her 770-strong ship's company with her, including the Commanding Officer, Captain Arthur Loxley. He had shown the kind of stiff upper lip and Nelsonian self-sacrifice so admired by the British people. His last words were: 'Keep cool and be British.'[4]

3   Stealthy, Inhuman Instruments

Weddigen's exploits, followed by Schneider's sinking of *Formidable*, demonstrated the devastating potential of the submarine–torpedo combination, advocated with such passion by Robert Fulton more than a century earlier. For all that, the Royal Navy still appeared to hold Germany's fate in the grip of its blockade.

Its diplomats in the USA raged against the hypocrisy of those labelling the use of submarines as inhumane and monstrous while the British starved women and children in Germany. Critics of submarine warfare were guilty of failing to visualise 'the spectacle of a hundred thousand, even a million, German children starving by slow degree as a result of the British blockade . . .'[1] Such emotional outbursts about the alleged impact of the blockade – at that early stage in the war actually having little effect – were designed to win American public sympathy.

Beyond claims of civilian suffering there was crushing disappointment in Berlin at the progress of the war so far. Hopes for a swift victory had lost their sheen by the opening months of 1915. All that had been achieved was an ugly, squalid scar of opposing trenches gouged across the face of Europe, from the English Channel to the Alps.

The Kaiser turned to his navy for the kind of decisive result the army had failed to achieve. While he did not at first regard a ruthless, unrestricted campaign against all shipping as a good idea, he was in the end persuaded by the naval high command. Yet even they did not necessarily have the backing of their own submariners. Prior to hostilities, analysis by the German Navy's submarine warfare experts delivered the unpalatable answer that 222 U-boats were needed for a successful counter-blockade of Britain. However, the Germans had 193 fewer operational boats than at the outbreak of war. Fewer than half a dozen would be on patrol at any one time, owing to the need for repairs and maintenance, shore leave for crews and also training.

The Germans were resorting to a kind of warfare the majority of people still thought abhorrent, including the First Lord of the Admiralty, Winston Churchill. Prior to the war he had stated: 'I do not believe this would ever be done by a civilised power. If there were a nation vile enough to adopt systematically such methods, it would be justified and indeed necessary, to employ the extreme resources of science against them . . .'

To gain retribution he advocated unleashing 'pestilence' and even moves to 'poison the water of great cities, and, if convenient, proceed by the assassination of individuals'.[2]

The Germans were now seeking to cripple the largest merchant fleet in the world – Britain's. Strategic impact would be the goal rather than a civilised observing of the Prize Laws, as had been the case so far.

Known by the Germans as *Handelskrieg* – 'trade war' – the prospect of it even horrified and deeply perturbed many in the upper echelons of the military–political machine. Among them was the Chancellor, Theobald von Bethmann-Hollweg, who feared that neutral shipping – and lives – would be lost. Sacrificed along with them would be Germany's cause in the non-aligned world, especially in the USA.

It was impossible for Bethmann-Hollweg's wise counsel to win the day when the majority of Germans regarded the enemy blockade as illegal, unjust and evil, aimed only at preserving Britain's hold on world trade.

The British, on the other hand, in March 1915 expressly forbade their submarines from waging unrestricted warfare against enemy merchant shipping, though their surface blockade did skirt the edges of legality.

Apart from their moral outrage, strategically the Germans were extremely frustrated that the Royal Navy was not offering itself up for destruction. It did not sally forth to attack the enemy fleet in its home bases, which were by now well shielded by minefields, with U-boats ready to strike.

The British were not stupid enough to serve themselves up. Had they done so, Churchill felt 'the German equalization policy would have had a very good chance . . .'[3]

Otto Weddigen was awarded the *Pour le Mérite*, the famed Blue Max, for sinking the three old cruisers and given command of the brand new ocean-going submarine *U-29*. He was dubbed the 'Polite Pirate' by the British press, for striving to ensure the crew and passengers of the ships he sank were in the lifeboats and given a good start towards safety. Weddigen was, nonetheless, a prodigious taker of lives.

On 18 March 1915, a battle squadron of the Grand Fleet processing through the Pentland Firth filled his periscope view. He fired a torpedo, hoping to sink the super-dreadnought *Neptune*, but the eel went wide of the mark. More torpedoes were about to be launched when the roar of thrashing propellers and a massive, metallic bang announced doom. The boat's periscope had been spotted and what followed was a lethal repeat of an earlier episode, where Weddigen was almost sunk by a hard-charging destroyer. This time he did not get away with it and the bow of the battleship *Dreadnought* carved Weddigen's boat up.

Dreadnought's massive 21,845-ton bulk easily sliced the 867-ton submarine in two. As the for'ard part of the U-boat lurched above the surface the large number '29' was clearly seen painted on her. Cross-checking with intelligence would later confirm that the British had taken a notable scalp. An oil patch, items of clothing and various other bits of floating debris fleetingly marked *U-29*'s grave. Weddigen, his submarine and her crew had been terminated by the primary exemplar of the new type of capital ship.

Dreadnought appeared to be the standard-bearer for the supposed continuing supremacy of the battleship. Yet she was the only battleship ever to sink a submarine by ramming and the destruction of *U-29* would be *Dreadnought*'s only taste of combat in her entire 14-year lifespan.

The Germans mourned Weddigen's demise as the snuffing out of 'a meteor'. Having sent to the bottom a total of 56,284 tons of shipping,[4] he is memorialised as the first of Germany's submarine aces. Even the

British authorities during his brief career referred to him as a 'brilliant submarine officer'.[5]

The loss of its star U-boat captain would not deter Germany and it declared the waters around the British Isles a war zone. The official warning to shipping issued by Berlin advised that 'every merchant-ship met in this War Zone will be destroyed, nor will it be possible to obviate the danger with which passengers and crew are thereby threatened'. Neutrals were fair game too, owing to 'the misuse of neutral flags by the British Government' and because of the hazardous nature of naval warfare, it 'may not always be possible to prevent the attacks meant for hostile ships from being directed against neutral ships'.[6]

The unrestricted campaign seemed to reap excellent dividends for little loss, with 115 merchant vessels sunk and only five U-boats lost between March and May 1915. The British had sent out hundreds of auxiliary patrol vessels to work with destroyers, yet between 16 February 1915 and 5 October 900,000 tons of shipping working for the Allied cause was lost.

Since sinking *Pathfinder* Otto Hersing had been active off the French coast. Having begun his war knocking on the enemy's front door, in late January 1915 he took *U-21* into the enemy's backyard, making history as the first enemy submarine to operate in the Irish Sea. This was something previously deemed impossible owing to U-boats allegedly lacking the range. Hersing went via the shorter southern route, through the Straits of Dover and St George's Channel, rather than attempt the long way, around the top of Scotland. He successfully dodged anti-submarine nets, mines and patrol vessels. When *U-21* made a shore bombardment it was, with typical audacity, against Barrow-in-Furness, where Royal Navy submarines were constructed, but the target was not the shipyard. Surfacing and sending his gun crew into action, Hersing's objective was an assault against an airship station located on Walney Island, just across the Channel from Barrow.

U-21's shots fell well short of the massive airship sheds but the shock of an enemy vessel suddenly appearing out of the Irish Sea to hurl shells onto British soil was profound. Shore batteries soon sprang into action and plumes of water spouted close to the submarine, but she dived and escaped.

The same day, *U-21* attacked the 6,000-ton collier *Ben Cruachan* off Morecambe. When a torpedo failed to do the job, she sent a boarding party across to order the crew off and set scuttling charges.

It gratified Hersing that *Ben Cruachan* was carrying coal to Scapa Flow, for he robbed the Grand Fleet of fuel supplies that would have powered warships blockading Germany. Two more vessels, the *Linda Blanche* and *Kilcuan*, were sent to the bottom before *U-21* headed home.

The most important, and far-reaching, aspect of Hersing's achievement was the impact his activities had on a ship that he did not sink, the British-flagged *Lusitania*, 32,000-ton, 785ft-long pride of the Cunard Line.

On hearing an enemy submarine was active in the Irish Sea – into which he would soon take the liner – her captain, Commander William Turner, decided the presence of many American citizens on his passenger list justified hoisting the US flag. He hoped to deter U-boats, as the Kaiser's submarines were forbidden from attacking neutrals.

When news of this ruse reached Germany, there was fury that a British merchant ship had opted for such tactics. It was ersatz anger, for in late 1914 two German capital ships took refuge in neutral Turkish waters and hoisted the Ottoman flag while retaining their original crews.

No matter, Germany was determined to let those who chanced a transatlantic crossing know they were at risk, regardless of which flag they sailed under. On 1 May an advertisement placed by the Imperial German Embassy in the *New York Times* under the header 'NOTICE!' made things abundantly clear. It warned: 'travelers sailing in the war zone on ships of Great Britain or her allies do so at their own risk.'[7]

Published in the Ocean Travel section of the newspaper, it was situated right next to another notice advertising liner departures. These included *Lusitania*, sailing to 'Europe via Liverpool', casting off at 10.00 a.m. The advertisement boasted that she was the 'Fastest and Largest Steamer now in Atlantic Service'. Confidence was high that *Lusitania* would come to no harm and be back in New York a few weeks later.

Having proved that she could evade and outpace enemy surface cruisers on her previous run from New York, where she had eluded a German ship, the threat from submarines was felt to be minimal. Even if hit, thanks to her excellent internal buoyancy *Lusitania* still stood a good chance of reaching Liverpool. Despite the unrestricted campaign, the idea that a U-boat would strike without mercy or warning, instantly sending a passenger liner, along with her crew, passengers and cargo to destruction, was too outlandish.

Yet the Germans thought they had just cause to target the liner, for aboard *Lusitania* when she left New York – her fifth transatlantic dash in defiance of the U-boats – were more than 1,000 cases of 3-inch shells, nearly 5,000 boxes of small arms ammunition and ten tons of explosive powder.

On the day *Lusitania* sailed from New York the *Gulflight*, a fully-laden American-flagged oil tanker heading for France was attacked by *U-30* off the Scilly Isles. Although salvaged, three Americans were killed, including the ship's captain, who suffered a fatal heart attack.[8]

Patrolling the same waters was 33-year-old Kapitänleutnant Walther Schwieger, in *U-20*. She had already sunk a steamer and a sailing vessel, both flying the British flag.

With only a pair of torpedoes left, fuel running low, and the onset of thick fog hiding likely targets, Schwieger was persuaded *U-20* should head home. He also feared his submarine might be caught unawares by a destroyer lunging out of the murk, while the prevailing sea conditions were rather lively and making surface transit uncomfortable.

Schwieger ordered the boat dived to 60ft and 90 minutes later heard the sound of powerful propellers thrashing the water, his finely-tuned hearing assessing it was not a destroyer. Bringing the boat up to periscope depth Schwieger took a swift look, discovering a heavy cruiser had passed overheard but was now beyond range. Cursing a missed opportunity to claim a major enemy unit, Schwieger was consoled by seeing blue sky. He ordered the boat surfaced, aiming to recharge the battery.

At 2.20 p.m. on 7 May, four tall funnels and masts were sighted.

U-20 was by then off the Old Head of Kinsale. At first thinking it might be more than one vessel, Schwieger's sighting took shape as a large ocean liner, coming from south-southwest and heading in the direction of Galley Head. *U-20* dived, hoping the target would sail close enough for an attack. Schwieger watched the liner turn away and cursed his luck.

Then she turned back. To make sure his two remaining torpedoes hit, Schwieger took *U-20* in as close as he dared, firing one at 3.10 p.m., from a range of 700 yards.

The 'eel' ran at 9ft, set at that depth to ensure it hit square below the waterline. Schwieger saw an 'unusually great detonation . . . a large cloud of smoke and debris shot above the funnels'.

He judged 'a second explosion must have taken place. (Boiler, coal, or powder?) Bridge and part of the ship where the torpedo hit are torn apart, and the fire follows'.[9]

The ship stopped very quickly after the hit, listing to starboard and going down by the bow. Schwieger called over a merchant marine officer embarked specifically for the purpose of identifying such targets. Making a periscope inspection, this man cried out: 'My God, it's the *Lusitania!*'[10]

Schwieger thought the *Lusitania* would soon roll over and was persuaded not to launch the second torpedo. He didn't want to send it 'into the crowd of those passengers who were trying to save themselves'.[11]

Lusitania sank within 20 minutes. A later investigation of the wreck concluded that while the magazine was not breached, coal dust igniting in a confined space caused a secondary explosion. It was this that ripped the side of the ship out.

Of the 1,198 people who lost their lives 124 were Americans. The casualties also included German saboteurs who had boarded the liner at New York, intending to sink her en route with bombs placed in her holds. They had been arrested and put in the ship's cells.

This truly was war against the people – injuring or killing defenceless civilians. It was not formalised warfare by armies on battlefields distant from cities and towns or even rules-bound interception of merchant vessels, with all the attendant care for the lives of non-combatants.

The torpedo from *U-20* struck without warning, with civilians a deliberate target. The same could be said of the British blockade but there was something about submarine attack that made it a more heinous crime in many people's eyes, both on the Allied side and in the newspapers of neutral nations. They described the *Lusitania* sinking as a foul crime.

According to the *Morgenbladet* in Norway *Lusitania*'s sinking aroused 'a feeling of horror'.[12] It added: 'The Germans have meant to terrify. They have terrified their friends and terror breeds hate.'

In Britain there were riots on the streets. Business premises that had owners with Germanic names were burned down and shops looted. Liverpool – *Lusitania*'s homeport – was host to some of the largest and most violent rampages. People of German or Austrian origin fled the city. Admiral Battenberg, the former First Sea Lord – forced by anti-German sentiment to resign in October 1914 – changed his name to Mountbatten.

For all the global outrage, the sinking of *Lusitania* or some other vessel carrying many Americans had been a matter of when, rather than if. Winston Churchill had actively encouraged neutral shipping into the danger zone in the hope of an attack that would turn America against Germany. Churchill hoped U-boat depredations would so infuriate the USA that it would join the Allied side. This did not happen in the aftermath of *Lusitania*, though it did take the edge off the USA's stance on the Royal Navy's actions. America was uncomfortable with aspects of the British blockade and Admiralty interference with neutral shipping but it did not aggressively oppose it.

In Germany the sinking of *Lusitania* appeared a great achievement, with the *Frankfurter Zeitung* newspaper boasting of 'an extraordinary success'.

It expressed no pity for *Lusitania*'s passengers when Germany's sons, husbands, fathers and other menfolk were being killed or maimed by the tens of thousands, fighting in the trenches. The people wanted a swift victory and for the British to suffer.

To celebrate the *Lusitania*'s sinking, postcards were printed depicting the brilliant achievement and ghoulish medals were struck.

It turned out not to be such a triumph.

One of the medals was copied in Britain and widely distributed as an example of brutal Germany exulting in the loss of innocent civilian lives. In the face of American protests Berlin expressed regret but pointed out the liner was a legitimate target because she was carrying munitions.

Kapitänleutnant Schwieger returned home in *U-20* thinking the majority of the *Lusitania*'s passengers were rescued by vessels dashing to her aid and was appalled by the scale of the deaths. He shrank before the international outrage, which made him into 'an object of odium and loathing'[13] around the world. With one torpedo a U-boat captain had risked bringing the USA into the war and potentially undermining his nation's entire war strategy. How long before another split-second error of judgement – a target rapidly approaching within the narrow field of vision offered by a periscope – led to even greater

loss of American lives? Schwieger and the other U-boat captains continued their grim work, believing the destiny of their nation depended
on them prevailing. The sinking of another vessel, this time with far
fewer Americans killed, would force the Germans into a rethink on
unrestricted submarine warfare.

On 19 August, Kapitänleutnant Rudolf Schneider's boat sank the
15,800-ton *Arabic*, a liner of the Liverpool-based White Star Line, to
the south of Ireland. Forty-four of those aboard lost their lives, among
them three US citizens. Even in the face of more American protests the
naval high command wanted no pause, but politicians and the Kaiser
feared further unrestricted submarine warfare would bring the USA
into the war on the side of the Entente powers. Following much heated
debate the unrestricted campaign was suspended in mid-September.
No passenger liners would be attacked in the English Channel or in seas
west of Britain. Attacks would still be made against commerce in the
North Sea, but under Prize Rules. The suspension of the unrestricted
campaign in the Irish Sea and the Atlantic – where it most hurt the
British – was not popular among the German people.

Tactical reality was forcing the change anyway. By October 1915 the
Germans would only be able to keep four boats at a time in the hunting grounds and in November this was reduced to three. Crews and
submarines needed to rest and recuperate. It was the Flanders Flotilla
based in Belgium that shouldered the burden, using its much less capable coastal boats.

In 1915 U-boats sank 1,307,996 tons of shipping – a shocking total
bearing in mind there had never been anything like submarine warfare
before. It included 855,721 tons of British shipping.

Britain's share of world shipping was so great that it made little difference and so it was manageable. In April 1915, for example, U-boats
sank only 23 ships out of 6,000 arrivals in, and departures from, the UK.
German and Austrian submarines would, though, still prey voraciously
on commerce in the Mediterranean, where there was less chance of
hitting American vessels. U-boats carried on laying mines in the North
Sea. In the meantime there were those in Germany still agitating for a
return to unrestricted submarine warfare.

The first warship sunk by a submersible war vessel: the sloop USS *Housatonic*.

A bearded George Garrett at the helm of a Nordenfelt submarine boat. He both designed and supervised the construction of it in Sweden during the 1880s. Note the collapsible funnel.

A Whitehead Mk I torpedo in a US Navy shore base, October 1892.

The third Holland Class boat built for the Royal Navy making a transit (probabaly of the Solent) in the early 1900s. Officers and the helmsman enjoy smoking their pipes while other ratings ride on the aft part of the casings.

HMS *Pathfinder*, the first ship sunk by a submarine using a self-propelled torpedo.

The Royal Navy boat *B4* in Portsmouth Harbour, with antennae rigged for radio communicaton — a time-consuming process that might make her sailors less happy in war conditions.

German war artist Claus Bergen created this painting, 'U-boat 53 in the Atlantic', after spending time abroad the submarine on a war patrol during the First World War.

The Cunard Line's RMS *Lusitania* departing New York at the start of her ill-fated final voyage in May 1915. A few days later, while off southern Ireland heading for Liverpool, she was torpedoed and sunk by *U-20*.

The British Union Castle Line SS *Gloucester Castle* battling heavy seas, wearing a dazzle paint scheme to try to confuse the aim of U-boat captains. The *Gloucester Castle* was torpedoed in 1917 by *UB-32* off the Isle of Wight. After being salvaged she sailed on through the inter-war years before being sunk by the German surface raider *Michel* off Ascension Island in June 1942.

British steam-powered fleet submarine *K6* running full speed trials at Scapa Flow, smoke billowing from funnels.

Aboard a British anti-submarine patrol craft patrolling the North Sea, an officer scans the seascape for periscopes while a sailor listens in on a primitive hydrophone for sounds of the enemy below.

The large, heavily armed U-cruiser *U-151* in spring 1918 stopping the *Isabel De Bourbon* for cargo inspection. The Spanish passenger steamer was allowed to go on her way unharmed, but in the summer *U-151* attacked twenty-four vessels and sank twenty-one of them.

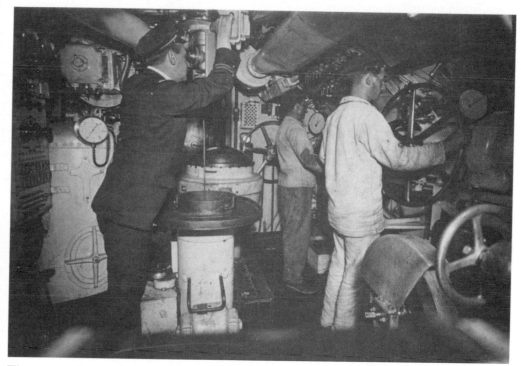

The cramped control room of the French First World War submarine *Andromaque*, with her captain on the periscope (left) and two of her sailors operating equiptment.

The extraordinary British submarine cruiser *M1*, which mounted a 12-inch gun previously carried by a pre-dreadnought battleship. Towards the end of the First World War, Max Horton commanded this large boat.

The mine-laying submarine *UC-5* is seen here after surrendering to the Royal Navy in November 1918. Her capitulation is signalled by the White Ensign flying superior to the Imperial German Navy flag.

4   No Surety of Survival

Just as the Germans tried to break the deadlock on the Western Front via unrestricted U-boat warfare against Allied sea trade, so submarines would become a major part of a British scheme with the same objective.

In considering where to help the Russians – and in that way assist the Allied cause in the West – the best pressure point seemed to be the weakest of the Central Powers, the soft underbelly of the enemy coalition. The aim was to break the strategic impasse by knocking the Turks out of the war.

The Allies needed to keep Russia in the fight in the east and to increase the strain of fighting on two fronts imposed on Germany. That meant ensuring supplies and even troop reinforcements got through to the Russians, who were themselves showing signs of collapse in the Caucasus. In return the British would be able to receive wheat, while the Russians benefited from much-needed hard currency. There might even be a new front opened up against the Central Powers along the axis of the Danube.

Access to the Black Sea was entirely controlled by the Ottomans, with the Turkish Straits a major highway for exporting Russian grain prior to the war. With the Ottomans joining the Central Powers – declaring war on the Allies on 1 November 1914 – nothing could now be imported or exported.

Nearly 40 per cent of all Russia's trade before the conflict passed through the Dardanelles and open access to the sea elsewhere was also restricted. Wherever you looked, Russia was at the mercy of other nations – or the weather – for its access to the sea. In the far north the primary port of Archangel was closed by Arctic ice for five months of the year. By 1915 a railway was being built in order to try to establish a major new warm water port at Murmansk, in the Kola Peninsula.

There was no possibility at all of troop reinforcements or supplies coming from the Western Allies via the Baltic, the entrance to which was controlled by neutral nations or heavily patrolled by the enemy.

In the Pacific, Vladivostok was ice-bound for four months of the year, in addition to being very far away from the scene of the action, lying at the end of a single-track 5,000-mile railway connecting it to Moscow. And so, Allied eyes fixed on the Black Sea.

By the time the Ottomans declared war an Allied force was already in position to mount a blockade, while plans were being devised to barnstorm an Anglo-French fleet through the Dardanelles into the Sea of Marmara. Allied battleships would make Turkey capitulate thanks to a terrifying display off Constantinople, threatening to reduce the Ottoman capital to rubble. The new super-dreadnought HMS *Queen Elizabeth* reinforced the prospective bombardment fleet, mainly composed of old pre-dreadnoughts from both the French and British navies. *Queen Elizabeth* packed an unprecedented main gun armament of eight 15-inch guns, the most powerful weapons afloat at the time. While the battleships readied themselves for their grand adventure, Allied submarines would attempt to carry the fight to the Turks.

British submarines had been poised to act off the Dardanelles within weeks of the war starting. The depot ship *Hindu Kush* was sent to the Aegean with three B Class submarines – *B9*, *B10* and *B11* – the auxiliary vessel *Blenheim* providing additional support. Just getting submarines designed only for coastal defence around the British Isles to the Eastern Mediterranean was an incredible achievement – a 3,000-mile voyage with a pause at Malta. Establishing themselves at Tenedos, a Greek island lying just to the south of the Dardanelles, the British boats were joined by the French submarines *Le Vernier*, *Faraday*, *Coulomb* and *Circe*.

Twenty-six-year-old Lieutenant Norman Holbrook commanded *B11*. His boat and other Allied submarines were second division and their limitations would make realising operational objectives a big challenge. The B Class boats did not have the range when dived to make it all the way to the Sea of Marmara, so that meant they could only manage brief forays up the Dardanelles.

By December the plan was to send submarines beyond Turkish minefields to explore opportunities off the port of Çannakkale on the Asian side. It was a considerable challenge that would require every ounce of skill, for the current flowing towards the Mediterranean – 1.5 knots in the broader parts and around 4 knots in the Narrows themselves – was almost too strong for feeble B Class boats. They were hard to handle, whether surfaced or dived, with a displacement surfaced of 285 tons and a length of 143ft. *B11* was the last of the type to be completed (in 1906). With a crew of two officers and 13 ratings, *B11* boasted four torpedoes – a pair up the tubes with two reloads. Capable of 6.5 knots maximum when dived, she could stay down for 3.5 hours – at that speed covering 22 miles in best conditions. By reducing her rate of advance by two knots, *B11* might manage 50 miles on a single battery charge.

At 12 knots maximum speed on the diesels while surfaced, *B11* could hope for a range of 740 miles.

B Class boats were fitted with petrol engines, prompting one distinguished submariner-turned-historian to describe them as 'a little like living inside the bonnet of a motor car'.[1] Even when the boat was running on the surface, with the hatch open, those inside were invariably intoxicated, giving the appearance of being drunk. While the battery did not give off poisonous fumes, after a short time submerged the air soon became foul and all but minimal physical exertion was unwise. Even if the boat did surface safely there might not be enough oxygen to immediately start the engines.

Potentially, the biggest hazard during *B11*'s voyage would be mines tethered to the bottom by cables or chains. If snagged on the submarine they could be pulled down onto the hull. Highly sensitive prongs would detonate the explosives contained within. To fend them off, tubular steel fenders were constructed around *B11*'s hydroplanes and other protuberances.

Holbrook intended squeezing every second of life out of the new battery cells, as surfacing in the Dardanelles, particularly in the Narrows themselves, would invite destruction. Both sides of the Dardanelles bristled with gun batteries, whose crews were highly trained and commanded by Germans. Destroyers and patrol boats were constantly on the prowl. Should dodgy handling qualities accidentally expose *B11* they would eagerly seize any opportunity to fire at her periscope or try ramming.

Searchlights scanned the surface at night, so even the cloak of darkness was no surety of survival. Room for manoeuvre was restricted and there were anti-submarine nets arrayed at various points and a wire to try to snare submarines.

Holbrook took *B11* through the narrow waters between Cape Helles and Kum Kale in the early hours of 13 December with his luck holding, though there was trouble with a guard on one of the hydroplanes.

As *B11* passed through the mix of fresh and salt water, the boat's depth varied from around 15ft to 40ft – and this was without any alteration in speed or helm.

The current that flows out of the Sea of Marmara into the Dardanelles not only varies in speed – between 3 and 4 knots – but the mixture of fresh and salt water offers different densities. This makes things even more treacherous for a submarine, as fresh water offers less buoyancy than salt water. If a boat is trimmed for submerged passage in fresh water and then enters a patch of salt water it might suddenly shoot to the surface and be exposed to attack.

After negotiating the Kephez minefield successfully, *B11* went deeper, intending to bump along the seabed if necessary. Old and small she might be, but *B11* was very robust. In common with other boats of the era, she could handle knocks and scrapes as she pushed aside mine cables, successfully passing through five rows.

With only the background hum of the battery and minimal machinery turning, it was very quiet inside the boat. As a mine cable scraped along her hull the sound reverberated with bowel-loosening loudness. After four hours of slithering along Holbrook risked a periscope look and found the old battleship *Messudieh* in his sights, a very large and tempting target.

In making his attack, Holbrook edged *B11* in close, going deeper and then coming up to periscope depth when 1,000 yards out. He ordered *B11* down to 80ft and altered course, which put him beam on to the tide rather than pointing his bows into it.

After blowing the auxiliary ballast tanks he managed to get back up again, but even then *B11* was subjected to sudden changes in depth that made ensuring the torpedo would run to target very tricky. One moment Holbrook had a clear view through the periscope and the next the boat suddenly plunged to 40ft. As soon as the torpedo was fired Holbrook ordered some of his men to run forward to compensate for the sudden loss of weight. He feared *B11*'s bows would poke above the surface.

The torpedo took 30 seconds to hit target, with Holbrook ordering the boat back up for a periscope look, giving the Turkish battleship's guns something to fire at. Through the spray – with shells dropping close, but not near enough to cause harm – *B11*'s captain could see *Messudieh* was done for. Holbrook ordered the auxiliary tanks flooded to gain depth, feeling his way out of the bay into the main current of the Dardanelles, *B11* bumping along the bottom, glancing off reefs. At 10.20 a.m. Holbrook risked another periscope look, for, with his compass refusing to work, any visual information he could get was vital. Pushed along by the current on the return journey out of the Dardanelles, *B11* at one point grounded and was left with her stubby conning tower exposed. Keeping his nerve, Holbrook managed to unstick his submarine and escape, sliding away into deeper water. With battery power finally exhausted, *B11* surfaced well west of Cape Helles, in safe waters.

Holbrook's Victoria Cross citation would declare it had been awarded for 'most conspicuous bravery'. *B11*'s First Lieutenant, Sydney Winn, was awarded the Distinguished Service Order (DSO) while the rest of the crew received either the Distinguished Service Cross or the Distinguished Service Medal (DSM), depending on rank. Other accolades included a town in New South Wales, Australia, changing its name from Germantown to Holbrook.

The Prize Court in London eventually made an award of £3,500 to the crew of *B11*. After the prize agents had taken their cut, Holbrook received £601 10s 1d, Winn benefiting to the tune of £481 4s 2d, with £240 12s 1d going to each of the Chief Petty Officers and each Able Seaman getting £120 6s 1d, the equivalent of three years' pay for the latter.

Even the enemy was full of admiration for Holbrook's exploit, with Vice Admiral Johannes Merten – the German commander of Turkey's coastal defences – calling it 'a mighty clever piece of work'.[2] Officially the Turks described *Messudieh*'s loss as 'the result of a leak' but the jingoistic British pointed out gleefully that 'it was caused by the explosion of two hundred pounds of British gun-cotton'.[3]

While it was a brilliant piece of propaganda – confirming the Royal Navy's submariners were to be reckoned with – in strategic terms Holbrook's success did little to alter the state of play. Despite being the hero of the hour, his own assessment was more or less the same. 'I feel that the great distinction conferred upon me, is too much for the small service I have rendered,' he wrote to Roger Keyes about his award, 'as the Messudiyeh [*sic*] was a very old ship and not much of a loss to the Turks.'[4]

In fact, it had a derogatory impact on later operations by Allied battleships, the Turks populating the Dardanelles even more thickly with mines, which would exact a dreadful toll. They also ensured that their major vessels stayed away from the Narrows. To get at them in their boltholes in the Sea of Marmara and off Constantinople would require a more modern submarine type with the required range and endurance and capable of carrying more torpedoes.

5   The Finest Feat

A major naval assault to force the Narrows on 15 March ran into serious trouble. Mines sank the British pre-dreadnought battleships *Irresistible* and *Ocean* – also claiming their French equivalent, *Bouvet* – while other ships were damaged. Throwing good money after bad, the Allies decided to land troops on the Gallipoli peninsula to effect the destruction of the forts, hoping this would ensure control of the Straits as a precursor to moving forcefully against the Turkish capital. Once the forts were destroyed the Allies aimed to sweep aside the mines and enemy naval forces to subjugate the Ottomans and open the route to Russia.

In late April 1915 the Allies landed 70,000 troops, mainly British but including 25,000 from the Australian and New Zealand Army Corps (ANZAC). Submarines were destined to play an important role because the only way the Turks could get enough supplies and reinforcements to their own troops in the remote Gallipoli peninsula was to ship them by sea. The roads were atrocious and there was no railway, so if Allied submarines could make the enemy's maritime transport untenable they might be starved into submission. Submarines might even venture into the Sea of Marmara and attack shipping off Constantinople itself. The same effect achieved by a line of battleships could now be supplied by striking suddenly from beneath the sea, potentially terrorising the Ottomans into surrender.

The B Class craft were incapable of providing deep penetration of the Sea of Marmara, so four E Class submarines were ordered to the Eastern

Mediterranean. Roger Keyes, who had been posted to the Aegean as the Chief of Staff to the naval force commander, was a prime mover in persuading the Admiralty that the E Class potentially offered a decisive effect. The first attempt by one of these vessels was not a success, with *E15* running aground, being subjected to heavy enemy fire and ending up scuttled. The *E15* experience and equally ill-fated attempts by French boats threw into doubt the whole idea of submarines getting through the Narrows, but Keyes decided it was worth persevering.

The honour of next attempting a passage of the Dardanelles would fall to the Australian boat HMAS *AE2*, which had a mixed British and Aussie crew. Her captain, Lt Cdr Henry Stoker, had put himself and his 32 men in the frame by lobbying energetically to have a go.

Volunteering was something of a habit for Stoker. When an opportunity to command one of two new E Class submarines constructed for the recently established Royal Australian Navy (RAN) cropped up he had eagerly stepped forward. A Dublin doctor's son and a cousin of *Dracula* author Bram Stoker, in early 1914 the 31-year-old took his British-built submarine to the other side of the world. A distance of 35,000 miles, the epic 83-day voyage brought him fame in Australia.

Sister vessel *AE1* vanished early in the war – during operations against German forces in New Guinea – and so, with his boat the only RAN submarine left and the enemy surface threat in the Pacific eliminated, Stoker lobbied the Australian government to contribute *AE2* to operations in European waters. He felt she could have a worthwhile effect on the war working under RN command but still acting as a standard-bearer for Australia.

In mid-December 1914, *AE2* sailed from Australia with a convoy, the boat under tow to preserve the battery and rest her crew. *AE2* was the sole protection for vulnerable troop ships – the first time a submarine had ever been used as an escort vessel. If any likely enemy raiders were sighted *AE2* was to slip her tow and go off to attack them. The convoy was unmolested and after reaching Port Said on 28 January Stoker received new orders, directing his submarine to join the British flotilla in the Aegean.

Going aboard HMS *Queen Elizabeth* to meet Roger Keyes, Stoker proposed *AE2* should have a crack at a passage of the Narrows and was taken straight in to see the boss of the Mediterranean Fleet, Vice Admiral Sir John de Robeck.

Even the urbane Stoker must have been rocked on his heels to be told that if he succeeded 'there is no calculating the result it will cause, and it may well be that you have done more to finish the war than any other act accomplished'.[1]

After a false start on 24 April, *AE2* departed properly in the early hours of 25 April, just as Allied ships carrying troops approached the landing beaches. The ANZACs were soon in a perilous position. Hard pressed by determined defenders and demoralised under heavy fire in a narrow beachhead, there was talk of evacuating them.

A British submarine officer on the command staff interrupted an emergency meeting aboard *Queen Elizabeth* with a transcript of a message from *AE2*, which revealed she had broken through into Marmara.

Roger Keyes, whose eyes lit up with delight, couldn't resist revealing the good news by announcing *AE2* had achieved 'the finest feat in Submarine History'. Keyes hoped she would now 'torpedo all the ships bringing reinforcements, provisions, ammunition etc, making for Gallipoli'.[2]

He told Australian senior officers they had to go ashore and tell their men the good news, to put new fire in them and avoid a humiliating defeat.

Two days after *AE2* had departed for her attempt to get through the Narrows, HMS *E14*, under the command of 33-year-old Lieutenant Commander Edward Boyle, sailed out to repeat the feat.

As *E14* passed Nagara, Boyle risked a periscope look and found a likely looking target, a gunboat. The disturbance caused by the torpedo discharge attracted a lot of enemy attention, shells crashing into the sea all around *E14*, making sharp cracks. Boyle fired another torpedo, keeping the periscope up to watch the run to target. There was a satisfying eruption of water and filthy brown smoke up the side of his victim. *E14* had sunk the enemy gunboat *Berki-Satvet*.

Boyle's scrutiny ended when his attack periscope view went black. Putting the larger observation scope up, he was astonished to find an enterprising Turk leaning out of a small boat, covering the attack periscope's window with both hands. Boyle gave the order to go deeper and it was torn from the man's grasp.

After more than five hours submerged *E14* left Gallipoli itself behind and entered the Sea of Marmara, finding numerous Turkish patrol vessels scurrying around.

Boyle next found his periscope view filled with an enticing pair of transport ships, but with three destroyers in attendance. With consummate skill – and great good luck – he managed to sneak within 800 yards of them and fire a torpedo. The enemy destroyers raced to ram *E14*'s periscope, opening fire with their guns for good measure. The torpedo missed, so Boyle fired another then took his boat deep, just avoiding the bows of a destroyer but with the top window of his attack scope shattered by shrapnel.

A large explosion was both heard and felt in *E14*. Taking the submarine back up for a look, Boyle was delighted to find one of the transport vessels belching a lot of yellow and white smoke. She was sinking but making a desperate attempt to beach herself. Having prevented some supplies (or even troop reinforcements) reaching the Gallipoli peninsula, *E14* resumed her patrol, heading east. By 29 April *E14* had clocked up 45 hours dived out of 64 since making her passage of the Narrows.

After *E14* and *AE2* met up to let their captains discuss tactics, the Australian boat was caught on the surface by two Turkish patrol vessels off Kara Burnu Point. On diving, *AE2* went out of control and broke the surface, the torpedo boat *Sultanhisar* pouncing. Neither the torpedoes she launched nor her shells hit the Australian submarine, which submerged only to lose control again. Stoker ordered full astern, with *AE2* 'slowly and reluctantly'[3] responding, pulling out of the dive and ascending. Now she was going up too fast as, with most of the ballast blown, she was too light. Breaking surface the submarine was subjected to intense enemy fire and dived again.

This time *AE2* 'seemed to be trying to stand on her nose ... everything moveable tumbling down forward, men slipping and struggling', reported 21-year-old engine room rating Charles Suckling. *AE2*'s men were 'Holding on to valves and pipes, anything to keep themselves on their diving stations'. Suckling had no confidence of ever seeing the surface again. '. . . this time we were gone for good,' he thought, 'everyone's eyes were on the sides of the boat waiting for it to cave in.' *AE2* shot up, emerging stern first, propellers thrashing the air, water cascading off her casing. Within moments three shell holes were punched in the hull, knocking out the engines. 'We were finished,' judged Suckling. 'She could no longer dive. All hands were ordered over the side, the officers remaining aboard to sink the boat.'

The submariners waved their shirts and hats to indicate surrender but it didn't initially work. 'The two gun boats continued firing at us after we had taken to the water,' said Suckling. One of the torpedo boats realised the enemy was giving up and steamed around the mortally wounded submarine to stop the other firing. *AE2*'s men were picked up and while this was going on Stoker, the last man to leave the vessel, climbed to the top of *AE2*'s conning tower and pulled down the White Ensign. Stoker's cool actions earned the admiration of the enemy, with *Sultanhisar*'s captain, Yuzbasi Riza Efendi, and his men saluting. Stoker jumped into the water and swam away, turning around to watch his beloved *AE2* disappear, feeling she went 'gracefully, like the lady she was, without sound or sigh, without causing an eddy or ripple on the water'.[4]

For the men of *AE2* capture was not the end of their troubles.

'Then began a life for us which was nothing but a sorry existence,' Suckling related, 'and I don't think if we had known what was ahead of us, that one of us would of [sic] left the boat. And when we were released from Turkey, three and a half years later, leaving four of our number behind, we were nothing more than living skeletons.'[5]

The *AE2*'s ratings were used to construct a railway through the Taurus Mountains to ensure Turkish troops fighting the British in the Levant and Arabia could be reinforced and resupplied. Stoker and the officers of *AE2* were treated rather differently but suffered all the same. He made several attempts to escape, sometimes using elaborate disguises, which never convinced anyone that he was a Turk. As punishment he was cast into small, dank prison cells where light did not penetrate and his only companions were 'bugs, fleas and rats'.[6]

Turkish officers often gathered by Stoker's cell door to hurl verbal abuse at him, enraged by alleged British maltreatment of their own soldiers in captivity. This turned out to be false and on Stoker's release in 1918 they apologised for their behaviour.

Replacing *E14* in the Sea of Marmara was sister vessel *E11*, commanded by 32-year-old Lieutenant Commander Martin Nasmith, a hard but fair captain who appreciated the absurdities of life in a submarine. This was just as well, for during an attempt to sink the paddle steamer SS *Kismit* his boat was attacked by cavalry.

The *Kismit* first of all tried to ram the surfaced *E11* and then ran herself aground, the crew jumping overboard and swimming to shore. Determined to get her, Nasmith realised the waters were too shallow to fire a torpedo. Trimming *E11* down as much as possible, to make her a smaller target, Nasmith intended putting a boarding party across to destroy *Kismit* with demolition charges. As *E11* edged in a pair of Turkish cavalrymen spurred their horses along the top of the cliffs overlooking the beach and were soon joined by around a hundred comrades-in-arms. They dismounted and began firing their carbines at *E11*. Withdrawing, *E11* fired a torpedo at *Kismit* after all, but it was a wasted shot.

The headline event of *E11*'s first patrol in the Sea of Marmara was a daring early morning penetration of Constantinople harbour on 25 May.

To provide conclusive evidence that he'd really managed to pull it off – the first enemy intrusion into those waters for more than a century – Nasmith fitted a camera on the periscope. He took photographs in which the Grand Mosque was clearly visible but also nearly covered himself in failure rather than glory.

Firing both port and starboard bow tubes at a gaggle of craft alongside the Arsenal Wharf, one of the weapons turned around and came back at *E11*, only just missing. The torpedo that ran true hit some lighters alongside merchant vessels, with an explosion that blew a massive hole in the side of the troop transport *Stamboul*. A wave of panic swept through Constantinople, for it was feared Allied battleships would now appear in the Bosphorus.

6   An Embrace of Death

Nasmith's great feat at Constantinople was achieved on the same day a German U-boat captain delivered a big shock to the Allies, sinking a battleship within sight of troops fighting ashore.

There had already been a submarine scare, with periscope sightings thinning out the more important major warships off Cape Helles, the main British beachhead, and also those in support of the ANZACs. Dead mules floating in the water, their legs pointing stiffly into the air, were mistaken for submarine periscopes while even playful dolphins caused jitters. It was all very disquieting for the troops, who felt their spirits sag as ships melted away.

The pre-dreadnoughts *Majestic*, *Swiftsure* and *Triumph* were among those remaining to provide gunfire support and act as command vessels. Residing aboard *Swiftsure* was *Daily Telegraph* war correspondent and former army officer Ellis Ashmead-Bartlett, who regularly visited troops in the beachhead. As he sat down to lunch in *Swiftsure*'s wardroom, at around 12.30 p.m. on 25 May, a young sailor appeared at the door, asking permission to come in with a verbal message for the commander, the second in command of the battleship.

'Beg pardon, sir, the *Triumph* is listing,' the youngster said.[1]

U-21, commanded by Otto Hersing, had struck – the same captain and submarine that had claimed HMS *Pathfinder* off Scotland.

Since the early days of the war major warship targets had become few and far between, yet the Dardanelles potentially offered a very happy hunting ground for *U-21*.

After more than four hours of creeping into the best attack position, Hersing was ready and the target was perfectly presented – broadside on, at a range of 300 yards. He ordered: 'Torpedo – fire!'[2] Deciding to keep the scope up, Hersing watched the torpedo streak to target. Guns aboard *Triumph* fired in vain after a lookout spotted the periscope.

There was a massive eruption of smoke and spray up the battleship's side, with water and coal raining down on her, a 'dry, metallic concussion' being felt in the submarine followed by a big explosion. 'It was a fascinating and appalling sight to see,' Hersing thought.[3]

From the upper deck of the nearby *Swiftsure* everybody looked on with mounting horror as the doomed battleship slowly turned turtle, a destroyer and other vessels taking off as many men as they could. *Triumph* made her last salute, bows down with her stern in the air amid an eruption of bubbles, smoke and steam.

The most senior officer present, Rear Admiral Stuart Nicholson, who had been watching events unfold from aboard *Swiftsure* using a telescope, observed sombrely: 'Gentlemen, the *Triumph* has gone.'[4]

For the *Daily Telegraph* war correspondent – already dismayed at the incompetent management of the land campaign – it seemed submarines ruled the waters off the beaches.

By supreme irony, the Royal Navy's mission to protect trade was turned on its head by Hersing's actions. For example, HMS *Majestic* only risked going to anchor amid a cluster of merchant vessels and smaller, similarly sacrificial naval craft. The *Arcadian*, which was carrying the general in command of the whole land operation – General Sir Ian Hamilton – and his staff, even had a liner secured either side as a shield.

Using merchant vessels to protect valuable major units against submarine attack was not a new tactic, for when the Grand Fleet suffered periscopeitis in 1914 colliers were berthed alongside battleships at Scapa Flow. In time most key capital ships would be constructed with 'torpedo bulges' – outer compartments filled with water or air – that, theoretically, could be penetrated without the ship being sunk.

In 1915, off Gallipoli, no such integral protection was available to *Majestic*, completed in December 1895.

At 6.40 a.m. on 27 May *U-21*'s torpedo cut through *Majestic*'s nets and slammed into her below the waterline on the port side. While there was an explosion, the battleship did not initially seem mortally wounded.

When *Majestic*'s steam whistle let out a blood-chilling scream, a soldier bathing in the sea just off the beach watched in astonishment as the battleship rolled over, 'with men jumping into the water'.[5] A wave of jubilation swept along the Turkish trenches.

An Australian soldier who witnessed the loss of both *Triumph* and *Majestic* felt 'an uneasy feeling' was planted in the minds of the troops. Submarines were, he felt, responsible for 'a hideous type of warfare'.[6]

Submarine action in the Mediterranean theatre of war was not just restricted to waters off Turkey, for the Adriatic provided a stage for an ace practitioner of the deadly trade.

Today it seems distinctly strange that land-locked Austria would possess a battle fleet, but in the early 20th century it fielded a powerful navy that included four modern dreadnought battleships.

That the Austrians were able to exert ascendancy in the Adriatic was not due to their ceaseless presence at sea, but rather to a failure by the

Italians. After joining the Allied cause in May 1915 their naval performance was lacklustre although help would come from the British and the
French, the former sending obsolete battleships and submarines well
past their prime.

The Allies more or less conceded the Adriatic to Austria, putting
their main effort into bottling up enemy forces to stop them from getting into the main part of the Mediterranean.

The leading submarine operator of the Austro-Hungarian Navy was
Lieutenant Georg von Trapp, who used an old Holland-type boat and a
captured French vessel to rack up an impressive score. Thirty-five years
old, the son of a naval officer and born at Zara, von Trapp was educated
at Graz and attended the naval academy in Fiume. On receiving his
commission he was immediately appointed to the Whitehead works,
where he got to know how both submarines and torpedoes were put
together and functioned. He also met his future wife, the extremely
wealthy Agathe Whitehead, grand-daughter of the British torpedo
inventor.[7] When Agathe christened a newly-built submarine in 1909,
Georg was there as her consort. That submarine was *U-V*, which von
Trapp would one day command.

Lieutenant Georg von Trapp, the Austro-Hungarian Navy's top submarine
captain. (*Imagno/OMB/TopFoto*)

Four of the Austro-Hungarian Navy's seven U-boats were based at Cattaro. A pair – obsolete types of little if any operational worth – guarded Trieste, in the north-eastern corner of the Adriatic with the remaining boat at Pola on the Istrian Peninsula. All the Austrian boats were actually past their prime and difficult to keep going but their crews were resourceful and talented at keeping tired old machinery in harness. The rest of the navy looked down on them and even the submariners thought of themselves as 'neglected stepchildren'.[8] They were not even trusted with the maintenance of their own torpedoes, which was done ashore. On being returned to the submarines these weapons often 'ran crooked' and sabotage was suspected.[9]

Another handicap was provided by the rules of war.

In early May 1915, with likely enemy warship targets scarce throughout most of the Adriatic, Lt von Trapp was furious at rules of engagement that forbade him from attacking neutral cargo vessels running supplies for the enemy. He decided U-V must search to the south, even though other Austro-Hungarian submarines had failed to find much there. There was, however, recent intelligence of a French cruiser patrolling in the Strait of Otranto, while enemy warships were thought to be using harbours in the Ionian Islands.

Passing Corfu and heading for Ithaca, von Trapp found and stalked the cruiser, eventually catching his target at night and making a submerged attack. He watched the bubbles of the torpedoes' compressed air propulsion gleaming in the moonlight as they sped away at 40 knots. Ten seconds later, he heard 'a dull, hard sound' as the first hit and then the second, 'as if a knuckle hit an iron plate'.[10] Von Trapp saw smoke erupt 'far above the topmasts' while all around him submariners exclaimed: 'Hurrah!' Torpedo one hit the cruiser in the port dynamo compartment and the other exploded in the aft boiler room. Von Trapp shouted for more torpedoes to be readied, so that U-V could deliver the *coup de grâce*.

The *Léon Gambetta* was already doomed, listing dramatically to port with von Trapp watching as efforts were made to launch lifeboats. He had no trouble imagining the terror and the panic aboard a ship without power, all decks plunged into darkness as waters rose.

Nine minutes after the torpedoes were fired *Léon Gambetta* was gone and U-V surfaced. Von Trapp later claimed five lifeboats were sighted and he calculated there were too many people in the water for his small submarine to carry safely. The extra weight would make the boat dangerous to handle and while picking them up she would be vulnerable to attack. He was surprised the cruiser had been without an escort to come and rescue survivors.

The same explosion that deprived *Léon Gambetta* of lighting also knocked out her wireless, so she could not send a Mayday message. Italian warships were fortunately patrolling close by and there were also neutral vessels near at hand. On spotting the cruiser in trouble, they raced to the scene, picking up survivors. Despite this only 137 of the cruiser's men survived,[11] with 684 officers and ratings, including an admiral, killed.

Six months later von Trapp was appointed to command *U-XIV*, the former French boat *Curie*, which had been captured after getting stuck in anti-submarine nets. Following a refit she was commissioned into the Austrian fleet. Across 19 war patrols in two submarines von Trapp would sink the Italian submarine *Nereide* and 11 cargo ships, total tonnage 47,653.[12]

As von Trapp was building his reputation at sea, the Germans entered the Adriatic and made their own presence felt. In the summer of 1915 26-year-old Oberleutnant Heino von Heimburg was a newly minted submarine captain given command of *UB-15* to learn his craft. Von Heimburg's boat was a coastal submarine constructed at Bremen that had been sent by rail to operate from Pola. The UB-Is were designed to be broken down and easily reassembled after being transported to whatever operating area they were required in. They were the product of an emergency requirement, ideal for protecting the seaward flank of the German forces on the Western Front by operating from Flanders. Short patrols in the lower North Sea and English Channel to destroy enemy vessels were envisaged, but they soon proved themselves in the Adriatic, Aegean, Sea of Marmara and Black Sea.

Small and lightweight, at 127 tons (surfaced) and 92ft long with a beam of 10ft, it took just 75 days from start to finish to construct the first UB boat and 17 were built by May 1915. A follow-on class of 30 bigger, better UB-IIs was ordered shortly thereafter, with 93 even more effective UB-IIIs constructed by the end of the war. Such was their simplicity the crews of UB-Is called them 'sewing machines'.[13] With a crew of only 14, they had a range of just 45 nautical miles dived at 4 knots before a battery charge was essential. Despite being coastal vessels they could sail 1,650 nautical miles surfaced (at 5 knots) but their sting was not that powerful. With an armament of only two torpedoes, and no reloads, each shot had to count.

Von Heimburg took *UB-15* out from Pola to patrol off Venice on 10 June, risking a periscope look astern to find an Italian submarine not far away on the surface. Without a stern tube, Heimburg had to do an about turn to bring his bow tubes to bear. No sooner was a torpedo fired than *UB-15*'s bows lurched upwards. Men not required at their action stations were ordered for'ard to increase the weight and while all that was going on an explosion was heard.

With that drama over Heimburg did a quick periscope look to make sure the coast was clear and surfaced the boat. There was no enemy vessel left – only smoke and bits of debris, with a few survivors swimming around who were picked up. Von Heimburg had destroyed *Medusa*, a 245-ton boat commissioned into the Italian Navy in 1911. That a German submarine had carried out the deed was a violation of neutrality laws, for at the time Germany was not at war with Italy (and wouldn't be until 28 August 1916). To get around that technicality von Heimburg's boat flew the Austro-Hungarian ensign – Italy and Austria had been at war since May – and carried an Austrian officer as an advisor.

Von Heimburg soon switched his crew to the recently assembled *UB-14*, also operating as an Austro-Hungarian boat under cover of the fictitious pennant number *U-XXVI*. On 7 July 1915, again off Venice, he encountered the 10,000-ton pre-dreadnought *Amalfi*, one of the most modern warships in the Italian fleet, which had been using her 10-inch and 7.5-inch guns to bombard Trieste. Once again, it took just one torpedo to inflict destruction. One hundred and fifty of *Amalfi*'s 550-strong complement died, the rest picked up by escort vessels.

Captain Herbert Richmond, a British naval officer sent to liaise with the Italian battle fleet based at Taranto, moaned that his hosts had admitted that 'the Austrians have command of the sea in spite of their inferior force and without fighting an action' with their battle fleet. Richmond suggested the answer was some British submarines and, until then, 'it will be the enemy who commands'.[14]

All the Royal Navy could release in the autumn of 1915 was half a dozen second-line boats of the B Class. These operated from Venice, with an elderly 24-year-old Italian cruiser named *Marco Polo* as their mother ship. The British boats' commitment was ill-starred and achieved little, if anything.

A major handicap was presented by environmental conditions, for waters off the enemy coast were clearer than those off Italy, where many major rivers drained into the sea. That meant lots of silt, which created cloudy waters Austrian boats could use to avoid being spotted from the air.

The Otranto Barrage was established in September 1915 as an alternative to a blockade by warships. Nets and mines were strung across the 44 miles between Otranto and the island of Fano, on the Greek side of the Ionian Sea. Patrolling anti-submarine ships and Italian and French submarines assisted by scouting aircraft reinforced this and the nets were kept in place by 60 drifters supplied by Britain. Despite a lack of hard evidence to show it was a success the Allies believed the Otranto Barrage was effective. In retrospect it was more of a sieve than a barrier, as there were many gaps through which enemy submarines frequently slipped. Italian warships meant to provide back-up were rarely at sea and poor relations between the French and the Italians meant patchy co-ordination.

Otto von Heimburg took *U-14* out of the Adriatic before the Barrage was introduced and by mid-August 1915 was operating from Bodrum in south-western Turkey and under the Turkish flag. He sank the 11,000-ton troop ship *Royal Edward* as she headed from Egypt to Mudros carrying reinforcements for the British 29th Division. Hit aft, *Royal Edward* took just six minutes to sink and out of 1,400 troops aboard 600 survived. Von Heimburg later remarked, in horrified awe at what he had done: '. . . with one lone torpedo we not only had destroyed a ship of great value, but we had also wiped out a complete enemy battalion.'[15] His next notable exploit was the assassination of *E20*, a deed made possible by an Allied submarine commander's lethal blunder.

Turquoise was the first French submarine to make it into Marmara but her achievement ended with an unfortunate twist. Just over a week after breaking through, she suffered mechanical problems, her captain, Lt Léon Ravenel, reluctantly conceding it was best to head home.

Approaching Nagara on 30 October, the French boat ran aground and was fired on by Turkish shore batteries, which hit the periscope. Ravenel decided to surrender and was captured along with his crew.

In the process, the destruction of secret documents – including note-books and charts – was overlooked. These were seized by the Turks and passed on to their German advisors. Among the things revealed was the location and time of a planned rendezvous with *E20*.

Von Heimburg was sent to add another submarine kill to his tally and on 6 November off Rodosto spotted *E20*'s conning tower. He watched the moment of torpedo impact, seeing a 'tremendous explosion, a cloud of smoke on the water. When the smoke disappeared no submarine was to be seen, only men swimming around in the water.'[16]

UB-14 surfaced and nine survivors out of *E20*'s crew of 30 were picked up, including Lieutenant Commander Clyfford Warren, the captain.

Warren had been brushing his teeth when his boat was blown up and was in a rather stunned condition when pulled from the sea.

'I say, that was a neat shot!' he exclaimed.[17] Taken below, Warren asked for a toothbrush. As for the French submarine captain whose failure to destroy secret documents cost British submariners their lives, he would face a court martial back home when released from captivity in 1918. Ravenel was acquitted and his feat of reaching Marmara lauded.

Despite such telling blows against the Allies, the amount of damage British submarines were causing was beginning seriously to concern Turkey's high command and its German advisors. With so much shipping – both big and small – being lost, it was feared that Turkish troops fighting in the Gallipoli peninsula would soon find it hard to carry on.

General Liman von Sanders, the German commander of the Turkish Fifth Army of 60,000 troops, said: 'Had the British managed to increase their undersea offensive the Fifth Army would have starved.'[18] Notwithstanding the German general's verdict – and despite all the damage caused by British submarines and the incredible heroism of their crews – the strategic objective at sea was not achieved. Turkish maritime supply lines were never completely severed.

The Turks ran a convoy system that proved effective, putting their ammunition supplies into barges that were heavily escorted by gunboats as they sailed through coastal waters. British submarines were wary of straying into the littoral as torpedoes often failed to run in such conditions and deep water was always preferred in case a boat needed to escape.

Nasmith above all posed the greatest threat to enemy supply lines.

Over the course of three patrols, *E11* spent a total of two months waging war in Marmara, sinking 35,000 tons of enemy shipping. The founder of the modern Turkish state, Mustafa Kemal Atatürk – himself a combat veteran of Gallipoli – would describe Nasmith as 'the King of the Marmara'.[19]

Roger Keyes pressed hard for the example of Nasmith and other daring submarine captains to be followed by the surface navy via another bid to break through the Narrows.

He thought it likely Turkish coastal defences were weakened, with guns taken away to support land forces and their supplies depleted. Allied minesweeping capabilities were also now better.

A sustained effort by battleships, cruisers and destroyers might tip the balance in favour of the Allies and cause the collapse of the Turkish Army. With Allied troops bleeding to death in their tens of thousands, was it right to let old battleships stay in harbour?

The Admiralty was happy to back whatever course of action was chosen by commanders on the spot but Admiral de Robeck, ever cautious, with his nerves frayed, refused to go along with the Keyes proposal. The example of the submariners was not followed and the dreadful and pointless sacrifice continued ashore. By the end of October 1915, infantry units were seriously under strength, while British divisional artillery was allowed to fire no more than two shells a day. There was no cold-weather clothing even with winter fast approaching.[20]

By autumn 1915 half the 100,000 British troops fighting on the peninsula were not fit for combat.[21] Britain had suffered 21,255 killed and 52,230 wounded, while the French lost 10,000 dead and 17,000 wounded. The Australians paid a butcher's bill of 8,709 killed and 19,441 wounded, with 2,779 New Zealanders killed and 5,212 wounded. India suffered 1,358 dead and 3,421 wounded and Newfoundland 49 dead and 93 wounded.

Yet, despite their want of water and better food, the Allied troops were still more fortunate than the enemy, who had been denied significant supplies by British submarines. Turkey's blood price was 86,692 killed in battle with 164,617 wounded, those figures including Arabs conscripted into the fight.[22]

The evacuation of Allied troops began on the night of December 18/19, the eight-month campaign having seen terrible slaughter ashore along with intensive and varied submarine warfare. The British boats sank two battleships, a destroyer and five gunboats, along with nine transport vessels, 30 steam ships, and seven vessels carrying ammunition and various supplies. More than 180 small vessels were sent to the bottom.

Numerous extraordinary exploits had pushed the limits of the submarine warfare envelope. On the other side, the German boats, too, had scored some notable achievements, delivering some hammer blows – such as sinking old battleships – that helped ensure the failure of an Allied campaign.

7   Baltic Gatecrashers

British submarines were at the forefront of another attempt to help the Russians and get around deadlock on the Western Front. It was, likewise, a theatre of war in an enclosed sea that was equally challenging to sneak into.

In autumn 1914, First Lord Winston Churchill and Jacky Fisher – the latter soon to be pulled out of retirement to fill the First Sea Lord slot again – saw sending submarines into the Baltic as a mere precursor for the entry of a battle fleet and a large landing force of British and Russian troops. The essential first step was the destruction of the enemy High Sea Fleet, to clear the ocean avenues, and that was a rather tall order. Also needed was a major victory on land by the Russians to weaken the Germans in the east, while the British and French armies pressed from the west. The big Baltic venture did not happen, so the Anglo-French forces instead mounted their doomed Dardanelles campaign. British submarines were still sent into the Baltic where, as the agony of Gallipoli unfolded, they had an effect out of all proportion to their numbers.

On 15 October 1914, *E1*, commanded by Lt Cdr Noel Laurence, and *E9* (Lt Cdr Max Horton) set sail from England's east coast, aiming to slip into the Baltic. The British submarines faced considerable enemy defences, combined with treacherous sea conditions and tricky interlocking neutral waters. An attempt to reconnoitre the route had been detected by the Germans, who were more vigilant than ever. Once through, after seeking to attack enemy vessels, the submarines would head for the Russian naval base at Libau, though nobody had yet informed the hosts they were coming. They were sent with little or no thought as to how they might be resupplied or maintained once in theatre. For the submarines themselves it was a one-way ticket, as it would be unwise to try to sail them back out again. As and when necessary the men would travel home through Archangel (or covertly via Sweden and Norway).

E1 and *E9* attempted their Baltic breakthroughs with a separation of three hours between each one on the night of 17 October. Going fast on the surface in the darkness, *E1* cut through the Skagerrak and made it into the Kattegat with no problem, avoiding all shipping. The sea was calm and there was no moon to expose the British submarine.

Beyond Saltholm Island the waters were very shallow and diving was near impossible in some places. Naturally, the Germans mounted intensive patrols of these spots and Laurence and Lt Ronald Blacklock, *E1*'s second in command, had agreed that if caught their only option was to blow up the submarine. It would be a great disgrace for *E1* to fall into enemy hands intact, so explosive charges were already fitted to torpedoes and a wire passed back up through the boat to Blacklock on the bridge. It was connected to a detonator switch. The hatches on the fore and aft parts of the casing were open to allow the crew to bale out before the officers on the bridge blew the submarine up 'and no doubt ourselves too', as Blacklock later reflected.[1]

In order to avoid attracting attention the submarine had switched to quieter battery drive and, as *E1* crept along, lighthouse beams, one on each side, swept the water but missed the boat. There were three close shaves with German destroyers, one passing so close Blacklock felt he could have tossed his cap onto her upper deck.

The very able commander of Russian naval forces in the Baltic, Admiral Nikolai von Essen, was, meanwhile, expressing his surprise and pleasure at getting naval assistance from Britain. 'Under whose command will they come?' Admiral von Essen enquired of Cdr Hugh Grenfell, the British Naval Attaché in Petrograd. Grenfell assured the admiral British submarines would 'produce considerable effect'.[2]

E1 and *E9*, plus any others that soon joined them, were to work under Admiral von Essen's command, so long as that remained in line with the overall strategic objectives of Britain. The defeat of Germany was the common aim, so that should be simple.

When *E1* arrived off Libau she was met by one of the Russian Navy's small steam vessels. Aboard was a young officer named Lt Chaplin, who spoke perfect English. He revealed to Laurence that he was liaison officer to the submarine. Chaplin cheerfully observed that *E1* was in the middle of a Russian minefield and offered to identify a safe route through.

In *E9* Horton had a fraught time getting into the Baltic, but handled it with his usual coolness. Reaching Libau on 21 October, *E9* flew a huge White Ensign and launched distress rockets to make sure the Russians knew she was friendly. A tugboat led the way through the minefield and *E9* berthed to find the Russians in the process of destroying the port in order to deny its use to the Germans, who were advancing rapidly.

Within a few days, *E1* and *E9* were out looking for targets, the former heading for waters off Danzig. In spite of finding a harbour stuffed with masts and funnels, no vessels came out to offer themselves up for destruction. With both boats ordered north to a naval base in the Gulf of Finland, an elderly corvette named *Rhinda* was assigned for submarine crews to live aboard while their boats were in harbour.

By early November the submarines and *Rhinda* were at Reval – today Tallinn, capital of Estonia – where there was a dockyard for repair and maintenance. The British found Reval a strange experience, not least due to the fact that its ruling classes were of German ethnicity and some families contributed men to both sides in the war. The only true Russians in the place were military imports and many locals spoke only German even though it had officially been banned.[3] There were Britons living in Reval, some employed as foremen in factories, and they were more than happy to entertain the submariners in their homes.

Despite the onset of winter the Royal Navy's boats persevered with operations, defying severe conditions. Patrolling on the surface, spray would freeze on hitting the hull and sometimes it even froze in the air after breaking over the boat.

When watch-keepers went below after a spell on the bridge it would take ten minutes chipping away gently with a hammer before overcoats could be taken off. There was always a hammer and chisel handy to remove ice from the conning tower hatch in case an emergency dive was needed. After all, a boat could not submerge if ice froze the hatch open.

A canvas screen attached to the bridge lip was meant to shelter lookouts from bitter weather. Frozen stiff, possibly with a layer of ice six inches thick, it proved a pain to dismantle before diving.[4]

One benefit of the cold was that fresh food, including meat and bread, kept for a lot longer aboard submarines than it might usually. It was just as well, for tinned provisions were unavailable from any source in Reval.

In late November 1914, *E9* deployed with the aid of a Russian ice-breaker that carved a clear path to the open sea, though the submarine's exterior was soon well covered in ice. Ballast tank vents were sealed shut and some valves were frozen. Yet, despite the potential risk of *E9* sinking like a stone, Horton decided to dive, discovering – just as he suspected – that things quickly thawed out in the warmer water under the ice. The British submarines would achieve little that winter, but they at least dared to venture out, while the Russians laid their boats up and waited for spring.

In one encounter with the enemy *E1* nearly came off worse while patrolling on the surface. Pulling watch on the bridge, Blacklock was alarmed to see a periscope around 500 yards away on *E1*'s quarter, immediately ordering the boat to point her stern towards the threat. This would narrow *E1*'s target profile and give her a chance to shoot back with the stern tube.

Cdr Laurence leapt up the ladder to the bridge, emerging just in time to see two torpedoes pass, one on each side of the boat. Blacklock's order to put the helm over had saved them. *E1* promptly dived and then, as Blacklock put it, 'hung round the area hoping that the German submarine would surface before dark . . .'[5] The enemy did not oblige.

Admiral von Essen was, meanwhile, fascinated to read a report on how the British boats managed to keep going despite the winter. He assembled his own submarine captains and gave them a telling-off for lacking the kind of spirit displayed by the Royal Navy. It created 'considerable friction'[6] between British and Russian submariners.

*

When they could be spared from the main effort in the Atlantic, Mediterranean and Aegean, U-boats were active in the Baltic, as *E1* had discovered at the end of 1914.

A German submarine scored a success on 11 October 1914, when *U-26*, commanded by 33-year-old Kapitänleutnant Egewolf von Berckheim, torpedoed the armoured cruiser *Pallada*, off Hanko. She was the first major Russian warship destroyed in the First World War, the entire 568-strong crew being killed when she exploded. The only sign *Pallada* existed was her ceremonial icon floating on the water. Six days later a Russian mine sank the German cruiser *Friedrich Carl* off East Prussia, evening the score, while the cruisers *Gazelle* and *Augsburg* were damaged by mines.

The boldest and most successful of Germany's submarines operating in the Baltic, *U-26* also sank the minelayer *Yenisei* and steam merchant ship *Frack*. She stalked and sank the 2,000-ton Russian transport ship *Pechora* on 25 August[7] and was sighted on the surface off Dagerort on 30 August, the same day sinking the 869-ton steamship *Zemlya*. Some time thereafter *U-26* was lost with all hands in the Gulf of Finland.[8]

A major objective for British submarines was to stop iron ore shipments from Sweden to Germany. Iron ore was vital in the manufacture of armaments and while the Germans had a domestic source, from mines in Silesia and Alsace-Lorraine, the Swedish reserves were the richest in the world. They were as important, if not more so, than domestic supplies and the Allies also needed Swedish iron ore, exported via Narvik.

During the winter, with much of the northern Baltic frozen, shipments for both sides started out overland from northern Sweden to Narvik. From there they went either over the North Sea to the UK or south through the littoral waters of Scandinavia and across to Germany. With the ice thawing from late April and iron ore shipments and other sea traffic resuming in the Baltic, Horton and Laurence began to hunt again.

South of the Swedish island of Gotland, *E1* caught three German naval auxiliary vessels, firing two torpedoes at one of them. Surfacing, *E1* looked for survivors but there were none. This was the first ship the submarine had destroyed.

In late May 1915 Horton, who would sink eight enemy destroyers in total and numerous merchant vessels, set about a convoy, claiming one cargo carrier. In early June, while still on the same patrol, *E9* bagged a collier transferring coal to destroyers and also sank one of her customers.

Returning from patrol, Laurence's *E1* went into refit but the dockyard at Reval proved incapable of manufacturing the replacement shafts needed to transmit power from the diesels to the electric motors. The enemy provided the solution. In a complex and deeply mysterious deal the new shafts were made in Germany, allegedly for a Swedish power station.

This was just one example of the fashion in which the warring sides actually carried on trading with each other in back-door secret deals, throughout the war.

On 14 August 1915, *E13*, commanded by 31-year-old Lt Cdr Geoffrey Layton, and *E8*, commanded by 31-year-old Lt Cdr Francis Goodhart, departed from Harwich as reinforcements for the Baltic effort.

Goodhart had already conducted a number of patrols in the Heligoland Bight and was eager to prove himself, but while *E8* made it through, on the night of 18 August *E13* ran aground inside Denmark's territorial waters, on the island of Saltholm. Even though the boat was lightened by fuel being pumped over the side she could not be floated off.

E13's presence put Denmark in a very awkward position, for while it sympathised with the Allied cause, it was wary of its powerful neighbour. A policy of robust neutrality was pursued by the Danes, enforcing the integrity of their territorial waters via an active naval presence. Should a foreign warship stray into Danish waters then it would have 24 hours to exit, or both vessel and crew would be interned for the duration of the war. Denmark's navy would, if necessary, enforce the security of any vessel finding itself stranded.

Aboard *E13* attempts to contact the Admiralty by wireless to ask for advice came to nothing, so Lt Cdr Layton decided it was time to make preparations for abandoning ship, giving orders to burn secret documents and charts. After dawn on 19 August Danish naval forces discovered *E13* and, on receiving this information, Denmark's high command ordered a task force to the scene. In the meantime four torpedo boats arranged themselves around *E13* to protect her at a distance.

The Germans also spotted the stranded submarine and sent a torpedo boat in as close as possible, but without straying into Danish territorial waters. Submariners on *E13*'s casing could hear enemy sailors screaming insults.

8 The Submarine Officer's Dream

On the same morning that *E13* was discovered stranded on Saltholm, inside the Baltic, off Riga, Cdr Laurence in *E1* was able to put himself across the path of the High Sea Fleet's battlecruiser squadron.

The Germans normally only operated older, expendable cruisers and destroyers in the Baltic but they wanted to support a move to outflank the Russian Army with an assault on the Latvian port.

With intelligence that something big was about to happen, three elderly Russian submarines had placed themselves in the Gulf of Riga itself while *E1* and *E9* waited in waters just outside.

While Laurence got some rest, Lt Blacklock was on periscope watch. With visibility no more than three miles, out of the mist, just after 8.00 a.m., emerged the huge black shape of an enemy battlecruiser. Laurence was called from his bunk and took over the scope, seeing more German capital ships following the first, all in the ideal position for an attack. 'This was the moment we had all longed for,' related Blacklock, 'the submarine officer's dream come true.'[1]

Just as Laurence was about to fire, *Derfflinger* received a periscope sighting report from another ship and turned towards *E1* – presenting a narrower target. Keeping his nerve, at 8.20 a.m. Laurence snapped off a single torpedo in 'a split second attack'[2] targeting *Moltke*, the second ship in the line. *E1* did not hang around to watch the impact, going deep and right under *Derfflinger*, avoiding her by a mere six feet, the noise of the massive screws overhead very loud and frightening. On the surface there was a flash in the mist and the sound of an explosion rolled across the water. Hearing this, *E1*'s men 'were mad with joy'.[3] A hole had been punched in the battlecruiser's forward torpedo room, letting

Commander Noel Laurence, who, while in command of the British submarine
E1, managed to damage the German battlecruiser *Moltke* with decisive effect.
(*Central News / TopFoto.co.uk*)

in 450 tons of water and killing eight men. *Moltke* was a comparatively
new battlecruiser ship, only commissioned in March 1912, and had a
large number of watertight compartments, so was difficult to sink. She
brushed off *E1*'s attack and kept going.

Bringing his boat up to periscope depth to inspect his handiwork
and, if possible, get off another shot, Laurence found the battlecruisers
withdrawing.

Their escorting destroyers were coming in to attack. Such vessels
still had no means of hitting back at a submarine, other than ramming
or firing their guns. If a boat stayed submerged it was unlikely to be
detected unless it showed a periscope or came very close to the surface,
but the Germans did trawl for submarines using small contact mines
on the ends of wires. On this occasion they exploded too far away to
damage *E1*, aside from a few broken light bulbs.

'We last sighted the *Moltke*, steaming slowly away to the westward
with a heavy list to starboard,' noted Blacklock. *Moltke* had to complete
the voyage home stern first to avoid taking in even more water and
would be under repair for six months.

E1 may not have sunk the enemy vessel, yet her actions had a massive impact, the incident leading to the failure of the enemy's push on Riga. The German naval force was meant to supply firepower to help subdue the enemy's defences from seaward and land troops but the whole thing was called off for fear of more submarine attacks. This was an extraordinary effect for one hit that killed fewer than a dozen people.

The capital vessels of the High Sea Fleet were of vast importance and a subsequent Imperial Decree from the Kaiser instructed that, should a serious submarine threat be confirmed, the battle fleet – or any of its constituent squadrons – should immediately retire to a safe port.

The High Sea Fleet would from then on, unless there was some exceptional circumstance, stay out of the Baltic and the German Army did not make another move against Riga for 14 months.

As with Otto Hersing in the Dardanelles and Nasmith off Constantinople, such a major strategic success ironically removed from reach (and potential destruction) the submariners' most desired targets, leaving behind only cruisers, destroyers, merchant ships and tiddlers.

The Germans did, though, have one enemy vessel at their mercy they could immediately make pay for the attack on *Moltke* and the failure of the Riga offensive.

Impotent though they might feel in the face of submerged British submarines, in *E13* stranded at Saltholm there was a ready-made and ideally exposed scapegoat. At 9.28 a.m. on the day *E1* attacked *Moltke*, two German torpedo boats, *G132* and *G134*, were sent to take revenge, after receiving orders to act directly from Berlin. As they charged into Danish territorial waters, the international signal for 'abandon ship immediately' flew from their halyards.[4] *G132* launched a torpedo but it hit the seabed and detonated, so closing to less than 400 yards the torpedo boats opened fire with their guns. Within three minutes *E13* was ablaze, with water gushing in to reach her battery cells and create chlorine gas and, as the submarine's ammunition began exploding, Lt Cdr Layton gave the abandon ship order.

E13's men leapt into the sea to escape the inferno their boat had become but the Germans shot at them. Still the nearby Danish warships held their fire despite their own navy's standing orders, though the torpedo boat *Soulven* sped towards the Germans after despatching a lifeboat to go to the aid of *E13*'s men. Two Danish vessels managed to halt the slaughter by placing themselves between the German guns and *E13*. The torpedo boats withdrew at speed to the south. It was not even five minutes since they had begun their attack. Fourteen of *E13*'s 29-strong crew were dead, nine of them drowned or shot in the water, while another two were injured. The Danish naval commander on the scene had feared an exchange of fire might provoke war between his nation and Germany. In the aftermath of the incident Copenhagen did at least lodge a complaint with Berlin but no apology was forthcoming.

Since Max Horton's arrival in the Baltic, the Germans had become fixated on his almost magical ship-killing abilities.

They blamed his exploits in *E9* for the failure of their grand strategy to move north up the eastern shores of the Baltic and swing along the Gulf of Finland to take Petrograd. The Germans even referred to the Baltic as 'Horton's Sea', such was his effect on their psychology. They dared not even run sea trials with newly launched warships for fear of his sending them to the bottom. As summer 1915 set in, chilling news of a bounty being placed on the heads of the two leading British submarine captains by the Germans reached Reval. '. . . a big reward had been offered to murder Laurence or Horton,' related Blacklock. 'Queer things happen in war.'[5]

It was Horton who was the arch pirate and must be eliminated above all others, and German sympathisers in Reval hired a beautiful young woman to put an end to him, so that it might please Berlin (and benefit their wallets).

They gave her a phial containing poison and she conspired to receive an invitation to a party Horton was attending. She spoke English perfectly and on meeting the British submarine captain the conversation flowed easily. The would-be assassin suggested they should find a quiet spot and a waiter duly delivered two cups of coffee. Horton was momentarily distracted and his companion put the poison into his coffee, but when he picked it up she placed a hand on his sleeve. 'Don't!' she exclaimed. 'It might be poisoned!'

Thoroughly charmed by Horton, the young woman had changed her mind about her mission and now eagerly supplied the names of those who had commissioned the assassination. The Russian secret police arrested them and they faced a firing squad but Horton refused to give up the young woman. He presented her with a gold cigarette case that had his signature engraved on it, which she would later use as a passport to escape across Scandinavia to England.[6]

There are no yarns about beautiful female assassins being sent to kill Noel Laurence but Horton liked to be one up on him anyway. The fact that Laurence was ahead of Horton on the Navy List – and therefore senior even though they held the same rank – aggravated E9's captain. He didn't like playing second fiddle to anyone.

There was tension between the two British submarine captains throughout their time in the Baltic and Horton didn't fancy being told what to do by foreign officers either. Enjoying a run of successes in late September 1915, sinking three large cargo vessels – *Pernambuco*, *Söderhamn* and *Johannes-Russ* – Horton attacked *Dal Afoen*. Despite carrying heavy Swedish iron ore for Germany's arms manufacturers, *Dal Afoen* stubbornly refused to go down after the first torpedo hit. Horton resolved to finish the job after the merchant ship's crew got away safely, but the Swedish destroyer *Wale* intervened.

Her captain told E9 by light signal:

'You are in Swedish waters.'

'I make myself six miles from land,' Horton flashed back.

'I make you five,' *Wale* insisted, implying E9 was trespassing.

Horton was absolutely confident of his boat's position both on the chart and in international law. He ordered his yeoman to signal: 'The neutral limit is three miles. Please stand clear while I sink this ship.'

Receiving no further communication from the Swedish destroyer, Horton ordered another torpedo fired, this time from E9's stern tube. *Dal Afoen* finally succumbed.[7]

The British effort in the Baltic was never a one-man show, no matter how much the Germans credited Horton with achieving.

For example, Lt Cdr Goodhart in E8 enjoyed a very successful run, on 5 October 1915 sinking the steam cargo vessel *Margarette* off Konigsberg using gunfire and by 19 October the boat was loitering with intent off Libau. Making careful periscope observations, Goodhart subsequently noted in his diary: 'Thursday Oct 21st (Trafalgar Day). Wish we could celebrate it by sinking a Dreadnought but fear there is nothing [going on] to bring them out.'

He did score a major success, though not against an enemy battleship but rather the cruiser *Prinz Adalbert*. She was nearly sunk some months earlier when Horton's boat attacked her, causing serious damage. Now *Prinz Adalbert* met her nemesis.

Goodhart kept his periscope up during his attack and saw 'a red line of flame along her waterline under the fore bridge . . . There was a terrific crash . . . I hardly realised I had "blown up" a ship. Poor devils in her, they can't have known anything about it . . . the flash knocked me back from the periscope, I thought at the time that a 12" shell had burst just in front of the periscope.' Hot, jagged metal plate and fragments of machinery and human beings plunged into the sea all around the British submarine. On hearing their attack had succeeded, *E8*'s crew were 'very bucked [up] & clapped!!'

Goodhart took the boat down to 50ft and withdrew while enemy destroyers searched the spot where the submarine had been.

To celebrate *E8*'s success, her officers popped the cork on a bottle of champagne they had been saving for just such an opportunity. '. . . feeling more & more pleased with life somehow,' remarked Goodhart in his diary. It was not all fizz and grins, though, and he reflected: 'It's awful to think of the personal loss of life, but looking at it from the proper war point of view it is a good bit of work, & everybody in the boat deserves it.'[8]

Only three men out of the *Prinz Adalbart*'s ship's company of 675 were saved. Sources in Petrograd soon confirmed a British submarine had sunk the cruiser and it was the most devastating knock to German naval fortunes in the Baltic so far. Old, slow and less well-protected cruisers were no longer to be risked. All such vessels were paid off and their crews sent to the U-boat service to man new submarines. It was a fine, if grim, tribute to the growing reputation of Britain's pursuit of the deadly trade in the Baltic.

While the submarines and the majority of their crews stayed in the Baltic, the key officers of *E1* and *E9* were ordered home for a rest and to prepare for new commands. Horton and Laurence would take the covert route back, via Sweden and Norway.

Horton didn't want to go, and the Russians had protested vigorously against his recall. Horton suggested he should stay on as Senior Naval Officer in the Baltic, which he rather fancied. The British Ambassador also protested that Horton must not go, as he was brilliant with the Russians. A senior officer on the Admiralty staff in London, who probably disapproved of submariners in general and Horton in particular, rejected the proposition. 'I understand Commander Horton is something of a pirate and not at all fitted for the position of S.N.O. in the Baltic,' he sneered.[9] Horton's gambler's luck and ability to hold his drink had mightily impressed his hosts, so they sent him back to England after a grand banquet, with both British and Russian officers escorting him to his train.

Horton wore an enormous sable coat possessing a rank odour, a gift from his grateful hosts. He puffed on foul-smelling Russian cigarettes, waving goodbye from the steps of the carriage, his face wreathed in misty breath, cigarette smoke and vodka fumes. Some of Horton's colleagues were, however, glad to see the back of him, for he was too generous with criticism of those he felt did not meet his exacting standards. Not everybody in the Russian Navy was warm towards the British either, whose exemplary record at sea, especially Horton's, rankled. A new commander for the British forces might find it easier to be tactful.

Another welcome returnee via the neutral nations route was the captain of the ill-fated *E13*. While his Danish captors were very friendly and hospitable, Lt Cdr Layton decided after a few weeks he ought to get back to England. Escaping from the naval barracks in Copenhagen one night, dressed as a Danish sailor – leaving a dummy under the bedclothes – Layton soon changed into civilian clothes. He caught a ferry to Sweden and once safely in pro-British Norway picked up false papers, including an American passport.

Layton boarded a Norwegian mail ship for the final leg of the journey to Newcastle and imagined he would be greeted with disapproval at the Admiralty and censured for losing his boat. That was far from being the case. Experienced captains were valued highly, at least within the Submarine Service itself. They had shown that tiny vessels could achieve big things and while a new submarine could be easily built, men who had the guts to command them were hard to replace.

9 Setting the Traps

In 1914 the majority of the world's merchant vessels were British – 3,063 out of 4,881 – representing a massive fleet that, in essence, controlled world trade. Meanwhile, the Royal Navy's warships cleared the shipping of the Central Powers from the seas, eliminating the other side's means of oceanic supply. Via blockade it could try to lock surviving enemy merchant ships in port while intercepting neutral vessels carrying cargo to Germany and keeping the Kaiser's navy penned in.

On the other hand, the commitment of so many British and imperial troops to the Western Front created a vulnerability the enemy's submarines could prey on. Britain needed vast amounts of material to maintain its massive military effort, offering U-boats a chance of starving Allied troops of munitions and other supplies. They could deny enemy war industries the raw materials needed to make the tools of war and sink food shipments to the troops, while also fermenting discontent and even revolt among a starving British population. Or so the Germans hoped. The idea that U-boats could even win the war was taking root.

The fact that the British failed to follow the pattern of their successful Great War of 1792–1815 – by convoying merchant vessels – enhanced the U-boats' opportunities. In keeping the Baltic trade going, for example, in the late eighteenth and early nineteenth centuries the Royal Navy provided escorts for convoys that often numbered hundreds of ships. Even in heavy weather the majority of them reached British ports. A hundred years on, with the nation even more dependent on overseas trade, Britain failed to adopt this proven system.

This was because of a mindset in the Admiralty that recoiled from the passive business of waiting for the enemy to attack groups of merchant ships. It favoured searching out and destroying surface raiders, though submarines posed a somewhat different challenge. They could only be attacked if they chose to give themselves away.

In the Napoleonic Wars, with all merchant vessels under sail, they more or less went at the same speed. In the new world war, in which there were large numbers of steamships of various sizes, types and ages, it was felt impossible to marshal them. Some shipping firms were not keen on slowing down vessels that might otherwise easily outpace a U-boat (whether dived or surfaced). Besides, the scale of the threat posed by U-boats was still not fully appreciated and it was felt losses could be easily replaced or worked around.

The opponents of convoys in the Allied camp claimed they would tie up thousands of warships that might be better employed aggressively hunting down the enemy. The business of arranging convoys was too much trouble: especially getting the ships to assemble. Then there was offloading a mass of vessels in Liverpool or some other port all at the same time. This would, it was suggested, disrupt global trade and clog up the supply system. Finally, didn't convoys make the enemy's job easier by presenting them with a mass of targets in the same place? The Admiralty decided it was best to stick with independent sailings, while its warships continued hunting and killing the enemy where possible. The fact that the convoy system was used to successfully transport troops to Gallipoli and also for cargo shipments across the English Channel was felt to be irrelevant.

On the other side, the issue of convoys was not predominant.

The Central Powers did not, or rather could not, rely entirely on sea trade to sustain them. Their vast lands had to feed their populations, for better or worse, but they still went overseas to seek out additional specialist materials for war manufacturing, which was not an easy task.

By contrast, due to their maritime supremacy, whatever the Allies needed they could get from wherever they wanted in the world. Merchant vessels carried many millions of people, animals and all kind of munitions and other items essential for the Allied war effort, largely without contest from the enemy's surface fleet. It was confined to poking its nose out of port on occasional raids.

Among those striving to secure munitions for Germany from sources in the USA was a 36-year-old naval intelligence officer attached to the *Admiralstab* (the Admiralty Staff) in Berlin, Kapitänleutnant Franz von Rintelen. From an aristocratic background, he had before the war worked as a merchant banker in New York. He now found that neutral America responded to complaints about its arms manufacturers too eagerly supplying the Allies by suggesting Germany, too, could place orders for the same goods. Von Rintelen reflected bitterly that cargo vessels destined for Germany did not enjoy the same protection as those from Britain, France and Russia – courtesy of the oceanic supremacy of the Royal Navy. He described this as 'no foe whose trenches could be taken by storm; it was a spectre, an intangible phantom, against which strategy, tactics, and all the courage of the German soldier were helpless'.[1]

The Germans grew to loathe the Americans for their criticism of Old Europe's warlike ways while at the same time making billions of dollars from fuelling the conflict with munitions sales. Neutrality as defined by the USA seemed to be a rather biased affair, with US-manufactured bullets, shells and weapons slaughtering the pride of Germany.

As the war slid into its third summer, the Germans could tell an enormous ground offensive was about to be launched by the Allies on the Western Front. It was crucial something was done about it. The generals were keen for unrestricted submarine warfare as were certain admirals and politicians, but in some quarters there was still reluctance about completely unleashing the submarines. The risk of bringing the USA into the conflict remained a concern. The overall head of the navy, Admiral Henning von Holtzendorff, had come around to the view that unrestricted submarine warfare was necessary but Chancellor Bethmann-Hollweg still feared the consequences.

For their part, the British were not unaware of the growing U-boat threat and again considered launching a major amphibious assault against Zeebrugge to wipe out the Flanders Flotilla. It was proposed the British and French armies should make a concerted big push into Belgium, including along the coastal zone. The Royal Navy would provide protection and firepower from the seaward flank. That plan was called off, as the French needed all their strength to hold the Germans back at Verdun. The British still went ahead with their offensive but in France, launching a massive assault on the Somme in July 1916.

For Germany the tools for achieving a decisive strategic effect at sea were finally at hand. Before the war various submarines of the overseas variety had been ordered, but while those construction programmes gathered pace the new classes of smaller, less sophisticated, submarines had to carry the weight. Aside from the UB coastal patrol boats there were UCs (minelaying submarines). During the period February 1915 to February 1916 the Germans managed to double the size of their submarine force, to 50. One hundred and fifty-seven U-boats would be constructed in 1916.[2]

The number of vessels deployed to sea fluctuated, though a maximum of 20 on patrol at any one time was possible by mid-1916.

The growing size of the submarine force provided more options for the new Commander-in-Chief of the High Sea Fleet, Admiral Reinhardt Scheer. He controlled half of it, the ocean-going boats.

Renewal of a limited campaign was agreed in March 1916, despite a lingering anxiety over America, and began in the middle of that month. Full-scale unrestricted submarine warfare would start within a fortnight if there were no signs of the British blockade loosening.

The restrictions were duly lifted fully and over the next few weeks 250,000 tons of Allied shipping was destroyed, but an incident in which American lives were lost forced an about turn in German policy.

The French-flagged 1,350-ton cross-Channel packet *Sussex*, running from Dieppe to Folkestone with 380 passengers aboard, was torpedoed by *UB-29* on 24 March 1916. The submarine's 27-year-old captain, Oberleutnant Herbert Pustkuchen, claimed she was a legitimate target and that periscope observation revealed people in military uniform on the vessel's upper deck. Although badly damaged, *Sussex* did not sink. Eighty lives were lost and people were badly injured, the fatalities including 25 Americans. The Germans tried to claim *Sussex* hit a mine but evidence of a torpedo was found.

After stewing over the *Sussex* attack for around a month, the Americans lodged an official note of protest, warning that if Germany did not cease unrestricted submarine attacks against merchant shipping Washington would cut all diplomatic ties with Berlin. Even the Pope intervened. British foreign minister Sir Edward Grey revealed in Parliament that the Vatican was making 'representations to Germany in order to induce her to abandon submarine warfare'.[3] The Holy Father was also seeking an end to the British blockade, but the Vatican secretary of state, Cardinal Pietro Gasparri, had in late 1915 described submarine warfare as 'appalling and immoral'.[4]

The Germans angrily reminded the world that millions of civilians were being starved by the Royal Navy's blockade. Even so, they ordered U-boat captains again to observe Prize Rules, while unrestricted warfare was still pursued in the Mediterranean and U-boats continued laying mines in British waters. Furious at the latest flip-flop, Admiral

Scheer and the commander of the Flanders Flotilla issued withdrawal orders to their deployed U-boats.

Advocates of unrestricted submarine warfare bent all the harder to the task of winning the case for a sustained and unflinching campaign. Within weeks, the only major clash between the German and British main battle fleets in the war would play right into the hands of admirals and generals pushing hard for the U-boats to be unleashed.

It was Winston Churchill who famously described Admiral Sir John Jellicoe, the 57-year-old commander of the Grand Fleet, as 'the only man on either side who could lose the war in an afternoon'.

This oft-quoted description of the person in charge of the world's mightiest man-made destructive force was prefaced by Churchill explaining that Jellicoe bore responsibilities 'on a different scale' from any other war leader. It was the Grand Fleet that ensured Britain stayed in the war by ruling the waves. To lose that supremacy would release the Germans from the Allied naval vice to run rampant.

The thing that, above all else, weighed heavily on Jellicoe's mind was the threat from under the sea – mines sown by German surface ships and submarines along with torpedoes launched by enemy submarines and destroyers. The loss of a brand new battleship – *Audacious*, which sank after striking a German mine off northern Ireland – along with cruisers and pre-dreadnought battleships in the first two years of conflict, planted the seeds of a nightmare scenario in Jellicoe's mind. Should the enemy manage to lure the Grand Fleet – or a significant part of it – into a minefield or a submarine ambush, Britain's supremacy could be dealt a devastating blow.

Added to this pressure was that Britons hungered for another Trafalgar, an epic naval clash to settle things in Britannia's favour for a hundred years – just as Nelson and his Jack Tars had in 1805. England (and the rest of Britain and the Empire) expected it, but it had not yet been delivered. The likelihood of a new Trafalgar was slim, and Jellicoe knew it. He was not likely to hazard the Grand Fleet in anything but the most favourable conditions and laid down fighting instructions in exhaustive detail. He explained in a memorandum to the Admiralty that should the enemy fleet turn away from the Grand Fleet he would 'assume the intention was to lead us over mines and submarines, and should decline to be so drawn'.[5]

*

For Admiral Scheer the abandonment of unrestricted submarine warfare at the end of April was not all bad news. While it meant a key
means of forcing the British out of the war had been discarded, it also
released assets he might now use to great effect. Anyway, he refused to
allow the submarines under his command to be used in actions against
commerce if it meant they must observe Prize Laws. This was wasting
scarce assets and exposing them to undue risk for little gain.

Scheer did plan on using U-boats to ambush British battleships,
though not quite in the fashion Jellicoe feared, but rather like muggers
waiting in a dark alley for unsuspecting pedestrians.

U-boats would be carefully placed to catch British capital ships both
as they came out from their main bases at Rosyth and Scapa Flow and
as they headed back home or diverted to the Tyne for battle damage
repairs.

The German scheme involved mounting a bombardment using
battlecruisers against Sunderland on the north-east coast of England. It
was hoped this would bring Beatty's battlecruisers charging down from
the Firth of Forth and tease the Grand Fleet out of Scapa Flow. Furthermore, German battlecruisers would turn away and lead the enemy
to Dogger Bank, where the main force would be poised to envelop and
destroy Beatty's ships before the Grand Fleet could intervene.

The British were at the same time working on a plan to tempt the
Germans out. Their trap would be sprung on 2 June, with light cruisers
as the prime lure. The Grand Fleet and the RN's Battle Cruiser Fleet
(BCF) would be a hammer to smash the enemy against an anvil composed of submarines and freshly placed mines.

Due to some vessels needing repairs and strong north-easterly winds
preventing scouting by Zeppelins over the North Sea, the Germans delayed and modified their plan. It would now involve their battlecruiser
squadron making a show of itself off Norway, hoping the BCF would
chase it south into the fatal embrace of the High Sea Fleet.

As with German submarines, the main aim for the Royal Navy's
boats was to ambush a major enemy warship either leaving home base
or returning to it. The tedium of waiting for something to show itself
would be compounded by turbulent sea states, which made conditions
inside the boats most unpleasant.

In late May 1916, as part of its own ambush plan, the Admiralty had instructed three boats – *D1*, *E26* and *E55* – to lurk near Horns Reef, on the main approach route to the German North Sea naval bases. They were told to ensure they were alert during the period 1–3 June, staying well hidden until then, and so they spent most of their time sitting on the seabed. As they did this, off the Jutland Peninsula 110,000 men were locked in combat on 31 May and 1 June. Three British battlecruisers and 11 other vessels were sunk while their foe lost 11 ships. Total British casualties were 6,094 killed while the Germans suffered 2,551. There were concerted torpedo attacks made by the destroyer squadrons of both sides and it has been argued that the fourth such German assault was the key moment. It forced Jellicoe to turn his force away at the precise moment when the High Sea Fleet was in its most perilous state.[6]

The fear of torpedoes and Jellicoe's reaction gave the German fleet the time it needed to slip away into the swiftly gathering darkness. It went secure in the knowledge that British night-fighting skills were poor.

British torpedoes – all fired by cruisers and destroyers – claimed two German cruisers (*Frauenlob* and *Rostock*) and the pre-dreadnought *Pommern* (already heavily damaged by shells), also inflicting slight damage on the German battlecruiser *Seydlitz* and possibly sinking a German destroyer.

Apart from *Invincible*, during the afternoon fight the most shocking British losses were the battlecruisers *Queen Mary* and *Indefatigable* (both blown apart by German heavy shells). HMS *Marlborough* was the only British battleship hit by a torpedo, with major flooding and two men killed. During the battle the British believed the guilty party was an enemy submarine or mine. *Marlborough*'s captain related that 'a periscope was observed by witnesses about 1,000 yards on the starboard beam'.[7] But it was more likely to have been fired by a German surface warship – possibly the severely damaged cruiser *Wiesbaden* or the equally badly knocked about destroyer *V48*.

The *Revenge* was one of several other British battleships reporting a periscope and there were claims of U-boats being rammed and suspicious oil patches supposedly indicating enemy submarine activity. During the running fight between British and German battlecruisers that opened proceedings, torpedo tracks and near misses were reported by Royal Navy ships along with a periscope sighting. Admiral Beatty mistakenly thought his vessels were passing over a line of specially placed U-boats but it was the battlecruiser *Moltke* – *E1*'s victim in the Baltic and now back in service – that was responsible. She had fired torpedoes shortly before the British sightings and all the submarine sightings in the main clashes were phantoms.

German submarines had no success in catching British warships either before or after the battle and U-boats sent misleading sighting reports of RN units, which proved no use at all in springing the trap.

In the end no submarines of any kind were directly engaged in the main fight but a tiny combat vessel so long derided by the battleship faction had exerted a powerful influence on the course of the war's greatest naval battle, even though it wasn't there.

10   Turning the Screw

In its immediate aftermath Jutland seemed to be one thing, when in fact it was quite another. The Germans saw it as their triumph, trumpeting it to the world in the neutral press. One German newspaper mounted a huge placard on its offices displaying the incredible words: 'Trafalgar is Wiped Out.'[1]

The British public regarded Jutland as a shameful failure but their nation's naval supremacy held even though it was not a clear-cut tactical victory. The huge Grand Fleet soaked up the damage and remained the predominant maritime force, but Jutland did end any chance of an outflanking move by the British through the Baltic, ensuring hopes of getting supplies and troop reinforcements to the Russians via that route were stillborn.

The Jutland result froze in place the brutal dynamic of the war: bloody stalemate on the Western Front and an unyielding British naval blockade. After near-hysterical jubilation in the battle's immediate aftermath, the strategic failure of the High Sea Fleet sank in for the Germans. Their navy's heavily damaged ships would take months to repair and would not be ready for action again until August. Some key vessels were non-operational for the rest of the year. Jutland had proved Germany's battleships were inadequate for the job of taking Britain out of the war and Admiral Scheer was not afraid to admit this. He told the Kaiser: 'A victorious termination of the war within measurable time can only be obtained by destroying the economic resources of Great Britain, namely, by the employment of submarines against British commerce.'[2] It was a double-edged sword, for a return to unrestricted submarine warfare risked America entering the struggle on the Allied side. With Scheer and others pressing for unrestricted submarine warfare immediately, Bethmann-Hollweg resisted while the Kaiser still wavered.

As a sequel to Jutland, in mid-August 1916 Admiral Scheer decided on a bombardment of a port on England's north-east coast, again trying to tempt British battlecruisers out for annihilation. He was determined to use submarines as key players in the scheme. Five capital ships would form Scheer's bait for a raid on Sunderland, including the *Moltke*. Fifteen dreadnoughts were to hang back, waiting to pounce. It was hoped that in seeking to close with *Moltke* and the other four ships, Beatty's battlecruisers would blunder into two lines of U-boats (12 submarines) before the main German force weighed in and smashed them to pieces. Eight Zeppelins would be aloft, keeping watch for the Grand Fleet entering from the north.

Once again the submarine trap failed though two British cruisers were sunk, while the German fleet found itself almost trapped by the Grand Fleet and had to withdraw. The British submarine picket off the German bases similarly failed to sink anything as the High Sea Fleet emerged from its lair.

Alas, poor Jellicoe would not get an opportunity to wipe away the stain on his reputation for not delivering a new Trafalgar. Nor would the Royal Navy receive another chance to destroy an entire enemy battle fleet at sea. In August 1916 Zeppelins gave the game away – spotting the RN's Harwich Force – and, acting on their reports, the High Sea Fleet slipped through the noose tightening around it. A U-boat also reported the British battle fleet approaching from the north and that confirmed the wisdom of the retreat. Admiral Jellicoe withdrew too, anxious not to risk either the Grand Fleet or the BCF when there was no chance of a fleet-versus-fleet action and he remained extremely wary of both mines and U-boats.

The failure of the German submarine trap was evidence of an ailment. The recent focus on attacking enemy trade had not prepared the U-boats well for a different kind of effort. Their captains were both inexperienced in attacking an enemy battle fleet through its protective screen and co-ordinating their movements with surface units.

In the aftermath of this deeply frustrating episode, Jellicoe informed the Admiralty that he felt it most unwise for light cruisers – even if moving fast and undertaking evasive manoeuvres – to stray unescorted into waters where submarines were operating. Jellicoe was not surprised by the enemy's attempt to lay a submarine trap for the Grand Fleet but rather that it had not been tried more often.

It was decided not to send the Grand Fleet main force into the southern North Sea unless there were plentiful destroyers to act as a screen, though if the nation was in peril it would still take the risk.

Admiral Scheer was also very concerned about submarine ambushes, evidence of which was provided when battlecruiser *Derfflinger* was attacked in the early hours of 20 August as she returned home.

Both torpedoes fired by *E23* missed but it was an unsettling demonstration of hidden dangers. When German major units next ventured out, eight weeks later, *E38* scored a torpedo hit on the cruiser *München*, forcing Scheer to withdraw. The following month Noel Laurence, who had already managed to persuade the enemy not to risk capital ships in the Baltic, played his part in achieving the same state of affairs in the North Sea.

His latest command was *J1*, first-in-class of a new type of large, 1,820-ton fast boat with three propellers. *J1* also had four bow tubes, enabling a powerful torpedo salvo.

She was an example of battleship admirals trying to bend submarines to suit their old-fashioned needs. Possessing a large flat upper deck and surface ship style bow, she was designed to run ahead of the Grand Fleet like a torpedo boat and then dive for the attack.

Cdr Laurence found *J1* hard to handle when submerged and keeping her stable at periscope depth for anything but short periods was very difficult. His boat's idiosyncrasies didn't stop Laurence from pulling off a remarkable achievement in heavy seas as *J1* prowled up and down off Denmark. At ten minutes to noon on 5 November, during one of his brief excursions to periscope depth, Laurence was delighted to find fat targets. It was a quartet of Kaiser Class battleships and his old friend *Moltke*.

They were providing cover for a rescue mission on behalf of *U-30* and *U-20*, which had run aground on the Danish coast. They were notorious submarines that had outraged America with their activities. While *U-30*, which sank the *Gulflight* in May 1915, managed to get herself afloat again, *U-20* – the boat that torpedoed *Lusitania*, and which was still under the command of Kapitänleutnant Schwieger – would not budge. Her crew blew her up.

Stalking the battleships sent on a vain mission to rescue the U-boats, despite the rough conditions and only fleeting periscope looks, with *J1* even exposing herself on the surface momentarily, Laurence took his chance. When *J1* was around 4,000 yards to port of the German line, he fired a full spread of torpedoes, scoring a hit each on the *Kronprinz* and the *Grosser Kurfürst*. They ended up in dry dock for a considerable time though Laurence wished that he'd aimed all four torpedoes at a single ship and sunk it.

The Kaiser was furious, telling Scheer it was 'disproportionate' to risk battleships to save U-boats, and banned him from doing so again. Scheer explained that it would have been 'glad tidings for the British Government' had two U-boats been destroyed by Royal Navy action or interned by the Danes.[3] Scheer explained the importance of U-boat crews knowing their own navy would do its utmost to protect them if they got into difficulties. This was needed in order to preserve their 'ardour'[4] for risky work. With no major deployments then planned, the battleships had nothing better to do anyway and, as Scheer proudly stated: 'English torpedoes have never yet proved fatal to our big ships . . .'[5] Scheer had, however, gone cold on venturing across to the North Sea to trap British battlecruisers. He now saw Germany's submarines as potentially succeeding where the surface fleet had failed. Calling the U-boat force a 'sharp blade', he was frustrated by reluctance in the political leadership about a return to unrestricted submarine warfare. The Kaiser, too, remained opposed, quailing at the idea of U-boats firing torpedoes into ships carrying women and children, but Scheer and other senior naval officers advocating unrestricted submarine warfare had powerful allies in the German Army.

Both Paul von Hindenburg and Erich Ludendorff, the men in

command of the main effort on the Western Front, believed the war could not be won on land. By 1916 the scale of bloodletting had reached staggering proportions. The horror of Verdun was drawn out almost from the beginning to the end of the year, with 550,000 Frenchmen killed and wounded while more than 430,000 Germans were sent to their graves or injured. Meanwhile, the Somme offensive cost the British heavily – 19,240 dead and 35,493 wounded on 1 July 1916 alone. The sixteen-week offensive would see a total of 620,000 Allied casualties (420,000 of them British and Empire troops).[6]

It also drained away the core strength and morale of the German Army, which suffered equally during August counter-attacks – around half a million dead and wounded, including thousands of irreplaceable junior officers and non-commissioned officers. This vain sacrifice was a major reason why admirals and generals believed the only road to an outcome favourable for Germany was unrestricted submarine warfare. The wonder weapon must be fully unsheathed, to force Britain to the negotiating table.

On the Allied side, in late November the Marquess of Lansdowne pushed for a negotiated peace in order to avoid 'the ruin of the civilised world'.[7] He suggested the 'peace party' in Germany should be assisted by reassurances that the Allies did not 'desire annihilation of Germany as a great power' and that 'freedom of the seas' should be safeguarded.

Bethmann-Hollweg was still making efforts to find a means to end the war, suggesting in late 1916 that peace talks could be held in a neutral country. His proposals came to nothing, strengthening the hand of the unrestricted submarine warfare faction.

Those in the German political leadership who opposed it did not do so because they cared about the loss of civilian life per se. It was the potential *for American lives to be lost* that horrified Bethmann-Hollweg and his fellow peace advocates; the more Americans were killed by German submarines, the more likely the USA was to enter the war on the side of the enemy.

Against the determined resolve of senior officers to have unrestricted submarine warfare imposed, and with the Chancellor getting no traction with his peace proposals, the Kaiser caved in. It was, anyway, impossible to resist the public pressure for U-boats to be freed from restrictions.

The realisation that there would be no quick, glorious victory had dawned most cruelly, with casualty lists extending into the hundreds of thousands and starvation at home.

In the autumn of 1916, British intelligence agents in Central Powers nations sent reports to London of real hardship among the enemy civilian population. While the troops on the front line were necessarily kept well fed to carry on fighting, on the home front the winter of 1916–17 was dubbed 'the turnip winter' as the root vegetable had become the staple. In one Berlin restaurant boiled crow was also on the menu.[8] Austro-Hungary was in a similarly poor situation, if not worse, so how could the leadership possibly restrain the U-boats?

A further driver was the impact of the British blockade on the war industries. Supplies of iron ore, nickel, rubber and copper remained short and this in turn made arms manufacturing problematic, including the construction of warships and submarines. One or the other had to get priority and – recognising the surface fleet had failed to break Britain's grip on the oceans – it would be U-boats. Yet, as naval construction took precedence over merchant ships, the more cargo-carrying ships the British sank or captured, or were interned by the neutral powers, the worse the situation got.

To help break the British stranglehold scarce resources were devoted to constructing two large merchant submarines, in order to sneak essential war supplies through the Royal Navy's cordon of steel.

The first of these was *U-Deutschland*, which was not officially a naval vessel, at least not at that stage of her career, and there would also be a sister, *U-Bremen*. In the context of Germany's overall dire position, the amount of cargo *U-Deutschland* brought back during two transatlantic voyages was modest while sister vessel *U-Bremen* never even completed her maiden transatlantic crossing. She disappeared along with her entire crew. With an urgent need to field as many U-boats as possible in the unrestricted campaign, *U-Deutschland* would ultimately be converted into a fully-fledged offensive weapon fitted with torpedo tubes and guns.

The U-boat force sent its vessels to prey on enemy trade off the east coast of the USA, and at the centre of one drama would be a young officer who had trained the merchant submarine crews for their voyages.

Though he was a late starter – not receiving his first front line

Kapitänleutnant Hans Rose, captain of *U-53*. (*NHHC*)

submarine command until April 1916, when *U-53* was commissioned into service – 31-year-old Kapitänleutnant Hans Rose would become one of Germany's foremost submarine aces.

He was handpicked for *U-53*'s ground-breaking transatlantic mission by the head of the U-boat service, Kommodore Hermann Bauer, who valued Rose's cool head and maturity. No U-boat captain had ever conducted a solo mission at such a distance. Australian and British boats may have sailed thousands of miles but they made port calls along the way or sailed in convoy. This would be the first unsupported transoceanic projection of power by any submarine.

In weighing up the challenge ahead, Rose told Bauer that *U-53* would, as she was then configured, find it very difficult to pull it off, if not impossible. For example, *U-53* could manage a range of 5,600 nautical miles[9] at most, but would need longer legs than that. Modifications were essential and the improvements were made within a fortnight, with some buoyancy tanks converted to take additional oil. Even a range of 7,600nm was on the margins for such a round trip – most of it run on the surface to conduct the passage as swiftly as possible while also preserving battery power, which would only be used when it was necessary to dive to avoid trouble.

During the mission *U-53* was to call at an American port to let US Navy officers visit a state-of-the-art submarine. This would put a human face on Germany's U-boat campaign, to offset Allied propaganda about so-called pirates; with Rose and his men explaining how the Germans were only resorting to submarine warfare to loosen the British blockade garrotting their nation. Fully ready for the task ahead, *U-53* sailed from Wilhelmshaven on 15 September, with three months' supplies aboard. After a very brief visit to fly the flag at Newport, Rhode Island, where the openness of the Germans surprised American visitors to the boat, *U-53* headed back out to sea late in the afternoon on 7 October. She set course for waters around the Nantucket Lightship, just outside the three-mile limit of US territorial waters. Staying off the coast for a day, *U-53* sank five ships in short order and then set course for home, leaving behind a deeply shocked USA. *The New York Times* remarked ruefully in an editorial on the U-boat's activities: 'No one had thought of the long gray visitor as a destroyer of shipping and perhaps of lives.'[10]

During his mini campaign Rose was careful to take measures to avoid loss of life, going as far as towing lifeboats over to the lightship.

With maydays filling the airwaves, 15 American warships made for the scene, including the destroyer USS *Fanning*, whose sailors watched incredulously as *U-53* unhurriedly went about her business. 'It was an unbelievable sight,' said Lt George Fort.[11] As it was all happening within international waters, the crews of the American warships could do nothing but look on 'helpless, like spectators at a dog fight '.[12]

In one case, the ship in question stubbornly stayed afloat, even after charges in her hold detonated. Rose decided he would have to take decisive action, signalling to a USN destroyer: 'Get out of my way. I'm going to torpedo the ship!'[13] Finally, before sinking the Norwegian-flagged oil tanker *Christian Knudsen*, the submarine went alongside her to refuel. Having finished a good day's work, Rose gave orders to dive and *U-53* made her exit.

Canadian newspapers claimed that American inaction aided and abetted German aggression but Assistant Secretary of the Navy Franklin D. Roosevelt maintained that the USN had acted under the remit of international law. Intervening would have been a violation of the USA's neutrality.[14]

U-53's assault on shipping had a significant impact on Wall Street, wiping $500 million off the value of shares in a quarter of an hour.[15]

The cost of marine insurance skyrocketed.

Theodore Roosevelt – former Navy Secretary and President as well as being F.D.R.'s cousin – warned: 'War has been creeping nearer and nearer, until it stares at us from just beyond our three-mile limit . . .'[16]

Realising the utter vulnerability of North American littoral waters, the Admiralty put pressure on Canadian authorities to create a coastal patrol force of armed trawlers and other small vessels. Guns to arm these vessels and experienced sailors to both command and help operate them were also promised, to try to protect shipping using Canadian ports.

As far as the Germans were concerned *U-53*'s brief foray fulfilled its objective of providing a deterrent to American intervention in the war on the Allied side, proving no part of the Atlantic Ocean was safe from U-boats.

Meanwhile, submarine warfare in waters around the British Isles was being pursued with vigour. Due to more U-boats both in commission and deployed on operations – many of them newer craft possessing greater offensive capabilities and range – the latest campaign was achieving much more impact than that of 1915.

Though not always sticking to Prize Rules, the Germans tried to conduct themselves within its strictures. They sent 341,360 tons to the bottom in October 1916 and in January 1917 would sink 328,390 tons of neutral and enemy shipping.[17]

A sense of crisis grew in Britain. Aside from trying to import enough for its own needs, it was keeping France in the fight with supplies of coal and other vital goods. It was feared the activities of U-boats could, if they proved wildly successful, end the war and force a negotiated peace on terms favourable to the enemy.

An official list of merchant vessels published in the *Daily Chronicle* would claim that between 26 October 1916 and 23 January 1917 some 470 vessels were sunk, including 187 British.[18] This was an intolerable casualty rate and proof that Scheer's 'sharp blade' was beginning to cut deep.

11   An Impossible Task

In late November 1916 Admiral Jellicoe reluctantly yielded command of the Grand Fleet to become First Sea Lord, primarily to lead the fight against the U-boats.

His new appointment followed an emergency meeting in London held earlier in the month and called at Jellicoe's instigation. He outlined his anxiety over 'the ever-growing danger of the submarine' and recommended 'adoption of the most energetic measures'. If the navy was not able to destroy enemy submarines and protect 'sea communications' – the routes used by merchant vessels to reach Britain – Jellicoe feared 'there was undoubted risk of our being forced into making an unsatisfactory peace'.

His fears were provoked by intelligence reports of the Germans 'making special efforts' to expand their submarine force. There was, Jellicoe felt, no chance of destroying enemy craft at a faster rate than Germany could build them. Existing anti-submarine measures were not up to the job. He felt the Admiralty lacked focus and drive even though there was 'insufficient reserve of food in the country to provide against the consequences of successful action by enemy submarines'. Construction of merchant ships to replace those sunk by U-boats was inadequate.

Jellicoe proposed to the First Sea Lord, Admiral Sir Henry Jackson, whom he would shortly replace, that a committee or even a new department in the Admiralty, should be established in order to tackle 'the serious danger confronting us'. It should be staffed by 'clever and young officers who had shown marked ability in studying new ideas'.[1] They would analyse how best to protect merchant shipping and galvanise development of anti-submarine weapons.

Jellicoe judged that the Germans would not risk their battle fleet in action again before the U-boats had been given a chance to succeed (or fail) in the task of destroying Britain's trade. He therefore proposed taking destroyers away from Grand Fleet duties to operate against submarines.

He maintained that the U-boat threat must be dealt with 'at all costs, and without delay, since the existence of armies as well as that of the civilian population depended on merchant shipping'.[2]

Having lit a fire under the Admiralty, and, he hoped, the government too, Jellicoe returned to the Grand Fleet on Guy Fawkes night. On 24 November he was handed a telegram from the First Lord, Arthur Balfour, offering him the job of First Sea Lord. The 61-year-old Admiral Jackson had confessed it was time he 'made way for a more energetic and more experienced Admiral than I can claim to be . . .'[3]

Jellicoe was under no illusions about leaping from the frying pan into the fire. There had been widespread attacks in the press and Parliament on Jackson, along with other senior officers and politicians, for failing to suppress the U-boats or prevent the bombardment of east coast towns. Jellicoe felt the latter was impossible to stop, unless major British units happened to be in the same stretch of sea. The battle against submarines needed six months to a year at least, until new equipment and tactics bore fruit. It was with a heavy heart that Jellicoe departed his flagship *Iron Duke* on 28 November, cheered by the roars of thousands of his sailors, many of whom wept to see him go.

Heads continued to roll, with the First Lord also exiting and being replaced by Sir Edward Carson, a former leader of the anti-Home Rule movement in Ulster and latterly attorney general. Prime Minister Herbert Asquith quit on 5 December, partly due to his failure to combat the submarine menace, and was replaced by Lloyd George at the head of a new coalition.

Looking on aghast was Admiral Fisher, forced into retirement again after the Dardanelles debacle. 'The British Empire and the German submarine cannot co-exist,' he wrote to Reginald McKenna, a former First Lord of the Admiralty who was similarly out of favour. '. . . one or the other must shortly be destroyed.'[4]

By late January 1917 Jellicoe's health was buckling under the burden of his new task and he was confined to bed 'with neuritis'. Fisher rushed to his bedside but was banned by Lady Jellicoe from spending more than ten minutes with her poorly husband. He stayed an hour, with Jellicoe revealing his 'one and only terror is the German submarine menace' and moaning that it was a threat that 18 months of 'Admiralty apathy has made so prodigious as to be almost beyond cure!' In Fisher's view civilised warfare was a thing of the past, but he felt Jellicoe was not 'Satanic' enough to vanquish the uncivilised U-boats.[5]

For the submariners tasked with bringing Britain to its knees the boot seemed to be very much on the other foot. The war artist Claus Bergen, who had volunteered to capture life at sea in the famous *U-53*, felt the German people were being consigned 'to starve like rats in a trap' and the U-boats were engaged in a 'sacred fight to cut off the enemy's supplies as well'.[6]

U-53 submariners who went aboard British vessels to sink them with charges discovered a cornucopia of goods now unknown in Germany. These included 'cocoa, coffee and expensive tea' along with 'fine white English bread, English marmalade, ham and bully-beef, bacon and beans ... good soap ... tobacco ... oilskins [and] rubber boots that did not fit the crew'.[7] This discarded surplus footwear seemed most outrageous of all.

U-53 senior rating Roman Bader raged against an enemy 'system of war that thrust into the hands of innocent German children a slice of raw onion for their supper'. The British were 'inhuman' for turning his fellow Germans into 'skin and bone'.[8] Sinking cargo vessels engaged in feeding the enemy seemed entirely justified.

In Britain the popular war papers still branded German submariners 'pirates' and 'outlaws', with the notorious *U-53* allegedly a prime example. According to one illustrated journal of the war's events, her previous exploits off the coast of the USA demonstrated that submarines represented an unprecedented danger. Never before, so it claimed, 'had the whole civilised world been menaced with such horrors, with indiscriminate massacre at sea on so colossal a scale'.[9]

This was even before unrestricted submarine warfare fully resumed.

It duly came on 1 February 1917 and by then Germany had 105 U-boats in commission. Deployed strength at sea was variable, with 44 across all theatres. Of these vessels, only a small proportion accounted for the majority of the enemy's losses. Germany's top aces were Lothar von Arnauld de la Perière (*U-35*), Walther Forstmann (*U-39*), Max Valentiner (*U-38*), Otto Steinbrink (*U-34*), Hans Rose (*U-53*) and Walther von Schwieger (*U-20*).

During one Mediterranean patrol by *U-35*, from 26 July to 20 August 1916 de la Perière sank 54 vessels, notching up a total of 90,350 gross tons of shipping. By war's end his overall total would be 453,700 tons, which has never been bettered.

*

Among the dirty tricks already used by the Admiralty against U-boats were the notorious Q-ships. These vessels even worked with Royal Navy submarines to trump the stealth of the enemy via their own brand of covert lethality. The idea for Q-ships sprang from a conversation in September 1914 between Winston Churchill and the naval commander at Portsmouth, Admiral Sir Hedworth Meux. The latter complained of an incident in which a German submarine attacked a ship carrying fruit and vegetables from France to Southampton. The admiral and Churchill, at the time First Lord of the Admiralty, agreed it would be wonderful if a gun could be hidden aboard the vessel.[10] Although a weapon was fitted, an opportunity to blaze away from amid the spuds and carrots never arose, at least not for that particular ship.

When the Germans expanded their submarine operations early in 1915, Churchill authorised the introduction of more vessels that could possibly sink U-boats by surprise. It seemed as a good an idea as any other at a time when anti-submarine measures actually remained few and far between.

Originally dubbed Special Service Ships, they were mainly small cargo ships or trawlers taken up from trade, though some were purpose-built. Their weaponry usually consisted of a 4-inch gun, at least a pair of 12pdrs and also depth charges, though the larger ones were more heavily armed.

The guns were concealed under bogus lifeboats or behind fake superstructure with hinged drop-down panels. With the benefit of hidden flotation measures, such as empty barrels in their holds, they also had a pretty good chance of surviving a torpedo hit.

The point was to get U-boats to expose themselves on the surface – as they would be disinclined to waste a torpedo on a target apparently so modest – and then lure them within point blank range of the guns.

The existence of Q-ships became known to the Germans quite soon after they were introduced, partly thanks to spies in British and Irish ports reporting mysterious craft under conversion, or construction. Queenstown, in the south-west of Ireland, was particularly active (which is perhaps why the vessels ended up being called Q-ships).

Commissioned by both the British and French navies, the first Q-ships began operations in November 1914 and over the next three years sank eleven U-boats. For a time at the beginning some trawlers were used as decoys for accompanying submarines, the Royal Navy assigning elderly C Class coastal boats to work with them. The submarine was connected to the Q-ship via an underwater cable (for towing) and a telephone line, both of which would be disconnected on contact with the enemy.

The first German submarine to be sunk by a Q-ship was *UC-40*, which encountered the converted steam trawler *Taranaki* in late June 1915, around 50 miles off Aberdeen. Both *Taranaki* and *C24* had called at the Scottish port but kept well away from each other in order to avoid giving the game away. Once out at sea and under cover of night they linked up. Securely attached to *Taranaki*, the submarine maintained a depth of 40ft, with someone telephoning the trawler at regular intervals to ensure the link functioned. Two hours into the patrol – the first of its kind ever – the phone rang in *C24*. A voice on the other end said a German submarine had surfaced close by and was firing at *Taranaki*.

The Q-ship obeyed the U-boat's heave-to order, with members of her crew pretending to abandon ship, but the tow failed to disconnect properly, leaving 540ft of cable hanging from *C24*'s nose. The British submarine was able to manoeuvre to prevent it entangling the propeller. Lt George Mackness of *C24* recalled that his boat was gifted 'an absolutely sitting shot at the German as she was stopped beam on to us'.[11] *C24*'s torpedo hit the U-boat square on and only the Commanding Officer, Kapitänleutnant Gerhardt Fürbringer, a junior officer and a rating survived, because they had all been on the submarine's bridge. They were picked up by *Taranaki* with Fürbringer accusing the British of using 'a dirty trick'.[12] The torpedo fired by *C24* was a Mk5, one of the oldest types in the Royal Navy inventory, with a relatively small warhead, and Fürbringer initially believed it was an internal explosion. The other German officer was very angry with Fürbringer 'for not having kept on the move when on the surface'.[13]

Around three weeks later, also in waters off Scotland, *U-23* was caught in the same kind of trap. Pretending to be Norwegian, the decoy trawler *Princess Louise* distracted the German while *C27* torpedoed her. Ten men were saved, including the captain and members of the gun crew.

These would be the only enemy submarines confirmed sunk by British submarines working with Q-ships.

While it is the activities of British Q-ships that are most famous, the French operated 15, the Russians and Italians deployed them and both the Turks and the Germans employed their own versions. The Turks used a Q-ship named *Dare* disguised as a schooner and she tried to ambush the Russian submarine *Tyulen* on 13 August 1915, but failed to sink her.

Allied Q-ships did not rack up a huge score of victims. While only 11 submarines were sunk for the loss of 61 British and three French Q-ships between 1914 and 1918. Yet the psychological impact of their activities on U-boat crews was significant. Many innocent merchant vessels plying their trade escaped attack because a German submarine captain feared he was looking at a potential Q-ship and was deterred. A number of U-boats were damaged during encounters with Q-ships and this took them out of action. As news of the disguised war vessels spread, U-boat captains became even more wary. Also, as unrestricted submarine warfare became the norm, with torpedoes more frequently used, so the likelihood of a Q-ship success declined.

In late February 1917 the British pulled off a masterstroke by unveiling the infamous Zimmermann Note. A telegraphic message sent by newly appointed German foreign minister Arthur Zimmermann, it communicated the resumption of unrestricted submarine warfare to Count Johann von Bernstorff, Germany's Ambassador in Washington DC.

This was not news to the Americans. On 31 January – the day before the new campaign began – their ambassador in Berlin, James Gerard, had been told as much by Zimmermann. As would soon be discovered, this was *after* the note had been sent. It had actually been intercepted by Room 40 on 16 January, but the British chose not to immediately reveal their explosive intelligence until it would have greatest effect.

During the Berlin meeting Zimmermann boasted to Gerard that the war would be over within months and the Allies driven to the negotiating table, the oceans graveyards for their merchant vessels. Zimmermann explained that unrestricted submarine warfare was necessary as the German people were being starved to death by the British blockade.

What the Americans did not know, until a transcript of the Zimmermann Note was delivered to them, was that – should it come to hostilities between the USA and Germany – Berlin was willing to assist Mexico with a land grab. The German Admiralty had also previously offered U-boats and auxiliary cruisers to operate in the Gulf of Mexico in support of an invasion. To transmit his note Zimmermann added insult to injury. In addition to using other routes of signals communication, he utilised a secure telegraph line the Germans had been authorised to use by the US State Department *only* for peace proposals.

The Zimmermann Note began by explaining it was Germany's intent to 'endeavour . . . to keep the U.S.A. neutral' but also advised: 'In the event of this not succeeding we [should] make Mexico a proposal of alliance on the following basis: Make war together. Make peace together.'[14] This was what made the note so incendiary.

The ultimate recipient of the details contained within the Zimmermann Note was the German Minister in Mexico, Heinrich von Eckhard. If an invitation for Mexico to invade the USA was not enough to inflame the majority of Americans against Germany, there was also a suggestion of Japan being asked to join the fight (by switching sides).

Had the Germans suspected the British were tapping transatlantic cables carrying telegrams – and had penetrated their codes – the Zimmermann Note might also have gone via another method. The use of a diplomatic pouch carried by the cargo submarine *U-Deutschland* had been mooted. According to naval intelligence officer Franz von Rintelen, sending it via submarine seemed to offer an 'absolutely safe way' of conveying the message[15] and *U-Deutschland* was due to depart Bremerhaven on 17 January 1917 for another cargo run to the USA.[16] But the submarine option was slow and at any moment there might be an incident in which a U-boat sinking, or sinkings, tipped America over the edge into war.

Had the *U-Deutschland* option alone been used, the Zimmermann Note might have remained secret and American opinion might not have swung so violently, or swiftly, in favour of war with Germany.

In any event, several U-boat attacks tipped the American public even more against the Germans. The 16-year-old freighter *Housatonic* was the first US-flagged ship sunk in the new unrestricted campaign, on 3 February, the same day Washington severed diplomatic relations with Berlin.

Sharing her name with the first ship sunk by a submarine, the 3,143-ton *Housatonic* was in February 1917 carrying wheat to London when intercepted by *U-53* off the Scilly Isles. To show that she was neutral a massive Stars and Stripes was painted on each side of her hull, but this did not save the merchant ship. The submarine, still commanded by

Hans Rose, surfaced and put some shots across *Housatonic*'s bows. Rose ordered papers detailing the cargo brought to him, with contraband revealed to be aboard.

'I have orders to sink every vessel coming to England,' Rose told the captain of *Housatonic*, Thomas Ensor, 'and though I am sorry, it is my duty to sink you.' The *Housatonic*'s crew was given an hour to abandon ship, with *U-53*'s boarding party delighted to purloin soap, which was now impossible to get in Germany.[17]

Showing his customary humanity, Rose kept *U-53* on the surface for 90 minutes to tow the lifeboats closer to the Cornish coast. Spotting a Royal Navy patrol vessel, *U-53* attracted attention by firing a couple of shots. Casting off the lifeboats, the submarine dived and left the area.

It was felt in the USA that while the Germans would show such humanity at the outset of their new campaign – especially towards vessels that sailed prior to the start date – as the weeks went by they would become more ruthless. In the period 3 February to 4 April ten American merchant ships were sunk by U-boats and of the 64 merchant mariners killed, 24 were US citizens. Three of the ships were sunk in the Mediterranean and the rest in waters stretching from Ireland to Brittany.

The sinking of three American vessels on 16 and 17 March – the freighters *Vigilancia* and *City of Memphis* along with tanker *Illinois* – off Plymouth, Ireland and the Channel Islands, respectively, caused deep disquiet in the USA. Fifteen of the 45-strong crew of the *Vigilancia* were killed, half a dozen of them Americans, *The New York Times* reporting on 19 March that she 'was torpedoed without warning'.

It was the sinking of a Cunard liner that had the most impact. Departing New York on 17 February, the 18,099-ton RMS *Laconia* was bound for Liverpool carrying both cargo and 73 passengers, with a crew of 216 composed of both British and American mariners. In her holds were thousands of empty shell casings, 3,000 tons of steel, bales of cotton and mail. *Laconia* was also carrying treasure: 132 boxes of silver coins along with 852 bars of silver. She was sunk on the night of 25 February. In one damaged, waterlogged lifeboat two American women – 59-year-old Mary Hoy and her 34-year-old daughter, Elizabeth, both from Chicago but latterly residents of London – grew steadily weaker from exposure. Although transferred into another lifeboat, they both died, the mother expiring in the arms of the daughter who let her slip away into the ocean. Within minutes the daughter allowed herself to be taken by the big waves sweeping over the boat. In all six passengers and six members of the ship's crew were claimed, one of the latter a US citizen. Several hours later HMS *Laburnum* appeared, bringing salvation.

Going ashore in Queenstown, survivors were escorted away to be given hot baths followed by a meal of broth, salmon, turkey and champagne. Among the *Laconia* survivors was eager young war reporter Floyd Gibbons, of the *Chicago Tribune*, who had been ordered to join the newspaper's London bureau. Gibbons decided to hunt for a typewriter and, after finding one in a nearby office, pounded out a 4,000-word report, which he cabled to his newspaper immediately. It was the revelation of how the two American women lost their lives that caused the greatest stir in the USA. Mrs Hoy's 33-year-old son, Austin, who worked for an American engineering firm in London, sent an angry telegram to President Wilson describing his mother and sister as 'foully murdered on the high seas'.[18]

Of the toll in US shipping and lives during such a short period *The New York Times* observed: '. . . it was unofficially admitted here [in Washington DC] tonight that virtually a state of war exists between the United States and Germany.' Less than three weeks later that virtual state of war became an actual fact.

12   Struggle by Hunger

After being removed from his position as First Lord of the Admiralty, Arthur Balfour was made Foreign Secretary and in April 1917 embarked on the fast liner RMS *Olympic* to make a risky transatlantic crossing for a summit meeting in the USA.

It had been arranged immediately after the USA declared war on Germany on 6 April 1917, with Balfour due to sail from Liverpool a week later. The Balfour Mission would discuss with President Wilson and other top officials how the USA could best co-ordinate with Britain in pursuit of Germany's defeat.

When President Wilson told Congress on 3 April that he wished it to declare war Balfour had described that event as 'a great day for the world'.[1] He felt the prospects of victory were good, provided the menace of the U-boats could be overcome. Along with specially selected top brass and others in his mission, Balfour embarked aboard the 46,359-ton sister vessel to the ill-fated *Titanic* feeling a mixture of excitement and trepidation. Now sporting dazzle paint, to try and confuse U-boat captains about what she was – and even which way she was heading – the six-year-old *Olympic* would be followed closely by the ten-year-old fast liner *Adriatic*.

Like *Olympic* requisitioned for Admiralty service, the 24,000-ton *Adriatic* could manage a top speed of 17 knots. This was enough to outrun a U-boat, while *Olympic* boasted an impressive 24 knots. The enemy submarine threat still put a chill into the warm optimism surrounding the Balfour Mission. Despite a host of escorting cruisers and destroyers, the two liners turned back to Liverpool, such was the prevailing U-boat anxiety.

Eventually they got underway properly, with escorts coursing ahead and all around at top speed. Once the warships reached the end of their range, *Olympic* and *Adriatic* went on alone, placing their best defence in sheer speed. Aboard *Olympic* Balfour fell into a dark mood during 'a terrible week we spent at sea in that voyage to the United States'. He felt the German submarine campaign was succeeding, with U-boats 'destroying our shipping and we had no means of preventing it. I could not help thinking that we were facing the defeat of Great Britain.'[2]

Among those in *Adriatic* was naval officer spy Franz von Rintelen. He was being shipped back to the USA, where authorities wanted to prosecute him for running a sabotage campaign against merchant vessels sailing from American ports (and even blowing up warehouses). Von Rintelen had been arrested by the British when the neutral merchant vessel in which he was travelling back to Germany was boarded in the English Channel. At one stage it was mistakenly reported in newspapers that von Rintelen had been executed by firing squad. Once the USA entered the conflict the British decided to send him back across the Atlantic to face justice, despite his status as a prisoner of war.

For the majority of the voyage von Rintelen wore civilian clothes, his assigned British naval officer escort never more than a few feet from his side. He was less than amused to be locked into his cabin at night, protesting that if a U-boat torpedoed *Adriatic* he would be 'drowned like a rat'.³ Von Rintelen's cabin door was thereafter left unlocked but he was put on his honour not to get up to any mischief. This was quite a risk with a man whose speciality had been sabotaging merchant ships.

As the voyage progressed, periscopeitis asserted itself and even the cool von Rintelen got twitchy. Considering it likely that *Adriatic* and *Olympic* would meet a U-boat and be boarded, he went to elaborate lengths to indicate he was a German. He secretly made a flag by stitching together material in the national colours of black, white and red. Fearing he would be prevented from speaking by his escort, von Rintelen planned to wrap it around his waist under his jacket. He would leave it unbuttoned to flash the flag at any U-boat boarding party. Von Rintelen and the Balfour Mission were safely delivered to the USA and the naval spy's trial began in May 1917. He was arraigned before the judge alongside other German agents, officials, saboteurs and sympathisers arrested by the authorities, evading the death sentence but receiving four years in prison.

Arthur Balfour was quite overwhelmed by the reception he received from crowds of jubilant, cheering Americans, but there was serious business to be settled. Pressing issues Balfour would raise with President Wilson included a means to increase ships carrying material to Europe and the construction of merchant vessels to replace those lost to U-boat action. It was estimated that the British mercantile marine was 400 ships short of what it required to meet the needs of feeding the nation while also supplying the armed forces and assisting allies.

Balfour intended requesting that the USA's wheat surpluses should be shipped across the Atlantic, while the British and French wanted to relieve pressure on their own food supplies by having the Americans train their troops at home before shipping them to Europe.

Should the Americans provide even 500,000 tons of shipping, it would barely make up for what was being lost *each month*, and to help him lobby for help Balfour received an alarming running tally of losses. Deep gloom descended on receiving news that U-boats had sunk 420,000 tons of Allied shipping between 1 and 19 April. Losses that month, from the Mediterranean to the Atlantic, would peak at 860,344 tons of shipping (810 vessels) of which 545,282 tons were British.[4] Only two U-boats were sunk in the same period.

The German naval leadership had calculated that their submarines needed to sink around 600,000 tons of shipping a month to starve the British into capitulation. April 1917 gave them a deeply gratifying total of 802 tons of shipping sunk 'per U-boat day'.[5]

In March U-boats had claimed more than 593,000 tons of shipping (353,478 tons British) and in May would notch up over 596,000 tons (353,289 tons British) for seven U-boats sunk. In June more than 687,000 tons (477,925 tons British) were sunk, while the Germans lost just two submarines.[6]

The primary killing grounds were the narrower waters where merchant vessels inevitably clustered as they sailed up the English Channel and entered the Irish Sea or the Clyde, heading for ports such as Southampton, Liverpool, Glasgow or London. Of the 272 ships sunk by U-boats in June 1917 it transpired that 66 per cent were attacked in the South West Approaches.

The losses may have been terrible, but even with April's horrific spike the Americans were reluctant to allow their new war partners unfettered access to shipping. They feared their core stock might be sacrificed to preserve Britain's.

The US Ambassador to London did his bit to convey the impact the U-boats were having, writing to a senior official in the State Department in early May 1917 that even he and his staff were on rations.

'There are no potatoes,' Walter Hines Page revealed. 'We have meatless days. Good wheat meantime is sunk every day. The submarine must be knocked out. Else the earth will be ruled by the German bayonet and natural living will be verboten.'[7]

Ground zero for the whole Allied cause was an urgent necessity for credit in the USA to purchase supplies. In early March 1917 Ambassador Page provided President Wilson with a doom-laden summary of the crisis. 'England has not only to pay her own war bills, but is obliged to finance her Allies as well,' he told the President.[8]

There was great danger that orders from the British and French would all but dry up, with transatlantic trade ceasing. There would be financial and commercial damage in the USA almost as serious as that inflicted on Europe. Without credit the whole global trading system could collapse. By July the situation was even worse and Ambassador

Page warned that Allied financial resources were all but exhausted.

An influx of American troops would help buck things up at the front eventually, but there was still great fear the French might collapse. By the beginning of April 1917 Britain was in the red on its account with J.P. Morgan to the tune of $400,000,000[9] and it had no means of repaying it. With payments due, if no further credit were made available the Allied war effort could grind to a halt just as the Americans were joining the fray. The Balfour Mission worked hard to find a solution and the US government agreed to advances from its own Treasury to cover the British overdraft. This was a great, if militarily unspectacular, victory over the U-boats, guaranteeing the lifeblood of supplies would continue to flow across the Atlantic. Now the crucial battle was on to prevent the U-boats cutting the artery, for it was one thing to make the payments and quite another to secure delivery of the goods.

In late March 1917, a distinguished-looking gentleman, silver of beard and hair, had boarded the steamship *New York* in an American port and set sail for Liverpool. Though he wore civilian clothes, and carried no uniform at all in his luggage, this was 58-year-old Rear Admiral William Sims, on a secret mission under the assumed name S.W. Davidson. His task was to discover how his country might best help Britain's navy once a state of hostilities existed between the USA and Germany.

By the time Sims reached British waters America was at war and he found a mood of optimism abroad in England that the submarine peril could not seriously endanger the Empire. The American admiral was a long-time friend of Jellicoe, whom he had first encountered when both were serving ashore to put down the Boxer Rebellion in China in 1901. Sixteen years later, on entering the First Sea Lord's office in Whitehall, Sims expected to receive upbeat confirmation that Germany's submarine offensive was mastered. While Jellicoe greeted Sims cheerfully, after the American sat down he pulled out a sheet of paper and slid it across the desk. Sims scanned it and was shocked to his core. The true scale of Allied and neutral merchant vessel losses due to U-boats was staggering and was predicted to reach 900,000 tons that month. In response to Sims's expression of deep concern, Jellicoe replied calmly, 'as though he was discussing the weather',[10] that the rate of losses seemed likely to force an end to the war.

Sims asked what was being done and was told by Jellicoe: 'Everything

The remarkable Admiral William S. Sims who worked closely with British counterparts in the darkest days of the anti-submarine campaign during the First World War. (*NHHC*)

that we can.' Anti-submarine forces had already been increased, while Britain was, according to Jellicoe, building 'destroyers, trawlers, and other like craft as fast as we can'.[11] He indicated that any and all assistance offered would be eagerly embraced, while Sims observed that it looked as if the Germans were winning the war. 'They will win,' the British admiral admitted, 'unless we can stop these losses – and stop them soon.'[12]

Jellicoe told Sims he believed the terrible situation confronting the Allied cause was about to get even worse. The summer months would provide more daylight and calmer seas – a great slaughter may unfold.

Sims asked if there was a solution. Jellicoe told him there was none in sight, despite the best efforts of anti-submarine forces, while press reports of submarine sinkings were grossly exaggerated. There had been only 54 confirmed U-boat sinkings since 1914. Sims soon heard from other British senior officers that it was estimated the Germans were building submarines 'at a rate of three a week'. In fact, it was seven a month.

Widely believed reports of U-boats voluntarily surrendering without a fight were rubbish, a deliberate falsehood spread by the British to lower enemy morale. Bizarrely, even some senior British naval officers and politicians believed there were rows of surrendered U-boats secreted in far corners of naval dockyards at Plymouth and Portsmouth.

Admiral Sims exited the Admiralty and went to make a report to Ambassador Page, delivering the bleak assessment that with losses 'now approaching a million tons a month' the Allied effort was about to fold. Sims observed: 'the limit of endurance would be reached about November 1, 1917; in other words, unless some method of successfully fighting submarines could be discovered almost immediately, Great Britain would have to lay down her arms before a victorious Germany.'[13]

Rear Admiral Alexander Duff, whom Jellicoe had appointed as the head of the Anti-Submarine Division within the Naval Staff, had proposed convoys, but Jellicoe told him there were not enough escort vessels.

Jellicoe's inability to delegate meant he was invariably buried under paperwork, while red tape entangled him, hampering his ability to make the obvious decision. His fragile constitution and unbending dedication to doing his duty by his nation – ensuring the buck stopped with him no matter how small the matter – threatened paralysis. The argument over convoys was already well underway even during the 1916 restricted submarine warfare campaign (and therefore prior to his arrival in Whitehall). As the commander of the Grand Fleet, one of Jellicoe's necessary obsessions had been achieving superiority in numbers of battleships as well as firepower over the enemy's High Sea Fleet. The numbers game became the focus for Jellicoe now, too. In addition to more destroyers there needed to be hundreds, if not thousands, of smaller patrol vessels. Ideally these should be backed up by expansive minefields and miles of anti-submarine nets to pin down every inch of ocean. It was necessary to smother the U-boats under an anti-submarine blanket, but that would take time, a commodity that was in short supply. Meanwhile, it was estimated that the efficiency of the shipping system had declined by 30 per cent since the beginning of the war. This was due to not having enough labourers to load and unload the ships, the inevitable back-up of heavily laden ships waiting to discharge or take aboard their cargoes and bureaucratic delays in issuing sailing orders.

Replacing what was lost to enemy submarine attacks was not easy either. The British had managed to build two million tons of new shipping since the beginning of the war, but industrial relations in the shipyards were not always good and led to disruption. Although strikes were made illegal under the Munitions of War Act, they still happened, including a serious one at the Fairfields Yard on the Clyde in August 1915.

In early 1917, Jellicoe used a public speech to plead with shipyard workers not to go on strike, but rather to work hard and clock in on time. In addition to strikes, other delays were caused due to shipyards working with reduced materials. Timber was scarce (though wood was more essential in building merchant vessels than for warships). Steel supplies were under pressure. Ironically, a major source of steel for the British shipbuilding industry prior to the war had been Germany. The navy was also competing with the army for steel to create the tools of war. Aside from replacement merchantmen, Britain built 1,000 vessels of war during the conflict, ranging from battleships to destroyers and small patrol craft, including 155 destroyers and 36 submarines on the Clyde alone.[14] Adding to the problems, many skilled shipyard workers had joined up to fight and were replaced by women or men without the same level of skills or experience as their predecessors.

The shortage of cargo-carrying vessels was partly tackled by converting some ships to suit specific needs, including dry goods freighters into oil carriers. Vessels that had previously worked on rivers were made into ocean-going ships. The processes in the shipyard were altered to be more efficient and less of a draw on resources. Pneumatic tools for riveting and caulking were introduced and speeded things up while also making it easier for women to work in shipyards. Electricity was used to operate machinery rather than steam, and this reduced the pressure on coal. Despite this, it remained very much a coal-fuelled and steam-powered world. The Germans relentlessly targeted coal supplies, for British fields supplied the whole Allied effort. Sinking as many vessels as possible carrying pit props was another way to undermine the very foundations of the enemy's campaign.

General Ludendorff was hopeful Allied coal supplies would be disrupted enough to force the British and the French to cancel plans for a summer 1917 offensive. It didn't happen and an Allied offensive was launched in the spring. The situation on land remained very gloomy, for the major Allied offensive of April and May failed, with 350,000 casualties, and the French Army subsequently mutinied.

Confronted with the potential defeat of the side his country had just joined, Admiral Sims rolled up his sleeves and became an integral part of the Admiralty's efforts to beat the U-boats. Appointed commander of American naval forces in Europe, he immediately worked up a plan that would see a strong force of US Navy destroyers based in Ireland.

When Sims met the relentlessly upbeat Prime Minister, he was not convinced Lloyd George was being honest with himself, let alone the nation. The PM acknowledged the situation was bad, yet with a smile declared: 'But we shall get the best of the submarines – never fear!'[15] On the German side there was growing confidence, with the Kaiser making boastful speeches about his submarines winning a decisive battle that would 'break our enemy's war will'.[16]

The concept of the U-boat as a terror weapon had been fully recognised during planning for the new unrestricted campaign and was now proven, much to the fury of the British. Many merchant ships belonging to neutral nations refused to even set sail. In the first month of the new unrestricted campaign, the masters of several hundred vessels chose to stay in port.

Describing it as a 'life and death struggle by hunger', a senior German politician crowed that England was facing 'a situation unparalleled in her history'.[17] The Germans were betting the war would be over by August.

In London, Sims asked himself: 'How, then, could we defeat the submarine?'[18] The answer was the tried and tested convoy system, if only entrenched opposition could be overcome. There was little faith in it to be found in either the Royal Navy or US Navy – or indeed in the merchant marine. The biggest enemy the Allies now faced in their battle for survival was themselves.

13   Demands Upon the World

Convoying of merchant vessels actually stretches back to the Middle Ages. In 1225 a dozen vessels were specially assigned to escort a shipment of King Henry III's coins across the Channel. By the late 1300s the practice of sailing ships under escort of war galleys commanded by specially appointed officers was a regular occurrence. In the Napoleonic Wars convoying actually became compulsory by law (from 1798) for most merchant vessels, which was a response to the high casualty rate of 1797 when the French took advantage of too many ships sailing solo.

Opposition to convoying also went back a long way. In the seventeenth century one English naval officer raged against the passivity of it as a means to protect trade against voracious North African pirates, describing it as 'a very ill way of carrying on the war'.[1]

By the early twentieth century, many of the same doubts about the war-fighting efficacy of convoys had planted themselves again in the minds of aggressive naval officers. Modern warships were built to move fast and hit hard, with the men who crewed and commanded them specially trained for offensive warfare. They hated being tied to slow, fat merchant vessels when they could be racing off to find and sink the enemy, but a somewhat different mindset and tactics were required to beat U-boats.

It was true, as Admiral Sims willingly admitted, that the Royal Navy of 1917 enjoyed supremacy *over the surface of the sea*, as it had done for a very long time. The problem was, maintained Sims, that modern naval warfare required 'far more than controlling the top of the water'.[2] It was, Sims suggested, 'absurd to say that a belligerent which was losing 800,000 or 900,000 tons of shipping a month, as was the case with the Allies in the spring of 1917, was the undisputed mistress of the seas'.[3]

Submarines were not just making battleship commanders afraid to sail in certain waters, but their refusal even to show themselves while going about their heinous business neutralised the speed and hitting power of the latest destroyers and cruisers. Those people in the Admiralty who saw the illogicality of the traditional offensive mindset against such a slippery foe eagerly pointed out the futility of dashing about the ocean. Wasn't it far better to let the enemy come to you, by putting merchant vessels in convoys and providing them with a strong escort?

That, according to the offensive warfare faction, would merely deliver up scores of targets for the submarines. The anti-convoy faction suggested the crews of most cargo vessels were unlikely to have the skills needed to keep station or follow sailing orders precisely. They also claimed that fast merchant vessels would be required to travel at the same speed as slow ones, making them vulnerable to attack.

These arguments were not new, while convoy operations already running continued to show why they actually worked and the fears about the merchant marine's capabilities hardly, if ever, proved to be correct. Ships in convoys, should they be unlucky enough to be found by a U-boat, still stood a good chance of getting through unscathed. Vessels carrying soldiers and coal across the English Channel were still being escorted in convoy, as were troopships from Australia and India to the Middle East and Europe. There remained few losses despite growing numbers of U-boats. Between 1914 and 1918 there would be 39,352 transits by coal-carrying vessels in convoy across the Channel and only 53 ships were lost.[4]

A submarine would probably only manage to fire one torpedo before escort vessels chased down the track and dropped depth charges (which were now an effective weapon). Should a U-boat be unwise enough to surface in order to use guns, then a hot fire from warships and armed merchant vessels could be expected.

Some people refused to wait for the Admiralty to issue universal convoy orders. Angry at a refusal to introduce convoying for the Scandinavian trade, Admiral Beatty insisted on a trial run. The results were impressive and casualties plummeted to less than a quarter of a per cent of previous losses.[5] That was in April 1917, when overall losses from U-boat attacks peaked, but still Jellicoe was not sure about universal convoys.

Behind the façade of certainty he projected about the submarine threat being mastered, the Prime Minister, if his *War Memoirs* are to be believed, suffered a collapse in confidence.

He saw Jellicoe and other naval top brass as dinosaurs determined to achieve a new Trafalgar with battleships, while the war was lost to

U-boats. In January 1917, he was especially unimpressed by an official Admiralty edict that 'vessels should sail singly, escorted as considered necessary'. It also stated that 'several ships sailing together in a convoy is not recommended in any area where submarine attack is a possibility'.[6]

Admiralty practice funnelled merchant vessels towards zones where warships regularly patrolled and in the PM's view this clearly signposted to U-boats where they should lie in wait. Lloyd George claimed wireless instructions to merchant vessels – about rendezvous points with escorts – were intercepted by the Germans, decrypted and tip-offs sent to U-boats. The merchant vessels 'found not a guide, but a pirate waiting their arrival', observed Lloyd George.[7] He could barely contain his fury: 'In fact, by this egregious plan, our ships were in effect often shepherded into the abattoir where the slaughterers lay in wait for them.'[8] Fuelling the Prime Minister's anger was how well the Grand Fleet was protected. It was, in effect, convoyed under escort from destroyers and cruisers (on the rare occasions it went to sea).

Such massive protection was not available to the men who sailed in the merchant ships upon which the fate of the nation and the entire Allied war effort depended. The Prime Minister encountered one valiant mariner while returning aboard a passenger ship from a summit with French political leaders. Lloyd George asked 'the grizzled skipper' why he was making the Channel crossing. The man told him that he'd just been torpedoed for the sixth time 'and was now making his way to Liverpool to take charge of another ship and face the U-boats again'.[9]

On 13 February Lloyd George invited Admiral Jellicoe and Admiral Duff to a breakfast meeting in Downing Street to discuss the crisis.

A convincing and well-balanced case for convoys was put forward in a memorandum by Sir Maurice Hankey, Cabinet Secretary (the Prime Minister's foremost aide). Neither admiral would, even after two hours of discussion, change his stance. The PM pushed hard for the convoy system to be applied globally during a War Cabinet meeting on 23 April but again Jellicoe refused to accept it was the answer; the PM asked him to reconsider. Lloyd George decided to visit the Admiralty on 30 April to have it out with Jellicoe and Duff but on his arrival found they had decided to give universal convoys a try.

The PM undoubtedly played a pivotal role in getting widespread convoying, but his depiction of himself as a heroic, determined politician forcing the obdurate, anti-convoy admirals to do the right thing was labelled 'the biggest lie ever told' by Edward Carson.

A number of factors, not least the promise of American destroyers and the success of convoying coal shipments across the Channel, tipped the balance in the Admiralty. The coal ships had been subjected to a determined assault at the end of 1916 but between early February and May 1917 only nine out of 4,013 vessels convoyed on the route were sunk.

The first new trial of the convoy system was to be from Gibraltar to Plymouth, departing the Rock on 10 May. Sixteen vessels were escorted by a pair of Q-ships, *Mavis* and *Rule*, along with a trio of armed yachts, at an average speed of just over 6 knots. On 18 May a destroyer escort squadron from Devonport met the convoy and two days later all the merchant vessels were safely delivered. The next success was a convoy of a dozen merchant ships departing Hampton Roads for Britain on 24 May. Under escort from the cruiser HMS *Roxburgh*, destroyers reinforced its protection as it passed through submarine killing grounds off the British Isles. No ships were lost.

The truth was that a submarine searching for a convoy was as likely to miss 40 ships through the narrow aperture of a periscope as it was to discover a single ship. Convoying forced the enemy – if he could find and keep up with the ships long enough to mount an attack – to fight on terms more favourable to escorts. They no longer needed to go and search for the U-boat needle in the haystack.

The Allies were also improving their countermeasures and a big effort was made to ensure hydrophones were more effective. The early models were put over the sides of ships and only if the vessel stopped could they pick up the sound of a surfaced submarine's diesels (or possibly a U-boat dived on battery power). They did not have the ability to say exactly where the enemy vessel was, as no bearing or range was yielded.

By 1917 it was possible to tell both range and bearing, but the hydrophone was still far from accurate and results could often send the hunter in the wrong direction. The way to fix a target was for three or more hydrophone-equipped patrol vessels to compare their results, achieving a triangulation. Hopes were high, but only three U-boats were actually destroyed during the First World War thanks to the ship-mounted hydrophone.[10]

Escorts got their chance at bloodletting once the U-boat delivered itself to them but they still mostly acted as babysitters that deterred attack rather than actively hunting down and destroying the enemy's forces.

Capt. Herbert Richmond summed the dilemma up succinctly: 'A pack cannot hunt without a scent.'[11] Furthermore, he said, it was 'idle to talk of an offensive against an enemy when the means of finding him, or, if found of destroying him, are lacking'. Yet, instead of devoting their entire resources towards the anti-submarine war, the British were diverted into attempts to find roles for their own submarines that were dead ends, no matter how admirable in terms of technological innovation.

While U-boats may have been achieving astonishing totals in tonnage sunk, Britain's combat-proven submarine captains had discovered a major problem. There were hardly any enemy targets. There might be thousands of Allied merchant vessels to hunt on the high seas but there were few enemy freighters, or even surface warships, out there by 1917.

This led to submarines and their crews being employed in missions far removed from the harbour protection and anti-shipping roles envisaged for them before the war. Like their German opposite numbers they had adapted to laying mines and were useful for bombarding targets ashore with their guns. British submarines were also tasked with trying to shoot down Zeppelins over the North Sea, where and when they could. There were several encounters in which the Zeppelins did not take kindly to being shot at and sometimes hung around for hours dropping bombs, making life very uncomfortable for the submarine in question.

In a bid to create vessels that would fit into conventional naval warfare, sometimes deeply flawed designs were tried out by the British. These were efforts to make the submarine into something that it wasn't – like taking a car and trying to make it swim or fly.

Generally, the innovative submarines were large, such as the K Class, which was really a submersible light cruiser. Ordered in August 1915, in the quest for high speed the Ks were driven by steam turbines. Their role was to forge ahead of the British main battle fleet on the surface, scouting out the enemy and diving to mount attacks. Large and difficult to control, they could manage 25 knots on the surface and 9 knots submerged.

One of the reasons the K Class had been introduced was to trump a rumoured new class of U-boats allegedly capable of 22 knots surfaced. No such German submarine ever existed and many in the RN wished the same of the notorious Ks.

It is never a good idea to punch massive holes into the hull of a submarine and the rule of thumb, if you must, is the fewer the better. The Ks flouted this wisdom. Hatches were bad enough, but adding funnels that had to be 'swung down'[12] by a complex mechanism each time a boat dived was fraught with potential for disaster. So it proved, with various mishaps due to water ingress and also disastrous collisions with other K-boats and surface vessels at high speed. The most notorious K Class incident was the so-called Battle of May Island in January 1918, off the Firth of Forth.

Several K Class boats were sent out like greyhounds coursing ahead of huntsmen, in this case capital ships on a rare foray. On what was a pitch-black winter's night a U-boat sighting threw the entire fleet formation into confusion. *K22* collided with *K14* and the battlecruiser *Inflexible* then crunched into *K22*. While those two submarines limped back to port, *K17* collided with the destroyer *Fearless* and sank. *K6*, meanwhile, became embedded in *K4*. The latter managed to free herself, but *K4* was taken down and there were no survivors, though some of *K17*'s men survived. More than 100 men had been killed.

The Battle of May Island was hushed up at the time, but across the navy the Ks were loathed, though some of them lingered on until the 1920s with further mishaps, which claimed more lives. The K Class boats were an example of the envelope being pushed so hard the design aspiration outpaced operational reality and practical wisdom.

The manic pursuit of innovation to try to make submarines conform to familiar roles threw up another outlandish example. Called the M Class, with a length of 296ft and a displacement of 1,950 tons dived (and a safe diving depth of 200ft), they could submerge in just 90 seconds. *M1*, *M2* and *M3* were each fitted with a shortened 12-inch gun taken from reserve weaponry stocks for Formidable Class pre-dreadnought battleships.[13] This weapon was mounted on the front of the large fin and the M Class boats were intended to work as big gun anti-shipping units, though they still had four bow tubes and a 3-inch anti-aircraft gun. In an extraordinary tactic – called the dip-chick manoeuvre – the captain would order the boat to surface with gun elevated, until the fin and gun housing were partially exposed and the muzzle was about 6ft above the surface. As the captain used the periscope to scrutinise his target, a lid on the muzzle would open. With the 12-inch gun belching smoke and flame, the submarine would dive and go deep while the shell was still in flight to target. This could theoretically reduce the exposure time to a mere 35 seconds, though in practice it was more likely to be around 70. The vessel would have to surface later, in order to load the gun – an action that would increase the risk of being sighted by the enemy. Submarine *M1* entered service in the summer of 1918, with Cdr Max Horton as her captain. Had there been any German surface ships to target there is no doubt he would have trained his crew relentlessly to hit hard and disappear. As it was *M1* was never allowed to operate off hostile shores, for the Admiralty feared she could be captured and employed to carry out bombardments of British towns and ports. It also feared *M1*'s design would be copied.

The Ks and Ms were wasteful diversions from the main effort. The Admiralty should have maintained focus on combating the U-boat menace rather than go chasing radical solutions for problems that really didn't exist.

There remained within the British submarine force a feeling of crisis, a nagging anxiety that the Royal Navy's boats were not being used properly and doing enough, or in the most effective fashion.

The hard-working E Class submarines had at least earned a justified reputation as effective anti-shipping platforms. Like predecessor boats they were designed to sink large vessels from close range, relying on a single torpedo fired from a bow tube. As the war progressed they were modified, with broadside tubes and an additional tube fitted in the bow. One shot, one kill was rare in practice, especially against big ships, the warhead of a single torpedo proving incapable of sinking a well-built vessel with plenty of watertight compartments.

Although potentially wasteful in scarce torpedoes, one way to ensure a devastating blow was to fire multiple torpedoes in a salvo, known as a spread. With only one or two bow tubes, salvoes were not possible with the E Class. A proper salvo required new kinds of submarine with more bow tubes, like the J Class and the L Class, the latter a patrol submarine intended to supplant the E Class. The L Class had a quartet of torpedo tubes in the bow, though later batches had an additional two, along with a pair of beam torpedo tubes. With the push on to improve the more conventional submarine type, it seemed to some that the best antidote to the U-boat virus was another submarine – a gamekeeper-turned-poacher arrangement.

The first purpose-built hunter-killer submarine was the R Class, the design of which was first proposed in March 1917 as the U-boat crisis peaked. After a pause, during which the case for the R Class was assessed and confirmed by the head of the Submarine Service, the design was finalised. An order to construct a dozen was placed with various yards.

With an impressive submerged speed of between 14 and 15 knots, thanks to two powerful electric motors, the R Class was designed to chase down U-boats and even overtake them to lie in wait. The high speed of the R Class was aided by a sleek hydrodynamic, spindle-type hull form and there was no gun mounted on the outer casing, as that would have created too much hydrodynamic drag.

A small boat of only 500 tons (dived) displacement, the R Class offered poor performance on the surface, tending to roll with alacrity. Despite such flaws, the R Class's underwater performance was the ace card. The maximum submerged speed of 15 knots could be sustained for an hour and was actually not bettered by any submarine until the latter days of the Second World War.

Careful handling was needed at speed when submerged, for with planes angled at 30 degrees bow-down, the crush depth could be reached within 20 seconds. Even shallower angles could see a boat crash through the safe diving depth of 250ft within a minute.[14]

Given that the requirement for such a boat was propelled by a desperate need to provide an effective and sure way of killing enemy submarines, an ability to actually find the opposition was paramount. The hydrophone set fitted to the R Class proved so effective during sea trials it was possible to find a target without needing a visual sighting. This created the possibility of sneaking up on a surfaced, or even submerged, U-boat.

Nine R Class boats were constructed, all in 1918, with *R1* and *R2* launched at Chatham Dockyard on 25 April. With half a dozen commissioned by war's end they would be too late into service to have any impact in the role for which they were designed. Only one attack on an enemy submarine was recorded, in October 1918. Having used her high speed to make a 20-minute sprint at 60ft, *R7* obtained a good position to kill a surfaced U-boat until the appearance of a merchant vessel caused the target to make a crash dive. *R7* let loose an entire salvo of six torpedoes but failed to score a single hit.[15]

In the last two years of the war it fell to other types of submarine to carry the hunter-killer trident. The L Class boats were also armed with 18-inch torpedoes, though in later variants 21-inch torpedo tubes were fitted in the bow. Their favoured tactic against a U-boat was to sneak up on it while ballasted down to leave only the fin and the 4-inch gun platform showing. It was hoped the enemy would stand little chance of spotting such a low and slim profile. Action would be joined beyond torpedo range, with the element of surprise and well-aimed shells hopefully destroying the target.

Regardless of the tools created by each side for submarine warfare, what really made the difference was the skill of the man who commanded the vessel. Some submarine captains displayed a greater knack for the trade than others. Evidence for this was provided on the German side by the relatively small number of men being responsible for the majority of sinkings. Out of Germany's 400 U-boat captains 22 sank or captured 60 per cent of the merchant vessels lost by the Allies and neutral nations.[16]

The British, lacking the same level of opportunity for individual high scores, sank 346 enemy vessels of all kinds. Martin Nasmith and seven other captains reaped 281 of that total. Nasmith sank four enemy warships while Max Horton got three.[17] Six U-boats would be sunk by British submarines between March 1917 and the end of the year, with a total of 17 accounted for by the service across the entire war. Only two British captains sank more than one U-boat (Cdr Robert H.T. Raikes and Cdr Philip Philips), which was perhaps slim pickings for a navy that considered itself the world's most professional and aggressive armed force.

14   Paradise for U-boats

The Germans and Austrians almost from the start of the war had waged an energetic submarine campaign in the Mediterranean. While sinking

enemy naval vessels and merchant ships supporting the Gallipoli campaign was the major focus for these boats, that commitment had ended
in early 1916. Even so, by the end of the year – with Italy now at war
with both the leading Central Powers – 22 U-boats were operating from
bases in the Adriatic.

A new hunting ground for them had been created in October 1915
when the Allies put ashore a substantial expeditionary force at the Greek
port of Salonika in the Aegean. The British and French, supported by
the Italians, hoped to push into Serbia, to support its defence against
a German and Bulgarian onslaught. By spring 1916 the 160,000-strong
landing force was surrounded, with its back against the sea, and within
nine months 600,000 Allied troops were sucked into the Salonika front.
It was a major drain on men and resources, with disease rampant and
rendering many thousands of troops combat ineffective. The Salonika
effort required massive assistance from the sea with warships, including
elderly battleships and cruisers, again committed to loitering off shore
to provide naval gunfire support. There was a constant feed of troop
transports carrying reinforcements and also cargo vessels with supplies.
Mines were frequently sown off Salonika and while attempts to sink
troop transports were thwarted, U-boats preyed on general merchant
traffic.

At the same time the Allied score sheet against U-boats in the
Mediterranean had few entries. The much-vaunted Otranto Barrage,
for example, sank a solitary enemy submarine (UB-44) in the last six
months of 1916. Elsewhere in the Mediterranean theatre, during the
same period, the Allies accounted for a mere three U-boats. Against
this, between June and December 1916, they lost 256 ships (including
96 British), making 662,131 tons of shipping in total.[1] It was British merchant traffic that inevitably suffered the most, being more numerous
than other nations' and with generally larger vessels, which offered
more tempting targets.

For the U-boats gunfire continued to be the preferred means of
attack. The top-scoring German ace – Lothar von Arnauld de la Perière,
in U-35 – enhanced his effectiveness during his successful summer of
1916 patrol by carrying a gunnery expert specially assigned from the
High Sea Fleet.

By September a trio of long-range large U-boats were simultaneously deployed in the western basin of the Mediterranean, while the

less profitable eastern basin was left to smaller craft. By the end of the year, at any one time there were half a dozen long-range U-boats in the Western Med.[2]

A combination of factors, but particularly a lack of Allied tactical focus, made the Mediterranean, as historian John Terraine memorably labelled it, 'a U-boat paradise'.[3]

Convoying was even later in being introduced across the Mediterranean than elsewhere, while the alternative system of protected routes again just signposted where targets could be found. After using their periscopes to watch Allied patrol vessels sail by – confirming they were in the right location – U-boats surfaced and got to work with their guns.

A request by the British commander in Malta to introduce the convoy system came to nothing, as the obdurate Admiralty told him it was up to the French to agree to such a scheme. It was a neat piece of buck passing, for the French were as sceptical of convoying in the Mediterranean as the British naval high command was of using it elsewhere.

Whereas around the British Isles the Admiralty entirely ran the show – one single authority co-ordinating the anti-submarine effort, for better or worse – in the Mediterranean there were three nations. Consequently, there was corresponding number of zones of operation, with different nations in charge. Taking the lead in waters off Tunisia and Algeria, in addition to those off southern France and to the south and west of Greece, were the French. The British, using Malta as their operational hub, protected seas between the island and Egypt while the Italians were in charge of their home seas.

It was not always an easy partnership. There were occasionally dead zones between jurisdictions where patrol vessels were sometimes not provided for close escort of vital ships, such as those carrying troops or ammunition. The U-boats took advantage and a notable cock-up was the loss of the 26-year-old 2,964-ton Italian-flagged troop carrier *Minas* in early 1917. Carrying Italian, Serbian and French reinforcements to Salonika from Taranto, *Minas* received a close destroyer escort from the Italians while sailing in their zone. This warship turned back before sighting the expected British destroyer and conducting a formal handover.

Meanwhile, the Royal Navy had not been told of any escort requirement, so no ship was sent out from Malta. Proceeding unprotected, the *Minas* was off Cape Matapan when she was spotted by *U-39*, commanded by Kapitänleutnant Walther Forstmann.

The fatal attack took place shortly before dawn on 15 February, under 'a livid sky and [on] an icy sea'.[4] On being hit by the first torpedo *Minas* 'gave a tremendous lurch like some wounded monster'.[5] A second torpedo struck the ship while hundreds of men were still crowded on the upper deck. With lethal rapidity *Minas* went down stern first, taking 870 with her. Italy shrank in dismay at the loss of so many lives in one ship.

When the unrestricted campaign was initiated in February 1917, U-boats operating in the Mediterranean numbered 18 – four less than the previous year – but Allied losses still climbed steeply.

Fifty ships, including neutral vessels, were sunk in February alone. In late April 1917 the Suez route was abandoned, with shipping from the Far East to Europe sent around the southern tip of Africa rather than risk a passage across the Mediterranean.

Eventually the situation became so serious that a summit was held at Corfu, where France had a naval headquarters. It was decided the French Navy would keep an eye on the Austro-Hungarian battle fleet in the Adriatic while the British took control of introducing more anti-submarine patrols and running a convoy system. By the end of the war there would be 42 destroyers and more than 30 sloops committed to escort work in the Mediterranean. With America and Japan weighing in, reinforcements for the anti-submarine campaign were forthcoming and the U-boats began to feel the pressure. Casualties rose as 1918 progressed – four submarines sunk in May alone – while their victims were reduced.

The Germans also deployed U-boats into waters beyond Constantinople and if the Med was, at least initially, a paradise, then the Black Sea soon turned into a kind of hell. It was an arena of frustration and high casualties.

U-boats initially operated from the Ottoman capital and then from Varna after October 1915, when Bulgaria joined the war on the side of the Central Powers. The Turks had no seagoing submarines while the Bulgarians operated a single ex-German U-boat.

Germany's submarines were tasked with giving the Turks some parity with the Russians, or even superiority, if that was at all possible. Russia's submarines were eventually active, too, achieving some successes in attacking enemy convoys in a theatre where the Black Sea Fleet (BSF), with its main base at Sevastopol, retained the upper hand. Pre-dreadnoughts and the brand new battleships *Imperatritsa Ekaterina* and *Imperatritsa Maria* spearheaded Russia's powerful surface force. The most serious blow of the war for the BSF was the loss of the *Imperatritsa Maria*, which was destroyed on 20 October 1916 owing to her own ammunition detonating while she was in Sevastopol harbour.

At the beginning of the war the BSF fielded a quartet of submarines, reinforced by two elderly boats transferred from the Pacific Fleet via the trans-Siberian railway. They didn't have the range necessary for sustained war patrols off the enemy coast, especially in the key choke point of the Bosphorus, so remained dormant. Things would not change until newer craft arrived. In the meantime there were no effective anti-submarine countermeasures and when U-boats sank a few vessels off Odessa there was no retribution. The minelaying boat *UC-13* ranged off the shores of the Caucasus in the eastern Black Sea, but in late November ran aground in a storm off the Bosphorus and was abandoned and destroyed.

For the Russians, interrupting coal supplies from the Zonguldak region and disrupting maritime traffic into and out of the Turkish Straits were key objectives. As in the Gallipoli campaign, the lack of a decent road system or railway link to the front line in the Caucasus forced the Turks to transport troop reinforcements and supplies by sea, offering a vulnerability to be exploited. They were also compelled to bring coal supplies essential to their industry and fuel for their warships by ship, too, creating another Achilles heel. A combined assault by the new Russian submarine *Nerpa* and two destroyers in September 1915 saw four Turkish merchant ships driven ashore and destroyed by guns. Steaming into action, the Turkish *Yavuz* (the former German battlecruiser *Goeben*) caught the *Nerpa* on the surface, unleashing a barrage of 11-inch shells, but the Russian crash-dived and got away. As the Turkish fleet flagship *Yavuz* was a prize target throughout the war in the Black Sea and, in mid-November, off the Bosphorus, the submarine *Morzh* fired torpedoes at her, but they ran wide.

Morzh was sister to *Nerpa*. Completed in 1914 and large compared to earlier Russian boats, they had two bow tubes and two aft, along with eight externally mounted torpedoes and a pair of guns. Designed to attain 16 knots top speed on the surface, the lack of German engines (as originally intended) meant using some taken from gunboats, which un-fortunately fell short of the power needed. The minelaying submarine *Krab* was also less than perfect. She could potentially cause serious disruption in enemy sea lanes if she laid her 60 mines, but was difficult to operate and took 20 minutes to submerge, which was achingly slow and therefore risky.

The quality of Russian submarine crews was poor, which made achieving good results in a very new and highly technical form of warfare a real challenge. The majority of the ratings were illiterate peasants and their commanders were not generally blessed with offen-sive spirit. In the opinion of Lt Norman Archer, a British liaison officer posted to Sevastopol, when it came to a torpedo many Russians did not know 'which is the arse and which is the elbow'.[6] Despite a general lack of technical prowess, the Russians at least fitted their boats with long-range wireless sets, which enabled them to communicate with surface warships acting as scouts for potential targets.

As time went on the BSF's submarine force improved and became the most effective of all such formations within the Russian Navy. It held its own against its German counterpart and hampered the Turkish war effort.

A notable success for the Germans in a theatre with not many enemy merchant vessels at large was *UB-7* sinking the British steamship *Pata-gonia*, ten miles to the north-east of Odessa on 15 September 1915. On 27 October the same year both *UB-7* and *UB-8* were sent out to attack a parade of Russian warships lining up to bombard Varna, including the elderly pre-dreadnought *Panteleimon* (the former revolutionary hotbed *Potemkin*). *UB-8* could not manage to get a shot in against *Panteleimon* though *UB-7* did, but it detonated prematurely.

The Russian Navy's skill with mines, so evident in the Baltic, was re-peated in the Black Sea, though they were more likely to have been laid by surface vessels than by the unreliable *Krab*, which spent a lot of time under repair. *UB-45*, which had managed to sink four Allied ships in her short career, was lost on 6 November 1916, claimed by a Russian mine that blew her up as she left Varna. All but five of her 23 crew were lost.

For the Turks the coal shortage was so severe that their warships were hardly ever at sea, while by late 1916 the German-manned *Yavuz* and cruiser *Breslau* (renamed *Midilli* in Ottoman service) were seldom active. Hungry for something to do, Russian submariners were cock-a-hoop to capture the armed merchant ship *Rodosto* in October 1916 after she engaged in a gunfight with the *Tyulen*.

Apart from sowing their own mines off Russian bases, especially Sevastopol, to try to catch enemy boats, U-boats were sent to hunt and kill their opposite numbers. On 21 August 1916, *Nerpa* was attacked by *UB-7* off the Bosphorus, one torpedo glancing off her with a resounding clang but no explosion.

The German submarine force in the Black Sea experienced a grim period at the end of 1916. *UC-15*, operating out of Constantinople, was sent to sow mines off Romania and was possibly destroyed by one of them. *UB-7* was sunk in early October 1916. While it has been claimed a Russian aircraft sent her to the bottom under a hail of bombs off Sevastopol, no sure cause has ever been established. *UB-46* was sunk on 7 December 1916, another Varna-based U-boat that hit a mine while returning from a deployment. There were no survivors.

The Russians lost only one submarine in the Black Sea, the *Morzh*, which departed on her twenty-fifth patrol in mid-May 1917 and never came back. She was lost either due to a mine (possibly Russian) or air attack. The last enemy vessel claimed by a Russian submarine was a Turkish freighter, in late October. The *Gagara* lobbed shells at her until she ran aground in panic. Hostilities ended in the Black Sea in early November after the Bolsheviks seized control in Petrograd. The end of conflict at sea in the Baltic would not be so neat, with British submariners embroiled in the chaos of revolution.

15 Out Like a Lion

Though it was a sideshow, the Baltic was still crucial for two reasons. Firstly, it remained the main conduit for supplies of iron ore to German war industries. Secondly, for the Allies it was essential Russia stayed in the fight, to ensure Germany's full might couldn't be brought to bear on the Western Front.

The new senior British submariner charged with overseeing the

Royal Navy's part in this effort was 33-year-old Francis Cromie, a tall and very self-assured individual.

A stylish fellow, he favoured long sideburns and a uniform coat with a luxurious astrakhan collar, but at sea roughed it in typical sub-mariner's piratical style – tousle-headed, dirty and clad in a roll-neck jumper. Despite his refusal to drink alcohol or smoke, Cromie won the admiration of the Russians as the epitome of the English officer. Submariners under his command in *E19* liked his daring, but worried about occasional lack of attention to detail, not least the correct running depth for torpedoes and avoiding collisions with harbour defence booms. While Cromie's record in the attack did not quite match that of Horton, it was still impressive, including disposing of five merchant vessels in a single day. Thanks to Cromie's religious observation of Prize Rules, not a single merchant mariner was killed. The following day Cromie captured a Swedish vessel, the *Nike*, carrying iron ore to a German port. He took her as a prize to Reval under escort where, afraid of offending the Swedes, the Russians handed both the vessel and her ore back to her owners. Hearing that his exploits over two days had paralysed traffic in the Baltic, with neutral shipping refusing to leave port, consoled Cromie.

Cromie distinguished himself further on 7 November 1915 by sink-ing the German light cruiser *Undine*, with *E19* getting the first shot in from 1,000 yards. Having crippled the cruiser – stopped dead, con-sumed by smoke and flame – Cromie sent another torpedo into his victim. It must have planted itself in an ammunition magazine, which exploded.

With spring 1916 and a new campaigning season, the British sought to use their five boats along with the Russian Navy's dozen long-range submarines to good effect. Canadian-built AG-Class boats had also ar-rived and the Russians were working them up for operations.

Faced with this, in April the Germans introduced convoys, with mer-chant vessels additionally ordered to take advantage of Swedish territor-ial waters as much as possible. The primary Allied objective remained attacking enemy warships, with opportunities against merchant ships taken where and when possible, within Prize Rules if possible.

In May 1916 the Russian boat *Volk* managed an impressive score in a single day, sinking three German cargo ships off southern Sweden. A few days later a German Q-ship rammed *Gepard* as she prepared for a surface torpedo attack against another convoy. Despite substantial damage the Russian boat made it home.

With fresh supplies of torpedoes taking a while to arrive – the main supply route from the UK was by cargo vessel up around northern Norway to Murmansk – British submarines were forced to try Russian weapons, which proved capricious. This contributed to the overall record for 1916 being poor, especially in comparison with 1915, which had gone out like a lion. The Russians would not yield to Cromie's pleas for a more aggressive policy, but the British decided to boost submarine numbers in the Baltic by transporting additional craft into the theatre of operations.

C26, *C27*, *C32* and *C35* departed Chatham under tow on 3 August 1916, taking the long voyage round the top of Norway, their initial destination Archangel. They passed through seas where mines laid by German auxiliary cruisers and submarines were not unknown, but reached port safely on 22 August. They were next put on barges and transported by canals and rivers to Petrograd, which they reached on 9 September, and then moved to Kronstadt. To save on weight, batteries and other removable items of equipment were sent separately aboard merchant vessels but these were sunk off northern Russia on the first attempt.

A second batch of batteries was sent aboard a cargo vessel called *Slavonic* by the same route, but on reaching Petrograd they were found to be defective. Despite this, the C Class boats were by mid-October on the move again, to Reval, with *C32* and *C35* overcoming the battery problems to conduct patrols before the ice made operations impossible. Switched to the Gulf of Riga, they operated from Rogekul in Moon Sound, where the other C Class boats soon joined them.

During September 1916 the U-boats had better luck than Allied submarines, sinking a trio of merchant ships, including the British-flagged *Kennet*. They laid mines in the Gulf of Finland, which later claimed several Russian warships, but the winter brought a halt to their activities. It was a particularly severe one that would not fully release its grip until May 1917. Once the thaw set in German submarines were first off the mark, laying mines off Russian naval bases while sinking and capturing ships in the Gulf of Bothnia. Four Russian submarines sailed in late May 1917 to strike back, but *Bars* was sunk by depth-charging and a pair of boats deployed the following month suffered misfortune. *Pantera* was attacked by a Zeppelin and was so badly damaged she had to head home while the other, *Lvitsa*, hit a mine. The run of bad luck continued, with the brand new Canadian-built boat *AG-14* lost in July off Libau (probably sunk by a mine).

With huge civil unrest and under intense political pressure, the Tsar abdicated in March 1917, to be replaced by a weak and chaotic Provisional Government. The Russian Navy became rudderless, with mutinies at Kronstadt and Helsingfors, inactivity due to the frozen Baltic making things even worse as the sailors could not be sent to sea. They had nothing to do but become even more rebellious.

Reval, where British submarines were based, remained relatively peaceful, though committees were elected to convey the needs of sailors to officers and tell them what to do. Living aboard the depot ship *Pamiat Azova* (the former *Dvina*) one British officer found Russian sailors who before the turmoil had been 'kindly, simple people' suddenly 'transformed . . . into ravening savages'[1] by casting off oppressive Tsarist naval discipline.

Within a month of the Tsar abdicating, vengeance-seeking sailors had murdered more than 1,000 of their officers. This led to fears for the safety of both Royal Navy submarine crews and Russian officers assigned to work with them. Cromie was forced to intercede to save the lives of some who were needed by the British flotilla.

Amid all this tumult, somehow submarines still got to sea, the last achievement by a Russian boat in the Baltic being *Vepr*'s sinking of the 873-ton German-flagged *Friedrich Carow*, in August 1917.

The operating base was switched to Helsingfors in October, with Cromie assuming command of both British and Russian submarine forces. By now he doubted anything but an all-out enemy attack would stir his allies and when the Germans made their big move, it was three British boats that tried to bar their way.

The focus of war in the Baltic was the Irben Strait, the southern entrance to the Gulf of Riga. The Germans were seeking a breakthrough on the Kurland front so they could directly threaten Petrograd and knock the Russians out of the war. To do that they needed to take Riga and control sea access, to safeguard the flank of any advance on the enemy capital. By 4 September 1917 the city had fallen and this was followed by a major move to control the mouth of the Bay of

Riga via Operation Albion, occupying the islands of Osel and Dago.

Taking maritime risks they had been shy of since 1915, due to the British submarine threat, the Germans assembled a powerful invasion fleet to transport 25,000 troops. Eleven High Sea Fleet battleships with a screen of destroyers and cruisers spearheaded its escort. More than 70 minesweepers preceded these and at the heart of it all were 19 troop ships and 21 supply vessels. Submarines *UC-57* and *UC-78* were also part of the plan, having arrived at Riga shortly after its capture to use the port as their operating base.

The bombardment to cover the amphibious assault opened in the early hours of 12 October, the battleships *Bayern* and *Grosser Kurfürst* hitting mines but suffering only minor damage. A German task group was sent into the gulf itself to attack enemy naval forces, the dreadnoughts *König* and *Kronprinz* clashing with the old battleship *Slava* off Moon Island, an indecisive scrap.

Over subsequent days various skirmishes between light and heavy units of both fleets erupted while German troops were put ashore. British submarines were sent to intervene, but their attacks came to nothing and they sustained serious damage during counter-attacks, with *C32* run aground and her crew escaping with the assistance of Cossacks. She was later blown up to prevent the enemy taking possession.

On 7 November the Bolsheviks seized power in Petrograd and, as Russia slid into civil war, they sought to end hostilities with Germany in lieu of permanent peace terms, which were to be negotiated during talks at Brest-Litovsk. The delicate position of the British grew even trickier when the government of Finland called on Germany to help it resist a Bolshevik coup. The Finns ordered all Russian naval units to withdraw and while surface vessels soon quit Helsingfors seven British and four Russian submarines remained. By January 1918 the Germans had closed off the Gulf of Finland and the Admiralty, with the permission of the Bolsheviks, brought the majority of the RN submariners home via Petrograd and Murmansk.

Twenty-five men stayed behind to maintain the boats until the vessels' fate was decided. Nobody was in any doubt that they would have to be destroyed to prevent them falling into German or Bolshevik hands.

They were duly scuttled off Helsingfors in early April 1918, shortly after German troops landed at Hangö, less than 80 miles to the west.

With the exception of Cromie, the remaining British submariners now also went home.

The Germans were delighted to finally see the end of the British menace in the Baltic, one of their admirals admitting during the Brest-Litovsk talks that 'the English [submarine] Flotilla' had been 'a constant anxiety . . . in fact the only one'. The Royal Navy's submarines were 'pests'.[2]

Cromie, meanwhile, took up residence in the British Embassy at Petrograd. He was assigned by then to the Naval Intelligence Division and running various espionage operations.

Britain and other Western powers intervened militarily against the Bolsheviks in the summer of 1918 and among troops inserted into northern Russia was a field force of Royal Marines. Its objective was to ensure the Germans did not start operating submarines from a base on the Barents Sea. This made Cromie's position even more precarious, as the Bolsheviks broke off friendly relations with Britain.

Heavily engaged in organising an uprising to overthrow the embattled communist regime, on 31 August 1918 Cromie was gunned down during an incursion into the Petrograd embassy by Bolshevik shock troops. Many thought Cromie, the only British naval attaché ever to lose his life in combat – suffering a fate unique for a submariner – should have been awarded the Victoria Cross. The covert nature of his activities on Russian soil, and the controversial and politically sensitive manner of his death, ruled that out.[3] Plenty of naval VCs would soon be won elsewhere during a spectacular venture that sought to eliminate the U-boat threat.

16   A Damned Good Twist

Despite introduction of the convoy system, the situation at the beginning of 1918 was far from assured for the Allies, even with the USA's entry into the war. Merchant vessel sinkings remained well in excess of new ship construction and the Germans were convinced they could

still achieve victory by means of U-boat warfare, despite their submarine losses climbing steeply, from 22 destroyed in 1916 to 63 in 1917.[1]

Admiral Scheer won agreement for more resources to be poured
into submarine construction, with a U-boat Office established in December 1917 to co-ordinate this. That month it placed orders for 120
boats, followed by another order in the New Year for 220. The completion of submarines was still far short of Scheer's ambitions, for the
navy received only three new U-boats in January 1918. The maximum
number of submarines delivered in a month that year would be 12 (in
June). It was estimated by the U-boat Office that it would take until late
1919 for output to reach 23 per month.

The situation was not helped by the Supreme Army Command refusing to release skilled workmen for submarine construction and telling the navy its own requirements must take priority. The navy would
have to make better use of the workmen it already had.

When it came to U-boat crews a critical point had been reached,
due to exhaustion and the difficulty of replacing those killed, including many highly skilled veterans. Other parts of the Fleet were being
denuded to supply new officers and men for the U-boats but several
months were needed to train them in operating submarines and gaining proficiency with weaponry.

A major part of German hopes at sea rested on the efforts of the
Flanders-based U-boats, operating from the Zeebrugge–Ostend–Bruges
triangle, which was a formidable operating centre with a dockyard,
heavily protected submarine pens and ammunition bunkers. Crucially,
it was 300 miles closer to the Dover Straits than the North Sea bases –
offering a swift breakout into the Channel and beyond.

On the Allied side the idea of delivering a direct knock-out blow
against the U-boats in Flanders was given impetus by a speech from
President Woodrow Wilson. 'Why don't the British shut up the hornets
in their nests?' he enquired in the spring of 1917. 'We are hunting hornets all over the farm and letting the nest alone.'[2]

Wilson was actually thinking of the ultimate expression of Fulton's
torpedoes – an impenetrable shield of sea mines stretching from British
shores to Norway to complement the Dover Barrage, thereby sealing
up 'the nest'. The US Navy's boss in Europe had reservations about
the effectiveness of such a Northern Barrage, although those who
did not know the reality of combating U-boats thought it an obvious

solution. Some newspapers claimed a North Sea mine barrage 'would blow to pieces any submarine which attempted to force a way across'.[3] There were even naval officers who backed the idea. The invention of a revolutionary kind of mine by an enterprising American solved one of the major Northern Barrage challenges, namely how to anchor one in such deep waters while still being effective. It could be tethered at great depth, but was connected to a long copper wire, which was in turn attached to a float. Should a submarine – even at a depth of around 200ft – touch the wire then the mine was electrically detonated. Such a weapon – felt to be more effective than traditional designs – also meant fewer mines were required (a mere 100,000 compared to 400,000 conventional types), with a consequent reduction in manufacturing resources. There would also be less strain on ships and men needed to put the mines in place and maintain them. The British and US governments agreed to proceed with the Northern Barrage on 2 November 1917, the Americans estimating it would cost $40 million.

In the end, like all minefields, while it did make life difficult for German submarines the Northern Barrage did not prevent them from reaching their hunting grounds. Admiral Beatty was not a fan either, thinking it a diversion of scarce resources and a hindrance to free movement of the Grand Fleet. The U-boats would also, he judged correctly, use Norwegian territorial waters to get past the mines. A direct assault on the 'hornet's nest' itself might be a better means to bring about a decisive result in the struggle against the U-boats. Just such a plan had been dusted off – yet again – and was being worked up for action.

The British estimated there were between 40 and 50 U-boats based at Bruges, just over six miles inland, which were using canals to reach either Ostend or Zeebrugge. In fact, only 37 U-boats had ever belonged to the Flanders Flotilla at its peak but they were still a big threat. German destroyers and torpedo boats based at Ostend and Zeebrugge were also becoming increasingly aggressive and successful and so needed neutralising too.

Admiral Sims thought proposals for attacking the submarine bases, 'did not greatly impress naval strategists, but they certainly sounded a note which was popular in England'.[4]

Admiral Reginald Bacon, the former boss of the Submarine Service, felt it was better to try to knock the canal lock gates out via a bombardment using battleship guns. Jellicoe disagreed, in June 1917 labelling it a scheme that 'no responsible naval officer would recommend'.[5] Achieving a hit on the small lock gates from a dozen miles out to sea was thought impossible and there was intelligence they could even be withdrawn into protective revetments.

Still sceptical about convoys working, Jellicoe was open to the idea of assaulting the submarine menace in Flanders as part of a massive effort in 1917 to push the Germans back on the Western Front. A proposal for a spectacular combined operation was floated, which envisaged a big push at Ypres – about 70km to the south-west of Bruges – accompanied by assaults from the sea at Ostend and Zeebrugge.

The navy would be tasked with putting ashore an entire division of troops along with tanks and artillery. For Admiral Fisher, smouldering in retirement at the failure so far of the navy to beat the U-boats, this sort of venture was the only suitable medicine. Hunting down U-boats at sea was, he felt, 'looking for them, like a needle in a bundle of hay on the wide ocean!'[6] The prescription for what ailed the Allied cause was the old plan he and Churchill had advocated in late 1914. He repeatedly told whoever would listen 'the one and only way of dealing with the German submarine menace' was to capture the bases. 'When you have a plague of wasps, you don't send little boys with butterfly nets to catch individual wasps,' he grumbled, possibly inspired by President Wilson's remarks. 'YOU TAKE THE WASPS' NEST!'[7]

While the old First Sea Lord might have thunderously cheered on a big push against the 'wasps' nest', Admiral Beatty was alarmed by the prospect of battlecruisers and battleships pulled in to provide heavy-weight covering fire. This potentially gave the Germans the very thing they had desired for so long: a major part of the British battle fleet detached from the main body, which could be destroyed by a stronger enemy force. Beatty thought the whole concept ill-advised, especially as not enough time was being allowed to train for such a large and complex operation. He suggested somebody needed to talk to those who had been heavily involved on the naval side in the last major British amphibious assault. The casualty rate among old battleships on bombardment duty off Gallipoli showed the likely outcome.

Apart from the adjacent threat of the High Sea Fleet, even if the Bruges submarines were bottled up there were U-boats operating from Heligoland and other North Sea bases that could intervene. It would be the sort of opportunity not gifted to enemy submarines since the early months of the war. Beatty thought that blocking the entrance to the canals might succeed if an innovative approach were adopted. He suggested sending in concrete blockships fitted with some means of cutting through minefields and guided via radio control from aircraft. It was beyond the capability of technology available at the time and the plan for a large combined assault was put on ice when the Ypres offensive faltered in late September.

Rear Admiral Keyes was made boss of the Dover Command, taking up his new job on New Year's Day 1918, and he energised the Zeebrugge raid idea while improving the Dover Barrage.

The latter had so far proved ineffective, its nets and mines preventing hardly any Flanders-based U-boats from breaking out via the Channel. Keyes made sure enemy submarines could not so easily dive under the Barrage and avoid mines. A U-boat was soon destroyed while trying to sneak through in the dark. Caught in a searchlight and forced to dive, it hit a mine and was blown apart.

The appointment of Keyes to the Dover Command came as part of a changing of the guard, with Admiral Jellicoe – perceived to have resisted new ideas, primarily convoys, for too long – replaced by Admiral Sir Rosslyn Wemyss, and it was he who sent Keyes to defend the Channel.

Keyes was determined to ensure the forthcoming raids on Zeebrugge and Ostend were a fully naval affair, feeling that should he turn to the army for assault troops it would offend the navy. In the Grand Fleet's battleships – swinging at anchor while the army did the bulk of the fighting and dying – there were many frustrated sailors itching to get at the enemy. The call for suitable men had gone out at year's end, asking for volunteers from among those who were physically fit and likely to be brave too, along with officers possessing exceptional leadership abilities. Ahead lay four months of secret training, which was described as for 'hazardous service'.

The final plans for the Zeebrugge and Ostend assaults were settled and approved by the Admiralty in late February 1918. That month the Germans sank 307,000 tons of shipping. While not the most serious level of losses – 540,000 tons were sunk in the corresponding month of 1917 and it was 574,000 tons *less* than in April 1917[8] – if the war was to be won it had to be reduced even further.

The Zeebrugge and Ostend assaults seemed an ideal stratagem to achieve this, but could not happen until mid-April 1918, when there would be a suitable moonless night, accompanied by the necessary high water between midnight and 1.30 a.m. The wind would, according to forecasts, also be blowing in the right direction to preserve a smoke-screen. Without those conditions the whole enterprise would probably not stand a chance.

Even as preparations for the raids entered their final period the Germans launched the first of three massive offensives on the Western Front, the so-called *Kaiserschlacht* – the Emperor's Battle – which was a bid to achieve victory before the American Expeditionary Force could add its full weight to the contest.

The U-boats having failed to deliver the decisive blow so far, this seemed to be the next best option – a knock-out punch on land in the west using extra troops released from the Eastern Front.

The British sectors of the Western Front were the main pressure points, as the German high command had assessed that Britain's army was exhausted after its very costly efforts in 1917. The offensive against the Somme was launched on 21 March while in England training for the Zeebrugge and Ostend raids continued.

The main assault troops for the raid on the Flanders ports were the 4th Marine Battalion (500 men) and three companies of sailors (around 200 men). They would be carried into action by the specially adapted cruiser *Vindictive* and two converted Mersey ferries – *Daffodil* and *Iris* – which were the spearhead of a task force totalling 165 vessels, with 10,000 men at sea.

The role of actually blocking the canals fell to old cruisers of the Apollo Class – *Brilliant* and *Sirius* at Ostend with *Thetis*, *Intrepid* and *Iphigenia* at Zeebrugge. Should they succeed in making it across the harbour, *Thetis* was to go up the canal and ram the lock gates, with the other two vessels sunk in the canal entrance, between the pier heads. At Ostend, *Sirius* and *Brilliant* would plant themselves in the entrance of the canal.

A Mole that also masked the entrance to the canal protected the harbour at Zeebrugge. It was an impressive, heavily fortified structure made from stone, but it had a weak point. This was a wooden and steel viaduct that carried a train line, which would be the special target of two explosive-packed submarines, *C3* and *C1*. They would ram it and be blown up, in order to prevent the Germans from sending reinforcements along the Mole.

As well as gun batteries and various stores sheds along its top, the Mole hosted within its protective embrace accommodation for U-boat crews, shelters for submarines and moorings for torpedo boats. The troops from *Vindictive* and the ferries would capture the far end of the Mole and take out gun batteries, killing as many enemy troops as possible, hopefully improving chances of the blockships getting past. *Vindictive* had 'clips' that were meant to go across the Mole and hold her in place. Should they not work, the ferries, aside from landing their own troops, were to keep the cruiser pressed against the Mole.

Finally the time came for the assault units aboard their assigned ships to be let in on the big secret. The demolition parties were tasked with destroying gun batteries on the Mole along with a lighthouse at its end, cranes, warehouses and stores. Smokescreens would obscure them from the view of German gunners and there would be special recall signals for them to get back to their respective ships. Former Grand Fleet sailor and now demolition squad member, H.E. Adams, noted incredulously that '*all* this [is] to be completed within an hour'.[9] The enormity of the task and the slim chance of survival sank in. 'There was a funny feeling running through our veins by this time, I don't think we spoke much, just ready – set for the "go" – and the sooner we got stuck into it, the better.' The men made up little packages of keepsakes to be sent to their families if they did not return and wrote last letters and postcards home. These would be sent out after the raid whether they were dead or alive.

It was towards evening on 11 April when the vessels committed to the assault force assembled off the Goodwin Sands. 'What an honour, and what a Mission for a law-abiding peaceful Liverpool ferry boat,' thought Adams aboard *Daffodil*. 'So our mixed squadron of "Crocks" – obsolete, dejected and to all appearances disgusting, not even fit to boast "H.M.S." – set out down the Medway on a job unparalleled in Naval History.'

Forming into three columns, the task force headed east. Rear Admiral Keyes originally intended leading from aboard *Vindictive* but realised this was not the best place from which to co-ordinate the overall operation. Instead he embarked in the destroyer HMS *Warwick*, which had an enormous silk White Ensign flying from her stern.

As the ships sailed, in France the situation was desperate. Since 21 March 100,000 casualties a week had been suffered, with the British sector under severe pressure along a 50-mile battlefront. It seemed all might be lost.

The Commander of the BEF, Field Marshal Sir Douglas Haig, issued an order calling for his men to give their all. 'With our backs to the wall and believing in the justice of our cause each one of us must fight on to the end,' Haig told the troops. 'The safety of our homes and the Freedom of mankind alike depend upon the conduct of each one of us at this critical moment.'[10]

The ultimate objective of the German assault was to cut the BEF off from the Channel ports, then surround and destroy it, while also threatening England directly. 'If we reached the Channel Coast we should lay hands directly on England's vital arteries,' explained General Paul von Hindenburg, the overall commander of the Kaiser's forces in the west.[11]

The Germans hoped their U-boats would simultaneously reap a deadly harvest, for as Hindenburg later admitted, 'the moment was coming nearer when America would begin to come on the scene fully equipped. If before that time our U-boats had not succeeded in making the transport of large masses of troops with their supplies highly questionable, our position would become serious.'[12]

The Royal Navy's attack on the Flanders ports could not come at a more opportune time for the hard-pressed Allies, but the 11 April venture was a false start. It was called off due to an unfavourable wind making an effective smokescreen impossible.

After Keyes lobbied hard in the Admiralty for another go, the assault force again set sail on the afternoon of 22 April. Keyes was mindful that the next day belonged to England's patron saint and sent a suitably rousing signal by semaphore to his ships: 'St. George for England.'

Vindictive's CO, Capt. Alfred Carpenter, signalled back: 'May we give the dragon's tail a damned good twist.'[13]

By 11.50 p.m., *Vindictive* was less than a mile from the Mole, but the enemy showed no sign of waking up. Not even the noise of British monitors *Terror* and *Erebus* shelling German positions along the coast worried them, for such bombardments were routine.

When British motor torpedo boats raced into Zeebrugge harbour, engines roaring, the enemy could not help but twig. Within moments the sky was alive with bursting star shells, but the smokescreen remained impenetrable. With her assault troops still hidden from view, *Vindictive* slid in towards the Mole, aiming to come alongside by the lighthouse. A gust of wind cleared the smoke, like a theatre curtain suddenly torn aside. The enemy's searchlights no longer probed the swirling opaqueness of smoke but fell on the shocking sight of an enemy cruiser just 600ft away.

All hell broke loose, with every German gun capable of bearing on the cruiser firing. Fortunately for *Vindictive*, she was already too close to the cover of the Mole for her hull to be penetrated fatally, though her upperworks were mercilessly hammered.

17   Glorified Trench Raid

Vindictive's 6-inch guns spat back and she crunched alongside the Mole. It was one minute past midnight. Casualties aboard the cruiser were already heavy and her sudden burst of speed at the end had put her further down the Mole than planned, against a part the assault troops had not been trained to tackle.

They had rehearsed using carefully constructed Mole mock-ups, but not for this section. It was festooned with machine gun nests and barricades and *Vindictive* was also unable to secure herself – the swell was so high as she came in that she rolled heavily and the specially designed clips were damaged. Most of the gangways designed to enable men to swarm ashore were wrecked by both enemy shells and the force of the ship hitting the Mole. *Daffodil* came to *Vindictive*'s rescue – a contingency that was well rehearsed – pressing her bow to the cruiser's side and putting on full power to hold her in place.

Aboard *Daffodil* the sailors stood ready for action, clad in their unfamiliar khaki combat clothes and tin hats, 'armed with cutlass, revolver, plenty of ammunition . . .'[1]

Vindictive was clearly having a terrible time and demolition party member H.E. Adams saw 'heaps of men were killed'. As *Daffodil* rose and fell, scraping up and down *Vindictive*'s hull, Adams caught momentary flashes of the hellish conditions inside the cruiser through the other vessel's scuttles. He saw red water sloshing about the mess deck, which, he felt, was 'Blood of British Seamen – who until a moment or so ago, were alive and well. Their heads – arms – legs and trunks torn to bits and separate, mixed up with the loaves, potatoes, stools, mess utensils, and so it went on – the guns still craving for more victims . . . it was terrible – made you very sick at heart . . .'

It seemed like half an hour must have gone by when there was 'a terrible deafening explosion a thud that shook Heaven and Earth. The ships shivered and trembled – the nearest approach to an earthquake one could imagine. We had been warned to expect it, but among all this it had passed from one's mind – the concussion threw you to the deck.' This was submarine *C3* detonating.

During the early stages of developing the attack plan, it had been proposed that a floating pontoon laden with high explosive should be placed next to the viaduct. Lt Cdr F.H. Sandford suggested it would be better to load an elderly submarine with H.E. and then drive it deep into the structure, right between the piers that supported it. This would ensure the full force of the explosion went up and into the viaduct – like a gigantic torpedo exploding under the hull of a ship.

It was a risky proposition for whoever took the chosen submarine to its final destination, for the vessel would have to stay on the surface all the way in, exposed to the fire of dozens of enemy guns. The chances of success and survival for the crew were low and it was decided that two vessels would be needed, to provide an element of back-up if one was sunk.

Despite the extreme risk, there was no shortage of volunteers, though married men were barred. Command of *C3* was awarded to Lt Richard Sandford, the 27-year-old younger brother of the man who came up with the idea, while *C1* was to be commanded by Lt A.C. Newbold. Planning for the submarines' part in the attack included intensive studies of pre-war photographs, recent aerial imagery of the viaduct and even drawings provided by its designers.

Efforts were made to give the two officers and four ratings crewing each submarine – loaded with five tons of Amatol H.E. – at least a chance of escape. There would be a skiff in tow, into which the submariners would tumble in the final moments of the approach, leaving a gyro steering device to take the boat at maximum speed to the point of impact. A time-fuse would detonate the Amatol five minutes after it detected forward momentum had ceased. Should the skiffs be wrecked by enemy fire an alternative means of escape was via specially embarked ladders. The submariners were expected to use these for climbing up onto the Mole in order to make a suicidal dash to *Vindictive* or one of the other vessels.

Both *C1* and *C3* departed Dover as planned on the afternoon of 22 April, each under tow from a destroyer. Lt Cdr Sandford decided to try to ensure his brother survived by taking across a steam picket boat that was also towed by a destroyer. Once off Zeebrugge, the elder Sandford intended laying smoke floats in an effort to help obscure the approach of the submarines and then pick up the crews after they abandoned ship.

On the way across *C1* lost her tow and fell behind, but proceeding as planned *C3* let go her tow at 11.26 p.m. and headed for the viaduct without the benefit of a dedicated smokescreen or back-up submarine.

When star shells lit up the night sky heavy firing from coastal gun batteries tore through the air, but this was heading towards the task force at sea. *C3* was, as yet, left alone, skirting the edge of the main smokescreen, which cleared to reveal *Vindictive* coming alongside the Mole to a hot reception. As his own rendezvous with the enemy approached, Lt Sandford activated his smoke-making machine but its output was pathetic and easily dispersed. One or two shells smashed into the water nearby but *C3* still did not seem to warrant much attention.

Having decided he would steer the submarine all the way in to target rather than rely on the gyro gear, Sandford called his men up onto the casing. He also decided to light the fuse himself. A searchlight caught them, but then switched off – *C3* had been mistaken for a U-boat blundering about.

At just over 9 knots, the British boat crashed into the viaduct, burying her bow deep. As Sandford lit the fuse and his men tumbled into the skiff, overhead could be heard German voices and even some laughter. The skiff's propeller chewed into *C3* as a current swept it onto the submarine, while the Germans opened fire, wounding two of the submariners. Robbed of mechanical propulsion, *C3*'s men had just over two minutes to row themselves to a safe distance but holes had been punched into the skiff, probably by shrapnel from the near misses.

The sinking skiff crawled away as a massive explosion ripped 100ft out of the viaduct, atomising many of the Germans who had earlier scoffed at the stupid submarine. Shattered wooden piles, girders and other wreckage splashed into the sea all around but by some miracle did not hit the skiff.

Out of the night came salvation in the form of the elder Sandford and his steam picket boat. The submariners were soon hauled aboard, Lt Sandford by now badly wounded. The picket boat headed for the destroyer *Phoebe* where her doctor would soon be tending to the submariners' injuries. All the men who had taken *C3* on her last voyage would be decorated for valour, with Sandford himself receiving the VC.

Vindictive's captain, Carpenter, was also decorated with the VC, and the medal was awarded to four others for their heroic exploits on St George's Day 1918. Carpenter was keenly aware of the daily sacrifice made by the British Army and would later describe the Zeebrugge operation as 'merely a glorified trench raid'.[2] Overall casualties were 637 killed, wounded and missing in action, a very high price to pay during little more than an hour's action.

At the same time as the assault force set sail, the Germans decided to deploy their battle fleet, but fortunately not to destroy the British raiders. Their objective was to ravage an Allied convoy off the coast of Norway and sink its escorting warships. This would add another blow to punches delivered against the British at Ypres, where the Germans had unleashed the second stage of their spring offensive.

Maintaining strict radio silence, late on 23 April the High Sea Fleet was spotted by a British submarine. It did not attack or send a sighting report – the boat's captain mistakenly believed the ships were part of the covering force for Allied vessels laying the Northern Barrage.

Knowing nothing, the Grand Fleet did not at that point deploy from its new main base at Rosyth. The move south from Scapa had been instituted by Admiral Beatty to enable it to take advantage of just such a foray off Norway by the enemy battle fleet. Failing to find the convoy, which reached the Forth unmolested, elements of the German group continued to look for victims but found none. Indiscreet wireless use finally revealed their presence to the British and on 24 April Beatty sailed with 32 battleships, four battlecruisers, 26 cruisers and 85 destroyers, all steaming hard.

The High Sea Fleet was by then too far south and close to home to be caught. For the Royal Navy it was a golden opportunity missed. With shell problems fixed, better anti-flash discipline in its ships and even more powerful than it had been two years earlier, the Grand Fleet might well have achieved the new Trafalgar.

Royal Navy submarines were, however, lying in wait by the entrance of the swept channel through the German minefields in the Bight. The battlecruiser *Moltke* had suffered a mechanical breakdown and was being towed home by the battleship *Oldenburg* when they strayed within sight of *E42*. The British boat's captain, Lieutenant Charles Allen, put a torpedo into *Moltke*, which showed her customary ability to soak up damage and limped away. It was the last opportunity offered to an Allied submarine to torpedo a German capital ship at sea during the First World War

For the rest of the war the High Sea Fleet stayed in port. Its sailors grew restless, mutinous and unfit, with many of them recruited to the cause of world revolution espoused by the Bolsheviks. The best officers and ratings were sent to serve in the ever-expanding U-boat force.

The Ostend side of the raid could be considered a mere footnote to the venture at Zeebrugge, perhaps because it was an even bigger example of heroic futility. Lacking any diversionary attack to distract the enemy, the blockships were more exposed to fire, especially when their smokescreen dispersed too soon. There was also confusion over the exact route to the channel they were required to block. The Germans had moved a marker buoy a mile to the east and the blockships were well off target.

In early May another attempt was made to block Ostend, this time using *Vindictive* and the old cruiser *Sappho*, the latter failing even to make the Belgian coast. *Vindictive* soldiered on alone, coming under intense enemy fire as she approached the port and only partially blocking the channel, with the raiders suffering 48 killed and wounded. During the Zeebrugge and Ostend raids the Germans suffered fewer than 40 casualties.

In the final analysis British attempts to bottle up the U-boats were a tactical failure – disruption to U-boat activities was fleeting – but having learned the lesson of Jutland the British turned them into a strategic (public relations) victory.

That both the Zeebrugge and Ostend endeavours were heroic was never in doubt, with Winston Churchill hailing the former as 'the finest feat of arms in the Great War, and certainly as an episode unsurpassed in the history of the Royal Navy'.[3]

Churchill's old comrade-in-arms, Jacky Fisher, was less impressed. He decried attempts by the Admiralty to 'make the episode rank with the siege of Troy'. The British had not captured Zeebrugge and held on to it, which, Fisher felt, was the point – to permanently deny the Germans use of a Flanders submarine base. He felt bitterly the loss of young lives and feared U-boats might yet inflict starvation on Britain.[4]

Lloyd George disagreed and later described the Zeebrugge raid as 'the one naval exploit of the War that moved and still moves the imagination of the Nation'.[5]

It was a welcome example of extreme valour by a service widely perceived by many politicians and members of the public to have fallen short so far in the war. The vital – but comparatively boring – job of winning via convoying merchant vessels and blockading Germany did not set their imaginations on fire. Coming as the British sector of the Western Front recoiled under heavy enemy attack, the navy's raid appeared to deliver a dynamic blow against the hated submarines. It made the navy feel better about itself, harking back to the sort of daring actions it had specialised in during the Age of Fighting Sail when it was Britannia's unchallenged defence.

Admiral Scheer, while admitting the British effort was 'made with great pluck', felt it failed because blockships were not sunk in the actual lock gates, which remained operational. He explained that the 'connection between the harbour at Zeebrugge and the shipyard at Bruges was never interrupted even for a day'.[6] In April 1918 Germany's U-boats actually increased their tally, sinking 343,000 tons of shipping, including 216,000 tons of British vessels.[7] The loss of Bruges as an operating base would have been 'a very disagreeable blow to the U-boat campaign' according to Scheer, though he felt switching back to German bases would have got around it.

A new channel had actually been dredged around the blockships at

Zeebrugge by early May and was used by large U-boats to reach the sea.

It was the more effective Dover Barrage, along with the constant harassment by RAF, US Navy and Marine Corps aircraft of submarines deploying from, or returning to, Flanders that ultimately made it an increasingly unattractive operational base. Bombing raids by Allied aircraft never penetrated the submarine pens – huge enclosed concrete shelters at Bruges – though they did cause havoc elsewhere in the city. There was concern in London that civilians were being killed un-necessarily, but despite that air attacks were stepped up due to 'the vital importance of exploiting to the full the present unique opportunity of destroying enemy submarines and other craft in Bruges Dock'.[8]

While the Bruges bombing campaign may have achieved limited material impact on submarine operations, the psychological effect on the U-boat crews and their support personnel of never being able to rest must have been considerable. By September 1918, only 13 U-boats were operating from Flanders, 24 fewer than had sailed from there to prey on Allied shipping during their peak period.

By autumn 1918, submarines operating from Flanders had, over three years of activities, used their guns and torpedoes to account for 3,342,000 tons of enemy shipping, 23 per cent of the total sunk by U-boats during the conflict.[9]

18   Until Exhaustion

The High Sea Fleet might never set sail on a war mission again, but the U-boats sailing from North Sea bases continued to fight, though the overall figure for monthly Allied shipping losses declined steadily. It went from 296,000 tons in May 1918 to 119,000 tons by October.[1] Allied countermeasures were becoming increasingly effective and both air and sea forces, along with better anti-submarine weaponry, were dom-inating the oceans.

UB-72 was hounded from beginning to end of her deployment, the boat's fate illustrating that the Admiralty had finally got its act together. Under the command of 24-year-old Oberleutnant Friedrich Träger, *UB-72* departed Heligoland on 1 May, taking the northern route around the top of Scotland. Träger intended hunting in the North Channel and the northern zone of the Irish Sea. On 7 May a British airship spotted *UB-72* off Anglesey and that was when her troubles started, with three bombs dropped but missing by a wide margin. It was nonetheless a frightening experience.

That evening the U-boat's periscope was spotted by a destroyer, which over the course of two hours dropped 23 depth charges. These shook *UB-72* so much she sprang a leak in her No. 2 port ballast tank, which was actually full of oil to increase patrol range. It resulted in a very clear trail on the surface for the enemy to follow. Sure enough, at dawn on 8 May keen-eyed lookouts in another destroyer spotted the oil. A further 20 depth charges were dropped, putting the U-boat's lights out. The submarine was being shaken to pieces and armed trawlers joined in, but *UB-72* evaded destruction and also shook off a patrol boat that dropped five depth charges.

The German boat had so far failed spectacularly to achieve the objective of her patrol – sinking enemy shipping – and instead had been harassed constantly. For the next few days *UB-72* concentrated on avoiding enemy patrols. Heading south – still licking her wounds – at 5.50 a.m. on 12 May she was patrolling on the surface off Portland, crossing paths with the submarine *D4*. The British boat fired two torpedoes at *UB-72*, one going wide but the other crashing into the engine room, the explosion tearing the vessel apart. She sank almost instantly, though three of her crew survived. *D4*'s successful attack was remarkable for being the first instance of a new technology being applied to the hunter-killer role.

Capt. Nasmith of Dardanelles fame had invented the IS-WAS, a special instrument used to calculate a simple firing solution, by fixing where the target *is* going to be based on *where* it was (and using bearing, heading and speed of advance). It enabled submarine captains to use deflection when firing torpedoes to hit small targets at long range. All the leading submarine navies would within a few years employ the IS-WAS and over the years more advanced fire control computers would be created.

*

The biggest challenge for U-boats operating alone during the closing months of the First World War was to actually find merchant shipping in the vast ocean. Even when a vessel was attacked, often the U-boat came off worse. While the submarine may have delivered a serious blow it would not necessarily get away with it, at least not as easily as might have been the case previously. This was illustrated by the fate of the brand new *UB-124*, whose novice captain was 25-year-old Ober-leutnant Hans Wutsdorff.

After a bungled attack on a 4,000-ton steamship, *UB-124* reached her desired hunting ground off northern Ireland. Early on the morning of 20 July, in the entrance to the North Channel, she found a prestigious target. It was the 740ft-long, 32,284-ton displacement liner SS *Justicia*, sporting a new dazzle paint scheme to try to confuse predators.

The liner was on her way from Belfast to New York to pick up more US troops, having already transported 10,000 across the Atlantic. The previous day she had been hit by four torpedoes fired by *UB-64*, com-manded by 30-year-old Kapitänleutnant Otto von Schrader. *Justicia* was now heading for Lough Swilly under tow from an Admiralty tug.

By the time *UB-124* found *Justicia*, the liner was managing barely 4 knots and was closely guarded by 17 destroyers. As Wutsdorff scru-tinised his target, somewhere in the distance patrolling aircraft were busy dropping bombs on phantom submarines, the distraction helping *UB-124* to penetrate the protective screen. Coming in on the beam, Wutsdorff fired two torpedoes at *Justicia* from a range of 650 yards.

Both hit, one aft and one for'ard, but the inexperienced U-boat cap-tain made a basic error. Wutsdorff had failed to allow for the sudden loss of weight in his boat, with *UB-124*'s bows breaking surface right in the middle of an angry swarm of escorts. Wutsdorff bellowed an order for some of his submariners to run forward, but the sudden increase in weight took the boat into an uncontrolled dive. *UB-124* hit the seabed 280ft down, but did not fall apart or become crushed into nothing, des-pite being well below safe depth.

In silence on the bottom, the lull allowed the crew to regain their composure but at 11.30 a.m. enemy destroyers found the U-boat due to an oil leak. Into the sea tumbled an intense and terrifying depth-charge barrage, with 50 in all dropped. At 2.00 p.m. there was a short burst of five more, this time causing serious structural damage and more leaks. Wutsdorff gave the order to surface, with *UB-124*'s ascent as uncontrolled as her dive, the submarine bursting into the open amid enemy vessels. The U-boat was set upon by a pack of British destroyers with the unlikely names *Nutbrook*, *Marne* and *Pigeon*, whose gunfire was lethally accurate. Wutsdorff gave the scuttling order and told his men to abandon ship. The Chief Engineer Officer and Officer of the Watch volunteered to scuttle the boat and paid for it with their lives, disappearing into the deep along with *UB-124*. The submarine went down for the last time not far from where *Justicia* finally succumbed to her damage, the second largest vessel to be sunk by a submarine in the conflict.[2]

By this stage of the war in the Atlantic, liners carrying US troops were the most desired targets, but so far few were being attacked. Often, as was the case with *Justicia*, they were not actually carrying any American soldiers. Some in Germany wondered if the navy was still pulling its punches, for fear of further enraging the USA. The point where it mattered had passed. The U-boat force's excuse for not inflicting more pain on American shipping was that the Atlantic was vast and ships were really quite small. Of those encountered and attacked it was inevitable only a proportion would be carrying American troops. Three hundred thousand were reaching European shores each month but most were carried by British-flagged and ex-German liners with up to 10,000 troops in each ship.

Liners sometimes hit back. The *Olympic*, of the White Star Line, was one that did so. She shot at, then rammed *U-103* on the night of 12 May 1918. *Olympic*'s attack was in express contravention of her actual stated purpose – carrying troops safely to Cherbourg. The American destroyer USS *Davis* saved the majority of *U-103*'s crew.

If they couldn't find and sink cargo vessels in convoy, or catch fast liners carrying troops to Europe, the Germans thought they might be able to sink them while they were gathering to make a crossing. Alternatively, they could mine the exit points from ports on the Eastern Seaboard of North America.

A number of U-cruisers were sent across the Atlantic to achieve these ends, following in the footsteps of *U-53* and the former *U-Deutschland*. The U-cruisers would also venture as far south as the Equator and into the Mediterranean. Seven former merchant submarines were converted and used off the US coast and a further pair were constructed from the outset for combat operations but their efforts against shipping were too little to stem the flow of troops and supplies across the Atlantic, nor did they seriously harm convoys.

The brand new, purpose-built U-cruiser *U-154*, commissioned in December 1917, was sent to operate off West Africa. Korvettenkapitän Hermann Gercke's first submarine command, *U-154* was to work with sister vessel *U-153*. Gercke opened his tonnage account on 12 March, off Morocco, by sinking a 3,244-ton Norwegian-flagged cargo vessel carrying wheat from the USA to Gibraltar.

On 25 April 1918 *U-154* and *U-153* used their guns to subdue and sink the Q-ship HMS *Bombola*, a 3,140-ton ex-collier, fitted with a pair of concealed 14pdr guns, off the Cape Verde Islands. *Bombola* put up a good fight, lasting two-and-a-half-hours, and there were no survivors, though the corpses of some of her men were allegedly found on a West African beach.

While *U-153* decided to sail back to Germany *U-154* stayed on patrol but the destruction of *Bombola* had prompted the Admiralty to order submarine *E35* out from Gibraltar, tasked with patrolling one area while *J1* prowled another. Both were to see if they could hunt down and kill the culprit, or culprits, assisted by intelligence garnered from intercepts of enemy wireless signals. It was *E35* that exacted revenge for *Bombola* on 11 May, hitting *U-154* with two fish and detonating the German boat's own torpedoes. Wreckage was hurled 100ft into the air and the shockwave rocked *E35*, shattering some of her light bulbs. There were no survivors in the U-boat, with five British merchant mariners earlier taken prisoner also losing their lives.

In the final weeks of the conflict a young officer destined to one day revolutionise submarine tactics received a lesson in the futility of the solo submarine attack. In early October, *UB-68*, commanded by 26-year-old Oberleutnant Karl Dönitz, an engineer's son from the outskirts of Berlin, was operating from Pola in the Adriatic.

By the autumn of 1918 returns for U-boat patrols in the Mediterranean were declining dramatically, with just 49,000 tons of Allied shipping sunk in September.[3]

Dönitz aimed to reverse the trend and on his latest foray sought to take advantage of a new moon, attacking at night on the surface. He hoped the low silhouette of his boat would reduce the chances of being seen while she inserted herself between long lines of merchant vessels.

First sighting of a convoy came at 1.00 a.m. on 4 October, 50 miles from Cape Passero, off south-east Sicily, a lookout spotting an observation balloon towed by a destroyer. More and more shadowy outlines loomed out of the darkness – merchant vessels, all heavily laden with cargo, followed destroyers and other escorts. Suddenly the ships turned directly towards the submarine, part of a carefully timed zigzagging manoeuvre. Dönitz's boat was nearly in collision with one of them, but passed by a few feet astern.

Finally, Dönitz got into a good position and lit up the night with the explosion of a torpedo ripping into a cargo ship. This instantly drew the attention of a destroyer's crew. Crash-diving, Dönitz waited tensely for a depth-charge attack, which didn't come, probably due to the enemy holding off for fear of blast-damaging friendly vessels.

Dönitz pulled back, surfaced and prepared to attack again. As he brought UB-68 back up he was careful to show only the submarine's conning tower. Climbing up the ladder to open the hatch, he alone crept onto the bridge, taking a peek over the rim just after it broke the surface.

Assured he wasn't in imminent danger, Dönitz ordered the U-boat fully surfaced and set off in pursuit of the convoy, which was threatening to slip his grasp.

By the time he was in a position to attack again it was dawn, so Dönitz decided to make a submerged run. It was then that gremlins struck.

A type of boat with unstable tendencies longitudinally, for which it had already received modifications that did not work, UB-68 suddenly went nose down, almost vertical. Chaos was all around, with battery acid spilling over and lighting lost. With up to 1,500 fathoms (9,000 feet approx.) of water below, the chances of death were strong, for the maximum diving depth of UB-68 before the hull was crushed was around 200ft. Dönitz ordered all tanks blown and motors full astern with 'rudder hard over'. The descent was finally halted 'between 270 feet and 300 feet',[4] still well beyond the crush depth. The boat then started to rise, but rather too rapidly, leaping from the sea into daylight.

Dönitz was again first up the ladder, eager to see how dire the situation was, but found his boat surrounded by the convoy. The air was filled with the hellish noise of numerous ships' sirens. Furious flag signals flew from various halyards. Every gun able to bear, whether in a warship or a cargo vessel, was fired at the unlucky U-boat. Several destroyers were moving in to ram. Diving was a course of action not open to Dönitz, for *UB-68* had no compressed air left and was now being hit, with water gushing in at various points. 'I realised that this was the end,' Dönitz would recall, 'and I gave the order "All hands abandon ship!".'[5] A destroyer saved all but seven of the submarine's crew and Dönitz was headed for Malta, to be followed by a year as a prisoner in England.

He had plenty of time to reflect on how the convoy system had all but nullified any advantage submarines once enjoyed. Dönitz would one day write that solo U-boats would for long stretches 'see nothing at all; and then suddenly up would loom a huge concourse of ships . . . The solitary U-boat, which most probably had sighted the convoy purely by chance, would then attack . . . for perhaps several days and nights, until the physical exhaustion of both commander and crew called a halt.'[6]

A single U-boat could probably sink a couple of ships, but no matter how many they sent to the bottom, by 1918 the percentage loss for the Allies was negligible compared to what reached Britain unseen and unmolested.

The Allied armies went on the offensive along the Western Front that August and so began the final defeat of the demoralised, severely weakened German Army. The submarine bases in Flanders were abandoned and most of the U-boats sailed for Germany, with only four left behind due to mechanical problems.

The British, meanwhile, sent their own boats to stake out the remaining enemy submarine bases in the North Sea. On the afternoon of 16 October the brand new *L12* was involved in a short but very violent action off the northern tip of Denmark. Her victim, *UB-90*, was heading home to Kiel on the surface after experiencing engine and hydroplane defects when *L12* fired a spread of four 21-inch torpedoes at a range of 1,500 yards. There was a deep, rumbling explosion and when *L12* reached the scene she found only a large oil patch, a German sailor's cap and what appeared to be 'half a man's body'.[7]

Even when the chiefs of the army, the politicians and the Kaiser realised that terms had to be agreed with the enemy, the navy still wanted to carry on. The Germans sent their proposals for an armistice on 4

October 1918 – the day Dönitz was sunk off Sicily – but the navy urged prosecution of the U-boat campaign regardless. This included the unrealistically ambitious Scheer Programme for building lots of submarines to win the war in 1919. 'The Navy does not need an Armistice,'[8] suggested an officer on Admiral Scheer's staff.

A direct assault on Scapa Flow was recommended, in order to restore honour to the navy. An alternative, and rather familiar, proposal was luring the Royal Navy to destruction in the North Sea. Admiral Scheer agreed that the High Sea Fleet should do something. 'It must be deployed,' he ventured.[9]

So determined was the navy to go out in a blaze of glory it decided not to tell anyone what it was up to, though it did on 21/22 October issue a cease order for unrestricted submarine warfare:

Commence return cruise immediately. Because of current negotiations. All manner of merchant warfare forbidden. U-boats already returning. Attack warships only by day. Admiralty Staff of the Navy. Berlin.[10]

The Germans did not want another submarine outrage during the delicate process of armistice discussions, but for the naval leadership the decision was also tactically sound. The secret final assault would require the participation of at least two dozen U-boats and these must come home to be made ready.

As a precursor to whatever the heroic final gesture turned out to be, *UB-116*, commanded by 26-year-old Oberleutnant Hans Emsmann, sailed from Heligoland on 25 October. Emsmann's task was to penetrate Scapa Flow and sink either RN or US Navy heavy units, even though the key Allied capital ships had moved to Rosyth.

UB-116 sneaked into Hoxa Sound on 28 October, her telltale sounds picked up by British seabed hydrophones not long after 11.30 p.m. and her periscope also spotted. When a galvanometer indicated a disturbance in the earth's magnetic field as a submarine passed over its cable, mines were triggered. *UB-116* was the first, last and only submarine destroyed by shore-detonated mines in the First World War. She may well have been the final U-boat destroyed in the conflict, though that dubious honour possibly belongs to another vessel, depending on which source you consult.

Between the middle of October and 4 November, the Admiralty

estimated three enemy submarines were 'definitely known to have been sunk'. Otherwise, U-boats appeared to be returning home and 'no further hostile action had been reported'.[11]

That would not be an end of the matter, though, for action at sea would continue until the last gasp, a breakout of U-boats from the Adriatic provoking combat. On the night of 21 October the local U-boat commander in the Adriatic sent a wireless signal to his submarines ordering those on patrol to head straight for Germany, provided they had the diesel and the food supplies to make it. Alternatively they should return to Pola or Cattaro to take on fuel and food before making a run home.

By the end of October the Austro-Hungarian empire was no more and the constituent parts of its armed forces were being divided between the new nations emerging from the wreckage.

That meant naval bases had to be handed over to states that were not at war with the Allies and German submarines were no longer welcome. Having scuttled or otherwise rendered inoperable those that could not make it home, 14 vessels in all would try to reach Germany.

The most dangerous part of the voyage was the Strait of Gibraltar, which was packed with patrolling warships. A submerged passage was essential, with one U-boat captain recalling: 'We could hear the propellers of the vessels above, a steady hum, like a swarm of angry bees. The noise was our guide. When it had died away we would know that we were through the Strait.'[12]

Even then the U-boats could not guarantee being safe and might be attacked. U-34 was one boat that did not make it and may be the alternative bearer of the title of last U-boat sunk during the war.

According to British sources she was attacked on 8/9 November and sunk by gunfire from the Q-ship *Privet*, by that stage of the war operating overtly as an anti-submarine vessel. Post-war German investigations could only ascertain U-34 was lost some time after 25 October.

The final British warship victim of a U-boat during the conflict bore a highly significant name. *UB-50*, commanded by 27-year-old Oberleutnant Heinrich Kukat, sank the 14-year-old HMS *Britannia* off Cape Trafalgar, on 9 November. The old pre-dreadnought had for some months been engaged in escorting convoys to and from Sierra Leone, and Kukat missed with his first two torpedoes but the third hit. It detonated the contents of an ammunition magazine and so *Britannia* joined the long list of obsolete British battleships sunk by German sub-marines. *Britannia* took more than three hours to sink, with 50 of her 762 crew killed, most of them suffocated by the toxic fumes given off by burning cordite as they struggled to save her.

This one last hurrah for Germany's submarine force did not provide much by way of cheer. When a U-boat next had a battleship in its sights it would be a German one, with a red flag flying from it rather than the imperial ensign.

19 Immunity Lost

The day after *UB-116* was destroyed at Scapa Flow, mutiny gripped the German Navy, with its sailors refusing to undertake a suicide mission to preserve their admirals' pride. The naval command claimed all it wanted was 'a vigorous final stroke'[1] against the British, hoping to lure Royal Navy capital ships onto lines of U-boats, into fresh minefields and an ambush by the High Sea Fleet.

The German ratings were having none of it and so it fell to Kapitän-leutnant Johannes Spiess – Weddigen's second in command when he sank the three British cruisers in 1914 – to help subdue the mutineers. On 31 October, senior officers in a confidential interview asked Spiess if his men were loyal to him and would follow his orders. He replied that they would.

The crews of the battleships *Thüringen* and *Ostfriesland* were particu-larly rebellious so Spiess positioned his brand-new submarine, *U-135*, between them. Bow tubes were primed to fire at one battleship and stern tubes at the other.

Spiess watched as a torpedo boat approached at speed, seemingly ready to attack one of the battleships but at the last moment turning away and going alongside to put marines aboard.

The marines arrested the mutiny leaders but another battleship, *Heligoland*, still defiantly flew the red flag, so *U-135* was ordered to go and threaten her. It seemed to do the trick and her rebels surrendered.

Rather than isolate the mutineers, the navy made the mistake of allowing them ashore at Kiel, where they resumed their revolutionary activities. As had happened in Russia, sailors were at the forefront of major uprisings, taking control of Hamburg and Bremen. Spiess thought the mutineers should have been handled as harshly as the British dealt with theirs at the Nore in 1797, by hanging them. This was, however, a different time and Germany's collapse was complete.

In the Adriatic, Georg von Trapp, who remained Austria's leading submarine ace, found the navy he loved ceased to exist altogether. By then based ashore as a squadron commander, he had watched submarines return to Cattaro with their Austrian colours flying, including his old command *U-XIV*. When the ensign was pulled down for the last time there were tears and sobbing. 'Tirelessly, the U-boats have held out to the end in their sworn duty,' von Trapp recorded proudly. 'To the last salute of our flag.'[2]

The victorious Allies declared the U-boat menace vanquished. St George had slain the dragon and 176 German submarines were surrendered to the Allies. The majority of them sailed to British ports to be interned along with their crews. The Royal Navy's battleships escorted in the surrendered High Sea Fleet to linger under guard at Scapa Flow, where, in a final act of defiance, Germany's sailors scuttled their vessels at anchor on 21 June 1919. The supremacy of Britannia's big guns seemed assured, but when exactly did the Germans lose the war and what bearing did submarines, in the end, actually have on it?

The tipping point may have been the decision by the Germans to abandon their 'Sitzkrieg' on the Western Front, launching the Kaiser offensives rather than using divisions released by Brest-Litvosk to reinforce their position and then daring the Allies to break through.

Ludendorff's series of massive attacks failed to give German troops strategic objectives. Their indiscipline and underlying poor morale too often diverted them into pillaging Allied supply dumps where they found food and drink of a rich variety they had not seen for years. These were supplies brought to France that U-boats had failed to stop getting through. Meanwhile, the British naval blockade denied German soldiers and their loved ones even basic sustenance. Once they realised they were not going to beat the British or the French, their morale totally collapsed while Ludendorff had a mental breakdown.

If that exhausting big push – using up the last reserves, wasting the remaining military muscle – was not the tipping point, was it the French counter-attack on the Marne in July 1918? Or was it the huge, all-arms offensive to secure the Amiens railhead by the British that August, where tanks, aircraft and artillery were interwoven masterfully?

Ludendorff called the Amiens attack 'the black day of the German Army'[3] and the Kaiser was deeply shocked by his army's losses, along with the ability of the British Army, spearheaded by Canadian and Australian shock troops, to bounce back from the spring reverses. He suggested immediate peace talks. The famous interwar military historian Basil Liddell Hart considered each of the above events significant but traced the decisive moment that saw a critical 'decline in Germany's military power' right back to the beginning of the war.

Liddell Hart maintained that 'if the historian of the future has to select one day as decisive for the outcome of the World War he will probably choose August 2nd, 1914'. This was two days before hostilities between Germany and Britain commenced, when 'Mr Winston Churchill, at 1.25AM, sent the order to mobilize the British Navy'.[4]

The Royal Navy did not achieve a second Trafalgar but, according to Liddell Hart, its blockade of Germany contributed more than anything else to Allied victory, as 'the decisive agency in the struggle'.[5]

Like a straitjacket, the more the Germans struggled, the tighter the blockade became until they suffered utter powerlessness and were suffocated.

Therefore, and this was not highlighted by Liddell Hart, the decisive counter-struggle was the U-boat campaign. The German submarine effort sought to do what the battleships and cruisers of the High Sea Fleet could not do: break the ties that bound the blockade straitjacket tight.

Cutting the supply lines to Britain – which were sustaining the entire Allied effort on land by 1916 – and strangling the British nation would have created collapse. Yet the German decision to wage unrestricted submarine warfare brought the Americans into the war, meaning no chance of victory for the Central Powers. They toppled like dominoes as 1918 progressed, but the crucial prop was Germany. Once her military power had spent itself that was it. The whole thing collapsed and it was rotten from the inside due to the naval blockade and the failure of the U-boats.

222 THE DEADLY DEEP

The Allies, of course, did not get away scot-free. The landmark BBC TV documentary series *The Great War* – screened on the 50th anniversary of the beginning of the conflict – pointed out: 'Britain had also lost something that no Continental nation had ever possessed: A century's old sense of immunity . . .' The U-boats delivered 'a blow at Britain's lifelines, which struck at every citizen.'[6]

Between 1914 and 1918, the U-boat force sank 5,000 ships for a total of more than twelve million tons. This included the efforts of ninety-six UB boats, which sank 1,456 ships (2,289,704 tons) and 73 UC boats that claimed 2,042 ships (2,789,910 tons). German submarines sank ten battleships, seven heavy cruisers, six light cruisers and 21 destroyers. The butcher's bill for this was 4,744 men killed in 178 submarines lost,[7] but despite this high cost the strategic failure of the U-boats caused much bitterness and criticism of the Germany Navy. While the promises of victory turned out to be hollow, the bravery, the guts and endurance – the sheer sacrifice – of the U-boat men surely could not be denied?

On the Allied side nobody could – if they were honest about the nature of their triumph – overestimate the massive effort needed to combat the menace posed by a couple of hundred enemy submarines.

Just as the Germans made the wrong decisions, so the British made the right one – to convoy – though it was a close-run thing. It was Britain's merchant marine that was the essential component of Allied land victory and the defence of it was *the* key battle.

More than 3,000 surface ships, several hundred aircraft and almost 100 airships, assisted by hunter-killer submarines and Q-ships, were involved in defeating the U-boats. Mines reaped their share of kills, too, and even merchant vessels claimed to have sunk seven U-boats,[8] though some of them may actually have been Allied craft.

Of the U-boats lost, 55 were accounted for by warships, with another 48 probably sunk by mines, 18 destroyed by submarines, 11 by Q-ships and only one by an aircraft. A further 45 U-boats were sunk accidentally by their own side, ran aground or were lost due to other causes.[9] Balanced against this the British lost 60 submarines (to all causes), the Italians seven (to enemy action) and the Austrians eight (all causes). The Russians only admitted to one boat lost (due to accidental causes). The Americans lost only two submarines, which was due to their late entry into the war and limited deployment in the war zones.[10]

Overall, it was a case of going from one extreme to the other. At the outbreak of war submarines had been dismissed as craft of little value, but with the shocking losses of old battleships and cruisers in the early days of the conflict – along with escalating losses in merchant ships – there was a process of creeping paralysis in the British naval high command.

Its prejudices and refusal to give up surface vessel hunter-killer efforts – and take the less spectacular route of convoying – gave the U-boats licence to kill. A lot of time, resources and energy were wasted on the wrong solutions.

The Germans made their share of mistakes, too, while trying to figure out how to wield their new weapon. Above all, for Germany the idea that a conflict could be won by firing a silver bullet into the heart of the enemy war effort proved a chimera. Submarine warfare was an adjunct to other efforts, though it could still potentially be decisive in tipping the balance from victory to defeat, or vice versa.

How close did the U-boats actually come to bringing Britain and the whole Allied war effort to its knees?

The distinguished naval historian Arthur Marder judged that they failed to inflict 'widespread privation in Britain'.[11] The Germans never had enough submarines, nor were their tactics adequate once universal convoying was introduced. Victory was achieved for the Allies by safely escorting merchant ships to British ports and every one that got through was another nail in the coffin of the German cause.

Other components played their part in closing the ring of destruction. Aircraft and airships kept U-boats down, slowed their progress to a crawl and spotted them for attack. As with airships and convoying, the mere presence of so many destroyers and other ships was a weapon in itself. Keep a U-boat down all the time, on slow battery power, and you stood a very good chance of escaping.

Wireless intercepts also helped indicate where U-boats were – the British had cracked the German naval codes and exploited that to the full. There was also convoy re-routing away from areas where U-boats were detected, their activities charted. Only 39 out of 219 convoys were ever spotted by U-boats.[12]

Even with the defeat of the U-boats, the belief persisted that Germany constructed the best submarines, that theirs were the technological marvels. Had enough been built, might they have won?

By the end of the war the latest U-boats were huge in comparison to what had gone before – *U-139* was 400ft long and the size of a light cruiser, with a dived displacement of 2,500 tons.

Some boats had two decks, capacity for 20 torpedoes and 1,000 shells for two 150mm and a pair of 88mm guns. *U-139* and her two sisters possessed four torpedo tubes in the bows and two stern tubes. They could attain a dived top speed of just under 8 knots and surfaced of around 16 knots. While such boats could dive in just 120 seconds, with a maximum depth close to 250ft, they were big and unwieldy and could not manoeuvre well. Even so, the captain of *U-139* called his boat 'a real warship, one capable of conducting a respectable naval action by gunfire as well as by torpedo'.[13]

Despite this, the latest U-boats did not deliver on their potential and some British submarines were actually better war vessels. Aside from the criminally underdeveloped R Class hunter-killer boats, the British ordered an improved batch of L Class boats in early 1917. Known as L50s, they had six 21-inch torpedo tubes in the bow and two 4-inch guns. Fast craft, once their design had been tweaked, the L50s were capable of 10.5 knots submerged and up to 14 knots surfaced. They had a safe diving depth of 250ft. The L50 design was considered formidable even by the US Navy, one of whose experts called it 'the equal if not the superior' of the U-boat even though the British engines were not as powerful. While some Royal Navy submarines were better than German offerings, the RN's boats could not acquire the same deadly reputation because, as the late D.K. Brown pointed out: 'The only great advantage possessed by the U-boats was plenty of targets.'[14]

The final casualty of the first major submarine war would not come until long after the guns had fallen silent. In January 1919 mines laid by U-boats during the conflict claimed two merchant ships.

Six months later there was a solemn memorial service at Dover-court in Essex for Charles Fryatt, a 44-year-old merchant marine officer captured, put on trial and then executed by German firing squad two years earlier. His crime was trying to ram a U-boat in the English Channel.

Fryatt's remains were returned home shortly after the Treaty of Versailles was signed and he was accorded the honour of a state funeral at St Paul's Cathedral in London, attended by the Prime Minister and other high officials. Surrounding streets were packed with thousands of people paying their respects. A guard of honour from the Royal Navy and the merchant marine pulled a gun carriage carrying Fryatt's coffin. It was later taken by rail to Dovercourt to be interred.

Despite their perceived failure – and the revulsion some of their activities created – the story of the U-boats was not over. The seeds of a new war in which they would once again reach for victory were planted by the imperfect Versailles Treaty, which banned Germany from even possessing submarines. Marshal Ferdinand Foch, the overall Allied land forces commander, felt that punitive – yet for the French not punishing enough – treaty was a failure that would lead to future conflict.

'This is not a peace,' he said, 'it is an armistice for twenty years.'[15] He was right and in the next major conflict submarines would again reap a harvest of death and destruction, only this time they seemed to offer the promise of success on a truly global scale.

PART THREE

CONTAGION

1920 to 1945

'Such is the U-boat war – hard, widespread and bitter, a war of groping and drowning, a war of ambuscade and stratagem, a war of science and seamanship.'

Winston Churchill, September 1939

1 Secret Seedcorn

In the 1920s there were calls for the submarine to be outlawed entirely, with its opponents putting it on a par with poison gas – an uncivilised, disgusting outrage.

It was Germany that bore the brunt of the wrath with its former U-boat captains potentially facing prosecution. Some sought escape through employment as lumberjacks in Canada or eked out a living in the Scandinavian Arctic. Others stayed in Germany and became potato farmers while one or two even remained in the navy, including Lothar von Arnauld de la Perière. He served in the few old battleships permitted to the fleet of the new Weimar Republic and after apparently retiring went to Turkey, teaching in its naval academy until 1938.

In some cases, pursuing former U-boat captains for war crimes was justifiable in retribution for what President Wilson labelled the 'inhumanity of submarine warfare'.[1] Among outrages committed was the sinking in June 1918 of the hospital ship *Llandovery Castle* by *U-86*, which allegedly attacked survivors and rammed lifeboats.

Kapitänleutnant Helmut Patzig, along with two of his officers, was charged and a trial was due to take place in summer 1921. Before he could be put in the dock Patzig disappeared and while his fellow officers were convicted, they too somehow managed to flee justice. Patzig was later given amnesty by the German government and even saw service in the U-boat force during the Second World War, though only as a training flotilla boss.

A monstrous allegation was laid against Kapitänleutnant Wilhelm Werner of *U-55*. It was claimed that in April 1917 he had survivors from MV *Torrington* (sunk to the south-west of the Scillies) paraded on *U-55*'s casing and then ordered the submarine submerged, leaving 20 men to drown, though *Torrington*'s captain was taken prisoner rather than killed. He would in 1921 give a full statement on the incident to a British court. Werner was charged with the homicide of *Torrington*'s crew, but again he too was able to escape justice, turning up in Brazil working on a coffee plantation.

On the German side there remained bitterness about the alleged war crimes of Britain's Q-ships. For the vanquished there was also the perceived inhumanity of the Allied blockade, but the victor decides the peace terms and who should, or should not, be considered for prosecution.

The conduct of one famous British destroyer captain especially outraged the Germans. Charles Lightoller was Second Officer of the *Titanic* on her fateful voyage to disaster in 1912, famously making sure women and children escaped in the ship's lifeboats ahead of men. Lightoller was sucked down with *Titanic* and then blown to the surface when the boilers exploded. By 1918 he was captain of the destroyer *Garry*, which on 19 July sank *UB-110*, commanded by Kapitänleutnant Werner Fürbringer.

UB-110 was moving in to make an attack on a convoy when the periscope was spotted. Various patrol craft attacked with depth charges, forcing the U-boat to the surface. *Garry* rammed *UB-110* twice, the destroyer causing such severe damage to herself that she was forced to limp home stern first to avoid sinking.

Fürbringer survived and later accused Lt Cdr Lightoller of committing a war crime by ordering his men to shoot German submariners in the water. Far from putting Lightoller on trial for the deaths of 13 German submariners, the British decided no crime had been committed and even decorated him for sinking *UB-110*.

In September 1920, Capt. Max Horton was questioned about his conduct in the Baltic during 1915, possibly as part of an effort to ensure Britain's submarine captains had not blotted their copybooks. He was asked in writing to confirm what exactly happened when he was in command of *E9*. The Admiralty Secretary enquired if 'due warning was given to all the unarmed merchant ships which were dealt with by the vessel under your Command before any offensive action was taken against them'.[2] Horton sent back assurances that he had taken care to ensure lifeboats were well provisioned and stood an excellent chance of reaching land safely. As far as he was aware they all made it.

On both sides the vast majority of submarine and surface warship captains acted with humanity and did their best to avoid the deaths of civilians. It was inevitable there would be mistakes and occasional acts of cruelty – especially when passions ran so high on the Allied side about 'submarine pirates' and on the other about war by starvation.

In the conflict's aftermath submarine warfare was broadly viewed with horror in Britain and the United States but other victors – the French, Italians and Japanese – felt differently. The lesson they drew was that submarines stood a pretty good chance of defeating, or at least sorely weakening, even the most powerful navy.

In early 1920 Rear Admiral Ernle Chatfield became Assistant Chief of the Naval Staff (ACNS), a key appointment which involved shaping the Royal Navy's management and generally acting as troubleshooter for the Chief of the Naval Staff (the First Sea Lord).

As a product of the big gun battleship world Chatfield instinctively disliked submarines, but was not a dinosaur set in his ways against technical advances. He was keen on the navy's technology working better and felt equipment should be produced to meet the needs of the end-user, not created in isolation. Chatfield believed front-line sailors should not be expected to find a way of working with equipment 'in whose design they had no part'. One of the headline issues of concern for the new ACNS was 'how to deal with the submarine menace'. This would, hopefully, ensure the submarine crisis of 1917 never happened again for Britain, and Chatfield felt this could be achieved via 'scientific research'.[3] A Director of Scientific Research was appointed to preside over a special laboratory in Teddington, London while work was also carried out at Portsmouth, developing ideas produced by the laboratory in a practical naval setting.

Chatfield asked the First Sea Lord – since the end of 1919 his old friend and boss Admiral Beatty – to put anti-submarine technology development at the top of the agenda. By 1926 a centre for anti-submarine warfare (ASW) had been created at Portland in Dorset, not far from the old Whitehead torpedo factory (which was now run by Vickers). The Admiralty's ASW scientists worked alongside personnel from the navy's anti-submarine branch. With such an on-site partnership – practitioners and boffins working in a tightly integrated fashion – progress was impressive.

The new centre was officially named the Anti-Submarine Establishment, while warships were fitted with 'new detection apparatus', as Chatfield termed it.[4] This was Asdic, which stood for Allied Submarine Detection Investigation Committee – after the body formed to devise it during the recent war – which made a bland enough cover name for something today known as sonar (Sound Navigation and Ranging).

Asdic was a shipboard set that used audible sound impulses to try to find submerged submarines. It was fixed under the bows and could be rotated to send out a pulse of sound – a 'ping' – on a particular bearing. If it hit an object then it was reflected back to be picked up by hydrophones as a different sounding ping. The time interval between sending and hearing a returning echo – and whether or not the reflector changed position – enabled the distance and bearing of the target to be assessed. Also, the change in tone indicated if the object was going away from or towards the hydrophones.

This is called the Doppler shift, with a falling tone indicating that a target is receding and a rising one that it is getting closer, or as one naval officer has explained: 'This can be quite aurally dramatic with a rapidly closing target, as the pitch gets higher and the interval between transmission and echo shorter with closing range.'[5]

To reduce interference from the hunting warship's own water flow, Asdic was put inside a protective, water-filled dome but, in general, the faster the warship the lower the chance of Asdic working as desired.

Water flow noise could conceal the echo, so speed was usually curtailed, the warship following a search pattern, stabbing into the darkness with pings, listening for an echo and slowing down every now and then to improve chances of detection.

Chatfield was the primary Royal Navy representative at the Washington Conference (1921–22) where, after much arguing, agreements were made about how many battleships and other surface warships the leading naval powers could have. Britain was allowed to modify its major warships 'against air and submarine attack'.[6]

It also made a bid to get rid of submarines altogether, but that caused a great deal of friction with the French, Japanese and Italians. Though some of the US Navy's officers were ambivalent about submarines, the Americans did not support the British proposal and it failed.

Under the terms of the Versailles Treaty Germany had surrendered all submarines, support vessels and even the floating docks in which they were repaired. Article 191 of the treaty stated: 'The Construction or acquisition of any submarine, even for commercial purposes, shall be forbidden in Germany.'[7] While the Germans may have been banned from constructing and operating U-boats *on their own territory*, as soon as the early 1920s they began a secret programme to ensure submarine expertise did not wither.

A key element of this was a company established in the Netherlands involving pivotal players who were German and with appropriate naval and/or shipbuilding expertise. Covert funds from the navy and sponsorship by German industrial concerns helped the enterprise get off the ground. Ingenieurskantoor voor Scheepsbow (IvS) was a submarine design bureau that worked in tandem with a Berlin company, Mentor Bilanze. The latter was allegedly just a firm of accountants, but its real purpose was to seek submarine construction contracts. From the late 1920s Ingenieurbüro für Wirtschaft und Technik (Igewit) laid the foundations for reviving U-boat production in Germany itself.

To keep busy, in the meantime the Germans built submarines for several foreign navies – sending designs and technicians to Japan, for example, in the 1920s. Three minelaying boats were built in a yard at Kobe (a joint venture with Blohm & Voss). Using foreign-designed boats was nothing new for Japan, which had operated a variant of the British C and L classes and French submarines, as well as Italian origin craft.

Other nations that showed an interest in Germany's submarine building skills included Argentina and Sweden. Its experts also oversaw construction of U-boats for Turkey in the Netherlands. These were taken through sea trials and then sailed to the client by German crews, while in the early 1930s a U-boat was even constructed for Turkey in Spain, also under the aegis of IvS. The Finns commissioned U-boats with assistance from German engineers, designers and submariners, except they were not built in Iberia but in Finland.[8]

The vessels so far built abroad were old pattern U-boats, more or less as used in the First World War though some of the work did pave the way for future types. For any future war a new design of U-boat altogether would be needed to match and exceed those produced by likely enemies. By the early 1930s, the Germans were laying down firm plans to reconstitute their submarine arm while prototypes of new boats were developed as small coastal designs for overseas customers.

Other nations had not been idle of course, with or without German assistance. For all its pretensions to democracy and fealty to a divine emperor, Japan was a military fascist state by the 1930s and was determined not to let internationally agreed restrictions hamper a naval and military build-up. Immediately post-war the Japanese saw the British as their main ally. They admired the Royal Navy greatly, basing many of the Imperial Japanese Navy's (IJN) customs on the RN (Nelson was their ultimate hero). They had purchased numerous warships from the UK but were alienated in the 1920s when the Americans persuaded the British to repudiate their alliance with Japan.

Reflecting traditional thinking on their utility, the Japanese – who founded their Submarine School in 1920 – saw submarines primarily as a means to erode an enemy battle fleet rather than to attack merchant vessels.

With vast distances across the Pacific to cover in order to reach waters off the principal naval bases of their most likely enemy – the USA – the Japanese were by the late 1920s building large submarines with very long range. Their first vessels of this type were based on German U-cruisers and were able to sail faster on the surface than Royal Navy and US Navy battleships, with speeds of up to 23 knots. They could reach Hawaii or even prowl off the coast of California if necessary, with enough fuel to get there and back without the need to replenish. They had good habitability and endurance, in order to loiter while seeking out targets. As early as 1925 the IJN was sending submarines to reconnoitre American naval bases.

The man who formulated an IJN 'attrition strategy' was Rear Admiral Nobumasa Suetsugu. He was not a submariner, but as an official naval observer attached to the Allied forces during the First World War he had studied the submarine and destroyer tactics of the Western navies. He believed the way to shorten any conflict with the USA was to destroy 30 per cent of USN forces via attacks by IJN submarines.

It was anticipated that a threat to the Philippines would provoke the USN into sailing its Pacific Fleet from Pearl Harbor to Manila. During this voyage Japanese boats would strike, along with naval aircraft, aiming to catch the Americans in submarine traps similar to those that the Germans tried to set for the Grand Fleet.

Aware it would have to cover huge distances to counter the Japanese threat, USN efforts to design a version of the IJN's long-range boat were initially undermined by the failure of its own industry to produce a suitably capable and reliable diesel engine. Development of new types was sluggish and the USN would enter the Second World

War with too many old boats. The British, also realising their most likely future enemy was Japan, proposed using Hong Kong-based submarines to stake out Japanese naval bases. At home they felt the European threat was minimal, though the Italians from the early 1920s pursued an energetic submarine construction programme, producing some impressive boats. The French, who also possessed colonies in the Far East potentially vulnerable to Japanese assault, had strongly resisted moves to abolish submarines at various naval arms limitation conferences. They still regarded them as coastal defence vessels but saw submarines as a useful inhibition on those who might wish to attack convoys – a hidden deterrent to enemy surface raiders. By 1930 the French were planning to construct large cruiser submarines to patrol Sea Lines of Communication (SLOC) between their Indian Ocean and Asian colonies.

In 1931 – before the Nazi menace manifested itself as a maritime threat – Britain had 53 submarines in service with a further half dozen being constructed. The French had 61, with 41 building, and Italy 75. The Americans had 81 in commission (four building) while Japan operated 72 submarines.[9] The Germans, of course, officially had none, although they did have the makings of a future submarine arm due to their secret submarine seedcorn initiatives.

In February 1932 the World Disarmament Conference, held at Geneva under the auspices of the League of Nations, began its long and arduous deliberations. There was a British push to get rid of offensive weaponry, including all submarines, along with heavy tanks and heavy artillery. The Germans suggested other nations should disarm and bring themselves down to the same demilitarised level as themselves. Should that kind of agreement not be forthcoming, they wanted all arms restrictions lifted. In November 1932 a secret plan to revive the German military – including 16 new U-boats – was approved by the last pre-Nazi government, showing that the intent to revive Germany's military power did not begin with Hitler.

The Geneva conference dragged on into 1933 and, after they took power, the Nazis sent Dr Joseph Goebbels as their main representative. Failing to gain the 'equality' they felt had been promised them by the other powers, the Germans withdrew from the conference that October. At the same time they announced their intention to leave the

League of Nations, a move described by one French diplomat as the 'gravest news in 20 years'.[10]

While all this was going on, despite the Nazis' loathing of communists they were quite happily allowing Russian naval engineers to work with IvS on the design of submarines for the Red Navy. In 1934, construction of three German-designed boats got underway at a shipyard in Leningrad (formerly Petrograd).

Some of those involved in sailing U-boats built abroad returned home to pass on their seagoing experience. Among instructors at a new Submarine School was Werner Fürbringer who, after his release from captivity, had been engaged as a civilian naval instructor for several years. He was sent to Turkey in 1928, along with at least two other former U-boat captains, to train the host nation's submariners, particularly at sea (in the IvS-built boats). Fürbringer officially joined the German Navy again in late 1933, with the rank of Korvettenkapitän and was soon appointed to command the Submarine School.[11] While men like Fürbringer were very useful in keeping alive the spirit and ethos of the U-boat force, no new story could be written without submarines in the water under German colours.

2   It Shall be Attacked

It has been hailed by some as the greatest con game of the inter-war years, a precursor of the British appeasement and gullibility that Adolf Hitler would later exploit to push his luck and annex chunks of Czechoslovakia.

For there is nothing that more encourages a gambler to be audacious than placing a bet on something and winning big. The Germans had already flouted Versailles to construct the new battlecruisers *Scharnhorst* and *Gneisenau*, which they claimed were within allowed limits (but which were well beyond).

Seeking to create a new U-boat force, Berlin assured London that should it be allowed to build submarines they would not be used against merchant vessels. Churchill – a lone voice in the political wilderness warning of danger – scoffed, labelling it 'the acme of gullibility', for if there was one mission U-boats would inevitably be charged with it was attacking sea trade.[1] In any war with Britain, why would the Germans keep their best weapon sheathed when a Royal Navy blockade might again inflict starvation?

They were finally edging towards coming out of the closet and while it was true they had not built *complete* submarines on their territory, the Naval Intelligence Division (NID) of the Royal Navy believed they had been working on *various sections* of new U-boats. These were ready (in different secret locations) for assembly as and when the right time came.

In negotiating a naval agreement with Britain the Germans admitted they wanted to build 12 submarines, along with cruisers, destroyers and battleships. They desired a naval strength that was 35 per cent of Britain's, but there was to be one exception. Should submarines not ultimately be abolished – or restricted in displacement per boat by international agreement – they would claim the right to construct 45 per cent of the British submarine tonnage. Furthermore, Germany wanted the right to seek parity in submarines should it be necessary. As First Sea Lord from January 1933 to September 1938 Chatfield was deeply embedded in negotiating the agreement and was sure the German caveat would only be enacted 'if subsequent circumstances rendered it imperative' and that it would be 'by friendly negotiation with us'.[2]

To calm fears of what the rearmament entailed, Hitler claimed Germany had no wish to invade anyone – not France, not Poland, nor were there any intentions towards Austria. He claimed it was all about restoring self-respect and about enabling Germany to play an equal part in ensuring Europe stayed at peace. In London *The Times* buttressed this falsehood with an editorial stating that Herr Hitler only wanted 'a free, equal and strong Germany instead of the prostrate Germany upon whom peace was imposed sixteen years ago . . .'[3]

The British pressed on with the bilateral naval agreement with Germany – not bothering to consult the French and Italians. Nor did they inform the League of Nations (the very organisation charged with ensuring the Versailles conditions were upheld).

It was an excellent deal for the Germans, especially as the RN was spread around the world while their own fleet would be concentrated in European waters (and with no sea lanes to distant colonies requiring protection). Germany's navy would be big enough to provide pause for thought in any crisis.[4]

'It was thus not a limitation on German rearmament but an encouragement to expand it,' decided the Berlin-based American radio correspondent William Shirer, who reported on the rise of the Nazis and their duping of Britain.

Admiral Chatfield felt the Anglo-German Naval Agreement (AGNA) acknowledged the hard reality that Germany was determined to rearm no matter what. Unless it wished to join France in going to war over the matter, Britain had 'no power in practice to prevent Germany building submarines as she wished, either in secret, or in fabricated parts ready for rapid assembly'.[5] In the short term the Germans could not possibly build more than 35 per cent of the Royal Navy's strength, at least not in surface warships. For Berlin the main purpose of seeking the agreement was to enable the construction of submarines. The commander of the new U-boat force (or U-boot-Waffe) was Fregattenkapitän Karl Dönitz. Following his release from an English PoW camp in July 1919, he had served ashore and in the surface fleet, by the early 1930s rising to command a cruiser. In 1935 he and fellow cruiser captain Günther Lütjens were called in by their boss and given important new assignments. Dönitz was made Führer der Uboote while Lütjens was to command surface raiders.

Once in post, Dönitz had an uncomfortable relationship with the boss of the Kriegsmarine, Admiral Erich Raeder, who advocated large, heavily armed big gun ships to prey on commerce rather than submarines.

It did not prevent Dönitz from drawing up ambitious proposals for U-boat construction. He ideally wanted 300 submarines, but the Kriegsmarine's Z Plan – its blueprint for major regeneration – granted him 233 (and only by 1948). The focus of the Kriegsmarine was on controlling the Baltic and supporting a war against the French or Russians, not fighting the British, so a campaign against high seas trade was not top priority.

The backbone of the new U-boat force was to be the Type VII, displacing 753 tons (surfaced), which was introduced into service in 1936. It had been produced under AGNA restrictions (complying with the minimum tonnage possible per boat while still remaining a viable ocean-going craft). Just over 218ft long and with a beam of around 20ft, the Type VII's surface cruising top speed was 17 knots, with 8 knots possible under the water. The Type VII had four bow torpedo tubes and one stern (for 21-inch torpedoes), a 3.5-inch gun and a single 20mm anti-aircraft gun.

In July 1937 the Germans made their first move to raise the bar on U-boat construction, confirming they would aspire to 45 per cent of the Royal Navy's submarine force and in 1938 they decided on parity with the British.

In the meantime the training of the men who would crew the submarines was accelerating, with six veteran officers visiting Turkey to receive refresher time in its U-boats. They were able to rehearse attack techniques against obliging surface warship targets.

Among them was Max Valentiner, responsible for sinking 144 vessels during the war, notching up the third highest tonnage total (299,473 tons). Valentiner would continue to train U-boat crews back home in the Baltic for some years to come, also overseeing acceptance trials of new submarines. He would be joined by luminaries such as Hans Rose, the gentlemanly captain who cheekily sank several vessels just outside American waters in 1916. Among visitors to Turkey in 1935 was Dönitz, gaining insight into how the training regime in the Turkish boats might be improved.

Nothing could hone the edge of the new U-boat force better than war itself, or operational conditions as close as possible to it. Such an opportunity soon arose, with at least two Type VIIA U-boats – *U-33* and *U-34* – deployed in 1936 to cruise waters off Iberia during the Spanish Civil War, supporting General Francisco Franco's fascist forces.

On station by the end of November, the German submarines lurked close to Alicante and Cartagena, looking for warships of the Republican government's navy and merchant vessels carrying supplies to Franco's enemies. Not long before their U-boats started hunting off the coast of Spain, the Germans signed the London Submarine Agreement, a confirmation of internationally agreed rules of conduct established in the London Naval Agreement of 1930.

By doing so, they and other signatories accepted a code of conduct requiring submarine captains to ensure the safety of a ship's passengers and crew before sinking a vessel. Under this so-called Submarine Protocol, if the target vessel was far from land, or seas were not placid, not even a ship's lifeboats were to be considered 'a place of safety'.[6] Submarine captains should also strive to ensure a neutral merchant vessel was close at hand to take survivors aboard. If those conditions were not satisfied the submarine herself was required to host passengers and crew.

The first three submerged torpedo attacks by U-34 missed their warship targets while U-33's attempts against cargo vessels in convoy were deterred by Republican destroyers. Such was the poor performance of the U-boats that it was an embarrassment to Germany, with the deployment cancelled on 10 December. Two days later, while still in Spanish waters, the submerged U-34 attacked and sank the Republican submarine C3 off Malaga, with only three survivors from the 36-strong crew.

Following this success patrols were conducted by 14 different U-boats[7] off Spain. Their activities were ostensibly part of an embargo by the international community to ensure arms did not get through to the warring factions. Italian submarines were also deployed and likewise operated in the interests of Franco. To avoid attacking German submarines, it was agreed the Italians should keep to the Mediterranean, while U-boats would operate in the Atlantic. From June 1937 Italian boats waged war from Gibraltar to the Dardanelles. They were not acknowledged publicly by Rome, with their attacks on merchant vessels blamed on 'pirate submarines',[8] though the nationality of the guilty parties was suspected.

On 31 August 1937, *Iride* attacked the British destroyer *Havock* off Alicante. When a torpedo skimmed past, *Havock* did not immediately respond, as nobody aboard could believe it. From the nearby cruiser *Galatea* the local commander of British naval forces, Rear Admiral James Somerville, blasted *Havock* with a sharp signal. He urged her to get on with hunting down the attacker 'to make up for your astounding lack of initiative'.[9]

Depth charges were dropped, but on reading Somerville's wireless signal the less pugilistic Admiralty intervened, ordering *Havock* to cease for fear of destroying an 'innocent' submarine.[10] It was an unwelcome example of back seat driving and it rather vexed Somerville. He had been pressing the Admiralty for some weeks for stronger action, as it was clear there were no British or other friendly boats operating in the locale. Spanish fascists had no submarines of their own while the crews of Republican boats had murdered their officers and would not put to sea.

After the incident with *Havock*, Somerville suggested to the Admiralty that his ships must not wait until they were targeted but should attack any submarine detected with full force. The admirals and politicians in Whitehall refused to authorise a change to the Rules of Engagement.

It led to bizarre situations where British destroyers would find and hold contact with dived submarines for some hours, making attack runs but only dropping the occasional warning depth charge at a safe distance. During one episode that stretched across 148 nautical miles, from waters off Valencia to Majorca, a presumed Italian submarine was detected, pursued and kept down for a punishingly long time.

The Italians for a period stopped operating their boats in close proximity to foreign warships, after an agreement for the British and French navies to be reinforced by Italian surface vessels in policing the arms embargo in the Western Mediterranean. This included joint operations against 'pirate submarines'. The Italians waited a few months and then resumed submarine attacks on merchant vessels, sinking the 887-ton British-flagged coal carrier *Endymion* on 31 January 1938, off Cartagena. Press reports blamed it on 'a Spanish rebel submarine'.[11] The ship's captain and his wife were among 11 killed and nobody aboard saw any signs of a submarine beforehand, not even the torpedo as it sped towards them. The coal-carrying ship did not have a radio and was unable to call for help. It took only four minutes for *Endymion* to sink and RN destroyers saved just four people.

In the incident's wake the British government said it would not 'tolerate submarines being submerged in this zone [the Western Mediterranean], and orders have accordingly been given to His Majesty's warships that if a submarine is found so submerged henceforth it shall be attacked'.[12] *Endymion* would be the last ship sunk by a submarine before the joint operation ended, though another British merchant vessel was claimed by air attack a few days later. Both *Endymion* and the other ship were but a foretaste of what was to come. Events in the autumn of 1939 would prove that merchant vessels were easy prey when sailing alone and submarines had lost none of their stealthy lethality.

3   Battle Stations Immediate

Dönitz began the new conflict with just 57 boats in commission, though not all were immediately available for operations, which was far from ideal, especially to take on the naval colossus that was the Royal Navy.

After Britain guaranteed Poland's security Dönitz decided that to gain any kind of advantage at all he must deploy submarines ahead of hostilities. On 15 August 1939 all but three of the 24 U-boats capable of long-range patrols in the Atlantic were ready to sail for war stations. Four days later the orders were issued, with submarines departing Kiel and other bases to take up position in the Western Approaches, English Channel and off north-west Scotland. They were also ready in the Baltic to sink any Polish warships that dared to come out.

It was not the first time German submarines had been deployed pre-emptively in recent times. During the Munich Crisis of 1938, when it looked likely that both France and Britain might go to war with Germany over Czechoslovakia's dismemberment, U-boats headed for the same war stations. A year later Britain and France declared their intention to enter a state of war with Germany following the latter's 1 September invasion of Poland.

The Royal Navy had 43 operationally deployable submarines, with a further eight devoted to training duties. Of these 15 were obsolete or so unreliable they could not safely be sent on patrol.

Britain's submarines were also spread thinly across the globe. Thirteen boats were on the China Station to face the Japanese threat while in home waters there were 18, of which 14 were modern. Devoted to the Mediterranean were ten submarines, with a further two allocated to operating in the Atlantic.[1]

Both German and British boats were meant to operate against merchant vessels under restrictions that stripped a submarine of its greatest protection – the ability to strike from below the sea and remain unseen and therefore (comparatively) safe. Rather than rely on what he could see through the periscope and then fire torpedoes, the submarine captain would – as was the case for much of the First World War – be required first of all to surface, stop the merchant ship in question and inspect cargo and papers, before assisting in the safe escape of those onboard. Should enemy submarines stay dived, there was great confidence in the Royal Navy that Asdic could find them and they would be destroyed by depth-charging.

Having persuaded itself that it had sewn up the submarine threat, the Admiralty did not like to think otherwise, even though the HMS *Basilisk* incident of 4 October 1937 showed that Asdic might not be perfect.

Sailing in broad daylight off the coast of Spain, men aboard the destroyer claimed to have seen a torpedo pass down her starboard side, yet there had been no confirmed submarine contact beforehand. Depth charges were dropped as a precaution anyway during attacks on what subsequently looked like submarine contacts. Unsubstantiated press reports later said oil was seen on the surface of the sea and also 'items of personal belongings' were retrieved – though they did not say by whom – while fishermen allegedly found an expended Italian torpedo.[2]

In Germany the *Deutsche Allgemeine-Zeitung* criticised the British for 'attempting to sink a submarine which had not attacked them'.

Despite all this, a week after the incident an unidentified Admiralty official told the press: 'It is true that depth charges were dropped when a submarine supposedly attacked the *Basilisk*, but, after a full investigation, we've changed our minds. We cannot tell what it was that appeared to be a torpedo. It might have been a porpoise.'[3] Rather than admit that Asdic might be imperfect – and in some circumstances might fail to pick up a submarine before it could fire torpedoes – the incumbent First Sea Lord, Admiral Chatfield, decided: 'No action required since the *Basilisk* incident did not take place.'[4]

The self-deceiving Royal Navy therefore went into the Second World War with an unjustified faith in the infallibility of Asdic – it would never fail to pick up a U-boat hence whatever it was had menaced *Basilisk* could not have been a submarine. Unfortunately for the British, the quarry was a most formidable breed of submariner, using tactics that sought to defeat Asdic by not conforming to expectations.

Yet they had their problems, too. One barrier to the effective utilisation of submarine forces by Germany was the attitude of its own naval high command. In 1939 the Commander-in-Chief of the Kriegsmarine thought surface raiders stood a better chance of success than submarines against the British. A veteran of Jutland, Raeder was not at all pleased to be going to war before the Z Plan could be completed. He complained in his war diary that he had been told there would be no need to worry about conflict until 1944. As things stood Raeder felt the German Navy was 'in no way adequately equipped for the great struggle with Great Britain . . . the submarine arm is still much too weak to have any decisive effect on the war'. The Kriegsmarine's surface warships were similarly likely to be outclassed, being 'so inferior in number and strength to those of the British Fleet that, even at full strength, they can do no more than show they know how to die gallantly . . .'[5]

Even First World War submarine ace Walter Fürbringer regarded the chances of winning any future conflict against Britain by means of the submarine as slim. Dönitz was more confident. In a book published before the war – ignored and unread by many of those in Britain who should really have paid attention – he provided useful clues about how his U-boats would be wielded. He recommended surface attack, building on inter-war research and exercises with torpedo boats at a time when Germany could not operate its own submarines. He proposed that U-boats should dive only when they needed to get out of trouble, or avoid detection. Dönitz also secretly worked on how to use groups of submarines in co-ordinated attacks – to divide escort forces and sow confusion that could be exploited. Crucially, by staying on the surface the enemy's Asdic could be nullified, and attacking at night would further improve chances of success.

Surface night attack was predicted by a British submarine officer nearly a year before the war, but his analysis was suppressed. Lt Ian McGeoch was serving in the submarine HMS *Clyde* when in early 1938 he drafted a paper called 'The Offensive Value of the Modern Submarine'.

It was revised and submitted to the *Royal United Services Institution (RUSI) Journal* in December 1938 but the Admiralty refused permission to publish. In his paper, McGeoch suggested: 'A subsidiary but very important tactical capability of the submarine is surface night attack: the small silhouette of a submarine gives her an advantage at night over all but the smallest of vessels . . .'[6] The Royal Navy did conduct night manoeuvres with its own submarines playing the role of the enemy, but submerged to deliberately hamper their effectiveness. Lt McGeoch was under no illusions about serving in a fighting arm that was the orphan, unwanted child of the Royal Navy.

So cocky were the British about defeating submarines with Asdic that in 1937 the Admiralty declared 'the U-boat will never again be capable of confronting us with the problem with which we found ourselves faced in 1917'.[7] The serving First Lord of the Admiralty, Sir Samuel Hoare, even claimed 'today we are justified in saying that . . . the submarine is no longer a danger to the security of the British Empire'.[8]

Such blithe ignorance was not restricted to Britain, for Dönitz felt the officers of many navies found it difficult to 'to appreciate and assimilate the importance of any other method of fighting, such as submarine warfare'.[9]

Horton's opponent: Admiral Karl Dönitz, who put U-boats on the cutting edge of the Third Reich's bid for victory and rose to command the entire Kriegsmarine and ultimately replaced Hitler as Führer. (*BArchiv, Bild 134-C1948/o.Ang*)

First blood in the new submarine war was taken by 26-year-old Oberleutnant Fritz-Julius Lemp in command of *U-30*, one of several U-boats strung out across the North-Western Approaches to the British Isles.

Lemp was a German born outside the Reich, at the port of Tsingtao in China, which was at the time part of the Imperial German territory of Kiaochow. His father was an army officer and on the outbreak of war in 1914 the family returned to Germany. Joining the navy in 1931, seven years later Fritz-Julius was awarded command of his first submarine.[10]

Lemp's boat received news that a state of war existed between his country and Britain at noon on 3 September, when U-30 was patrolling waters to the south of Rockall. The signal flashed to all U-boats at sea instructed: 'Battle Stations Immediate, in accordance with Battle Instructions for the navy already promulgated.'[11]

That same evening U-30 attacked the liner *Athenia*, of 13,581 tons displacement, to the west of Ireland. She was the first Allied ship loss of the Second World War, carrying 1,013 passengers including many refugees, among them 246 American citizens desperate to get home, while a number of those aboard were children being sent to safety.

Departing the Clyde the day Hitler's troops invaded Poland, *Athenia* called at Liverpool before sailing from there on 2 September, next picking up passengers at Belfast. Leaving Ulster waters on the morning of 3 September, she was finally underway properly for Canada, steaming at 12 knots and taking submarine countermeasures by zigzagging.

These did not deter Lemp, who thought his target was an Armed Merchant Cruiser (AMC) and therefore permitted, or so he later claimed. The ship was certainly large and, as far as Lemp could tell, showing no lights. *Athenia* had adopted black-out conditions and she was also outside the usual route used by transatlantic liners.

Lemp fired two torpedoes, which almost proved fatal for his own vessel as one of them went haywire and came back on itself. The hydrophone operator called out that one of the 'eels' had gone rogue, so Lemp quickly ordered U-30 deeper to avoid it. Some accounts say that orders were given to fire another torpedo, but it refused to leave the tube.[12] Whatever happened, at least one of U-30's weapons ran true and inflicted a mortal wound on the liner.

Aboard *Athenia* a fireman – one of the men whose job it was to keep the burners in the engine room boilers going – had climbed up through several decks and was waiting his turn to abandon ship when he saw a submarine break the surface 'about a hundred yards off'.[13]

The U-boat's radioman meanwhile heard *Athenia* sending the message 'SSS', which was code for a vessel under attack from a submarine.

Lemp ordered his gun crew to shoot at the liner's wireless mast and aerials in a bid to curtail the signal. It took two shells to silence *Athenia* and *U-30* sailed around for a short while, with Lemp guiltily pondering what his next move should be. He realised that he'd just violated international law by making a torpedo attack on a passenger liner and should assist the survivors.

If he did so the world would know for sure that a German submarine had committed the deed, so Lemp decided to withdraw *U-30* without offering assistance.

In the meantime British warships and merchant vessels of various nations made for the scene to rescue survivors. In all 119 people were killed – 93 passengers and 26 crew, including 28 Americans. A number of those who lost their lives were trapped below decks. The survivors were landed in Scotland and on the west coast of Ireland, making a pathetic sight as they came ashore, 'with their clothes torn off their backs, black with grease, barefooted and penniless . . . after a night of horror without precedent '.[14]

When Hitler's propaganda ministry asked the German naval high command if British reports of a liner being torpedoed could be true, it was told it was not possible. There were no U-boats in the relevant area, and it would be against standing orders. The nagging suspicion remained, however, that a German submarine was responsible.

At 4.55 p.m. on 4 September Dönitz sent a general signal to his U-boat captains: 'Existing orders for mercantile warfare remain in force.' Adolf Hitler was fearful of American casualties, so another was sent, just to make sure. 'By order of the Führer,' it stressed, 'passenger ships until further notice will not be attacked even if in convoy.'[15]

That a U-boat was the most likely guilty party did not prevent Berlin suggesting *Athenia* had been sunk by a drifting mine or by explosives planted in her hold by the British to blacken the German reputation. The Admiralty denied the sabotage charge or that it had done anything else to *Athenia*.

German officials branded suggestions of a U-boat attack 'an infamous, shameless lie, a criminal attempt to influence United States opinion and make a new *Lusitania* case'. Furthermore, it was 'out of the question that a German warship torpedoed the steamer. All German warships and U-boats have the strictest orders to capture, not to sink merchantmen.' The Reich's spokesmen suggested some other cause such as 'boiler explosion'.[16] Admiral Raeder told the Naval Attaché at the US Embassy in Berlin it had 'definitely [been] established that the *Athenia* had not been sunk by a German U-boat'.[17] While some neutral nations may have been taken in, the Americans were not fooled. The State Department issued a statement on 6 September saying it believed 'the ship was submarined'.[18] From London, US Ambassador Joseph Kennedy conveyed a report by an American passenger who had 'seen the submarine which had torpedoed the *Athenia*'.[19]

4 Slow off the Mark

The first British warship to be attacked in the Second World War was the submarine *Spearfish*, in circumstances that greatly angered her 29-year-old captain, Lt John Eaden.

Like her predecessors a quarter of a century earlier, *Spearfish* was tasked with giving advance warning of enemy ship movements. She and other boats were unfortunately sent too late to catch the deployment of U-boats to their war stations or the exit of the pocket battleships *Admiral Graf Spee* and *Deutschland*.

On 3 September, at 21 minutes past the 11.00 a.m. deadline for Germany to withdraw from Poland, *Spearfish* was on the surface, heading for a new patrol position. From the bridge Lt Eaden spotted 'two tracks approaching from the port bow' and initially thought they were dolphins. As they sped past his boat, leaving a trail of bubbles, Eaden realised they were torpedoes.

Spearfish made a crash dive and Eaden waited for his hydrophone operator to report telltale sounds indicating the bearing of the attacker. The search for what he felt sure was a U-boat proved futile. After surfacing, *Spearfish* received a signal from the Admiralty revealing hostilities with Germany. 'I was annoyed,' Eaden confessed, 'because it did appear to me that the German[s] had got the information that the war had commenced before we had. I felt that we had been a bit slow off the mark.'[1]

A week later there was an even bigger cock-up, with the first British naval vessel to be destroyed in the conflict falling victim not to the enemy but to another Royal Navy submarine.

HM Submarines *Oxley* and *Triton* were both on the surface in the Norwegian Sea on the night of 10 September, the former an elderly boat that had proved too expensive for the Royal Australian Navy to run. She had been handed back to Britain in 1931 and eight years later was sent to her war station towards the end of August, one of a number of boats on a picket line off southern Norway.

In bad weather on 10 September *Oxley* drifted into a box of sea assigned to *Triton*, a new boat commissioned in late 1938, whose captain was Commander H.P. de C. Steel.

Off Norway it was often difficult to make an accurate navigational fix owing to mist obscuring the sun during the day and hiding the stars at night. It was also rare to sight the coast, and taking soundings to compare them with a chart proved of little assistance as the seabed was flat for miles. On the fateful evening *Triton* interrogated the other boat by light signal – sending the accepted challenge – but got no response.

Aware that *Oxley* was close by, and the mystery vessel might be her, *Triton* tried to provoke a response by firing a rifle grenade to explode on the sea. Again there was no visible reaction from what might, after all, be a U-boat. *Triton* fired two torpedoes, but just before they hit, light signals winked from the other submarine's bridge. There was a blinding flash as the torpedoes exploded. *Triton* swept the heaving surface of the sea with her searchlights, catching three men struggling to keep their heads above the water amid debris and oil. Safety lines were put around two of *Triton*'s junior officers who each managed to pull a survivor from the sea.

Any satisfaction felt at sinking a U-boat disappeared when the rescued men turned out to be British. One of them was *Oxley*'s captain, Lt Cdr H.G. Bowerman. At a subsequent inquiry it was decided navigational error by *Oxley* was compounded by lookouts failing to spot *Triton*'s light signal challenges. When they did respond – firing their own rifle grenade into the sea – it failed to detonate. Bowerman was only advised of the presence of another submarine when it was too late.

The cause of *Oxley*'s loss was covered up at the time, with the British claiming she was sunk during a collision between submarines.[2]

Revealing that the first Royal Navy warship destroyed in the conflict – and with 53 men killed – was a self-inflicted casualty would have been a major propaganda gift to the enemy.

The loss of *Oxley* was only the latest frustration for the Royal Navy's submarine force. On 6 September *Seahorse* and *Sturgeon* were bombed by British aircraft but escaped serious damage. A failure to brief *Sturgeon* fully on the disposition of British submarine forces off the hostile shore also led to her firing torpedoes at sister vessel *Swordfish*. Fortunately they missed. Three days later *U-35* dodged torpedoes from the surfaced *Ursula*. Not long after, another U-boat offered itself up for attack, but the range was too close for *Ursula*'s torpedoes to arm.

When the Germans suffered their first U-boat loss, on 14 September, it was not at the hands of either a friendly or an unfriendly submarine but rather Royal Navy surface ships. It came at the end of a chain of events involving Lemp's *U-30*, which encountered the 5,200-ton freighter *Fanad Head* around 300 miles to the north-west of Ireland.

Breakfast was being served to the ship's nine passengers when the sound of running feet in the passageway outside the dining room and the 'continuous ringing of the ship's bells'[3] indicated something was wrong.

The captain of *Fanad Head*, Capt. G. Pinkerton, had spotted a submarine five miles off the starboard bow, coming on at high speed. The ship changed course to try to evade it but the U-boat remained dead astern, 'a black speck surrounded by large white bow-waves and with dense black smoke pouring from it'.[4]

Both the U-boat and *Fanad Head* were being 'driven to their utmost capacity'[5] but the submarine was faster and bound to catch up and after 90 minutes of being pursued Pinkerton decided to order abandon ship. The lifeboats were being prepared for lowering when the bosun cried out: 'He's going to fire!'[6] A shell screamed in but missed and, meanwhile, the radio operator was sending 'SSS'. He also managed to contact a US-flagged vessel, the *American Merchant*, which was altering course to pick up survivors.

As all this unfolded HMS *Ark Royal* was about 200 miles away to the north-east. On picking up the SSS call, she decided to launch Skua dive-bombers to investigate and ordered three of her six escorting destroyers into action. Britain's only fully modern aircraft carrier had been sent out to hunt submarines in the North-West Approaches, one of three such hunter-killer groups centred on fleet carriers. It was felt escorts fitted with Asdic and carrier-borne aircraft with special anti-submarine bombs could combine to give the Royal Navy an edge it did not have in the First World War.

As events would soon show, it was a flawed tactic – the weapons were ineffective and the carriers too few (and valuable) to deliberately risk in the same waters as U-boats. Yet it was something the Admiralty felt compelled to try as the RN had a mere 180 destroyers in commission on the outbreak of war. This was too few to cope with fleet work around the globe and trade protection duties, at least not without major help.

Within four days of *Athenia*'s sinking, newly appointed First Lord of the Admiralty Winston Churchill – called back to his old job on the day hostilities commenced – had issued orders for the convoy system to be introduced. To their credit, whereas in the First World War shipping companies were reluctant to tie themselves to the Royal Navy's convoy apron strings, in this conflict they immediately realised it was better to join the gang. For all that, in those early days of war there were still many ships sailing solo as they headed for friendly ports. So it was that just after 3.00 p.m. on a fine, sunny afternoon, with calm weather and clear vision away to the horizon – the Atlantic swell long and languid – *Ark Royal* sought to fulfil her duties by catching and sinking the U-boat attacking *Fanad Head*.

As the carrier turned into the wind and piled on the knots, needing to maintain a straight course at high speed to launch aircraft, she made herself somewhat vulnerable to a stalking U-boat.

Seeking an escape from the noise of the flight deck and looking out to sea from the carrier's juddering quarterdeck, a young officer noticed a torpedo leaping in and out of the water, heading straight for *Ark Royal*. He dashed over to a telephone and tried to get through to the bridge, but failed.[7] Fortunately, a lookout had also spotted the torpedo and the carrier's helm was immediately put hard over. Sailors aboard escorting destroyer *Firedrake* saw the carrier make 'a sudden violent turn to port and as she did so two torpedoes passed astern of her'.[8]

Kapitänleutnant Gerhard Glattes of *U-39* had actually fired three torpedoes, all armed with magnetic pistols, but they either missed or detonated prematurely in *Ark*'s wake, sending up plumes of water and black smoke. *U-39* was assailed by *Firedrake* and two sister ships, *Faulknor* and

Foxhound, while *Ark* immediately exited the scene, removing herself from danger.

With Asdic pinging, the destroyers worked in a tight hunting partnership, *Foxhound* obtaining a strong echo. A signal flag indicating an attack flew from a halyard, depth charges tumbling off her stern and smoke billowing from throwers hurling charges out on the ship's beam.

The destroyers all obtained good contacts and bracketed the U-boat with depth charges set initially between 100ft and 300ft, but then as deep as 500ft. The explosions caused flooding in *U-39*, with salt water hitting the battery to produce chlorine gas.

Realising his boat was beyond redemption Glattes ordered ballast tanks blown and preparations made to scuttle after surfacing. Amid eruptions caused by detonating depth charges, the U-boat broke surface. *Firedrake*'s B turret 4.7-inch gun opened fire, a shell exploding just beyond the U-boat. *Faulknor* joined in the bombardment and *Firedrake*'s X turret also barked. *Faulknor* got the first hit, while *Foxhound* dashed in at ramming speed. The sea curled away high on each side of her sharp bow, the props at her stern throwing out a huge, cockerel-tail wake.

Before she could crash into the U-boat, men started popping out of the submarine's hatches and jumping into the sea. Figures on the bridge shouted and waved their hands in the air.

Foxhound turned away, while the other two destroyers slowly went in close, launching sea boats to pick up 44 men in all – the entire submarine crew. The scuttling charges ripped holes in *U-39*'s hull and down she went. In service less than a year, *U-39* was a serious loss for the German submarine force as she was a Type IX boat, a large, long-range vessel. Eight had been ordered in 1936, with seven of them in commission by late August 1939. Taken aboard one of the British destroyers, a submarine officer in shock at losing his boat was determined not to let the enemy see he was beaten. Asking for his men to be assembled on the quarterdeck, once they were at attention facing him he threw his arm up into a Nazi salute and exclaimed: 'Heil Hitler!' British ratings manning the aft guns couldn't help but guffaw and snort derisively[9] while their shipmates got on with handing out dry clothes and cigarettes and offering mugs of hot, strong cocoa or tea.

5   Like Hungry Gulls

The crew and passengers of *Fanad Head* had by now embarked in the lifeboats, which, thought one of them, was 'a feat none too easy in the heavy sea, as they were rising and falling a distance of about ten feet'.[1]

The American rescue ship was not expected for around 20 hours, so everyone took at least one blanket each to get through a night in an open boat.

They rowed away from *Fanad Head* but hadn't got too far when a submarine with a yellowish green hull and dark green conning tower approached. Oberleutnant Lemp was on *U-30*'s bridge while several of his crew clambered around on the submarine's casing doing various tasks.

'All of them were bearded and unshaven (*sic*) but they looked decent young Germans, just carrying out orders,' thought the *Fanad Head* passenger. 'The Commander ordered us to row alongside and told us in perfect English that it was unlucky for us that he was faster than we were, a statement with which we all agreed.' Lemp asked *Fanad Head*'s Capt. Pinkerton what his ship's cargo was and 'appeared somewhat disappointed when he learned it was grain'.[2] He'd rather sink a cargo of war materials, like munitions, iron ore or coal. Pinkerton mentioned the American steamer coming to pick them up, so Lemp said he would tow the lifeboat over to *Fanad Head*'s other one, which was about 400 yards away. After doing so, Lemp announced he was off to sink *Fanad Head* and promised to come back and give both lifeboats a tow towards the American ship. Seeking to conserve shells and torpedoes, Lemp decided to send two of his men aboard *Fanad Head* with scuttling charges, the U-boat going alongside, partially submerged under the stern of the merchant ship to hide her presence.

There was a heavy swell and both passengers and crew in the lifeboats were steadily becoming more and more seasick. Even grizzled sea officers with 20 years' service were distinctly queasy. They scanned the skies, seeing the occasional gull and stormy petrel, but then, 'suddenly [we] got the surprise of our lives,' said the passenger. 'In the distance beyond the ship we heard a low hum and saw a dark speck that resolved itself into an aeroplane. At first we thought it was a transatlantic flying boat, but as it rapidly approached we saw that it was a Blackburn Skua monoplane, the latest type of aeroplane used by the British Fleet Air Arm.'

This aircraft was piloted by Lt R.P. Thurston, with Petty Officer James Simpson as Observer, and it went into a shallow dive towards the stern of the merchant ship. Thurston released four bombs, which to the 'hopeful and optimistic eyes' of the crew and passengers in the *Fanad Head*'s lifeboats 'appeared to hit the submarine'.

Skuas were only armed with a single 100lb bomb and four 20lb bombs each and[3] such weapons were too small to do more than mildly damage a U-boat, even if they landed right on top of it. Should they explode while the Skua was still low overhead they might pepper the aircraft with hot shrapnel and cause serious damage. That is what happened, causing the fuel tank of Thurston's Skua to burst into flame.

The U-boat dived immediately, but the dinghy used by the boarding team was still attached by a kind of umbilical cord. It was dragged along behind the submerged *U-30*, giving away the boat's exact position. Ten minutes later another Skua appeared, piloted by Lt Cdr Dennis Campbell, with Lt Charles Hanson as Observer. It headed for *Fanad Head*, with Campbell and Hanson spotting two people in the water. This was the crew of the downed Skua, which had flopped in flames onto the sea. Seeing what appeared to be a U-boat just under the surface – below a shimmering patch of oil – Campbell dropped bombs, but it was actually the wreckage of the first Skua.[4]

Onlookers in the lifeboats had high hopes the U-boat was sunk, but these were dashed when they saw *U-30* surface. Despite a Skua still being overhead, Lemp decided he had to cut the yellow dinghy free. A brave volunteer was ready below the hatch and the moment the conning tower emerged from the sea, this man threw it back and leapt out to detach the dinghy. The remaining Skua swooped, but, having no bombs left, machine-gunned the U-boat. In the short period in which *U-30*'s tower was visible it was hosed down with hundreds of bullets from wing-mounted machine guns, slightly wounding the sailor cutting away the dinghy. With fuel running low and ammunition gone, Campbell's Skua headed back to *Ark Royal*, flying low over the lifeboats, sending a light signal message.

'HELP COMING HELP COMING'[5]

Unaware of the earlier dramas and having covered his original search area, 23-year-old Lieutenant Guy Griffiths, a Royal Marine pilot, was taking his Skua back to *Ark*. In the back of the aircraft, scanning the sea below, Petty Officer George McKay remarked over the intercom: 'There is a merchant ship over there, let's go and look at it.' [6]

Taking the aircraft down to 20ft above the sea, Griffiths intended going around the vessel's stern to check the name and port of registry. He was astonished to find a U-boat conning tower poking out of the sea below the overhang, so climbed and kicked the Skua into a 180-degree stall turn.

Aboard *U-30* Lemp ordered a crash dive.

The submarine disappeared under the nose of the aircraft, which was right on target with Griffiths dropping bombs at 'no feet at all', as he later described it, rather ruefully.

As the Skua pulled up 'there was a terrific crash . . .' As had happened with Thurston's bombs the fuses had been set to explode instantaneously the moment they hit something.

With his submarine now dived and moving away from the *Fanad Head*, through his periscope Lemp watched the self-inflicted demise of the enemy aircraft: the blast of its own bombs tearing part of the Skua's tail off before it dropped into the sea. Those watching from the *Fanad Head* lifeboats saw 'a long triangular splash of water'. [7]

The Skua's engine was ripped out and Griffiths, who had been struggling to open his canopy, was sucked through the hole in the nose. Air bubbles from the aircraft carried him to the surface, his only injury a damaged right hand and a watch driven painfully into his left wrist. Petty Officer McKay was trapped in the back of the aircraft and was drowned or killed by the impact.

Griffiths swam a mile and a half to the stern of *Fanad Head*, which appeared to be totally abandoned, pulling himself up a rope ladder hanging down the side of the ship. Aboard he discovered two armed Germans, who took him prisoner. [8] There was also a badly burned man lying on the deck. Griffiths only realised this was a brother pilot from the *Ark Royal* because of the man's flying suit. Both Thurston and Petty Officer Simpson had made it out of their wrecked aircraft but Simpson was overcome and drowned before he could get to *Fanad Head*.

U-30 had by now come back to *Fanad Head*, but this time stood off a short distance. Lemp called up to his men that if they had not yet set scuttling charges he was going to torpedo the ship. The Germans told the British aviators there was no alternative if they wanted to live but to jump into the water and swim to the submarine. The U-boatmen and British aviators were helped out of the water onto the submarine's casing, watched anxiously by Lemp. He wondered how long he had before more enemy aircraft appeared overhead. The prisoners were hurried down a hatch and *U-30* dived. Lemp fired four bow torpedoes at *Fanad Head*, which either ran wide, too deep or otherwise failed for technical reasons. He finally hit her with a torpedo from the stern tube.

This coincided with the arrival overhead of half a dozen Swordfish Torpedo-Spotter-Reconnaissance aircraft (TSR) packing 100lb anti-submarine bombs. Their aircrews saw the track of the German torpedo and made out the smudgy shape of a submarine under the sea. They pounced, their actions applauded by those in the *Fanad Head* lifeboats. '. . . the six planes immediately swooped down on an area of the sea about half a mile from the ship . . . like a lot of gulls hungry for a piece of bread – and dropped many bombs, we could easily see the explosions . . .'[9]

The bombs gave Lemp's boat a good shake, shattering many lights, providing a new experience for the captured British pilots; they were being attacked not just by their own side, but by fellow naval aviators from *Ark Royal*. As the ghostly green outline of *U-30* melted away to nothingness and set course north-west, on the surface the occupants of the lifeboats watched *Fanad Head* break up and sink. 'First the masts slowly canted towards each other, then the funnel gradually sank in the water. The two boilers exploded one after the other. The bows and stern slowly rose out of the water and finally disappeared from view as the ship sank to the bottom of the sea.'[10]

The *Fanad Head* survivors were later picked up by a pair of British destroyers that had steamed hard to rescue them, covering 200 miles in just five hours.

Royal Marine pilot Guy Griffiths found his incarceration aboard *U-30* a fascinating experience, even if he was not pleased at being in the hands of the enemy. '. . . they were exactly the same as us,' he decided and, far from being Nazi brutes as rumoured, 'they had treated us extremely well, just as we would have treated their officers.'[11] Griffiths thought both Lemp and his First Lieutenant, Peter Hinsch, 'had a great sense of humour . . . like all submariners'. The British naval aviator spent two weeks aboard *U-30* in all, with the injured Thurston well cared for. Realising his serious burns would need to be kept free from infection, the U-boatmen volunteered 'one by one' to give Thurston fresh pyjamas and clothes every few hours.[12]

While the Germans were keeping the details of their activities secret from the enemy aviators, Lemp explained to Griffiths that when the submarine got in he would make his patrol report. Thurston would go immediately to hospital, while Griffiths would be sent to prison camp.

After a fortnight of sailing together – during which the prisoners learned nothing of the *Athenia* sinking – Lemp decided on reaching home port that his remaining British guest could not be handed over without an appropriate farewell. 'We will have a pleasant party,' the U-boat captain suggested. A bottle of schnapps and some glasses were produced, Lemp filling them to make a toast. 'Wishing you a short prisoner of war time,' he said, handing a glass to Griffiths. 'We will drink to the war ending.'[13]

At that exact moment, three black uniformed officers of the SS made their entrance, barging into Lemp's cabin and knocking the drinks out their hands. They ordered him to 'stop drinking with the enemy', warning Lemp his behaviour 'would be reported'.[14] The SS men escorted Griffiths off the submarine, putting him in the back of a Horch opened-topped saloon car. An SS man sat on either side, each with a pistol pointed at him. The driver was told to take them to the German naval headquarters.

On arrival they put Griffiths in a room, locking him in. Inspecting his surroundings the British pilot discovered it was some form of operations centre, showing the location of every U-boat. 'Suddenly an admiral arrived and ordered me out and then tried to explain to these astonished SS "you can't lock this chap up in a top secret room".'[15]

Griffiths was taken to a German naval detention centre rather than a prisoner of war camp. In November 1939 he wrote to his wife from the Oflag IX camp, using a secret code[16] to embed details of how the British anti-submarine bombs were defective and did more harm to the aircraft that carried them than to the U-boats. She passed this letter on to the Admiralty who asked her not to talk about it to anyone except her immediate family.[17]

Of vital interest to the Germans on U-30's return from her first war patrol was the final confirmation, or otherwise, of whether or not she had sunk the *Athenia*. Lemp was flown to Berlin to brief the naval high command and Dönitz was subsequently advised that the episode was to be kept secret. Lemp was not court-martialled, for it was felt he had acted properly and in good faith. Dönitz ordered the relevant page of U-30's log to be removed and replaced with a doctored one. While it confirmed attacks on *Blairlogie* and *Fanad Head*, on the day *Athenia* was sunk it showed U-30 100 miles away.

On the other side of the conflict the *Fanad Head* episode might appear to suggest hunter-killer groups were an ideal solution to the U-boat menace at a time when German submarines were sinking a merchant ship a day.

It actually revealed serious deficiencies.

Apart from claiming one U-boat – which only failed to sink *Ark Royal* due to her own faulty weapons – the chain of events saw several brilliant opportunities to sink another (U-30) frustrated.

Worse still, two of the carrier's own aircraft were brought down by their own bombs and valuable aircrews lost at a time when there were shortages in aviators. For Vice Admiral L.V. Wells, in charge of the *Ark Royal* hunting group, there was definite room for improvement.

He suggested the current philosophy on attack was flawed. Dropping lots of small bombs on a target was not as effective as one or two big ones. Wells suggested arming Swordfish with three powerful depth charges.[18]

For the Germans, the lesson was recorded in the U-boat force War Log, which argued that it showed 'how very difficult it is for U-boats to have to act according to prize law, especially with a/c [aircraft in the area]. They make themselves vulnerable and lose their strength, which lies in being able to surprise and to dive.'[19]

For the Admiralty, another flaw in the hunter-killer group strategy was within days exposed by the fate of HMS *Courageous*, which was sunk thanks to one of her own aircraft. It was spotted by Kapitänleutnant Otto Schuhart, who had been feeling increasingly angry about the

Aboard *U-30* at Wilhelmshaven in August 1940, Kapitänleutnant Fritz-Julius Lemp (left, with white cap) stares intently at his boss, Admiral Karl Dönitz, shortly after the latter has presented the former with the Knight's Cross. (*BArchiv, Bild 101 II-MN-1365-27A/Peter Rudolf*)

lack of targets to be found in the South West Approaches.

On the afternoon of 17 September, while scanning the horizon with *U-29's* periscope, Schuhart spotted a biplane circling a merchant ship, which he felt had to be a Swordfish from a carrier.

That would be a target well worth finding, so despite his submarine running short of fuel and needing to turn for home soon, Schuhart went on the hunt. Around 6.00 p.m. the submariner pulling watch duty on the periscope spotted smoke on the horizon and called Schuhart over.

Studying a shape poking up over the horizon, *U-29's* captain realised it was the towering bridge structure of a British carrier. The ship was too far away for a realistic shot, but U-29 hung on until the carrier got bigger and was coming straight towards her invisible would-be assassin.

It was a gift of a shot, as the target was maintaining a steady course to recover aircraft. Schuhart's task was made difficult by the setting sun but, firing from 3,000 yards, a spread of three torpedoes was sent on its way.

British destroyers soon found U-29 and made several depth-charge attacks but she got away. Tuning in to the BBC World Service the following day, Schuhart was elated to discover he had sunk HMS *Courageous*. Out of the 1,260 men in the ship's company and embarked air squadrons, only 519 survived, picked up by destroyers and passing merchant ships. The policy of sending out carriers to hunt down submarines was clearly deeply flawed, for all it did was deliver unto the enemy the kind of target they so desired.

Churchill hid his shock by promising merchant vessels would soon be armed and issuing reassurances that warships were well equipped and trained to tackle the submarine menace.

The British believed up to seven U-boats had by then been destroyed but in reality just two had been sunk: U-39 by *Ark Royal*'s escorts and U-27 to the west of the Hebrides on 20 September. The First Lord was publicly upbeat, remarking to MPs just under a week later that 'the British attack upon the U-boat is only just beginning'.[20]

Further cheer was provided by a decline in merchant shipping sunk by the enemy, from 65,000 tons in the first week of the war to 46,000 tons in the second and 21,000 tons in the third.

The fight against the opposition's submarine force was still shaping up as a difficult enterprise. 'Such is the U-boat war,' admitted Churchill to Parliament, 'hard, widespread and bitter, a war of groping and drowning, a war of ambuscade and stratagem, a war of science and seamanship.'[21]

An important element of the struggle was breaking the other side's wireless signal ciphers. In that respect the Germans gained an early upper hand. It resulted in a punishing ordeal for the same submarine that had narrowly avoided being sunk on the first day of hostilities.

The Admiralty had received intelligence about an alleged sonic indicator buoy that marked a swept passage through the enemy's defensive minefields in the approaches to Wilhelmshaven. This could open the gate to sinking German warships in their safe harbour. Alternatively, the buoy might be some new form of anti-submarine device.

It was decided *Spearfish* should be sent to sniff around the area and determine exactly what it was. The submarine's captain, Lt John Eaden, considered it 'a difficult and dangerous patrol' with instructions to 'go and sit on the position where this indicator device was reported to be and see what happened'.[22]

An S Class boat, completed in 1936, with a crew of 39 *Spearfish* was specially designed to operate in the two parts of the world crucial to British security – the North Sea and the Mediterranean. Britain would build more S Class submarines between the early 1930s and 1944 than any other type, 63 in total.

A reliable and sturdy submarine, at 208ft long and with a beam of 24ft, displacing 761 tons surfaced and 960 tons dived, the S-boat was comparable to the enemy's Type VII, though not so long or as fast on the surface. The S-boats could go as deep as 300ft and make 15 knots on the surface and ten dived. They had six torpedo tubes, though some of those built during the war would boast seven. Their armament was completed with a 3-inch deck gun and machine guns.

Spearfish departed Dundee on 20 September and two days later was off the coast of Denmark, with the boat's Asdic – mounted on the bottom of the hull – quite useless in such shallow waters. Active pinging was not advisable anyway, as the sound could be picked up by the enemy's hydrophones.

At 7.13 a.m. on 24 September a loud explosion was heard in the water and *Spearfish* bottomed at a depth of 84ft with all machinery stopped. As nothing further was heard, at 9.00 a.m. Eaden cautiously brought the boat to periscope depth and took a look. Within seconds 'a heavy charge was exploded quite close', reported Eaden. 'This shook the submarine and did some minor damage. It was now apparent that we were being hunted by the Germans.'

Eaden was sure his periscope had not been spotted. He wondered how the Germans knew exactly where to place themselves in order to pick *Spearfish* up immediately on their hydrophones. The only option was to go ultra stealthy.

'My orders to the men were to keep quiet and to lie down and rest. This, of course, was to conserve oxygen we'd got and also to limit the amount of carbon dioxide which was exhaled.'

The only people active aside from Eaden were an officer in the control room, an Engine Room Artificer overseeing the opening and shutting of vents and high pressure air, two men on the hydroplanes and ratings in the engine room and torpedo space; a dozen men in total.

More depth charges were dropped between 2.50 p.m. and 4.10 p.m., but not as close as before. Eaden counted 25 detonations in all, some of which gave *Spearfish* 'a good thump but did no damage'. At 5.20 p.m. some form of wire or grapple was passed over the after jumping stay – the latter was part of a wire stretched from stern to conning tower and to the bow for fending off any nets or wires encountered while dived.

There was then an ominous bump on the after casing followed by a series of lesser bumps moving aft. It was a depth charge, which exploded 'with the most appalling crash'.

Eaden saw the submarine 'spring inwards and then open out again. Nearly all lights were smashed . . . In the darkness the spurting of water and hissing of escaping air could be heard . . . I sat still for a moment as I rather expected a wall of water to descend, flooding up the submarine.'

The primary damage had been to the engine room pressure hull and frames, which were bent. The port main motor cooler had burst and the port main motor switchboard was covered in water, rendering it useless. There were serious HP air leaks and the main battery ventilation drain was filled with running water. Throughout *Spearfish* makeshift repairs were applied, but the most pressing problem were engine room leaks. These could eventually prove fatal if they weren't stopped, but a fortuitous piece of forward planning saved the boat. Inspired by reading about submarine operations and damage control practice in the First World War, some of the *Spearfish* submariners had before departing made lots of wooden plugs of various sizes. Wood was preferred to stop leaks, as it expanded when it got wet and these assorted plugs were now hammered into cracks and gaps.

It wasn't the end of the enemy assault, as more depth charges exploded around *Spearfish*. While they shook the boat they did not make matters any worse than they were already. At 6.00 p.m. Lt Eaden ordered a tot of rum issued to bolster morale then instructed his men to lie down or sit to conserve air. The atmosphere in the boat was getting really foul, with some finding it difficult to breathe – particularly two of the older ratings. People were getting severe headaches and the lack of oxygen made it very difficult to think logically. In case the boat was captured or salvaged, Eaden ordered the ship recognition manual, memos, cipher books, war orders and other secret documents placed under bilge plates in the machinery space. This would put them out of sight and, hopefully, make sure they were almost instantly destroyed by water immersion. While all was not lost, the situation was far from ideal and Eaden realised there was only one course of action. Mustering all hands in the control room he congratulated them on 'their great steadiness and behaviour'. He then explained that he intended to blow the ballast tanks and surface. 'If there was any enemy in sight we would engage them. If not we would make our way home via Danish territorial waters.'

Such was the scale of damage to the boat it was by no means guaranteed she would be able to surface again.

At 8.45 p.m. all hands went to diving stations and *Spearfish* rose from the seabed. Due to the HP leaks making air pressure in the submarine greater than normal Eaden got a Leading Seaman to hold onto his legs as he opened the top hatch. This ensured he didn't pop out like a cork. Much to his surprise, he found the enemy did not surround *Spearfish*.

The British submarine limped across the North Sea unable to dive and halfway home met a Home Fleet escort force that at one stage had to fight off a Luftwaffe attack.

Reaching Rosyth Dockyard on the morning of 27 September, *Spearfish* would be under repair until spring 1940. In the meantime, her captain puzzled over how the Germans had gained such precise contact with his boat in the first place, especially without the aid of Asdic to help them. He was sure he had taken the utmost care 'and yet within hours of reaching my patrol position they were within contact of me'.

Some years later the mystery would be solved, for Eaden learned that the enemy had actually broken the British naval cipher. He was told this meant 'they knew exactly where I was going. They had simply been waiting for me rather like setting a mouse trap [and] waiting for the mouse.' The enemy knew his patrol area if not the exact objective of his mission.

At that point of the war German naval codes had not been penetrated but the B-Dienst naval intelligence code-breaking organisation passed the fruits of its labours on to friendly units operating in enemy territory so they could try to avoid British patrols. Similar information could be utilised in Germany's backyard to intercept and attack trespassers.

Penetration of Admiralty signals traffic began as far back as 1935, when B-Dienst cut its teeth cracking signals sent between the warships of a Royal Navy task group stationed in the Red Sea. Waiting in vain to intervene on behalf of the League of Nations against Italy's subjugation of Abyssinia, the British ships had switched to using war codes and ciphers. The Germans twigged and so over the course of several months began working on the British system.

The basis of a new Admiralty code introduced on the outbreak of hostilities was therefore familiar to the Germans and that is why they soon cracked it. Prior to the war Cdr Louis Mountbatten was among those who struggled to persuade the Admiralty it should follow the American lead and introduce machines to constantly generate new, safer encrypted signals.

Trials with encryption machines were arranged but it was decided they were impractical in bad weather and so complex they were bound to go wrong even in calm seas. Mountbatten suspected that this was far from the case, and the navy just couldn't be bothered to change its ways.[23]

With battle joined, B-Dienst was to give German naval forces, including U-boats, a potentially decisive edge. Over subsequent months, and into the summer of 1940, the British would suffer a crisis of confidence not only in their own submarine forces but also in their ability to destroy the enemy's. One particular enemy exploit provided a real shock.

6 Boldest of Bold Enterprises

Admiral Dönitz had been mulling over the prospects of getting into the enemy's main war anchorage of Scapa Flow for some time. He pondered the failed attempts by von Henning in *U-18* (November 1914) and Emsmann in *UB-116* (October 1918) along with the 'very great difficulties involved, from the point of view of both seamanship and navigation . . .'[1]

The strong currents of the Pentland Firth in the approaches to Scapa were faster than a submerged U-boat could manage (10 knots versus 7 knots), leaving the boat at the mercy of the sea. It was also likely that anti-submarine nets would be arranged across the anchorage entrances and there had to be carefully sited defensive minefields, not to mention patrolling warships. Dönitz considered such a mission 'the boldest of bold enterprises'.[2] That it could be achieved was never doubted by Kapitänleutnant Viktor Oehrn, the admiral's Staff Officer, Operations who told Dönitz: 'I'm pretty sure we could find a way to get in.'[3]

Intelligence reports and recent naval high command feasibility reports were studied along with aerial reconnaissance photographs showing enemy capital ships in Scapa. It seemed a submarine might be able to enter via Hoxa Sound when the nets were drawn aside to let a vessel in.

The Luftwaffe's very high-flying photoreconnaissance aircraft were sent specifically to photograph Scapa's entrances and when these photos came back it was clear that Hoxa was a no-go. Neither would a submarine stand a chance of getting in via Switha Sound or Clesstrom Sound. Other likely entrances had blockships in their channels but there was one with shallows on each side that could allow access.

It would require a submarine captain with exceptional skills. Weighing up a list of likely candidates, the admiral decided 31-year-old Kapitänleutnant Günther Prien 'possessed all the personal qualities and professional ability required'.

The son of a judge from the Hanseatic port of Lübeck and originally a merchant marine officer by trade, Prien had joined the navy in 1933. After seamanship training as a rating he transferred to the submarine force and became an officer, seeing service in U-26 during Spanish Civil War patrols. After passing his submarine Commanding Officer course, Prien became captain of U-47 in 1938. With the outbreak of war he soon achieved success, sinking three merchant vessels in as many days.

A few weeks later, on entering the admiral's cabin aboard the submarine depot ship Weichsel, Prien was confronted by Dönitz and a group of other officers studying various documents. There were charts of Scapa Flow laid out on a large table and Dönitz asked him: 'Do you think a determined commander could get his U-boat inside Scapa Flow and attack enemy forces?'[4] Suddenly realising what he was being asked to take on, Prien did not know what to say. Dönitz suggested he should

Kapitänleutnant Günther Prien in 1940, after his legendary attack on HMS *Royal Oak* in Scapa Flow. (*BArchiv, Bild 183-2006-1130-500/Annelise Schulze*)

think things over before giving an answer. Should he decline the honour it 'would not affect the high opinion we have of you'.[5]

Overnight Prien studied charts, navigation books and intelligence reports, deciding to accept the challenge. At a subsequent meeting Dönitz asked if Prien fully understood the risks, in light of the previous failures to get into Scapa. Prien said he did. Dönitz shook his hand and told him to make *U-47* ready to sail.

On 12 October an air reconnaissance flight photographed major units of the Home Fleet at Scapa, ideally placed for an attack. Prien by now knew charts of Scapa intimately and he combined that with intelligence provided by *U-14*. She had been sent on a scouting mission in September to gather information on tides and frequency of enemy patrols. The intention was for Prien to enter via Holm Sound, squeezing by blockships if need be. The night of 13/14 October was felt to be the best opportunity, as if *U-47* needed to go in on the surface she would be guaranteed minimum visibility, especially with a new moon, which meant next to no light. In advance of *U-47* embarking on her venture all other U-boats were directed away from waters around the Orkneys in order to avoid provoking an alarm and making the enemy more vigilant.

After steering across the North Sea, using dead reckoning and taking soundings of the seabed, Prien edged closer to Scapa, keeping up a pattern of lying on the seabed during the day and surfacing at night to get air and charge the battery. Until 13 October the crew did not know exactly what their mission was, though they guessed something big was imminent. Prien gathered them in the forward torpedo room and told them they were about to go into Scapa Flow itself. They seemed to accept it with equanimity, the silence broken only by 'a soft gentle crunching sound as the boat shifted on the sea bed'.[6]

U-47 rested on the bottom all day, in 270ft of water, the men taking it in turns to climb into the bunks and draw the curtains to try to sleep. All but a few lights and other systems were shut down to preserve battery juice.

The boat surfaced at 7.15 p.m. and a hot meal was served – roast ribs of salt pork with cabbage – and then the voyage to death or glory began. There was a heart-stopping moment when at 11.07 p.m. the black silhouette of a ship materialised out of the night. It was a merchant vessel and Prien dived U-47 to slip by unobserved.

When they surfaced again, Kirk Sound was visible ahead, and U-47 prepared to make her appearance on stage. Prien was presented with what he later described as 'a very eerie sight. On land everything is dark, high in the sky are the flickering Northern Lights, so that the bay, surrounded by English [sic] mountains, is directly lit up from above. The blockships lie in the sound, ghostly as the wings of a theatre.'[7]

He decided to squeeze past the blockships on their northern side and, as the U-boat got closer to the anchorage where he hoped to discover some juicy targets, Prien found it 'disgustingly light. The whole bay is lit up.' Heading north he spotted the big, bulky silhouettes of 'two battleships' along with what he thought were destroyers lying beyond.[8]

At 12.58 a.m., with just 22ft below the boat's keel Prien fired one torpedo at what he referred to as 'the northern' ship and two at 'the southern'. All had impact exploders. 'After a good 3½ minutes, a torpedo detonates on the northern ship,' reported Prien, 'of the other two nothing is to be seen.'[9]

Disappointed, but with no interference from the enemy as yet, Prien swung U-47 around and fired a torpedo from the stern tube, then turned the boat to fire three more torpedoes from the bow tubes, some with magnetic exploders.

'After three tense minutes comes the detonation on the nearer ship,' said Prien. 'There is a loud explosion, roar, and rumbling. Then come columns of water, followed by columns of fire, and splinters fly through the air. The harbour springs to life. Destroyers are lit up, signalling starts on every side, and on land 200 metres away from me cars roar along the roads. A battleship has been sunk, a second damaged, and the other three torpedoes have gone to blazes. All the tubes are empty. I decide to withdraw . . .'[10]

U-47 made off at high speed – still on the surface – headed to exit by Skildaenoy Point. Finally, after a few more tricky manoeuvres, *U-47* broke through to the open sea and went as fast as she could, heading south-east for home. With daylight fast approaching, Prien decided *U-47* would be advised to dive and sit on the seabed for a few hours to let the fuss die down. As he left the bridge Prien took a last look over his shoulder: 'The glow from Scapa is still visible . . . Apparently they are still dropping depth charges.'[11]

On 15 October *U-47* sent a signal to U-boat headquarters: 'Operation successfully completed. "ROYAL OAK" sunk. "REPULSE" damaged.'[12]

Prien thought he had scored a hit for'ard on *Repulse* and that another blew *Royal Oak* up. In truth he only hit *Royal Oak* (and *Repulse* was not even there). Aboard the British battlewagon the first torpedo impact was dismissed as a near miss bomb dropped by a Luftwaffe raider or even some form of small explosion aboard ship.[13] It just seemed too incredible to the battleship's officers that a submarine could have sneaked into Scapa. Three subsequent torpedo hits tore open *Royal Oak*'s hull and she capsized within two minutes, sinking 13 minutes later, with the loss of 833 sailors and marines.

Returning to Wilhelmshaven on 17 October, Prien was an instant superstar of the newsreels. Both he and his crew were whisked away to Berlin for a congratulatory audience with Adolf Hitler, who presented the submarine captain with the Knight's Cross.

In Britain even the First Lord of the Admiralty admitted Prien had pulled off 'a feat of arms'.[14] Within two weeks Churchill was at Scapa for an emergency meeting aboard the battleship HMS *Nelson*, galvanising efforts to secure the anchorage against both U-boat and air attack. It was thought the Home Fleet would not return to use Scapa until

March 1940, a prolonged absence that was a major achievement for the Germans.

Away from the daring exploits of Günther Prien, certain German submarines were already creating grimly impressive score sheets, none more so than *U-48*, commanded by 31-year-old Kapitänleutnant Herbert Schultze. Since her first patrol in September 1939 the Type VIIB boat had managed to sink ten merchant ships, totalling 64,934 tons.

On 8 December *U-48* was subjected to prolonged depth-charging after attacking a convoy, suffering serious damage which took several hours to repair. Early the following morning, with the boat back on patrol, the dark shape of a vessel with no lights showing was spotted. It was the *San Alberto*, an Eagle Oil ship of 8,000 tons displacement. Poor visibility meant the first two torpedoes missed, but the third hit *San Alberto* right in the middle, breaking her back, though she did not immediately tear in two. *U-48*'s radio operator heard the distress signal go out but no position was broadcast. 'This success is our revenge for the evil depth charging,' Schultze observed in his war journal.[15]

U-48 resumed her patrol, leaving *San Alberto* to break up, but while the fore part turned turtle and sank the aft portion stayed afloat. Aboard was apprentice Merchant Navy officer Yves Dias, aged 17, who was very grateful the ship was outward bound to Tampico in the Gulf of Mexico and therefore unladen. Had she been carrying oil, *San Alberto* might well have exploded. 'First thing I knew I was chucked out of my bunk onto the deck,' said Dias. 'We rushed about to get the lifeboats lowered but there were only lifeboats on the one side as on the other they had been destroyed by the explosion.'[16]

One man trying to climb into a lifeboat fell into the sea and was swept away. Two lifeboats were successfully lowered, with Dias in the one with the ship's captain aboard. They soon lost sight of the other boat, which 'didn't get picked up for 14 days, but they were all alright', recalled Dias. Someone in the lifeboat spotted signs of life aboard the remains of the ship. 'We noticed the ensign going up and down and so realised there was somebody left onboard, and it looked as if it might float for a bit. So, we rowed back – with difficulty, as it took about three or four hours. There was a big sea running but we got back onboard. About a third of the tanker was left afloat, including the galley, and we had plenty to eat because the food for Christmas was onboard.

Unfortunately it was breaking up and gradually we were sinking and we hadn't any lifeboats left.'

Heavy seas had smashed up the boat in which they'd come back alongside and though various merchant ships passed by they acknowledged neither distress lights nor the ship's ensign going up and down. At one point a survivor decided he would swim to one of these vessels and jumped overboard. 'Of course in the water he was very small,' said Dias, 'and was just blown away, so he drowned.'

They fired the ship's gun to attract the attention of another vessel, but it retreated, thinking it was being shot at. There was a gale blowing and it was increasingly uncomfortable aboard the fragile remnants of *San Alberto*. Fortunately a Belgian tanker spotted the distress signals and sent a message to the Admiralty, which ordered the destroyer *Mackay* to the rescue.

'They realised they couldn't come alongside us because the sea was too rough,' said Dias, 'so they had fired a rope to us and we pulled a carley raft over. We had to jump overboard and swim for the raft and get onboard it. They then heaved us back to the *Mackay*. Oddly enough it was warmer in the water than it was on *San Alberto*'s upper deck. Once aboard *Mackay* we were bunged down below decks and some of the ship's company gave up their bunks for us as they realised we'd had a hard time.'

Also out on another patrol in December 1939 was Fritz-Julius Lemp in *U-30*, and he would ensure the year went out on a sour note for the Royal Navy. Following the loss of *Royal Oak* the elderly battlewagon *Barham* was among vessels withdrawn from the Mediterranean Fleet to boost forces at home, joining patrols to stop surface raiders breaking out into the Atlantic. Late on the afternoon of 28 December Lemp caught sight above the horizon of the tall superstructures of *Barham* and battlecruiser *Repulse*.

Dipping under the escort destroyers *Nubian* and *Isis*, Lemp fired a pair of torpedoes at each target with three missing but one hitting *Barham*. Exploding close to the shell rooms of A and B main 15-inch gun turrets, it failed to blow the ship up, but four men were killed. Seriously down by the bows due to flooding, *Barham* set course for Liverpool where she would be in dry dock for six months.

Back in Germany B-Dienst was able to tell Dönitz that Lemp had scored an impressive hit before the submarine captain could get around to sending his own signal. This was because B-Dienst had detected heavy Admiralty signals traffic, including a request for destroyers to escort *Barham* back to Britain.

Though the Germans did not know which of their submarines was responsible, a subsequent British U-boat warning signal was intercepted and decrypted. Lemp finally reported his attack on 30 December, telling U-boat command he had torpedoed 'a battleship of the Queen Elizabeth Class'.[17] After attacking *Barham* Lemp headed south into the Irish Sea and *U-30* laid a dozen mines off Liverpool. Within the span of a month they sank four merchant ships, including one blown apart, and damaged another. Until local waters could be made safe the British were forced to divert shipping elsewhere, a serious inconvenience.

Heading for Germany via St George's Channel, *U-30* was caught by the destroyer *Vesper*, which gained a solid contact. One of the submarine's crew recorded this frightening experience in his diary. 'Alarm! . . . Attacked by depth charges . . .' wrote Oberleutnant Eichelborn. 'We all turned pale. Nothing was broken but we are being hunted. Damage to diving gear.'[18]

U-30 got home despite the damage.

7   Cheated of Certain Success

Of the 114 merchant vessels sunk by U-boats between September 1939 and the end of the year, 110 were sailing solo. Compared to the 5,500 ships that got through unmolested by sailing in convoy, such losses were not serious. Mines, including those laid by Lemp in *U-30*, also took their toll on shipping, sinking 79 vessels – both British and neutral – along with some from Allied nations. The Royal Navy had lost an aircraft carrier, a battleship, an AMC (*Rawalpindi*) and two destroyers to aggressive enemy action or mines, with a total of 1,609 sailors and marines killed.

Despite the paucity of enemy submarine sinkings, in a radio

broadcast on 20 January 1940 Winston Churchill couldn't help boasting of Britain's alleged U-boat killing prowess, making unfounded claims for the purpose of boosting public morale. He said half the U-boat force had been sunk and was infuriated by the Royal Navy trying to tell him that both its Asdic-equipped warships and the RAF's sub-hunting aircraft were not delivering quite the devastation on enemy forces he claimed. The British had not actually eliminated 33 U-boats (out of 66) as the First Lord of the Admiralty suggested, but rather nine (out of 57) by the end of 1939. This disparity between Churchill's claim and reality would become a huge bone of contention.

Captain Arthur Talbot, a 48-year-old, straight-talking Yorkshireman, was Director of the Anti-Submarine Warfare Division and provoked the ire of Churchill over this very issue when the latter was serving as First Lord and after he became Prime Minister and Defence Minister.

Talbot was a seasoned warrior, having served in European waters during the First World War as a junior officer. What's more, he knew what he was talking about from front line experience in the new conflict.

He had started the conflict in command of the 3rd Destroyer Flotilla and his ships had picked up survivors from *Courageous*. Just under a month later, on 14 October, the 3rd Flotilla, with Talbot aboard HMS *Inglefield*, engaged in a hunt for U-boats that were trying to use wolf pack tactics in combat for the first time.

Like a grand master moving his pieces around a chessboard, Dönitz had long wanted to use wireless signals, combined with sighting reports from aircraft and surface ships plus other intelligence, to marshal several submarines against a convoy. German naval code-breakers had managed to penetrate wireless traffic about an Anglo-French convoy of 27 merchant ships, codename KJF-3, which was coming to Europe from Jamaica. Its escort included the giant French submarine *Surcouf*, a cousin of the British M Class with a pair of 8-inch guns mounted forward. The impressive silhouette of *Surcouf* on the surface deterred the German pocket battleship *Deutschland* from attacking the convoy on 9 October, but there was also a strong British cruiser presence.

Dönitz sent out the so-called Hartmann Wolfpack, named after its leader, 36-year-old Korvettenkapitän Werner Hartmann, in *U-37*, to lie in wait in the Western Approaches, which was the likely route of the convoy as it approached British waters.

Though four U-boats were meant to attack KJF-3 only two were involved, *U-48* and *U-45*, the latter commanded by 30-year-old Kapitän-leutnant Alexander Gelhaar. *U-48* sank two cargo vessels, while *U-45* claimed two more, one of them the French liner *Bretagne*, of 10,000 tons. She was attacked – despite extant orders not to sink liners – with three hundred passengers rescued.

U-45 was pursuing another ship on the surface, shelling it from a distance, when she was caught and attacked by Talbot's four destroyers, which had picked up distress signals.

The U-boat dived but Asdic contact was soon made. Thirty depth charges were dropped, Talbot recording: 'After one attack a large blow of air was seen, and after the last attack oil . . .'[1]

Pieces of grey painted wood were spotted on the surface – but this was still not absolute confirmation in 900 fathoms and contact was lost. 'I can see no reason for contact not being regained,' reported Talbot, 'other than that the U-boat was out of range on the bottom . . . I left two destroyers on the spot for twenty-four hours and they reported that there was a patch of oil near the position of the last attack and that, on the windward edge of it, large bubbles of oil were still appearing.'

That was about as much confirmation as the Admiralty would get for a destroyed, submerged submarine in such deep water – unless it had been forced to the surface before the death plunge. Corpses, or body parts, invariably helped to pin down the fate of the target, while oil could be collected and analysed to determine if it was of the sort used by U-boats. Hard proof was always better than circumstantial evidence. *U-45* had actually been destroyed, with Gelhaar and all his crew lost, but this would not be confirmed until German records were inspected after the war.

In early 1940 the Admiralty wanted the battle against the U-boats to be based on confirmed kills and proper analysis. Best, or over-optimistic, estimates would not do for the experienced Capt. Talbot. Former newspaper journalist and soldier-turned-politician Winston Churchill believed that in the battle for national survival other factors were important. He recognised that public morale – the vital buttress of the war effort – needed boosting by good news stories, hence his radio speech. Admitting that Asdic wasn't always reliable in sniffing out U-boats was not good for morale. That roving groups of warships were more often than not achieving little more than making themselves potential targets was not what he wanted to hear.

Behind the scenes the First Sea Lord, Admiral Sir Dudley Pound, was concerned the RAF was also getting carried away with itself. On 29 December 1939 he wrote to Air Chief Marshal Sir Cyril Newall, Chief of the Air Staff, outlining the risks of exaggerating successes against U-boats.

Coastal Command had reported that during 26,220 flying hours its aircraft attacked 55 submarines. It assessed that 20 had 'probably been destroyed or damaged' and this included 'two attacks in co-operation with naval vessels'.[2]

Attacks on enemy submarines by British aircraft were thoroughly investigated by the U-Boat Assessment Committee, whose President was Capt. Talbot, and he was assisted by, among others, an expert from Coastal Command. Pound informed Newall 'the committee's assessment is that, of the 55 submarines attacked, only seven have been hit with the following results:

a) 1 probably sunk.
b) 2 probably seriously damaged.
c) 4 probably slightly damaged.'

The RAF representative on the committee agreed with this analysis.

'I only call your attention to the above,' Pound added, 'because there is a danger that if any one weapon is credited with being more successful than it really is there is not the same incentive to improve it.'[3] Pound had cut straight to the heart of the matter. If the Prime Minister's delusions of an easy victory over the U-boats were believed, and if the airmen (or the navy) swallowed their own propaganda Britain could be defeated.

On the other side of the North Sea, Admiral Dönitz was equally wary of erroneous claims being exploited for propaganda purposes. When U-47 reported in late November 1939 that she had torpedoed and badly damaged a British cruiser off Shetland, the Reich's propagandists leapt on it. They claimed a confirmed sinking in a triumphant radio broadcast to the world. This was, after all, the legendary Günther Prien's boat. He had immediately transmitted the supposed sinking to U-boat headquarters, yet before any proper confirmation it was broadcast as fact. The

German public were hungry for more daring exploits by the glorious ace who sank *Royal Oak*, but his target this time was unharmed. The British were soon able to demonstrate that fact via their own news broadcast, explaining HMS *Norfolk* had returned safely to port.

'From the service-man's point of view,' noted Dönitz in the U-boat force War Log, 'such inaccuracies and exaggerations are undesirable.'[4]

Raising morale with falsehoods ran the risk of a devastating plunge when the facts emerged.

On the British side one of those who harboured deep misgivings about disregarding the facts was Rear Admiral John Godfrey, the head of the Naval Intelligence Division, whose Personal Assistant was Lt Cdr Ian Fleming. Godfrey, whom Fleming would use as his model for 'M' in the James Bond novels, thought a very careful balance needed to be observed between what he called 'Truth, Reality and Publicity'.

Truth was what NID 'thought was the truth', explained Godfrey. '"Reality" is actually what happened, undiscoverable in its entirety until we had access to German Records after the war. "Publicity" is what the world, the country, the Navy, Admiralty departments, and the First Lord [Churchill and his successor, A.V. Alexander], C.N.S. [the Chief of Naval Staff, Admiral Pound] and D.C.N.S [Deputy Chief of the Naval Staff], were told at the time.'[5] By spring 1940 NID believed 11 or 12 U-boats had been sunk, agreeing more or less with Talbot's analysis. At the beginning of the year 'only 9 out of 57 were *known* to have been sunk', revealed Godfrey, yet 'the First Lord was telling the world that we had sunk half the German U/Boat force'.

Certain people who needed to know the 'Truth' were kept in the dark and in early 1940 the First Lord – Churchill – had insisted on a limited awareness of the facts. Shipbuilders and weapons manufacturers were kept out of the loop, along with most senior naval officers. Shipyards were not fully aware of the scale of the threat facing Britain – and the consequent need to build more warships and merchant vessels as quickly as possible. Those expected to produce the weapons to destroy enemy submarines were not perhaps as motivated as they should have been, due to a lack of 'Reality'. If they believed the fight against the U-boat was going Britain's way, as Churchill had claimed on the radio, it could only have a detrimental effect on the war effort.

Rosy optimism might also lead to a lack of focus and urgency in the training of anti-submarine personnel. Worse than that, according to

Godfrey, 'the Cabinet must also have been misinformed'. In the war of 'Truth, Reality and Publicity' Godfrey found: 'Pressure from all sides to combine "knowns" and "probables" had become almost irresistible . . .' Godfrey quietly gave face-to-face briefings on the facts about U-boat sinkings to certain key people. The enemy were certainly not fooled for, as Godfrey noted, 'the real facts . . . were, of course, known to the German Admiralty'.[6]

While in Britain there may have been controversy and discomfort about the lack of enemy submarine losses, in Germany Admiral Dönitz and his captains were outraged at the neutering of their efforts through incompetent torpedo production. Günther Prien was so disheartened that he moaned to Dönitz that he was expected 'to fight with a dummy rifle'.[7]

This was due to the Norwegian campaign of April–June 1940 being a debacle for the Kriegsmarine. Despite safely transporting thousands of troops, sinking the old British carrier *Glorious* and claiming a few other Allied warships, the German fleet did not cover itself in glory. Across several battles with the Royal Navy, and also at the hands of the Norwegians, its surface force was denuded of many valuable units. Even the ability to read Admiralty signals did not help it greatly. It could not avoid sending ships and submarines into the restricted waters off Norway and up fjords and in such an environment the British could not help but capitalise. For Germany's submariners, Norway was a particularly bad experience. The U-boats were taken away from their increasingly fruitful campaign in the Atlantic and sent to waters where they failed to sink a single British or French warship. They sent only a few merchant vessels to the bottom while Dönitz lost *U-49* and *U-64*, the latter in a milestone episode.

On 10 April there was a fierce battle between British and German destroyers after the latter landed troops to try to seize the important iron ore exporting port of Narvik.

During what became known as the First Battle of Narvik the Royal Navy flotilla fought valiantly but came off worse. For round two, in order to eliminate eight German warships still at the port, a hunting pack of nine RN destroyers was assembled around battleship *Warspite*.

In bitterly cold weather on 13 April, with an uncomfortable swell and ice coating vessels' decks, the British headed for the Ofotfjord. Three destroyers steamed ahead of *Warspite*, using minesweeping gear to clear the way, while others were posted evenly around her.

Waiting for the British were enemy destroyers and three U-boats. *U-48*, still commanded by Herbert Schultze, was caught on the surface and the destroyer *Eskimo* raced over to send the hastily dived submarine away under a shower of depth charges. It was the opening action of the Second Battle of Narvik.

With oppressive clouds pressing tightly down and snow flurries swirling off the steep sides of the Ofotfjord, visibility was around ten miles at best. A Swordfish floatplane from the battleship was launched to scout ahead for the enemy. It soon reported by radio that two German destroyers were not far away. These greeted the plane with a storm of anti-aircraft fire but failed to score any hits.

Skimming over Narvik, the Swordfish, piloted by Petty Officer Frederick 'Ben' Rice, sighted another enemy destroyer in harbour. Having passed this intelligence on, Rice took the plane up the Herjangsfjord, to the north. Finding nothing obvious Lt Cdr W.L. Brown, the Observer and aircraft commander, suggested turning around and returning to *Warspite*.

As he banked, Rice spotted something.

'Hang on, there's a U-boat!' he shouted down the voicepipe to Brown.[8] It was *U-64*, a large Type IXB, just moving away from a jetty at the village of Bjerkvik. When Lt Cdr Brown asked him what he felt the plan should be, Rice replied: 'Let's bomb the bastards!' With floats attached it wasn't possible for a Swordfish to carry a torpedo, as it weighed too much and was tricky to drop. The *Warspite*'s aircraft was consequently carrying two 50lb armour-piercing bombs, a pair of 100lb bombs and a single ASW bomb. Rice, who had recently completed a special dive-bombing course with the RAF, decided to use the armour-piercing weapons.

As the Swordfish swooped, the 37mm anti-aircraft gun mounted on *U-64*'s conning tower threw up fiery shells but the only damage sustained by the aircraft was a pierced float. Rice released the bombs, pulled the stick back and the aircraft climbed away. Telegraphist Air Gunner M.G. Pacey, the rearmost man in the cockpit, fired at the U-boat with his machine gun.

One of the bombs hit at the base of *U-64*'s conning tower and the submarine sank by the bows in less than 30 seconds, drowning eight of her crew. 'It was lucky anyone got out all,' Rice reflected. 'Fortunately they had their watertight doors shut and it was those who were in the front compartments that didn't make it.'

U-64 was the first German submarine sunk by a British or Allied aircraft in the Second World War and the only U-boat destroyed by a battleship-based aircraft in the conflict. During the Second Battle of Narvik all eight German destroyers were also sunk or forced to run themselves aground.

Another major misfortune to befall the Kriegsmarine during the German invasion and occupation of Norway was the capture of secret documents from a submarine sunk in the Vaags Fjord.

The loss of *U-49* on 15 April was an amazing coup for the Allied side in the intelligence war and 34-year-old Oberleutnant Kurt von Gossler was notably unlucky. Prior to his Norwegian mission he sank just one ship between September 1939 and April 1940 – the British-flagged steam grain carrier *Pensilva* – despite four patrols and 59 days at sea.[9]

In the Vaags Fjord *U-49* was subjected to a furious depth-charge attack by the destroyers *Brazen* and *Fearless*, which were escorting a convoy of ships carrying Allied troops. After a particularly shattering explosion next to the conning tower von Gossler ordered all tanks blown. Once *U-49* surfaced her crew abandoned ship in a chaotic fashion. The bags containing the boat's secret documents were not weighted down properly and so failed to sink and were retrieved by the British.

When von Gossler was interrogated, he recalled that his boat had been attacked in November 1939 about 250 miles off Ushant. To evade destruction *U-49* had been forced down to a nerve-shattering 557ft.[10] Von Gossler said his submarine had suffered serious damage but managed to 'struggle back to Germany'. The whole experience possibly adversely affected his nerve, though von Gossler, his Chief Engineer and his Boatswain were awarded the Iron Cross for 'good work on effecting repairs to make the boat sea-worthy'.[11]

Had Hitler known what a gift *U-49* presented to the British he might well have revoked those medals. The recovered (and dried out) documents were sent to the NID, who were especially delighted with charts that showed where all the U-boats were off Norway and further afield. Also captured were operational orders for 10 March 1940 that detailed 31 U-boats and provided information on how they were dispersed, if in port or at sea.

Capt. Talbot produced an assessment document branded 'Most

Secret' on 24 April, which was sent to Churchill and a few others. 'If the captured operation orders are authentic,' wrote Talbot, 'it means, among other things, that all the first 13 U-boats [so far in the war] which have been assessed as "probably sunk" were, in fact, not so. The difference between the estimated numbers sunk which I gave you a fortnight ago and in this paper is ten.'

Having assessed all his sources of information along with the *U-49* haul, Talbot concluded that on 10 March 1940 the U-boat fleet status was 19 destroyed, two under repair and 45 available for operations. This was still some way short of the figure sunk as claimed by the First Lord during his January radio broadcast. By February Churchill was claiming 45 U-boats had been sunk while Admiral Pound hedged his bets by suggesting 35.[10] After receiving the 24 April papers on U-boat kills, Churchill remarked bitterly that 'it might be a good thing if Captain Talbot went to sea as soon as possible'.[12]

What stung the German submariners most in April 1940 were the numerous failed attacks against various British warships in Norwegian waters. *Warspite* was attacked unsuccessfully four times including by *U-25* and *U-47*. Günther Prien's frustrations during the Norwegian campaign were perhaps the keenest felt, as so much was expected of him and he delivered nothing. At one stage his periscope view was stuffed with French and British warships and troop ships, yet not one of the four torpedoes *U-47* fired claimed a victim. U-boat headquarters received an anguished wireless message from *U-47* reporting this serial failure. Dönitz recorded in the War Log that Germany's 'best U-boat commander' was suffering unsuccessful shot after unsuccessful shot but it could not be his fault.

The problem had actually dogged the U-boat force since the beginning of the war, including *U-39*'s impotent attack on *Ark Royal*. *U-27* was sunk by destroyers after firing useless torpedoes that detonated prematurely and gave away her position. These two failures had not been reported back to Germany by wireless as there had been no time before their crews abandoned ship and were captured. *U-39*'s captain was able to send a coded message back in a letter to his wife that indicated a problem with torpedoes. It persisted despite the U-boat arm's protestations that something was badly wrong and that proper rectification must be introduced.

Suggestions were noted and tweaks applied. *Perhaps torpedoes were simply being set to run too deep?* Depth-keeping adjustments were made. The Reich's torpedo boffins also advised not using magnetic pistol torpedoes in areas where the earth's magnetic field was likely to be more powerful; locations where this might be the case – such as rocky Norwegian waters – were marked off on charts and appropriate instructions issued to U-boat captains.

After they had done all that, and decreed only contact pistol weapons should be used off Norway, the torpedoes were still no good. On 18 April Dönitz fulminated in the War Log: 'All operational and tactical questions are again and again coloured by the intolerable state of the torpedo . . . The problem of where to operate the boats depends not only on the usual conditions, but in every case the question: "Will the torpedo work?" has to be considered.'

In listing his priorities for changes in operating procedures, Dönitz put 'Torpedo situation' at the top of his to do list, labelling it the 'most urgent requirement'.

Dönitz also asked for greater effort in finding countermeasures to the enemy's Asdic, which, he pointed out, was even in peacetime 'a most urgent requirement . . .' Asdic countermeasures were 'essential to the success of future U-boat warfare'. Dönitz pleaded that 'the best sonic technicians, chemists and physicists, be set to evolve a countermeasure'. In summing up the Norwegian campaign from the U-boat force's point of view, Dönitz suggested 'torpedo failures cheated the boats of certain successes, even after all doubtful shots and misses had been subtracted'.[13]

8   Magnificent Days

In stark contrast to the miserable time had by the Kriegsmarine, one Royal Navy officer described the Norwegian campaign as 'magnificent days in the story of British submariners'.[1]

What gave them their edge was the appointment in early January

1940 of Vice Admiral Sir Max Horton as Flag Officer Submarines (FOSM). He brought to bear dynamism, determination to succeed and also excellent strategic and tactical instinct born of war experience in the same seas and against the same foe. It meant that Karl Dönitz was now facing a man every bit as gritty and technically aware – and also as battle-hardened – as himself. Horton was a whirlwind, or as one staff officer put it, 'a tiger' with a bite and a growl, keen to shake things up. He drove himself as hard as his subordinates and while honest errors were tolerated 'slackness'[2] was not. His arrival came at the end of a gloomy period that could be traced back to the self-inflicted loss of *Oxley* and included the subsequent destruction of half a dozen boats at the hands of the enemy.

News of losses was flashed around the world via the Admiralty signals network. Among submariners reading of three boats lost in quick succession was Lt Alastair Mars, serving in *Regulus*, patrolling on the fringe of the ice zone near Vladivostok to keep an eye on the Japanese. The news drove Mars and other officers in *Regulus* 'almost to tears; then to anger. Someone had blundered.'[3]

It is likely B-Dienst code-breakers managed to provide advance warning of the three British submarines and, similar to *Spearfish* the previous September, the enemy placed anti-submarine patrol forces in advance. In the case of *Undine*, a German boarding party had managed to get aboard in the brief period before she sank, allegedly scooping up codebooks.

B-Dienst's success in reading British naval codes was unknown at the time, and certainly Admiralty laxness in encryption was a corporate problem. There was also a tendency to attribute unknown losses to mines, something that possibly slowed the introduction of improved countermeasures against enemy ASW forces, such as better hydrophones.

The three losses came just as Horton was picking up the reins. It made for a few black days, but while it was a knock, such things were more likely to create 'a desire for revenge'.[4] Horton immediately decided it was pointless deploying submarines too deep into the enemy's front yard, where defences were locked so tight.

There had been some British successes in late 1939, though nothing to match the spectacular results achieved by U-boats. *U-36* was the first German submarine destroyed by a British boat – *Salmon*, commanded by 30-year-old Lt Cdr Edward Bickford.

Though not yet delivering commensurate payback for the loss of *Courageous* and *Royal Oak*, British submarines did manage to damage some key units of the Kriegsmarine. While German cruisers may not have been sent to the bottom they were put out of action for some time. *Leipzig* was in dockyard hands for a year and *Nürnberg* for five months, Lt Cdr Bickford playing his part in the attacks that put them there. Added to the loss of the pocket battleship *Graf Spee* on the River Plate, Germany's surface force was experiencing a grim time and it helped lift the mood in the RN's submarine force.

As part of his house-cleaning exercise, Horton decided one handicap was the relative maturity of too many submarine captains. Drawing on his own insight into the rigours of command in war, he ordered a review of their ages. He felt only young men would be able to handle a long, hard conflict. The optimum age for submarine command was deemed to be 25, and some British submarine captains during the conflict would be as young as 22.

Ben Bryant, who commanded *Sealion* from early 1940 to October 1941, thought that 'probably the best years of a submarine CO's life are 25 to 30 – old enough to have experience, self confidence, and judgement; young enough not to think too much'.[5] Bryant himself broke that rule, as in 1940 he was 35. It didn't stop him sinking merchant ships and attacking a U-boat, nor did he lose his nerve under attack. Some men of exceptional ability – such as Bryant – could indeed handle the rigours of wartime submarine command well into their thirties (though he would not command a submarine past the age of 37).

A number of older British submarine captains were transferred out of their boats and into shore appointments or the surface navy. Bickford was among those who survived the cull. He was, after all, a national hero and globally renowned, with his exploits even featuring in *Life* magazine.

When it came to the enemy, in early 1940 Horton carefully studied what the next move might be and correctly guessed Germany would intervene in Scandinavia. Timing of deployments – knowing when to surge submarines in certain sea areas to catch the foe – was vital, and Horton judged it perfectly.

In early April intelligence indicated an invasion fleet was setting sail and it was better to sink those vessels on their way to Norway rather than wait until they were putting troops and equipment ashore. There would not be time to stop each vessel, search it and make sure it was being used for military purposes under Prize Rules. British submarine captains must be able to sink invasion ships without exposing themselves to enemy escort forces. Several recent interceptions in the North Sea of merchant shipping, including iron ore carriers, had proved tricky, almost leading to the loss of the submarines. Attacking with torpedoes while dived was the best solution but the Admiralty was still trying to occupy the moral high ground by observing Prize Rules.

Horton was a forceful character and fortunately his headquarters was in the Northways apartment block, Swiss Cottage, north London (rather than at some remote naval base). It meant he was close enough to Whitehall to obtain face-to-face meetings with senior admirals and politicians, where he exerted pressure for a change in the rules. As the Norwegian operation ramped up Horton explained that many of the likely targets were false-flag invasion vessels (troop ships flying neutral colours to deceive the British). On 9 April the War Cabinet gave the green light to sinking transport vessels heading north from Germany on sight, even if apparently neutrals.

A wireless signal was sent to all submarine captains on the picket line, which Lt Jack Slaughter, in *Sunfish*, received just as he spotted a suspicious Norway-bound German merchant ship. Eyes pressed to the periscope cups he asked for the signal to be read out to him – just to be absolutely sure – then ordered torpedoes fired. *Sunfish* bagged the *Amasis*, 7,129 tons, though it later turned out she was not an invasion vessel but was carrying coal to Oslo.

The *Orzel*, a very fast and capable Polish submarine now working under FOSM's direction, did score a devastating blow against the invader. She sank the 5,261-ton *Rio de Janeiro*, carrying hundreds of troops, artillery, horses and vehicles along with military supplies.

By 4 May British submarines had managed to sink 75,869 tons of enemy shipping. Of the 21 vessels sunk, 18 were merchant ships. In addition, the 2,400-ton gunnery training ship *Brummer* was sunk off Denmark by *Sterlet*.

On top of that, in April and May a further dozen enemy craft, including four armed trawlers and three minesweepers, totalling 10,257 tons, were sunk courtesy of mines laid by the British submarines *Narwhal* and *Seal* and the French boat *Rubis*.

The Allied successes against transport vessels off Norway were a welcome boost, but it was sinking or damaging German naval units that was the ultimate goal. *Truant*, commanded by Lt Cdr Christopher Hutchinson, managed to hit the light cruiser *Karlsruhe* off southern Norway on 10 April, damaging her so badly she had to be put down by her own escort forces.

The pocket battleship *Lützow* was attacked by *Spearfish*, which had been repaired since her torrid time in September 1939 and was now commanded by Lt Cdr John Forbes. The *Spearfish* torpedo hit caused severe damage to *Lützow*'s stern and put her out of action for a year. This was all much to the credit of the British submarine force, but there were also debits.

Tarpon was sunk in the Norwegian Sea and her entire crew killed on 10 April, the same day that *Thistle* was lost along with her men. *Thistle* had engaged *U-4* in the Norwegian Sea, close to the coast off Skudenes, but the British boat's torpedoes missed. *U-4* waited patiently for her chance to strike back, launching torpedoes that destroyed *Thistle* not long after midnight. Only a large oil patch was found when *U-4* surfaced to look for survivors. *Tarpon*'s end was unique as she was the only British submarine sunk by a German Q-ship, *Schiff 40*. She had not managed to deceive *Tarpon* but gained the upper hand after the submarine's attack on her failed. The sonar-equipped *Schiff 40* undertook a three-hour hunt for *Tarpon* and, after successive depth-charge barrages, wreckage was blown to the surface, along with human remains and documents.

A week later *Sterlet* was lost in the Skagerrak and again there were no survivors. On 5 May came the controversial loss of the large Porpoise Class minelaying submarine *Seal* in the Kattegat, which struck a mine, though none of her men was killed. They were captured along with the submarine and *Seal* was later pressed into service as the training boat *U-B*.

An ominous discovery was made at the end of May after the small Type IIB boat *U-13* was attacked and sunk by the sloop HMS *Weston* off the east coast of England. Charts retrieved from *Seal* had been used to enable *U-13* to thread her way through minefields off Suffolk, where she was determined to lie in wait for targets. Forced to the surface, *U-13*'s entire crew were saved, including her captain, 24-year-old Oberleutnant Max Schulte.

When a Royal Navy diver went down to the submarine wreck a sheaf of standing orders from Karl Dönitz was retrieved. Among them was an instruction banning U-boat captains from rescuing survivors from ships attacked off the British Isles. Dönitz felt they were unwisely risking their boats and crews in waters heavily patrolled by the Royal Navy and where there was plenty of enemy air cover.

In his Standing Order Number 154, issued in late November 1939, Dönitz, stated: 'Do not pick up survivors and take them with you. Do not worry about the merchant-ship's boats. Weather conditions and distance from land play no part. Have a care only for your own ship and strive only to attain your next success as soon as possible. We must be harsh in this war. The enemy began the war in order to destroy us, so nothing else matters.'[6]

9   Last Stand of the *Shark*

In the summer of 1940, with the Battle of Britain raging in the skies over southern England, *Shark* deployed yet again to patrol off the coast of occupied Norway. As the S Class boat headed across the North Sea to relieve *Sealion* off Stavanger she encountered bad weather. Forced to take a star fix at night in rough seas on 5 July, in order to be sure of her position, *Shark* had not long been on the surface – at a time of year when there was no true darkness in the Arctic – when a lookout spotted an aircraft.

The boat made a crash dive and it was then, as 28-year-old Signaller Eric Eaton would colourfully describe it, 'this bloody great bomb hit the stern of us'.[1] In fact two or three depth charges had exploded around the boat, the first time German aircraft had used them in anger against a submarine.

Shark plunged to over 450ft, 'which in those days was pretty dodgy', suggested Eaton – especially when the maximum test dive ever conducted by the boat was 200ft. '. . . the telemotor system packed up, the [hydro]planes were stuck hard to dive [there was] a big hole in us,' he said, 'water was pouring in. All the lights went out. A big pot of stew on the [cooking] range tipped over ... we were going sliding down at an angle of about 45 degrees, pretty fast ... everybody was hanging on to what they could ... just couldn't get the boat under control at all.'

Radical action was needed and the captain, 30-year-old Lt Peter Buckley, ordered the boat's ten-ton drop keel to be released. Suddenly much lighter, the badly injured *Shark* shot to the surface.

The worst of several serious problems was damaged propulsion and a jammed rudder, which meant *Shark* could only go in circles and there was no possibility of diving. One of the battery sections was also creating smoke and fumes despite not being connected to the drive. A wireless message was sent to FOSM explaining where the boat was and that she was stuck on the surface.

In the dangerous, exposed Arctic summer twilight the likelihood of escaping further attention was slim. Before climbing up onto the bridge, Buckley briefed his men on the inevitability of having to fight it out using small arms and the boat's 3-inch gun.

Most of *Shark*'s men went up to the bridge and casing while the others set about destroying equipment or ditching secret materials over the side in the weighted bag. Scuttling charges were prepared in the torpedo room and wireless cabin. Eaton and Lt Buckley manhandled the Lewis machine gun up the ladder. Others armed themselves with rifles while some helped get shells for the 3-inch gun up via another hatch and onto the gun platform.

It was around midnight, with *Shark*'s men finding 'half the German air force waiting for us', according to Eaton. 'I fitted it [the Lewis gun] in the brass tube screwed to the side of the bridge ...'

He had just done this when he saw 'this plane coming. About 100 yards away he opened fire and so did I and I felt a wave of bullets whisk past my head ...'

Various types of German aircraft joined the assault, cannon shells ripping holes in a ballast tank, making the submarine list to starboard. Two men either fell into the sea or were washed off the casing, never to be seen again.

Shark's plucky few did their hopeless best, with Eaton on the machine gun and six submariners shooting back with rifles from the bridge. A well-aimed shot from the 3-inch gun exploded close enough to a German bomber to see it off, emitting smoke and sparks from an engine.

Despite all this, it was clear who would ultimately triumph.

'We were just a sitting duck,' thought Eaton. 'I don't know what good we did apart from boosting our morale and keeping busy.'

A young stoker said to Eaton: 'Give me a bloody rifle and I'll have a go!' Before the lad could pull the trigger a Messerschmitt Me-109 strafed *Shark*. Everything but the stoker's legs disappeared in a red mist. Another submariner had his arm ripped off.

Buckley told Eaton to cease firing and climb down from the conning tower to the casing. 'I think the boat is going to sink,' he explained.

Eaton did as ordered but was blown off into the sea when a bomb exploded nearby. Blacking out for a few seconds, he regained his senses to find *Shark* still going around in a circle. Someone threw him a heaving line, which he grabbed, and he was pulled back aboard just as more enemy aircraft swooped.

By that time all the ammunition was spent, so *Shark*'s men were utterly defenceless. 'We couldn't do anything short of chucking nuts and bolts at them,' said Eaton, 'another bloke got blown overboard and drowned.'

They had no alternative but to surrender. Someone was sent down to the wardroom to fetch a tablecloth, which was the only large white thing aboard. This was waved at a circling Dornier, which sent back a light signal, instructing *Shark* to heave to or head for Stavanger.

Buckley ordered all stop. The secret material had been disposed of and the boat wouldn't stay afloat for much longer, so scuttling was not needed.

An Arado seaplane landed and taxied alongside the submarine, two crewmen jumping out of the cockpit. They climbed down from their aircraft and clambered across to *Shark*, revolvers in hand.

Eaton's Lewis gun must have riddled one of the floats on their aircraft with bullets because the Arado toppled over and sank. This left the two Germans surrounded by bloodied, fierce-looking British submariners.

Eaton observed: 'they were most uneasy.'

Fortunately for the enemy aviators a large Dornier seaplane landed and sent over some men in an inflatable dinghy to take Lt Buckley and the submarine's First Lieutenant away to Stavanger.

An enemy armed trawler took the *Shark*'s men off the sinking submarine. With the wounded taken to a hospital, the rest of the British were held prisoner at a schoolhouse in Stavanger while a decision was taken on what to do with them.[2] A German officer came visiting, congratulating the submariners on their five-hour fight. 'You are all brave men,' he told them, 'but bloody fools. I salute you.'[3]

Shark's fate showed how aircraft with effective weaponry could swiftly overwhelm, incapacitate and sink a submarine that had discarded its primary defensive cloak of invisibility.

The attack on *U-30* by *Ark Royal*'s Skuas failed due to defective tactics and weaponry, but the Swordfish of *Warspite* had proved lethal with just one well-placed, armour-piercing bomb. The Germans had now used a swarm of aircraft – some armed with depth charges and cannons – to demonstrate conclusively that the war at sea now had to be fought in three dimensions: on the surface, under it and in the air.

It would take some time for certain senior officers to admit that even the strongest battleship was vulnerable to such an assault, never mind a submarine. After the loss of *U-64* in the Norwegian campaign Admiral Dönitz was already aware of the potential threat, but one of his fellow First World War veteran U-boat commanders had years earlier predicted such a situation would come to pass. In 1927 Korvettenkapitän Heino von Heimburg completed a study into future submarine types and tactics, which observed, among other things, that submarine captains would have to grasp 'that in all seas and at any moment they can be spotted and attacked from the air'. Furthermore, U-boats should 'accept battle on the surface against aircraft only rarely and reluctantly'.[4]

Von Heimburg felt submarines should not reveal themselves above the surface in daylight conditions. The submariners of *Shark* would heartily agree and no doubt say Amen to that. *Shark*'s last stand ranks in its own small way as high as Rorke's Drift or Little Big Horn in the annals of courageous defiance. Instead of a grassy hill or a remote mission station in South Africa her men fought it out from the conning tower and casing of their boat.

When devising how to counter a potential U-boat menace during a future war, British naval planners had not envisaged Germany gaining possession of Atlantic ports. They had hoped to bottle up the Kriegsmarine in its North Sea and Baltic boltholes, but that strategy was blown away when France was conquered with lightning speed in the summer of 1940.

The subsequent Dunkirk evacuation in late May and early June – codenamed Operation Dynamo – also seriously undermined Britain's ability to counter the U-boat threat. Destroyers badly needed to escort convoys and sink submarines were pitched into the effort and suffered badly.

Even before Dynamo got fully underway escorts were taken away from the anti-submarine effort to support British troops hemmed in by German invaders. Some took reinforcements across the Channel, even providing artillery support with their guns.

More than 40 destroyers were committed to lifting troops from Dunkirk, sometimes carrying 1,000 men at a time back to England, often weathering merciless enemy air attack.

Between 19 May and 1 June eight destroyers were sunk and numerous warships were damaged. A cruiser, 19 destroyers and seven minesweepers were put out of action for some time.

That U-boats did not intervene in strength to attack enemy warships when they were extremely vulnerable off Dunkirk and loaded with troops is perhaps surprising. This failure was due to the need for U-boat crews to be rested and vessels to receive maintenance after Norway.

One boat did enter the fray, *U-62*, which played a part in the sinking of the destroyer *Grafton* on 29 May, 13 miles to the north of Nieuport during a wild, confusing night fight. Silhouetted by explosions, *Grafton* made a wonderful target for *U-62*, commanded by Oberleutnant Hans-Bernhard Michalowski. He fired a torpedo that blew off the destroyer's stern and a subsequent S-boat torpedo hit compounded the damage. Observing the end of *Grafton* through his periscope, Michalowski spotted the menacing shape of what appeared to be a British destroyer coming towards him and withdrew.

The punishment inflicted on Britain's destroyer force during Operation Dynamo was so severe – and on 1 June casualties included *Basilisk* – the First Sea Lord ordered the most modern ships withdrawn for fear of losing them for convoy escort work.[5]

Just as the U-boats had been spent after Norway, so their main foe was debilitated by Dunkirk and there would be a knock-on effect when escorts were needed again to combat the revived German submarine force.

The capture of the French Atlantic ports presented an opportunity to Admiral Dönitz for launching an oceanic variant of the Blitzkrieg, and in the second half of 1940 up to 16 U-boats were deployed into the Atlantic simultaneously.

They could cut straight into the convoy routes, their journey to the most important hunting grounds shortened by 1,000 miles. It increased their reach and endurance on patrol, with U-boats not having to go around the north of Scotland unless they absolutely needed to. The Channel could be avoided altogether.

When it came to the troublesome 'eels', for the time being – until other types of torpedo could be made equally trustworthy – only contact pistol torpedoes would be used. Torpedoes with contact pistols captured aboard HMS *Seal* had been tested and found to be very reliable, so Dönitz suggested they should be copied. The pace of U-boat construction also accelerated.

Dönitz would be the theatre director, aiming when the time was right to finally unleash his wolf packs onto the stage, building on the small-scale experiment of autumn 1939. He would co-ordinate the entire effort via wireless communications from a new headquarters in France.

The U-boat force boss planned to allocate roles to his star players and supporting actors, bringing to fruition a new form of submarine warfare that he had first concocted in 1918, while brooding over his fate in a prison camp.

The British, meanwhile, were increasingly anxious as it dawned on them that nowhere like enough U-boats were being destroyed. Yet the tendency to blame the messenger persisted, rather than double down on efforts to improve tactics and anti-submarine technology.

Under heavy pressure to justify his approach to deciding how many enemy submarines had been sunk, in mid-September 1940 Capt. Talbot submitted a paper citing a number of instances where U-boat kills turned out to be nothing of the sort. He wanted to outline how exacting detective work was necessary.

Sometimes old wrecks were detected on Asdic and attacked. On 11 October 1939 the destroyer *Winchelsea* and the anti-submarine trawler *Loch Tulla* made an attack after getting a good contact in Liverpool Bay. The sighting of oil on the surface was thought evidence of a submarine sunk. When divers went down in January 1940 they found 'the old wreck of a small coasting vessel, lying bottom up, with a hole through it, apparently made quite recently. The wreck was still exuding oil.'[6]

Ships that had fallen victim to U-boats could also waste the efforts of anti-submarine vessels. Talbot presented a particularly poignant example: 'On the 5th February, 1940, HMS *Antelope* attacked a contact . . . and the ship and Commander-in-Chief, Western Approaches both considered that a U-Boat was destroyed. The Asdic evidence was not good, and the Assessment Committee came to the conclusion that *Antelope* had probably attacked the after part of the S.S. *San Alberto*, which had been torpedoed in the vicinity about 7 weeks previously; the wreck was known to have broken in two, and the after part had drifted some 12 miles before finally sinking.'[7]

Sometimes the errors were made by over-eager naval aviators, like the Swordfish flight who said they made a torpedo attack on a U-boat at 8.00 p.m. on 5 July 1940, claiming two hits. Unfortunately they had picked on one of their own. The British submarine *Tetrarch* 'reported she had been attacked by aircraft at the time and position sighted, and that she was undamaged'.

Talbot felt that his department was doing excellent work in uncovering the true state of affairs, for spies in Germany confirmed the accuracy of its assessments. By July 1940 the Germans had lost 27 submarines and so Capt. Talbot by his own analysis reckoned 25 had been destroyed since 3 September 1939. Despite being correct, Talbot 'was nevertheless relieved of his appointment',[8] not an uncommon fate for naval staff officers who contradicted Churchill. The PM still felt many more enemy submarines *must* have been destroyed.

Sinking U-boats remained fundamental to keeping Britain in the war, as it was so reliant on sea trade for its survival. Raw materials and products flowed to Britain from all corners of the globe while its own goods were traditionally exported around the world, especially to the markets of the Empire.

As remains the case today, sending things by sea was far cheaper than any other means of transportation. The Merchant Navy that carried things to and from Britain along the ocean highways was still vast, numbering 1,900 ships, and when war broke out in September 1939 55 million tons of foodstuffs and raw materials were being imported to the UK annually.[9] In the summer before war broke out Britain was consuming 30 per cent of the world's wheat, 25 per cent of its beef and 40 per cent of its tea. It devoured a 40 per cent share of the world's exported oil, 25 per cent of its copper and a quarter of its pig iron. Britain took 50 per cent of Canada's wheat exports and most of Australia's. Germany, Belgium and Italy combined imported less wheat than Britain. Sugar – to go with all the tea imported primarily from Ceylon and India – came to British shores from 27 countries. The British even outdid the Germans in tobacco imports.[10]

While imports from far across the sea were vital, trade with Europe – especially aboard the vessels of the large Scandinavian merchant fleets – was crucial, while exports and imports carried by non-British vessels could not be overlooked. It all made Britain the hub of a vast globalised trading system and per head of population the 48 million Britons possessed the highest income of any European state.[11]

Prior to the war, Britain imported 22 million tons of foodstuffs but by the end of November 1940 it would be less than 12 million.[12] Next to food, space in ships' holds was mostly taken up by timber, not least pit props for the coal industry.

Rationing of oil, petrol and coal, along with clothes and food, started in early 1940, with limits per person placed on the consumption of sugar, bacon, butter and ham. Other things were restricted as the war went on, with adults permitted up to three pints of milk a week and three eggs a month. Certain types of food (including imported fruits) were still available off ration, but were rare and expensive. It was a case of eking out certain foods while not restricting those that were plentiful – there was no limit on bread or vegetables, so people would not starve, though they might lack certain elements of a balanced diet. While the British people were not in imminent danger of starving, the war effort might grind to a halt if the convoys didn't get through.

Priority was put on ensuring the armed forces were well fed throughout the conflict, along with providing the essential war materials. If the troops couldn't be fed or armed then Britain's capitulation might be achieved. It was obvious the best means of knocking the British out of the war remained destroying their sea trade – cutting lifelines to the Empire and other sources of supply. While the Royal Navy reigned supreme above the waves its Achilles heel remained how well it had – or had not – prepared for anti-submarine warfare and how many warships it could devote to that effort.

Of vital importance was President Franklin D. Roosevelt's achievement in getting the Neutrality Act of 1939 passed by Congress. This amended earlier legislation that had required the USA to impose a blanket ban on supplying belligerents with weaponry and munitions. The Neutrality Act, approved on 4 November, allowed other nations to procure war materials in the USA, so long as they put cash down and then carried them away in their own ships. This automatically favoured Britain and her allies, who controlled the majority of the world's merchant shipping, while Germany possessed none of those advantages.

It was a pretty good deal for America too. It meant that it was not in the business of extending credit in lieu of payment to nations that might well run out of the means to pay it back.

Securing a source of war materials and other supplies was one thing, but the problem of scarce escorts continued to dog Britain's efforts. The Royal Navy's destroyers – hard-hit during the evacuation from France – were also kept close to home during the summer 1940 invasion scare. New vessels, most notably Flower Class corvettes, were gradually supplementing them but they would take some months to enter service in significant numbers.

Meanwhile a ragbag of pre-war sloops and armed trawlers were far from ideal stopgaps, while older V and W Class destroyers from the First World War were pulled out of reserve. Britain was also negotiating with the hard-nosed Americans to take over 50 obsolete Town Class destroyers the US Navy felt it did not need.

Aside from the scarcity of available ships and aircraft, from the summer of 1940 pressure was exerted strategically in the Mediterranean. After France surrendered and the Vichy regime gained control in the south, its fleet was no longer available to patrol the western basin.

With the entry of Italy into the war a new Royal Navy task group called Force H had to be formed, based at Gibraltar under Admiral Somerville, to handle the Western Med and operations out into the Atlantic.

Italy possessed a powerful and modern battle fleet along with the biggest submarine force in the world prior to the war, even if its 115 boats were not always the best, nor their crews the most aggressive.

A squadron of large, ocean-going Italian submarines was sent to operate from Bordeaux against the Atlantic convoys, while in the

Mediterranean Italian anti-submarine units were very active. They sank a series of British submarines in a short space of time: *Odin* (13 June 1940), *Grampus* (16 June), *Orpheus* (19 June) and *Phoenix* (16 July) were all lost without a single survivor, though *Parthian* sank the Italian submarine *Diamante* on 20 June.

British submarine casualties mounted elsewhere, too. *Narwhal* was lost to enemy air attack in the North Sea on 23 July, while *Spearfish* was sunk off Norway on 1 August by *U-34*. There was just one survivor.

Meanwhile, tension also mounted in the Far East with the Japanese taking advantage of events in Europe to occupy French Indochina. Another consequence of the French capitulation was a strange confrontation aboard the *Surcouf* at Devonport in July 1940. Having only returned to European waters with the Kingston, Jamaica convoy in late 1939, *Surcouf* had no experience of operating with the Royal Navy and therefore no rapport with the host service. Her crew were hostile towards the idea of fighting under British command and when, in July 1940, the RN insisted on taking her over, they resisted. Three British sailors were killed and one Frenchman. By contrast with that bloodletting, *Rubis* came over peacefully to continue working with the British as a Free French submarine.

Apart from worrying about unreliable former comrades-in-arms there was continuing anxiety in Britain about Ireland being used for U-boat operations. During the First World War the Royal Navy had bases in the south of Ireland, but now only Londonderry and Belfast, the main ports of Ulster, remained British. Until 1938 Treaty Ports in Ireland had been open to use by the Royal Navy but in a rash act the British government had given up that right.

Rear Admiral Godfrey was among those who worried about ensuring neutral Ireland did not actively assist the Germans, particularly their submarines. U-boats might exploit bleak, remote, jagged inlets to refuel and resupply from replenishment ships. Ireland realised that it could not seal itself hermetically from the war and it certainly didn't want to alienate its much larger, more powerful neighbour by allowing U-boats to use its harbours.

The Irish anxiety would resurface at various times during the war, though Ireland's military was keen not to see its nation's hospitality abused. There was a measure of unofficial co-operation, including British air reconnaissance of the west coast.

U-boats did actually venture into Irish bays. In the first month of the war *U-35* visited Ventry to offload 28 Greek mariners rescued after sinking their ship. Abwehr agent Walter Simon was landed at Dingle Bay, County Kerry on 13 June 1940 by *U-38*. His objective was to spy on British ship movements but Simon was captured after getting drunk in a pub and ranting about the Irish being liberated by Hitler. He was sentenced to three years in prison for entering Ireland illegally.

Stories circulated of German submarines allegedly visiting Irish harbours so their crews could buy fresh eggs and vegetables, with one U-boat captain supposedly shouting: 'Come on, Maggie, hurry up with those cabbages!'[13] The veracity of these yarns was dubious. As one Irish newspaper observed, 'most of the German subs were actually seen in pubs'.[14]

10 Wolves Unleashed

Once again Germany's young submariners were faced with shouldering a great responsibility and pulling off a feat their fathers' generation failed to deliver.

Despite the scale of the challenge Dönitz sensed the initiative could decisively swing towards Germany and that needed as many U-boats at sea as possible with the Luftwaffe weighing in more heavily to help find convoys and mark them down for attack.

The Führer was enthusiastic about the campaign, for the success of Prien above all persuaded Hitler that the U-boat was a weapon of real strategic potency. This was being translated into resources for submarine construction.

It was very troubling for the Admiralty that, even with a small number of craft, the Germans seemed to be gaining the upper hand. Stalking U-boats were especially good at picking off stragglers as they fell behind. Or they preyed on those vessels that forged ahead of convoys, which at the time generally contained ships capable of between 9 and 14.9 knots.[1] Ships faster than 15 knots sailed solo, while special convoys were arranged for those that could only manage 6 or 7 knots.

On making a convoy sighting a U-boat did not immediately attack but would send a signal to the submarine force headquarters, which then directed other boats into an interception position. The wolf packs would, under long-range direction from Dönitz, place themselves in a line ahead of the convoy – on its anticipated route – ideally waiting for night to fall. They would surface to make their attack runs, following motor torpedo boat-style tactics laid down by Dönitz, hoping to penetrate between slow-moving merchant vessels, getting right inside the convoy. If a torpedo failed to hit an intended victim, there was a good chance it would get another.

With a surfaced top speed of around 17 knots Type VII U-boats could escape retribution from much slower escort vessels, diving only if they looked likely to be caught. Once removed from immediate danger they would surface again and try to make another attack run before dawn. On 30 August the code-breakers of B-Dienst managed to provide key intelligence. They had picked up Admiralty wireless messages giving away the co-ordinates of where a convoy would link up with escort vessels for the final leg of the voyage to the UK.

Having tried to make the wolf pack concept work in the autumn of 1940 – and failing against convoy KJ-3 – the attack on convoy SC-2 would be another serious bid to prove it could work.

Convoy designations indicated points of departure and which direction they were running. The primary convoy routes were Halifax to Britain (HX, a fast convoy); Gibraltar to Britain (HG); Sierra Leone to Britain (SL). SC-2 was made up of 53 vessels and assembled at Sydney, Nova Scotia, hence the name SC, though inevitably convoys departing from there were colloquially known as Slow Convoys.

Departing on 25 August, SC-2 was spread out across several miles of sea, crawling along at around 6 knots. Most of the ships were elderly and some were older than the century. For the majority of the voyage across the Atlantic, SC-2 would have no escort, with warships protecting it only for the last 400 miles. The route had changed from that followed during the First World War, in order to place convoys as far away from the U-boats as possible. Convoys still headed for major ports on the west coast of Britain but came in via the North-West Approaches.

It was standard practice for convoys to be commanded by a commodore, who might be a retired Royal Navy senior officer – in his fifties or sixties, often with experience of command in battle – or a senior merchant marine officer drafted into the Royal Naval Reserve (RNR).

After being reactivated these men attended a course at the naval staff college in Greenwich, learning how to manage convoys from aboard a designated merchant vessel, using a small staff of naval personnel. The subjects studied included contemporary communications techniques, weaponry fitted to merchant ships, how convoys were formed and organised in port and how they should conduct themselves on the high seas, plus how to work with escort commanders.

One of the early convoy commodores, though not on SC-2, was Frederic Dreyer who had only recently retired as a full admiral. By 1939 he was 61 years old but had the energy of a much younger man and plenty of opinions. Dreyer had served as Assistant Director of ASW in the Admiralty in 1917 and held very senior posts in the inter-war RN.

For years he had been telling the Admiralty it was unwisely putting all its anti-submarine eggs in the Asdic basket. His warnings had been ignored.

He explained that numbers mattered, reminding the RN top brass of the 1930s that when convoys started properly in 1917 the British had 339 destroyers and by November the following year the figure was 433. In September 1939 the British were down to 184 destroyers. By November 1918 the RN fielded 3,100 other patrol vessels whereas in September 1939 it had 63.

Dreyer warned that the anti-submarine problem was 'extraordinarily difficult and is particularly so for those who are unaccustomed to handling ships in all weathers and use of all manner of weapons and instruments at sea'.[2]

In 1936 the First Sea Lord (Ernle Chatfield) told Dreyer that Britain would not require 'anything like the number of ships to protect our trade against submarine attack that we required in 1917 because our anti-submarine methods are far advanced beyond what they were at that date'.[3] So much confidence had been placed in Asdic that between the wars it was even thought unnecessary to rehearse the skills of convoying.

Roderick Macdonald, a future British admiral, but a very junior officer serving in a battleship in 1940, claimed there was 'no record of any exercise in the protection of a slow convoy against submarine or air attack between 1919 and 1939'. This was, Macdonald felt, due to 'unjustifiable reliance on a primitive underwater sound detection system [Asdic] even though U-boats had attacked on the surface at night in World War One – escorts [were] designed for a second Jutland and not for anti-submarine work in the Atlantic'.[4]

In comparison to other skills and trades, such as gunnery, signals and torpedoes, the ASW specialisation 'was thought of as second class'.

Macdonald found that when he and other junior officers went on training courses they 'suffered more time on the parade ground than we spent in the anti-submarine trainer'. These errors were the product not of ignorant politicians, felt Macdonald, but the navy's attitude. It bore responsibility for 'undeniably professional cock ups'.

In autumn 1940 the hard reality of 'professional cock-ups' was about to hit convoy SC-2 – and the deficiencies highlighted by Dreyer and Macdonald were to be cruelly exposed.

By the night of 6 September it had reached the rendezvous point with its escorts, to the south and west of Iceland. The Northern Escort Force was led by the sloop *Lowestoft*, whose captain was 40-year-old Cdr Arthur Knapp. Also at his disposal were *Scarborough*, another sloop built in the mid-1930s, the 1920s vintage Canadian destroyer *Skeena*, and *Westcott*, an unmodernised First World War-era destroyer. There was also *Periwinkle*, one of the new Flower Class corvettes (only commissioned in April 1940) and a pair of trawlers adapted for anti-submarine work, *St Apollo* and *Berkshire*. With the exception of *Skeena* and *Westcott* none of these ships was fast enough to catch a U-boat on the surface.

That the convoy had got so far without a single ship lost was a miracle. A gale brought some security, as rough seas precluded an effective U-boat attack, but it couldn't last for ever and plumes of smoke from the funnels of the ancient coal burners were a dead giveaway.

Though this was their first time on Atlantic escort duty, Cdr Knapp and *Lowestoft*'s crew were at least battle hardened, having faced the enemy numerous times while escorting convoys off the east coast of Britain.

The foe in that combat arena had been enemy torpedo boats and aircraft and while *Lowestoft* now had Asdic, she was not yet fitted with surface search radar, which would prove to be a critical handicap.

Dönitz had ordered three submarines to arrange themselves to the south west of Iceland. Günther Prien in *U-47* was to work with *U-65* and *U-101*, the latter making the first contact but soon being spotted by *Skeena* and *Periwinkle* and forced to dive. The weather deteriorated again, but once it cleared *U-65* acted as a marker, trailing the convoy on the surface, an indicator beacon declaring her position to other U-boats and Dönitz. On the night of 7 September Prien came in first, on the surface – unseen by any of the escorts – making short work of three merchant ships.

The 5,017-ton *José de Larrinaga* was carrying scrap metal and linseed oil. Of her 40-strong crew none survived, for ships carrying iron, steel ingots, oil or ammunition were the worst to sail in. They either burned (tankers), sank in seconds (ore and metal carriers) or blew up (ammunition ships). Forty-seven men lost their lives in Prien's other victims, the grain carrier *Gro* and *Neptunian*, with a cargo of sugar.

RAF Sunderland flying boats were overhead by 8 September, forcing the U-boats to remain submerged during daylight hours and fall behind, but under cover of night they surfaced and made speed to catch up.

Prien added to his tally by sinking the Greek-flagged *Possidon* (carrying sulphur phosphate) with 17 of her crew killed. *U-28* and *U-99* also attacked, with the former sinking the cargo carrier *Mardinian*. In the face of this onslaught no submarines were sunk, though some of their lunges were parried.

For the captain of *U-99*, Kapitänleutnant Otto Kretschmer, SC-2 was a dismal failure, which was not something he was used to or could tolerate.

A tough but decent man, the 28-year-old Kretschmer would be described by one of his sailors as 'cold blooded'.[5] Others thought him 'a quiet, deliberate man' who 'looked more like a student than a U-Boat Captain'.[6] His sailors were very loyal to him and swelled with pride at being national heroes, especially when their captain joined Prien and other top scorers in receiving the Knight's Cross for 100,000 tons of shipping sunk. Kretschmer disliked the fuss and attention the Reich showered on him, and the label 'Tonnage King', but put up with the brass bands, the girls throwing garlands around his neck and glittering public relations events where flashbulbs crackled. It was good for crew morale.

Kretschmer was ruthless in the moment of attack but when possible showed kindness to the survivors of the ships he sank, which he was obliged to do of course by international law. He did not hate the British, for he had studied English literature at Exeter in Devon for a year in the late 1920s and understood the character of the foe perhaps better than many of his contemporaries.

Kapitänleutnant Otto Kretschmer in November 1940. (*BArchiv, Bild 183-L22207/ Alwin Tölle*)

He gained the nickname 'Silent Otto' because he disliked the need for Admiral Dönitz to communicate all the time with his U-boats and refused to play along. He correctly judged that too much to and fro with signals – many of them operationally unnecessary – was unwise, as it might signpost a boat's location. Kretschmer preferred to keep wireless communications minimal and 'take advantage of whatever the passing moment offered and made no elaborate plans for attacking convoys',[7] which was the very antithesis of the Dönitz method.

Having started the war in *U-23*, Krestchmer took command of the brand-new Type VIIB *U-99* in February 1940. After a period of sea trials and crew work-up the boat set out from Kiel on her first patrol in June 1940. She had a gold-painted horseshoe fixed to each side of her conning tower to bring her luck, which they did, but the leadership of her exceptional captain was key to the boat's survival during some very close calls when depth-charged on earlier patrols.

What unfolded during the attack on SC-2 took the shine off Kretschmer's recently presented Knight's Cross, with *U-99* achieving no sinkings. Regardless of Kretschmer's bad luck, the successful assembly and attack by a wolf pack and the sinking of five ships out of SC-2's 53, although not a serious loss for the British, was a forewarning of an even bigger assault.

11   The Quiet Fury of Silent Otto

Departing Liverpool in mid-September 1940 and heading for Canada was the cargo liner *City of Benares* and among those aboard were 90 children being sent overseas to safety.

By 17 September *City of Benares* was 250 miles to the west of the Hebrides, one of 20 vessels in convoy OB-213. At 10.00 p.m. a torpedo fired by *U-48*, now commanded by 31-year-old Kapitänleutnant Heinrich Bleichrodt, hit the liner in the stern.

There had been regular abandon ship drills aboard *City of Benares*, with the children rehearsing how to put on and take off their lifejackets, although by the time *U-48* sighted the convoy it was believed the submarine danger had passed. Some children were killed in the initial explosion, as the torpedo detonated under their cabins, while others were trapped aboard ship or died when lifeboats smashed into the side of the liner and they were tipped into the sea.

City of Benares took an hour to sink and if they did not get into lifeboats survivors clung on to rafts, many of them perishing. One man lost five of his ten children in the *City of Benares*,[1] while only 13 of the evacuee children who had boarded the ship four days earlier on the Mersey would be rescued.

The *City of Benares* sinking shocked the world. The children had been sent away to escape death at the hands of Luftwaffe bombers only to be killed by a U-boat, *The Times* labelling it a 'brutal and barbarous slaughter'.[2] US Secretary of State Cordell Hull branded it 'a most dastardly act'.[3] The Germans denied they bore any responsibility, claiming no U-boat had torpedoed a British ship marked as a passenger vessel. It was suggested by one 'semi-official source' in Berlin that *City of Benares* hit a British mine. If it was true, said this source, 'that British children went down with a British steamship it would naturally be regretted in German quarters'.[4] Still squirming, the Nazi spokesmen said Germany was entitled to attack armed merchant vessels anyway.

The *City of Benares* torpedoing hardened attitudes in Britain. Lt Cdr Joseph Braithwaite, MP for Holderness, told Parliament: 'the time has come to blast the enemy and destroy his homes as he has destroyed ours'.

Braithwaite recalled that on the outbreak of hostilities Neville Chamberlain had remarked, 'we had no quarrel with the German people'.

The MP felt that was 'not true now', and he went on: 'After 18 months of the bombing of civilians, the machine-gunning of refugees on the roads, the attacks on merchant seamen and passengers in open boats, the sinking of the "City of Benares," and the bombing of our ancient buildings, all gloated over by the German people, the time for that kind of talk has gone.'[5]

The kind of total war at sea exemplified by the torpedoing of the *City of Benares* required the net of destruction to be cast across a huge area of ocean. The stripe of U-boats across the likely intended route of a convoy could be up to 100 miles broad and lookouts in the evenly spaced submarines would hopefully be able to spot the ships. Their watch was combined with the efforts of hydrophone operators, who could pick up the sound of merchant vessels approaching from between 80 and 100 miles away.[6] A U-boat trailing the merchant ships continued transmitting information on the course and speed of the target.

There is, however, no tougher test of a plan than actual contact with the enemy, and the period 21–22 September 1940 would put both sides under pressure. The attempt to form a stripe across the path of convoy

The backbone of Germany's second attempt to win a war with a submarine campaign, the Type VII U-boat. This one was caught on the surface in July 1943 and is under attack from Allied aircraft.

A painting entitled 'Going to England', Claus Bergen's highly evocative depiction of a U-boat going forth to attack and defeat Britain in 1939, with Luftwaffe bombers overhead.

The prime target of Germany's U-boats in the Second World War: a North Atlantic convoy.

Senior Axis officers watch as an Italian submarine of the Liuzzi Class returns to Bordeaux after completing a war patrol.

The top-scoring Allied submarine captain in the Second World War and CO of HMS *Upholder*, Lt Cdr Malcolm David Wanklyn, pictured at Malta on 24 May 1941. On the right is his First Lieutenant, Lt J. R. D. Drummond.

A First World War regenerated V&W Class destroyer, HMS *Wolverine* may or may not have destroyed *U-47*, along with the boat's captain, Gunther Prien, and her entire crew. *Wolverine* shared in the destruction of *U-76* and, while under the command of Peter Gretton, sank the Italian submarine *Dagabur*.

HMS *Seawolf*, which Lt Dick Raikes commanded while operating out of a Soviet base in the Kola Peninsula during the Second World War.

Ensign Kazuo Sakamaki's midget submarine aground in the surf on Waimanalo Beach following the Pearl Harbor attack.

The famous periscope shot of the Japanese destroyer HIJMS *Yamakaze* sinking on 25 June 1942 after being torpedoed by USS *Nautilus*, about 75 miles southwest of Yokohama.

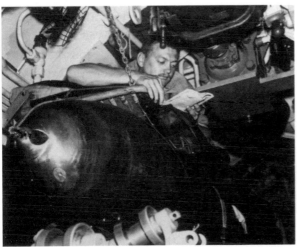

(*left*) Aboard the American submarine *Bullhead*, a submariner spends off-duty time reading in his bunk, nestled atop a torpedo-loading rack.

USS *Wahoo* in August 1942 off Mare Island Navy Shipyard, California, where she was built.

A post-war shot of US Navy destroyer sailors loading hedgehog projectiles on the starboard projector of their ship — it was a weapon system first proven in combat by the British during the Battle of the Atlantic and used into the Cold War.

Wearing his combat dress, the legendary U-boat hunter Captain Frederic 'Johnny' Walker gives orders via a loud hailer system from the bridge of HMS *Starling* in early 1944. He is watching HMS *Woodpecker* close in for the kill.

An image taken by an aviator in a US Navy aircraft attacking *U-848* southwest of Ascension Island on 5 November 1943. German submariners take cover wherever they can. *U-848* was ultimately sunk with the loss of all but one of her 63 men.

The legendary Black Swan Class sloop HMS *Starling*, in which Captain Frederic 'Johnny' Walker led his 2nd Escort Group on its early 1944 killing spree. Commissioned in the spring of 1943, by the end of the war *Starling* had played a decisive role in sinking more than a dozen enemy submarines, a total unrivalled by an escort in any navy. She destroyed three of them solo.

(*left*) In the latter phase of the Battle of the Atlantic, a depth charge explodes astern of the US Coast Guard Cutter *Duane*.

The Type IXC/40 submarine *U-534*, which was sunk by British aircraft in the Baltic at the end of the war in Europe but in 1993 raised. Today *U-534* is preserved as a tourist attraction called 'U-boat Story' at Woodside, Birkenhead, just across the River Mersey from what was the RN's main escort base in the Battle of the Atlantic.

U-858 is brought to anchor off Cape Henlopen, Delaware, in May 1945 after being surrendered at sea, with a Sikorsky HNS-I helicopter and US Navy blimp overhead.

HX-72 did not work, so U-boats had to be guided by the latest location and heading reports provided by Prien in *U-47*, performing the trailing job.

Kretschmer headed for the convoy as ordered, not feeling the need to send a signal by way of acknowledgement to U-boat headquarters, but a novice captain's habits sent him into a fury. This officer had first of all transmitted a wireless message to Dönitz confirming he had joined the unsuccessful 'stripe', then let him know he'd left it and was well underway to intercepting the convoy. Even though the British could not read what the signals actually said, Kretschmer feared they would triangulate the point of origin, alerting the convoy to the presence of enemy submarines. He was tempted to send a signal telling the other captain to stop his damned broadcasting.

U-99 made a fast surface transit to the likely interception point but found nothing there, Kretschmer feeling certain the convoy had altered course due to an Admiralty U-boat warning. It had actually done so as a standard precaution.

In a bid to find the quarry *U-99* dived, removing the noise interference of her own diesel engines. The trusty ears of Jupp Kassel, the senior rating hydrophone operator, picked up a faint hydrophone effect to the south. Surfacing again, *U-99* endeavoured to catch the convoy, at 2.30 a.m. on 21 September, finding the merchant ships heading east.

It was a moonlit night and edging around HX-72 Kretschmer picked out the low, dark outline of a submarine dawdling along. He decided to cut his own speed to sneak up on the other boat, with *U-99* on top of this craft before somebody spotted her. Amid frantic orders the other boat accelerated away, churning up a boiling phosphorescent wake and turning around to send a light signal challenge. Kretschmer ordered his boat's identity to be flashed by light signal, the other submarine came back and the two U-boats nestled alongside each other. Kretschmer had surprised *U-47*, with Prien shouting across that had he not been absent from the bridge there was no way his friend's submarine would have been able get that close. 'You need to get some lookouts,' Kretschmer warned. After discussing tactics the two aces parted company and the slaughter of HX-72 began.

The convoy was several hundred miles to the west of Ireland and there would be no escort for another 20 hours. Prien and Kretschmer's boats were initially joined by U-48, fresh from sinking the *City of Benares*, along with U-65, U-46 and U-43.

The first victim fell to Kretschmer, who torpedoed the oil tanker *Invershannon* not long after 3.00 a.m. Just over an hour later he sank *Baron Blythswood*, which disappeared in 40 seconds. The U-boat men were astonished at the rapidity of her demise, which was due to her cargo of iron ore. Next came the *Elmbank*, a 5,156-ton vegetable oil tanker.

A cargo of timber kept her afloat so both U-99 and U-47 had to pour shells into *Elmbank* before she succumbed. With all torpedoes gone, Kretschmer's boat set course for home following Prien, who had departed a few hours earlier having finally used up all his ammunition. On the way, U-99's radio was tuned to a Berlin station that proudly boasted of U-48 sinking two British ships, the *Invershannon* and the *Elmbank*. Noting his boat's work being attributed to another submarine Silent Otto felt considerable irritation, but declined breaking radio silence to send a correction to U-boat headquarters.

Even though Prien and Kretschmer had quit the field of battle, the attacks on HX-72 continued into daylight on 21 September, with the 4,409-ton cargo ship *Blairangus* – fatally lagging behind – claimed by U-48.

After the British escort arrived the submarines withdrew to wait for night, when the convoy was subjected to a dreadful mauling.

The late-arriving U-100, commanded by Kapitänleutnant Joachim Schepke, another of the Reich's much-celebrated aces, racked up an astonishing six vessels sunk, three of them in the space of an hour. U-32 damaged one ship and U-48 another, the 5,136-ton cargo carrier *Broompark*. Among the vital supplies lost to the British war effort were pit props, iron ore, fuel oil, grain and steel.

'The escort [ships] were in fact completely in the wrong place,' said *Lowestoft*'s 20-year-old Sub Lt Michael Irwin, 'proceeding away from the convoy, to the stern . . . when the submarines were *inside* the convoy . . . which was quite unbelievable at the time from the British point of view.'[7]

Trying to illuminate the attackers – the wolves on the rampage *among* his flock of sheep – escort force leader Cdr Knapp's actions proved counterproductive, serving to reveal more targets. 'We were firing star shells most of the time, which was completely ineffective' said Irwin, 'and I suppose [as they were] near the convoy [they] illuminated the convoy. [U-boats] would go inside the convoy on the surface or trimmed down and they would torpedo ships right, left and centre.'

By 10.45 p.m. the Anglo-French corvette *La Malouine*, which was on her first patrol with the Northern Escort Force, had already taken on board survivors from the *Canonesa* and *Dalcairn*. Next, according to her captain, 39-year-old Lt Cdr Ronald Keymer, she 'ran into a mass of small wreckage supporting a dozen scattered survivors of the *Empire Airman*'.[8]

This vessel was carrying iron ore so hadn't stayed afloat for long after a torpedo from Schepke's *U-100* holed her.

To pick up *Empire Airman*'s men *La Malouine's* captain ordered his ship slowed 'and survivors [were] hailed to the effect that [scrambling] nets were down to [the] water port and starboard forward and aft – that I could only remained [*sic*] stopped for five minutes . . . Six or seven men reached the nets, but all but two were too panic-stricken or dazed to do more than continue swimming up and down the ship's side.'

The two *Empire Airman* survivors picked up by *La Malouine* were among just four that would be saved from that merchant vessel's crew. To stop any longer than five minutes would have opened up *La Malouine* to being torpedoed. As she got underway again the corvette dropped a raft over the side with a calcium flare burning. Anyone who climbed aboard could, theoretically, be found later and picked up.

At 11.51 p.m. *La Malouine* herself was attacked, her Asdic operator picking up the sound of a torpedo coming straight at the ship. Lt Cdr Keymer decided the best course of action was to make an aggressive, high-speed turn towards it. The torpedo was avoided and there was a fleeting Asdic contact on a U-boat wake, with *La Malouine* firing illumination rockets to see if she could spot a submarine on the surface. She found nothing.

With the convoy scattered over miles of sea in the dark, *Lowestoft's* radio room picked up distress calls as ships were picked off. In the early hours of 22 September *Simla* was close enough for *Lowestoft's* Sub Lt Irwin to watch as 'she blew up in a sheet of flame but you didn't always see ships blow up, you just heard it . . .'

In the aftermath of HX-72, Cdr Knapp would draft a report to the Admiralty on how the U-boats had penetrated the convoy rather than just attacking from the exterior. He recommended that an escort ship should sail in the centre of a convoy but received no acknowledgement for his report. Irwin thought it had probably provoked only 'complete bafflement'.

La Malouine's Lt Cdr Keymer speculated in his post-action report, for Western Approaches Command in Plymouth, that German submarines had a special night torpedo sight 'consisting of a camera capable of taking a rapid succession of films in what is almost complete darkness'. No such device existed per se, though the Germans did have an excellent conventional sight for night action. Keymer was not convinced that Asdic was as infallible as some might think. The U-boats were defeating it 'probably by means of either jet propulsion, bubble protection, detachable decoy, or a combination of one or more, being greatly reduced in efficacy'. In reality they simply attacked on the surface, where Asdic could not detect them.

If HX-72 was bad, worse was to come in mid-October, especially during carnage dubbed by the Germans 'Night of the Long Knives'.[9]

Convoy SC-7, composed of 49 vessels, sailed from Nova Scotia on 8 October, protected by five escorts for the final 400 miles to the UK, and was met by a wolf pack of seven U-boats. Panic set in and the merchant vessels scattered. U-boats sank four merchant ships on 16–17 October, but it was 18–19 October when they really savaged SC-7. In the space of just six hours, they claimed a further 16 merchant vessels.

Reeling from the disaster of SC-7, the British sent 11 escorts out to protect follow-on convoy HX-79 as it completed its passage across the Atlantic but even so, of 49 merchant vessels a dozen were lost on 19–20 October. Five U-boats were involved in the well-coordinated attack, four of which had also attacked SC-7, switching to join *U-47* against HX-79. Prien had been shadowing, with the other boats homing in on his locator beacon. Jumping into the fight alongside Prien was Oberleutnant Engelbert Endrass in *U-46*, along with Schepke in *U-100* and *U-48*.

So many torpedoes were fired in the tonnage-feeding frenzy, the Germans did not know exactly which U-boat was responsible for each sinking. Admiral Dönitz concluded that during the attack on SC-7 alone half a dozen boats had sent 30 ships to the bottom (for a total tonnage of 197,100). Post-war analysis by a German naval historian, also drawing on British records, suggested it was actually 20 ships, totalling

79,646 tons. Similarly, Dönitz decided 17 ships from HX-79 had been sunk, for a total tonnage of 113,100 tons. Post-war it was judged the true figure was 12 ships totalling 75,063 tons.[10] For Dönitz the attack on the two convoys was proof the wolf pack system could reap incredible dividends. On 20 October, he noted in the War Log that it was a 'colossal success'[11] that proved the tactic of 'countering concentration in convoys with a concentration of U-boats' was correct. Unfortunately, there were self-imposed handicaps. There were only enough U-boats in the operational area 'from time to time' to form wolf packs. Dönitz added: 'The more U-boats there are in [the] operations area the more frequently such operations will be possible.'

In a final tribute to his men Dönitz noted: 'The main thing however will always be the ability of the CO.' His carefully nurtured young submarine captains were proving to be expert ship killers and the second half of 1940 was dubbed 'The Happy Time' for the U-boats, with around three million tons of Allied shipping sunk.

12   Prime Minister's Peril

The staggering level of losses injected real foreboding into the mind of Winston Churchill. He would later confess that while he felt, even before the Battle of Britain, that any German invasion attempt would fail, the struggle against the U-boats made him 'even more anxious'.

It was the gravest of dangers and not even the threat from Nazi capital ships marauding in the sea lanes concerned him as much: 'The only thing that ever really frightened me during the war was the U-boat peril.' He noted of convoy SC-7 that it was 'massacred by U-boats' and in its aftermath 'a shadow hung over the Admiralty'.[1]

There were a few glimmers of hope, not least escort vessel reinforcements, including more Flower Class corvettes entering service. Nevertheless, convoy HX-90 in early December 1940 was another calamity for the British, with Prien and U-47 at work again, in a wolf pack of six boats. Once more the number of ships sunk claimed by Dönitz and the

Reich's propagandists was wide of the mark, with 18 (totalling 120,698 tons) trumpeted erroneously. The real figure was 11 ships (73,495 tons), but that was bad enough.

In Britain there were naval officers calling for the Royal Air Force to do more but Coastal Command was its Cinderella branch, cursed with obsolete aircraft. These included the large Saro London and Stranraer (both biplane flying boats). It also operated a massive, lumbering torpedo-bomber called the Wildebeeste (another biplane). Only the new Sunderland flying boat was any good, with the Anson a poor second (both were monoplanes). Coastal Command was forced to borrow aircraft designed to pound strategic land targets but as Bomber Command ramped up its campaign against Germany these were withdrawn from maritime operations.

It would take until 1942 for the RAF to operationally deploy an effective depth charge. Using depth charges was far better than bombs, as the Fleet Air Arm had discovered. In sinking *Shark* off Norway the enemy had already proved the effectiveness of aircraft against even dived submarines, especially using depth charges.

The Germans, on the other hand, were managing to field a formidable long-range bomber over the ocean. The Focke-Wulf (Fw 200) Condor would for a period become the scourge of Allied convoys. Kampfgruppe 40 (KG 40) was based at an airfield near Bordeaux, flying sorties from the summer of 1940. A typical mission would take a Condor out across the Bay of Biscay into the Atlantic, to the south and west of Ireland, then it would head north and turn east south of Iceland to land in Norway. With the aircraft refuelled and re-armed the mission was then repeated in reverse. Between August and October 1940 Condors sank 90,000 tons of shipping.

Lobbying by Dönitz, Kretschmer and others for more assistance from the Luftwaffe seemed to work, as from early 1941 Condors would provide reconnaissance for U-boats. Acting as flying beacons, they avoided direct communication with a gathering wolf pack for fear of giving away its location to the enemy. They sent their reconnaissance reports to the U-boat headquarters and the necessary information was then forwarded.

Condors were particularly effective against convoys from Gibraltar to the UK, which had to pass well within their range. One such was HG-53, which sailed from the Rock on 6 February 1941. Enemy spies at

Algeciras in Spain saw its 21 merchant vessels depart with heavy escort provided by Force H – the battlecruiser HMS *Renown*, carrier *Ark Royal*, cruiser *Sheffield* and eight destroyers – in addition to the sloop *Deptford* and destroyer *Velox*. Force H was actually using HG-53 as a bluff. After accompanying the merchant ships through the Strait and out into the Atlantic, after night had fallen it headed back into the Mediterranean. Its true objective was a bombardment of the Italian port of Genoa.[2]

HG-53 was twice cursed. Firstly, it lost that impressive escort force, which would have guaranteed its safety from enemy air, surface raider and submarine attacks. Secondly, the size of the original escort persuaded the enemy it was an important convoy that should be attacked with all available units. HG-53 was the first ever targeted by German air and submarine forces in a successfully co-ordinated fashion.

The first casualties came early on 9 February, with the torpedoing of the *Estrellano* and *Courland* by *U-37*, which had been directed towards the convoy by a B-Dienst radio intercept.

Twelve hours later, homing in on the beacon of *U-37*, five Condors attacked, flying at only 150ft as they approached from astern.

That kind of low-level assault by such large aircraft would never have been attempted had carrier-based fighter planes been present, or even destroyers bristling with AA guns.

Despite the best efforts of *Deptford* and *Velox*, assisted by the paltry fire of merchant vessels, four ships were sunk – *Britannic, Jura, Tejo* and *Dagmar 1* – with the *Varna* and *Raina* damaged but still steaming. *Deptford*'s guns did manage to hit one Condor, which was forced to land in Portugal.

U-37 sank the *Brandenburg* on 10 February while the enemy heavy cruiser *Admiral Hipper*, which had been diverted to attack HG-53 at the invitation of Admiral Dönitz, came across SLS-64 first and sank seven of that convoy's 19 vessels.

Varna succumbed to her torpedo damage, her crew rescued by the *Empire Tern*, but the convoy reached Liverpool on 24 February without any further attention from the enemy.

In France Admiral Dönitz was very satisfied with the co-ordination between air and submarine forces. '. . . it proves for the first time that even at this early stage co-operation between U-boats and G.A.F. [German Air Force] can lead to considerable success,' he noted in the U-boat War Log.[3]

*

With the Germans already proving adept at interpreting radio trans-missions to aid the attack on HG-53, the British were getting into the same game at the tactical level. Even if you couldn't read exactly what a wireless transmission (W/T) said it could still tell you a lot. In addi-tion to revealing the location of the sender and receiver, the amount of traffic could indicate whether an attack was imminent. Signalman William Pollock, a young Scot who had volunteered for the navy in the autumn of 1938 during the Munich Crisis, was part of a highly secret W/T Party.

Aiming to equip escorts and convoys with the ability to avoid trouble, its members were sent from destroyer to destroyer, spending a few weeks at sea in each one. They installed equipment and trained radio operators in how to detect enemy transmissions and determine their point of origin. In the W/T office of a destroyer Pollock and his trainees would sit at the controls of an elementary Very High Frequency (VHF) receiving unit trying to tune in to various transmissions, listening out for German. Although to begin with he couldn't speak German, Pollock 'tried to make some sense of the nature' of enemy transmissions. If they picked up German, they would try to hold the frequency.

Based ashore in a large house at Liverpool, during training members of the W/T Party would go to various points in a neighbouring park to see if they could pick up each other's transmissions. They learned how to understand the nature of what the enemy might be saying and could tell the difference between encrypted German and British signals. The maximum range of the Radio Direction Finding (RDF) equipment fitted to destroyers in the early part of the war was only about three to five miles, so Pollock found that 'when it got loud you knew it [the point of origin] wasn't that far away'.[4]

Often the transmissions picked up were 'marred by static and the weather conditions and sometimes', he said, 'you just had to assume it was an enemy transmission, especially if it was close'.

There was never a shortage of something for Pollock and others to listen out for. U-boats were able to receive wireless transmissions even when submerged, via an aerial they could poke above the surface, while Ultra Long Wave radio messages could be picked up when they were were fully dived, though not too deep.[5] Daily position reports sent to Admiral Dönitz were most useful. Signals on attacks even included how many torpedoes were left, so Dönitz could organise U-boat dispositions and act on the latest information.

Aboard a destroyer on convoy duty, determining whether potential enemy threats were ahead, astern or on either flank was critical in order to configure units to fend off an assault.

Pollock learned to recognise the distinctive transmissions of an enemy submarine sighting a convoy, which would 'call up its friends' and send a message to the U-boat headquarters. He also knew the sort of transmission the enemy headquarters made in order to 'tell the U-boats at sea that U-so-and-so has been in touch with a convoy bearing of so-and-so . . .' Pollock was amazed at the enemy's lack of caution, though he was always wary about the Germans listening in to British wireless signals. Royal Navy W/T discipline was generally good, with as few transmissions as possible made by its units. If line-of-sight messaging were possible light signals and semaphore would be used to maintain radio silence.

Once a destroyer's operator was proficient in detecting enemy transmissions Pollock would move on to another ship, but he spent enough time on the convoys to see things that would always haunt him.

These included 'ships being blown up all over the place . . .' While aboard HMS *Hesperus* Pollock saw a Greek-flagged merchantman torpedoed. 'I recall the lads in the water from the ship . . . and going down the rope ladder and helping one aboard. When he did [finally] get aboard he seemed to just give up. I gave him artificial respiration until one of the Petty Officers said "give up . . . the man is dead".'

Almost as disturbing was seeing the ship's mascot, an Alsatian, 'prancing up and down the foc'sle' as the vessel went down by the stern 'and the last you saw of it [the dog] was still staggering, keeping its balance'.

As the year drew to a close, U-boat commanders were looking forward to further happy times in 1941, ravaging British convoys. The top submarine captains and their crews were given extended leave over Christmas while their boats received essential repairs.

Impressive though the achievements of the German submariners were during 1940, buried below the surface of their incredible success lay the seeds of decline and destruction. Though the pace of U-boat construction was being increased, it was still not enough to replace

31 U-boats lost since the war's beginning. Force levels fell to 22 boats available for operations, which was fewer than Dönitz had in September 1939. The aces were being pushed hard, some might say too hard. Among their enemies was the sea itself, which that winter at least imposed a temporary lull.

Even if dreadful conditions meant the U-boats could not deploy to sink merchant vessels, numerous British ships were sunk off Liverpool and elsewhere. Their agents of destruction were magnetic sea mines laid by German submarines over some months, which remained dormant until a vessel passed over them, triggering a detonation.

The Luftwaffe dropped mines in the approaches to British ports, which became a serious problem, requiring both merchant ships and warships to have their hulls demagnetised, a process called degaussing.

The magnetic mine problem was so severe that in late 1939 it led to merchant traffic being diverted entirely away from London, to the Mersey and also Bristol. By the end of 1941 about 400 merchant ships belonging to Britain, the Allied nations or neutrals had been sunk by mines in British waters. It was one of several reasons why the hub of the anti-U-boat war could no longer be Plymouth, which was ideally placed to cover the South West Approaches, but now far too exposed. From the summer of 1940 the Devon naval city was also subjected to a series of devastating air raids, growing in intensity to mass firebombings in March and April 1941. In choosing a new headquarters for the fight against the U-boats, the Admiralty looked to the Mersey.

Taking a detour a short way inland from Liverpool waterfront, you can easily find Derby House, a pretty anonymous-looking office block behind the Old Town Hall. From early 1941 it became home to the Western Approaches Command (WAC) which made sense due to a number of factors. In the Second World War the fight was much further out into the Atlantic than it had been in the previous struggle and about four convoys reached the Mersey each week, creating the huge and complex task of unloading ships. More than 30 per cent of all UK sea trade flowed into the UK via Manchester and Liverpool, representing 4.2 millions tons of cargo out of a total of 12.9 million tons (a low figure in itself compared to the pre-war figure) handled from April 1940 to April 1941. The reward for the area's prominence in the fight for national survival was 68 bombing raids on Liverpool between summer

1940 and the beginning of 1942, a longer sustained air assault than at any other UK port, with the exception of London, during the Second World War.[6]

Derby House was by late 1940 being subjected to major work, with a bunker complex constructed below it that could withstand direct bomb hits and shock and which was sealed against gas attack.

Known informally as 'The Citadel' – or, in less complimentary fashion, 'The Dungeon'[7] – at its heart was the cavernous Map Room featuring massive maps of the Atlantic (the 'plots') and other charts spread across entire walls. The Citadel also housed communications equipment and the many staff who ran it all. Admiral Percy Noble, a surface navy officer, began co-ordination of the fight against the U-boats from Derby House in February 1941. Aged 61 when he took over as Commander-in-Chief, Western Approaches,[8] Noble worked in collegiate style, a consummate diplomat welding together all the different aspects of the fight.

Noble needed considerable physical stamina, for like the captain of a warship he might be needed to handle some crisis or other at any time of day or night. He spent his waking hours in an office with a large window that enabled him to merely turn his head and study the huge plots of the Atlantic on the walls of the Map Room. He could see various situation reports, also displayed on the walls, as they were updated. Just above the office was the small bedroom, or cabin (as the navy called it even though ashore), where Noble slept. It meant he was able to return within minutes, or even seconds, to the office or go down onto the floor of the Map Room.

Signals were brought to Admiral Noble, whether he was in the office or his cabin, for immediate action. Over a period of 22 months he had only four days off from this punishing existence, though he did visit major ports and the Admiralty for conferences and to gather facts. For this purpose he used an Airspeed twin-engine Envoy III aircraft piloted by his Flag Lieutenant, with the Admiral's flag painted on its nose.

Working underground for long stretches without any sight of the outside world, even though Noble's mind might be alert and concentrating on the campaign in the Atlantic, physical fitness declined. Each day, to try to offset this, he endeavoured to go for at least a half-hour walk in a local park. There were private, personal pressures too, for beyond his concerns about the waging of the anti-U-boat war, Noble had two sons in warships, a worry he shared with Dönitz. The German submarine boss had one son serving in U-boats and the other was also in the naval service. Both admirals possessed a single-minded determination to endure, no matter what.

13   This Horrible Foe

In the winter months following the great German successes of October 1940 – 103 merchant ships sunk, totalling 443,000 tons and about 70 per cent of them by U-boats – numbers of submarines available for operations fell dramatically. Mountainous seas and dreadful weather made life aboard the U-boats almost unbearable and it was impossible to successfully attack shipping.

Following the New Year lull, U-boats accounted for 21 ships (126,792 tons) while the Luftwaffe sank 20 (78,597 tons). Even though there were just 22 operational craft, the U-boat force and the Luftwaffe managed to destroy 1,971,294 tons of shipping (557 ships sunk) in the first half of 1941, with 1,220,322 tons of it (263 ships) attributed to submarines.[1] Casualties on this scale outstripped the ability of the Allies' shipyards to replace lost merchant vessels.

The surface raiders, capital ships and disguised AMC were also finally delivering the kind of results Germany's admirals desired. Yet a single U-boat that cost a fraction of the price of a heavy cruiser to build and maintain in service – crewed by 142 men as opposed to nearly 1,200 – could in a matter of a few hours sink more ships than a surface raider. This was a message that, even now, Dönitz found hard to get across to the navy's surface fleet-biased leadership.

In London, pondering how to master the threat to British trade, Churchill waded through mountains of paperwork, trying to grasp 'this shapeless, measureless peril, expressed in charts, curves, and statistics!'[2]

It appeared that what mattered, actually, was the amount, by weight and kind, of cargo safely imported to Britain. Surveying the statistics of cargo landed in February 1941, the First Sea Lord informed Churchill that 'entrances of ships with cargo in January were less than half what they were last January'.[3]

It was after a gloomy War Cabinet meeting in early March that Churchill took Admiral Pound to one side and told him: 'We have got to lift this business to the highest plane, over everything else. I am going to proclaim "the Battle of the Atlantic".'[4] He issued a Battle of the Atlantic directive on 6 March. A secret sermon on requirements to triumph in the face of adversity, it was Biblical in its portent – and actually delivered in Churchill's capacity as Minister of Defence. The directive, however, was less a Jeremiah-like girding up of the loins than a Peter-like call for Britain and her allies to prepare their minds for action.

Giving four months to get things under control, Churchill allocated top priority to hunting down U-boats wherever they could be found and also eliminating the Condors. Furthermore, he stressed, U-boats should be both attacked at sea and bombed in the construction yards and dockyards. Thousands of British workers were also to be switched to repairing damaged merchant vessels and warships. When it came to offloading cargo, cranes that were not needed in the less important ports should be moved to those that were the busiest and a concerted effort made to reduce congestion during offloading and loading.

The Battle of the Atlantic concept was, felt Churchill, a logical follow-on from the Battle of Britain. A committee was formed, composed of relevant ministers, senior armed forces officers and key officials from agencies, government departments and organisations. Churchill chaired it and at each meeting, he said, 'everything was thrashed out; nothing was held up for want of decision'.[5]

Between 19 March and 8 May 1941 the Battle of the Atlantic committee met every week and from then on until 22 October approximately fortnightly. Churchill never lost sight of the terrible challenge Britain was confronted with. 'It was the kind of battle, which, in the cruel conditions of war, one ought to be content to fight,' he felt. 'But now our life-line, even across the broad oceans, and especially in the entrances to the Island, was endangered.' Two days after Churchill issued his secret Battle of the Atlantic directive 'the horrible foe',[6] as he described the U-boat force, received the first of a series of body blows.

For the Royal Navy the V & W Class escorts – those old First World War-era destroyers given a new lease of life – were proving to be a success and HMS *Wolverine* was among vessels of the type that would garner a reputation for lethal efficiency. She was heavily engaged in early March 1941, as convoy OB 293 (composed of 37 ships, heading for Canada and the USA) was threatened by a wolf pack as it passed to the south of Iceland.

The attackers included Günther Prien's *U-47*. Working with the destroyer *Verity*, alongside corvettes *Arbutus* and *Camellia*, *Wolverine* drove off *U-47* and *U-95*, but Kretschmer in *U-99* was also on the scene.

Despite heavy seas, *U-99* accounted for the large whale ship *Terje Viken* and the tanker *Athelbeach*, while five other ships were sunk by U-boats. In return the two British corvettes destroyed *U-70*.

At 23 minutes past midnight on 8 March a lookout aboard *Wolverine* reported smoke on the water. The Asdic operator picked up something on an identical bearing and, judging by the distinctive sound of diesel engines and props, it was likely to be a U-boat on the surface.

The captain of *Wolverine* was 38-year-old Lt Cdr James Rowland, who had previously served in the RN's submarines for six years. As someone with special insight into how best to combat submersible opponents, he chose not to give away the destroyer's position by firing a star shell.

Wolverine chased down the bearing of the noise, while a light signal silently flashed news of a contact to *Verity*. Three minutes later the glowing phosphorescence of a wake was spotted, with *Wolverine* raising her speed to 22 knots. Another 60 seconds passed before the dim silhouette of a U-boat was sighted in the distance.

It was zigzagging and at 12.30 a.m. HMS *Verity* fired star shells, which starkly lit up the scene. The U-boat, not surprisingly, made a crash dive. Slowing, to reduce her own noise generation, *Wolverine* tried to pick up an Asdic contact, working with *Verity* to fix the target.

Depth charges went tumbling in and the U-boat fired a torpedo to distract her pursuers, but they were too clever for that and refused to follow it. Next the U-boat tried to outrun them on the surface, but the fugitive was spotted off *Wolverine's* starboard bow at 5.18 a.m.

A minute later, Lt Cdr Rowland himself sighted the enemy craft, which was trimmed down to show only the conning tower. Changing course to port, the order 'full speed' rang out, followed by 'stand by to ram'.[7]

The U-boat started to fully submerge and once dived was heard on the hydrophones turning to starboard, props spinning ever faster.

Wolverine was overhauling her and Rowland found he was 'aided by phosphorescence and crystal clear water' which enabled him 'to estimate the U-boat's position with considerable accuracy'.

With *Wolverine's* bridge directly over a large patch of bubbles, Rowland calmly issued an order down the voice pipe: 'Fire one.'

The first depth charge went into the water.

'Hard a port,' Rowland ordered, then: 'Fire two . . .'

Rowland dashed across the bridge and watched a depth charge being hurled by a starboard thrower.

Darting back to the voice pipe he shouted: 'Fire three!'

A mere four seconds separated salvo two from salvo three and ten charges were dropped in all, some on the shallow depth setting.

By 5.41 a.m. the contact was strong and two minutes later Rowland noted: 'Faint orange light sighted on the starboard side in approximate position of the pattern, but was lost after about 10 seconds.'

This indicated the U-boat had blown up, but *Wolverine* continued to pursue Asdic contacts. At about 7.00 a.m., Rowland began to doubt he was still chasing a submarine. The contacts were 'behaving erratically' rather than using deliberate evasion tactics. By 8.15 a.m. Rowland felt they could not be a submarine and even appeared to be circling in a fashion inconsistent with a U-boat.

'Perhaps the amber-coloured light was in fact the key to the whole secret,' Rowland concluded, 'as we never carried out a really thorough search of the actual scene of the attack, being led away, I fear, by a school of fish.'

In the war's aftermath, the collation of enemy records and prisoner interrogation transcripts led the British to conclude the orange glow was most likely *U-47* blowing up under the sea. That has since been challenged. Those who propose *Wolverine* did not sink *U-47* contend the boat was lost not long after due to other causes. Tantalisingly, the U-boat force War Log reports that on 10 March a fragment of a position report was picked up, possibly from *U-70* or *U-47*, though the former was definitely sunk three days earlier. *U-47* did have a faulty radio, so this may have been Prien's last bid to contact headquarters. On 7 and 9 March an attempt was made to contact *U-47* and *U-70*, asking for situation reports. When they did not reply it created 'great anxiety'. A position report request on 10 March likewise received no response.[8]

Whether *U-47* suffered a structural failure – and was turned into twisted metal – or was sunk by a haywire torpedo or destroyed due to British attack, the most famous submarine ace produced so far by Germany in the Second World War was no more. With such a magnificent legend built around Prien it was difficult for the Nazis to admit he was a mere mortal and had been killed. News of his likely death was suppressed by order of Hitler for fear of damaging national morale. It was even kept from Prien's wife for some time. Various conspiracy theories about what happened sprang up, including that Prien and his crew mutinied; that he refused to take a dodgy U-boat out and was sent to a concentration camp and shot; that Prien and his men were drafted to an army penal battalion and were all killed. It was even suggested that he brought his damaged submarine into a Norwegian port and then disappeared. After the war Prien's comrades set out to debunk these myths[9] by visiting each eyewitness who saw 'Prien' on the Eastern Front or claimed to know where he was buried. Prien's fellow submariners concluded in the end that he and his men had no known grave except the ocean.

14   Phantom of Destruction

Convoy HX-112, composed of 41 ships, had departed Halifax, Nova Scotia two weeks earlier, destined for Liverpool, with 20 of its vessels carrying cargoes of vital oil, petrol and aviation spirit.

Now, on the night of 15 March, the jagged silhouettes of merchant ships were lit up sharply by an explosion. A torpedo fired from the stern tube of *U-110*, commanded by Fritz-Julius Lemp, had slammed into the 6,207-ton tanker *Erodona*, carrying benzene.

Lookouts aboard the destroyer *Walker* snapped their heads around, realising the battle was now on. Leaping sheets of flame showed where the *Erodona* had been claimed, followed seconds later by a rumbling explosion.

Turning at speed, *Walker* zigzagged across the gap between herself and *Erodona*, the scene lit by the ghastly glow of the tanker's burning wreckage and the slicks of blazing fuel floating on the sea. It made the faces of the destroyer's men glow satanically as they searched in vain for the guilty party. HX-112's other escorts – destroyers *Vanoc*, *Volunteer*, *Sardonyx* and *Scimitar*, along with six corvettes, including *Bluebell* and *Hydrangea* – were disposed ahead and astern and on the flanks, searching for signs of the enemy.

As commander of the Liverpool-based 5th Escort Group, only established that February, it was down to Cdr Donald Macintyre to lead the fight back while also trying to save lives. From *Walker* he signalled *Bluebell* to go and pick up survivors, though he privately doubted there could have been any. While a search was made, none of the 32 merchant mariners that made up *Erodona*'s crew survived nor did the four army artillerymen put aboard to man her guns.[1]

Catching a fleeting Asdic echo that might be a U-boat, *Vanoc* and *Volunteer* dropped two dozen depth charges, the explosions hurling spray into the sky but not bringing up a submarine. The escorts waited tensely for another attack, trying to spot the low outline of a predatory U-boat on the fringes of the convoy or even among its columns.

Again, they found nothing, not even *Vanoc* with her radar. Very few British destroyers were fitted with the kind of equipment that could detect a surfaced submarine, but just a few weeks earlier *Vanoc* had received a Type 286M set. Originally devised for the RAF's Coastal Command to mount in aircraft searching the surface of the sea it had been adapted to try and 'see' U-boats and other targets in the dark or through mist.

With a fixed antenna it would only 'look' in the direction the ship was heading, on a fixed bearing. It was, though, potentially a game changer, removing a surfaced U-boat's advantage over Asdic – but the Type 286M had yet to prove itself.

Among those on the other side responding to the call for action was Joachim Schepke in *U-100*. Schepke was tall and extremely handsome with an ego to match and was a formidable ship killer, as he had proved during his attack on HX-72 the previous autumn.

A dedicated Nazi, Schepke had become the hero of propaganda newsreels churned out by order of Reich Minister Goebbels. At public appearances Schepke was mobbed, with women throwing themselves at his feet, while young boys idolised him and wanted to be U-boat captains when they grew up. Just a few weeks earlier the 29-year-old Kapitänleutnant had addressed a massive rally of young Germans in Berlin. Surrounded by top brass and proudly throwing aloft a stiff-armed Nazi salute, Schepke mounted the stage. Hands grasping either side of the lectern, he spoke of the glorious and important work U-boats were doing for the Fatherland.

Schepke was well known for inflating his tonnage claims, but even so he had fully earned his ace status. Adolf Hitler himself had presented the Knight's Cross with Oak Leaves to Schepke, the highest award for bravery in the face of the enemy that Germany could give. He was based at Lorient, alongside Kretschmer and Prien, and the Kriegsmarine's three top submarine aces often went for dinner. They made a bet with each other. Whoever first attained the total of 200,000 tons of shipping would buy the other two dinner with champagne.

By the time Lemp discovered HX-112 Prien was gone (though not confirmed dead yet), but Kretschmer and Schepke were still out there and would now bare their teeth.

For the British, dawn on 16 March came as a deep relief but Cdr Macintyre still felt as if a shadow 'of impending doom' hung above the convoy, especially as his team was new to the game and inexperienced at fighting off U-boats.

As dusk fell a signal lamp flashed from *Scimitar*, the Yeoman on *Walker's* bridge swiftly taking down a message on his pad. He tore the sheet off and handed it to the captain. It said:

'Submarine in sight six miles ahead.'²

Now the issue of life or death for the convoy would be decided. Macintyre ordered *Scimitar* and *Vanoc* to join *Walker* in a full speed charge towards the U-boat. It was Schepke in *U-100* and he didn't hang around, diving while the enemy warships were still three miles away. The destroyers were spread out in a line, their Asdic pinging, hopefully catching the U-boat in overlapping cones, rather than allowing their quarry to sneak into a blind spot. They failed to find anything and *U-100* got away, surfaced and continued to trail HX-112.

At 10.06 p.m. there was an explosion as a U-boat claimed a victim within the convoy. Before the clock reached 11.00 p.m. another five merchant vessels would be sunk. Asdic still picked up nothing, so the lookouts of the escorts tried to spot phosphorescent trails. Cdr Macintyre prayed for deliverance from the awful slaughter.

Suddenly, just visible in the dark, slowly dissipating, was a white streak: the wake of a surfaced German submarine moving in for the kill.

Macintyre yelled down the voice pipe to the engine room, ordering full speed ahead, 34 knots. *Walker* sped down the wake, hoping to force the submarine to dive.

On the bridge of *U-100* lookouts realised to their horror that a destroyer was charging straight at them.

Schepke's vessel crash-dived again.

Nine depth charges set to detonate deep tumbled from *Walker's* stern, but the explosions were too far away to cause serious damage to *U-100*. Letting the convoy and its escorts pass ahead, the submarine surfaced.

Lunging in from the starboard side, Schepke was soon spotted again and it was *U-100's* bad luck to be discovered by *Vanoc*. It was the first time in history a warship had successfully used surface search radar to detect an enemy submarine in action. Diving with all haste, *U-100* was subjected to two depth-charge attacks, including a pattern of five exploding close alongside.

The combined force of the explosions grabbed the boat like a gigantic hand and shook it. Light bulbs shattered, plunging *U-100* into darkness and cracking depth gauges. More charges tumbled in, this time closer and causing further damage; the boat's bilge pumps were knocked out and instruments failed. Without the pumps clearing water out of internal ballast tanks and bilges – to create positive buoyancy – the boat would become heavier and heavier until she sank below crush depth.

Most frightening of all, high pressure air bottles under the casing had been damaged and were leaking, the noise so loud Schepke was convinced the British would hear it. He was right. The earphones of the Asdic operator in *Vanoc* were filled with a bubbling sound.

Aboard *U-100* even the deck plates beneath Schepke's feet were wrenched from their mountings and the hydroplanes seemed not to respond, leaving Schepke without a means to control the boat's destiny.

U-100 began what Schepke feared was a long slide to a grim death.

The inside of the boat got colder and colder, the hull itself groaning and creaking as the submarine approached 750ft. It was the very limit of what she could tolerate.

Soon *U-100* would be crushed, along with everyone in her.

The freezing water would rush in, their mangled bodies becoming entwined in twisted wreckage.

Schepke decided on a last, desperate throw of the dice – he would blow all the compressed air they had left to surface the boat. He felt there was no alternative if he was to save *U-100* and his men. As soon as they broke the surface *U-100* would fight it out with her persecutor. His heart sank when, on asking the torpedo compartment if the forward tubes were loaded and ready to fire, he was told that it would need time.

U-100 successfully surfaced and, after climbing up to the bridge, Schepke was able to make out an enemy destroyer only 500 yards away. It was closing *very* fast. *U-100* needed the diesel engines to fire up and power her out of peril, but they wouldn't start due to damaged fuel lines. Schepke ordered the electric motors to be engaged again, but even they were temperamental and did not kick in.

Becoming flustered as the enemy destroyer sprang in for the kill, Schepke gave an order that sealed his submarine's fate. He told the engine room to go *astern* on the starboard electric motor – but this took *U-100* right into the path of the charging HMS *Vanoc* rather than *ahead* and out of danger. Schepke realised with chill dread that he'd made a terrible error.

Lookouts screamed in panic that the Tommy warship was about to hit them. In defiance – in one last attempt to deny reality – Schepke tried to reassure them. 'Alright, do not panic he will miss us and pass astern.'

Submariners whose nerves had been shredded by the earlier depth-charging jumped overboard to save their skins, though they probably drowned. Finally realising his boat was done for, Schepke shouted down the open conning tower hatch: 'Abandon ship!'

Men rushed up from below, pulling on their life vests. A group of submariners made for the 88mm gun on the forward casing, intending to train it and blast the enemy destroyer. Realising it would be impossible to bring it into action, others made for the 20mm cannon on the conning tower platform. Some of their shipmates shouted at them not to do so. If they did that the Tommies would refuse to pick them up from the water.

Vanoc's captain ordered stop on the engines five seconds before impact, her bows crunching into the U-boat just ahead of the conning tower. The bows rode up onto the submarine, twisting the conning tower platform guardrails with a jarring metallic screech. Schepke was pinned against the periscope stand – his legs sliced off at the thighs. Though the violent impact hurled other submariners from the tower and casing into the sea, Schepke remained upright. As *Vanoc* went astern, tearing herself free from the U-boat, Schepke's torso toppled into the Atlantic. Still alive, he thrashed about. Absurdly, his white cap was still clamped on his head, set with its peak at the dashing, devil-may-care angle he always affected. The black sea closed over him.

As searchlights from *Vanoc* and *Walker* swept across the surface, the ocean also swallowed up *U-100*. Of the submarine's 41-strong crew only six would be saved, the others killed in the impact of the collision, drowned, trapped inside the boat or carried away into the depths.

As if the death of two superstar U-boat aces was not enough that month, Kretschmer also met his nemesis during the battle for HX-112.

His submarine had carefully shadowed the convoy until dark on 16 March and then struck, sinking six ships in quick succession. The first expired in 'a sheet of flame [that] shot out of the tanker turning the night into daylight'.[3] This was the 6,593-ton Norwegian oil carrier *Ferm*, with the 5,728-ton British tanker *Venetia* next. The casualty rate was so severe – five ships torpedoed within the space of an hour – that Cdr Macintyre was 'near to despair' as his escorts rushed about trying to catch the phantom responsible for such terrible destruction. 'I racked my brains to find some way to stop the holocaust,' he said.[4]

U-99 provided the solution herself, for at 3.00 a.m. she ran out of torpedoes. It was dangerously time-consuming amid an escorted convoy to use the gun, even at night, and so – with no realistic alternative to carry on killing – Kretschmer decided to take his boat back to Lorient.

A cock-up on the bridge of *U-99* sealed her fate, with a lookout failing to spot the slowly moving *Vanoc* looming out of the darkness. The senior rating Officer of the Watch compounded the error. As *U-99* almost collided with the enemy ship, in a panic he ordered a crash dive.

At 3.37 a.m. *Walker* picked up an Asdic contact, but initially dismissed it. Right underneath *Vanoc*, it was presumed to be water disturbance rather than a U-boat, 'but as the asdic operator insisted the contact was firm and the echo rapidly improved, the Captain [Macintyre] decided to attack'.[5]

Aboard U-99, a very peeved Kretschmer asked the senior rating: 'Are you sure we could not have got away on the surface?'[6] The senior rating said he didn't think it would have been possible, as the destroyer must have spotted them. Instead they were now at the mercy of the enemy, with Kassel on the hydrophones calling out that two destroyers were moving in.

Walker passed right overhead, dropping half a dozen depth charges, while Kretschmer took U-99 down to 393ft. There was a series of deafening explosions, shattering light bulbs and glass in gauges. A water pipe burst in the forward bunk space. Fuel oil from a cracked tank flooded the control room, mixing with water that was now ankle deep.

It was hard to be sure of depth without a functioning depth gauge in the control room, but a secondary one in the torpedo compartment indicated they were going past 600ft. Kretschmer ordered the tanks blown to surface, but nothing happened. The valve that let compressed air into the tanks would not open, even though two men were struggling with it.

The boat slid past 700ft, but then the valve finally opened and U-99 slowed her rate of descent. She started to rise. Kretschmer tried to get the boat under control at 200ft, so he could crawl away while still dived, but it seemed the propellers were damaged. U-99's ascent picked up pace and she leapt from the sea. Wrecked steering and electric motors stymied the possibility of still getting away at high speed on the surface.

Vanoc reported to Walker that a U-boat had surfaced close by.

Macintyre, whose view was blocked by the other warship, flashed back a testy light signal: 'Well, get out of the way.'[7]

However, he would not ram the U-boat. With a convoy to escort to the UK, Macintyre could not risk damaging his ship, especially as Vanoc had already suffered a seriously crumpled bow.

U-99 was mortally wounded anyway, wallowing with a list on amid a rapidly spreading slick of oil and surrounded by enemy shell splashes. Kretschmer cursed his luck at not even being able to fire off a last, defiant torpedo at the enemy.

The submarine's final signal was sent to U-boat force HQ: 'Two destroyers – sunk – depth charges – 53,000 tons [a reference to shipping U-99 claimed] – capture – Kretschmer.'[8] This message was heard by U-37, which forwarded it to Dönitz, who mistakenly assumed Kretschmer had sunk two destroyers in his last stand.

The majority of *U-99*'s crew were already on the casing, sheltering from the enemy's fire on the starboard side. Smoking a cigar while shells thunked in, Kretschmer considered his next move. He estimated *U-99* would stay afloat for about a quarter of an hour – time for the enemy to potentially send across boarding parties. Kretschmer ordered *U-99*'s scuttling and sent some men to do the job.

Both *Walker* and *Vanoc* stopped their bombardment after a couple of minutes, while aboard the U-boat scuttling charges could not be set as it was impossible to gain access to the compartment where they were stored. Kretschmer ordered all hatches opened and everybody out, except for the Engineer Officer who was sent below to flood the ballast tanks and open the galley hatch wide to let in more water. Until now there had been no fatalities, but suddenly *U-99*'s demise accelerated. Men on the aft casing were thrown off as the boat lurched and began to sink stern first. The Engineer Officer was still inside the submarine and would lose his life.

At Kretschmer's request one of the German senior ratings sent a light signal message to *Walker*, revealing: 'We are sinking.'[9] It also stated that some of the U-boat's crew were in the water and asked for them to be picked up.[10]

As the boat slid into the deep the rest of *U-99*'s men were swept off the conning tower and into the water. *Walker* picked up 35 but two more men were lost, drowning after abandoning ship.

Kassel was nearly thrown back into the water as he appeared to be dead, but instead he was taken below decks and thawed out in the warmth of *Walker*'s galley. With his sea boots full of water, Kretschmer found it difficult to haul himself up the scrambling net onto the destroyer's upper deck. *Walker* was picking up speed, just in case there were any other U-boats around, and Kretschmer thought he would soon have to let go. That would be the end of him, but one of his men reached down to help him up the last few feet.

A grinning British sailor welcomed him aboard by poking a pistol in his face. The U-boat captain couldn't help laughing, but this stopped when he saw the man's eyes fixed covetously on the binoculars hanging around his neck. Before Kretschmer could deny the binoculars to him by flinging them overboard another sailor grabbed them. They would eventually end up in the hands of Cdr Macintyre, who used them for the rest of the war.

As Walker and the other escorts returned to shepherding the merchant ships, *U-99*'s men were treated well by their captors, with Macintyre and Kretschmer having a few chats, though the German remained guarded.

Macintyre knew about Kretschmer's impressive war record anyway, while a sketch retrieved from a captured submariner depicted a U-boat among merchant ships firing torpedoes. The British escort commander reflected that a lot of his dashing about outside the convoy during the battle had been in vain.

Considering the British sank no U-boats between late November 1940 and early March 1941, to lose four in the space of a fortnight – including two in the same place on the same night – was a pretty heavy blow for the Germans. Churchill saluted the captains of *U-99* and *U-100* as 'outstanding officers', remarking that 'elimination of these three able men [including Prien] had a marked effect on the progress of the struggle. Few U-boat commanders who followed them were their equals in ruthless ability and daring.'[11]

The removal of the three aces was made possible due to a variety of factors. There were errors made by the U-boat captains themselves, including Schepke's wrong order when trying to get out of *Vanoc*'s way. The aces were also facing experienced captains who would make determined depth-charge attacks. In *Walker*, Cdr Macintyre was blessed with a particularly talented Asdic operator, further illustrating the right man in the right place could have a decisive effect. Instinct was also a valuable attribute in hunting U-boats and the best Asdic operators developed a sixth sense about whether a contact was a submarine or a shoal of fish (and also what the quarry might do next). The top escort captains possessed the same uncanny ability, especially if they were former submariners.

The ships they commanded were by now somewhat more formidable (in the right hands) than the corvettes and sloops U-boats had often faced. It is true that they were old – *Walker*, *Wolverine* and *Vanoc* had all been completed towards the end of the First World War. After seeing active service for a decade they were put into mothballs, but were taken out of reserve and commissioned back into service not long

A powerful depiction by the artist Leslie Carr of the destroyer HMS *Viscount*, which sank U-boats in both world wars, showing *U-87* being rammed. *Viscount* did not actually destroy a submarine with that name in either conflict but it remains a good illustration of a favoured method of eliminating surfaced U-boats. (*VT Collection/AJAX*)

before the outbreak of war. Most useful was the top speed of the V&W destroyers, which was twice that of the Flower Class. They were armed with four 4-inch or 4.7-inch guns and carried up to 45 depth charges, and their combination of speed and a displacement of 1,400 tons meant they could cause a lot of damage when ramming.

With such ships and men entering the fray, spring 1941 marked the end of the so-called Happy Time for the German submarine force. That didn't mean things were not grim for the British. While they sank seven U-boats in the North Atlantic that March, there were still heavy losses in merchant ships: 243,000 tons (due to U-boats) and 113,000 tons (Luftwaffe bombers). The upward momentum would continue into April, but the British tightened their game even more.

15   The Enigma of Fritz-Julius Lemp

March 1941 was perhaps when the odds really began to stack up against Germany winning the war at sea, due to the loss of the leading aces and the difficulty in replacing them.

The fate of U-110 two months later could be described as the moment all hope was gone, though the Germans did not know it. It was not a matter of its significance being lost in the fog of war, but rather being hidden by the British behind a veil of secrecy designed to ensure nobody knew quite how decisive and shattering the blow was. The turn of events was decided by the actions of a few young men on both sides, bearing the heavy burden of command in the vastness of the ocean. Chief among them was Fritz-Julius Lemp, who had been presented with his Knight's Cross in August 1940 by Dönitz, the admiral also rewarding him with command of U-110, which was a new Type IXB submarine launched at the end of the same month.

By spring 1941, even though he had enjoyed great success in that boat, Lemp was fraying at the edges. Indicators of this included his response to an order requiring him to switch to weather reporting duties during one patrol. Aware his boat needed some serious dockyard

A portrait of Kapitänleutnant Fritz-Julius Lemp wearing his Knight's Cross. (*BArchiv, Bild 134-B2630/o. Ang*)

attention, *U-110*'s captain responded grumpily: 'Shit, Lemp.'[1]

Well aware of the strain on his crew – and their need to blow off steam – he tolerated hard-drinking runs ashore and also his youngsters' love of American jazz and British popular tunes. Though banned by the Nazis, they were played on the boat's record player and broadcast throughout the vessel when not in high-threat zones.

In navies there are happy ships and unhappy ones and while Lemp did his best to strike the right balance – for he was father to his boat's family – *U-110* was in the latter category. His newly promoted second in command was Oberleutnant Dietrich Loewe, an ardent Nazi in an arm of the German military in which any formal membership of a political party was prohibited. Loewe would 'tolerate no criticism'[2] of the regime according to *U-110*'s men, who regarded him as a Jonah, as before joining the submarine service he had served in two surface ships that were sunk. *U-110*'s men 'thought him brainless and inefficient'.[3] Furthermore, they despised him as 'narrow-minded, callous, brutal and a bully'.[4]

Junior lieutenant Ulrich Wehrhöfer did not improve the mood in *U-110*, for he was another Nazi intensely disliked by the men, especially the senior ratings.[5] Lemp was not a fan of the Nazis for he disliked their rigid lack of humour but was loyal to his country and its government. However, his contempt for Wehrhöfer was obvious. He once allowed other officers to play a trick on the lieutenant by fixing a piece of bacon to his bunk while he slept. Prone to seasickness, on waking and smelling the bacon Wehrhöfer threw up.[6] Problems with Lemp's crew were compounded by the quality of the personnel becoming diluted as the submarine force expanded. What had been a tight, highly trained elite service became much less so and U-110 got new people who were not so resilient or well trained as their predecessors.

By April 1941 the number of boats available for deployment against the British had increased to 30 and by July 1941 it would be 60. Up to a dozen new boats a month were joining the force, most of them improved variants of the trusty Type VII. It meant more and more men were needed as quickly as possible and in some cases the training regime suffered, with a reduction in the preparation time in the Baltic. One new submarine captain had to make his own arrangements for a vessel to be made available for attack training. In the past one would have been provided for him as part of the normal process.

The need for experienced mariners was so desperate that a known communist sympathiser and even a former inmate of a concentration camp were among U-110's crew. The latter was a highly experienced former merchant marine officer who, along with his family, had suffered terribly at the hands of the Nazis and was implacably opposed to their cause. Yet he was made a Petty Officer and navigator of the boat. This man spoke little of his own incarceration, but other members of U-110's crew swapped stories about alleged outrages perpetrated in the concentration camps against political prisoners.

Joining U-110 along with some other veterans from Lemp's previous command, U-30, was that boat's former radio operator Georg Hogel.

A newcomer was Leutnant Helmuth Ecke, a war correspondent from the Propaganda Kompanie. Ecke had never been to sea in a submarine before but had seen his share of action on land. His job was to take photographs of life aboard and write up a story extolling the heroic efforts of the U-boat force. Determined not to be more of a burden than possible, Ecke volunteered to pull duty as a lookout when the submarine was on the surface.

As U-110 departed Lorient on 15 April, on what was only her second war cruise, Lemp considered his crew good enough for whatever might lie ahead, though some of his *U-30* veterans begged to differ. They thought too many of the youngsters were prone to panic.[7]

By now U-boats were being pushed further and further west into the Atlantic, to exploit the vulnerability of convoys in the gap between their Iceland-based escorts leaving them and Canada-based forces coming out to provide protection (and vice versa).

On the morning of 9 May *U-110* made a surface rendezvous with *U-201*, a Type VIIC commanded by Oberleutnant Adalbert Schnee. Using megaphones the two captains held a brief discussion about tactics, deciding convoy OB-318 should be attacked as soon as possible.

Lemp would go in first, with Schnee's boat coming in about half an hour later. As they were attacking further west than had ever been attempted by any U-boat in the current war it was hoped the convoy would by then be naked of protection.

It was soon realised that the OB-318 escorts had not gone, with one of Lemp's officers urging him to 'postpone the attack, as he felt sure that the escort were about to leave the convoy which would therefore become an easy prey'.[8] Lemp doubted *U-110* had enough fuel left to stay out much longer and guarantee getting home.

To prepare for a daylight attack, Lemp made sure the four torpedoes loaded in the bow tubes were all electric rather than compressed air. The track created by the bubbles of a compressed air-propelled torpedo might not be observable in the dark, but during the day it would be a real giveaway.

Ready to strike, *U-110* dived to make the attack around noon, firing three torpedoes with an interval of 30 seconds between each one, subsequently hearing a corresponding number of explosions.

Two ships were sunk, the 4,976-ton *Esmond* and the 2,609-ton *Bengore Head*. The former went down in spectacularly horrific fashion, the stern lifting vertically into the air, with vehicles carried as deck cargo tumbling into the sea.[9] When Lemp tried to add another ship to his tally things went badly wrong. Fixing his sights on a large tanker Lemp ordered a fourth torpedo to be fired but it failed to leave the tube, which sparked a blazing row between the First Lieutenant and the Engineer Officer.

As a consequence of three torpedoes being fired rather than four, the ballast pumped forward – to compensate for the sudden lessening of weight – turned out to be too much. The nose dropped dramatically and the boat went into an uncontrolled dive, while the two arguing officers furiously tried to assign blame.

After control was restored Lemp took *U-110* back up for a look at what was happening on the surface, but left the periscope up for too long and found an escort charging straight at him.

This was the corvette *Aubretia*, but she lost contact, though her captain, Lt Cdr Vivian Smith, used instinct to place ten charges set to explode at 100ft and 225ft.[10] They didn't cause *U-110* any structural damage but the psychological effect was severe. The explosions created 'a feeling of depression in the boat', as one of *U-110*'s older men noted in his private diary. 'From our listening apparatus we establish the fact that we are being hunted by three destroyers.'[11]

As Lemp held the three-dimensional tactical picture in his head, trying to figure out what to do next, he appeared utterly calm. Taking the boat deeper he ordered a sharp turn to starboard. Lemp's dark sense of humour did not desert him. He tried to reassure his men with a joke that may have been a reference to the *Athenia* incident. 'You don't think I'm going to let them catch me and shoot me, do you?'[12]

From aboard HMS *Bulldog*, Escort Group 3 boss Commander A.J. 'Joe' Baker-Cresswell signalled the rest of his ships to maintain over-watch on the convoy, while he took his destroyer across to join *Aubretia* and the Town Class destroyer *Broadway* in hunting the U-boat.

Aubretia dropped a second pattern of depth charges, set to explode at 150ft and 385ft with[13] Ecke, the war correspondent, finding this attack to be 'far louder and more terrifying than anything he had ever heard on the Western Front, the explosion of Stuka aeroplane bombs included'.[14] This time *U-110* was mortally injured and there was 'a certain degree of panic among the crew, most of whom rushed forward as the U-Boat went down somewhat by the stern'.[15]

U-110's interior was wrecked, hydroplanes no longer functioning and rudder rendered useless, with vital instruments knocked out. Thanks to a damaged fuel tank oil was seeping into the submarine by the galley. Lemp thought *U-110* might still crawl away, but the electric motors had also been wrecked. The battery was so badly damaged it was possibly producing chlorine gas, with some of the men complaining about difficulty breathing. Lemp ordered *U-110* surfaced but the wheel that controlled the valve – enabling compressed air to be blown into the ballast tanks – had actually been sheared off. It was lying on the deck. Then the most incredible thing happened, for the explosions either somehow released compressed air into the tanks or blew the boat to the surface. Waiting for the submarine were the three warships eager for the kill, with *U-110* coming up less than 1,000 yards from *Bulldog*.

Lemp was first up the ladder and exclaimed: 'Uhlandstrasse, last stop, all change!'[16] Throwing back the upper hatch, he took a quick, cautious look at the situation and then shouted down the conning tower: 'We're surrounded . . . all hands abandon ship!'[17]

The control room looked like 'a wrecked kitchen' thought Ecke as he stumbled through, 'it really was the end'.[18]

Lemp trusted Engineer Lieutenant Eichelborn would open the main ballast tank vents to take the boat down while setting scuttling charges. Heinz Wilde was the last man out of the boat and as he emerged on the bridge he told Lemp: 'The secret things are still down there.'

'Leave it Wilde,' Lemp responded, ushering him over the side, 'the boat's sinking anyway.'[19]

As the enemy submariners poured out of *U-110*, it seemed to the British that some were going to her deck gun and intended fighting back. *Bull-dog* and *Broadway* opened fire with their cannons. Some of the Germans were hideously maimed or decapitated while others leapt off to drown in the sea. Cdr Baker-Cresswell realised there might be a good chance of capturing the U-boat and her secret materials, so he ordered *Bulldog* into full astern, bringing her to a halt 300 yards from the submarine. He also signalled *Broadway* not to ram but her CO, Lt Cdr Tom Taylor, did not see the light signal. Baker-Cresswell resorted to using a radio megaphone, bellowing: 'Do not ram!'[20]

Broadway ended up hitting *U-110* a glancing blow, with the submarine's foreplane slicing open the plating on the destroyer's bows below the waterline and then knocking off the port propeller.[21]

Cdr Baker-Cresswell ordered Sub Lieutenant David Balme, *Bulldog*'s navigating officer, to take the warship's seaboat and a boarding party to capture the enemy submarine.

Balme thundered down the ladders to the spot below decks where the boarding party was already being assembled. The Chief Gunner's mate was handing out revolvers and webbing, with the men putting

Sub Lt David Balme on the bridge of HMS *Bulldog* in 1941. (*Sue Balme*)

their lifejackets on, then weapons in holsters on top. Balme had seven seamen at his disposal, each with particular skills that could be used to keep the U-boat afloat.

Selected for his specialist knowledge of secret W/T technology was William Pollock, who had recently been sent to *Bulldog* to carry out the usual installation of wireless detection equipment and training of personnel. Pollock had witnessed the action from the bridge, where Balme turned to him and suggested: 'I would like you to volunteer.'[22]

Pollock felt he had no choice but to go.

Once aboard the whaler Balme took the tiller, with five people rowing – three on one side, two on the other – and with a man in the bow to jump off and secure the boat to the casing of the submarine.

'Speed was so essential,' explained Balme. 'I just went straight for the U-boat, which was the windward side and brought the whaler along-side and my bowman jumped off with the painter [rope], held the boat steady. I had to climb over all the oarsmen . . . and jumped onboard the U-boat. A U-boat is of course a terribly round slippery thing . . . not like getting onboard an ordinary ship.'[23] Successfully gaining purchase on the casing, Balme pulled his revolver out and walked along to the conning tower.

While 15 of U-110's men lost their lives, 32 of them would survive.

Lemp was not among them and the enigma of what exactly happened to him has provoked controversy.

According to one account Lemp was concussed and manhandled up the ladder to the bridge and essentially pushed overboard to drown.[24] This prognosis seems unlikely, due to some of his men conversing with him in the water and the testimony about him being first up the ladder while cracking a joke. Dietrich Loewe and Lemp were for a while swimming next to each other and noticed U-110 stubbornly remaining afloat. According to Loewe, U-110's captain called out that they should swim back to the submarine and board it to make sure she sank.[25] The sea was too strong and the U-boat was too far away, so Loewe instead decided to swim for a British corvette that was stopped in the water. He had no idea what happened to Lemp.

Did Lemp realise that a terrible error had been made and he had put his men's survival before state secrets? Did he turn around and swim back towards the submarine but was drowned? Alternatively, did Lemp commit suicide by throwing his arms up in the air and letting the sea overwhelm him, fearing that he would be put on trial as a war criminal for the Athenia sinking?

There have even been claims that Lemp was shot trying to get back aboard U-110. David Balme denied them and pointed out: 'Nobody would be shot swimming in the sea. We never did that in the Navy.'

Curiously, Pollock is on the record as stating that Lemp was 'one of the people killed when he was trying to get back . . . to try and set the scuttling charges again'.[26] However, Pollock admitted he did not actually see Lemp being killed. Balme thought Lemp allowed himself to drown. 'I have always said that the shock to him . . . when he realised the ship wasn't sinking – and he may have seen the boarding party coming – [was so great] that he committed suicide. Had he been an older man you might have said a heart attack [killed him], but he was only 30 or something.'

However he met his fate, Fritz-Julius Lemp remains a bit of an enigma. Some have depicted his sinking of Athenia as the act of a heartless Nazi but it seems likely to have been a genuine mistake about which he felt very badly. The Nazi characterisation seems off target. While a dedicated submarine captain and patriot, he showed no special sign of enthusiasm for the regime's ideology, either to captured British naval aviators in 1939 or to his own men.

As one of the last surviving members of the 'Old Gang' still at sea in 1941, Lemp was probably overtired by the rigours of war. Dönitz had offered him a shore job, which he refused, and so he stayed at sea to make mistakes that cost him his life and also killed 14 of his crew. Whatever redemption Lemp was reaching for it remained beyond his grasp and his final errors would ultimately prove extremely costly for his nation's entire war effort.

U-110 crippled on the surface as HMS *Bulldog* lowers a boat to capture the German submarine. (*Sue Balme*)

16 Look at this, Sir

After climbing up a ladder fixed to the outside of *U-110*'s conning tower – an action that forced him to holster his pistol – David Balme was surprised to find the hatch shut. He wondered if this indicated that somebody was still on board? Surely all the hatches should have been left open to accelerate the scuttling process?

Screwing up his courage, Balme opened it and climbed down into the upper conning tower compartment. Finding this deserted, his next barrier was the shut lower hatch that opened directly into the control room.

Praying there would be no nasty surprises on the other side of it, Balme opened it. An act replete with potential risk, Balme would later describe it as 'the worst moment of my life . . . I waved my revolver around in case anybody was there, just to have a shot at him if he appeared, but there wasn't anybody visibly down at the bottom . . .'[1]

Forced to use both hands going down the ladder into the control room, Balme again holstered his weapon. Landing on the deck, he got his revolver out and took a good look in both ends of the boat.

Throughout the vessel lights were still on, with a loud humming noise caused by the generators. It also appeared the port engine was still going, but on slow ahead. Finding the submarine entirely deserted was 'a very great relief'. Balme shouted back up the conning tower to Pollock, who was poised on the bridge, semaphore flags at the ready to send a message to *Bulldog*. Balme told him to signal all was clear, while calling the rest of the boarding party down into the submarine. He was keenly aware it was a race against time to harvest secret materials. Scuttling charges could detonate at any moment or the submarine might sink due to water flowing into some unseen part of the craft.

Pollock climbed down from the bridge. It was his first time inside a submarine and he scanned his surroundings with great curiosity. '. . . just below the periscope there was a table, a navigational plot where they had been tracing their course. There was [sic] the wheels and that for the planes where the operators sat before them. To their left, further aft, was the officers' quarters, their wardroom and just opposite that was the W/T office.'[2]

Sub Lt Balme decided they should make a human chain and pass all the secret material – codebooks, signal books, navigation manuals – up onto the casing for transfer to one of the escorts.

There was a setback when *Bulldog*'s whaler was smashed against the U-boat, leaving them with no immediate means of escape except to leap into the sea. Made aware of this, Baker-Cresswell told *Broadway* to send over her motor cutter. This acted as a ferry for taking materials to

Bulldog and by some miracle everything went over dry. If the codebooks got even the slightest bit wet it would spell disaster as the ink used in them was soluble. Balme asked Pollock to go to the W/T cabin and note down all the German wireless settings. The W/T sets themselves were fairly well secured – built into the frames – but there was also what appeared to be a portable typewriter. Its keys lit up when pressed and there were numerous, very intriguing wires plugged into it. There were also rotor disks incorporated into the machine. It looked similar to a British coding machine but the Royal Navy did not have many of them at sea yet, nor were they as complex.

Pollock called out: 'Look at this, Sir!'

He and Balme agreed it was definitely something worth removing. It appeared to be secured to the desktop only by a few screws. 'It was like [un]screwing something in your own home,' explained Balme.

It was carefully manhandled up ladders, passed down from the conning tower and taken across the casing to be placed in the cutter. The rotor disks – eight in all – were also soon on their way to *Broadway*.

At the time, though, it was other material that seemed of greater importance, including charts of the approaches to Lorient, with heavy black lines marked on them. These appeared to indicate German minefields, showing safe routes through them. There was also a grid map, with U-boat patrol squares indicated on it, which looked to be the most valuable find of all. Balme instructed his team to gather up anything that looked likely to be important. This could include notebooks, reference books, 'anything . . . that was portable and [that] we could carry and take away'.[3]

He told them to use their imaginations about where stuff might be secreted. Going into the captain's cabin, Pollock broke open a drawer and found sheaves of documents and various other items, which he 'popped into a briefcase that was there'.[4] He also found a book of naked pinups and was inspecting it closely when Balme looked over his shoulder and quipped, 'it is the naked truth we want'.[5]

It took several hours to ferret everything out and pass it up to the casing and to keep morale up sandwiches were sent over from *Bulldog*. Another team of sailors was put onto the boat's forward casing to place *U-110* under tow, though the submarine seemed to be getting heavier in the stern, which was ominous.

The U-boat was to be taken to Iceland and Balme got Pollock to send a semaphore message to *Bulldog* asking for some specialist help in getting the engine running. *Broadway*'s Engineer Officer and a couple of stokers came over by cutter, along with the ship's gunnery officer, for a look at the submarine's weaponry.

'We were all nervous of turning handles too much,' Balme later confessed.[6] 'We didn't understand the German writing on the handles and on the levers. The engineer officer and myself thought "if we tamper with things we could even set off the charges".'

It was decided not to get the engines running after all, just in case.

The trickiest moment during the whole episode was when *Bulldog* slipped the tow and raced off with other escorts to depth-charge a potential submarine. Balme found this 'a very forlorn moment' and aboard *U-110* they could feel the shock of the explosions reverberating through the water. They worried about detonating the scuttling charges. Despite such moments there were no serious gripes from anyone in the boarding team. Everyone seemed excited to be doing a really worthwhile job of plunder. 'Having cleared out the U-boat of all the books and charts and any interesting movable equipment, we decided to batten [the submarine] down [and exit] because there wasn't anything else we could do down below. When *Bulldog* came back from hunting this other U-boat we were very, very glad to see her . . .'

The tow was put across successfully and at 6.30 p.m. Baker-Cresswell ordered the boarding party back to *Bulldog*. *U-110* stayed afloat the whole night and into the following morning, by which time there was a strong wind blowing. Suddenly she went down by the stern rather dramatically, her bows rearing up. The tow had to be cut and Lemp's boat slid below the waves to join him.

The process of getting the *U-110* survivors aboard *Aubretia* and below decks had been done with amazing speed and efficiency. It was important they did not know their submarine and its secret materials had been captured.

They would later be permitted to write home to relatives and some would undoubtedly do their best to convey vital intelligence by code, just as British PoWs did the other way around. The only means of ensuring absolute secrecy was to keep them completely in the dark, or in *Aubretia*'s case cooped up below decks in compartments with no scuttles. Heinz Wilde saw *U-110* had not yet sunk as he was hurried along the corvette's upper deck and he also saw a rowing boat of some kind alongside the submarine, but never thought to mention it in a letter.

It was perhaps just as well that *U-110* was lost while under tow, for Iceland was host to numerous German spies who David Balme felt sure would have passed information on to Berlin. As it was, *Bulldog* and the other escorts pulled in to Hvalfjordur and did their usual refuelling and resupply routine. *Bulldog* went alongside the cruiser *Birmingham*, also taking the U-boat prisoners aboard from *Aubretia*. In *Bulldog* they were kept in a compartment right next door to all the secret materials taken off *U-110*. Balme was most amused, as the Germans 'had no idea they were sleeping and eating within feet of all their secrets'.

Bulldog was ordered straight back to Scapa Flow, which took 36 hours at her top speed of 35 knots. A relatively small and very fast target, she was very unlikely to be spotted and sunk by an enemy submarine.

So important was the cargo that when *Bulldog* came across a downed Walrus flying boat – it had experienced a mechanical failure while transporting an admiral to Scapa – she steamed right by, much to the fury of those in the aircraft. They had to wait for someone else to rescue them, but had *Bulldog* stopped she might well have made a perfect target for a U-boat.

Once at Scapa, *Bulldog* offloaded the Germans as quickly as possible. Not long after that an expert from the Admiralty came aboard to go through the secrets haul. Every single page of every codebook was photographed in case it was lost when going by plane or train to London. It turned out the 'typewriter' was an Enigma encryption machine. Discovering it, along with all of its rotors, made the expert beam with delight.

Sub Lt Balme spent 'a very exciting day' going through the materials with the expert, who told him 'we've never had any of these things – we have always wanted them . . .' Not only was he handling much-prized German cipher books and the Enigma machine, he was also presented with a list of the settings. One particularly brilliant prize was the officers-only cipher book, which would never be captured again in the war.[7]

Packed into suitcases, the secret materials were loaded onto a trawler and taken across to mainland Scotland and then went by train to London.

Afterwards Cdr Baker-Cresswell told his men they must never breathe a word of it, not to their families or anyone else. 'It was the most closely guarded secret ever,' said Balme.

In August 1941 Balme would join his CO and some of the others for a trip to London, where they received medals from the King, who was one of the few outside the Admiralty and intelligence services who was let in on the scale of the *U-110* capture. The King told Balme as he made the award: 'This is the most important event of the whole war at sea and I wish I was giving you a much higher decoration but we can't for security.' The award of the Victoria Cross to Balme and others – the proper reward for their heroic deeds – would have drawn too much attention to the significance of their actions.

17   The Suspicions of Admiral Dönitz

The German submarine force boss would be unaware of *U-110*'s capture for many years, but even before it happened he still believed British intelligence services had somehow penetrated the German military.

Dönitz noted in the War Log on 18 April: 'The impression is given that the English [convoy] traffic is being deliberately routed to avoid the attacking disposition. It is therefore suspected that by some means the enemy has obtained information of our attack areas.' This prompted him to issue orders that even within the U-boat force 'the number of persons having knowledge of U-boat operations is to be kept as small as possible'.[1]

Similarly, Dönitz decided no longer to provide daily reports on the position of U-boats to Group Command West of the army, the commander of the Atlantic Air Forces or the Naval Liaison Officer in Bordeaux.

Furthermore, naval bases and organisations outside the U-boat force using its radio frequencies must be 'restricted to the essential'. Dönitz ordered that 'listening-in on the U-boat radio wave by unauthorised persons' should be avoided. The true scale of British insight into exactly what the U-boats were doing – regardless of Bletchley's work on Enigma – was quite staggering.

Otto Kretschmer was given a hint of how effective it was when, shortly after his capture, he was taken to meet Capt. George Creasy, Talbot's successor as head of the Anti-Submarine Warfare Division. This highly unusual encounter occurred a fortnight before Dönitz noted his suspicions of a mole, or moles, within the German military.

The Ace and his men were being held in the Trent Park prison camp in Middlesex, with *U-99's* captain questioned for an entire week but giving little, if anything, away. Taken to Creasy's central London apartment, Kretschmer entered the sitting room to find a British naval officer with his hand stretched out. The German came to attention and saluted, Creasy introducing himself and suggesting, with a disarming smile, that they should sit, pouring them each a glass of port.

Kretschmer was no fool – he knew Creasy's charm offensive was a ploy to glean intelligence – but he cautiously played along, taking the port and seeing no harm in also accepting a cigar.

Creasy's opening ploy was to impress Kretschmer with unparalleled insight into his own life, such that he might conclude it was useless trying to hide anything. Creasy also revealed that *U-47* had been sunk five days before Kretschmer was captured. Though Kretschmer did not show any emotion it was hard to have Prien's death confirmed in this fashion and it made him extremely wary of what he might be asked next.

'I could give you almost as accurate an account of your trips as your War Diary shows,' boasted Creasy.

Kretschmer responded that he found that hard to believe.

Creasy proceeded to provide a detailed account of Kretschmer's patrols since arriving at Lorient with *U-99*. This stunned the German, who this time struggled to hide his shock, realising many of the French dockyard workers must be spying for the British. Even more unsettling was Creasy's easy knowledge of who the leading U-boat captains were, for the Germans had no idea who was in command of British surface warships or submarines. 'Poor Schepke,' observed Creasy, seemingly with real sympathy, adding: 'It was a horrible death for a bold com-mander.' Creasy said the British were glad to have sunk Schepke but 'we would have preferred him to have died differently'.[2]

Apart from human intelligence gathering in occupied Europe and wireless direction-finding technology, the Admiralty could now pluck the fruit of *Bulldog*'s secret capture of Enigma materials. It would enable Bletchley to crack open German naval codes and read the orders being sent to U-boat commanders. It is the fashion at the time of writing to laud the code-breakers of Bletchley as the real winners of the Second World War – as if the Allied cause would never have stood a chance without their efforts.

Although it would provide a decisive edge, one eminent historian of the effort to crack Enigma codes has observed that 'in the end, wars at sea have to be fought by people at sea'.[3]

For their part, aside from concerns about spies and leaks within their own military, the Germans suspected their radio transmissions were being heavily monitored and that a reduction in signals traffic would help.

They were right to exercise caution for Radio Direction Finding facilities had been established in Canada, Iceland and the UK, which picked up German transmissions and triangulated them. British and Canadian warships were also being fitted with a High-frequency direction-finding device (HF/DF, nicknamed Huff Duff), which worked on a tactical basis to tell escort groups where U-boats were by picking up their wireless transmissions.

Analysis of enemy signals traffic continued to be crucial.

In London the Admiralty's Operational Intelligence Centre (OIC) was the brain of Britain's global naval effort and within it was a Submarine Tracking Room, which performed the role of identifying the locations where U-boats were lurking, whether in their naval bases, dockyards, or deployed at sea. The OIC realised that the volume of signals traffic – the brevity, or otherwise, of the message – could indicate a lot without actually knowing what the wording was. Contact reports tended to be concise – especially if the U-boat was near the enemy and did not wish to risk prolonged exposure on the surface. A longer message might be one of the tonnage reports Dönitz insisted U-boat captains sent during a patrol.

It did not occur to the Germans that their ciphers had actually been broken, although Dönitz did fret about it, asking if it was possible Enigma had been compromised. He was reassured by his experts that it wasn't.

The U-boat force boss had plenty of other things to worry about, never mind anxiety over broken codes. The U-boats were now forced to lock horns with tenacious convoy escorts to get at the merchant shipping, while also going well within range of increasing numbers of enemy aircraft.

By April 1941 RAF Coastal Command was under Admiralty direction and being expanded by 15 squadrons. Reinforcements included 57 long-range Catalina flying boats that would operate from airbases in Scotland and Northern Ireland, giving them as much range as possible out into the Atlantic. Coastal Command was by May 1941 also operating a squadron of Hudsons and two squadrons of Sunderlands from Iceland.

Rather than scheduling air cover for every convoy, the RAF wouldn't provide it unless there was a specific threat (such as signals traffic analysis that indicated danger). One veteran Royal Navy escort group commander decried the RAF's failure to learn 'the lessons of the First World War', which was that 'the right place for aircraft was around the convoy, in escort'. Lt Cdr Peter Gretton, aged 29, and in summer 1941 captain of HMS *Sabre*, also felt that 'airmen much preferred to go out on long sweeps looking for U-boats' as doing this 'gave them the feeling of the offensive'. Except, as Gretton pointed out, 'in fact it was quite useless. It was like looking for a needle in a haystack . . .'[4]

Eventually the RAF would come to understand that it was better to wait for the U-boats to unmask themselves by attacking convoys rather than go searching the immense ocean. Air defence, when available at this stage in the war, was also passive – primarily keeping U-boats down, capitalising on their fear of being spotted – with Coastal Command yet to receive powerful enough depth charges.

The Germans had their handicaps too. Apart from overcoming the efforts of the British and Canadian escort forces, U-boats were hampered by fear of provoking the USA.

In spring 1941 the US Navy's involvement in patrolling a 'security zone' made U-boats wary of trespassing too close to North America. Things became trickier in July 1941 when the US military took over garrison duties in Iceland and the USN began escorting shipping to and from there. The risk of a U-boat sinking an American escort at night when lights were doused was considerable, so special instructions forbade German submarines from attacking a warship unless it was confirmed British or Canadian.

It was almost impossible to make such a distinction after sunset and, after lobbying by Raeder, the Führer agreed in August 1941 that U-boats could attack all escorting warships.

By August 1941, Dönitz had 198 submarines at his disposal with 80 available for deployment. With strength in the enemy's escort forces also growing, a stand-off developed. Sinkings declined dramatically but so did U-boat losses. There were signs that while some among the new generation of U-boat captains were made of formidable stuff, having earned their spurs while second in command of boats commanded by the 'Old Gang', others were not so determined. In the latter category was 31-year-old Kapitänleutnant Hans-Joachim Rahmlow, who took the brand new U-570 out on her maiden patrol only to find notoriety and disgrace. Rahmlow had only recently been transferred to the submarine force from the surface fleet. He was a harsh disciplinarian and U-570's very inexperienced crew did not respect him. Consequently, the boat's morale sank.

Sinking no ships at all, in late August 1941 U-570 surrendered to an RAF aircraft off Iceland after Rahmlow panicked on surfacing the boat to find it circling low overhead. It was the first ever capitulation by a U-boat to an aircraft. After capture, although Rahmlow was kept separately his officers were imprisoned with Kretschmer and other submariners at Grizedale PoW camp in the Lake District, North West England. Kretschmer had by then become leader of captured U-boat personnel in England and presided over secret Courts of Honour that sat in judgement on officers who it was felt surrendered their boats without putting up an adequate fight. The First Lieutenant of U-570, Oberleutnant Bernhard Berndt, was found not guilty of cowardice, but this was conditional on action to restore his honour. Berndt was required to escape and sink U-570, which was by then known to be at anchor in the Channel off Barrow-in-Furness. Breaking out of the camp on the night of 18/19 October 1941, Berndt was apprehended by a Home Guard patrol and later shot when trying to escape.[5]

While valour may have been lacking in U-570's captain, the war in the Mediterranean – where the Axis powers were under pressure – provided an opportunity for another to show his mettle.

General Erwin Rommel's Afrika Korps was in late 1941 running out of fuel, ammunition and reinforcements, in no small part due to the depredations of Malta-based British submarines.

In the final three months of the year the boats of the 10th Flotilla – the so-called Fighting Tenth – reaped a rich harvest. The figures were not huge compared to the Atlantic, but in the context of the Mediterranean struggle they were significant. More than 18,000 tons was sunk in October, 26,000 tons in November and 13,000 tons in December. Across the same three months 19,400 tons of Axis shipping was also damaged.[6] Overall less than 40 per cent of supplies sent to Rommel actually reached his troops.

On the other side of the coin, a particular target for Italian and German submarines were tankers that plied between the Levant and Egypt, transporting fuel for the Eighth Army and the RAF in North Africa. The Axis paid a heavy price for trying to cut this supply line, with five Italian and three German submarines lost in the first three months of 1941, most of them destroyed by British submarines.

A further five U-boats were sunk in the subsequent three months, while in the summer the Italians lost five boats, with *Perla* in early July captured and taken into Beirut.

To try to tip the balance in its favour, Germany ordered U-boats and Luftwaffe squadrons to the rescue. While the Luftwaffe pounded Malta relentlessly, the U-boats landed some shocking blows on the British, sinking ships that had been escorting convoys from the UK to Gibraltar (and vice versa) or across the Mediterranean to besieged Malta and Tobruk. *Cossack* was sunk by *U-563* to the west of the Rock on 23 October (and the majority of her crew killed) with *U-81* sinking the famous carrier *Ark Royal* off Gibraltar on 13 November (one man killed). *Ark* had just participated in a convoy to ferry fighter aircraft to Malta for the defence of the island.

The cruiser *Galatea*, which had already been damaged by Luftwaffe dive-bombers on 14 December, was finished off by *U-557* as she approached Alexandria (470 men killed). *U-557* didn't survive long herself, and was mistakenly rammed by an Italian surface warship with no survivors.

The greatest cause of celebrations in Berlin in late 1941 was the sinking of HMS *Barham*, for it was a long time since an enemy battleship had been sunk and it provided a new U-boat hero to boost morale.

U-331 was one of the six submarines sent into the Mediterranean as part of emergency measures. A Type VIIC boat, she was commanded by Oberleutnant Freiherr Hans-Diedrich von Tiesenhausen, a 28-year-old

Latvian-born aristocrat who had once served as a junior officer under Kretschmer.[7]

At 1.00 p.m. on 25 November *U-331*'s hydrophone operator picked up the noise of screws. Putting the attack periscope up, von Tiesenhausen was delighted to find the enemy battle fleet, recognising three battle-ships of the Queen Elizabeth Class – the modernised *Queen Elizabeth* and *Valiant* along with their unmodernised sister vessel *Barham* – which were protected by eight destroyers.

The Asdic of HMS *Jervis* caught a fleeting echo but this was not thought to be a submarine and *U-331* successfully sneaked through the destroyer screen. At a range of between 600 and 700 yards, the U-boat fired a spread of four torpedoes and then went deep and right under *Barham*.

Three torpedoes hit *Barham*, ripping her hull open, with the inrush of water creating a dramatic list to port. Within five minutes she blew apart, killing 862 out of the 1,312 sailors and marines aboard. *Jervis* and *Jackal* made a vain attempt to hunt down the perpetrator, while the destroyers *Nizam* and *Hotspur* picked up the 450 survivors.

'A very satisfactory result,'[8] Admiral Dönitz noted in the War Log for 26 November. After returning to Salamis, *U-331*'s operating base in occupied Greece, von Tiesenhausen was called home to be paraded in Berlin as the newest U-boat ace, and on 15 December made a radio broadcast describing his attack. The Germans had, however, not been able to ascertain which battleship exactly had been sunk and the Brit-ish denied it outright. The news blackout lasted until late January 1942 when it was felt impossible – with so many men killed – to keep it a secret.

Despite such successes, Dönitz recognised it was only so much window dressing. When it came to eroding the enemy's ability to use his own submarines to prey on supply lines to Rommel, nothing was achieved by U-boats in the last three months of 1941.

British submarines were lost due to mine strikes. *Tetrarch* was sunk somewhere off Sicily on 27 October while *Perseus* was claimed in waters near Cephalonia on 6 December. *Triumph* disappeared in the Aegean on 30 December. It didn't blunt the sharp edge of the Fighting Tenth or the RN's Alexandria-based submarine squadron. Likewise, although the air assault caused terrible damage to Malta and inflicted suffering on its people, their spirit was not broken.

*

For the Axis to prevail in the war, the crucial contest remained against convoys in the Atlantic. Among the new aces during late 1941 was 27-year-old Kapitänleutnant Erich Topp who commanded *U-552*, earning notoriety for sinking the destroyer *Reuben James* to the west of Iceland. The first American warship sunk in the Second World War – despite the USA still being nominally neutral – *Reuben James* was an elderly four-stacker assigned to the so-called Neutrality Patrol.

Her loss was the culmination of a series of events encouraged by the blurred lines between preserving the USA's neutrality while protecting merchant shipping. Should they detect a U-boat, USN escorts like the *Reuben James* were not meant to attack, unless they were themselves subjected to aggression. They were, however, permitted to advise British escorts of a submarine's location.

The USS *Greer*, which was said to be 'en route to Iceland with mail',[9] was attacked by *U-652* on 4 September. Evading destruction, *Greer* responded, as allowed by the Rules of Engagement, with depth charges.

Greer was the same kind of vessel as those provided to the UK via Lend-Lease, so commentators in the American press observed that her ensign might be the only way to 'distinguish her from the ships of her type which are hunting submarines for the British Navy'.[10] This distinction was not possible if visibility was less than perfect and especially in Arctic latitudes where at certain times of year there was little daylight.

Other types of American warships were also not safe. USS *Kearny* was a brand new destroyer that at 4.15 a.m. on 17 October 1941 was hit by a torpedo, the explosion killing 11 of her sailors but not sinking her. The captain of *U-568* had sighted a destroyer silhouetted against the flames of a burning merchant ship. Unable to check what ensign she flew, he decided it was too good a target to pass up.

It seemed to be only a matter of time before an American warship was sunk by a U-boat. That moment came around dawn on 31 October when the 21-year-old *Reuben James* was split in two by a torpedo explosion, taking 115 men down with her. There was speculation she might have been stalked by a wolf pack but it was just Erich Topp's boat. *U-552*'s captain thought restrictions placed on attacks in the security zone patrolled by the Americans to be utter nonsense. He could see nothing wrong with sinking *Reuben James*, and even President Roosevelt conceded it was an inevitable consequence of placing American warships in harm's way to protect convoys. Roosevelt, despite his bias towards the British, decided the loss of *Reuben James* was not a *casus belli* and diplomatic relations with Germany were maintained. Those in the USA who opposed the drift to war – or even supported the German cause – would find events overtaking them in early December, not in the Atlantic but on the other side of the world.

18   Prisoner of War No. 1

On 8 December 1941 Kazuo Sakamaki regarded himself as the unluckiest man alive. Given the supreme honour of attacking American battleships at Pearl Harbor he'd flunked the test. The 23-year-old Japanese midget submarine captain had failed to cover himself in glory and then failed to atone by committing suicide.

Corporal David Akui, of the Hawaii National Guard, was on patrol to safeguard a nearby airfield when he found the distressed Sakamaki on Waimanalo Beach. In the poor pre-dawn light Akui noticed a dark figure at the edge of the surf. Raising his rifle, he bellowed a challenge. Failing to get a recognised code word in return he shouted at the man to stop where he was and lie down. There was no need, for Sakamaki was unconscious. On coming around he found himself looking down the barrel of a gun.

It was hard to tell who or what the prisoner was exactly, for he wore only a loincloth, but Akui decided he was possibly Japanese. He marched the man along the beach and handed him over to some army officers, who took the suspected Japanese to a shack, sat him down and fetched a blanket. They also gave him some crackers and water. Despite his trauma and generally poor condition, Sakamaki's eyes sparked with the fire of defiance.

At first he declined to answer their questions but then, in halting English, requested paper and a pencil. He scribbled a note and handed it to one of the American officers. It explained he was a Japanese naval officer whose vessel had run aground on coral and after abandoning it he'd swum ashore. Sakamaki signed off with an unusual request: 'Kill me in an honourable way.'[1]

Much to Ensign Sakamaki's disappointment his captors did not oblige and he would find fame and notoriety as 'Prisoner of War No.1'.[2]

After daybreak things became clearer. Stranded around 150 yards off-shore was a small submarine. Someone swam out with a towline and it was hauled up onto the beach. The corpse of another Japanese was found washed up nearby, seemingly a crewman from the strange vessel. In fact Pearl Harbor had been attacked by five midget submarines early on the morning of 7 December.

The first shot fired by the US Navy during the Pacific war came from USS *Ward*, on patrol off Pearl Harbor. At 3.58 a.m. *Ward* received a signal from the minesweeper USS *Condor* about a suspicious submarine-like object, so the destroyer's captain, Lt William Outerbridge, ordered a sonar sweep, but nothing was found. Around two-and-a-half hours later, the captain of the fleet auxiliary support vessel *Antares* spotted the conning tower of a small submarine that appeared to be having problems staying submerged. He also alerted *Ward*. Meanwhile, an Observer aboard a naval Catalina flying boat spotted the long, thin shape of what seemed to be a submarine just below the surface. The aviators presumed it was an American vessel in trouble and so only dropped smoke bombs to mark its position.

Lt Outerbridge disagreed with this analysis and, having scrutinised the fast-moving object astern of *Antares*, felt it was either a German or a Japanese intruder. It was making an attack run against *Antares*, or trying to follow her through the anti-submarine net into Pearl Harbor.

'Captain, what are we going to do?' the senior rating in charge of the *Ward*'s gunnery department enquired. He received a very direct response: 'We are going to shoot.'[3]

Two of *Ward's* 4-inch guns fired. One shot missed but the other was right on target, punching a hole in the conning tower where it joined the hull. The submarine turned over and disappeared below the waves and, as *Ward* passed over the spot, she rolled depth charges in to finish the job. The Americans were not entirely sure they had destroyed the vessel, despite an oil slick on the water, so the Catalina dropped some bombs, too.[4] A message was sent to naval headquarters at 6.53 a.m. about *Ward*'s attack[5] but there had been so many similar incidents it wasn't felt worth sending the fleet to action stations.

At 7.55 a.m. hundreds of Japanese dive-bombers, torpedo-bombers and high-level bombers began their attacks on the USN's Pacific Fleet. They had been launched from six aircraft carriers 275 miles north of Hawaii.

The air assault was meant to be a precursor rather than the main event. Japanese fleet commanders thought that, while violent and destructive, it would be too brief to cause decisive damage. They felt that submarines would cause the enemy more harm.

Five of 24 I Class submarines stationed off Pearl Harbor were mother ships for the midgets ordered to penetrate the harbour. Lying in wait and perfectly placed, the large, well-armed I Class boats were initially ordered just to reconnoitre the situation off the American bases and trail warships. They were not to make any attacks until the bombs were falling. Thereafter they should ambush surviving enemy vessels – especially damaged battleships and carriers – as they attempted to make a break for the US mainland.

The overall objective of the Japanese assault on Pearl Harbor, both from the air and under the sea, was to cripple the USN's Pacific Fleet for at least six months. This was to remove the most serious impediment to a planned campaign of conquest to secure the oil, minerals and forced labour necessary for Japan's economy and war machine.

Japan imported the majority of its oil, scrap metal and tin from the USA but Washington had imposed a trade embargo as a protest at Japan's aggression in Asia – especially its brutal, long-running campaign in Manchuria and China. It increased the severity of trade restrictions after Japan's occupation of French Indochina in September 1940.

The course to conflict was set, but the Americans – despite well-rehearsed war plans and deep insight into Japanese naval codes – failed to respond adequately. All the pieces of the jigsaw were there – identified via signal intercepts – but they were slow to put them all together, hesitating to believe the Japanese actually meant to strike US territory. Nevertheless the Americans eventually concluded some form of attack would come at 1.00 p.m. EST on 7 December (about 7.50 a.m. in Pearl Harbor) – but most likely against the Philippines. The Japanese intended to declare war before striking, but decryption of the instructions by

Japan's embassy in Washington DC took so long that the declaration was delivered after the bombs started falling.

In September 1940 Japan joined the Axis, and its partners – Germany and Italy – had by mid-1941 invaded the Soviet Union and were intent on conquering Egypt, while the Battle of the Atlantic was at its height. If Japan was to assist them – and also benefit itself while the Russians and British were tied down – then it had to strike hard and fast.

Senior military officers were worried that if Japan did not act soon its war effort would be crippled – for a start the Imperial Japanese Navy's oil reserves were in danger of disappearing and the Americans must not be given time to complete an extensive warship construction programme. The campaign of conquest aimed to secure all the resources Japan needed before Tokyo negotiated peace from a position of strength.

Should the Americans prove to have some fight in them, the plan was to draw the main US fleet towards a climactic final battle. Forward bases would have been secured across the Pacific and a strong defensive outer perimeter established, to guard the Japanese empire's possessions. Japan would by then also have its own powerful new fleet in commission, ready for action.

The two dozen I Class submarines in the vanguard of the Pearl Harbor carrier strike force were deployed from Japan between 11 and 21 November. This was not undetected by the Americans, but they thought it was probably in support of a move against the East Indies.

By 6 December, all the IJN's assigned submarines were gathered in the waters off Hawaii. Success should have been assured, but it wasn't, which didn't reflect on the quality of the boats or their crews, but rather on flaws in tactical employment. The high volume of signals traffic between the senior Japanese fleet commander, based at Kwajalein, in the Marshall Islands, and the submarines made it easier for American direction finders to fix the locations of the boats and assess how many were likely to be off Hawaii. American ships were re-routed, while valuable units stayed in port or had a heavy escort. The Japanese had the fastest, most powerful and farthest-reaching torpedo then in existence, the Type 95, but it couldn't show its power if there were no targets.

A couple of cargo vessels were sunk by IJN submarines, but no USN warships. The Japanese also failed to co-ordinate their efforts, with some sea sectors left unattended for long periods while a boat went off in pursuit of a target. None of the midget submarines succeeded in attaining their objectives, though at least one did get into the middle of the American fleet anchorage.

During the air attack several American ships spotted a periscope and fired at it, with one 5-inch shell hitting the Japanese boat's commander and mashing him up. The craft still managed to fire a torpedo but it failed to strike any warships and blew up on hitting the shore.

The USS *Monaghan* was heading to join *Ward* on anti-submarine patrol when a lookout spotted something under the water – a strange, long, somewhat bent object lying ahead. The captain, Lt Cdr William Burford, remarked that he didn't know what it was but 'it shouldn't be there'.[6] Despite its damaged state, the midget submarine's commander tried to hit *Monaghan* with its remaining torpedo, which missed. The destroyer shoved the midget submarine down to its doom. As *Monaghan* passed over, depth charges were dropped, set at just 30ft, their explosions shaking the destroyer's stern violently.[7]

At 10.41 p.m. on the night after the air attack the commander of the midget submarine launched by *I-16* sent the wireless message 'Tora! Tora! Tora!' ('Tiger! Tiger! Tiger!'). This was the code word for a successful surprise attack, but there was no evidence of this. The mother submarines waited for the midgets to return, but by 11 December they gave up all hope of seeing them and headed back to base.

Reeling from the attack on Pearl Harbor, which killed or injured 3,500, the United States was bolstered by a fiery speech given by President Roosevelt to Congress on 8 December.

Labelling 7 December 1941 'a date which will live in infamy', Roosevelt said it was 'obvious that the attack was deliberately planned many days or even weeks ago' even as the USA was engaged in talks with the Japanese 'towards the maintenance of peace in the Pacific'.[8]

Congress declared war on Japan the same day while another part of the IJN's long-cultivated war plan was enacted, for within a fortnight of the Pearl Harbor assault there were nine Japanese submarines patrolling off the west coast of the USA.

Their desired targets failed to show up, for the USN's carriers continued operating from Hawaii and would soon reap a suitable revenge. Some retribution was achieved on 10 December when a Dauntless dive-bomber from USS *Enterprise* attacked and sank s *I-70*. She was the first full-size Japanese submarine sunk in the Second World War, with no survivors from her 93-strong crew.

If Japanese submarines were unlucky at Pearl Harbor, the US Navy's were equally cursed when they tried to defend the Philippines from invasion. In a repeat of the German U-boat force's misfortunes in Norwegian waters, chronic torpedo failure nullified the best efforts of American submariners.

Of the III submarines the USN had in commission on the outbreak of war, 28 operated from the Philippines. When Japan struck there on the same day as Pearl Harbor no serious resistance was provided by the motley collection of elderly cruisers and destroyers in the Asiatic Fleet, while fighter squadrons of the US Army Air Corps (USAAC) were wiped out on the ground. It fell to Asiatic Fleet's submarines to mount a defence and their crews were determined to inflict havoc on transport ships off-loading Japanese troops. They were to be frustrated, for even though the American boats successfully held enemy vessels in their crosshairs, the majority of their Mk X and Mk XIV torpedoes exploded shortly after launch, ran under the targets or simply failed to detonate. They sank just three vessels.

The Americans were having a tough time, but three days after Pearl Harbor the British were also to suffer a hard knock.

The loss of the battleship *Prince of Wales* and the battlecruiser *Repulse* on 10 December off Kuantan was the first open-ocean loss of capital ships to air attack. It might not have happened had it not been for IJN submarines, which both found and fixed the British ships for destruction.

As Japanese invasion forces landed on the Malay Peninsula on 8 December, the British sent out Force Z – composed of the two capital ships and destroyer escorts – from Singapore to try to destroy enemy shipping.

Sixteen IJN submarines had been assigned to cover the Japanese invasion of Malaya and at 2.15 p.m. on 9 December *I-65*, commanded by Lt Cdr Harada Hakue, sighted Force Z heading north-west and trailed the British ships. The Japanese had received intelligence of the enemy vessels being in the Far East but this was the first confirmed visual sighting and the IJN feared the two British capital ships would now attack invasion shipping.

I-65 lost them in bad weather during the afternoon but in the early hours of 10 December, I-58, commanded by Lt Cdr Sohichi Kitamura, fired a spread of torpedoes at Force Z, which missed.

During a subsequent high-speed chase at 14 knots I-58 managed to send a full sighting report, giving course, speed and location, though contact was soon broken. This report at least told air reconnaissance aircraft where to look for the enemy vessels. Once they were found, Japanese bombers were guided in and sank the two British capital ships, with 327 sailors and marines losing their lives in *Prince of Wales* and 513 in *Repulse*.

Thousands of British and American sailors and marines had died within the space of a few days, with momentum in the war running firmly in favour of the other side. Official British naval historian Capt. Stephen Roskill would describe it as 'the spring tide of Axis success'.[9]

19   Deadly Drumbeat

For much of 1942, the most savage sector in the Battle of the Atlantic was off the Eastern Seaboard of the USA, during a second Happy Time for the U-boats. What a deadly playground it was, for while German submarines had been deterred from preying on British shipping in US territorial waters until December 1941, now they ran rampant.

Far from easing the British predicament, the entry of the USA into the war for a while made it worse. Many American escort vessels were sent to the Pacific and those that remained were hopeless at anti-submarine warfare in littoral waters. The gift of 50 Lend-Lease destroyers and 10 former US Coast Guard cutters to the British and Canadians had also denuded the USN's own stock of potential ASW vessels.

The Royal Navy was able to protect British-flagged vessels during the transatlantic voyage but could not defend them while they were sailing within US waters – and it wasn't politic to tell the new allies how to organise things in their own front yard. The British did suggest that even a weakly escorted convoy was better than allowing ships to sail solo but it would take some months before the Americans paid heed.

At night the Eastern Seaboard was lit up like fairyland, the perfect backdrop for sighting and sinking shipping, within sight of funfairs and boardwalks. Some people thought the activities of U-boats might even boost the economy as a tourist draw. The civic leader of Baltimore forecast that resorts would thrive rather than decline.

A dozen German submarines at a time operated off the US coast, claiming a rich harvest of British-flagged tankers, described by one post-war historian as 'a holocaust'.[1] The Germans called it Operation *Paukenschlag* (Operation Drumbeat) and despite its grim toll of Allied shipping some holiday resorts along the Florida coast resisted pressure to turn off the lights until April, when the US Navy insisted it had to be done.

The head of the USN, Admiral Ernie King, loathed the British and initially, out of pride, refused to accept two dozen RN anti-submarine trawlers on loan for convoy escort work. The official reason was because the USN was worried it would lead to weaker protection on transatlantic convoys. In the end King did take them, such was the growing crisis of the second Happy Time. The British switched a pair of escort groups to operate from bases in North America, while Coastal Command sent some squadrons to fly from airfields on the western side of the Atlantic.

Service chiefs from both the USA and the UK met in early 1942 and it was decided that rather than just being an entirely Admiralty task, responsibility for organising and protecting convoys should be split between the two nations. The Atlantic was divided into an eastern zone (in which the RN held prime responsibility) and a western zone (where the USN led the fight). Responsibility switched between the two navies along a Change of Control (Chop) Line.

By May 1942 the convoy system off the east coast of the USA was properly established and so Dönitz – again following his policy of least cost for maximum return – sent long-range U-boats to attack less well-protected shipping in the Caribbean and the Gulf of Mexico.

The so-called Milch Cows, ten large Type XIV replenishment boats built from 1941 onwards, enabled this. Tasked with keeping hunting submarines deployed for longer and further out into the Atlantic, they supplied fuel, food and other supplies in mid-ocean. With that help, between January and June 1942 U-boats accounted for 585 Allied and neutral merchant ships – three million tons of shipping (including 492 sunk off the Atlantic coast of the USA). The price paid was 21 U-boats lost; including half a dozen destroyed in the far western Atlantic – but a hundred new submarines were brought into service.

While all this was going on the Royal Navy was trying to persuade the RAF's Bomber Command to release aircraft and aircrews to tip the balance back in favour of the Allies. It was reluctant to do so, for the RAF believed its best chance of contributing to the defeat of the enemy was through strategic bombing. The navy pointed out that without the flow of oil supplies across the Atlantic the RAF's bombers would be grounded, but such logic cut little ice with Bomber Command, that is until Churchill intervened and told the air force it had to help out.

It was true that air raids against U-boat construction sites were yielding some results, with reconnaissance photographs taken on 28 July revealing 'submarine ship-building yards have been severely damaged'.[2]

It still fell far short of being the sort of substantial effort needed and the Royal Navy's official historian would be extremely critical. In Roskill's withering analysis the failure of the RAF to better resource the Atlantic battle meant 'another year was to elapse, and further enormous losses of ships and cargoes were to be suffered, before Coastal Command's long-range aircraft began to play a decisive part in the struggle'.[3]

Of particular significance were Very Long Range (VLR) B-24 Liberator bombers, which would evolve into truly formidable anti-submarine aircraft. These at last began to enter the fray in 1942 and the first U-boat sunk by a VLR was U-597, attacked on the surface off Iceland on 12 October by an aircraft from No. 120 Squadron.

While they waited for more long-range aircraft, the main effort for the Allies was providing better weapons for destroyers, allied with improved tactics, development of escort carriers and more effective penetration of German naval codes.

*

In January 1942 Captain Gilbert Roberts had been sent to Liverpool to set up the Western Approaches Tactical Unit (WATU), to both distil and improve upon the tactical lessons.

Located on the top floor of the Exchange Building, adjoining Derby House, the WATU introduced new ways of training and fresh tactics and thinking. A one-time gunnery officer in the cruiser submarine *X1* during the late 1920s, Roberts made it his business to sit down with escort group commanders and ask how they reacted when under U-boat attack at night. He did not get a very reassuring response from most of them.

One remarked: 'Well, what can you do? It's a very difficult thing and we can't see them.'[4]

Roberts acknowledged that the radar sets then in service were 'very elementary' and not all warships had them. There was one escort group commander who, on being asked the standard question, gave a more positive response. He told Roberts 'when an attack . . . takes place all the escorts should do the same sort of thing on a planned schedule at exactly the same time' and in this way there would be 'maximum effect . . . around the convoy'.

This officer was Cdr Frederic 'Johnny' Walker, captain of the sloop *Stork* and commander of the 36th Escort Group, based at Liverpool.

Due to his long years specialising in ASW, Walker believed that only maximum simultaneous coverage (with no gaps to let a U-boat escape) would stand any chance of catching an enemy submarine. Walker called his night attack response plan 'Buttercup' (the codeword flashed to all warships in an the escort group under assault). On receiving the 'Buttercup'[5] signal the majority of the escorts would shoot off in various directions away from the convoy, firing illumination rockets and star shells.

The aim was to rip away the protective cloak of darkness from the U-boats as they withdrew. One of the escorts would stay close to any torpedoed ship as it fell behind the convoy – provided it was still afloat – hoping to catch a U-boat trying to finish it off. Walker could claim two U-boat kills thanks to this tactic.

It might seem incredible that such a tactically adept officer should just be a Cdr but he did not suffer fools gladly, which was why he had been passed over for promotion between the wars. He was too fond of telling senior officers what he really thought. His ASW specialisation further marginalised him and for the first two years of the war Walker was actually confined to shore jobs. Yet cometh the hour, cometh the man and Walker's aggression, determination and eye for tactical detail – and above all his amazing instinct and skills in hunting submarines – were just what Britain needed. There were other escort group commanders who would prove equally remorseless, including Macintyre who got Schepke and Kretschmer, but Walker was to be the most illustrious of them.

Capt. Roberts studied numerous convoy action reports from Walker and others, suggesting to Admiral Noble that serious losses happened when U-boats waited until escorts had raced off in pursuit of a contact and then got among a convoy. A different tactic to deal with that was required. With the admiral's agreement, Roberts started work on a new set of instructions called 'Raspberry'.

In 'Raspberry', on receiving the codeword the idea was, again, to turn night into day with rockets and star shells. This time one escort would race ahead of the convoy, zigzagging, while others fell back to carry out radar and Asdic sweeps behind it (where a daring U-boat commander might well be waiting to get among the merchant ships). There was also 'Pineapple', which was triggered on receipt of intelligence that a wolf pack was waiting across the path of the convoy. On receiving the signal, escorts would charge ahead – again firing star shells and rockets – to make the U-boat commanders scared of being revealed, so that they dived. Once this was achieved the escorts would turn back and a search pattern would be run, to try to find the bolder enemy boats. To perfect these tactics the WATU ran intensive war games during which officers of the Women's Royal Naval Service (WRNS), who did not serve in the fighting arms, proved tough taskmasters and expert ASW tacticians. They often humbled the less able escort captains.[6]

In essence, the plans to combat U-boats were all a variation on a theme – to take aggressive, co-ordinated action and deny enemy submarines their main advantages of surface speed (over slower escorts and merchant vessels) and cover of darkness. They would have to dive into an environment where they were slow and sonar could search them out.

20   Serve Some Tea

One place in which Asdic was particularly useless at seeking enemy craft was in harbour, where seabed clutter easily hid those intent on doing harm to surface vessels.

This offered the Italians a golden opportunity to strike a blow against the British that threatened to nullify the Royal Navy's dominance of the Mediterranean. For despite their lack of aggression and luck in major surface warship operations – and the less than stellar performance of their big submarines in the Atlantic – the young men of the Italian Navy excelled at less conventional forms of warfare.

These unconventional warriors on the night of 18/19 December 1941 penetrated the defences of Britain's main Mediterranean Fleet base at Alexandria. To enable the attack, the large submarine *Scirè* had transported three manned torpedoes called Pigs (fitted with detachable warheads) in containers fixed to her deck. Off Alexandria their crews climbed aboard and launched them.

The RN's Mediterranean Fleet had been warned via decrypted Italian signals that some kind of attack against Alexandria was imminent, but exactly how was not known. An alert was sent out across the fleet, but the Italians still managed to slip through the anti-submarine net when the gate was opened to let in British warships.

With their pilots picking a target each, the Pigs edged under the battleships *Queen Elizabeth* and *Valiant* and Norwegian-flagged fleet tanker *Sagona*, detaching their charges. The crew of one Pig, Lt Antonio Marceglia and Lt Spartaco Schergat, abandoned their craft after failing to get back through the net. They tried to escape across the desert to a pre-arranged rendezvous point with *Scirè* off the coast but were captured, as were Lt Luigi Durand de la Penne and Lt Emilio Bianchi, along with the third Pig crew, Lt Vincenzo Martellotta and Lt Mario Marino.

Bianchi and Durand de la Penne were found perched on a mooring buoy below *Valiant*'s bow and taken aboard the battleship, the vessel under which they had planted their explosive charge. Refusing to answer any questions, they were kept in a compartment deep inside *Valiant*, but at 6.00 a.m. de la Penne revealed that charges were due to detonate.

Sustaining serious damage, though not mortally injured, the British battleships settled on the bottom of the harbour. The extent of their damage was kept secret – aided by the fact that they remained upright in shallow water. A bonus victim of the attack for the Italians was the destroyer *Jervis*, which was taking on fuel from *Sagona* at the time of the explosions. She was put out of action for a month while the battleships would not be fully operational until July 1942 (*Valiant*) and June 1943 (*Queen Elizabeth*).

Seeking to press the Axis advantage in the Mediterranean, German naval boss Admiral Raeder pushed for Malta to be conquered, so eliminating the menace of British submarines preying on shipments to the Afrika Korps.

After this – with their flank protected and supply lines safeguarded – Axis forces could push on to conquer both Egypt and Iran. This might open up the possibility of linking with the Japanese.

In the face of a determined air assault on its island base, the Fighting Tenth endured and the brightest star of all the Malta-based submarine captains was 31-year-old Lieutenant Commander Malcolm Wanklyn, who commanded HMS *Upholder*. He destroyed more tonnage of enemy shipping than any other Allied submarine captain, notching up 140,000 tons. During 25 patrols in the central Mediterranean, making more than 36 attacks, Wanklyn's tally included two enemy submarines, a destroyer and an armed trawler. *Upholder* also damaged an enemy cruiser and a destroyer but, most importantly, sank 11 enemy supply ships, damaging four others.

Wanklyn won the Victoria Cross in waters south of Sicily during an attack on a troopship convoy sailing from Naples to Tripoli. It was the first VC awarded to a submariner in the Second World War.

Upholder's victim was the 17,800-ton *Conte Rosso*, a Glasgow-built former transatlantic liner of the Italian Line. So a British submarine commanded by a Scot attacked a liner that had once given Scottish shipyard workers gainful employment. *Conte Rosso* took with her 1,300 out of the 2,729 mariners and troops aboard.

The Italians exacted swift revenge by subjecting *Upholder* to a blistering depth-charge assault, the submarine's hull recoiling amid thunderous explosions. Men grabbed whatever they could to stop themselves from being toppled. Light bulbs shattered. Eardrums popped. Wanklyn tried his best to thread *Upholder* through the gauntlet of depth charges.

Even though he could hear enemy propellers, the lack of working hydrophones meant he had no idea if the enemy ships were going away from or coming towards his boat. Wanklyn took his guess, each time telling the coxswain to take *Upholder* to a certain depth and steer a course he hoped would edge them out of danger. Somehow he did it, with *Upholder* surviving the blast of 37 depth charges in the space of just 20 minutes. *Upholder* settled on the seabed for an hour, just to make sure the coast was clear. 'Serve some tea,' Wanklyn whispered to the submarine's cook, who rustled up steaming hot mugs of char, along with some cake and fruit salad. When *Upholder* surfaced and moved through an oil-covered sea, moonlight revealed shattered lifeboats and other debris. There was no sign of the enemy, not even corpses. The citation for his VC said Wanklyn handled the attack with the 'greatest courage, coolness and skill'.

When asked in January 1942 if he would like to be flown home for a rest, he responded: 'Thanks, but no. It's my ambition to sail back home in command of *Upholder*.'[1] Wanklyn even submitted a request to extend his boat's time on station for a further two months, but it was declined, so he took *Upholder* out on her 25th patrol. It would be her farewell to the Med before sailing for the UK.

The exact circumstances of how the boat and her men met their end somewhere off Libya are not clear but she was most likely destroyed on 14 April. According to one theory, *Upholder* was spotted by German aircraft and bombed while in shallow water, then depth-charged by an Italian motor torpedo boat.[2]

Two other VCs were awarded to daring British submarine captains in the Mediterranean. Among the boats operating from Alexandria was HMS *Torbay*, whose captain was the supremely aggressive 35-year-old Anthony Miers (another Scot). He won his VC for a daring penetration of Corfu harbour in March 1942, with *Torbay* sinking two supply vessels. She subsequently escaped the attentions of enemy warships that dropped 40 depth charges during a 17-hour pursuit.

Cdr John Linton, a 38-year-old Welshman, was captain of *Turbulent* and his VC was awarded to salute his courage in command of various submarines since 1939. A rugby-playing giant, Linton was a man of few words and nerves of steel. His record included sinking an enemy cruiser, a destroyer, a submarine and 100,000 tons' worth of merchant shipping, along with the destruction of three trains by gunfire.

In the last year of his life, Linton was at sea for 254 days, half the time submerged. *Turbulent* endured more than a dozen pursuits by enemy submarine hunters – surviving a total of 250 depth charges – but Linton, his men and the boat met their end in bitter circumstances. In February 1943 *Turbulent* was sunk not by a hard-charging destroyer – as might have befitted such a daring submarine captain and his courageous crew – but by a mine, somewhere between Sardinia and Corsica.

British submarines were by now also waging war in the frozen Arctic. With the Soviet Union in the war and requiring substantial military aid from the Allies, Murmansk, the port developed during the First World War as a gateway for supplies, was the main destination yet again. From August 1941 Allied merchant ships made the dangerous voyage to Murmansk in the Kola Peninsula and Archangel on the White Sea, the so-called Kola Run.

With German units operating from several bases in Norway, and even from Finland, there was an offensive to actually capture Murmansk, which failed. The port was subjected to intense aerial bombing, with the Kola Run itself hotly contested and made all the more arduous and hellish by two environmental factors. Firstly the Arctic ice during the winter months crept closer to the Russian shore, hemming the convoys in and shortening the range for U-boats and Luftwaffe bombers based in Norway. This increased their endurance and sortie rate. Secondly, during the summer months the Allies were forced to risk almost constant daylight as they sailed across the top of the world.

The Arctic convoys had run with few losses in early 1942, but in the Admiralty there was a fear that Germany's surviving surface raiders might emerge from hiding in the Norwegian fjords to attack Allied shipping. The U-boats began to take their toll of convoys in the spring, including the heavy cruiser *Edinburgh*, which was torpedoed by *U-456* before being finished off by enemy destroyers (though one of the enemy vessels was also lost). The U-boats failed against their desired targets, however, for 34 out of 38 ships in convoys PQ-15 and QP-11 got through unmolested. Convoys going to Russia carried the prefix PQ, while those coming the other way were labelled QP.

The ice edge in April was at its closest to land. Naval chiefs thought it would be better to temporarily abandon the Arctic convoy effort rather than suffer severe losses of warships and merchant ships which the

Allied cause could not afford. The political imperative overturned such objections. Soviet leader Josef Stalin was arguing for a second front to relieve pressure on Russia and the Arctic convoys were a means to show willing in lieu of invading north-west Europe.

PQ-16 in late May was composed of 35 merchant vessels – a visible demonstration of an increasing effort on the Kola Run. It departed the assembly point at Reykjavik, Iceland, on 21 May while QP-12, composed of 15 ships, sailed from the Kola Inlet. On 25 May Luftwaffe air attacks began with seven ships lost from PQ-16 while QP-12 suffered not a single loss. No surface raiders had appeared and enemy submarines failed to act either.

PQ-17, of 36 vessels, and QP-13, of 35 ships, which departed Reykjavik and Kola respectively at the end of June were a different story. It appeared *Tirpitz* was coming out and PQ-17 was ordered to scatter on 4 July. The main escort force, led by the cruiser HMS *London*, withdrew to the west in order to hold off the enemy battleship. It was a fool's errand, for while *Tirpitz* did come out, she did not depart her Norwegian fjord base until after the convoy was ordered to scatter.

Sighting reports from two Allied submarines and a Catalina patrol aircraft were intercepted by the Germans and decoded, persuading Admiral Raeder to call off the surface raider group attack on PQ-17.

This left the job of attacking the convoy to U-boats and the Luftwaffe. With PQ-17 losing collective protection and also nearly all of its escorts, bombers and U-boats were able to hunt down the merchant vessels with ease, sinking 23 out of 34 ships.

The Russians were distinctly unfriendly to their Allied supporters, only grudgingly allowing Royal Navy warships to work out of Murmansk and Archangel. Bitter memories of Western intervention at the end of the previous war were lodged deep. Fraternisation between Western sailors and local girls was actively discouraged. For their part the British sailors and marines who went ashore or, worst luck, were actually based there, found their surroundings bleak and squalid.

Into this uninspiring environment were sent Royal Navy submarines to see what they could do by mounting patrols from Kola. Thirty-year-old Lt Dick Raikes was captain of *Seawolf*, which from time to time operated out of the Polyarnoe inlet, near Murmansk, between October 1941 and August 1942. His first impression was 'wholly unfavourable' and he observed: 'The cold grey rocky sides of the Kola Inlet rose steeply from the cold sea, and they were snow-capped. The whole panorama was grey and white, with not even a building to break the bleakness of the scene until we turned the corner into Polyarnoe itself.'[3]

Relations with the Russians were characteristically frosty, but the hosts were delighted to join British submariners in watching Disney's cartoon movie *Snow White*. The Soviets liked it so much they requested multiple showings until it wore out.

There was a cultural surprise from the Soviets in return.

While Raikes was browsing the library of an officers' mess ashore, he was amazed to find an uncensored copy of the 'original unexpurgated complete edition' of Sir Richard Burton's *Arabian Nights*.

'What a thing to find, in English, in such a place!' exclaimed Raikes, while its 'sheer pornography . . . had to be read to be believed'.

At sea during the winter it was often snowing, or a bright moon rendered it 'like being on the surface by day'. *Seawolf* was frequently coated in ice but the gloom was lifted by the Northern Lights, which Raikes felt were 'like a gigantic fireworks display'. On one patrol a gauge froze at 40ft and Raikes only realised his submarine was beyond safe diving depth – and might soon implode – when the hull began to protest.

During gales those pulling a watch on the bridge had to be lashed to the periscope mast, so they weren't snatched away by angry seas, while in the deep, winter spray turned to ice in the air, slicing the skin of submariners' faces. Cooking was impossible in such rough seas, so Raikes and his men armed themselves with tin openers and used their fingers to consume the cold contents of cans.

The Russians customarily did not tell their allies where their submarines were operating, which led to *Seawolf* making what may have been an unwitting attack on a Soviet boat during the afternoon of 18 March 1942. *Seawolf* was 170 miles to the west of Trondheim, staking out approaches to the Norwegian fjord where *Tirpitz* lurked, when her hydrophones picked up a submarine. Inspection via the periscope revealed what looked to be a surfaced U-boat, which must have passed close to *Seawolf* while submerged.

'It was calm but with a very heavy swell,' Raikes explained, 'and I only had time to turn and fire on a very broad track indeed. After the correct firing interval one loud explosion was heard.'

The submarine's noise stopped and a quick look through the

periscope revealed a smudge of black smoke on the water. *Sealion* surfaced, Raikes climbing up to the bridge to find the prow of his boat cutting through a heavy oil slick. While at the time he reported a U-boat 'probably destroyed', German records captured at the end of the war did not substantiate the claim.

Discussing it with members of his crew in the 1980s, Raikes remained certain *Seawolf* had claimed a U-boat, but he also suggested 'the possibility must remain it was a Russian'.[4]

As the ships of PQ-17 were picked off, on the night of 5 July *K-21*, commanded by Lt Cdr N.A. Lunin, allegedly attacked and hit *Tirpitz*. Lunin reported that he spotted the German battleship along with the heavy cruiser *Hipper* and an escort of eight destroyers north-east of the Norwegian North Cape. Lunin claimed two hits on *Tirpitz*.

The British submarine *Unshaken* was also stalking the same group – indentifying them as *Tirpitz*, *Hipper* and *Scheer* plus escorts – and reported a *possible* hit by *K-21* on *Hipper*.[5] The Germans denied there had been any hits at all and claimed that *Tirpitz* was unaware torpedoes had been fired. Lunin got home to be hailed a hero, also claiming he sank an enemy destroyer. He was saluted with the Hero of the Soviet Union award.

21   Of Monstrosity and Mercy

The same sort of undeclared war at sea that had taken place in the North Atlantic during 1940–41 was also waged in the South Atlantic. This was primarily due to one of the United States' major suppliers of raw materials remaining non-aligned but antagonised by Axis actions.

The traffic from Brazil to the USA and the world beyond included rubber, iron ore, chrome and industrial diamonds with neutral Brazilian vessels inevitably suffering collateral damage as U-boats preyed on the ships of Allied nations sailing the same routes. The risk was increased by the internal transportation of Brazilian goods and people being so difficult, which meant a great deal of coastal traffic was not heading overseas but taking goods between different parts of Brazil.

Even while the country stayed neutral the Americans were allowed to develop air bases to fly anti-submarine aircraft on the trade routes off its coast, while USN escorts patrolled the broader South Atlantic and safeguarded all coastal traffic. In return for providing such protection, American naval forces were allowed access to Brazilian ports and dockyards.

Diplomatic relations were broken off between Berlin and Brazil in early 1942 and such was the increasingly blatant co-operation with the Allies that in June the Germans began an all-out campaign in the sea lanes emanating from Brazil.

With the waters off the Eastern Seaboard of the USA less fruitful due to convoying and improved anti-submarine tactics, the hunting grounds off Brazil were bound to become a major focus for both German and Italian submarines. Five Italian boats operating as group Da Vinci achieved considerable success in the Caribbean in February and March 1942, sinking 15 ships off the Windward Islands for a total of 93,000 tons.[1]

The warmer waters of the Atlantic were thought to favour the Italian submarines, being closer to the Mediterranean conditions they were constructed for. The sinking of the Brazilian-flagged cargo vessel *Cabedelo* – lost with all 57 onboard – by *Leonardo da Vinci* on 26 February 1942 was a big step on Brazil's path to conflict with the Axis. The *da Vinci*'s 34-year-old captain, Lt Luigi Longanesi-Cattani, knew he'd made an error with potentially serious consequences, for when he sent a wireless report on the sinking, he did not admit the name or the flag of the target.[2] In April the *Calvi*, commanded by Cdr Emilio Olivieri, sank five ships while working solo, adding a further 27,571 tons to the Italian total. Most damaging of all for the Allies was the loss of nine tankers. It was a high water mark for Italian submarines for they sank no more ships in the Atlantic during 1942.

Mexico had declared war on Germany in May 1942 after only two of its ships were sunk by U-boats but Brazil, which had a substantial pro-German lobby in its parliament, endured worse, though even its patience was not limitless. It was a killing spree within sight of Brazilian shores by *U-507*, commanded by 35-year-old Korvettenkapitän Harro Schacht, that led to anti-German riots on the streets of Brazil's cities. On 16/17 August Schacht sank five Brazilian-flagged merchant vessels.

As these ships went down one by one in the approaches to Bahia and Sergipe, the Brazilians were presented with their own variant of the *Lusitania* or *Athenia* outrages.

More than 140 officers and men of the Brazilian Army were among those who lost their lives in the *Baependi*. When another ship was torpedoed the death toll included pilgrims on their way to Sao Paulo.[3] A total of 500 people were killed in the five ships. Brazilian fury was further stoked by news that one ship Schacht sank was engaged in picking up survivors from another.

A local newspaper summed up the national mood: 'Truly monstrous are the acts which the Axis submarines have just perpetrated against helpless Brazilians . . . If Rome, Berlin and Tokyo think that they can intimidate us by such savage acts, they are completely mistaken.'[3]

On 22 August Brazil declared war on Germany and Italy, though not against Japan (for the simple reason that Tokyo's submarines had not committed any acts of aggression against its vessels).

In all, 36 merchant ships flying its flag – a not insignificant part of the Brazilian merchant marine – had been sunk before Brazil felt compelled to declare war. Once it was in the war American anti-submarine aircraft and surface warships were able to make even greater use of Brazil's bases, extending their range and coverage. The Brazilian Navy also joined the fight, while the Americans sent $100 million in military aid under Lend-Lease, with anti-submarine vessels among the first examples of this material support. In return, Brazil would eventually send an expeditionary force overseas to fight the Italians and the Germans.

For the Italian submarine force, success in the Caribbean was followed by bad news, when no quarter was given in the final fight of the *Calvi*, commanded by Captain Primo Longobardo (who had at one time sailed in Kretschmer's *U-99* to sharpen his warfare skills). The 40-year-old veteran officer was Italy's most successful submarine captain in the Atlantic, commanding two other boats prior to *Calvi*. Longobardo sank four ships during one patrol in waters off the west coast of Scotland (a tonnage total of 17,489 tons) and for this achievement he was awarded the Iron Cross by Adolf Hitler.

On 3 July 1942, *Calvi* was ordered to attack convoy SL-115, sailing from Freetown to the UK, which had an escort force composed of HMS *Lulworth* – a one-time US Coast Guard cutter transferred to the UK – and the sloops *Bideford*, *Hastings* and *Londonderry*.

Calvi was forced to the surface and put up a terrific fight before sinking, with her captain among the dead. Longobardo was posthumously awarded the Gold Medal for Valour, Italy's highest decoration for bravery in the face of the enemy.[4]

While some Axis submarine captains covered themselves in glory, paying the ultimate price for defiance, others became notorious for their incompetence and were reviled by the men they commanded.

One of these less than exemplary U-boat COs was 27-year-old Korvettenkapitän Rudolf Lemcke. A former surface fleet officer, he assumed command of *U-210* in February 1942, his men especially disliking his heavy drinking on patrol (brandy and champagne being his favourite tipples).[5] Lemcke also had the habit of ordering the boat dived when the sea was rough, so he could sleep off a hangover.

On 3 August 1942 *U-210* turned towards Greenland, with fuel running low but picking up homing signals from other U-boats. A wolf pack was being assembled to attack convoy SC-94 and *U-210* was instructed to join the party. *U-210* was soon found by the enemy, around 650 miles to the north-east of Cape Race, courtesy of keen Asdic operators in the Canadian destroyer *Assiniboine*. What unfolded became one of the legendary close quarters battles in the Battle of the Atlantic and (on the German side) among the most idiotic.

To start off, *U-210* received such a going-over with depth charges Lemcke felt compelled to surface and engage in a gunfight, a fatal tactical error. With a fuel tank holed by shellfire, *U-210* was unable to dive and eventually attempted to seek refuge in a fog bank. This tactic failed as the Canadian warship's radar held the submarine fast in its grip. Lemcke recognised this would be a fight to the death or a humiliating surrender and felt disinclined to choose either, so he let the agony go on.

With *Assiniboine* circling, guns blazing and the U-boat outgunned, in desperation *U-210* turned ever tighter. The destroyer's bridge received a hit, causing a fire and killing a man, but *Assiniboine* delivered the more devastating blows. A hit dead centre of *U-210*'s conning tower killed Lemcke and five of his men while also wrecking it, knocking out the submarine's anti-aircraft cannon.

Assiniboine rammed the U-boat, while inside *U-210* one of the officers lost his nerve, issuing contradictory orders. An engine room Petty Officer, who had cultivated a particular hatred for this man, armed himself with a very heavy wrench, intending to put a stop to the nonsense. The

Petty Officer stood behind the screaming officer, waiting for the lights to go out so he could bash the other man's brains in. The lighting held and so, without the cover of darkness, the Petty Officer thought better of it, especially when the order to abandon ship was finally given.

The German submariners scrambled out of the hatches and leapt into the sea, with *Assiniboine* and the British corvette *Dianthus* saving 37 of them. It was, though, a pyrrhic victory as *Assiniboine* had been very seriously damaged and was no longer much use. This gap in the anti-submarine screen presented the U-boats with an opportunity to break into the convoy.

With mayhem unleashed on SC-94, it was clear to the Admiralty that escort reinforcements would be needed. Orders to join the fight were sent to 43-year-old Cdr Arthur Layard in the destroyer HMS *Broke*, at the time teamed up with the Polish destroyer ORP *Blyskawica*.

Responding affirmative, as the two warships headed for the battle, Layard noted rather drily in his diary: 'From signals received S.C. 94 seems to be having quite a bit of trouble with U boats.'[6]

The weather worsened, with *Broke* jumping about so violently it made many of her ratings seasick. Progress was slow but Layard kept track of events as they unfolded by monitoring signals. He was aware that *Assiniboine* had disposed of one U-boat but there were plenty of others intent on causing trouble. Layard would be the senior officer in the escort once he arrived, something that filled him with trepidation.

When *Broke* met the convoy on the evening of 8 August, Layard was alarmed to find HMS *Primrose* the only escort vessel actually with it.

'All the rest were away hunting U-boats or standing by stragglers or picking up survivors,' Layard noted in his diary. 'The convoy had been attacked in daylight this afternoon & 5 ships sunk. Took up position on the starboard beam.'

Someone in the corvette *Dianthus* spotted a U-boat on the surface and lookouts aboard *Broke* saw a star shell exploding in the sky as the corvette raced in to attack. At 7.10 p.m. on 8 August the coxswain on the bridge of *Dianthus* had sighted what might be a submarine conning tower but a squall hid it before he could be sure. An hour later the lookout in the crow's nest on the masthead also fleetingly spotted something, about eight miles away. Less than an hour after that a lookout in *Dianthus* caught sight of two enemy submarines on the surface. Opening fire, the corvette dropped 12 shells around *U-379*.

Morale in the submarine was shaky even before the encounter with *Dianthus*, due to 30-year-old Korvetttenkapitän Paul-Hugo Kettner's poor command skills. Deeply superstitious, Kettner at one stage held a target vessel in his periscope sights but 'refused to fire . . . because it was Friday'. The crew of *U-379* considered him 'a lazy, inefficient martinet' who 'threatened his men with the death penalty for minor offences . . .'[7]

Apart from leaving notes around the U-boat ordering people to abide by certain petty rules and regulations, Kettner presided over an idiosyncratic daily routine, dictated by his own needs. He spent much of his time 'lounging in his bunk in pyjamas' listening to the radio. There would be no lolling about for *U-379*'s captain as *Dianthus*, commanded by Lt Cdr Clement Bridgman, closed in for the kill.

Kettner actually thought he'd managed to get away, despite the hydrophone operator – who could hear the propellers of the enemy warship getting louder – advising him to the contrary. He insisted that the hydrophone operator 'was talking nonsense', sending the man into such despair he angrily tore his headphones off and cast them aside.

The first depth-charge attack threw the submarine upwards, with the electricity failing, periscopes damaged and none of the gauges working. The boat remained watertight, however, with the Engineer Officer, Oberleutnant Max Lang, successfully blowing the tanks to surface.

Holding the enemy in her searchlights and loosing off Snowflake illumination rockets, *Dianthus* hurled in five more depth charges and opened fire with her 4-inch gun, winding herself up to ramming speed.

Smashing into the U-boat forward of the conning tower, the corvette pushed *U-379* down and rode over her. Once the stern was free *Dianthus* let go five more depth charges, set to explode at 50ft.

Inside the submarine Kettner panicked, leading a rush to abandon ship but struggling to open the conning tower's lower hatch. He shouted: 'I can't do it!' A senior rating stepped forward and, without saying a word, opened the hatch for the captain, who scrambled up, 'pushing others off the conning-tower ladder in his haste'. Remaining officers and senior ratings were left to organise the abandon ship procedure, with an order for married men to leave first.

Dianthus swung around and fired several 4-inch shells into the submarine, then charged again, ramming *U-379* three more times. Finally, the U-boat disappeared below the waves. The last anyone saw of Kettner he was 'swimming in the Atlantic, and asking who had his life-jacket'. He and the other 36 members of his crew drowned or died of exposure.

The SC-94 fight went on and, expecting a daylight attack on 11 August, the escort force was drawn tight around the convoy. The fog cleared, enabling air support from dawn, with warships directing aircraft onto Huff Duff contacts. Reading signals from his boats, Admiral Dönitz realised the chances of success were now minimal so cancelled planned attacks.

The five-day running fight drew in a total of 18 U-boats, with 11 merchant ships sunk, totalling 53,000 tons.[8] Three U-boats had been sunk (the two attacking the convoy and another on its way to join in). Four U-boats were damaged and forced to withdraw. Between 25 July and 10 August the total number of German submarines lost was ten, a sign that the initiative was passing to the Allied escorts.

22   Tipping Point

Almost at the same time as the hard-fought battle of convoy SC-94 unfolded in the Atlantic, the struggle for control of the Mediterranean spiked, and key to it was the fate of Malta.

The tiny island was a dusty anvil on which the mighty hammer of the Luftwaffe and the Italian air force was falling repeatedly, unloading more bombs on it than had been dropped on London during its Blitz.

For both the civilian and military population – including the submariners of the Fighting Tenth – it meant a troglodyte existence in cavernous shelters carved out of rock. The stresses and strains of action patrols were bad enough but even when back in Malta, thanks to the constant German air attacks, there was no rest for the submariners. The officers' quarters in the submarine base had been reduced to rubble and the barracks where the ratings went for a rest were strafed on a daily basis.

Four British submarines were damaged by air attack while alongside, so in March 1942 it was decreed boats should be dived in harbour during daylight hours. *Unbeaten* sustained damage while submerged. Boats receiving work could not be moved or dive, and found no refuge. The Polish-manned *Sokół* was damaged while alongside the wharf for repairs but was eventually made ready for patrol despite the air raids. *P39* was not so lucky. Hit more than once by bombs, she was declared a total loss.

April 1942 saw the most intense period of bombing, with the Greek submarine *Glaucos* sunk while under refit and the British *P36* suffering a similar fate. A special effort was made by the Germans to hit Malta's submerged submarines, even in deep water, and *P34* was so badly damaged she nearly couldn't surface.

In addition to the Axis possessing absolute air supremacy – bombing any ships that were spotted – aircraft and enemy torpedo boats sowed mines, often in the very routes submarines used to exit and enter Malta. There were no minesweepers left afloat to clear the channels, and submarine flotilla commander Captain George 'Shrimp' Simpson decided the Fighting Tenth should be disbanded until the channels could be swept. The process of transferring submarines and personnel to Alexandria, to be absorbed into the 1st Submarine Flotilla, was completed by early May.

When the Afrika Korps made its big push to reach Cairo in the summer of 1942, it was decided the Alexandria-based submarines and their depot ship *Medway* should switch to Haifa. *Medway* didn't get very far as she was torpedoed by *U-372* on 30 June just off the North African coast. This left British submarines without vital floating workshops, a resupply base, accommodation, mess decks or offices for flotilla staff. Fortunately only 30 of the 1,135 highly skilled personnel aboard *Medway* were killed and 47 torpedoes were recovered for future use. The guilty U-boat was on 4 August cornered by four British destroyers and sunk off Haifa.

Royal Navy submarines operated from Beirut for a short period but by late July the process of reforming the 10th Flotilla had started at Malta, as minesweepers had by then made the channels safe. At the same time a shake-up of RAF top brass, and fresh fighter aircraft, saw the British securing air superiority.

HMS *Unbroken* sailed from Malta on 30 July with a minesweeper clearing the way and fighter cover overhead, beginning her patrol by spending a week prowling in the Bay of Naples. Her captain was the highly experienced and aggressive 26-year-old Lieutenant Alastair Mars and his boat had been deployed to help protect an important convoy.

With food, fuel and other supplies running low, Malta was still dangerously close to being knocked out of the fight. In response, Operation Pedestal was being mounted, a convoy of 14 ships with the heaviest protection of any staged by the Royal Navy in the Second World War. There would be submarines guarding the flanks, while also distracting enemy naval forces, and so Lt Mars got war patrol orders.

He was to start off by using the boat's newly fitted 3-inch gun to bombard a railway line on the coast of Calabria while also looking for targets at sea. Thereafter, *Unbroken* would loiter off Messina, having reserved at least four of her eight torpedoes for any Italian cruisers trying to interfere with Pedestal. After unsuccessful attacks on merchant vessels that consumed four torpedoes, on the night of 8 August Lt Mars took *Unbroken* in towards the Italian coast and destroyed a goods train.

By dawn on 10 August, *Unbroken* was on her allotted patrol station off the Cape Milazzo lighthouse, about 18 miles from Messina. After diving she was harassed by Italian patrol craft, so Mars decided he would change the boat's patrol station unilaterally. This was a potentially serious breach of discipline but as absolute radio silence was needed in the enemy's home waters Mars could not inform the flotilla headquarters.

Mars placed his submarine between Stromboli and Salina, two of the Aeolian Islands, about 30 miles away from his originally assigned spot. *Unbroken*'s CO was aware enemy cruisers were to be found passing through these waters, heading out from or back to Messina.

On 11 August, just as the sun was coming over the horizon, *Unbroken* dived to await passing trade, Mars calculating the Pedestal convoy was by then off Ibiza.

Apart from *Unbroken*, six British submarines were strung out on a picket line to the south of Pantelleria while another was allocated waters off Cape St Vito. Like *Unbroken*, their job was to watch out for cruisers or any other enemy units trying to attack Pedestal.

On that day the elderly carrier *Eagle*, bringing up the rear of the convoy, which was already under heavy air attack, was attacked by *U-73*.

She had stalked the convoy for more than hour, a layer of cold water hiding the submarine from the Asdic of escorting destroyers. It enabled 29-year-old Kapitänleutnant Helmut Rosenbaum to follow his specific orders to sink enemy carriers and by this stage there were three with

Pedestal. For the Germans it was vital to prevent them from flying air-craft ashore to Malta, while the carriers' loss would also fatally weaken the convoy's defences.

Rosenbaum put four torpedoes into *Eagle* from a range of 500 yards, which tore out the port side of the carrier. She took on a severe list as thousands of tons of water poured in. Aircraft tumbled off her flight deck, while hundreds of men leapt into the sea.

Fighters preparing to land back aboard to refuel and rearm suddenly found they had no ship, so touched down on the more modern car-rier *Indomitable*. There was no room for them so they ended up being ditched over the side. Somehow 927 men from *Eagle* were saved, though 163 went down with her, the sea belching gigantic bubbles as the ship's boilers exploded.

A wild melee developed on 12 August as the convoy entered waters between North Africa and Sicily. Italian submarines were spoilt for choice when it came to targets while dive-bombers and low-level torpedo-bombers came on in swarms.

The Italian submarine *Axum* scored hits on the cruisers *Nigeria* and *Cairo*, along with the large oil tanker *Ohio*. The *Cairo* was so badly damaged – with her stern blown off – she had to be sunk by her own side. *Nigeria* headed for Gibraltar with a flooded boiler room and other severe damage below decks. The cruiser *Kenya* was also hit by a sub-marine torpedo but was able to stay with the convoy. So vital was her cargo that the *Ohio* carried on steaming towards Malta.

So many torpedoes were fired and so many bombs rained down that it was unclear whether submarines or aircraft, or a combination of both, sank some ships. The Italian submarines *Dessie* and *Alagi* claimed a share in sinking two merchant vessels, while *Bronzo* hit and damaged another, which later had to be sunk by a destroyer. Italian submarines did not have it all their own way. The *Cobalto*, a brand new boat on her first mission, was rammed and sunk by the destroyer HMS *Ithuriel*.

In *Unbroken* Alastair Mars estimated the convoy was covering 300 miles a day and would be through the Sicilian Channel on the night of 12/13 August. *Unbroken* spent the daylight hours of 12 August at peri-scope depth, patrolling slowly under a glassy sea to give her captain time to grab some sleep and her crew to rest.

Surfacing after dark, Mars found the night lit by the red glow of the volcano Stromboli, which glowered from the nearby island. In the early hours of 13 August, while still surfaced, *Unbroken* picked up a sighting report. A British reconnaissance aircraft had discovered an Italian cruiser force to the north of Palermo, heading east at 20 knots to pass south of the Aeolian Islands – not far from where *Unbroken* lay in wait.[1] The cruisers had been sent to attack the Pedestal convoy but Italian commanders were not satisfied they had enough air protection, so decided to withdraw them.

At 7.00 a.m. Mars sat down in the wardroom to a breakfast of bacon and eggs, but the hydrophone operator called out that he had picked up the sound of propellers ahead. Sending his breakfast plate and cutlery flying, Mars dashed to the periscope. Taking guidance on bearings from the hydrophone operator, *Unbroken* headed west towards the target but Mars saw nothing. He listened in on the hydrophone headset and decided it was heavy surface units. Returning to the periscope, Mars was delighted to spot the tall masts of large vessels on the horizon, emerging out of the morning mist.

He saw that it was four cruisers with a screen of eight destroyers and under an air protection umbrella. Mars estimated the enemy warships were making 25 knots. Taking the submarine deep enough not to be spotted from the air, Mars manoeuvred *Unbroken* into what he hoped would be a good firing position.

On each very brief look he made sure the scope poked no more than six inches above the surface. He also immediately checked for enemy aircraft, which fortunately were doing circuits on the other side of the task group.

An enemy destroyer passed over *Unbroken*, but its draught was not deep enough to strike any part of the submarine. With the destroyer gone, Mars fired a spread of four torpedoes. The range was 3,000 yards and two cruisers were hit, a torpedo slamming into each one. Mars took *Unbroken* deep and while destroyers carried out sonar sweeps and made depth-charge attacks – dropping more than 100 – the British submarine got away intact.

The *Bolzano* – a heavy cruiser of 13,883 tons displacement and armed with eight 8-inch guns – was so badly damaged she never saw service again. She was only saved by running herself aground on a nearby island while the *Muzio Attendolo* – a light cruiser of 8,994 tons – had 60ft of her bows blown off. *Bolzano* was refloated a month later and set off under tow for Naples, later heading for La Spezia, where she remained until sunk by an Allied attack in June 1944. *Muzio Attendolo* received temporary repairs at Messina, enabling her to sail for Naples. In early December 1942 Allied bombers finished the job Mars started.

The losses on the Pedestal convoy were substantial – a carrier and two cruisers along with nine merchant vessels – but four ships got through carrying supplies and *Ohio* limped in, shepherded by RN destroyers. Although she sank in Grand Harbour, *Ohio* remained upright and her aviation petrol and oil were retrieved. The Pedestal ships sustained Malta at the most critical point, ensuring its submarines and surface vessels continued launching attacks on Axis supply lines.

Rommel needed 70,000 tons of supplies a month to keep his army rolling[2] but a significant proportion of that was still not getting through. In August 1942 a quarter of the tanks, trucks and other vehicles sent by sea from Italy to North Africa, along with large amounts of ammunition and 41 per cent of the fuel, were sunk in transit. Most of the losses were due to British submarines.

It would get worse for the Axis in September, with 44 per cent of the ships sent to Rommel sunk before they reached North Africa.[3] Rommel's advance into Egypt stuttered and stalled on 30 August, partly due to his tanks being robbed of petrol. It seemed the tide of war was being turned against the Axis in North Africa, both on land and at sea, but in the Atlantic, the Far East and the Pacific the story was far from settled.

23 With all Battle Flags Flying

Having only 'seriously damaged the tools of a past war', as one US Navy historical analysis has termed it,[1] the Japanese hungered to sink the aircraft carriers they had failed to eliminate at Pearl Harbor.

To achieve that they aimed to force a major fleet battle, and part of it involved utilising submarine ambush techniques used without success at Jutland (and its near sequel) in 1916.

In early May 1942, during the Battle of the Coral Sea – historic for neither side's warships exchanging fire, with the engagement fought entirely with carrier-based aircraft – *Lexington* was sunk but the Japanese lost a carrier too, and another was damaged. The stage was set for an epic fight, with *Yorktown*, *Enterprise* and *Hornet* going up against a five-strong enemy carrier strike group and battle fleet (with 11 capital ships) accompanying an invasion force headed for Midway Island and the Aleutians.

American and Australian intelligence analysts had correctly assessed in mid-May that the Japanese would make this move in early June. US Pacific Fleet boss Admiral Chester Nimitz was a former submariner, so recognised his boats might take the edge off the enemy, provide early warning and even pull off something notable.

One of the first moves was to have the submarine *Gudgeon* on a patrol line to the north-west of the island, while a further two dozen submarines were positioned in the approaches to Midway.

The Japanese, meanwhile, aimed to put their own picket lines of submarines across the anticipated route of USN carriers responding to the attack. The Americans had already placed their carriers off Midway, so by the time Japanese submarines reached their allocated areas their targets had long gone. The IJN attempted to reconfigure submarine patrol lines, with boats surfacing to make fast surface transits, but failed to catch the enemy carriers, though *Yorktown* suffered serious damage due to air attack that left her a sitting duck.

Aboard submarine *I-168*[2] Lt Cdr Yahachi Tanabe was grateful for new orders. When aircraft earlier pounded Midway Island as a precursor to the planned invasion, *I-168*'s 35-year-old captain had watched through his periscope, giving reports of fuel tanks exploding to his excitable crew.[3] Subsequently carrying out a shore bombardment of Midway's defences, *I-168* was for a while subjected to air attack and depth-charging.

When the submarine's radio mast was extended it picked up wireless signals about four Japanese carriers being sunk and a sighting report from a reconnaissance aircraft. An enemy carrier appeared to be dead in the water and *I-168* received a direct order to 'locate and destroy . . .'[4]

It was the *Yorktown*, which had been abandoned but had not sunk as expected and efforts were being made to salvage her. *I-168* proceeded swiftly on the surface but not at top speed, for Tanabe was wary of missing his target in the darkness. He was mightily relieved when, at 5.30 a.m. on 6 June, a lookout sighted a black lump darker than the surrounding night, 11 miles away. 'It was the easiest intercept a submarine commander ever made,' said Tanabe. 'My course had not changed, from beginning to end.'[5]

Diving the boat, Tanabe slowed *I-168* right down to reduce noise, taking very careful periscope looks as he sneaked inside the destroyer screen. He estimated that up to seven enemy warships could be arrayed against him (with some possibly out of sight behind the carrier). A smaller vessel was nestled alongside the crippled ship.

I-168's men hardly dared move or breathe as she crept into a firing position, while through the scope Tanabe saw the sky was getting lighter. The enemy carrier actually seemed to be making modest headway – she was under tow from the fleet tug *Vireo*.

At 1.30 p.m. *I-168* fired a spread of four torpedoes from a range of 1,200 yards and less than sixty seconds later explosions were heard, provoking the submarine's men to yell an exuberant: 'Banzai!'[6]

Tanabe ordered full ahead and down to 200ft. In a daring move reminiscent of U-boat captains in the First World War, he took *I-168* right under the target. He didn't think the carrier would sink immediately and it would for a short while protect his boat. Tanabe also reasoned the Americans wouldn't want to drop depth charges with their own men in the water around the sinking ship. When Tanabe tried to creep away *I-168* was detected, with the destroyers *Monaghan*, *Gwin* and *Hughes* launching depth charge attacks that lasted until evening. *I-168* survived the assault, but only just.

Tanabe could chalk up two ships with his one spread, for while two torpedoes hit *Yorktown*, another ran shallow and hit a destroyer moored alongside. This was USS *Hammann*, which had two hoses connected to *Yorktown*, one for piping in fire-fighting foam and the other extracting oil to correct the carrier's list. The destroyer was also supplying food and coffee to a salvage party of 160 men led by *Yorktown*'s CO, Capt. Elliott Buckmaster. *Hammann* had received signals from other destroyers about a potential submarine presence, but before she could disconnect herself the four torpedo tracks were sighted, coming in on the starboard beam.

Hammann's 20mm cannons fired at the most shallow-running torpedo but missed and the subsequent explosion broke the ship's back. Debris, oil and water shot high into the air, raining down on *Yorktown* and *Hammann*; all lines and hoses were severed by the force of the ship being lifted up. The destroyer's captain, Cdr Arnold True, was hurled against a desk in the pilot house with such force it broke a rib. He was unable to speak, leaving the Executive Officer, Lt C.C. Hartigan, to give the obvious order: 'All hands abandon ship!'[7]

The destroyer sank less than four minutes after the first explosion, taking 15 of her men with her, although the majority of casualties were inflicted about a minute later when, according to a USN action report, 'there was a heavy explosion underwater'.[8]

It was most likely the destroyer's own depth charges reaching their preset depth as the stern sank, the massive second detonation killing or injuring dozens of men in the water. In all *Hammann* lost 81 out of her crew of 241. Aboard *Yorktown*, as soon as the torpedo tracks were spotted one of the ship's 20mm guns was fired to warn people throughout the vessel of an enemy attack. Two chilling words were passed along: 'Torpedo attack.'[9] Some sailors and marines were hurled around, breaking bones, while others were thrown into the sea by the massive *Hammann* explosion. The fresh torpedo damage combined with her already fragile state meant *Yorktown* was doomed, though Capt. Buckmaster remained reluctant to give up. The salvage team was taken off the ship by *Vireo* but Buckmaster wanted to go back aboard again in the morning, by which time a salvage tug would have arrived. It was not to be. Buckmaster recorded in his action report that just after 7.00 a.m. the following morning: '*Yorktown* turned over on her port side and sank in about 3000 fathoms of water with all battle flags flying.'[10]

When *I-168* reached home her men received a heroes' welcome, yet while Tanabe's sinking of *Yorktown* was celebrated, news of four Japanese carriers lost at Midway was kept from the civilian population for the rest of the war.

Overall, the performance of the American submarines at Midway was not marked by obvious success and the most effective boat bore the same name as Fulton's craft of the early 1800s. Prior to Midway, 37-year-old Lt Cdr William Brockman of the *Nautilus* trained his men hard to make up for the deficiencies of his elderly vessel (first commissioned in 1930). He also had the wireless set tuned to the same frequency as Catalina scout aircraft[11] to take advantage of up-to-the-minute information. On the morning of 4 June, after picking up a sighting report of enemy aircraft, he found a group of four enemy ships – the battleship *Kirishima* and the cruiser *Nagara* with two large destroyers.

A Zero fighter from one of the carriers strafed the American submarine's periscope, which was followed by depth-charging. Once this ceased, Brockman was able to insert his boat among the enemy, the Japanese battleship shooting at his periscope but missing. *Nautilus* fired a torpedo at *Kirishima* from 4,500 yards, which also missed. Next, a cruiser dodged a *Nautilus* torpedo and again the submarine weathered depth charges, this time from the destroyer *Arashi*.

While the other ships raced off, *Arashi* stayed behind to carry on hunting the submarine, but after a few hours departed to join the main Japanese carrier task force. *Arashi* was spotted by American dive-bombers and they followed her to the carriers, their subsequent attacks instrumental in destroying the pride of the Imperial Japanese Navy. Had *Arashi* not stayed behind to search for *Nautilus* she might never have been spotted and followed by the enemy aircraft. During the subsequent battle the Japanese lost their key strike force, with four carriers sunk by American dive-bombers and torpedo-bombers. The IJN also lost many highly experienced, irreplaceable aviators.

During the afternoon of 4 June *Nautilus* fired a spread of torpedoes at the crippled and furiously burning Japanese carrier *Kaga*, but the American submarine could not hang around to observe their impact as two destroyers pounced. Judging it was safe to take a periscope look, Brockman brought the boat back up. Having witnessed the destruction of the old battleship *Arizona* at Pearl Harbor on 7 December 1941, he now saw a similar smoke cloud towering over an enemy vessel.

Brockman mistakenly reported that he had finished off the *Soryu*. Later analysis revealed the ship's correct identity and the fact that none of his torpedoes contributed to her sinking. Nonetheless, Brockman was decorated with a well-earned Navy Star for valour while in command of *Nautilus* at Midway. In a strange twist it also emerged later that the air tank of a *Nautilus* torpedo that broke apart on hitting the carrier saved the lives of some Japanese survivors who clung to it until rescued.

Nautilus was the best performing of the American submarines, with other submarine captains blaming their boats' failure on the manner in which they had been deployed. Their bosses thought they were at fault by being too risk averse and lacking in skills. It didn't help that the majority of American boats were old, some dating back to the 1920s, but a huge problem was the number of torpedoes that were duds, either going astray, failing to detonate or exploding prematurely.

Rear Admiral Robert English, boss of the USN's Pacific-based submarines, suggested that during his next patrol Brockman should use his boat's two 6-inch guns to bombard Emperor Hirohito's summer palace on the coast near Tokyo. This would be a worthy follow-on to the Doolittle Raid, a spectacular, if largely ineffectual, air raid on Japan by 16 Army Air Corps B-25 bombers launched from the carrier *Hornet* in April 1942 (itself in retaliation for Pearl Harbor). A bombardment of mainland Japan would, so English thought, restore pride in the submarine force after its less than stellar performance at Midway.

English was asking Brockman to take his vessel into dangerous enemy home waters that would be hard to navigate safely in such a big old boat, never mind the danger posed by enemy anti-submarine patrols. After attacking and damaging a Japanese destroyer and missing a merchant ship on 22 June – receiving a depth-charge attack in return – Brockman scratched the idea of lobbing shells at Hirohito's palace.

Instead he stalked and fired two torpedoes at the destroyer *Yamakaze* on 25 June, finally achieving success. Trying to build on it, he also targeted a tanker, which escaped though damaged. For proof of *Yamakaze*'s end – and there were no survivors – Brockman took one of the most impressive periscope shots of the war, which showed the destroyer disappearing below the waves. A sinking rising sun flag emblazoned on a turret declared American retribution loud and clear.

English was very down in the mouth about Hirohito's palace not being shot up, but when Brockman produced his photo of *Yamakaze*'s demise he was delighted. The image was disseminated to the world's press and even ended up in *Life* magazine as its photo of the week. Brockman was rewarded with another Navy Cross.[12]

The Japanese may never have set foot on Midway but they did occupy two of the Aleutian Islands, though it was a strategic dead end. There was never any serious intention of using them as a stepping-stone to invade mainland Alaska. For both sides the battle for the Aleutians actually drew in military resources that could have been better used elsewhere. It did at least offer the USN's submarines a good opportunity to attack enemy vessels. On 4 July 1942 *Triton* sank the destroyer *Nenobi*, while on 5 July *Growler* destroyed another (*Arare*) and damaged two others (*Shiranubi* and *Kasumi*).

With the Japanese effort in the Alaskan Territory stymied, there was a bid by the IJN to spread terror in continental USA and Canada in retaliation for the Doolittle bombing raid and the exploits of *Nautilus*. On 20 June 1942 *I-26* fired two dozen shells at the Estevan Point Lighthouse, on the western side of Vancouver Island, in British Columbia. They shattered some windows but that was about it.

The next day *I-25* surfaced and carried out a bombardment of Fort Stevens, Oregon, causing no damage whatsoever except to the reputation of the coastal defence batteries. They did not understand what was happening and so did not fire back.

One Japanese naval aviator who specialised in operating from submarines twice carried out his own one-man blitz of the USA, the only occasions in history that an enemy aircraft has conducted bombing raids against targets in North America. Thirty-year-old Warrant Officer Nobuo Fujita was embarked in *I-25* to fly her Glen floatplane, having earlier suggested that submarine-based aircraft could be launched against the US Navy bases at San Diego and San Francisco or even be used to damage the Panama Canal lock system or attack Seattle.

Naval staff planners turned those proposed targets down but suggested he should drop incendiary bombs in forested areas. These might burn out of control and be impossible to douse, perhaps destroying entire towns. The first raid went ahead on 9 September, with Fujita launching from *I-25* before dawn. He dropped two 168lb incendiaries near the small logging town of Brookings.

Tokyo made plenty of propaganda capital out of the raid, with the *Asahi* newspaper boasting on 17 September: 'First Air Raid on Mainland America. Big Shock to Americans.'[13] It didn't cause a lot of damage but it did generate fear among the civilian population of the USA's west coast. Fujita was back in the Oregon skies on 29 September to drop more incendiaries, with his mother submarine aiming to further terrorise the USA by sinking some ships. The US government authorised a special flight of P-38 fighters deployed to an airstrip on the Oregon coast to try to shoot down the Japanese raider, but despite numerous alerts they never got their chance.

Fujita survived the war and was invited to Brookings in 1962 as part of efforts at post-war peace and reconciliation. He expressed his regret and shame at the raid, expecting an angry reception, possibly involving punitive egg throwing. The former naval aviator took along his Samurai sword, which had been passed down through his family for four hundred years, intending to atone by committing ritual suicide if required by his hosts. The visit went well and the sword was instead presented to the town library to be put on display. Fujita was made an honorary citizen and during several visits to Brookings was always greeted warmly.

24   Gaining the Edge

In the struggle between U-boats and the Allies in the North Atlantic, achieving victory depended on who gained – and then retained – the killer edge. For the Germans, while their submarines continued to rack up impressive tonnage totals, the enemy threatened this ability with growing air superiority. Admiral Dönitz noted that Allied aircraft had increased in number and variety and, he admitted, were fitted with 'an excellent Radar set [for use] against U-boats'. It was making the 'conduct of the U-boat war in the East Atlantic very difficult'. Boats sailing for patrols or returning from them were, while in the North Sea and the Bay of Biscay, 'exposed to grave danger by daily, even hourly, hunts by aircraft'.

Four U-boats had been sunk in July and August in the approaches to submarine bases, with others damaged. The mid-Atlantic air gap also appeared to be narrowing, with Allied aircraft ranging up to 800 miles to the west from British air bases. Dönitz felt such extended air cover for convoys, and harassment of submarines closer to home, made operations 'in some cases no longer worthwhile'. It could lead to 'irreparable losses, to a decline in successes and consequently to a decline in the chances of success of the U-boat war as a whole'. He demanded that the Luftwaffe provide a solution, using its long-range He-177 Greif heavy bomber, which the admiral felt was 'the only aircraft which has a range and fighting power capable of combating the enemy aircraft in Biscay and in the Atlantic against convoys'.[1]

A thousand He-177s had been built but only a few hundred were in service and their mechanical reliability was very poor. Though efforts would eventually be made to use them in an anti-shipping role, the He-177s would never try to hunt and kill enemy maritime patrol aircraft.

If the Germans could not reduce the Allied maritime air power edge with the He-177, work was at least underway to fit U-boats with equipment that hopefully would detect the radar of enemy aircraft.

On the other side of the contest there was a certain determination to achieve a decisive edge via another capture of secret materials, for seizing a U-boat was the ultimate prize.

Across the RN escort commanders cultivated plans, though none was devised with more clinical aggression than Johnny Walker's. His 'Operation "Haggis" for the Capture of a U-boat' was set down in July 1942 as the template for how things ought to be done.

While Capt. Walker felt U-boats forced to the surface would probably not be boarded and captured before scuttling charges, or other measures, took effect, it was worth having a well-thought-out plan. He observed, rather presciently, that even if a boarding party got aboard an enemy submarine it was 'unlikely . . . that they will come out alive'.[2]

Op Haggis bore all the Walker trademarks of decisive, even ruthless action. Distributed to his escort group ships it advised:

In broad outline the plan is:

a) *To ensure that no live German (or Italian) leaves the boat – any who may succeed in doing so are left to drown.*
b) *This intention is made outstandingly clear at the earliest possible moment both by deed (via small arms fire) and by word (via loud-hailer).*
c) *To send a boarding party over to enforce (a) above.*
d) *To keep the crew bottled up inside their boat: if they are to save their skins they will have to keep her afloat.*
e) *To tow the prize to a British port.*

When it came to 'Method of Execution', Walker, who had been promoted from Commander to Captain at the end of June 1942, pointed out: 'Seconds may make all the difference between success and failure.'

Op Haggis required the British warships involved to keep the U-boat's casing and conning tower 'under continuous fire' using cannons and machine guns. Walker also suggested they should 'keep up a continuous stream of orders and threats' via loudhailers. The enemy should be warned – in German or Italian, depending on which was relevant – that instructions must be 'carried out to the letter'.

The boarding party's primary objective would be to take control of the conning tower and bridge 'and from there to prevent any German from leaving the boat either by the conning tower or any other exit: briefly, to shoot anyone who shows his nose above the upper deck'.

Walker also decreed: 'Small arms fire should be directed down the conning tower hatch and Number 69 [reduced power] grenades thrown. Orders and threats . . . also bullets, should be freely used, bearing in mind that shooting, shouting and ruthless brutality is the only language that a Nazi really understands.' A high priority for the boarding party was 'to smash or securely cover both periscopes [using special canvas covers], so that the bottled-up crew are blinded as to what is really happening'.

It was stipulated that two warships should be involved in Op Haggis, with the boarding party coming from one and a towing party from the other. Of vital importance was 'a short length of chain', which Walker said was 'for hanging down the conning tower hatch, thus preventing it from being closed and the U-boat from diving'. He felt it might also be necessary to subdue the crew with 'an occasional stream of bullets [fired] from above ricocheting around their control-room'. The U-boat officers should be extracted from the submarine 'if possible, whilst leaving the ratings on board to keep her afloat'. He added: 'If a U-boat is brought to the surface in conditions favourable to the operation, ships in the vicinity are to take immediate action, as indicated above without waiting for orders.' Capt. Walker's escort group initiated Op Haggis in June 1943, after attacking and forcing *V-202* to the surface in the North Atlantic. However, since the submarine was so badly damaged and clearly sinking, Walker called off the attempt. It was not worth risking the lives of his men. Walker's ships rescued 30 German submariners.

When a feasible opportunity to capture Enigma materials presented itself, the ships involved did not conduct themselves with the sort of speed and efficiency Walker would have demanded.

Early on the morning of 30 October 1942, a Sunderland flying boat was conducting a routine search about 70 miles to the north of the Nile delta when its radar detected a U-boat on the surface.

The nearby destroyer *Hero* was ordered to find and attack the submarine, while at Port Said the 12th Destroyer Flotilla of four ships – *Pakenham, Hurworth, Dulverton* and *Petard* – was ordered to sail and join the hunt. Having made a good Asdic contact the pack of destroyers began their attacks shortly before 1.00 p.m. and, assisted by an RAF observation aircraft, kept the U-boat under assault for ten hours.

Three hundred depth charges were dropped, including some with soap squashed into their hydrostatic fuses to ensure they detonated beyond the maximum depth of 500ft. Forced to the surface, *U-559*, commanded by 28-year-old Kapitänleutnant Hans Heidtmann, was subjected to intense fire and her crew began to jump into the sea.

Petard did not have a boarding party standing by as she made her approach to *U-559* and had to call for volunteers, which wasted time. Two whalers were launched, with Seaman Stanley Reynolds given the job of putting the chain down the conning tower.

As his whaler approached the U-boat, German submariners who had leapt into the sea clung to its side, trying to get aboard. Instead of brushing them off and leaving them behind, the boarding party hauled them into the boat. This was all taking too long and Walker would no doubt have told them off severely, for in choosing to save the Germans *Petard*'s men were potentially losing an opportunity to save many more lives and supplies on the convoys.

An officer and a rating – *Petard*'s First Lieutenant Anthony Fasson and Able Seaman Colin Grazier – stripped off their clothes, dived off *Petard*'s other whaler and swam to the U-boat. The ship's teenage NAAFI canteen assistant, Tommy Brown, also dived in and swam across.

These three succeeded in getting inside the U-boat, with Brown given the job of taking material – including the latest Enigma settings – up the conning tower and handing it down to men on the casing, who then passed it on to eager hands in a whaler that had by then tied up alongside.

The whaler also took aboard a wounded German submariner who had been found 'shot up'.[3] In fact, seven U-boatmen had been killed in the battle, though Heidtmann survived.

From the whaler Reynolds saw that the U-boat was clearly 'in a precarious position', with water gushing in through holes ripped in the hull. Suddenly, to Reynolds' horror, the submarine 'just went down . . . disappeared'.

The men on the casing severed the lines and leapt into the whaler, which pulled away while Tommy Brown jumped off the conning tower and was hauled aboard. Asked about the men in the U-boat, he gasped: 'They are still down there.'[4] Fasson and Grazier stood no chance – fulfilling Capt. Walker's prediction about the risks – but even so the whaler rowed around hoping to spot them. As had happened with *Bulldog*'s capture, the George Cross was awarded to the men who had risked their lives and in this case lost them. Tommy Brown – actually only 15 years old at the time and too young for war service – was discharged ashore, but still received the George Medal. He was later killed in a house fire when trying to rescue his siblings, so his mother went to Buckingham Palace to collect the award. Among the documents recovered during 'the Petard Pinch' was the current short signal book and the latest weather reporting cipher. These gave Bletchley's boffins a start on finding a new way to crack a code produced using the new four-wheel Enigma machine, which had flummoxed the Admiralty for a while. With the aid of an electromechanical machine (the Bombe), by mid-December Bletchley was able to crack the Shark code then being used to communicate with U-boats in the Mediterranean and North Atlantic. Using this information the Submarine Tracking Room in the OIC ordered convoys to take appropriate evasive action and also sent warships and aircraft to attack the foe.

While the Bletchley code-breakers were busy capitalising on the material taken from *U-559*, in his headquarters at Liverpool, Admiral Noble had been studying the lessons of SC-94 and other engagements.

He decided that, in addition to dedicated escorts riding with convoys, Support Groups should be on standby. These extra warships would reinforce protection for a convoy under attack or be sent to guard one that intelligence indicated was facing an imminent U-boat threat. The advent of the Support Groups would hopefully secure the initiative for the Allies. It was not to be, at least not for a while. A need to protect the massive amount of shipping involved in Operation Torch – the invasion of North Africa – intervened to rob Western Approaches Command of destroyers, corvettes and escort carriers.

As it turned out, the Germans were poorly positioned to reap what might otherwise have been a rich harvest of vulnerable troop transports and supply vessels. The U-boats nearest to the invasion shipping were preying on traffic off West Africa and by the time they arrived off the landing beaches they found enemy defensive screens too strong. Results were meagre.

During Torch operations Allied land-based and carrier aircraft belatedly achieved a measure of revenge for the unfortunate *Barham*. On the afternoon of 17 November *U-331* – the boat that sank the old battleship in late 1941 – was spotted and sunk off the Algerian coast.

U-595 met her end three days earlier, off Cape Tenes, and air power was also decisive in that episode. Attacked by several RAF Hudsons, she sustained so much damage that Kapitänleutnant Jürgen Quaet-Faslem decided to head for the North African coast to put his crew ashore. He then intended to take *U-595* back out to deep water and scuttle her.

U-595 was under almost constant attack throughout four hours, remaining defiant and successfully damaging three of her attackers with AA fire. This was thanks to the courage of a rating ordered to man the boat's 20mm cannon. While he braved the fire of the enemy, *U-595*'s officers and senior ratings took cover inside the conning tower cowling. Throughout, Quaet-Faslem shouted advice until the enraged gunner shouted back: 'If you are so damned brave, come out here and help me with the ammunition!'[5] The boat's second in command did go to his aid but nobody else was brave, or foolhardy, enough.

The submarine's magnetic compass and the gyro compass were both out of action and the depth sounder functioned intermittently. When it revealed only eight metres of water under the keel, Quaet-Faslem gave the order for hard a'starboard and the submarine ran aground, approximately 70 miles to the north-east of Oran.

According to the testimony of *U-595* survivors: 'the captain then went to his locker, pinned his Iron Cross on his breast, wrapped the ship's flag about his neck, and gave the order to abandon ship, adding, "Every man for himself." The rubber boat was broken out, the crew gathered a few personal belongings, donned life jackets and jumped into the sea.'[6]

Allied air attacks on 15 November sank *U-259* off Algiers, while *U-98* was destroyed by HMS *Wrestler* on the same day, to the west of Gibraltar. Four more U-boats were sunk from 12 to 17 November.

Such losses were a shock to the system and Dönitz admitted his submarines were facing formidable opponents: 'The screening craft are destroyers of special skill, and experience . . .'[7]

The U-boats could not get near enough to cause serious losses among the invasion ships and Dönitz immediately deduced that to provide such strong escort forces off North Africa, the Allies must have stripped the North Atlantic convoys.

Yet his desire for a new massacre in the Atlantic was to be frustrated, for Admiral Raeder decreed that U-boats lost off North Africa must be replaced, with 20 in all assigned to prey on the invasion vessels. Robbing Peter (North Atlantic operations) to pay Paul (feed the North Africa Med effort) continued to undermine the wider aim of the U-boat force.

Dönitz was infuriated by his inability to take advantage of 'favourable conditions in the Atlantic . . . because of withdrawal of boats to the Mediterranean and the Gibraltar-Morocco area'.

U-boat losses in waters off North Africa and Gibraltar were six times those in the Atlantic, where one U-boat was lost for every 130,000 tons of Allied shipping sunk. Off North Africa, noted Dönitz, the loss rate was '1 boat for every 20,000 tons sunk and in addition a much higher percentage of boats heavily damaged'.[8]

Looking at the bigger picture, Dönitz felt that the efforts of U-boats in the Arctic did little to achieve victory, with their results 'of no numerical importance'. After the Allied invasion operations had ceased, additional U-boats diverted to the Mediterranean would discover fewer targets.

Dönitz was sure the U-boat force was still 'ready and willing to fight under most difficult conditions' but there remained the fundamental need to maximise tonnage sunk while minimising U-boat losses.[9]

For all the frustrations of Admiral Dönitz, the struggle remained finely balanced. Axis submarines were still taking advantage of Allied weakness in parts of the world where escort forces were scarcer and air cover lacking.

For example, in October a group of five U-boats set to work off Cape Town, achieving significant success by attacking troop convoys headed for the Middle East, sinking two dozen ships for a tonnage total of 161,000.[10] By late 1942 there were five Type IX long-range submarines on deployment in the Indian Ocean and among the most effective captains was Wolfgang Lüth, a Latvian German born into the Russian empire in 1913, who was devoutly religious and an ardent Nazi.

On 10 October 1942, Lüth returned home having completed a marathon deployment to the Indian Ocean in the Type IXD2 submarine *U-181*. During his absence on the seven-month deployment, Hitler bestowed upon Lüth the Knight's Cross with Oak Leaves and Sword – which previously only Kretschmer, Erich Topp and Kapitänleutnant Teddy Suhren had achieved – after being credited with 200,000 tons of Allied shipping sunk.

Once Britain reinforced the escort forces off southern Africa, the enemy boats moved to waters around Madagascar, while other long-range U-boats at the end of 1942 returned to hunting grounds off Brazil.

Dönitz remained doubtful about the worth of committing U-boats to the Arctic but it remained useful by creating a problem for the Allies that took away ships and men they badly needed elsewhere. In September 1942 convoy PQ-18, of 40 vessels, was set upon by a wolf pack of 12 U-boats, suffering modest losses (three merchant ships sunk). Massed air attacks by the Luftwaffe claimed a further ten. The Germans lost 41 planes to the anti-aircraft gunners and also to fighter aircraft from the escort carrier *Avenger*, while three U-boats were sunk.

The North African invasion led to a suspension of the Arctic convoys, though solo ships sailed without escort until they were resumed in November. The deterioration of the German situation in Russia, North Africa and Italy drew away Luftwaffe squadrons while Kola Run escorts grew ever more effective against the U-boats. The Allies continued to receive little or no direct help from the Russian naval forces throughout their Arctic convoy ordeal.

The Germans now had 365 U-boats, with 61 commissioned since the beginning of the year to make up for 32 sunk.[11]

By November 1942, there were 81 U-boats deployed across the Atlantic, with 42 attempting to find and attack North Atlantic convoys and those coming up from the south via Gibraltar. They sank 729,000 tons of shipping in November alone and with so many tankers lost it was feared the Allied gears of war could grind to a halt.

To try to turn the tide there was a change of command, with Max Horton appointed boss of Western Approaches Command the same month. Though Horton took control at the time of crisis, Admiral Noble had achieved great things in holding the line, despite a constant bleeding of escort vessels and their experienced crews to join the fight in other parts of the world. Now former submarine pirate and confirmed bachelor Max Horton was pitched against ascetic family man Karl Dönitz.

The work of the Liverpool-based tactical training unit would remain vital to the British effort, and among those officers who visited it frequently in late 1942 and early 1943 was the fiercely intelligent Peter Gretton. His proven aggression in command of the destroyer *Wolverine* had resulted in the Italian submarine *Dagabur* being sunk – by ramming – in the Mediterranean a few months earlier.

In recognition of his talents, the 30-year-old was promoted to Commander and given command of B7 escort group based at Londonderry. The calibre of officers appointed to warships in the Western Approaches Command had improved greatly since 1939 as the importance of the fight against the U-boat increased. However, Gretton was an exceptionally driven escort group leader, who was very demanding of his subordinates. According to one veteran convoy officer B7's boss was 'well known to be an arch-workaholic. When others went on leave he locked himself in an office at the base and devised new ways to sink U-boats.'[12] Gretton took over command of B7 in *Tay*, a River Class frigate functioning as escort leader, while he waited for the destroyer *Duncan* to come out of refit.

He kept everyone on their toes by, among other things, an idiosyncratic means of ensuring light signals or semaphore communications between ships possessed the kind of accuracy needed in the heat of combat.

'At first light at sea he would send signals around the escorts in Latin,' revealed one of B7's younger captains, 26-year-old Robert Atkinson, in command of the corvette *Pink*. '. . . you had to prove those signals when you returned to harbour, so it was easy for him to see where a mistake was made. It wasn't unknown for him to make a deliberate mistake and if your signals were not very good he would ask that you sent your signalman for further training instead of leave . . .'[13] Using Latin meant the signalmen had to take things down on their pads with absolute accuracy – they couldn't guess or abbreviate what was being said. Twinned with enhanced pre-deployment training for the British escort captains was a rapid increase in forces. The ships now entering service were more capable, namely the River, Loch and Castle classes. They were the product of modern requirements rather than leftovers from the First World War or the 1930s and made up for the Hunt Class, a new escort that couldn't handle Atlantic convoy work.

There was now an average of seven escorts per convoy, rather than five, while the Support Groups, returned to the North Atlantic fray from duties in support of Torch, were also proving their worth.

Allied boffins were doing their bit to turn the tide, with short-range radar that could detect surfaced enemy submarines at several miles distance. Fitted to increasing numbers of escorts, the new radar was not so easily detected by U-boats – in fact, the Germans were completely unaware of its existence. More sets were available from the spring of 1943, though only after Bomber Command had seen its own requirement for radar bombing equipment satisfied. Depth charges were now more powerful and capable of detonation at much shallower settings while the new Hedgehog anti-submarine weapon would prove an awesome killer. It hurled bombs ahead of a vessel to detonate on hitting a U-boat's hull, crucially while the target was still held in the Asdic cone of the attacking warship.

Previous to this, escorts would lose contact with a U-boat just before they attacked it with depth charges. They had to wait until they were above it. This meant the U-boat could tell exactly where the warship was and potentially dodge both the depth charges and the Asdic. Hedgehog, which had no depth settings, gave no such warning but, while just one hit with a bomb could destroy a U-boat, if it missed there was no detonation and therefore no shock damage to the target. Even a conventional depth charge that did not cause fatal injury to an enemy submarine could still shatter the nerve of a crew and cause enough harm to force it to the surface.

The follow-on to Hedgehog was Squid, which could hurl much heavier depth bombs that sank faster and could detonate at a set depth. Squid's detonation settings were transmitted direct from the Asdic set – not input by hand – and it was therefore quicker into action, had greater accuracy and sank onto target more rapidly.

A key innovation for aircraft hunting U-boats was the Leigh Light. The favoured tactic was to detect the submarine on the surface but not switch on the powerful searchlight until the aircraft was almost right on top of the enemy. By that time it was, hopefully, too late for a U-boat to evade destruction with a crash dive.

*

The few attacks by U-boats amid winter seas at the turn of the year were of a greater intensity, which prompted Admiralty experts to observe that the enemy was becoming 'bolder and more reckless'.[14] The bulk of Allied shipping losses were still in the North Atlantic and the Admiralty Monthly Anti-Submarine Report in January 1943 warned: 'the critical phase of the U-boat war in the Atlantic cannot long be postponed.'[15]

For Admiral Dönitz there came a personal triumph that showed his pressure for the submarine campaign to move front and centre of the Kriegsmarine's efforts had worked. After clashing with Hitler again, Raeder felt compelled to retire as head of the navy, with Dönitz appointed in his place on 30 January. Grand Admiral Dönitz retained his iron grip on the tiller of the U-boat force and hoped his desired strategy would never again be ruined, though day-to-day tactical oversight of submarine operations devolved to 42-year-old Rear Admiral Eberhard Godt. He had for some years been a key player in wielding the U-boats against convoys.[16] A modest man, preferring to stay out of the spotlight, Godt never forgot it was Dönitz who had the ultimate say.

Once established in the top job, Dönitz decided to decommission the majority of the Kriegsmarine's large vessels and break up their ship's companies, sending many of them to crew new U-boats. With more resources and people flowing to the construction yards and into the training schools – and with force levels rising to 300 submarines – a hundred U-boats could be deployed at any one time. The weapons the submarines carried were also improving. The *Federapparattorpedo* (FAT), first used in action in late 1942, could be set to take a turn to port or starboard after firing, then make fiendish zigzags in the midst of a convoy to ensure it hit something. Extra urgency was placed on developing another new torpedo which would home in on the noise created by a target vessel's propellers.

With Dönitz installed as the overall commander of the Kriegsmarine more resources and greater efforts flowed into the development of revolutionary U-boat types that were the brainchild of Hellmuth Walter. A submarine designer with a touch of genius, he was working on propulsion systems that, so he hoped, would make U-boats true underwater warriors and invincible. The new vessels would be a while coming and in the meantime more Type VII and Type IX U-boats were produced with design tweaks here and there.

The creation of devices that would give advance warning to U-boats of both enemy aircraft and warship radars was prioritised, but the Germans remained well behind the Allied development curve. The U-boats' radar detectors could pick up emissions by the enemy's 1.5 metre sets, but their foe now had the even more effective 10-centimetre radar. Worse still, the new Allied radar could even detect the thin stalk of a submarine's periscope.

25   Black March

As preparations for opening a second front by staging a landing in north-west Europe began in earnest, a key consideration was ensuring the transatlantic feed of supplies could be guaranteed.

In early 1943 a summit meeting of British and American war leaders at Casablanca considered, among other things, better organisation of Atlantic convoy protection. It came at a time of renewed crisis, for in February two Allied convoys suffered serious losses, again due to B-Dienst providing information of dates and routes. Things began to look very black for the Allies. Between 6 and 19 March U-boats savaged three convoys – SC-121, SC-122 and HX-229 – sinking 34 ships. SC-121 was attacked by 17 U-boats while the other two convoys were assaulted by a wolf pack of 38. Nothing on this scale had been achieved by the Germans since November 1942, and with only one submarine lost.

The bad weather made it difficult to keep convoys together. Throwing a protective cordon around them was almost impossible and air cover was not available as aircraft couldn't fly for much of the time.

The defenders of HX-228 did rather better during their battle on 10/11 March, losing a comparatively modest four merchant ships while sinking two U-boats. The episode illustrated that the days when U-boat captains could relax even for a second were long gone, though vulnerabilities on the Allied side were also severely punished.[1]

During the HX-228 fight, escort leader HMS *Harvester*, commanded by 38-year-old Cdr Arthur Tait, had rammed *U-444* in the early hours of 11 March and suffered severe damage, with the U-boat trapped under her stern.

U-444 broke free only to be chased by the Free French corvette *Aconit*, commanded by 32-year-old Lt Jean Levasseur. *Aconit* shelled *U-444* before ramming and finishing her off with shallow-set depth charges.

The severe damage suffered by *Harvester* meanwhile rendered her dead in the water while repairs were carried out. She was a perfect target for *U-432*, commanded by 26-year-old Kapitänleutnant Hermann Eckhardt. He spotted the British warship at noon and stealthily circled his target to make sure there were no other enemy vessels around. An hour later *U-432* fired one torpedo from a bow tube and then another from the stern tube, just to make sure. Both struck *Harvester*, which began to sink.

U-432 was Eckhardt's first front line command and after this triumph he suddenly lost his appetite for more action, though not for lunch. His First Lieutenant, 24-year-old Leutnant Josef Bröhl – a wolf pack veteran – urged Eckhardt to surface and pursue the convoy.

Eckhardt, over-confident yet lacking tactical wisdom, demurred. He suggested it would be better to take a meal break, with *U-432* maintaining a depth of 65ft. The First Lieutenant, who had even gone to fetch his camera so he could take some shots of the destroyer sinking after they surfaced, was exceedingly annoyed at remaining dived. Swallowing his anger, Bröhl gathered with the rest of the submarine's officers in the tiny wardroom to drink a champagne toast to their success. They also tried in vain to identify their victim in a ship recognition book while the boat's hydrophone operator left his post to wash up the champagne glasses. This proved to be fatal, for it meant nobody heard the returning *Aconit*, which was actually chasing down another U-boat but which soon detected the unwary *U-432*.

Depth-charge explosions shattered the complacency of the celebration lunch. As *U-432*'s men scrambled to their action stations – some spewing partially eaten food – the boat lost lighting and her electric motors while the main switchboard burst into flames. *U-432* went down by the stern in a terrifying 25-degree dive, not levelling off until she reached 1,017ft.

It was a record for a U-boat, though not recommended in a vessel with a crush depth of 700ft. Some of the boat's men were too scared to look at the depth gauge after it passed 984ft. As all tanks were blown to surface, Eckhardt ordered the crew to put on lifejackets and prepare to abandon ship. Dismayed, Bröhl suggested there was a chance the enemy might have departed and the boat should attempt to escape at full speed on the diesels.

Once *U-432* surfaced *Aconit* unleashed a storm of fire, which killed Eckhardt and several others as they emerged onto the bridge. *Aconit* then rammed the submarine, whose Engineer Officer had already initiated the scuttling procedure. The French warship picked up 20 men from *U-432*'s 72-strong crew, including Lt Bröhl, and also rescued *Harvester*'s survivors from various life rafts. As he recovered from his ordeal Lt Bröhl asked if he might send a message to his commanders in France, advising them of a record depth achieved for a U-boat. An Admiralty report on the action would later observe: 'The request was "Not Granted".'

The casualty level in March worked out at a dozen merchant ships per U-boat lost, a much better exchange rate for the Germans than the heavy losses off North Africa. In the Admiralty and the British government there was an air of crisis. It was being forecast by doom-mongers that in only two months Britain would be unable to meet war commitments or adequately feed itself due to the shortage of supplies. In some quarters there were serious doubts about the viability of the convoy system.

Wiser heads preferred to trust in calm analysis of the facts rather than give in to a few, inevitable, setbacks. The trend was still in favour of the Allies. The reality behind the terrible losses of March 1943 was that just 2.5 per cent of ships in convoy were lost. The U-boats only sank 3 per cent of all dry cargo vessels of more than 1,600 tons displacement available to the Allies. In April they would sink 1.6 per cent and in May 1.2 per cent. In June only 0.5 per cent of such ships were sunk. In the period December 1942 to June 1943, the average for such vessels sunk in each calendar month was 1.6 per cent.[2] Outside the hard-hit convoys, re-routing away from the danger zone had worked, with numerous convoys not spotted by even a single U-boat. Such success was a hidden, silent unseen killer blow to the Third Reich.

The sudden return to aparently significant losses was bound to be unnerving, especially as, for all its endeavours, Bletchley was still a few steps behind the Germans. The delay in breaking into certain enemy naval signals was one of the reasons the Germans were able to inflict such heavy damage on a few Allied convoys in March 1943.

B7 escort group boss Peter Gretton later reflected that B-Dienst's work at this time created 'one of those unpleasant periods of the war when the enemy were able to quickly decipher our codes and cyphers'.

The Germans therefore had 'a good idea of the position of most convoys in the Atlantic and made good use of this knowledge'.[3]

Such black periods had happened before and did not signify the death of the convoy system. The so-called Black March of 1943 did not, either. While 107 ships may have been sunk in the first 20 days of March in the North Atlantic – a total of 627,377 tons – only 15 were lost in the last 11 days.[4] Dreadful weather helped keep the total down.

April and May would see the struggle reach a new intensity, with B-Dienst still managing to intercept and decrypt crucial information contained within the 'U-Boat Situation Report' broadcast by the Admiralty.

This gave Godt and Dönitz an idea of what the British knew about their own dispositions, which they would then endeavour to counter by changing their plans. Dönitz recognised that re-routing was denying the U-boats their chances but was still mystified as to how it was, even when he re-directed U-boats, their targets remained elusive. It was also puzzling how both aircraft and escorts could be sent to intercept submarines with such precision. This was down to better co-ordinating of air and sea assets and also more effective use of Huff Duff, but above all it was due to a Bletchley breakthrough. They were now able to decipher intercepted W/T signals so fast they were almost reading them ahead of the U-boats.

Dönitz was still unaware of Enigma's vulnerability and believed the British were detecting U-boat locations via transmissions by the submarines' own 'radar search receivers'.[5] U-boat captains pulling out all the stops to reach a convoy would suddenly be forced to dive and were often attacked, with the target convoy slipping away.

A broad array of experts, but most notably former British naval officer (and Battle of Jutland veteran) Patrick Blackett, were also applying their considerable brainpower to defeating the U-boats by means other than depth charges and mortar bombs. In 1941 Blackett headed a team of boffins working on improving Coastal Command efficiency, but in early 1942 he switched to the Admiralty. By the autumn his team's statistical analysis demonstrated that a bigger convoy did not mean greater losses of ships.

U-boats armed with a finite number of torpedoes and a limited range of vision could only sink so many ships at any one time. This much was clear from the First World War and Blackett highlighted its enduring truth. He suggested that if a convoy of 32 vessels were increased to 54, it would not lose any more ships. It also had the added benefit of narrowing the number of convoys passing to and fro across the Atlantic, so reducing the U-boats' opportunities. This enabled more escorts to be concentrated on fewer convoys, raising the level of protection for each one.

Seasoned escort group commander Donald Macintyre further explained: 'Statistics showed that by increasing the number of escorts from six to nine, losses would be reduced by 25 per cent . . .' If air cover could be provided for eight hours a day, then losses could be reduced by 64 per cent.[6] Alternatively, if the fewer (but bigger) convoys were protected by the same levels of close escorts, warships could be released to form more of the trouble-shooting Support Groups. These could be on hand to assist a regular escort force and help it through the danger zones.

This was all well and good, but while the navy could apply their tweaks – reorganising the convoy system and rhythm, while reinforcing Support Groups – the RAF still refused to allocate more than VLR Liberators for use by Coastal Command in mid-Atlantic.

Often VLRs were not even used over convoys, but rather in the zones where the RAF felt U-boats were likely to be on the surface making fast surface transits to killing zones – the Bay of Biscay or between Iceland and Scotland. Yet when proper air cover was provided in the North Atlantic for convoys the results were much better. During its so-called 'Bay Offensive', in the Bay of Biscay, the RAF lost 100 aircraft for only seven enemy submarines destroyed between June 1942 and March 1943. At least one British submarine was also attacked and sunk by the RAF in Biscay. During the same period RAF aircraft helping to protect North Atlantic convoys sank 22 U-boats. Until May 1943 the RAF sank an average of one submarine a month in Biscay.

When both escort warships and aircraft protected convoys the U-boats were successfully neutered, managing to sink only 19 ships in such circumstances during the entire war. This effective solution to the

U-boat menace was not necessarily apparent – or even thought to be that important – in the corridors of power where many issues were at stake. The Bomber Command barons were fierce advocates of defeating the enemy by the merciless application of area bombing of the Reich itself.

Responding to the crying need for more resources in the Atlantic, the US Army Air Forces (USAAF) did at least establish a new anti-submarine group at Gander, Newfoundland, using Liberator aircraft, which significantly narrowed the so-called 'air gap'.

The Allied navies persevered with their own air power measures, and these included the greater deployment of organic air power, with the escort carriers that now formed a key part of convoy defence. Fleet carriers – big, expensive ships with large air groups – designed to fight enemy battle fleets or carry out bombing raids against land targets were capital ships ill-suited (and too few in number) for convoy escort work. Escort carriers (known as Carrier Vessel Escorts, or CVEs) were initially based on merchant vessel hulls. Many were swiftly and cheaply converted in US yards and transferred to Britain under Lend-Lease. American merchant vessels were used because the UK government would only release a few British-flagged ships. The Americans also offered to construct new-build escort carriers and could, anyway, turn them out far faster than any British yard.

HMS *Audacity* pioneered the CVE idea in the Royal Navy and was sunk off Portugal by *U-751* in December 1941 while working with Johnny Walker's escort group. *Audacity*'s fighter aircraft had shot down several Condors during convoy escort runs, and attacked *U-131*, but it took a while for the concept she had proved successful to be built upon. There were design problems, including a fuel system that led to one of the early British conversions, *Dasher*, blowing up off the west coast of Scotland. The flight decks also needed to be extended to cater for the slow take-off speed of the Swordfish.[7] With escort carriers being completed and commissioned in increasing numbers, the new type could really show what it could do. The British attached theirs to the escort groups, though they did experiment with hunting groups composed of CVEs and frigates. US Navy CVE hunter-killer groups were on the whole more effective, though that may have been down to luck. British escort carriers had also been diverted to cover the African invasions before they could make their impact felt in the North Atlantic. It fell to USS

Bogue to become the first escort carrier to accompany a transatlantic convoy all the way across. She did not on that mission score any U-boat kills, which was probably a testament to the deterrent effect of her air patrols.

26 The Fulcrum

In the Kriegsmarine's upper echelons March 1943 was greeted as a very encouraging upturn in the fortunes of the U-boat force but, as German commanders also knew only too well from past experience, such success always had a flipside.

'Convoy warfare in March has led to a considerable using up of U-boats,' the U-boat force War Log observed. 'A large number of boats have returned [home] owing to fuel and torpedo exhaustion and damage. The gaps thus produced must be filled as quickly as possible, if the monthly sinking figures are to be increased.'[1]

To fill them, Godt was forced to order the large, long-range Type IX U-boats into the North Atlantic rather than head for their usual hunting grounds in the Indian Ocean, the South Atlantic or the Caribbean. This was a sound move anyway, as the Allied demand on merchant vessels to support the North African campaign had denuded southern waters of many potential targets. It was a Milch Cow that found and then shadowed convoy HX-231 as it headed for the UK, also fulfilling the dual function of replenishing 16 other U-boats that would soon try to mount an attack.

On the Allied side, Peter Gretton and the B7 escort group would play an important role in the defence of HX-231 and two subsequent convoys that have come to be regarded as the fulcrum of the Battle of the Atlantic.

U-boats working as the *Löwenherz* (Lion Heart) wolf pack or in support of it, would attempt to attack HX-231 – composed of 61 merchant vessels – at various times between 4 and 7 April, in a fight stretching across 700 miles of ocean.

At 5.30 p.m. on the evening of 4 April, when the convoy was 27 miles south of Cape Farewell, Greenland, battling a gale, the Admiralty sent an electrifying signal to the B7 group. It stated: 'You are encircled by approximately 32 U-boats. You may expect attack from down moon at approximately 02.30.' As a well-blooded escort group, the men of B7 knew exactly what lay ahead and on the open bridge of HMS *Pink* Lt Atkinson awaited Cdr Gretton's instruction. It consisted of just one word by light signal: 'Anticipate'.[2] Atkinson was not worried by such terseness. 'We were so highly trained we knew exactly what to do.'

Assembling the crew in the main mess deck, Atkinson told them how things would play out. 'I am not sure how many of us will live to see daylight,' he told his men, 'but I intend to do so and this is what we will do. We will have hands to tea at six o' clock. We will have pipe down at seven o'clock. We will have action stations at one o' clock in the morning, dressed in Arctic clothing. Hot chocolate will be served at two o'clock and you can expect to be there the rest of the night.'

Atkinson found that some of his men couldn't get to sleep, while others had no problem. They got their alarm call courtesy of a U-boat.

'You could almost have set your clock,' said Atkinson. 'At half past two the first ship went up.'

The fight unfolded with U-boats making various lunges at the convoy over the coming hours and with Gretton's *Tay* attacking a submarine that crossed her bows in the pre-dawn darkness of 6 April, having not been detected by the ship's radar or spotted by lookouts. *Tay* got a good grip on the U-boat from a strong Asdic echo and dropped a pattern of charges, with 'a great red glow in the water, followed by a very heavy explosion'.[3] For years Gretton thought *Tay* had sunk *U-635*, but after his own post-war investigations concluded it was *U-306* and she was not destroyed but got away.[4] *U-635* had actually been sunk the previous day,[5] surprised on the surface by a VLR flying at 50ft. *U-632* suffered an identical death on 6 April.

A harrowing moment came when *Tay* passed through a group of survivors from an iron ore carrier that went down with terrible swiftness. The red lights of the survivors' lifejackets burned in the black but with no lifeboats they were unlikely to last very long in the cold sea.

'It was an appalling decision to make as to whether to stop or not,' reflected Gretton, 'but by leaving her place in the search to do so, the ship would leave a gap through which more attacks could be made, and more men drowned. We had to go on.'[6]

With the U-boat hunt concluded, *Pink* was sent to see if she could find any of these survivors. After searching for four hours she found nobody, so Gretton called her back.

Three ships were sunk in the convoy and three more after falling out of formation. Two of these had deliberately quit, preferring to take their chances on their own. Despite this, the German attack on the convoy was hesitant, infected by a justified fear of air attack. According to the U-boat force War Log entry for 7 April, 'very little success was achieved . . . probably due primarily to the inexperience of the young Commanding Officers'.[7] No credit was given to the stiff defence put up by the British escort group. For most of the U-boat captains it was their first war patrol and Dönitz had been so concerned about their potential timidity that he sent a signal as battle was joined exhorting them to deal the enemy 'a heavy blow'. Later in the month he would warn them not to allow their 'healthy warrior and hunter instincts to be humbugged' as that would rob them of their powers to resist 'present day enemy defences'.[8]

The Admiralty's interrogations of survivors from the 38 U-boats sunk since the turn of the year, and other intelligence, had revealed shaky morale in the U-boats. Some novice captains were shy of even deploying on patrol and eager to report defects in order to stay in port. Dönitz was not ignorant of this and as the situation grew worse his authoritarianism would begin to exert itself even more, with stiff penalties for shirkers. In spring 1943 he still held out hopes for a decisive blow, and so an even greater battle was to unfold a month later.

Gretton and B7 had about a week in port at Londonderry before embarking on the voyage to the next pitched battle. They were providing protection for convoy ONS-5, composed of 41 ships, the majority of which were old, slow unladen vessels heading for New York. By the time the convoy was to the south of Rockall the U-boats were already beginning to gather, and the weather was deteriorating.

An attack alert was sent on 24 April, which turned out to be a false alarm, but *U-710* was sunk by a Coastal Command B-17 Flying Fortress, right on the intended course of the convoy. *Could it now slip through a hole in the gathering wolf packs?* This was not something to bank on and

Gretton began to worry about the sheer difficulty of refuelling from two auxiliary tankers.

Small vessels like destroyers and corvettes burned a lot of fuel oil as they battled heavy seas to keep a convoy together. If a top-up could not be achieved there was the danger of running out during a battle. Gretton's fears grew when it proved impossible for *Duncan*, from which he now commanded B7, to maintain the hose connection by which the oil was to be transferred from the tanker *British Lady*. The merchant ships themselves were finding it really difficult to maintain headway, sometimes managing only a couple of knots, and began to fall out of formation. The warships found it hard to round them up, with two merchantmen even colliding.

With U-boats attacking HX-234, the convoy coming the other way, Gretton entertained the hope that his charges might yet avoid harassment. Early on the morning of 28 April a signal from a U-boat was detected by Huff Duff, less than 50 miles away. Gretton decided – with the weather marginally calmer – to again try to top up from *British Lady*. The *Duncan* succeeded this time, with *Vidette* and *Loosestrife* also replenishing.

Seven submarines of Group Star were arrayed against the convoy as it crawled across heaving seas to the south of Iceland. Several attempts were made to attack on the night of 28 April but were parried by escorts. In Liverpool, Max Horton watched the progress of ONS-5 on the massive operations maps in his headquarters bunker. Each encounter was marked on the track of the convoy and Horton realised reinforcements would be required. He ordered the 3rd Escort Group to sail from St John's Newfoundland, which it did at 11.00 a.m. on 29 April.

The first merchant vessel in ONS-5 to be torpedoed was the US-flagged, 6,198-ton *McKeesport*, loaded with sand ballast. At around 5.30 a.m. one of her lookouts saw what he fancied was a large fish leaping out of the water. It was a torpedo fired by *U-258*, whose previous attacks had been frustrated. This U-boat had raced ahead and dived to let the convoy pass overhead, risking a periscope look and firing two torpedoes at the nearest ship. *Duncan* and the anti-submarine/rescue trawler *Northern Gem* were instantly on the job, carrying out depth-charge attacks where they thought the guilty party might be.

U-258 was already at a safe distance, leaving behind *McKeesport* sinking very slowly, giving time for all 68 of the crew to safely abandon

Admiral Sir Max Horton, renowned First World War submariner who commanded the Royal Navy's submarine force in the Second World War and was
later Commander-in-Chief Western Approaches Command. Pictured here in
July 1943 in the Derby House bunker at Liverpool. (*IWM/A 18476*)

ship. They were picked up by *Northern Gem*, though one man who fell
into the freezing sea died later from shock. While abandoning ship the
Master of *McKeesport* had ditched confidential books over the side but
left aboard charts on which were marked the location of the Western
Ocean Meeting Point (where escorts were due to meet merchant
ships). Fearing a U-boat might send a boarding party aboard to snatch
this priceless intelligence, Gretton sent the frigate *Tay* back to sink
McKeesport.

At least four U-boats were estimated to be within striking distance
of the convoy and Gretton ordered various escorts away down the
bearings provided by Huff Duff to attack them. They made no positive
Asdic contacts, though they dropped a few deterrent depth charges.

Amid howling winds and mountainous seas – so huge even the
crow's nest on the top of *Snowflake*'s mast filled with water – there

were a couple of half-hearted attacks by U-boats. The rest of the night passed off without incident and by the following morning Group Star lost contact with the convoy, which had been scattered by the storm, the vessels spread far and wide. Only 20 were left in formation, so Gretton's ships set about rounding the others up.

Gretton was forced to leave, along with several other escort vessels, in order to refuel at Newfoundland. This left Lt Cdr Robert Sherwood – a veteran of the SC-7 fight of 1940 – aboard *Tay* in command of an escort force that was by now a mixed bag of B7 and 3rd Escort Group, with the 1st Escort Group soon ordered into the fight.

During the ONS-5 battle, between 28 April and 6 May, the Allied convoy was subjected to attack by up to 41 U-boats in various packs. Dönitz exhorted them to begin 'the Drum Roll' immediately darkness fell on 5 May, promising 'there will be nothing of the convoy left'.[9]

There was, however, limited time before ONS-5 got to safe waters where air cover would be even stiffer, but the U-boats managed to run up a good tally of merchant ships sunk.

'During the first night 8 boats were able to sink 13 ships straight away, probably mainly because of the suddenness of the attack,' noted the U-boat force War Log. The following day a further four vessels were sunk, or so Dönitz thought. The total number of merchant vessels sunk during the battle was actually 13, making a poor balance sheet for the Germans. Allied aircraft and warships made the U-boats pay a heavy penalty for modest success. Five U-boats were sunk during the ONS-5 battle, with no survivors from any of them, representing 255 men killed. A number of U-boats had also been damaged and would need major repairs, with a sixth lost to air attack. A gloomy U-boat command War Log noted that the casualty rate was 'very high and grave . . . enemy radar location is the worst enemy of our submarines' and efforts to both hide a submarine from it and improve its detection had be redoubled. 'Radar location is . . . robbing the submarine of her most important characteristic – [the] ability to remain undetected.'

For his part, Admiral Dönitz blamed thick fog for the failure of his U-boats to massacre ONS-5, once again giving the escort vessels little, if any, credit for their efforts.

If there was a glimmer of hope for the Germans it resided in the future development of anti-aircraft submarines, snorkel devices to enable boats to remain submerged for almost an entire deployment and the introduction of new U-boat types. The next convoy battle would, though, force Dönitz to make an unwelcome decision, to save his U-boat force from annihilation: withdrawal from the North Atlantic.

Once again defeat was primarily delivered by Gretton and the B7 group, with the wolf packs failing to sink any merchant ships in convoy SC-130 but losing four U-boats along with their crews. Those sunk included U-954, in which Leutnant Peter Dönitz, younger son of the U-boat force commander, was serving.

In the first 22 days of May 31 U-boats were sunk, which for Dönitz was 'a frightful total, which came as a hard and unexpected blow'.[10] Until then he held out hopes that the U-boats might be able to hold their own despite the Allied superiority in manpower and technology. In February, 19 U-boats had been sunk, followed by 15 in March and 16 in April, making a total of 81 lost in the first five months of 1943.[11]

There had been setbacks before, and also crises, but they had been overcome. This time Dönitz concluded: 'We had lost the Battle of the Atlantic.'[12] That being the case, the only logical choice was withdrawal. Writing some years removed, Dönitz described the May 1943 situation in bleak terms. 'Wolf pack operations against convoys in the North Atlantic, the main theatre of operations and at the same time the theatre in which air cover was strongest, were no longer possible. They could only be resumed if we succeeded in radically increasing the fighting power of the U-boats.'[13] Dönitz did not envision a total cessation of U-boat warfare at the time. He explained to Hitler that submarine warfare must be continued 'even if great successes are no longer possible' for it would tie down Allied forces that might otherwise be used elsewhere. The Führer agreed, stating: 'There can be no talk of slackening off . . .'[14]

The order to withdraw from the North Atlantic was issued on 24 May, two days after every ship of convoy SC-130 reached Liverpool. They brought, among things, vital cargoes of fuel oil, explosives, grain and lumber.

The war against the U-boats would in the short term mutate into a different kind of struggle, particularly in the mid-Atlantic around the Azores.

*

In a long, hard war it was easy to miss a turning point, especially when expressed in terms of how many cargo vessels and oil tankers got through rather than territory taken and armies destroyed.

The German surrender at Stalingrad in early February 1943, with 93,000 soldiers of the Sixth Army taken prisoner by the Red Army, was a spectacular reverse. So was the fall of Bizerte and Tunis on 7 May, that within days led to 275,000 Axis soldiers surrendering. On the other side of the world the Americans had triumphed at Guadalcanal in the Solomons and begun their grand offensive to try to drive the Japanese all the way back across the Pacific. The battles of HX-231, ONS-5 and SC-130 were elevated in hindsight, justly described by one admiral as 'preparing the way for the invasion of Europe'. Sir Roderick Macdonald also noted: 'Had this been a land battle – or a sea fight of old – its name would be in the history books, like Salamis or Trafalgar. This was no skirmish. The fight to defend convoy ONS5 was of more significance than Alamein.'[15]

The laurels worn by the victorious escort groups came in the form of slips of paper on which were typed decrypted messages. After ONS-5 each of the captains received a congratulatory signal from the Prime Minister, which Lt Cdr Atkinson, CO of *Pink*, thought 'rather a prize'. Even Max Horton sent a signal of appreciation – a rare thing indeed – prompting Atkinson to remark with a smile, 'he didn't send many letters of appreciation to anybody'.

During a speech at the Mansion House on 30 June, after being awarded the Freedom of the City of London, Churchill said the wolf packs had 'recoiled to lick their wounds and mourn their dead'. Furthermore, he revealed: 'Since the middle of May scarcely a single merchant ship has been lost in the whole of the north Atlantic.'

The fear of Britain being invaded – always far greater than the likelihood – or of being starved into defeat had finally been lifted. It was not actually the end of hard battles in the Atlantic and elsewhere against the U-boats. There would be some tricky moments for the Allies – but it was definitely some kind of turning point. 'I think we really felt that at last our training and technology had got on top of the U-boats,' said Lt Cdr Hart of HMS *Vidette*. [16]

While a British destroyer captain may have described it as such post-war, in 1943 the U-boat command had other ideas. It still nurtured hopes that once new anti-aircraft guns had been fitted and radar detectors improved the wolf packs could return to the North Atlantic. That the Germans could believe so was due only to their enemy's failure to fully exploit his own advantages.

27   The Führer is Watching

For the Allies, one aspect of the war against the U-boats that remained highly controversial was Bomber Command's refusal to release more aircraft for the fight earlier. It was only after the U-boats had been defeated in the North Atlantic that the RAF's maritime offensive began to achieve telling results, partly aided by Ultra (as the secret product of Allied code-breaking was known).

This was buttressed by the enemy's continuing inability to devise a truly effective radar detector and a tactical error by the Germans. To try to fend off Allied air attacks the U-boats' gun power was being improved and they were attempting to find safety in numbers by crossing Biscay on the surface in groups. U-boat captains claimed in July to have 'warded off' 18 Allied air attacks, but in August and September only six were deterred. Numerous U-boats were sunk. Whether it was new radar detectors or enhanced armament, success would only be achieved, thought the U-boat top brass, 'when the boats' armament permits them to remain on the surface to fight it out with the planes, or at any rate when it is essential for boats attacking a convoy to get ahead to make an attack despite enemy air escorts'.[1] To that end, there would be the new 'anti-aircraft submarines' with extra guns and armour. By May 1943 U-441 and U-256 were being reconstructed, but not even the so-called U-flak boats would prove capable of winning a fight with aircraft.

While Allied sailors and airmen in the firing line at sea, or over it, may have been successfully combined against their common foe, Britain's military leaders were far from united. They indulged in what Peter Gretton labelled 'stupid quarrels', which he regarded as 'a disgrace and a tragedy', adding: 'So many ships were sunk and so many lives were lost unnecessarily during those first two years [of war].'[2] The navy complained again and again that too many RAF aircraft were being used to bomb the enemy's impregnable, reinforced concrete submarine pens. Such raids were, said ace U-boat killer Donald Macintyre, 'entirely without result'.[3]

Achieving victory in the Battle of the Atlantic wasn't just about sinking U-boats. It was about preventing them from sinking merchant vessels. This required enemy submarines to be destroyed in the right place (the North Atlantic) at the right time – before they could get at the convoys carrying aviation fuel for bombers among other things, not on their way back to base.

Maintaining an air umbrella over the convoys themselves would keep U-boats down and prevent them from even trying to attack the merchant vessels. The Allied navies would themselves wield their own air power to great effect, particularly in the new battle zone around the Azores. The escort carriers were particularly effective, especially within US Navy hunter-killer groups. These fought a series of battles between July 1943 and the start of 1944, clearing the waters through which Allied shipping from the USA – with troops and supplies destined for the invasions of Sicily and then Italy itself – would sail, heading first for Gibraltar.

The CVEs *Bogue*, *Core* and *Santee* were assigned in the Support Group role for convoys that Ultra revealed were under threat. This was the crucial difference between the US and British use of similar hunter-killer groups in 1939. The US Navy escort carriers were sent by specific intelligence, assisted by Huff Duff to threat zones, rather than heading off into the unknown in the mere hope of finding a submarine.

The aircraft and ships, along with the weapons they carried, were also a lot more effective. Through July and August 1943 the USN's hunter-killer groups sank 13 U-boats, with destroyers reaping their fair share of that success. Among the casualties were four Milch Cows, including three that could also lay mines.

The Milch Cows were now a key means of enabling the Germans to maintain U-boat patrols beyond the North Atlantic, making them a top priority for the Allied hunter-killer groups. The Milch Cows were obliged to carry out their time-consuming replenishment on the surface, which inevitably exposed them. U-boat command also had to arrange rendezvous points with attack boats by wireless signals, which were intercepted and decrypted.

The slaughter of the Milch Cows was a serious blow to Germany's ability to wage long-distance U-boat warfare, leaving Dönitz with just three. Some operational U-boats had to be diverted to refuelling tasks so that patrolling submarines could make it home to the French ports.

In Allied circles there were concerns that such success might tip the enemy off to the fact that their signals were being read. However, German confidence in the unassailable nature of Enigma remained, despite renewed anxiety in August 1943 that it had been cracked. The main blame was still being placed on the Allies' ability to detect German radar emissions and their Huff Duff.

In the Admiralty's OIC, the grand wizard of the organisation, Cdr Rodger Winn, a QC in civilian life, read the runes and predicted Admiral Dönitz might yet seek to pull off a triumph in the North Atlantic.

'It would be the last dying struggle of the caged tiger for the enemy to send back in September and October into the North-Western Approaches, his main U-boat forces,' Winn wrote in July 1943.[4]

Winn felt that it could be handled, for Allied escorts were now strong, Merchant Navy morale was robust and even heavy losses could be absorbed. It would give the Allies an opportunity to destroy even more U-boats. The only slim hope the Germans might have was some form of wonder weapon to turn the tables on the Allies. Admiral Dönitz believed this to be the case and instituted a shake-up in tactics to reflect it. From now on the first priority would be eliminating enemy escorts using a new type of torpedo.

The G7ES *Zaunkönig*, or 'wren', was fitted with a crown of hydrophones in its nose, which steered it towards the target's primary source of noise, the propellers. The purpose of this escort killer was enabling U-boats to peel away a convoy's layers of protection before wiping out the merchant vessels. With electric propulsion, it did not produce any visible track of bubbles. Most crucial of all, it generated so little noise at optimum speed that its own 'ears' could easily pick up noise generated by enemy vessels.

The first acoustic homing torpedo produced by the Germans was the T4 *Falke*, or 'Falcon', which some U-boats had been armed with since the beginning of 1943. Only 30 were fired before the upgrade to *Zaunkönig*.

Originally it was not to be introduced into service until early 1944, but development was accelerated, with testing truncated. The G7ES, also known as the T5, was ready by 1 August 1943, with the 80 torpedoes manufactured by then sent to the French Atlantic U-boat bases. These enabled 20 submarines to be given four each, two loaded in the bow tubes and two allocated to the stern tube. With a top speed of 24.5 knots, the *Zaunkönig* – 'the anti-destroyer torpedo', as the U-boat force War Log put it – could be fired at a target from any angle, but the recommended average speed setting was between 10 and 18 knots. Any faster and the torpedo's ability to hear anything above its own noise was degraded. It could not be used in sea states stronger than six and armed itself after 400 metres.

U-boat captains had to be careful such torpedoes didn't lock onto their own boat. So, if a *Zaunkönig* was fired on the surface – and night attack on the surface was still favoured – it was suggested a U-boat should crash-dive (to become as quiet as possible by using electric drive). Putting extra distance between the firing U-boat and the weapon was also recommended.

The 19 submarines sent into the North Atlantic in September 1943 to attack convoys were also fitted with a quadruple 20mm AA gun and two twin 20mm cannons, along with the latest radar detection devices and even decoys known as Aphrodite (to seduce Allied radar away).

Their targets were to be convoys ONS-18 (27 ships) and ON-202 (42 vessels). The Submarine Tracking Room in the Admiralty assessed something ominous was brewing, fulfilling the prediction by Rodger Winn that U-boats would in the autumn go back into the North Atlantic. A suspicious lack of signals traffic by U-boats known to have deployed from the French ports had been picked up by the OIC. On 18 September Bletchley decrypted a signal from Godt telling the U-boats to establish a patrol line by 20 September, though the subsequent diversions for ONS-18 and ON-202 were not far enough north to avoid trouble.

The bombastic tendencies of Dönitz somewhat played into the hands of the Admiralty. He provided confirmation that battle was to be rejoined in the North Atlantic by sending a morale-boosting message to his U-boats.

Many of them were commanded by inexperienced captains and he obviously felt they needed bucking up. 'The Führer is watching every phase of your struggle,' Dönitz told them. 'Attack! Follow up! Sink!'[5]

This might work with youngsters but veteran U-boat captains at sea regarded that sort of address to the troops as 'Dönitz crap'[6] and bitterly applied themselves to their grim business with little enthusiasm.

The Dönitz messages prompted an increase in Allied air cover for the convoys and orders from Horton for a Support Group to make speed and join the escort forces – close protection was being provided by the B3 and C2 escort groups and they would now be supported by the 9th Group.

The escort groups had been warned on the afternoon of 19 September of wolf packs massing, and just before sunrise the *Zaunkönig* made its lethal debut, blowing off the stern of the frigate *Lagan*. She did not sink but was of no more use and had suffered 19 dead.

The Allies were already sinking U-boats. *U-341* was caught on 19 September by a VLR of the Royal Canadian Air Force (RCAF) and the following day *U-338* was assailed by an RAF Liberator, though it was the Canadian corvette *Drumheller* that actually destroyed *U-338*. Caught on the surface and hit by shells from the warship's 4-inch gun, she crash-dived. As *Drumheller* carried out an Asdic search there was a huge explosion below. It has been suggested that this was one of *U-338*'s own homing torpedoes detonating prematurely or *U-338* herself imploding due to damage. Whatever the exact nature of her fate, *U-338* and her 51 men never returned home.

After a pair of merchant ships were sent to the bottom Max Horton ordered both convoys combined along with their escort forces, a total of 17 warships.[7] A night of intense combat followed on 20 September, with the escort force constantly in action and frustrating numerous attacks. It paid the price: *Zaunkönig* sank the RN corvette *Polyanthus* and the RCN destroyer *St Croix*. Sixty-six out of the *St Croix*'s 147 crew were killed after the ship was hit by two torpedoes fired by *U-305*, while *U-952* sank *Polyanthus* with one hit, leaving a single survivor. The frigate *Itchen*, commanded by Lt Cdr Bridgman who had been captain of *Dianthus* during the SC-94 fight, picked up 82 men from both ships.

While the chances of the combined convoy getting through without further losses were aided by fog, it also made it difficult for the Merchant Aircraft Carrier (MAC) HMS *Empire MacAlpine* – a grain ship topped with a flight deck – to launch air patrols with her four Swordfish.

Fifteen U-boats continued to dog the convoy and early on the morning of 22 September the destroyer *Keppel* accounted for *U-229* by ramming and depth charges. According to B3 group commander Cdr M.J. Evans there was 'a black pit surrounded by the white froth of her wash' as *U-229* dived in a vain attempt to escape destruction. 'As we passed over, a ten-charge pattern set at 50 feet added insult to injury,' added Cdr Evans. 'A large patch of oil was soon spreading over the water but little time was spent in searching for survivors owing to my insistence on returning to the convoy.'[8]

The battle's climax came on 22/23 September. Assisted by Swordfish from *Empire MacAlpine* and RCAF Liberators, the escorts mounted a concerted effort against the U-boats, with three destroyed and others damaged, but six more merchant vessels were sunk.

In the early hours of 23 September a *Zaunkönig* fired by *U-666* blew *Itchen* apart, killing 147 men. Amid the confusing melee, in which several ships fired on a U-boat, Cdr Evans at first thought *Itchen*'s demise 'to be the submarine blowing up'. It was a very hard blow, for only three men survived, saved by SS *Wisła*, which stopped to fish them out of the water despite the grave risk of U-boat attack.[9]

Once things calmed down, confirmation of the terrible truth was obtained by Cdr Evans: 'I called all escorts on R/T and established the fact that only *Itchen* was not answering' and he learned she had been 'torpedoed in her foremost magazine'. The only consolation was that the U-boat 'was probably considerably shaken by the explosion and dived: its attack was frustrated and no ships of the convoy were torpedoed'. Fresh escort groups arrived on 25 September, with the combined convoy suffering no further losses. The U-boats were exhausted and withdrew.

In his Liverpool headquarters Admiral Horton had watched escort after escort marked sunk, realising that the Germans had changed tactics and possessed a new weapon. Using a hotline kept permanently open, he made a telephone call to the Admiralty asking what it was and why he had not been told about it earlier. Horton was informed that intelligence had picked up details of a more lethal acoustic homing torpedo type and countermeasures were being worked on. Horton signalled a warning about the new weapon to all his escort commanders, suggesting they should themselves adopt new tactics, while assuring them countermeasures were coming.

Dönitz and Godt mistakenly believed their submarines had 'eliminated'[10] between 12 and 15 destroyers, damaging two others, while also managing to sink nine merchant vessels and damaging another two. The main reason why they had not been even more successful was, so went the U-boat command narrative, the enemy's ability to bring up fresh escorts, and also the fog. The German naval chief still believed that the battle had proved that his men, their boats, weapons and tactics could achieve victory, with his young captains proceeding 'onwards and upwards to the crown of the U-boat career'.[11] He was wrong. There had been only ten merchant vessels sunk out of 90 and three out of 17 escorts sunk. Three U-boats had been lost, along with *U-386* and *U-270* damaged.

One of them fell victim to Fido, the Allies' own acoustic torpedo, which predated *Zaunkönig* by several months, though it was an air-dropped weapon. A US Navy Catalina had christened Fido by sinking a U-boat on 17 May 1943, the Americans also developing the Mk27 Cutie for use by aircraft.

In the aftermath of the convoy battle the British had a better assessment of the German homing torpedo's capabilities than Dönitz because, of course, they knew the actual scale of losses and the Grand Admiral did not. In Allied circles the new weapon would be called the German Naval Acoustic Torpedo, or GNAT, and the Admiralty's OIC soon had a pretty good idea of its qualities. This helped evolve the Foxer countermeasure, a noise generator to be trailed behind an escort, which aimed to distract the GNAT away. Though it was an unpopular encumbrance for warship captains, it worked well.

In reading German intentions and tactics, the continuing frequent use of signals remained very useful. When U-boats reported to Dönitz after attacks, they listed both the number and the types of torpedoes they had left. This enabled the OIC to calculate how long a submarine might stay out before turning for home and exactly what level of threat it might offer with its homing or other innovative torpedoes.[12]

The balance was now tipping even more in favour of the Allies than before. Twenty-three U-boats were destroyed for just 12 merchant vessels lost in September and October 1943. The new wonder weapon was a chimera. While the success of the *Zaunkönig* did momentarily send a shudder through the Allied command, its hit rate would actually prove to be a poor 6 per cent.[13] The OIC suggested the Allies should not publicly contradict claims of success with the *Zaunkönig*. When the weapon's limitations finally sank in on the German side it would be a serious psychological blow. The *Zaunkönig* could not turn the tide of the war but the Germans would still seek other means to create innovative tactics, weapons and submarines they hoped might do so. The British, meanwhile, unveiled their own attempt at a new type of undersea warfare. At exactly the same time as the Royal Navy was engaged in its bitter battle with the GNAT-armed U-boats a new kind of British submarine was attempting to deliver a devastating blow against the Kriegsmarine.

28   To Slay the Beast

Tirpitz, *Scharnhorst* and *Lützow* were the remnants of a demoralised German battle fleet, now largely confined to lurking in Norwegian fjords, hoping for a chance to attack convoys. They only survived because, after the majority of the heavy units were decommissioned and their men sent to the U-boats, Grand Admiral Dönitz softened his hardline stance about the entire capital ship force being axed. He decided some should be preserved to maintain a latent threat to the enemy's northern maritime flank. They would also tie down Allied naval forces that might otherwise be used elsewhere to decisive effect. This flip-flop provoked the ire of the Führer but Hitler gave in to the admiral's argument.

Winston Churchill was acutely aware of the residual danger posed by the *Tirpitz*. She was sister to the *Bismarck*, which had broken out into the Atlantic in May 1941 and caused much mayhem before being cornered and sunk. While *Tirpitz* and the other Nazi heavy surface units remained seaworthy, a repeat of that episode was always possible. The British resolved to go in and get the enemy's remaining capital ships and in late October 1942 there was an unsuccessful attempt to send in manned torpedoes to do the job. The British had developed their own variant of the Italian craft that crippled *Queen Elizabeth* and *Valiant* at

Alexandria. Some of these, which the RN called Chariots, were towed to Norwegian waters submerged behind a trawler. During bad weather they broke free and disappeared. The men who were to have piloted them into the German battleship's lair were forced to make an escape overland to neutral Sweden. One of the charioteers, Able Seaman Robert Evans, was caught by the Germans and executed.

Gaining the scalp of *Tirpitz* – Germany's last battleship, dubbed 'the beast' by Churchill – would be a terrific boost to the Allied cause, so the effort to sink her could not end there. In September 1943 the Soviets were demanding that convoys to Russia's Arctic ports be resumed, so removing the latent threat posed by *Tirpitz* and the other two vessels would be a useful precursor. With the majority of the surface forces tied up in the Mediterranean, the Admiralty was not keen on this addition to its work roster but Churchill insisted and fortunately the Submarine Service was still working on a plan.

It cannot have escaped the attention of FOSM – by now Rear Admiral Claud Barry – and his planners that the Japanese had managed to penetrate the defences of both Pearl Harbor and Sydney with midget submarines.

A veteran of two world wars, Barry had commanded submarine *D4* when she sank *UB-72* in May 1918. More recently he was CO of HMS *Queen Elizabeth* when the Italian-manned torpedoes at Alexandria attacked her. He therefore knew what it felt like to be in a battleship on the receiving end of an unconventional submarine attack.

The new attempt to sink *Tirpitz* would be made by X-craft midget submarines not unlike the old *Holland 1* in appearance and dimensions, except their main instrument of destruction were not torpedoes but explosive charges dropped under the target warship. This would be a way of achieving FOSM's stated objective of 'attacking capital ships in harbour and surrounded by net defences'.[1] The X-craft carried two large slabs of explosive, one either side of the hull, each one containing two tons of Amatol. They could be released from inside the boat to lie under the target vessel.

The origins of the X-craft went back some years, but in late 1940 the London Blitz threw a spanner in the works when the premises of Varley Engineering in Acton were burned down. Varley had been working on designs for a midget submarine and had even created a full-size wooden model. Relocating to Bursledon on the Hamble River, which runs into the Solent, the naval architects at Varley started again.

This time undisturbed by the Luftwaffe, orders were placed for modules that would be brought together on the Hamble to form a whole craft. The new vessel was to be named *X3* as the *X1* name had gone to the large cruiser submarine of the inter-war years and *X2* belonged to a captured Italian boat. Vickers at Barrow built the middle section of *X3*, while the company of Brigham and Cowan in Hull constructed the aft part and Thornycroft in Southampton handled manufacture of the fore end. Once launched, *X3* was sailed up and down the Hamble, diving and surfacing numerous times. Another prototype, *X4*, was put together at Portsmouth naval dockyard for basin trials. Both these boats would be assigned to training future crews composed of sailors who had responded to a call for volunteers to undertake 'special and hazardous duties'.[2]

An X-craft was 29 tons displacement (submerged), 51ft 7 inches long and could do a maximum of just over 6 knots (with the charges attached) on the surface and 5 knots top speed dived. A range of 80 miles was possible at 2 knots dived. It was reckoned an X-craft could deploy for up to a fortnight unsupported and reach a distance of 1,500 miles at 4 knots on the surface in ideal conditions. The maximum diving depth was 300ft and each crew was composed of four men: the captain, a navigator, a diver and an Engine Room Artificer (E.R.A.).

Such tiny submarines could not possibly reach Norwegian fjords under their own power all the way from their Scottish training base, especially when enemy activity could force them to dive and crawl along. There was a high possibility of them breaking down or sinking on the way, while the crews would be utterly exhausted and unfit to carry out the attack.

Vernon Coles, the E.R.A. in *X9*, painted a grim picture of life in an X-craft. First of all the crews couldn't eat very much food 'because the more you eat the more you've got to pass through [you] and that presented a problem', he said, of a potentially poisoned atmosphere. Much like any other submariners, the X-craft men did not wash, to save water, and 'it wasn't long before a lovely aroma spread throughout the boat and it smelled like new mown hay after it had passed through a horse . . .' The only space available to sleep was over the battery and, as Coles remarked, it was like being 'locked in a steel coffin'.[3]

★

The attack on *Tirpitz* was devised to take place at a time of year when daylight would be minimal or at least not of the almost continuous variety prevalent during the Arctic summer. It would also need to happen before the winter weather and gales set in.

Thanks to air reconnaissance of Arctic Norway, the targets were identified in the Alta Fjord or its offshoots, and the order was given to initiate Operation Source. The X-craft, known as the 12th Flotilla, were supported by a depot ship, HMS *Bonaventure*, at Loch Cairnbawn on a remote stretch of Scotland's west coast. Prior to the attack the entire area around the depot ship and the waters where the X-craft crews trained was sealed off. Only a specially selected few who could be guaranteed to keep their mouths shut, or had essential business elsewhere, were allowed to leave.

The X-craft departed Cairnbawn on 11 September 1943 under tow from six full-size ocean-going submarines: *Thrasher* (X5), *Truculent* (X6), *Stubborn* (X7), *Seanymph* (X8), *Syrtis* (X9) and *Sceptre* (X10).

There were three-man passage crews aboard each X-craft, which proceeded dived on the end of a 500ft tow rope, the mother submarines remaining on the surface to make best progress on the diesels.

The X-craft would surface three times a day to vent and charge their batteries, which was also a useful means of checking they were still attached.

Tow ropes broke twice. In the first incident, on 15 September, *Seanymph* left behind X8, commanded by Lt Jack B.M. McFarlane. *Seanymph* was for a couple of hours unaware that she and the smaller craft had parted company. It wasn't until the evening of 17 September that she found X8 and got her under tow again.

When X9 lost her tow from *Syrtis* the consequences were fatal. The X-craft did not surface as expected for her ventilation period. *Syrtis* turned around with E.R.A. Croker and the others aboard the mother craft 'full of apprehension' about their fellow submariners. All they found was a slick of diesel, which must have been released when X9 reached her crush depth and imploded, killing the passage crew.

X8 would encounter further difficulties. When she took on a list to starboard it was realised water had penetrated the charge on that side. The charges were safe unless Amatol came into contact with water, which made them dangerously unstable so, to avoid losing both X8 and

Seanymph, the starboard charge had to be ditched. This was duly done with both submarines dived and the charge set to 'safe'.

Even with this precaution it detonated 15 minutes later, when only 1,000 yards astern, but caused no harm to the submarines. *X8* now took on a list to port as buoyancy chambers in that side's charge were flooding. Both boats surfaced to ditch the charge, setting it to explode in two hours' time. The submarines were about four miles away when it exploded but this time *X8* suffered considerable damage and was no longer able to dive. There was no option but to scuttle her, which meant no attack would even be attempted on *Lützow* at her anchorage in the Langfjord branch of the Alta Fjord.

The distance between the release point and their targets was 50 miles. Once cast off from their big sisters the four remaining X-craft faced a two-day passage through a German minefield (off the island of Soroy) up the Alta Fjord before finally reaching the Kaa Fjord offshoot, where the *Tirpitz* and *Scharnhorst* lay.

The X-craft would have to sneak past thousands of troops and dozens of gun batteries in positions ashore before they even got to the submarine nets surrounding the enemy ships.

On the night of 21 September the X-craft surfaced to refresh their air and recharge their batteries. Perched on the casing of *X6*, John Lorimer – the boat's First Lieutenant – could actually see *Tirpitz* and she was nicely illuminated. 'I thought it was the most magnificent looking ship I have ever seen. It seemed an awful pity to blow her up.'[4]

The attack on *Tirpitz* took place in the early hours of 22 September, with *X10* assigned to attack *Scharnhorst*, also, hopefully, in the Kaa Fjord.

It was down to *X6*, commanded by 27-year-old Lt Donald Cameron – a former Merchant Navy officer cadet – and *X7*, commanded by 22-year-old Lt Godfrey Place, who at one time served in the Fighting Tenth at Malta, to make the main attack.

X6 penerated the submarine nets by the simple ruse of following a small coaster through the gate on the surface. Once in, *X6* dived and made straight for *Tirpitz*.

X7, meanwhile, attempted to slip under the nets, at first not succeeding. On the third try Lt Place 'managed to worm *X7* along the bottom under the nets'.[5] As *X6* moved in to place charges, she hit uncharted rocks and broached, a sailor aboard *Tirpitz* spotting her. He thought at first he was looking at 'a dolphin or a whale'. He then decided that somehow a submarine had got inside the nets. 'There's an enemy U-boat on the port side,' the sailor told his commander, who looked down at what appeared to be a 'long black submarine-like object' – but he decided it was merely a porpoise.[6] The alarm was sounded anyway and more than 2,000 sailors went to their action stations.

X6 lost her gyrocompass when she grounded while the periscope flooded and was useless. This did not deter Cameron. Running blind, he extracted X6 from trouble and took her under the *Tirpitz*, judging he had made it when he bumped into the battleship's hull.

Trapped momentarily by nets on the other side, X6 disentangled herself and after surfacing briefly, attracting enemy fire, he took her down, sliding under *Tirpitz* again. Cameron released one of the explosive slabs right under where he judged the bridge of the battleship was. After dropping the second charge X6's crew ensured certain items of secret equipment aboard the mini-sub were destroyed. X6 then surfaced and was scuttled.

After successfully abandoning ship, the British submariners were captured, put aboard *Tirpitz* and subjected to interrogation, but there were no English speakers aboard the battleship, so the anxious Germans got very little out of their prisoners. It was obvious that something untoward was about to happen, with the prisoners' frequent glancing at wristwatches indicating it would be soon. The CO of *Tirpitz*, Captain Hans Meyer, decided to shift the ship's position as a precaution, using cables to warp the bows to starboard.

X7 also managed to drop charges under *Tirpitz* – one aft and the other amidships, but she cut it rather fine and while making off was caught by the four explosions that lifted the 50,000-ton *Tirpitz* six feet out of the water.

Casualties aboard *Tirpitz* included men hurled into the air and slammed down again with their legs broken. The battleship's propulsion and electrics were badly damaged and she acquired a five-degree list, but this was corrected by counter flooding. Amid all the mayhem more Germans were killed by their own gunfire than by the British actions.[7]

After bottoming in 120ft of water for an hour Lt Place decided to surface X7, but she went out of control due to earlier damage and was fired on by the rather aggrieved enemy. Forced to dive again, there was very little HP air left to blow the tanks, so Place decided X7 would surface one more time for her men to abandon ship. Place and Lt Robert Aitken were the only members of X7's crew to survive the process.

On his arrival aboard *Tirpitz* Place made a peculiar sight, for he was clad in his usual X-craft at-sea dress of underpants and vest, plus a pair of socks and army boots. The furious Germans who found themselves confronted with this strange-looking character lost their tempers, threatening to shoot him if he did not reveal the locations where he had laid his 'mines'. Seeking to assert his dignity, Place informed them: 'I am an English naval officer and as such demand the courtesy entitled to my rank.'[8] All the 'mines' had already been detonated anyway.

The cool-headed Capt. Meyer reminded his crew that the prisoners were not to be harmed. The British submariners 'were well treated and given hot coffee and schnapps,' remarked FOSM's report on the attack. 'Everyone on board *Tirpitz* expressed great admiration of their bravery.'[9]

X5, commanded by Lt H. Henty-Creer, was thought to have come to grief about a mile down the fjord from *Tirpitz* while making an attack run. None of her crew was ever found, though wreckage was.

As for *X10*, after 16 hours dived, with neither the boat nor the crew in good condition, the chances of success for even a surface attack were thought to be zero. *Scharnhorst* was also nowhere to be seen.

X10 withdrew out to sea and after a few days of wandering along the coast was found by *Stubborn* and scuttled after her crew was taken off.

Rear Admiral Barry hailed the X-craft attack on *Tirpitz* as 'courage and enterprise of the very highest order', which would be regarded as 'one of the most courageous acts of all time'.[10] Both Cameron and Place were awarded the VC, with other participants also decorated for valour.

While *Tirpitz* survived despite serious damage, she would in the succeeding months be hammered again by Fleet Air Arm air attacks and be ultimately sunk by RAF heavy bombers on their third attempt (using a massive new type of bomb). The Home Fleet sank *Scharnhorst* during a night battle on Boxing Day 1943 off the North Norwegian Cape while *Lützow* ended her days scuttled in the Baltic.

For British submariners in late 1943, with the war in the Mediterranean won, more fighting lay ahead, both in north European waters and the Far East. They would join the US Navy's submariners in taking the battle to the enemy, though the Americans had so far suffered their share of problems in doing so.

29   Shooting Blind

Prior to the war the US Navy regarded periscope attacks as too risky. 'Periscopes were verboten,' explained one American submarine officer.[1] While not fixing the target visually, the USN boats did employ hydrophones or active sonar (Asdic) and 'trained assiduously' in the technique, though, as the same officer admitted, 'the people that did it realised it was largely phoney'.[2]

The drive not to use the periscope was prompted by air power paranoia. US Navy top brass were convinced aircraft would see and destroy any submarine operating at periscope depth. It was also assumed modern destroyers could easily find submarines with their sonar, so operating at (or below) 100ft would, theoretically, place a boat under a cold water layer that would bounce a ping.[3]

Officers caught showing their periscope during combat exercises had their promotion prospects damaged. To carry out an acceptable attack they had to find the target with active sonar or a hydrophone, firing torpedoes down the resulting bearing. With the technology then available this did not offer the kind of precision necessary to strike a target.[4] Out of 4,873 attacks by American submarines in the Second World War, just 31 were conducted by firing a torpedo down a hydrophone or sonar bearing. Not a single hit was achieved.[5]

Under such periscope restrictions, exercises prior to the war did not provide a realistic experience for submarine captains and their crews, who never heard or saw a torpedo exploding. This meant there was no feedback on how well – or badly – the torpedoes themselves performed, at least not from the submariners who fired them.

US Navy boats used two types of torpedo – the MkX and the MkIV

– both of which were propelled by steam turbines. Neither was much use for the first two years of America's war. Their depth-keeping was wayward – too often they ran under target vessels – while the means of detonating – the MkVI exploder – didn't work either. Neither the contact pistol nor the magnetic pistol back-up in each 'fish' functioned properly.

It took a long time to fix and even by August 1943 only three out of ten hits with American torpedoes actually detonated. Despite extensive work on the magnetic pistol it remained unreliable, so the USN had to stick with the modified (and eventually reliable) contact pistol warhead. It also persisted with a new magnetic detonator and introduced an electric torpedo, the MkXVIII. While initially unreliable it had the life-saving advantage of leaving no bubble trail.

In the early days of the Pacific war there were other problems aside from faulty torpedoes. Even in late 1942 the US Navy's submarine force was still handicapped by the quality of some officers. Too many captains were from the engineering side of the navy – technically highly proficient, but often not of the right stuff for combat command. Suitable operational doctrine was also a vacuum that had to be filled if there was to be any hope of success – the USN's submarines needed a clearly defined objective.

The idea that they were most usefully employed in reconnaissance for battleships rather than as offensive weapons in their own right lingered in the USN between the wars. A major impediment to American boats fully integrating into major fleet operations was the requirement for carriers and battleships to run at speeds of around 20 knots. Very few of the inter-war USN boats were capable of 20 knots surfaced and could manage at best around 8 knots dived.

America's submarines would have to evolve their own operational contribution and while some tasks were easily identifiable, the top brass felt they would not have a major effect on the course of the war. Submarines could be sent to specific points to lie in wait for certain targets, or could work as reconnaissance units to specific fleet orders in forward areas. They might also pick up flyers whose aircraft had crashed in the sea and land raiding parties on hostile shores. There remained no broader conviction within the USN that they had much strategic utility beyond trying to sink enemy capital ships to enhance the battle fleet's chances of success. Yet it was as weapons against Japan's trade that submarines could potentially be used to devastating effect, if only the USN leadership would have confidence in them.

Tackling all the aforementioned tasks, the USN's submarine war did not really get into its stride until late 1943. Until then all US forces were fighting a defensive war, but with the enemy's campaign of conquest finally running out of steam they could switch to the offensive. The Japanese now found themselves burdened with sustaining island bastions and captured territories spread across thousands of miles of ocean and protecting sea routes between them, and with Japan vulnerable to attack.

It might be thought that USN submarine force commanders would have devoured the lessons of the German experience in the Battle of the Atlantic. This was not necessarily the case. For example, prior to hostilities, USN submarines did not train in night combat despite ample evidence of its effectiveness provided by the European war between 1939 and 1941. As a result, the amount of shipping sunk by the American submarines in their first year of combat operations against the Japanese was equivalent to the tonnage sunk by U-boats in the Atlantic during a single (moderately successful) month.

The average kill rate for U-boats in mid-1942 was three ships a day but by then the USN's submarines were sinking zero vessels. Things did improve, and by year's end the average number of enemy vessels sunk per patrol was 1.94. This was not great but of course some USN boats sank more than others, although many sank none at all. While a lot of this was down to the chronic torpedo problem it was also due to the lack of aggression in certain captains. The USN was still striving to ensure the right men were in command of the submarines and that weapons worked. They also had to get rid of the old inter-war boats or remove them from the tip of the spear. The submarine force needed building up with the right kind of vessels in the right numbers to achieve any kind of telling presence in the enemy's waters. The introduction of fresh tactics was a gradual process, for, as one veteran submariner would confess: 'When the war came we had to learn our business all over again.'[6]

In early 1943 a new Commander Submarine Force, Pacific Fleet (COMSUBPAC) was appointed, following the death in an air accident of Rear Admiral English. A 53-year-old First World War veteran submariner, Vice Admiral Charles Lockwood had between February 1941 and March 1942 served as the US Naval Attaché at the Embassy in London. He gained some insights on modern submarine warfare from contacts in the Admiralty and also saw how the Germans tried to strangle British trade with their U-boats. He was promoted to Rear Admiral and brought back to command USN submarine forces in the south-west Pacific (operating from Australia).

On taking over as COMSUBPAC, Lockwood got rid of older, ineffectual submarine captains and decided that Japanese tankers should receive special attention. It was pointless sending submarines to patrol areas where enemy traffic was sparse, if non-existent. This had happened too much during the early days. Sometimes when Japanese Ultra – the product of labours by the USN's code-breakers – was used to direct a submarine to a more fruitful hunting ground the least well-placed boat was tasked with the job and failed to catch the target.

Rather than loiter off enemy naval bases – where the defences were bound to be stiff – Lockwood felt it was better to identify SLOC where the most targets might be found. He therefore sent submarines to prey on traffic between the East Indies and Borneo – where the oilfields were – and Japan. Tankers inevitably passed through the Luzon Strait, between Formosa and the Philippines, on their way to and from Japan. It would be a major battleground in the fighting to come.

The massive manufacturing capability of the USA was now swinging fully behind the war effort and when the time came to slash at the sinews of the enemy, new submarines would be the cutting edge – well before any US troops set eyes on the Japanese home islands.

These boats had welded hulls, whereas those made from riveted plates required the specialist skills of established shipyards and took longer to produce.

Welded boats could be mass-produced at numerous new yards established to churn them out. The USA would build 34 submarines in 1942 and 44 in 1943, while Japan constructed 61 and 37 respectively.

It may seem from those figures that Japan was holding its own, but the USA was in 1942/43 also building six battleships, 19 cruisers, 83 carriers (of various kinds) and 210 destroyers. By contrast, Japan in 1942/43 only produced six carriers, one battleship, seven cruisers and 22 destroyers (a good indication of its lesser capacity and lack of interest in anti-submarine forces). Between 1941 and 1945 the Japanese managed to turn out 63 destroyers, along with an unknown number of smaller anti-submarine craft. This compared very poorly with the USA's 349 destroyers and 498 other anti-submarine vessels.[7]

Altogether US naval war production represented a staggering effort that no other nation on earth could hope to match. The so-called 'arsenal of democracy', as President Roosevelt described America in a December 1940 address, was at the same time supplying both the British and Russian war machines.

Although the construction of modern submarines had begun in the late 1930s, the US programme really gathered pace with the Gato, Balao and Tench classes. The boats the USA produced to wage war were not just numerous – 203 submarines of all kinds added to USN submarine forces between 1941 and 1945 – but also excellent fighting vessels with plenty of torpedoes. They were large, designed to patrol the vast Pacific Ocean with the impressive surface speed necessary to make fast transits to hunting grounds, and had a 10,000-mile range.

The Gato, Balao and Tench classes could run at more than 20 knots on the surface and almost 9 knots dived. Gato and Tench had identical torpedo armament and capacity to earlier Tambor Class craft (six fore tubes and four stern). Balao Class boats had four bow tubes and four stern tubes. All three classes had a wartime crew of 80, which was large enough to maintain a watch system at sea for extended periods. The latest boats left the yards with 3-inch deck guns for attacking surface targets but were retrofitted with 4-inch or 5-inch guns. The original machine guns for self-defence were supplemented by 20mm and 40mm cannons. The Tambors would receive radar retrospectively but the other three classes had it when built. With full air conditioning and other mod cons, they were all spacious, comfortable boats, a world removed from the cramped, dank, comparatively small German and British submarines. The vessels may have been different but there was an aspect of the deadly trade as pursued by the Germans that would be adopted by the Americans, though not without some doubts to begin with.

30   Uncle Sam's Wolf Packs

The US Navy's Pacific submarine force shake-up and new boats were in marked contrast to the complacency of the enemy. Japan's navy failed to build enough destroyers, was poor in ASW techniques and was behind the curve when it came to radar technology.

Japanese convoys were getting bigger and escort forces were becoming stronger but there was still no IJN equivalent of Western Approaches Command to co-ordinate matters. There was also nothing that compared to Coastal Command providing aircraft to support the navy or protect convoys, whose administration suffered from the conflicting demands of the navy, army and Ministry of Munitions. Too often vessels sailed empty when they could very well have carried cargo to or from Japan.

There were no new weapons to compare with those the Allies developed, such as Hedgehog or Squid, and whereas Dönitz may have been assisted by the code-breakers of B-Dienst, the Japanese did not quite reap the same level of benefits from such input, even though they seemed to have a reasonably efficient intelligence-gathering ability.

IJN escort captains also deceived themselves, believing they were much more successful at ASW than they actually were and claiming sunk submarines when they were nothing of the sort. There was no dedicated analysis and questioning of claims to compare with the system in Britain.

The IJN battle fleet compounded the problems by declining to release more destroyers for convoy escort duty, disdaining such mundane work. Those escorts that were employed on ASW duties had no systemic means to prosecute the target and did not vary their depth charges between shallow and deep detonations – but rather set them all shallow.[1]

For all these faults, the Japanese were no pushover. It seemed by the end of 1942 that attacks by single US Navy submarines against their convoys would stand less chance of success than group efforts. Multiple co-ordinated assaults might throw a Japanese escort force into chaos and overwhelm a convoy's defence. Fortunately for the Americans, developments in crucial technologies were making it possible to adopt fresh tactics. The new submarines had both effective radar and radio-telephone technology. The latter potentially enabled commanders of attack groups to co-ordinate boats at the scene of the action. Code-breaking also provided a decisive edge, with the continuing provision of Japanese Ultra material to guide attacks. All this combined to make the idea of USN wolf packs a practical proposition, although they were officially called Co-ordinated Attack Groups (CAG).

There were important differences between the fashion in which the USN sought to wield its CAGs and German wolf packs. Even though hundreds of miles removed from the scene of the action, Dönitz and Godt still tried to exert control via signals but the Americans devolved control and initiative to the group commander. Dönitz did try out the concept of having an on-the-scene commander for a short while, but did not return to the idea. Under the usual German system there was no overall commander of a wolf pack actually at sea – no commodore to tightly co-ordinate attacks in the middle of the battle, adapting the plan minute by minute or even second by second in order to crack open the shell of escort force defence. The U-boat force chiefs held all the cards in deciding where the wolf packs should attempt to mount attacks, placing the groups in what they felt was the best position. The Kriegsmarine's boats were then left to stage their forays against the target convoy on an individual basis, as and when they could.

Within an American CAG the boss would be a former submarine officer in the rank of Captain, though temporarily made a commodore to provide the required authority over other COs. He was generally ten years or more older than his subordinate captains. Lockwood knew such men would have good tactical sense and mature judgement, though they were hand-picked not to be overly cautious.

By cutting the apron strings to distant, higher command – trusting the CAG commander on the spot – Lockwood hoped to effect greater destruction, to really hobble enemy trade. Above all, on-the-spot command kept signals traffic the enemy might intercept down to a minimum, denying the Japanese the same level of code-breaking – and hence convoy rerouting – advantage the Allies enjoyed in the Atlantic. The target for a CAG was, admittedly, less difficult to handle, for Japanese convoys were small, composed of at most a dozen vessels, whereas in the Atlantic U-boats would face dozens of ships spread across miles of ocean.

The first CAG deployment was staged in autumn 1943 under the command of 47-year-old Captain Charles 'Swede' Momsen, who was, despite his nickname, of Danish descent. The current boss of Submarine Squadron Two based at Pearl, Momsen had some months earlier worked on sorting out the torpedo problem, analysing the performance of exploders while conducting an investigation into 'an alarming number of duds'.[2] Now he would get to see how they worked in combat.

Lockwood had not initially been keen on wolf packs but both he and Rear Admiral Ralph Christie – boss of Submarine Forces South-West Pacific (SubSWPac), the Australian-based boats – were obliged by a directive from the head of the USN, Admiral King, to try them out.

Lockwood preferred to strike at the enemy's crucial sea trade rather than send wolf packs against enemy warship concentrations, so merchant shipping would be Momsen's primary target. Departing Pearl Harbor, the CAG was composed of *Cero*, *Shad* and *Grayback* (two Gatos and a Tambor respectively). Momsen, a war patrol virgin despite his high rank, was embarked in *Cero*, alongside veteran submarine captain Cdr David White. Key to tactical co-ordination was Talk Between Ships (TBS) short-range radio. The standard tactic was for one submarine to go in first, then withdraw astern of the convoy while the other two boats took it in turns to attack from the flanks, hoping to confuse and split up the escort. The convoy would be driven first one way then the other – each time into the eager arms of a waiting submarine.

The CAG was to use Japanese Ultra intelligence on convoy departures, arrivals and routes to assist in seeking out worthy targets – not just merchant vessels but also enemy submarines and even capital ships if the opportunity presented itself. On this first CAG deployment there were no tightly co-ordinated attacks in the fashion envisaged. Instead, the boats helped each other sight convoys and fix their positions for assault by individual submarines, though *Shad* and *Grayback* managed to attack one convoy simultaneously.

Momsen was at the time felt to have done a good job, for the boats he commanded reportedly sank 38,000 tons of enemy shipping (five vessels) and scored damage on eight others. In fact, as renowned submarine warfare historian Clay Blair has pointed out, the tally was not quite that high. Momsen's CAG actually sank three vessels, for a tonnage total of 23,500 tons. It nevertheless proved that modified American torpedoes could function when required.

There were still misgivings, even from Momsen. He wondered if Lockwood, blessed with the big picture, might be better off using intelligence sources to direct the CAG against selected targets, rather than the boats wasting time and diesel chasing after them. The CAG's submarine captains felt they should go about their business solo. *In gathering them together in one place might targets be slipping by elsewhere?*

Despite his earlier misgivings Lockwood became convinced the CAG concept could work. He was probably keen not to expose his own forces to the same level of signals interception and decryption that he must have known, from his time in London, that the Germans were suffering. His instinct was correct. According to senior Japanese submariner Capt. Tokuma Abe, who worked on countering the USN's wolf packs, his side could pick up messages between American boats and their bases, between submarines and even between boats and aircraft. 'We were able to intercept all such communications,' he revealed.[3]

The Japanese might well have been able to do so, but it was then a matter of breaking the American codes and using the resulting information to greatest effect. The IJN had comparatively little success in cracking Allied codes but signals traffic analysis and other interpretation did help them. 'We were able to foretell from statistical data where to expect enemy subs,' explained Lt Cdr Noriteru Yatsui, on the staff of the IJN's 7th Convoy Escort Group, 'and could even foretell the characteristics of such submarine groups – that is, whether they would be aggressive, daring, or otherwise.'[4]

None of that information was any good if the escort forces themselves were too small and not efficient enough to actually find and kill the enemy.

A second CAG was assembled in October 1943 and by November there had been such a general turnaround in American submarine force fortunes that 231,000 tons of enemy shipping was sunk that month.

Lockwood was so pleased with results that he was able to report on 22 November that American totals 'now compare favorably'[5] with those being achieved by the Germans. In comparison to the number of U-boats Dönitz was able to field when his own campaign peaked, the USN's force was still not huge. There were about 50 American submarines assigned to operations in the Pacific at the beginning of hostilities and the USN could only ever deploy about a dozen sub-marines at any one time in the region. The huge distances to be covered meant much of a boat's patrol was spent getting to waters where the targets might be and there was limited time on station. By mid-1944 there were 140 US submarines in the Pacific,[6] due to older ones being replaced with bigger, better boats, but Lockwood only controlled some of them. Despite this, 117 CAG were formed during the war.

While the Americans took the wolf pack model and shaped it for their own ends, the Japanese, who started hostilities with a submarine force larger than Germany's – 64 boats compared to 57 – failed to make anywhere near the same impact. This was almost entirely down to a rigid mindset in the high command.

31   A Ruinous Obsession

Japan's failure to properly capitalise on its submarine force in order to disrupt the enemy war machine was abundantly clear to a 47-year-old German naval officer sent to Tokyo to invigorate its naval campaign. Vice Admiral Paul Wenneker was Naval Attaché in the German Embassy, staying in post for the duration of the war. As such he gained great insight into how the Japanese conducted their submarine campaign.

Japan's naval top brass cold-shouldered his suggestion – conveyed specifically at the urging of the Naval Ministry in Berlin – that the IJN should 'exert their maximum effort in attack against U.S. merchant shipping in the Pacific'.[1]

Despite several similar pleas over subsequent years Japan's admirals would not budge, telling Wenneker they must preserve their submarines for action against enemy naval forces. Wenneker told his masters in Berlin that Japan's naval commanders felt merchant shipping 'could be easily replaced with the great American production capacity, but that naval vessels represented the real power against what they fought and that these vessels and their trained crews were most difficult to replace and hence were the one logical target'.

The Japanese Navy 'thought always of the U.S. carriers', said Wenneker. It obsessed over how many American carriers were being built, how many were in service in the Pacific, 'and that these must be sunk . . .' Next on the target list for Japanese submarines were battleships. Only after these had been tackled might submarines target 'lesser ships but never the merchantmen, except under most favourable conditions'.

This obsession extended to specific orders forbidding IJN submarine captains from taking on targets of opportunity if they had already been sent to attack major enemy naval units. Smaller warships and merchant ships were allowed to sail by unmolested. This did not please many Japanese submarine captains but they dared not disobey orders. They were even issued with strict instructions on how many torpedoes they might fire at given targets. A battleship rated all torpedoes, a cruiser no more than three and only one torpedo should be fired at an enemy destroyer or merchant ship.[2]

Aghast at the rigidity of their ally's conduct of submarine warfare, the Germans repeatedly pressed the point that the way to disable the enemy naval forces was to sink oil tankers. Once again Wenneker found 'the answer was negative; the mission was the American carriers and they could not be changed on this principle'.

Contrary to what Wenneker may have been told, some of Japan's submarines did attack merchant shipping whenever they got an opportunity. IJN boats in the second half of 1942 sent to the bottom 42 merchant vessels and damaged a further 11.[3] They also sank enemy submarines, including the USS *Corvina*, off Truk (by *I-176*) on 16 November.

The Royal Australian Navy did not get away without being attacked by Japanese submarines, with the cruiser HMAS *Hobart* torpedoed in July 1943, while part of a task force operating off the New Hebrides. Fourteen of *Hobart*'s men were killed or missing with a further 16 injured. *Hobart* did not return to service until 1945.

The Japanese submarine force paid a high price for such meagre success, with five boats operating in the South Pacific lost between 19 August and 15 September. USN destroyers sank three of them while aircraft assisted an American destroyer and a Royal New Zealand Navy patrol vessel in making the other two kills.[4] The following year the casualty rate would climb even higher.

When the IJN needed to obtain intelligence on whether the Americans would attempt to take the Philippines or the Mariana Islands, it established picket lines of scouting submarines.

The majority of them would be rolled up by a single destroyer, USS *England*, a product of the Bethlehem Steel Co. in San Francisco. Fitted with highly effective sonar, her armament included a trio of 3-inch guns, eight 20mm cannons, a Hedgehog, eight depth-charge throwers and two depth-charge racks. She had an impressive range of 6,000 nautical miles at 12 knots. Across the space of eight days in May 1944 *England* sank five enemy submarines, her crew pursuing their task with grim enthusiasm. Only one attack was carried out against a phantom target. Across her successful attacks, the *England* used Hedgehog to devastating effect, firing 13 salvoes of depth bombs and scoring seven hits.[5]

Aside from hydrophones picking up underwater explosions and rumblings – the shock of one knocking men on *England*'s fantail off their feet – further evidence of success was provided by oil slicks, bottle corks and fragments of polished wood. One of the latter bore evidence of candle tallow, while other bits of wreckage had Japanese writing on them.[6]

'It is doubted whether any other ship in this or any other war, has produced such a record,' remarked Rear Admiral J.L. Kauffman, Commander Destroyers, Pacific Fleet in his summary of the *England*'s exploits.[7]

Robbed of their submarine eyes, Japanese naval commanders placed their bets on the Philippines and got it wrong, leaving Marianas invasion forces to proceed unmolested. During the planning stage of the scouting operation the highly experienced Japanese submarine captain Lt Cdr Zenji Orita, of *I-177*, had urged his bosses not to place the boats in a straight picket line.[8] It was fortunate the American ships filled the air waves with celebratory radio signals about their submarine turkey shoot, for these were intercepted, decoded and warnings flashed to the surviving Japanese submarines, which made a hasty withdrawal.

Restricted though they might be by the top brass in their target choice, Japanese submarines frequently attacked convoys in waters around Australia, though they weren't very effective. IJN boats never sank more than five (merchant) ships a month off Australia. In March 1943 they sank no merchant vessels while eight attacks were reported in May and none at all in July, August and September. Targets were plentiful had Japanese submarines been unleashed in a determined and co-ordinated fashion. In July 1943 2,279,472 tons of shipping (504 ships) was convoyed across all routes adjacent to Australia.[9]

Often IJN boats were readied to search out victims off Australia but then diverted to other waters, especially to convey vital supplies and troops to besieged island outposts.

Japanese naval commanders were fiercely proud of and dedicated to using their submarines as transport vessels. This plunged some submariners into deep despair, complaining about carrying out 'such stupid work' when their real mission was to attack the enemy. Lt Cdr Orita complained to his boss that using submarines in this fashion was 'throwing away the reason for their construction'.[10]

The rationale behind this crippling misuse of boats was, according to senior naval staff officer Cdr Chikataka Nakajima, the result of too few submarines to handle both missions. Transportation was also considered a moral imperative 'because the Army . . . would have refused to send additional strength to the South Pacific if the Navy had left men to starve'. There were many discussions in the higher echelons of the IJN but in the end, admitted Cdr Nakajima, 'we were forced to let them be used for supply . . . because of the shortage of warships and supply ships of all types'. Utilising submarines as 'supply weapons' was also part of the strategy of 'fighting delaying actions on all islands'.[11]

Apart from Japan's faulty submarine strategy, Germany's Vice Admiral Wenneker was far from impressed with the boats themselves. He regarded them as 'poor types', which were 'too big for easy handling under water when under attack and consequently were too easily destroyed'. He found their Asdic, hydrophones and radar equipment 'very far behind in development'.[12]

Japanese submarine captains were desperate for effective radar. One of them complained that submariners in the front line were 'longing for radar as farmers look for rain in a long drought'.[13] Lt Cdr Orita did his very best to offset the unwieldy nature of Japanese boats. Moved from I-177 to command the even bigger I-47, he was well aware that his submarine was large and clumsy, qualities that could lead to the boat's destruction, especially if caught on the surface. He pursued efficiency relentlessly, especially in cutting down the time it took to clear the bridge for a crash dive, which could be a lifesaver.

In an effort to equip the IJN with long-range submarines that might stand a better chance of evading destruction, *U-511*, a Type IX, was sent to Japan. In September 1943 she was handed over by Kapitänleutnant Fritz Schneewind, and would be christened *RO-500*. The boat was given a thorough inspection and some equipment was removed for closer study at Kure naval dockyard to see if such a vessel could be produced in Japan. Wenneker was dismayed when the IJN came to the conclusion that it was 'too complicated for construction in Japan at this time'.[14]

With that option rejected it was arranged for an entire Japanese submarine crew under the command of Lt Cdr Sadatoshi Norita to receive training in Germany, to see if new tactics and procedures could be adopted by the IJN. The crew made a successful passage to the west coast of France in *I-8* and then went to the Baltic where, according to Admiral Wenneker, they undertook 'very good training in German boats and in German attack methods'. Norita and his men did not get to pass on their newly honed war-fighting skills, nor did they bring home a second U-boat gifted to Japan. Departing Kiel on 30 April 1944, the former *U-1224*, renamed *RO-501*, made it as far as the South Atlantic where the USS *Bogue* hunter-killer group caught her. The destroyer escort *Francis M. Robinson* was sent off to kill *RO-501* on the evening of 13 May, the unfortunate submarine being destroyed to the north-west of Cape Verde by a combination of Hedgehog and depth charges.

The to and fro of men and war materials between Japan and Germany continued, with U-boats also ordered to operate from Penang or Singapore, bringing out with them equipment that might prove useful in enhancing Japanese submarine operations. According to Wenneker the shipments included 'optical goods, plans for airplanes, and machine tool equipment. . . . special personnel . . .' Among items sent back to Germany in U-boats were quinine and tin. Very little reached Wenneker in Tokyo, as the US Navy's submarine blockade was too tight.

'It was terrible,' he remarked. 'Sometimes the entire convoy including all my material would be lost. It seemed that nothing could get through.'

Not a lot was getting through to the Germans from Japan either by the summer of 1944. Among the Japanese submarines that headed for Europe in 1944 was *I-52*, carrying rubber, tin, tungsten and quinine, along with two tons of gold (146 bars).

On 23 June, 850 miles to the west of Cape Verde, *I-52* made a night rendezvous with *U-530* to receive fresh food and other supplies. She also took aboard two German naval technicians with a radar set, to help the boat evade Allied aircraft in the Bay of Biscay as she neared Lorient.[15] They never got to set up the radar, for *I-52*'s voyage was well known thanks to Allied code-breaking, along with details of her meeting with *U-530*.

The *Bogue* group was tasked with finding and killing the Japanese boat, launching two Avenger torpedo-bombers equipped with surface search radar, each packing depth charges and a homing torpedo. They were to be aided in their hunt by a remarkable new device invented by Allied boffins, the sonobuoy (a floating Asdic). Sonobuoys could be sown across a wide or condensed area by aircraft, which could then listen for enemy submarines.

Successfully detecting the boats, the Avengers dropped sonobuoys. On picking up the propeller noise of a dived submarine one Avenger unleashed a Fido homing torpedo and two depth charges. The sonobuoys detected what sounded like a submarine being crushed by water pressure or snapping in two. Another Avenger was launched by *Bogue* and dropped its Fido over what was suspected to be the surviving submarine from the mid-ocean rendezvous, with an explosion heard 18 minutes later.[16]

Post-war analysis suggested that on both occasions *I-52* was the target, for *U-530* survived hostilities to be interned in Argentina. When *Bogue* sent destroyers from her task group to search the scene for evidence of a kill they found a sandal, some rolls of silk, bales of rubber and pieces of mahogany. Rubber was usually carried between the casing and the hull of a submarine, so it indicated the boat had been torn apart.

The Japanese submarine force in the Second World War never lost the talent for delivering shocks to the Americans, but often there was a sting in the tail. On 24 November 1943 *I-175* sank the escort carrier *Liscome Bay* off the Gilbert Islands but the USN boat *Sailfish* got revenge by sinking *Chuyo*, a Japanese escort carrier, off Japan on 4 December 1943. Therein lay the rub for the Japanese and their sink-the-carriers obsession. It didn't matter how many American warships they sank – carriers or destroyers – they would be replaced, thanks to the USA's awesome military-industrial power.

Gaps left by the loss of *Chuyo* and other Japanese carriers were not so easily filled. When they were, there was invariably a US Navy submarine waiting out there somewhere to try to sink the new vessels. The fate of the gigantic *Shinano* was a case in point. Lurking off Honshu on 2/3 December 1944 was the USS *Archerfish*, which spotted the 72,000-ton vessel on her maiden voyage. Earlier in the war the CO of *Archerfish*, 34-year-old Lt Cdr Joe Enright, while in command of USS *Dace*, missed an opportunity to sink the carrier *Shokaku* (well known by then as one of the ships that launched the attack on Pearl Harbor). Enright was so ashamed of his failure he asked to be relieved of command and was, but got a second chance in the *Archerfish*.

The American boat was actually sent into the waters off the Japanese home islands on stand-by, to rescue the aircrews of B-29 bombers shot down while blitzing Tokyo. On the evening of 28 November 1944, during a periscope look, Enright spotted a massive vessel with an escort of four destroyers exiting Tokyo Bay. This was the first ever sighting of the new ship by any American eyes, as there was no intelligence whatsoever to indicate she existed. Enright's target was originally laid down and constructed to be a sister vessel to the IJN's monster battleships *Yamato* and *Musashi*, but in the aftermath of the Midway losses Japan decided to complete *Shinano* as a carrier. Taking advantage of the darkness, for more than six hours *Archerfish* chased and then overhauled the enemy group on the surface. Once ahead, she dived and when the time was right fired six torpedoes. 'Moments later, a great glowing ball of fire climbed up the Japanese ship's side,' said one account, 'and the Americans soon heard a series of tremendous explosions while the enemy vessel disintegrated.'[17]

Enright had pulled off an amazing feat and *Shinano* remains the largest warship ever sunk in combat. *Archerfish* joined the ranks of the few USN boats to receive the ultimate accolade of a Presidential Unit Citation.

32 Captains Charismatic

While Japanese submariners were caught in a vice of their own navy's making, their American counterparts thrived. The USN's submarine force evolved into a finely tuned instrument of war, potentially capable of achieving decisive strategic effect.

This was due to a culture of training and command that created brave and resourceful submarine commanders who were then let off the leash – and guided by Japanese Ultra – to create havoc against the right kind of shipping, at the right time and in the right place. America's top undersea warriors were made of incredible stuff, with the best of them never lacking initiative and aggression. Superstars of a different order to Germany's gilded gods of Valhalla or the understated British with their stiff upper lips, they were products of the world's wealthiest, brashest and most glamorous nation. They were the children of a rising economic and military superpower – and they had something to prove.

The American submarine force had no laurels to rest on like its British and German equivalents, which had won their spurs in the First World War. In the aftermath of Pearl Harbor, with America's battleships on the bottom, the USN had to rely on the aviators, the US Marines and the submariners to hit back at Japan. The American submarine force established a reputation for courage in adversity, with its men often making the ultimate sacrifice. Three out of seven US submarine captains who won the Medal of Honor – the USA's highest award for valour in the face of the enemy – did not survive to collect their awards from the President.

The brave new breed of USN submarine commanders was leavened with leaders from an earlier generation, their older brothers who were no less courageous. Forty-year-old Cdr Howard Gilmore exemplified aggression and spirit. He had started out as an ordinary rating, but then passed the officer's exam and joined the submarine force. During a spell of pre-war shore leave in a Caribbean port he was beaten up and had his throat slit, but still survived, an indicator of his toughness. In March 1942 Gilmore took command of USS *Growler*, one of the new Gato Class submarines. She was blooded on 5 July that year off Kiska in the Aleutians, taking on the most formidable foe. It was not easy to hit a destroyer as they were fast, manoeuvrable and had a shallow draught – and unlike merchant ships they could dish out severe punishment to anyone who dared attack them.

Nonetheless, *Growler* took on a trio of Japanese destroyers, firing torpedoes while submerged and surfacing to use her 3-inch gun. Hitting the *Arare* and sinking her, *Growler's* torpedoes damaged the other two enemy destroyers, all while the American boat dodged enemy fish fired in retaliation. *Growler's* next deployment took her to waters off Formosa, where she sank four Japanese merchant ships in a fortnight, for a total of 15,000 tons.

Sailing from Brisbane again in mid-January 1943, in waters thick with enemy anti-submarine craft, *Growler* suffered a depth-charging, but it was her own defective torpedo that provided the worst scare by turning back on itself. On 7 February, after escaping an unusually determined depth-charge attack, *Growler* surfaced to make a run against a convoy. One of the escorts proved more spirited than the others by trying to ram the submarine. *Growler* narrowly avoided being hit and Gilmore gave the order for his boat to ram her would-be assailant, tearing into the enemy craft's port side at 17 knots.

Growler's bridge was doused by enemy fire as the submarine untangled herself, with two men killed and two others wounded. Gilmore gave the order to dive but was struck by bullets and mortally wounded himself, shouting: 'Take her down!' Everybody else evacuated the bridge and this saved the boat to fight another day. When *Growler* surfaced there was no sign of the enemy, Gilmore or the bodies of the other men. His last order became a slogan of the US Navy submarine force. Gilmore was posthumously awarded the Medal of Honor, the first one to a submariner in the Second World War.

The same day *Growler* had her tussle with an enemy escort, the Gato Class boat USS *Wahoo* returned to Pearl Harbor with a broom fixed to her periscope. She also flew pennants for sinking six merchant vessels and a pair of Japanese warships. It was the conclusion of her third war patrol and *Wahoo* proudly displayed another pennant, which was emblazoned with the suitably pugilistic slogan: 'Shoot the sunza bitches.'

It was all very much in line with the personality and way of waging war of *Wahoo's* 35-year-old captain, Lt Cdr Dudley 'Mush' Morton.

He possessed intense, tough-as-nails movie star charisma reminiscent of Burt Lancaster, gaining his 'Mushmouth' nickname due to a formidable capacity for spinning exciting yarns.

Morton was ultra aggressive, always looking for trouble and never content just to wait for passing trade. Having suffered frustration on two war patrols as Executive Officer to *Wahoo*'s first captain, Morton took over command on 31 December 1942. Right from the start he sought to make it clear things would be very different under him. '*Wahoo* is expendable,' he told his men. 'We will take every reasonable precaution, but our mission is to sink enemy shipping . . .'[1]

Morton said anyone who didn't want to accept that ethos could transfer out of the boat. Nobody did. One of his senior ratings would say of Morton that 'it took me one minute to realise that I would follow that man to the bottom of the ocean if necessary . . .' This was a submarine captain who 'knew his business inside and out'.[2]

When it came to sinking ships, Morton followed simple rules: 'Just sight, track, shoot and sink!'[3] He enthusiastically took up a suggestion for a new way of working put forward by Rear Admiral James Fife, who commanded the US Navy's Brisbane-based submarines at the time.

Having proved highly skilled on the periscope, Morton judged Fife's idea of splitting attack duties between the CO and the Executive Officer (XO, or second in command) potentially a good one. Provided he had an equally aggressive and skilled XO, he could take a step back and focus on the tactics, and the picture in his head. He would con the boat to place her in the best position and avoid danger, while the XO took care of business on the scope. Morton was especially fortunate to have Lt Richard O'Kane as his right-hand man for most of his war patrols in *Wahoo*. O'Kane was a master tactician and fully ready to command his own boat soon. The new way of attacking worked, but even so few submarine captains would have so much confidence in another officer that they could, as one history of the war put it, 'resist grabbing the scope in moments of crisis'.[4]

In mid-January 1943, *Wahoo* deployed from Brisbane and ventured to waters off Papua New Guinea, with Morton ordered to take a look at Wewak, a major enemy base on the north-east coast.

Its geography was fuzzy – available charts did not have much detail but one of *Wahoo*'s motor machinists came up with a solution. During

Lt Cdr Dudley Morton (right) with his Executive Officer, Lt Richard O'Kane, on USS *Wahoo*'s bridge at Pearl Harbor after her third war patrol. (*Photo: US National Archives/NHHC*)

shore leave in Australia he'd purchased a basic educational atlas and a map of New Guinea was in there, with an indentation labelled Wewak. Using this as his guide, Morton compared the atlas map with a naval chart, finding a stretch of coast with the same indentation. The naval chart was photographed and blown up. Using tracing paper and some sparse navigation notes a more detailed, if still somewhat rudimentary, chart was created.

Required to scout out the harbour, Morton was never going to venture in there without sinking anything. Diving the boat two miles out from Kairiu Island, which guarded the harbour entrance, on 26 January Morton edged *Wahoo* past its western shore and entered Victoria Bay. He found a destroyer with some enemy submarines moored alongside. The destroyer was departing and as she got underway Morton ordered three torpedoes fired, which missed astern. Keeping his nerve, with O'Kane on the scope feeding him information, Morton fired a fourth torpedo, which also missed as the destroyer turned towards *Wahoo*'s scope.

The enemy steamed into the attack, and Morton now had just one torpedo left loaded in the bow tubes. He kept his nerve, intent on trying what was called a down-the-throat shot. If he missed this time,

Wahoo and everybody in her was probably doomed. The destroyer was now just 800 yards away and O'Kane was astonished to see the entire upper works – masts, turrets, upper deck – were covered in Japanese sailors, all trying to spot the enemy periscope. The fifth torpedo hit the destroyer, seeming to break her in two with a massive explosion.

Despite vivid reports of the enemy's demise – and Morton's fierce insistence he had totally destroyed his foe – a confirmed sinking was not attributed to *Wahoo*. The *Harusame* was actually run ashore to prevent her from sinking. After major repairs she was returned to service, only to be subsequently sunk by American aircraft later in the war.

On the same patrol *Wahoo* used torpedoes and her gun to sink two cargo vessels, a troop ship and a tanker, Morton noting with satisfaction at the end of a signal to Pearl Harbor: '. . . all torpedoes expended'.[5]

And so *Wahoo* returned to Pearl Harbor with that broom fixed to the top of her periscope to indicate a clean sweep. Five ships sunk was at the time more than any other USN submarine had achieved on a single patrol. Later analysis would conclude that *Wahoo* actually sank three ships for a total of 11,300 tons.

The accolades poured in for Morton, with a Navy Cross and even a Distinguished Service Cross from the army, courtesy of General Douglas MacArthur. *Wahoo* was dubbed 'The One-Boat Wolf Pack'.[6]

Two more patrols were conducted in swift succession. Morton established a record for a USN submarine captain by taking just 25 patrol days to sink an estimated 93,281 tons of enemy shipping – supposedly damaging a further 30,880 tons – across all three deployments. More awards for Morton and *Wahoo*'s men followed and they were rewarded with a refit for the boat back in the States, at Mare Island, allowing them to spend some time with their families.

Back in the combat zone, in August 1943 Morton took *Wahoo* into the Sea of Japan itself but it proved an extremely frustrating experience, with all torpedoes missing or failing to detonate. There had been the occasional dud in previous patrols, but this was remarkable, for all the wrong reasons. Nine ships had been attacked and none sunk. 'Damn the torpedoes!' Morton wrote angrily in his War Log.[7] *Wahoo*'s men consoled themselves by sinking a few sampans with her gun and then headed home.

Returning to Pearl, Morton stormed down the gangway as soon as it was across and headed for Admiral Lockwood's office to give his boss the bad news. 'Well, Mush,' Admiral Lockwood enquired when Morton had blown off steam, 'what do you want to do?'

'I want to go right back to the Sea of Japan,' Morton told him, 'with a load of live fish this time.'[8]

Lockwood wondered if Morton didn't need a rest rather than another patrol straight away but he also knew *Wahoo*'s captain would not thank him for that. A successful patrol might be an equally good cure.

Wahoo went back into the Sea of Japan with a load of perfectly maintained fish and sank four ships, but her luck ran out. She was sunk on 11 October 1943 by Japanese ASW forces, which had been alerted to enemy submarines in the La Pérouse Strait by detecting USS *Sawfish* passing through on 9 October.

Wahoo was gone, credited with sinking 19 ships (55,000 tons) and damaging two more during six patrols.[9] *Time* magazine rated *Wahoo*'s penetration of the Sea of Japan 'a feat ranking with German Günther Prien's entry at Scapa flow . . .'[10] Like Prien and *U-47*, Morton and *Wahoo* ultimately could not outrun the Grim Reaper.

The entire USN submarine force was stunned that the seemingly invincible Morton could be dead, with Lockwood remarking: 'It just didn't seem possible . . .'[11]

Morton seemed to have become a little frayed around the edges prior to the last patrol of *Wahoo*. It has been claimed that some members of his crew were scared of how driven, yet exhausted, he had become. He was suffering from prostate problems and between patrols spent time in hospital and needed treatment for it at sea, which did not help his frame of mind. Also, some officers (including O'Kane) who knew him best – and would have advised Morton when not to take unwise risks – had moved on to other boats.

Morton would not be awarded the Medal of Honor, which perhaps seems strange. It is likely this was because of an incident in which his thirst for destroying the enemy got the better of him.

On 26 January 1943, the day after the Wewak venture, *Wahoo* sank the troop ship *Buyo Maru* off the coast of New Guinea. Surfacing *Wahoo* amid lifeboats containing hundreds of survivors, Morton seems to have rationalised that every Japanese soldier killed in the water would save a life ashore.[12] As the submarine passed among them every weapon *Wahoo* could muster, including the 4-inch gun, was used to destroy lifeboats and kill enemy soldiers. The Japanese started firing back and even throwing grenades at the submarine, actions that some of *Wahoo*'s sailors later claimed provoked Morton. One officer in his crew implied that Morton's deep and abiding loathing of the enemy was a motive. He possessed 'a biological hatred of the enemy' according to Lt George Grider and during the lifeboats attack stared about him 'with exultation at the carnage'.[13]

Nearly 90 Japanese troops were killed, though O'Kane would insist the boats were targeted rather than the men. Morton wanted to prevent them from reaching the shore to reinforce Japanese forces fighting in New Guinea.

Morton did not hide *Wahoo*'s actions, and wrote a full report on what had happened. In a further twist that illustrated the random cruelty of war, there were 491 Indian Army PoWs aboard *Buyo Maru* when she was sunk, with an estimated 195 losing their lives (many, it is alleged, due to *Wahoo*'s actions).[14] The majority of the 1,126 people aboard the ship were picked up by Japanese rescue vessels. Nobody could ever doubt Morton's courage and Lockwood did not censure him for his actions after sinking *Buyo Maru*, but many within the USN were deeply troubled.[15]

Morton may have been denied the Medal of Honor but he was awarded a fourth Navy Cross posthumously. Once Japanese records were available after the war it transpired that by the time she entered the La Pérouse Strait *Wahoo* had probably sustained damage to an oil tank. This forced Morton to gamble on a surface passage at full speed, early on the morning of 11 October.

Coming under fire from coastal artillery, the boat dived but Japanese aircraft and anti-submarine craft were called to the scene. They attacked the submerged boat with bombs and depth charges, blowing one of the submarine's propeller blades to the surface.

They may have been aided in their hunt for *Wahoo* by one advance in technology where the Japanese were keeping pace with their opponents. This was the Magnetic Anomaly Detector (MAD), which was fitted in some of their patrol aircraft. It picked up disturbance in the earth's magnetic field caused by the passage of something made of metal, such as a submarine, below the surface of the sea. The *Jikitanchiki*, as it was called, could find submarines down to 800ft – just beyond the crush depth of a USN boat – if the search aircraft flew close to the surface.

Regardless of exactly which piece of technology or units played the key part in *Wahoo*'s destruction, clear evidence of a submarine's demise was found on the surface. There was, according to a post-war USN account of her loss, 'an expanding oil slick of diesel fuel 200ft wide and three miles long [that] marked *Wahoo*'s grave'.[16] American submarines would not go back into the Sea of Japan until 1945. Admiral Lockwood remarked that *Wahoo*'s crew 'would follow their skipper to the Gates of Hell . . . and they did'.[17]

33   Hit 'em Harder

Cdr Sam Dealey was a smooth customer, a Texan and nephew of the man who established the *Dallas Morning News*, but he achieved such low grades at the naval academy he was forced to quit.

Dealey was readmitted and graduated in 1930 at the age of 24, and during the early years of his naval career served in the submarine *Nautilus* and was later Executive Officer of the destroyer *Reuben James*. Selection for the US Navy's submarine Prospective Commanding Officer course came in the spring of 1941. After passing the tests he was sent to Submarine Base New London, Connecticut, to oversee the fitting out of the brand new Gato Class submarine *Harder*, before taking command. Ordered to the Pacific, *Harder* narrowly escaped destruction by a US Navy aircraft while passing through the Caribbean.[1]

It was *Harder*'s fifth patrol in June 1944 that was to be her most famous. Probing the Sibutu Passage – a heavily patrolled stretch of water between Tawi-Tawi and northern Borneo – on the night of 6 June *Harder* happened upon a convoy composed of three oil tankers escorted by a pair of destroyers.

Dealey decided on a surface chase but ordered *Harder* to dive when she was exposed by bright moonlight.

Not long after that the destroyer *Minazuki* tried to find and attack

Harder, with Dealey turning the submarine's stern towards the enemy and, at a range of just over 1,000 yards, firing three torpedoes. Two of them hit *Minazuki*, which sank five minutes later. The other enemy escort was luckier, escaping an attack by *Harder* but suppressing the submarine until the tankers got away.[2]

When the destroyer *Hayanami* tried to find *Harder* the following morning Dealey stalked her and then blew her apart with two torpedoes. Withdrawing under depth-charge attack from enemy ASW vessels, Dealey headed for the coast of Borneo, where *Harder* took aboard a party of British commandos who had been on a raid. With these passengers embarked, it was on the night of 9 June, again in the Sibutu Passage, that Dealey struck again.

Cdr Sam Dealey wearing the Navy Cross presented to him by Vice Admiral Charles A. Lockwood for extraordinary heroism as captain of USS *Harder*. (*USN/US National Archives/NHHC*)

At 9.02 p.m., with *Harder* on the surface, a pair of zigzagging destroyers were sighted. *Harder* dived but still with the radar mast poking above the surface to track the enemy. Dealey took the boat to periscope depth and saw the destroyers were 'just what the doctor ordered'[3] and nicely lined up for attack.

With the range down to 1,000 yards, Dealey saw 'both destroyers were overlapping' and at 9.24 p.m. fired a spread of four torpedoes. One passed ahead of the nearest ship, *Tanikaze*, but the second hit close to the bow, while the third slammed into the warship below the bridge. The fourth torpedo missed astern. '. . . the sub was now swung hard right to avoid hitting the first destroyer and fire was held on the remaining tubes', reported Dealey. Calculations were made on attacking the second destroyer but, so Dealey believed at the time, events overtook that idea. 'About thirty seconds after turning, the second destroyer came into view just ahead of what was left of the first one, then burning furiously.'[4] Dealey was delighted to see the fourth torpedo from the first spread hit the other destroyer. He remarked, rather laconically: 'No more torpedoes were needed for either.'[5]

He reported that *Harder* was so close to her first target – a mere 400 yards – that when the destroyer's boiler exploded the submarine was 'heeled over by the concussion'. He went on: 'At almost the same time a blinding explosion took place on the second destroyer (probably the ammunition going off) and it took a quick nose dive.' It had been an incredible few minutes, which Dealey described as 'pandemonium'.[6]

He didn't stop there, for on 10 June *Harder* encountered a full task force including a trio of battleships, not least the gigantic vessels *Musashi* and *Yamato*, but the submarine's periscope was spotted by an enemy aircraft and marked with smoke. A destroyer was sent to attack and kill the interloper but again Dealey took up the gauntlet. He waited until the destroyer was about 1,000 yards away and fired a trio of torpedoes in a classic down-the-throat tactic. *Harder* went deep and a series of explosions occurred overhead, which Dealey thought was his target destroyed.

Harder was subjected to depth-charge attacks from escorts and enemy aircraft for some hours, but sneaked away. As soon as she could, *Harder* sent a sighting report on the enemy battleships. This, combined with other submarine intelligence, enabled the Americans to intercept the Japanese task force at the Battle of the Philippine Sea on 19/20 June and sink three carriers and damage a battleship.

After performing some further surveillance off Tawi-Tawi, *Harder* headed for Darwin, arriving on 21 June. Dealey had fully earned the nickname bestowed upon him – 'The Destroyer Killer' while the boat's motto – 'Hit 'Em Again, Harder' – was entirely fitting. He was not ultimately credited with the second destroyer sunk on 9 June, as post-war analysis could not confirm it, nor would the 10 June destroyer be confirmed. The overhead explosions were bombs or depth charges.

On 5 August *Harder*, *Haddo* and *Hake* were deployed from Freman-tle, on Australia's west coast, to conduct wolf pack operations, 16 days later joining forces with *Raton*, *Ray* and *Guitarra* to attack a convoy off Paluan Bay.

Harder possibly sank one cargo vessel, but on 22 August she reverted to her specialisation of killing warships by sinking a couple of enemy frigates, the *Hiburi* and the *Matsuwa*, off Bataan. On 24 August *Harder* and *Hake* mounted a joint submerged foray against two enemy war-ships. This time it was *Harder* that was destroyed, with no survivors, due to depth-charge attack. A Japanese action report mentioned 'much oil, wood chips, and cork floated [*sic*] in the vicinity'.[7] Dealey was awarded the Medal of Honor for his exploits in *Harder*, the citation paying tribute to him for 'conspicuous gallantry and intrepidity at the risk of his life above and beyond the call of duty . . .' Under Dealey's command, Harder sank 16 ships, for a tonnage total of 54,000 tons. When the loss of Dealey and *Harder* sank in, Rear Admiral Christie reflected: 'We can't bear this one.'[8]

When they set off for their fifth war patrol in autumn 1944, little did the men of USS *Tang* know that the agent of their destruction was actually nestled aboard their vessel.

Attacking an enemy transport ship off Formosa on the night of 24 October 1944 – a vessel she had crippled earlier – the surfaced *Tang* fired two further torpedoes, one of which went rogue and came back on her. The order for full speed ahead was given to try to dodge this weapon, but it struck the submarine in the stern, just 20 seconds after *Tang* fired it.

As she went down, Cdr O'Kane ordered *Tang*'s upper lid shut. Before this could happen the submarine suddenly jerked upwards, flinging everyone on the bridge into the sea. Of the nine men on the bridge only three would survive to be picked up by the enemy.

Tang, meanwhile, had sunk to the bottom, with three compartments flooded in 180ft of water. Fortunately the hatch between the con-ning tower and the control room had been shut. As Japanese patrol craft dropped depth charges, secret documents were destroyed and the crew prepared to try to escape using breathing apparatus.[9]

Further disaster struck when a fire broke out in the forward battery compartment killing many men, but 13 still managed to exit the submarine, though only five would live to be captured. That any made it to the surface was a miracle, for it was the deepest escape ever by American submariners in wartime. In all 78 of *Tang*'s men died.

It was the American submariners' great misfortune to be picked up by a destroyer that had saved the survivors of *Tang*'s previous attacks. Enraged Japanese mariners attacked *Tang*'s men, including O'Kane, beating them severely with clubs and kicking them. O'Kane would recall that when he and his men realised their torturers were the 'burned, mutilated survivors' of their boat's actions they found they could 'take it with less prejudice'.[10] With the exception of O'Kane, the crew were forced to remain on the upper deck of the destroyer in the hot sun. They were from time to time tortured, including having cigarettes stubbed out on their faces and being beaten with the broad side of a samurai sword by one IJN officer. When *Tang*'s men did not give the right kind of responses under interrogation they were hit on the head with a baseball bat.

It was bitterly ironic that *Tang* sank herself, for it brought to a close a record-breaking patrol in which O'Kane's boat sent 13 ships to the bottom. Despite going into captivity O'Kane remained the USN's tonnage king for a while, having sunk 24 Japanese ships to score a total of 93,824 tons.

He was awarded the Medal of Honor, a reward he deserved even more after enduring the privations of a Japanese PoW camp.[11]

Around the same time as *Tang* and her crew suffered a cruel fate off Formosa, the American invasion of the Philippines provoked the biggest fight in naval history, stretching across hundreds of miles. Submarines played a peripheral role but still managed to inflict significant damage.

On 23 October 1944 USS *Darter*, commanded by 32-year-old Cdr David McClintock, spotted an enemy strike force heading towards the Philippines, its mission to destroy the US invasion ships. Shortly before dawn *Darter* joined up with *Dace*, commanded by 31-year-old Cdr Bladen Claggett, and sank two cruisers – *Maya* and *Atago*, while damaging *Takao* – in the Palawan Passage. American boats also managed to sink a Japanese destroyer and another cruiser during the Battle of Leyte Gulf.

Gremlins struck on 24 October when *Darter* ran aground at Bombay Shoal, but *Dace* saved the stricken boat's crew. Several days later *Nautilus* shot *Darter* to pieces with 55 shells from her 6-inch guns, in order to ensure she was of no use to the enemy. Two previous attempts at shelling and torpedoing the stranded boat by other submarines had failed to make much visible impact. *Nautilus* reported that *Darter* had been successfully reduced to scrap and concluded: 'Estimated draft of *Darter* – 4 Feet.'[12]

This was a loss that could be borne, especially with American submarines scoring other telling blows, not least *Sealion*'s remarkable exploit in the early hours of 21 November. Attacking a pair of battleships and two escorting destroyers carving through the Formosa Strait at 16 knots, *Sealion*'s captain, 31-year-old Lt Cdr Eli T. Reich, fired nine torpedoes in two salvoes, ripping apart the destroyer *Urukaze* and sinking the battleship *Kongō*. Using the periscope to check his handiwork, Reich saw a 'tremendous explosion', which he thought lit up the sky 'like a sunset at midnight'.[13]

For the Japanese it was a heavy blow and, while average tonnage results for USN boats might still be modest by peak German standards, at around 200,000 tons a month, they were steady and devastating. Sixty-eight USN submarines were deployed in October 1944, managing to sink 30 per cent of Japan's tankers, with a tonnage total of 320,900 tons. Overall the Japanese lost 600 ships in 1944, a total of 2.7 million tons sunk. They could not by then replace the destroyed shipping and their vital sea trade was almost at a standstill by year's end.

American submarines would soon own the seas even around Japan – and losing at Leyte had more or less cut the jugular of oil supply from the East Indies to the Japanese home islands.

34 Ebb and Flow

By late 1943 not only had U-boats been pushed out of the North Atlantic, the Italians had capitulated, with their large and modern battle fleet neutralised. The Germans were on the defensive in occupied Italy and facing further defeats in Russia. The Japanese were still a formidable problem, but had peaked and were beginning to recoil almost everywhere under Allied pressure.

From March 1944 it was noticeable that Axis submarine activity declined in the Indian Ocean. Japanese boats sank only three merchant vessels and damaged one other before offensive IJN submarine operations ceased there altogether. The IJN's focus was switching to a fight for survival in the East Indies and the Pacific, for after Leyte Gulf the Japanese were forced to contract their outer defensive perimeter in a vain attempt to protect the SLOC between the oil fields in the East Indies and Japan. The IJN had failed during three years of war in the Indian Ocean to make any serious impact on Allied merchant traffic, despite most vessels sailing solo and without escorts.

That left the Germans to carry on the fight, though it was a minor effort compared to European operations and a by-product of a desperate need to obtain war materials for the Reich. The Italians occasionally sent submarines to sink ships in the Indian Ocean and played an important part in conveying supplies to Europe in order to feed both their nation's needs and Germany's.

Comandante Alfredo Cappellini was at Singapore being loaded with tungsten and rubber among other things, and preparing to depart for Bordeaux, when on 8 September 1943 news of the Italian surrender broke. While some Italian boats now joined the Allies to fight their former ally in the Mediterranean, those operating from Penang were taken over by the Germans. *Cappellini* became *UIT-214* (as in 'U-Italian'), while the ex-*Luigi Torelli* was christened *UIT-25*. The majority of their crews were made prisoners of the Japanese and endured brutal conditions every bit as bad as those suffered by Allied troops. Some Italians volunteered to help crew their old boats on the long supply run to Europe for the Germans.

U-boats sent to hunt in the Indian Ocean never inflicted the same level of carnage there as they did in other parts of the world and there was a bitter twist for the crew of one submarine patrolling the warm waters East of Suez. In September 1944 the men of *U-859* were feeling well satisfied at having sunk the 7,648-ton British-flagged *Troilus* along with the 6,255-ton Panamanian–flagged *Colin* and the 7,176-ton US-flagged *John Barry*.[1] That the submarine had managed to complete the majority of the outward-bound journey to Penang unseen was due to a new wonder device.

The snorkel, or snort mast, was a British invention created during the First World War but never pressed into service for Royal Navy submarines. Other nations experimented with it, producing their own variants.

The Italian Navy held trials but it was the Dutch who first made effective use of what they called the 'sniffer' (to draw in air while operating a boat at periscope depth). The Germans captured two Dutch submarines with 'sniffers' in 1940, adapting the technology as the *Schnorchel*, but they did not introduce it into front line service until early 1944.

It enabled the inhalation of fresh air and the expulsion of fumes, avoiding the need for a submarine to surface and expose itself in order to run diesels and charge the battery. Tricky to use, the *Schnorchel* required some skill, for if the valve shut it could create a vacuum and suffocate the crew, or there might be blowback of diesel fumes. Tactically, U-boat captains had to be careful not to show it above the surface when Allied units were known to be around, and the visible expulsion of fumes was an additional problem.

U-859 had proved adept at using the *Schnorchel* and demonstrated its worth, though not in a part of the world where enemy aircraft and escorts were numerous. When British submariners learned of U-boats seeking to complete almost an entire voyage submerged on *Schnorchel* – except for occasional night-time surface running – it provoked genuine admiration.

There was envy over the provision to such U-boats of 'large quantities of eau de Cologne for washing purposes'.[2] Royal Navy submariners were forced to use seawater to wash in (in order to preserve fresh water supplies). Cologne was a cure for prickly heat whereas bathing only in salt water encouraged it to become 'an exasperating tormentor' during voyages in the tropics.[3]

Despite her use of the *Schnorchel U-859* had given away her entry to the Indian Ocean by sinking the three merchant vessels and in early July was attacked by a Catalina flying boat.

Apart from this sighting, the British were also much obliged for the situation reports sent by the boat to U-boat headquarters, which confirmed a boat was on the loose.

The Type IXD2 was on her first patrol, but was commanded by a 28-year-old veteran of 16 patrols in various boats. Kapitänleutnant Johann Jebsen had distinguished himself as captain of *U-565* in March 1942 by sinking the British cruiser *Naiad* in the Mediterranean. His luck ran out when *U-859* strayed into the line of sight of the British submarine *Trenchant*, commanded by 30-year-old Lt Cdr Arthur 'Baldy' Hezlet.

The British boat had been sent into the Malacca Strait to stake out approaches to Penang. Informed by Ultra, the commander of RN submarines based in Ceylon sent a signal to Hezlet, instructing him to place *Trenchant* off the northern channel to the port on the morning of 23 September. Turning his boat's stern to *U-859* Hezlet decided to fire three torpedoes, hitting with one, the explosion breaking the enemy submarine in two. After picking up survivors, *Trenchant* dived again and set course for home. Hezlet inspected the prisoners, who seemed very grateful to be saved and not at all worried that for them the war was over. The only officer among them was the Second Engineer, Ober-leutnant Horst Klatt, who explained that he was alive because he had diarrhoea. He had been in the heads[4] at the time the torpedo hit, which killed the rest of the officers who were gathered in the wardroom for a discussion.

Trenchant returned to Trincomalee with a Jolly Roger flag flying to celebrate not only the U-boat sinking but also the successful covert insertion of commandos on a hostile shore and minelaying. *Trenchant*'s mines would sink two Japanese transport ships for a combined tonnage of 2,841 tons.

Meanwhile, U-boat command had received an erroneous report of *U-859* reaching Penang in late August, so it was a real shock when the truth emerged a month later. For the British, sinking *U-859* was vindica-tion of their decision to return substantial submarine forces to the Far East. By spring 1943 the modern depot ship *Adamant* was at Trincomalee offering engineering support and accommodation to submarine crews, but still only as mother ship to three Allied boats. With the British sub-marine construction programme accelerating, in autumn 1943 it was decided new T Class and S Class boats should be assigned to operations in the Far East. The British built up their strength rapidly and soon the 4th Submarine Flotilla, of half a dozen T Class submarines and an S Class boat, was in place.

By February 1944 there were seven T Class and five S Class sub-marines. When the depot ship *Maidstone* arrived she became the mother ship of the S Class boats, collectively known as the 8th Flotilla.

Before leaving the UK the British submarines were modified, with enhanced air conditioning, refrigeration for food and additional cap-acity for fresh water and oil.

A major problem was that the extra oil had to be kept in outer tanks. If they were punctured it could be fatal, with leaks potentially giving away the boat's position to the enemy. Before entering a danger zone, submarine captains made sure they had used up the oil in the outer tanks.

There was a clear dividing line between where the RN's submarines operated and the Americans. The Royal Navy was restricted to a British Zone, west of the Sunda Strait and stretching up into the Bay of Bengal. The USN got the run of a more target-rich American Zone east of that and all the way to Japan. The Americans even got the Gulf of Siam and the Java Sea, though the British had the Malacca Strait.

The Americans pursued a deep ocean campaign while the British were in the littorals – operating closer to shore and sometimes miles from the nearest water deep enough for them to dive, with numerous enemy minefields to deal with, too. The smaller British boats, with shorter periscopes, were better suited to patrols in shallower water and could operate in as little as 60ft, while the USN liked 180ft (and had longer periscopes).

There was also a different tactical philosophy. The USN was still keen to deploy wolf packs and use a tactic known as the end around. This was a high-speed surface transit to outflank a convoy, just out of sight over the horizon but still with eyes on the target via a fully-extended periscope. It needed plenty of room.

The Royal Navy's submarines were dedicated solo hunters, but a major problem was the paucity of significant targets. The British grumbled both about missing out on the big league east of the Sunda Strait and living conditions at sea, which were abominable. The 'stink-ing hot'[5] environment overpowered air conditioning and crews had to strip down to shorts and boots, while fresh food lasted hardly any time at all. With little chance of sinking anything of significance – a juicy battleship, cruiser or carrier – and the big, decisive actions unfolding either in the Pacific or in Europe, some British submarine captains with good war records decided the game was not worth it. They requested to be relieved of their commands after just a few frustrating, but very dangerous, patrols. Some of the men they commanded were not too keen on being in the Far East either. By summer 1944 many ratings only recently joined up were unhappy about swapping Europe, where the conflict seemed to be cooling down, for a dangerous part of the world far away from their families. Conversely, some seasoned submariner ratings complained of the war not burning hot enough in the British Zone.

Tactically using guns was a better choice in shallow coastal waters where getting torpedoes to run was problematic. The dip a fish took after leaving the tube, before straightening up and arming, meant it stood a good chance of burying itself in the mud. Consequently, most British submarines in the Far East were packed with shells in any nook and cranny that would accept them, all the better to feed the guns. It was a practice that alarmed the navy's ordnance experts back home when they heard about it. Bumping knees against stockpiles of shells under the tiny wardroom table of a submarine was bad enough but finding shells stored in engine room compartments – with excessive heat not recommended in case it made ammunition detonate – sent shudders through the Admiralty's munitions regulators. Yet no British submarines exploded and they rarely ran out of ammunition.

To better equip the British boats for surface actions they were given extra armour protection and bristled with machine guns, each of them also receiving a 20mm cannon. The Achilles heel remained the ballast tanks, which were easily punctured. Once that happened a boat would probably have no chance of escaping a persecutor by diving on reaching deep water.

By the end of 1944 there were 40 Royal Navy submarines in the Far East and frustration among their crews was even greater. With not much of any significance left to sink, even guns were not being used much.

The amount of action to be had in the British Zone was not enough to keep all the British submarines then based in Ceylon employed. Once the two established flotillas moved forward in spring 1945 another was to be established at Trincomalee for residual tasks.

The submarine depot ship *Adamant* went to Fremantle while *Maidstone* was based at Subic Bay in the Philippines, to act as mother for the Second Submarine Flotilla. The way was open for Royal Navy submarines to play their part in the Allied campaign against Japan to the end, even as the fighting in European waters continued and in some respects intensified.

35 No Lazy Sunday

The war against the U-boats is often depicted as ending with their withdrawal from the North Atlantic and the decline of the wolf pack menace. In fact all it did was mutate into another kind of struggle. If during the last major convoy assaults of May and September 1943 the U-boats were fighting to give Germany victory, thereafter they were trying to stave off defeat and deter an invasion of north-west Europe.

In the winter of 1943/44 there had been the usual pattern of terrible gales, forcing a lull, though as January neared its end the struggle intensified again. The British escorts would not let the enemy relax and if there was one man who never gave the foe any quarter it was Capt. Walker, who led the 2nd Escort Group on a killing spree.

Between 31 January and 19 February Walker's five warships destroyed six U-boats, with several hundred enemy submariners meeting their maker. At the time Dönitz had 26 submarines deployed in the North Atlantic and the mid-Atlantic. With convoy traffic building in the South West Approaches, some of them were given orders to move in and attack enemy shipping as it approached the Irish Sea via the southern channel.

As Dönitz reconfigured his boats via wireless signals, the Submarine Tracking Room in the OIC plotted the rapidly evolving threat and a commensurate build-up of Support Groups and air power was triggered. Walker's 2nd EG was part of the response and was positioned to the south-west of Ireland. His own ship, *Starling*, kicked things off by destroying *U-592* on 31 January. On the night of 8 February *Woodpecker* obliterated *U-762*, her end producing the usual grisly remains, which were revealed by a searchlight. Walker sent a light signal to *Woodpecker* inviting her to inspect the evidence. 'Come over here,' he ordered, 'and look at the mess you have made.'[1]

The key tactic was the creeping attack, which involved one ship – often *Starling* – slowing right down to make herself undetectable by the U-boat's hydrophones. This vessel would hold the submarine in her Asdic cone, while directing another escort in to carry out the kill. The rest of the group's ships would gather in a large circle all around the unfortunate U-boat, waiting their turn to rush in and attack if required.

Even with this ruthlessly efficient tactic, sometimes an enemy submarine could prove a very tricky customer. On 9 February *U-238*'s commander, 26-year-old Kapitänleutnant Horst Hepp, showed that he was a fast learner. Had he started his combat career in earlier times Hepp might have survived, but it was his tragedy to begin a third war patrol at the very moment Walker's group reached its peak.

After nearly colliding with one of the 2nd EG ships in fog on the surface, *U-238* dived and fended off several creeping attacks with tenacity. As she twisted and turned *U-238* used a *Pillenwerfer* ('Pill-thrower'), an underwater gun that fired carbide pellets. These effervesced, producing bubbles and noise when they came into contact with water, aiming to confuse Asdic and hydrophones. This countermeasure device could also launch a 'noise charge' – replicating the hum of electric motors – up to 100 yards away from a U-boat. Yet another variant released oil and was capable of ejecting 'old cap-bands and gym shoes'[2] to try to deceive the hunters into thinking a submarine had been blown apart.

Such ploys were why Walker's group, and others, only firmly believed they had destroyed a submerged U-boat when they saw a massive explosion or managed to pick up significant debris that could only have come from inside a submarine. Enemy body parts were considered incontrovertible proof (once confirmed as human by pathologists ashore).

In a bid to stave off her end *U-238* fired homing torpedoes at her tormentors, which missed. It took eight hours and 266 depth charges to destroy *U-238* and everyone in her. *U-734* was claimed soon after, while *Woodpecker* and *Wild Goose* made short work of *U-424* early on 11 February. Eight days later the ferocious *Woodpecker* pecked another enemy submarine to death during a joint attack with *Starling*.

U-264 was forced to the surface and then finished off with guns, forcing her to scuttle, all 52 of her men successfully abandoning ship.

Walker's escort group had scored a notable triumph, for this was the first ever kill of a *Schnorchel*-equipped submarine. The Germans were not without their own little victories and *Woodpecker's* career came to an end when a homing torpedo from *U-764* hit her stern. It caused such damage she capsized on 27 February, despite a valiant attempt to tow her home.

Whenever U-boat survivors were pulled up onto warships in Walker's group, to save themselves they had to abide by a strict rule, which required them to provide the number of their submarine and the captain's name. Failure to do this saw the U-boatmen left to the mercy of the sea.

Peter Eustace, a radar operator in *Starling*, held the arm of a young German in his right hand as an officer asked him to provide the required details. These were not forthcoming so the order was given to let the prisoner go. 'I can still feel this young boy's arm, or hand, sliding through my hand,' recalled Eustace decades later, 'and I would say that this lad was no more than 16-years-of-age. It is something which has haunted me . . .'[3]

Capt. Walker was not unusual for hating U-boats and the men who sailed in them. Many British escort captains shared his opinion, including Nicholas Monsarrat, who regarded the U-boat crews as being among 'the worst willing servants of world-enslavement' who, while brave, also engaged in 'killing by stealth without warning and without quarter'. Their trade was 'predominantly evil', said Monsarrat and 'cruel, treacherous, and revolting, under any flag'.[4]

Walker's ruthless zeal was perhaps fuelled by the fate of his submariner son. Timothy Walker had originally sought a career as a Catholic priest and after returning to Britain on the outbreak of war helped out at Dover Hospital as a stretcher bearer. He then joined the Royal Naval Volunteer Reserve (RNVR) as a rating. After officer selection and training he asked his father to help him get into the Submarine Service.

In mid-August 1943 Capt. Walker returned to Liverpool from one convoy escort mission to find a staff officer waiting for him on the lock gates at Gladstone Dock. Walker was told that his 23-year-old son was missing in action. His submarine, *Parthian*, had come to grief while on her way back to Beirut at the end of a patrol.

An old boat, *Parthian* had survived several scrapes during the war, sinking an Italian submarine in 1940. She had recently used her gun to bombard a railway line at the foot of Mount Olympus. Her nemesis was the same passive, killer that had claimed so many other submarines and their men: the sea mine.

While Sub Lieutenant Walker's death was not confirmed for some time, his father must have suspected the worst had occurred. In early July 1944 Capt. Walker was ashore in Liverpool, enjoying lunch at the Adelphi Hotel with his wife, Eileen, and some of his officers. One of them handed him a letter that had arrived in the ship earlier. It confirmed Timothy was dead. After watching a film at a local cinema, 48-year-old Walker fell ill and had to be taken to hospital, where he died a few days later. Officially the cause of death was cerebral thrombosis, but the immense strain placed on his body and mind by fighting the U-boats must have played a part in his demise, as must the news about his son.

Walker's escort group had already gone back to sea, expecting to be reunited with the boss when they called at Devonport. He would not be there on the wharf in the city of his birth to cast a critical, but fatherly eye over his 'chicks'[5] when they came alongside.

Although Walker could be ruthless with the enemy and was also a hard taskmaster, he was a hero to his men and to all in Western Approaches Command. His loss was a devastating blow. After a funeral service in Liverpool Cathedral he was buried at sea, appropriately enough taking his last voyage aboard the ace sub-killing destroyer HMS *Hesperus*.

Meanwhile, the ships that had at one time or another served under Walker's command continued their lethal harvest far and wide. The last U-boat scalp claimed by a Walker escort was *U-1063*, sunk by *Loch Killin* off Start Point in the Channel on 16 April 1945.[6]

By war's end the 2nd EG had destroyed 23 U-boats. Four ships that had served in the group were lost to enemy submarines, the last being the sloop *Kite*. She was sunk (by *U-344*) in the Barents Sea on 21 August 1944, with only nine survivors from her 226 crew. Within 24 hours *Kite*'s killer was herself destroyed, attacked by a Swordfish from an escort carrier. There were no survivors.

By the time of Walker's passing, the battle that he and so many others in the warships and merchant vessels fought so hard to win had yielded its prize – the invasion of north-west Europe.

British midget submarines played a key role in ensuring the Allied troops managed to get ashore safely, drawing some who crewed them from among those who had waged war on the U-boats.

Having served his time as a bridge watch-keeper in warships on North Sea and Atlantic convoy escort duty, 22-year-old Sub Lieutenant Jim Booth was recruited in late 1943 to a secret unit with an innocuous-sounding name, the Combined Operations Pilotage and Reconnais-sance Party, or COPP.

It masked a purpose of vital importance to the forthcoming invasion. To ensure any amphibious assault was successful the topography of proposed landing zones had to be surveyed, in addition to the shore's physical composition – sand or shale, whether or not it was steeply shelving, the gradient of the beach itself. This was very dangerous work, usually carried out at night under the noses of the enemy by commandos, who would come in on canoes from surfaced submarines that would pick them up again later.

Normandy was well defended by Hitler's much-vaunted Atlantic Wall of concrete gun emplacements and fortresses, its beaches thick with all sorts of obstacles and mines to negotiate. Most important of all for the COPP teams was avoiding the attention of the many radar stations embedded in the Atlantic Wall. These would easily pick up any surfaced submarine loitering offshore. Both the vessel and the com-mandos could be eliminated and the enemy alerted to the possibility of an invasion.

The solution was to use X-craft, which showed virtually nothing above the waves even when surfaced. *X20* and *X23* were assigned to COPP work, which is how Jim Booth found himself becoming a sub-mariner. He was made second in command to Lt George Honour in *X23*, but while *X20* carried out a beach survey *X23*'s was cancelled.

The two X-craft were not going to be idle, for their next task was to act as guides for landing craft on the day of the match, a mission called Operation Gambit. Positioned off the invasion beaches, when the time was right they would erect 18ft telescopic masts with lights on them and put up radar beacons. The guide lights were shaded on one side so they could not be seen from the land.

The crews were given small arms and ammunition in case they needed to defend themselves, but were bemused to receive a set of portrait photographs. 'These were to be used in the event of us having to abandon our craft and swim ashore,' said Booth, explaining that the pictures were for the manufacture of fake identity papers. 'I remember thinking this a pretty desperate measure and my own picture looked awfully English!'[7]

X23's sector was to be off Sword Beach, near Ouistreham at the far eastern end of the invasion sector, while *X20* would take care of guiding craft onto Juno Beach next door. With the date of the invasion set for 4 June, the X-craft were towed out of Portsmouth on the night of 2 June.

X23 was behind a trawler named *Grenadier*, the boat submerging as soon as possible to preserve secrecy. At a position to the south of the Isle of Wight the tow was slipped and *X23* proceeded solo, arriving off Sword Beach in darkness on 3 June. Once the sun came up, cautious periscope looks enabled a study of the coastline to ensure the boat was positioned properly. That job done, *X-23* sat on the bottom to wait the day out.

'We briefly came to periscope depth and were able to watch German soldiers enjoying lazy Sunday games on the beach,' recalled Booth. 'Little did they realise what was waiting for them. We dared not surface properly for air, which would have risked [us] being sighted and compromised the invasion. At precisely 23.15 [11.15 p.m.] on June 4, as were our orders, we surfaced and raised our aerial to receive a coded message [embedded in a BBC broadcast]. This would indicate whether the invasion was proceeding. The message, received by us at 01.00, in plain language revealed that the invasion had been postponed for 24 hours.'

X23's radio masts were taken down and the midget submarine settled again on the bottom. Its crew would have to endure more waiting, cooped up inside a hot, cramped, smelly submarine. Bad weather had forced the delay but finally, on 5 June, the invasion force vessels, carrying tens of thousands of troops and their equipment, departed UK waters for beaches stretching around 50 miles of the Seine Bay.

At 4.30 a.m. on 6 June, *X23* surfaced and erected the navigation aids. What stuck most vividly in Jim Booth's mind about the incredible events that unfolded was 'the aerial bombardment of the coast' with both the sea and the air reverberating to 'the noise of thousands of ships'. Finally, there came 'endless waves of landing craft and ships passing us by and the disgorging of the DD [amphibious] tanks'. The men of *X23* were deeply satisfied that their mission had been a success.

The cruiser USS *Indianapolis*, at Cold Bay, Alaska, October 1942, nearly three years before she was sunk.

In 2017 it was revealed that a team of civilian researchers led by Microsoft co-founder and noted philanthropist Paul G. Allen had discovered the wreck of USS *Indianapolis*. The survey team worked from aboard the Research Vessel *Petrel*, which is owned by Allen. He has led several other searches for lost historic vessels, including HMS *Hood*. An image shot from a remotely operated underwater vehicle shows a spare parts box on the floor of the Pacific Ocean in more than 16,000 feet of water.

Also shot from a remotely operated vehicle, this shows what appears to be the painted hull number '35'. Based on the curvature of the hull section, this seems to be the port side of the ship.

In a shot taken in early 1946, Japanese submariners unhappily pose for the camera in the forward torpedo room of *I-58*, the boat that sank USS *Indianapolis*.

USS *Perch* post-Korean War service, off Mare Island, with her drydeck shelter for launching raiding craft aft of the sail.

On 21 January 1954, the world's first nuclear-powered submarine *Nautilus* is launched.

The July 1960 first first firing of a Polaris test missile from USS *George Washington*, the world's first fully-fledged nuclear-powered ballistic missile submarine.

In July 1962, a Zulu Class diesel attack submarine of the Soviet Navy dives to escape observation but is caught and photographed by an American intelligence-gathering aircraft.

The US Navy nuclear-powered attack submarine *Scorpion* off Naples, Italy, on 10 April 1968. *Scorpion* was lost with all hands the following month while returning to the USA.

The decommissioned diesel submarine HMS *Onyx* is towed away form Birkenhead in 2006, after being preserved for some years as a museum to the Falklands War. She lingered for a while longer, moored alongside at Barrow-in-Furness but due to lack of funds was sent to the breakers in 2014.

The Soviet Navy ballistic missile submarine *K-219* off Bermuda in October 1986. The lid has been blown off one of her silos and a nuclear missile ejected into the sea.

Visible beyond some anglers was a considerable intelligence catch: a revolutionary kind of Russian craft called *Beluga*, captured on film for the first time by a Western visitor at Balaclava harbour in late 1991. The *Beluga* was created to see if the stealthy shape of a nuclear-powered attack boat could be combined with a new type of propulsion more silent than reactor machinery.

An imagining of the *Kursk* lying on the bottom of the Barents Sea in August 2000, with massive holes ripped in her bow and down her flank.

First in a new breed of British submarines: in the summer of 2007 the nuclear-powered attack submarine *Astute* emerges from Devonshire Dock Hall at Barrow-in-Furness where she has been built.

Images from the final homecoming of the Cold War warrior attack submarine HMS *Spectre*, Devonport, May 2010. The Swiftsure Class boat saw active service from the late 1970s, chasing the Soviets, into the 1980s deterring the Argentinians off the Falklands, right through to missions in the war against terrorism post 9/11.

In late 2015 the Improved Kilo Class submarine *Rostov-on-Don* passes through the Turkish Strait on her way to join Russia's Black Sea Fleet after firing Kalibr cruise missiles at targets in Syria.

An artist's concept of a converted Ohio Class guided-missile and Special Forces submarine launching cruise missiles.

During Exercise Saxon Warrior, held off the west coast of Scotland in August 2017, a RN Wildcat helicopter conducts a transfer of personnel from the British attack boat HMS *Trenchant*. Saxon Warrior was a massive demonstration of NATO maritime power. Spearheaded by American and British super-carriers and submarines, it was intended as a riposte to Putin's missile boat diplomacy in the Baltic.

RFS *Dmitriy Donskoy* — the last remaining commissioned example of the 26,000 tons (dived) Typhoon Class SSBN type in the Russian Navy — is led into the Baltic Sea in the summer of 2017 by another ocean-going giant, the 24,500 tons guided-missile battle-cruiser RFS *Peter the Great*.

In the summer of 2017 RFS *Dmitriy Donskoy* was deployed from her base in the Kola Peninsula and into the Baltic as a show of force aimed at NATO.

*

Having been forced to abandon regular wolf pack attacks against shipping in the North Atlantic, Germany's U-boat force now appeared to have lost the battle for the English Channel and the Bay of Biscay.

A single U-boat got through to the waters off the invasion beaches during June, managing to sink only one vessel – a Landing Ship Tank – on the 15th, despite thousands of potential targets. The wolves that had once ranged across the Atlantic to ravage convoys were now reduced to skulking on the bottom of the sea within a few miles of their besieged bases.

If conventional U-boats could not get right in among the invasion ships then a naval commando unit of the Kriegsmarine might. In the early hours of 6 July a signal was flashed to the Allied naval units warning that manned torpedoes or mini submarines were going to try to infiltrate anchorages. Their top target was the famous British battleship HMS *Rodney* – the vessel that sank *Bismarck* and battled her way through multiple U-boat attacks on the Pedestal convoy run to Malta. German panzer divisions ashore in Normandy especially hated *Rodney*, as her massive 16-inch guns had pummelled them on several occasions. The men of the Kleinkampfmittel-Verband, or K-Verband – a special operations unit established in 1943 – would dearly love to sink her.

Being at anchor, the mighty 35,000-ton *Rodney* was not well placed if one of the K-Verband craft broke through. Bad memories of the Italians crippling *Queen Elizabeth* and *Valiant* at Alexandria in late 1941 persisted and *Rodney* would need plenty of warning to get underway.

The K-Verband's V3 manned torpedo was actually composed of two torpedoes, one on top of the other. The pilot sat inside a tiny cockpit in the top one with a conventional torpedo slung underneath, which was fired at the chosen target. The V3 was first used against Allied shipping off Anzio in April 1944, sinking two small patrol boats and a merchant ship. During the 6 July scare off Normandy picket boats were sent out to patrol around *Rodney* and other vessels. They dropped small explosive charges at regular intervals, hoping to deter attacks. A Polish gunboat managed to snare both a V3 and its pilot, who claimed under interrogation that 50 were being readied for launch in factory buildings along the coast to the east. *Rodney* decided to take care of things herself with two short bombardments of her 16-inch guns, the massive shells eradicating the enemy base.

It wasn't the end of the menace, for the V3 was easily transportable by road on a trailer and could be launched from any suitable beach. The Germans sent out dozens at a time (with very few pilots surviving). The K-Verband claimed several successes for their various special warfare methods, not just with the V3 but also small explosive boats.

Two Allied destroyers were sunk, with another damaged, while four minesweepers were also blown up. The Polish cruiser *Dragon* was so badly damaged by a V3 attack that she had to be scuttled. Several other Allied vessels were claimed. Whether the V3s achieved quite the success attributed to them is open to question. Some of the Allied casualties may have been caused by mine strikes or torpedoes fired by conventional motor torpedo boats.

The Germans also created midget submarines called Biber ('Beaver') and Seehund ('Seal'). The Biber was a one-man craft and right up until the spring of 1945 dozens of them were operating out of Dutch ports against Channel shipping, but sank only a few vessels.

The Seehund, or Type XXVIIB, was a two-man vessel that, like the Biber, carried two torpedoes externally, or mines. Unlike the Biber, the Kriegsmarine considered it a proper submarine and gave each one a 'U' designation and number. Hard to handle and slow, the Seehunds also operated from the Netherlands. Dozens of Seehunds plagued waters off the east coast of England, achieving little except a high casualty rate among the unfortunate men asked to operate them.

Apart from being picked off by aircraft and naval patrol vessels, the Biber's use of a petrol engine could be lethal to its operator. One was discovered sinking off the English coast with its crewman slumped dead over the controls, killed by carbon monoxide poisoning.[8]

There were hundreds of Bibers and Seehunds manufactured, with plans to transport them piggyback on Type VII U-boats to remote combat zones. One such proposed mission saw Bibers taken to Arctic Norway in early 1945, to attack and sink a Russian battleship anchored at Murmansk, but it never went ahead. The Biber and the Seehund were weapons of desperation, but they were not the most amazing ploy considered by the Nazis.

36   Target New York

As the Third Reich staggered towards its Twilight of the Gods all manner
of strange schemes to deliver a sudden, devastating blow against the
Allies were put forward. Most desired of all was a strike against the
USA, that foe which had now entered two wars against Germany at the
critical point and swayed things in favour of the British in the Atlantic.

One unconventional proposal for using submarines to hit back came
in a circuitous fashion from famed Waffen SS commando Lieutenant
Colonel Otto Skorzeny. Like Hitler an Austrian by birth, he leapt to
fame by rescuing deposed Italian dictator Benito Mussolini from im-
prisonment during a daring glider assault on a mountaintop ski resort
in September 1943. In October 1944 he followed that up by kidnapping
the son of the Hungarian Regent, Admiral Nicholas Horthy. Skorzeny
hid Nicholas Jnr in a rolled-up carpet and flew him to Germany as a
hostage, making sure the Reich's unreliable central European ally
stayed in the Axis and did not sign a peace deal with the Russians.
Horthy abdicated and a new fascist government was installed, keeping
Hungary tied to the Axis wheel.

The advent of the V1 flying bomb – the first of the *Vergeltungswaffen*
or Vengeance weapons – sparked a new idea in Skorzeny's brain. In
the summer of 1944 he worked with Hanna Reitsch, the notorious avi-
atrix and fanatical Nazi, to try to perfect a sort of aerial version of the
manned torpedo, based on the V1.

The problem with the world's first cruise missile was that it was un-
guided. With a speed of 360 mph and a range of 148 miles it was launched
from ramps in France and Germany, pointed at England, flying across
the sea until its fuel ran out. It dropped out of the sky onto towns and
cities and exploded with terrifying effect. Skorzeny and Reitsch agreed
it would actually be possible to install a cockpit for someone to pilot a
V1 right to its target. They thought it would be fantastic if the Palace of
Westminster could be reduced to rubble. Even battleships and enemy
troop ships could be blown apart by such a guided missile. *There were
hundreds of Luftwaffe pilots without aircraft to fly, so why not send them on a
one-way ticket to glory in a V1?*

After flight trials with a manned V1 – in which two pilots were badly injured because they could not land the thing – Reitsch took one up and safely touched down again.

Even though Skorzeny recruited 100 fanatical flyers, drawn from the Waffen SS and the Luftwaffe, by the autumn of 1944 the air force had torpedoed the manned V1 project. It refused to give it any further technical or training support. Skorzeny secreted his V1 pilots at remote barracks and went to meet Heinrich Himmler, the head of the SS, at the Wolf's Lair, the Führer's military headquarters in the Prussian woods. Skorzeny suggested it might be possible to launch V1s from a U-boat and Himmler thought it an inspired suggestion. He declared: 'That's the way we can bombard New York!' It was, said the SS chief, 'a God-sent chance to punish America for bombing Germany.'[1]

Skorzeny put on a show of enthusiasm for the American angle but was a little daunted – he had been thinking more of attacking Britain or Channel shipping. Himmler insisted he set the New York project up immediately.

The SS Lt Col. was already worried about the practicality of ensuring accuracy after launch from the deck of a pitching and rolling submarine and believed the Americans would not react well to a V1 blitz of New York. It might only intensify their dedication to the Allied cause. Himmler, on the other hand, thought the Americans spineless and maintained they would cave in after such an attack. Skorzeny proposed spies should be sent ashore with some kind of electronic homing device, to be placed near strategically important targets. Alternatively suicide pilots might also suit the task of precision guidance.

When it came to this scheme, a precedent had already been set. In 1943 a plan had been developed by the Kriegsmarine and the Italians to send submarines carrying midget craft across the Atlantic to attack shipping at New York. Using either the large *Leonardo da Vinci*, or a similarly modified German boat, the mission was scheduled for December 1943, but due to the Italian surrender it was cancelled.[2]

The German submarine force had also for some years been conducting research into using small rockets fired by U-boats against convoy escorts. Successful tests were carried out from both surfaced and dived U-boats. A means of firing missiles while a U-boat was submerged at depth was devised, along with the technology to detect the target on the surface and guide the weapon against a destroyer.

U-511, commanded by 35-year-old Kapitänleutnant Friedrich Steinhoff, was the test platform and his brother Ernst was a V-weapon scientist. The scheme had been initiated after the two of them had discussed the possibility of launching rockets from submarines, but they were never used in action.

In November 1944 Allied intelligence officials informed the American government that V1s might be launched against New York, and warships were sent out to patrol seas up to 250 miles from the US coast. The alert was triggered after the FBI arrested German agents who had been landed on the US east coast by U-boats.[3] They yielded information of the plan, so FBI boss J. Edgar Hoover conveyed a warning to US Naval Intelligence.[4]

The Americans did not keep their fears of rocket attack under wraps. New York Mayor Fiorello La Guardia issued a warning on 10 December[5] and just under a month later Admiral Jonas Ingram, Commander-in-Chief of the Atlantic Fleet, staged a press conference about it. Ingram said the attack would probably happen sometime in the next two months, and that either New York or Washington DC would be the target.

Submarines, aircraft or warships would launch the missiles but U-boats were the most likely means of attack. The admiral said the Empire State Building might be a special target of 'robot bombs'.[6]

'The thing to do is not to get too excited about it,' Admiral Ingram advised. 'It might knock out a high building or two. It might create a fire hazard. It would certainly cause casualties in the limited area where it might hit. But it could not seriously affect the progress of the war.'[7]

If the admiral was seeking to reassure people it is unlikely that he succeeded. He also speculated that up to eight U-boats would mount the attack. Throwing oil on the fire, he explained that only areas within a 100-mile radius of the submarine launching point need worry.[8] The 'robot bombs' might come despite efforts to stop them, the admiral warned, with the approach of the submarines masked by snowstorms. He wanted everybody to be on the alert and that was why he was 'springing the cat from the bag to let the Huns know that we are ready for them'.[9]

Having thoroughly alarmed everyone the admiral pointed out that no U-boats had been sighted off the US coast for months. 'German submarines are no longer a menace – but they are not beaten yet,' added Ingram, in another masterful example of mixed-messaging.[10]

No robot missile attacks came at that time, but the US Navy remained on the alert, during a period when the conventional U-boat itself was causing renewed nervousness.

37   Total Underwater Warfare

By late 1944 the U-boat force had withdrawn from its French bases, with 30 Type VIIs making a 2,000-mile voyage to new homes in Norway. The U-boats appeared to be on the run, not just in waters off France but also in the Mediterranean, where their presence had been all but snuffed out. They were, as the Admiralty termed it with relish, 'virtually annihilated'.[1]

There were no U-boats operating in the Med by October 1944 and none managed to pass through the Strait of Gibraltar after May that year. Since 1941 62 German submarines had been sent to the Mediterranean and one by one they were eliminated.

Whereas Japanese use of MAD-equipped aircraft was not as effective as it could have been, the Allies possessed strength in depth, with plenty of modern planes and highly trained aircrews dedicated to hunting down enemy submarines. Allied aircraft fitted with M.A.D. flew out of Gibraltar, taking full advantage of the fashion in which the narrow strait between North Africa and Europe funnelled numerous U-boats to destruction. Once a submarine was found, patrol craft and escort vessels were never far away and soon made attacks. Their hunter-killer precision was aided by yet another secret capture, made two days before Allied troops went ashore in Normandy.

The Lorient-based Type IXC *U-505*, commanded by 42-year-old Oberleutnant Harald Lange, was cornered in the Atlantic 150 miles to the west of Dakar. *U-505* was already a jinxed boat – one of her previous captains blew his own brains out during a depth-charge attack and her luck had not changed.

It was Task Group 22.3, comprising the escort carrier *Guadalcanal* and five destroyers, that trapped *U-505*. As they surrounded the submarine and opened fire, hunter-killer group commander Capt. Dan Gallery flashed a salty restraining signal to his ships and aircraft: 'I would like to capture that bastard if at all possible!'[2]

Seizing a U-boat had long been an ambition of Gallery's and like Walker's his group had special boarding teams, with USS *Pillsbury*'s men taking the lead.

It was the first time since the War of 1812 that the USN had captured a warship during a conflict. Lt Albert David, who led the effort to salvage *U-505*, was awarded the Medal of Honor as it was felt he displayed true valour, especially with the submarine potentially sinking or blowing up at any moment. This was the only Medal of Honor won in the Battle of the Atlantic, but 43-year-old Lt David suffered a fatal heart attack in autumn 1945 before he could receive it, so his widow accepted it from the President.

The damaged U-boat was towed to Bermuda by a naval tug, while a destroyer raced ahead with all the secret documents and an Enigma machine with rotors. *U-505*'s crew remained in custody at Bermuda until the end of the conflict and all 3,000 of Task Group 22.3's men kept their lips buttoned about a German submarine being taken.[3] It became the US Navy's famous secret capture, though the material *U-505* yielded remained hush-hush for decades (the story of Ultra and Enigma not being admitted officially until the 1970s). Today *U-505* is a prize exhibit at the Chicago Museum of Science and Industry.

While the waters off southern England may have become known to German submariners by summer 1944 as the 'U-boat wrecking yard' – their vessels no more than 'iron coffins'[4] – in the Arctic, wolf packs displayed dogged persistence. There were still co-ordinated attacks on convoys to Russia and up to a dozen submarines at a time were sent out from the Norwegian bases, but again they faced escort carriers that scored their fair share of U-boat kills.

The Germans were still occasionally capable of vigour elsewhere and there were some painful losses for the Allies in the North Channel, between Ireland and Scotland. However, the U-boats were now unable to interrupt the flow of supplies across the Atlantic. The largest convoy of the war – HX-300, composed of 166 ships – reached Liverpool totally unmolested in July 1944. Just half a dozen corvettes and a single frigate escorted it for the majority of the voyage.

The struggle, such as it was, now took place around the British Isles – that great launch platform for armies and the source of their supplies as they advanced on the Reich. It was a contest that stretched from the Moray Firth in Scotland to waters off St Catherine's point in the Isle of Wight, and from off Halifax in north-east England to the approaches of Plymouth.

The U-boats sought to hide among rock pinnacles and the wrecks of past victims, waiting to sprint out and send torpedoes into the bellies of unsuspecting supply vessels or troop ships.

The Allied sub-hunters had to develop an even keener sense of U-boat sounds and also the difference between Asdic echoes reflected by sunken ships or a rock outcrop and submarines. It was fiendishly difficult work. Many depth charges and Hedgehog or Squid bombs were wasted on shoals of fish. The previously decisive, killer advantages of Huff Duff, land-based and carrier-based aircraft, Ultra intelligence, convoy re-routing and radar were of limited, if any, use.

Hardly any wolf pack deployments meant a lack of signals traffic between the submarines and U-boat headquarters giving away vessel locations and destinations.

The *Schnorchel* seemed to offer the enemy a chance of remaining invisible from aircraft for the majority of a patrol, if not all of it. In the view of the US Navy it was: 'Unquestionably . . . the most effective counter-device developed by the Germans in the Battle of the Atlantic.'[5] Other German countermeasures included APHRODITE – balloons trailing radar reflective metal strips released while a U-boat was on the surface, to distract the radars of Allied aircraft.

Both the *Schnorchel* and the *Pillenwerfer* were part of 'Total Underwater Warfare', a concept referred to in literature captured aboard *U-505*. According to USN analysis 'Total Underwater Warfare' required 'quick, effective and revolutionary measures', with the homing torpedo a key part. It sought to create pure underwater warfare, 'severing the tie which bound the U-boat to the surface . . .'[6]

In short, it was feared the *Schnorchel* made Allied air power impotent, for according to the USN analysis 'it greatly weakened one of the pillars on which our superiority over the U-boat had been built'.[7]

With U-boats rarely exposing themselves on the surface, escorts hunting the enemy in the inshore contest of 1944/45 often had no more to show for their efforts than dead fish. One attack in the English Channel did set off an enormous explosion, which was later thought to be an Allied ammunition truck that had plunged off a transport ship.[8] The Wolf Rock pinnacle off Land's End received a pretty severe depth-charge battering on several occasions. Despite all the time and effort wasted on phantom targets, in the end Allied naval forces were good goalkeepers. The fact that there were no U-boats down there showed the enemy had become surprisingly timid. It took the U-boats until August 1944 to get their nerve up and make a few serious forays against shipping but by then the Allied armies had broken out of Normandy.

At war's end there would be 37 escort groups operating in seas around Britain and northwest Europe, comprising 426 warships. Even the Baltic was no longer a safe haven, with Allied aircraft dropping copious amounts of mines to make even training and operational work-up of U-boats dangerous. In both European and Far Eastern waters there was a dramatic fall in merchant shipping losses, with the Admiralty claiming that October 1944 saw only one merchant ship lost to enemy submarine activity globally (the victim of a Japanese attack).[9]

For all that, nagging doubts remained in the Allied mind. New enemy vessels were being developed and the Admiralty feared Germany was preparing to launch another round of wolf pack attacks against the Atlantic convoys, only this time with the formidable new Type XXI U-boat.

Consolation was forthcoming from decrypted messages between the Japanese Naval Attaché in Berlin and his masters in Tokyo, confirming delays in getting the wonder boats to sea.

He also assisted the Allies by sending technical details of the new submarines to Tokyo, which were intercepted and helped in the process of preparing for what some in the Admiralty regarded as 'the second Battle of the Atlantic'.[10]

In addition to the Type XXI, the Germans, so it turned out, were also about to commission smaller, shorter-range Type XXIII U-boats. The Admiralty felt that when these submarines emerged the best cure was to destroy them all as quickly as possible. Should they escape into the vast ocean, their capabilities might make them very difficult to counter.

'Using his Type XXI boats, the enemy may yet attempt a resumption of pack tactics in ocean waters,' decided the Admiralty's expert ana-lysis, 'while keeping up his operations in inshore areas. Much, if not all, depends on the confidence which propaganda or successful operations can instil in the crew, and this, in turn, depends on how many captains return to tell of their exploits.'¹¹ In other words the crews should be killed in their boats if possible and any survivors captured.

The Type XXI would have a submerged range of 450 miles at 3 knots while the Type XXIII was capable of 250 miles at 2 knots dived. The top submerged speed of the Type XXI was 18 knots, with the Type XXIII reaching between 12 and 13 knots. According to the Japanese Naval Attaché, at 0.5 to 1 knots on the battery, the Type XXI would be completely silent.

When it came to hunting and killing the new enemy boats, the most the majority of British submarines could manage dived was around 10 knots – less than the R Class boats the RN had commissioned at the end of the First World War.

The Type XXI was another example of the Nazi regime's genius for sponsoring military-technical innovation of a potentially startling kind. With a sleek hull form, its cannons were mounted within the fin. It had a telescopic snort mast in its conning tower, rather than a clumsy, and far less effective, hinged mast, which had to pivot to upright from an eternal stowage. The Type XXI aspired to 50 hours submerged on the battery at full capacity, an endurance that could be doubled by reduc-ing energy consumption. Other submarines could only achieve half an hour at high speed submerged on battery power, or stay dived 24 hours at a few knots, provided they shut down almost all equipment.

The prime objective for a Type XXI was an entire patrol submerged and it would supposedly only take three hours to recharge the battery. The Type XXI also had 'creeping speed motors' on rubber mountings that absorbed noise, and it could safely dive to 440ft, which was 90ft deeper than the most modern British submarine and even more than the latest American boats. It allegedly had a crush depth beyond 1,000ft. A Type XXI supposedly did not have to surface to make an attack on a convoy. It could fire 18 torpedoes in 20 minutes and the reloads were conducted by machinery, with no human hands needed to haul the weapons around and shove them into tubes.

Dönitz told the Japanese a new submarine offensive in the Atlan-tic would be unleashed 'at one swoop', but it could only be achieved provided there were enough new boats to cause maximum damage. The earliest this could happen was March 1945, but this was soon pushed back to a start date of May or June. The Japanese were most anxious that the Germans remained in the fight, to prevent the full might of the Allies from being directed against them. If the new types of submarine could be unleashed along with Total Underwater Warfare, then so much the better for Japan.

Allied intelligence sources believed that by early 1945 50 Type XXIs were near completion. British submarines were unlikely to be able to do much to counter the Type XXI, due to their comparatively inferior performance, while even hardened, battle-proven escort groups might be impotent. According to one British submarine captain the Admiralty did not fancy the prospect at all and was 'pessimistic about coping with it'. The Type XXI 'with its high underwater speed . . . threatened to render counter attacking using asdic ineffective'.[12]

The newspapers were full of stories about the German wonder submarines and President Roosevelt felt it necessary on 9 January 1945 to address the issue in public. He explained in his State of the Union Address to Congress that the invasions of France – D-Day in Normandy and Operation Dragoon in the south – were made possible 'by success in the Battle of the Atlantic . . . Without this success over German submarines, we could not have built up our invasion forces or air forces in Great Britain, nor could we have kept a steady stream of supplies flowing to them after they had landed in France. The Nazis, however, may succeed in improving their submarines and their crews.' The President said that the battle for the Atlantic 'like all campaigns in this war demands eternal vigilance'.[13]

Even Max Horton was caught up in the scare and made gloomy predictions of terrible reverses that could see transatlantic and English Channel supply lines to Allied armies cut. After the war Horton would claim some British submarines were converted into Type XXI hunter-killers. These craft were, said Horton, 'stripped and adapted' in order to provide them with 'a very high speed'.[14]

The trials boat for this process was HMS *Seraph*, and in the summer of 1944 she was taken in hand with her propulsion improved, all external protuberances (including gun) removed, the conning tower made smaller and more streamlined and battery power boosted. On trials she proved she could manage 12 knots while dived for three-quarters of an hour. Her Achilles heel as a fighting boat against the Type XXI was not being able to recharge the battery at sea while dived, as she had no *Schnorchel*.[15]

Seraph was in the end used as a target boat to train escort commanders and Asdic operators to prepare for the new U-boats. She had limited utility beyond that, so which 'stripped down' boats was Horton on about?

The most likely candidates were V Class boats, 22 of which were built between 1943 and 1945. They had a submerged speed of 9 knots and could dive deeper than the similar U Class boats, but were not much of a match for the Type XXI unless radically modified. The modern S and T Class submarines had been sent to the Far East.

Horton also claimed escort groups were trained by the WATU in new tactics to tackle 'the special problems' the new German submarines would present.[16] At speed the Type XXIs would generate extra noise, so part of the solution was more effective use of Asdic and also greater precision with Hedgehog and Squid. No doubt rerouting convoys and the exploitation of Ultra to outfox the enemy would have remained powerful countermeasures, too.

For all the effort put into the Type XXI programme it was simply too late and Allied bombing of dockyards and construction sites kept the majority of 'electroboots' non-operational or prevented them from even coming together in the first place. Among the craft destroyed by an Allied air raid on a Baltic naval base was the prototype Type XXI, and along with it a chance of exhaustive testing to iron out problems before full production started. In the last six months of the war 17 complete Type XXIs were sunk at their berths in various naval bases.

The policy of building Type XXI modules at dozens of different sites – many with no previous experience in submarine construction – sometimes resulted in dire build quality. Modules often did not fit precisely, leading to a flawed pressure hull unable to cope with deep diving. Dispersed construction also threw a different spanner in the works. When American troops liberated Strasbourg they captured a construction yard on the River Rhine where 27 completed stern modules for Type XXIs were waiting to ship out. The boats they were intended for could not be completed.

The 'what if' gang – who like to speculate about what might have happened *if* the Nazis had perfected various wonder weapons – suggest that with dozens of Type XXI U-boats at sea the Germans could have won the Second World War.

There were other reasons why this would not have happened, aside from the sluggish Type XXI output rate and Allied bombing.

For a start, using the *Schnorchel* slowed U-boats down to a crawl, a handicap even the Type XXI would have suffered. A Type XXI on a noisy *Schnorchel* would have been unable to detect anything on her own hydrophones or even use periscopes effectively, due to vibration.

A poorly designed supercharger for the high-speed battery meant it wasn't possible to recharge in the short space of time desired. Key elements of the hydraulic gear to operate the diving planes, rudders and torpedo tube shutters were outside the pressure hull and vulnerable to damage.[7]

In practical warfare terms, despite its innovations, including a single all-welded hull, the other so-called wonder boat, the Type XXIII, was a pretty pointless craft. With a small crew (14) and only two torpedoes (and no reloads) the Type XXIII was bound to have limited endurance and minimal hitting power. There were 28 Type XXIIIs in service by the beginning of 1945 and, unlike their big sisters, the Type XXIs, they actually managed to attack ships – three boats of the class sank five merchant vessels between February and May 1945. Due to the pathetic weapon load that was about the most those boats could manage, even in the most favourable conditions. Like the small 'sewing machine' U-boats of the First World War, the Type XXIIIs had stability problems after they fired a torpedo and their *Schnorchels* were temperamental.

Only two Type XXIs ever deployed on combat patrol. Slow crew training – in fact, a lack of people due to the horrendous casualty rates in the U-boat force – was a severe handicap. So were teething problems associated with cutting-edge technology and a policy of sending trained submariners to fight on land. In the end no new wonder vessel could hide the cruel reality of the biggest mistake the Germans had made in submarine production, which was to persist too long with churning out variants of the Type VII. Herbert Werner received command of another after abandoning his previous submarine of the type during the retreat from Brest. He described *U-953* as an 'antique boat' that condemned himself and his men 'to almost certain death in the British shooting gallery'.[8]

★

As the Allies carried on knocking off U-boats in the West, in the East the Russians were tightening their grip. They had already secured superiority over the Black Sea where, until autumn 1944, a German submarine flotilla of small Type IIB boats had caused the Soviets some trouble. Six boats had been deconstructed and transported to Romania in 1941 via road, canals and the Danube. Once stitched back together they formed Combat Flotilla 30 at Constanta, sinking six Russian merchant ships and a few small vessels.

By the time Romania switched sides in late August 1944 there were three U-boats left, including Kretschmer's old *U-23*. Unwilling to surrender to the Russians, the German submariners scuttled their boats in Turkish waters and were interned.

In the Baltic there were no such lucky escapes for the thousands of Germans fleeing the Russians. On 30 January 1945 the Soviet submarine *S-13*, commanded by 31-year-old Captain 3rd Rank Alexander Marinesko, chalked up a grim milestone by sinking the 25,000-ton liner *Wilhelm Gustloff*.

She had for some years been used as an accommodation ship for U-boat crews under training but latterly had been pressed into service to evacuate people from East Prussia to the West. She was caught in the Bay of Danzig with only a torpedo boat for an escort, and it is reckoned 9,343 people lost their lives – almost ten times the number killed in the *Lusitania*.

It was the worst single death toll in maritime history, described by the German novelist Günter Grass as 'a collective death cry such as had never before been heard'.[19] Five thousand of those killed were children and the majority were refugees, though there were troops aboard – allegedly including U-boat crews. This made the ship a legitimate target for *S-13*.

On her way to Kiel after exercises in the Bay of Danzig, *U-2511* spotted people in the water. She surfaced to pick them up, finding they were some of the 1,230 survivors from the *Wilhelm Gustloff*,[20] though the heavy cruiser *Hipper*, already carrying refugees, did not stop to lend assistance. *S-13* struck again on 10 February, torpedoing the 14,700-ton liner *General Steuben*, which was on a similar evacuation mission, with 3,000 killed.

In the early hours of 17 April the Soviet boat *L-3* sank the troop ship *Goya*, killing nearly 6,000 military personnel and civilians. The Russian boats deployed into the southern Baltic then engaged in a feeding frenzy as the Red Army's advance forced the Germans to use the sea route to evacuate more troops and civilians, with at least another 12 transport vessels torpedoed, while mines sank four warships.

Marinesko was the Soviet Navy's tonnage king, having accumulated 42,000 tons sunk during the war, but he was not made a Hero of the Soviet Union as nobody believed his claims of sinking huge liners. He was a heavy drinker and insolent towards senior officers and in September 1945 he lost command of *S-13* for various offences. Marinesko was demoted to Lieutenant and in the late 1940s ended up in the Gulag. After release in the early 1950s he was restored to the rank of Captain 3rd Rank – the authorities finally believed his claims about sinking the liners – and awarded a full naval pension. Marinesko died at Leningrad in 1963 after a long fight against cancer.[21]

38 Endgame Europa

Despite such adversity the Reich would have 450 submarines in commission by mid-February[1] – more U-boats than at any time in the German Navy's history. But their chances of surviving and creating any kind of decisive effect had never looked bleaker.

The Germans were not just fleeing a red storm in the east aboard liners and troop ships. Key personnel, technology, weapons blueprints and even chemical elements crucial to munitions manufacturing were being smuggled overseas in U-boats. This was organised under Operation Caesar from December 1944, with the ultimate destination of many shipments being Japan. The frequency and sheer variety of materials and people carried was another definite sign the Thousand Year Reich was months from collapse.

U-864, commanded by 32-year-old Korvettenkapitän Ralf-Reimar Wolfram, was an Operation Caesar boat. Among the items in her special cargo were blueprints for Germany's new Me 262 fighter jet and Me 163 rocket-propelled interceptor and 60 tons of mercury along with specially trained engineers to assist the Japanese in using it all. A capacious Type IXD2 submarine, *U-864*, was also carrying missile components and other weapons technology, including BMW jet engines in crates,[2] along with plans for Italian-design mini submarines.

U-864 sailed from Kiel on 1 January 1945 but as she skirted Norway ran aground, the shock damaging her diesels and forcing the boat to seek repairs at Bergen. Reaching there on 5 January, *U-864*'s message to U-boat headquarters was intercepted and deciphered at Bletchley. It had earlier intercepted communications detailing the submarine's cargo. The British submarine *Venturer*, commanded by 26-year-old Lieutenant James Launders, was tasked with loitering off Norway around *U-864*'s anticipated departure date, close to the route she would probably take.

Venturer deployed from Lerwick on 2 February – three days before *U-864* sailed from Norway – the British guessing that the U-boat would pass the island of Fedje, which guards the north-west entrance to Bergen.[3]

On 8 February *U-864* suffered a further mishap that sealed her fate, when one of her engines broke down. Repairs to it made a racket and not far away was *Venturer*, which had now been ordered by the Admiralty to position herself off the Hellisøy Lighthouse.[4] At 9.32 a.m. on 9 February *Venturer*'s hydrophone operator picked up noise. At first the British submariners wondered if it was a trawler in trouble but then decided it could be a U-boat. *Venturer*'s Officer of the Watch, Sub Lt John Watson, took a periscope look down the indicated bearing and saw nothing. After coming on duty and taking over from Watson, the boat's First Lieutenant, Andy Chalmers, spotted *U-864*'s periscope. At 11.22 a.m. the U-boat's raised periscope and wireless mast were sighted. Launders would later observe that the German submarine commander was fatally careless.[5] *U-864* was also following a regular zigzag pattern and just as other submarine captains had used such predictability to sink surface ships so Launders now capitalised on it. He used *Venturer*'s hydrophone to gain an accurate target bearing and at 12.12 p.m., from a range of 3,000 yards, fired four torpedoes in a hosepipe pattern to intercept the predicted track. Each of the fish ran at 40ft,[6] with 17-second gaps between them. The hosepipe worked by firing all torpedoes down the same bearing, the gap between each one giving the target time to run into at least one of them. Launders timed it perfectly. *U-864* managed to evade three torpedoes, but steered into the path of the fourth.

The explosion tore the U-boat in two, *Venturer*'s hydrophone operator hearing *U-864* breaking up.

For *Venturer* it was mission accomplished and it remains the only time in history that one submarine has sunk another while both were submerged. Lt Launders was also notable for being the only RN submarine captain in the Second World War to destroy more than one German submarine (on 11 November 1944 *Venturer* sank *U-771* off Norway). Everybody aboard both boats perished.

One more milestone in the war came on the morning of 12 April 1945 when a submerged *Tapir* – commanded by 26-year-old Lt John Roxburgh – caught *U-486* on the surface north-west of Bergen. At 7.53 a.m. *Tapir* fired a torpedo salvo from a range of 3,200 yards.

'An explosion was heard two minutes after firing when I saw the U-Boat hit amidships and literally explode,' wrote Roxburgh in his patrol report. 'Bits of the U-Boat could be clearly seen flying through the air . . . and a large column of brownish smoke rose straight into the air to a height of some 500ft. This was most unexpected and very impressive. Further explosions were heard three minutes after firing, when two torpedoes were seen to explode at the foot of the Helliso [*sic*] Lighthouse . . .'

U-486 was the last German naval vessel sunk by a British submarine in European waters.[7]

When Allied intelligence organisations learned in March 1945 that Dönitz had ordered seven U-boats based in Norway to head for waters off the USA it was feared the long-awaited V-bomb blitz was about to be unleashed. Adding grist to the rumour mill were reports from spies in Norway about U-boats with launch rails fitted to their decks.

The leader of the Seewolf group deployed from Norway was also none other than Kapitänleutnant Steinhoff, now commanding *U-873*. Allied intelligence was aware of his rocket trials in *U-511* and also his brother's V-weapon work.

The USN countered the Seewolf group with the top secret Operation Teardrop. This involved the deployment of two hunter-killer groups centred on escort carriers. Each had 25 escorts and set out to eliminate the U-boats with ruthless efficiency in mid-Atlantic, so keeping the USA well beyond the likely range of cruise missiles or rockets.[8]

U-1235 was the first Seewolf boat destroyed, and was found by the most northerly placed hunter-killer group, led by the escort carriers *Croatan* and *Mission Bay*. Caught on the surface at night in thick fog on 16 April, around 350 miles east of Newfoundland, *U-1235* was picked out by a searchlight. After she dived Hedgehog attacks by the destroyers *Frost* and *Stanton* blew *U-1235* apart.

Less than an hour later *U-880* was destroyed by the same ships (again with no survivors). On 24 April *U-546* was not so easy to kill. She sank the destroyer *Frederick C. Davis*, killing most of her crew. A pack of USN warships hounded *U-546* for ten hours, USS *Flaherty* crumpling the submarine's forward compartments with depth charges. Forced to the surface, *U-546* was shot to pieces and slid below the waves, but with 47 of her 72 crew picked up by the Americans.

The boat's 30-year-old commander, Kapitänleutnant Paul Just, and seven of his men were not classified as PoWs, so they could be subjected to tough interrogation about the rocket attack plan. Receiving brutal beatings, they protested they had no idea what the Americans were talking about. This treatment continued for two weeks, despite the recovery of a diary from a *U-546* submariner, providing ample evidence there were no missiles aboard the boat. The captain of the destroyer USS *Varian*, which had taken aboard *U-546* survivors, was so appalled when he heard about their rough handling by the interrogators that he made a formal complaint.[9]

The final victim of Operation Teardrop was *U-881*, depth-charged to destruction by USS *Farquhar* to the south-east of Cape Race on 6 May. She was the last German submarine to be sunk by the USN in the Second World War.[10] The boats of the Seewolf group were actually equipped with nothing more special than *Schnorchels* and homing torpedoes. No sea-launched missile for U-boats was ever perfected by the Kriegsmarine, though rocket tests are thought to have continued until early 1945. The Bergen-based Type VIIC boat *U-1053* was lost during deep-diving trials in February 1945, possibly conducted as part of the programme.[11]

The Royal Navy never thought it likely the Germans could mount a rocket blitz on America, due to a lack of suitable submarines. Many in the USN hierarchy were also sceptical, with one admiral scoffing at the suggestion of buzz-bomb attacks on the USA. Aside from lacking the right kind of U-boats, there were also too many parts and players to be co-ordinated within a German system buckling under massive military pressure from East and West. What actually sank the sea-launched V1 project before it could ever get going was, yet again, the unco-operative Luftwaffe. It owned and operated the V1s and was not willing to release any of them for Skorzeny's scheme.[12]

As the German house of cards collapsed in early May 1945, those U-boats that might still escape to Norway were ordered to make a run for it.

By the time this instruction was issued, Dönitz had become the new Führer. Before Adolf Hitler killed himself he left a will declaring the former submarine captain to be at the helm of the ruined Reich.

Dönitz had proved a loyal servant of the Führer and his U-boat force had exerted itself to the utmost, making great sacrifices, which may explain why the admiral ended up as Hitler's successor. The Grand Admiral saw it as a sacred duty to try to negotiate a favourable peace with the Western Allies while ensuring as many people as possible escaped the grip of the Soviets as they rolled ever deeper into Germany.

Among the boats breaking out to head for Norway was *U-534*, a Type IXC commissioned in December 1942. Her first and only captain was 26-year-old Oberleutnant Herbert Nollau. The majority of the vessel's operational life, and Nollau's naval career, had been spent on training duties in the Baltic. In 1944 she was fitted with a *Schnorchel* and conducted front line patrols, but sank no ships, narrowly avoiding destruction when attacked by an RAF Wellington bomber. On 2 May 1945 *U-534* was the last U-boat to leave Kiel, joining up with a pair of Type XXIs, *U-3523* and *U-3503*.

There has been repeated speculation through the years that they were making a run to South America, but there is no evidence of this. On 5 May, two days before Germany unconditionally surrendered, while cruising on the surface all three submarines were attacked in the Kattegat by two RAF Liberator bombers, one of which was shot down.

While the other U-boats dived, *U-534* stayed on the surface too long. She tried to shoot it out, and was sunk by depth charges from the surviving Liberator but somehow only three men out of the submarine's 52-strong crew were killed, the remainder being taken prisoner.[13] As for the other two boats, an RAF Liberator sank *U-3523* on 6 May, while two days later *U-3503* was scuttled in the Kattegat, her crew seeking internment in Sweden.

Under the surrender terms all surviving U-boats were to be handed over intact to the Allies, but in defiance of that 218 were either scuttled or otherwise destroyed. In the end 154 U-boats were surrendered to the Allies, with the majority sailed by their crews to British ports for internment.

Lt Cdr Nicholas Monsarrat, captain of the frigate HMS *Perim* at war's end, thought it an odd finale for men who had fought so hard and for so long: '. . . all over the Atlantic, the fighting died – a strangely tame finish, after five and a half years of bitter struggle.'[14]

39   *U-977* & the Stowaway Führer

A few U-boats did indeed head for South America, including *U-977*. Later thought by some to have carried Adolf Hitler to Argentina, it would have been a most unlikely means of escape for a man who thought himself a coward at sea and could not set foot on a boat or a ship without feeling queasy. By April 1945 the Führer was a mental and physical wreck, not capable of enduring such a voyage, never mind the impossibility of getting him out of besieged Berlin and across war-torn Germany to Kiel.

U-977's captain was 24-year-old Oberleutnant Heinz Schaeffer, who, as a naval cadet, had watched German forces prepare for a potential invasion of England in the summer of 1940. Since then he had been second in command of a U-boat on war patrols, but had never commanded one before being appointed to *U-977* in December 1944.

She was a boat with a chequered history, having suffered severe damage during collisions in the Baltic, and even after repairs her hull remained fragile. *U-977* had to be confined to training duties and this made the Type VIIC boat an even more unlikely escape vehicle for the leader of the Third Reich or any other high official. As *U-977* was being prepared to go out on her final war patrol, her captain assessed that she was 'not fit for active service in any respect whatever'.[1]

Taking advantage of a visit to Kiel by Grand Admiral Dönitz, Schaeffer requested a meeting, hoping to persuade his boss not to deploy

U-977. He was disappointed, the admiral telling him the U-boats would 'fight on till victory' and would win 'whatever the cost'.[2]

After calling in for supplies and fuel in Norway, the boat headed out into the Atlantic, picking up a radio broadcast revealing Germany's surrender. Apparently U-boats must now obey Allied orders, which appalled Schaeffer, and so he devised a plan of escape to South America. *U-977* approached the Norwegian coast on 10 May to drop off 16 members of the crew who had voted to stay in Europe rather than go to Argentina. To ensure *U-977*'s intended voyage stayed secret, on being taken prisoner they were to describe themselves as survivors of a U-boat that had been sunk. The 32 who stayed aboard *U-977* had decided they would rather be interned in South America and seek a new life in a country where, so they hoped, Germans might be allowed to live peacefully.

Taking the northern route around Scotland, *U-977*'s men endured an extended period of more than a month submerged – using the *Schnorchel* for four hours a day. Conditions got so grim that Schaeffer felt that he and his men were 'on the verge of nervous breakdowns'.[3] There was trash and filth everywhere and they took to firing the rubbish out of the torpedo tubes.

Finally surfacing north of Cape Verde, *U-977* called at a remote bay on Branco Island for a few hours, with Schaeffer allowing the men to feel the sun on their skin and have a swim while dolphins played around them.

After a singsong to boost the mens' spirits the boat resumed her voyage, risking a surface passage thereafter, on one engine to eke out the fuel. Detours were taken to avoid being sighted by a merchant vessel and two aircraft but on crossing the Equator the usual ceremonies were held.

U-977 picked up a radio news broadcast that *U-530* had already sought refuge in Argentina, but that both the boat and her men had been handed over to the Americans. There was a discussion about scuttling *U-977* off the coast and then disappearing ashore, but Schaeffer realised that his men would soon be rounded up. He told them the best option was for *U-977* to head for the naval base at Mar del Plata. Accompanied by a low-skimming albatross for part of the way, they entered Argentinian territorial waters on 17 August to be met by an escort composed of a patrol boat and two submarines. *U-977* had completed

107 days at sea – 66 of them accounted for by one submerged stretch – and had covered more than 7,644 miles since leaving Germany. The submarine had started from Norway with 85 tonnes of diesel fuel and by the time she reached the waters off South America it was down to five.[4]

When interrogated at Mar del Plata U-977's captain provided a simple explanation for his actions: 'I no longer considered my ship as a man-of-war, but as a means of escape, and I tried to act for the best interests of all aboard. I respected the wishes of members of my crew insofar as they did not imperil the ship or cause damage to it.'[5]

To prove good faith U-977 had retained her full outfit of torpedoes, rather than making more space for her crew by ditching them. This was to prove no attacks had been made during the voyage.

It was a Uruguayan newspaper that started the story of U-977 bringing Hitler to South America and soon it was headline news around the world, especially as at the time it was uncertain if Hitler really was dead. Conspiracy theories abounded due to the lack of a body, though the Soviets did find a charred jaw bone that surviving dental X-rays proved was Hitler's.

He and Eva Braun had most likely committed suicide in the Berlin bunker and their petrol-drenched corpses were then burned above ground in a shell hole, with Goebbels tossing the match onto them.[6] The majority of Hitler and Braun's remains were lost amid the hellfire and chaos of the final moments in the battle for Berlin, but the Russians took some to Moscow.

Stories of body doubles being burned and the real Hitler escaping by submarine proved fireproof and ran wild in the war's aftermath. Schaeffer soon found himself before a special Anglo-American Commission that quizzed him about the possibility of his boat carrying a fugitive Hitler.

'Come on, where is he?' the incredulous U-boat captain was asked.[7]

Such an idea was nonsense and Schaeffer was insulted even to be asked, especially as he would rather see his submarine's incredible voyage making headlines.

In time the Americans released Schaeffer and he was shipped back to Europe where, instead of being freed, he ended up in British hands. The questions about Hitler started all over again. Eventually they believed him and so Schaeffer was released from captivity and became a civilian in a war-shattered Germany, though he later went to live in Argentina.

U-977 was sunk as a target by the submarine USS *Atule* on 13 November 1946 during torpedo firing trials, but the Hitler yarn refused to lie down. The Argentina-based Hungarian exile Ladislas Szabo wrote a book in the late 1940s about either *U-977* or *U-530* taking Hitler, Eva Braun and Martin Bormann to safety. He claimed there was a submarine convoy that transported the Nazi bigwigs to a hideout in Antarctica, constructed by order of Admiral Dönitz. According to this story the Nazis decided they preferred Argentina, so a diversion was made.

Schaeffer obtained a copy of Szabo's book and could scarcely believe his eyes. His boat had barely made it to South America, never mind venturing towards the South Pole. *U-977* had no ability to voyage under or through ice, especially with her already damaged hull. *U-530* was a long-range Type IX already off the Eastern Seaboard of the USA when the surrender was announced. The idea that this boat had sailed back to Germany undetected – through seas crowded with Allied warships and watched over by aircraft – to pick up Hitler was utterly preposterous. Szabo's suggestion that ample supplies of cigarettes aboard *U-977* were evidence of passengers was similarly ridiculous. He claimed U-boat crews were not permitted to smoke, so the cigarettes must have belonged to someone else, but U-boatmen were allowed to do so, just not while their boat was dived. Schaeffer felt Szabo knew as much about U-boats 'as an Eskimo about Central America'.[8]

The myth of Hitler escaping to South America persists to this day, fuelled by website blogs, books, newspaper articles and television documentaries. That people believed a crock like *U-977* could have transported him there – or even to Antarctica – is a testament to an enduring belief in the almost mystical power of submarines. Some of the U-boats' reputation was warranted, but quite a lot of it was not, as had been proved in the heat of combat. There was one theatre of war where the power of the submarine was actually under-appreciated, which was the Pacific. Even as Hitler's body burned outside his bunker months of fighting between the Allies and Japan were still to come.

40   Fires on a Darkening Shore

As the so-called New Order in East Asia collapsed the Japanese were hanging on by their fingertips to the territories they had conquered.

To weaken their grip in the Dutch East Indies, Malaya and Singapore, British submarines that had not forward-deployed to operate from Australia and the Philippines continued to act as launch vehicles for raiding sorties.

They also provided extractions for coast watchers who had been spying on Japanese shipping movements, and retrieved commandos after various missions behind enemy lines.

These were the kind of tasks that demanded the utmost skill from British submariners. While proud of their work – showing off superb seamanship – it was a job that continued to arouse dislike among the crews, due to the necessity for going into very shallow waters, which broadened the risks while narrowing the options of escape.

Alastair Mars was by then in the Far East and in command of *Thule*, while conducting such operations. For Mars it was essential that final judgement calls were the province of the submarine captain rather than the commander of the embarked raiders. He wasn't the sort of character who liked being told what to do anyway.

His navigator was 21-year-old Sub Lt Matthew Todd. He had joined *Thule* after serving in *Syrtis*, which later ran into a mine off Norway (on 28 March 1944) with no survivors. *Syrtis* had been almost brand-new, but as Todd reflected 'there is nothing you can do about a mine' so going to *Thule* 'was handy, as if I had gone out with *Syrtis* again, I would have lost my life'.[1] Once again serving in a new submarine, this time with Mars, Todd found that his captain's strong opinions often rubbed people up the wrong way. Mars, in common with many other wartime submarine captains, disliked the spit and polish mentality of certain peacetime naval officers, while having no time for endless form filling. As the war neared its end the autocrats and bureaucrats were trying to reassert their authority. They had a habit of mounting surprise submarine inspections and insisting on tropical white uniforms in the depot ship wardroom, and other such nonsense. Mars thumbed his nose at them with the deliberate aim of making it all too much trouble to impose formal naval discipline on his boat. 'Thule was, as a result, a bit of a black sheep,' confessed Todd, 'as people were wary of Mars and thought "Oh my God, here he is" when we fetched up at Trincomalee.' Even though Mars was 'very difficult', in the end Todd would consider his time in Thule to have been happy.

Thule did two patrols in the Malacca Strait laying mines in a channel just off Langkawi and attacked a Japanese submarine approaching Penang. Mars watched three torpedoes speed towards the target, with one exploding right in front of the enemy boat's conning tower. His instinct that it had detonated prematurely was eventually confirmed by an intelligence source, which revealed the enemy craft had not been hit.

The Triton Class boat undertook four special operations, landing commandos to work with local guerrilla forces, as part of preparations for the future British effort to kick the Japanese occupiers out of Malaya.

The most exhausting of these missions was called Carpenter-Mint, involving two voyages from Trincomalee to landing points in east Malaya, one of them only 20 miles from Singapore Naval Base. To reach them with the best chance of being unobserved required a passage via the Sunda Strait, about 4,600 nautical miles there and back.

Thule's usual complement was 64, but for the Carpenter-Mint mission of late May 1945 there would be a platoon of 19 Royal Marine commandos aboard. The submarine was required to 'provide for all that lot for five weeks or more', according to Todd. To get all the necessary food and other supplies aboard, a false deck was created for people to walk on – not unknown in submarines. The tinned food and ammunition was underfoot and there were the usual bumps, due to less headroom. Additional cargo was somewhat out of the ordinary: 14 rubber boats, with a corresponding number of engines and cans of petrol, large wireless sets and all their associated spare parts plus more than four tons of stores to put ashore. After stuffing all that aboard, Thule set off south across the Indian Ocean, heading for the Sunda Strait, with Sub Lt Todd plotting the course. The majority of the transit would be surfaced, even during the day, only diving the boat on sighting enemy aircraft or patrol vessels. Should any likely-looking targets cross Thule's path, her fire was to be held, as the security of the Carpenter-Mint mission was paramount.

'The Japanese were supposed to have a listening post in the strait [using hydrophones] and a controlled minefield,' explained Todd. 'We had to shut down almost everything for 15–20 hours: no fans, no air purification and it became atrocious, with 83 people on board. It was very hot and the humidity was extreme.'

While the food and fuel situation held up, water supplies got short and required careful rationing. Once through the strait the boat surfaced and again made speed, keeping well out of sight from land.

The Japanese did not once spot *Thule* during the whole five weeks of her epic voyage and Todd did all the navigation, spending two hours on watch, then four hours off, but always available for fixes.

Todd's navigation was on target and so they arrived safely off the correct landing beach, 35 miles from Singapore. *Thule* stayed submerged until after the sun went down and then surfaced and edged in towards the shore, all gun crews closed up for action. The hydrophone operator listened out for approaching patrol craft and a watch was also kept for any potential enemy radar transmissions.

The water offshore was a maximum of 19ft deep, which meant high exposure on the surface during the delicate (and prolonged) offloading task. There were lots of fishing craft around, but Mars reasoned they would not interfere or tip off the Japanese, as guerrillas controlled the local area. The Royal Marines found their way to and from the submarine while offloading by clever use of an infrared light on the conning tower and special goggles.

Waiting ashore to be taken off by *Thule* was an assortment of people, including a trio of British Army signals specialists who had been in the jungle for three years. Originally sent in to spy on enemy troop movements, they ended up with the guerrillas and helped them fight the Japanese, experiencing many brushes with death and disease. There were also the three surviving members of an American B-29 bomber crew. Their aircraft had been shot down while attacking Singapore. Two of the five airmen who parachuted to safety were captured by the Japanese, paraded around Singapore and then publicly beheaded.[2]

During one of her patrols in the Malacca Straits, *Thule* nearly suffered the same fate as quite a few other Allied submarines – being sunk by her own side's aircraft. The flotilla headquarters at Trincomalee failed to notify a Royal Navy strike carrier force of the British boat operating in adjacent waters. After receiving a sighting report of an unidentified submarine, aircraft were launched to go and sink what was presumed to be a Japanese craft. Fortunately Mars decided it was time to dive the boat for a tea break while checking her submerged trim and so she wasn't attacked.

Seeking to avoid further commando operations, Mars lobbied the flotilla commander for a normal anti-shipping patrol, but there was very little by way of enemy vessels to be had. Sometimes when something did appear it was not a suitable target. In the Java Sea a Japanese hospital ship 'all lit up' was sighted by *Thule*. Taking a periscope look, Mars decided he would not attack as the vessel was 'a pleasant reminder that if man is to remain civilised he must have rules'.[3]

On another patrol *Thule* was reduced to preying on junks. Todd, who would finish his time in the boat as her First Lieutenant, thought such encounters were counter-productive and also potentially rather dangerous.

Sometimes he would be sent aboard an intercepted junk to ask for papers and make a quick inspection of the cargo. At the forefront of his mind was the cautionary tale of a junk that made off with a submarine officer still aboard who was never seen again.

If that did happen to Todd the junk would probably head into shallower waters where *Thule* could not follow. In a case like that a submarine crew would not want to open fire in case it killed the man being held hostage. For that reason, when Todd went aboard a junk to inspect papers he was attached to *Thule* by a long rope, so that if the vessel suddenly broke away he could be pulled off and hauled back.

Many crews of junks were bemused about why their modest cargoes were of interest. Todd thought sinking even those that were carrying material for the Japanese was unfairly antagonistic to locals who lost their means of making a living. Even if they did sink a junk carrying enemy materials Todd thought 'it didn't make much difference to the Japanese war effort'. Mars usually rammed junks or small wooden craft, a method that let the crews go in peace – and in one piece – even if somewhat disgruntled.

Small motorboats packed with Japanese troops and armed with multiple cannons and machine guns were a different matter. Mars showed them no mercy. Spotting one of these out of the water on a slipway by a cluster of boathouses, Mars sneaked a dived *Thule* in close to the shore. The Japanese patrol vessel looked freshly painted, possibly even recently constructed. Mars decided to wait until after dark before surfacing and shooting the place up. *Thule*'s gunners set about the task with relish, using slow, deliberate aim to hit the enemy base with dozens of 4-inch shells while shredding it with 20mm cannon fire. Destruction delivered, *Thule* withdrew out to sea and dived, Mars using the boat's periscope to take a satisfied look at 'a funeral pyre on the darkening shore'.[4]

When the end came for the Germans in Europe, the Reich's collapse stranded both submarines and submariners in the Far East.

Among them was 38-year-old Fregattenkapitän Wilhelm Dommes, another former Merchant Navy officer who became a U-boat captain. Having taken *U-178* out to the Indian Ocean in August 1943 he was put in charge of all submarines operating from Penang. He was eventually taken prisoner by British forces and not released until 1947.

In the final months of the Reich, two U-boats were sunk in the Java Sea by American submarines. On the morning of 10 November 1944 torpedoes fired by *Flounder* hit *U-537*, with no survivors. On 23 April 1945, *U-183* was claimed by *Besugo*, with her commander, 28-year-old Kapitänleutnant Fritz Schneewind, killed along with the rest of the boat's crew.

The curtain fell on the last theatre of war for the Axis, which was never a mutual appreciation society. Even though allies, the Japanese and the Germans never had a warm working relationship. For example, unless permission had been obtained well in advance, no visits were permitted by Japanese officers to U-boats, while Tokyo and Berlin directed their submarines separately, with no joint operations co-ordinated by commanders on the scene. Many in the Japanese military loathed Europeans and the simmering hatred was reciprocated. One German submariner captured by the Allies in the Far East said that if Japan was not beaten there would eventually be a war between 'the white race and the yellow race'.[5]

The Germans and the Japanese might have been unable to work as a team operationally, but the British and the Americans – sharing a language, heritage and some cultural roots – seemed to find it less of a problem.

The Royal Navy's submarines even tried to adopt the wolf pack model. Hezlet's *Trenchant* sailed from Fremantle on 13 May 1945, along with sister vessels *Thorough* and *Taciturn*, to destroy enemy shipping in the Java Sea and the South China Sea. Known as Task Unit 71.7.19, over the next five days the three boats kept close company and rehearsed gunnery techniques, Asdic skills and conducted torpedo exercises.

It was 1,500 miles to the borders of the zones where the targets lay, which was a long way, taking seven days to get there. British submarines usually took on fuel at Exmouth Bay, on the very north-west edge of Australia, before striking out across the Indian Ocean.

On the way, Royal Navy boats might meet up with the large USN submarines to receive fresh fruit and other victuals, along with mail from home. British submariners – and those of other nations – used to write numerous letters while on a patrol, saving them up and sending them as a batch when the opportunity arose. Packages of letters they received from loved ones back home were, according to Alistair Mars, 'a constant reminder of the things we were fighting for . . .' Without letters from home, Mars reckoned, the 'determination and sense of purpose would certainly have weakened, if not withered away'.[6]

Striving to find something to sink, British submarines would often venture into shallow waters, acting on intelligence provided by American boats that dared not go in due to their larger size.

In early June 1945, *Trenchant* was sent into the Banka Strait, hunting for an enemy heavy cruiser making a run from Batavia to Singapore. At 11.48 a.m. on 7 June the 12,700-ton *Ashigara* – a warship celebrated in the IJN for participating in many actions – hove into *Trenchant*'s periscope view. She was steaming at 17 knots and was six miles away to the south, with 1,200 troops aboard. *Ashigara* seemed entirely without any escort, either aircraft overhead or destroyers, and was not making zigzags. The destroyer *Kamikaze* had earlier been on the scene – engaging in a surface tussle with *Trenchant* – but she was now busy elsewhere harassing *Stygian*, another British submarine.

As she got bigger and bigger in Hezlet's scope, he could see the Rising Sun flag fluttering proudly from *Ashigara*'s topmast and soldiers packing her upper decks, unaware their ride was hurtling into danger.

For Hezlet, the enemy cruiser presented 'a submariner's dream'.[7] With the range closed down to 3,000 yards he fired eight torpedoes in a spread that aimed to hit all the way down the cruiser's side. Hezlet hoped at least five would strike his victim and his prediction was bang on the money.

Part of the cruiser's bow was blown off, while steam came out of various places and she was gripped by fire. To try and save his ship, *Ashigara*'s captain attempted to run her aground on the Klippen Shoal, but she never made it, rolling over and sinking.

The absent *Kamikaze* now entered the drama and after dropping some poorly placed depth charges moved away to begin picking up survivors. *Trenchant* in the meantime exited to the east.

Hezlet was well pleased with his day's work. 'Triumphalism is now a dirty word,' he reflected some years later, 'but [back] then it was certainly not. We particularly thought of the [British cruiser] *Exeter*, whose destruction had been wrought mainly by the *Ashigara*.'[8]

41 Sink the *Takao*

Having by now gained considerable expertise in operating midget submarines successfully, the British were keen to find them further employment while also wanting to play a greater part in the defeat of Japan.

In February 1945 submarine depot ship *Bonaventure* was sent out to Australia carrying half a dozen X-craft to seek opportunities for action.

The flotilla commander, Capt. William Fell, flew all around the Pacific theatre meeting various US senior officers to ask them what his midget submarines could do to help the cause. He was 'determined to get some sort of an operation', explained one of his X-craft captains,[1] but it proved far from easy as there wasn't a lot left to sink. Eventually it was agreed that the X-craft should be sent to cut telegraph links between Japanese commanders in Singapore and Saigon and those between Saigon and Hong Kong. On the same day an effort would be mounted at Singapore to attack *Takao*, the last survivor from a class of four heavy cruisers, and *Myoko* (another cruiser).

Myoko was a sister of *Ashigara* and *Haguro*, the latter sunk on 16 May by four British destroyers in a brutal little scrap. USN submarines had sunk two of *Takao*'s sisters at Leyte Gulf in October 1944 while a third was so badly damaged she had to be scuttled.

The British decided to call the Singapore venture Operation Struggle, because it had been so hard to find something to attack, while the bid to cut Japanese communications was Operation Sabre. The X-craft and their crews were worked up for their missions in waters behind the Great Barrier Reef, rehearsing how to get under large warships and also cut seabed telegraph cables.

Once they were fully prepared *Bonaventure* took them back aboard and sailed for Labuan, Borneo, which would be the forward base for the attacks. To reach the target area required a tow of 600 miles. *XE1* and *XE3* were towed by *Spark* and *Stygian*, respectively, to a launch point off the Horsburgh Lighthouse at the entrance to the Singapore Strait. From there they would head off on their own to attack the heavy cruisers.

XE3 would tackle *Takao* while *XE1* was to target *Myoko*. Both the Japanese cruisers had earlier been damaged by American submarine attack – *Myoko* by *Bergall* the previous December and *Takao* by *Darter*, during the Battle of Leyte Gulf. They now hid in harbour behind anti-submarine nets but it was feared their 8-inch guns might bombard Allied troops making a future assault to liberate Singapore.

Privately, the Americans thought the effort to get at the Japanese cruisers was hardly worth it. They were not exactly a threat on the same level as *Tirpitz* and could be dealt with as and when they dared venture out. However, the Americans did appreciate the British desire to deliver a blow against an enemy to whom they had surrendered Singapore in 1942.

The 24-year-old captain of *XE3* was Lt Ian Fraser, while her diver was 26-year-old Leading Seaman James Magennis, who was part of the passage crew for *X7* during the attack on *Tirpitz* in September 1943.

To reach *Takao* meant going 12 miles up a narrow channel half a mile wide in the Johore Strait, which separates Singapore from the Malayan Peninsula. Dodging a few patrols, on the morning of 31 July *XE3* slipped through the anti-submarine net, whose gate was wide open. Fraser wondered if it was ever actually shut by the Japanese, who seemed not at all vigilant.

He used the periscope to inspect *Takao*, which was stern on to

Singapore Island, her bows pointing towards the Malay Peninsula and in very shallow water with the tide going out.

Her situation – with guns pointed in the direction any British land assault would come from – was exactly what made the higher command nervous. Operation Mailfist – the campaign to kick the Japanese out of Singapore – was due to begin in December.

Before taking the boat in to attack, Fraser let members of his crew take a look at their objective. She was pretty impressive, with a pile of three twin 8-inch gun turrets forward and two more aft, a tall pagoda control tower and more than 630ft long, with a draught of 20ft and a displacement of around 10,000 tons. *Takao*'s hull was camouflaged with blotches of different shades of grey-blue, which did nothing to hide the ship in her current location.

Despite crystal clear waters and it being an afternoon attack, *XE3* was not spotted as she approached. *Takao*'s bows and stern were between four and six feet off the muddy bottom but there was a pocket of water 18ft deep under the mid-section into which *XE3* soon wriggled. Even the thumping and bumping under her hull caused by this did not stir any of the several hundred men aboard *Takao*.

There was a porthole in the top of the X-craft through which daylight filtered down and as the submarine slid under the cruiser it dimmed. Once their eyes adjusted to the gloom the British submariners were able to see crustaceans on *Takao*'s bottom and weeds hanging down.

With *XE3* settled on the mud Magennis climbed into his diving suit, pulling on the breathing apparatus and mask. As he exited the boat via the lock-out chamber he was forced to squeeze through a narrow gap, for the hatch would not open fully underneath the ship. Magennis extracted magnetic limpet mines from a transportation container on the port side of *XE3*. The process of attaching them was made difficult by barnacles on *Takao*'s hull, so he used his diver's knife to scrape them off. It took 40 minutes to affix half a dozen mines, Magennis making double sure with some rope. There was a counter-mining device in each mine that would detonate it if somebody tried to prise it off.

Once Magennis was back inside, *XE3* dropped the large slab of explosive attached to the starboard side of her hull and made to ditch the container that contained the mines. Presuming this had all worked, Fraser ordered the boat's electric motors started up, but the tide was going out and *Takao* was now resting her bulk on the midget submarine.

'We flooded down and we couldn't get out,' recalled Fraser. 'We were in a very narrow hole under this thing.' Suppressing growing anxiety, for 20 minutes Fraser wriggled the boat, 'going full ahead, full astern, blowing tanks, filling tanks, just trying to nudge a hole in the seabed so we could climb out . . .'

It wouldn't be long before the battery juice ran out – and the mines and the explosive were due to go off in around six hours' time. Should she remain stuck *XE3* would be blown up along with *Takao*.

If they abandoned ship the prospect of being captured was equally grim, with the enemy sure to mete out brutal treatment (or even execution). Giving it another try, by some miracle the submarine had pushed enough mud out of the way to shoot from under the cruiser, creating a huge splash. Still those aboard *Takao* failed to notice.

Bottoming the boat in 50 feet of water around 16 yards from *Takao*, the mine container, which had, in fact, not ditched, caused further alarm. Its continued presence on the outside was putting a strain on the boat, making *XE3* lopsided and difficult to handle.

Magennis went out again, successfully levering it off. All the time this was going on there was the danger of somebody aboard *Takao* noticing a commotion. It was 'very clear water, anyone looking down must have been able to see a black shape', thought Fraser. Magennis's suit was also leaking air, creating a stream of bubbles, which was another giveaway.

Somehow *XE3*'s luck held and she got away unseen.

In the meantime Lt John Smart, commanding *XE1*, had given up on trying to get at *Myoko*, his boat having sneaked through the net gate later than scheduled, delayed by dodging mines and numerous criss-crossing patrol craft. *Myoko* was two miles further in than *Takao* and the tide was getting so low Smart feared *XE1* would be exposed and give away the entire operation. *XE1* sneaked over to *Takao*, and, finding no gap to get under, dropped her slab of explosive next to the cruiser.

Both X-craft made a safe exit, by which time their crews had been awake for more than 50 hours and the boats dived for around 20. Benzedrine pills were keeping them going,[3] but the air in *XE3*, despite the best efforts of purifiers, was pretty foul. Fraser surfaced the boat once *XE3* was beyond the lighthouse, his crew taking it in turns to go up for fresh air and stretch their aching limbs.

At 9.00 p.m. Fraser ordered the boat stopped and got everyone on the casing to see the anticipated explosions. There was a very loud bang and a flash over on the other side of Singapore Island and *XE3*'s weary submariners thought it 'magnificent'.[4]

XE3 got underway and successfully met up with her mother submarine, but *XE1* missed hers and had to make a rendezvous the following night. Each of the larger submarines shone its infrared light, which was picked up by the captain of each midget submarine as he scanned the darkness while wearing the required special goggles.

At the same time as *XE3* and *XE1* were taking on *Takao* the others were making their bid to cut enemy communications links in Operation Sabre. The captain of *XE4* was Lt Max Shean who, like a number of other Australian naval officers, had journeyed to Britain to join the mother country's fight.

The two telegraph cables that Shean's boat would be targeting off Saigon offered a form of communication that was not vulnerable to interception by airwave eavesdroppers. Severing them would force the Japanese to send wireless messages, which could then be intercepted and decrypted, giving the Allies priceless foresight of enemy operations.

Once set free from the mother submarine, finding cables that had been laid as long ago as the 1870s was a challenge in itself, and a special grapple-hook had been devised. This was dragged back and forth across the likely spot where they lay. To enable that to work the submarine had to be manoeuvred just a few feet above the seabed. It was a very tricky procedure due to salt water mixing with fresh from the Mekong Delta and causing fluctuations in buoyancy. Shean also had to keep a very careful periscope watch, which put a further demand on precise depth-keeping.[5]

Nonetheless the Saigon–Singapore cables were hooked and at 12.29 p.m. the first diver, Sub Lieutenant Ken Briggs, another Aussie, went out. He took seven minutes to cut through one of them with powered shears.[6]

XE4's other diver, Sub Lieutenant Adam Bergius, tackled the second cable but the shears broke before he'd finished. Bergius had to go back and get a spare cutter. The whole process was not made easy by the depth – 60ft, twice that at which naval frogmen usually worked, using oxygen – along with strong currents and tides. Each diver brought back a section of the cable as proof of job done, marked off at each end with hair ribbon.[7]

After cutting the second cable Bergius was plucked off his feet and tumbled away, but thanks to his safety line he managed to pull himself back hand-over-hand to *XE4* and climb inside. The X-craft returned safely to her mother submarine and was soon under tow and heading for Borneo.

The simultaneous attempt by *XE5*, commanded by Lt Herbert West-macott, to cut a communications cable off Hong Kong appeared to have failed. Post-war investigations revealed the cable had been damaged after all.

After returning to *Bonaventure* Lt Fraser joined Capt. Fell to look at aerial reconnaissance photographs of *Takao*. Despite the explosions, she was still upright with Fraser dismayed to see 'she hadn't been blown into smithereens'.

Capt. Fell was not amused either. 'We've got to do something about this,' he told Fraser. 'You'll have to go back.'

Fraser was understandably not too keen on this. They might not be so lucky the second time around, especially as the enemy was now fully alert to the threat. The prospect 'really did upset me', said Fraser, 'having done what I considered a successful attack . . .'

The new one was scheduled for around a week later and in the meantime the men prepared themselves and tried to relax. Fraser and the others were sitting on *Bonaventure*'s upper deck watching a film when without warning it ground to a halt. '. . . the Captain came out and told us they had dropped a nuclear bomb . . .'

Fell explained that the new operation against *Takao* had been delayed, but three days later there was a new twist. '. . . they dropped the second bomb and the Japanese capitulated,' said Fraser, 'so we didn't have to go back to Singapore. I was very grateful for that.' He joked: 'That is why I am so fond of nuclear bombs.'

Never mind Fraser being let off attacking the *Takao* again, it probably saved the lives of hundreds of thousands of Allied servicemen who no longer had to invade Japan.

42 The Road to Tokyo Bay

There are those who say dropping atom bombs on Hiroshima and Nagasaki was unnecessary, as was the firebombing of other Japanese cities. The US Navy's submarines had already defeated Japan and there was no military point in using the world's first nuclear weapons. An island nation, like Britain – and similarly dependent on sea imports to survive – Japan had failed to create the naval forces and technology necessary to fight back against a devastating submarine offensive.

The IJN was reduced almost to insignificance well before hostilities ceased. By June 1944, the Japanese submarine force was down to just 26 operational boats, though some were still operating off California where *I-12* was sunk on 13 November that year.

After the Battle of Leyte Gulf many Japanese vessels were pulled back to home waters and paid off, their men sent to the maritime air forces or the army. A number manned new *kamikaze* (divine wind) midget submarines and suicide torpedoes called *Kaiten* (return to heaven), the final throw of the dice for a service that had been mismanaged and frittered away.

Despite American supremacy at sea, one last victory was achieved by a Japanese submarine and the victim was a cruiser that had been in the thick of the action all the way across the Pacific.

A pre-war favourite of President Theodore Roosevelt, who used her as his 'yacht' for summer cruises, the *Indianapolis* in July 1945 delivered enriched uranium and other components for the Little Boy atomic bomb to the island airbase of Tinian. On 6 August Little Boy was dropped on Hiroshima by the B-29 Superfortress *Enola Gay*, immediately killing at least 80,000 people. By then *Indianapolis* had already met a cruel fate, but the sinking was only the beginning of the horror for her men.

Departing Tinian, *Indianapolis* headed for Guam and then for Leyte but was spotted by *I-58*, whose captain, 36-year-old Cdr Mochitsura Hashimoto, brought his boat up to periscope depth and then surfaced to get a better look. Climbing up to the bridge Hashimoto discerned a black shape moving across the ocean and gave the order to crash-dive. Hashimoto swung *I-58* around to head in the direction of what he later described as a 'dark object', which did not appear to be zigzagging.[1] It had to be an enemy ship, for Hashimoto had been advised before leaving Kure that a warning signal would be sent if any Japanese vessels strayed into his general patrol area. No such message had been received.

When setting up his attack Hashimoto was presented with the option of using four *Kaiten* torpedoes mounted on the boat's outer hull. Two of them were linked by an access tunnel, so could be manned when *I-58* was submerged. Specially selected young officers – unmarried, with no elderly dependants – who had volunteered to die for the emperor piloted the *Kaiten*, steering it from inside a tiny cockpit.

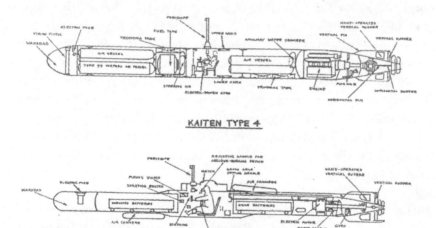

Line drawings of Japanese human torpedoes, in this case a Kaiten Type 4 (above) and Kaiten Type 10 (below). (*NHHC*)

Kaiten were only used if a target was at a great distance or a submarine wished to remain beyond sonar detection range. The IJN's submarine captains were not keen on launching manned torpedoes if close to enemy warships as the sudden loss of weight affected the trim of the launch boat, which might break the surface and be attacked. 'The operator was one hundred per cent expendable,' Hashimoto explained, '[but] most Japanese submarine commanders preferred impact-type exploders [conventional torpedoes]. Human torpedoes were only used as emergency weapons.'[2]

To attack *Indianapolis*, Hashimoto selected Type 95 oxygen-powered conventional torpedoes with combination impact-magnet detonators. Slowing *I-58* down to 3 knots, through the scope Hashimoto observed *Indianapolis* approaching off his boat's starboard bow. He ordered the helmsman to turn the boat so the forward tubes were pointed at the target. From the silhouette in the moonlight Hashimoto thought that his target was a big old Idaho Class battleship with a draught of 51ft. *I-58*'s torpedoes were therefore set to run at 12ft and he calculated the target's speed to be around 12 knots, range 1,500 yards.

Pulling the scope down Hashimoto ordered the first torpedo in a spread of six fired shortly after midnight on 30 July. Putting the scope back up, he saw hits on the target and heard another explosion, but did not see the flash. Two torpedoes hit *Indianapolis* at 12.14 a.m. – one blowing the cruiser's bows off while the other struck amidships on the ship's starboard side, triggering an explosion that made a huge tear in the hull. Within 12 minutes the remains of *Indianapolis* had vanished below the surface. While an attempt had been made by radio operators to send a distress signal, the swift loss of all power meant it failed to transmit.[3] Of the cruiser's 1,196 sailors and marines, 896 survived and made it into the water.

Due to an administrative cock-up at naval operational headquarters in the Marianas and Leyte, the *Indianapolis* was not expected at Leyte and so nobody noticed she was overdue.[4]

What happened next was immortalised in the 1970s Hollywood movie *Jaws* in which a grizzled character called Quint (played by Robert Shaw) reveals to his fellow shark hunters that he had served in *Indianapolis*. Quint explains that to defend themselves the survivors formed 'into tight groups', like squares of infantry facing enemy cavalry at Waterloo. They made a noise and hit the water and 'sometimes the shark would go away and sometimes he wouldn't'.

When a shark snatches a man, so Quint tells his companions, 'you hear that terrible high-pitched screaming. The ocean turns red and despite all the pounding and the hollering they all come in and they rip you to pieces . . .'[5] *Jaws* wasn't far off the truth. Real-life *Indianapolis* survivor Lyle Umenhoffer said of the shark attacks: 'You could see the fins coming and watch them and they would get up close to you like that and you would reach out to them and try to kick them real quick.'[6]

Some men drank seawater and they rapidly became dehydrated and started hallucinating, swimming away from their groups towards mirages of land or phantom rescue ships. '. . . as soon as they get [sic] about 10 or 15 feet . . . a shark would take them,' said Umenhoffer.

Those that went mad but didn't get attacked would roll over and let themselves drown. Other men became aggressive or were stricken by panic, drowning both themselves and the shipmates who tried to calm them down.

Nearly four days after the *Indianapolis* sank an American aircraft spotted people in the sea but had no idea who they might be, so radioed headquarters with a report. A Catalina flying boat was sent out to drop food, water and life rafts to whoever it was. The Catalina's crew saw the thrashing, circling sharks and decided to land and pick up as many people as they could. Just 316 men were left alive and to get them away from the sharks some were tied to the Catalina's wings. The Catalina stayed on the sea until the destroyer *Cecil J. Doyle* arrived and began taking survivors aboard. The *Doyle* shone a searchlight into the sky to guide in other rescue vessels.

There was a lot of soul-searching in the American naval high command, especially as thanks to Japanese Ultra a select group of senior officers were aware of *I-58*'s deployment.

The man who carried the can was the CO of *Indianapolis*, Captain Charles McVay, who faced a court martial in December 1945 for endangering his ship by not zigzagging. Cdr Hashimoto gave evidence at the hearing in the Washington Navy Yard and was asked if zigzagging by *Indianapolis* would have affected his attack plan. Hashimoto replied that it 'would have involved no change in the method of firing the torpedoes, but some changes in manoeuvring [by *I-58*]'.[7]

It was pointed out during the court martial that though it was up to McVay to decide on zigzagging, depending on the perceived level of threat, such a tactic was not compulsory. The USN justified not alerting McVay to Ultra intelligence on *I-58* because penetration of Japanese codes was a very closely guarded secret. It would only be utilised if it brought a major strategic advantage to the war effort.

Had the threat been present when *Indianapolis* was heading for

Tinian with the atom bomb components that might have been the case, but her subsequent voyage from Guam to Leyte did not fall into that category.

Although McVay was found guilty and suffered loss of seniority, the decision was revoked due to his fine combat record and he retired as a Rear Admiral in 1949. McVay never escaped feelings of guilt and shame over what happened and in 1968 killed himself, the last victim of Japanese submarine *I-58*. US Congress exonerated him in 2001.

On 14 August 1945, five days after the atom bomb was dropped on Nagasaki and the day Japan acquiesced to unconditional surrender, USS *Spikefish* sank *I-373* off Shanghai.[8] She was the last Japanese submarine to be sunk during the Second World War.

The formal surrender took place in Tokyo Bay on 2 September and a dozen American submarines were there, in recognition of their part in the strategic defeat of Japan. The British Pacific Fleet (BPF) had 29 submarines and six X-craft assigned to it by then but none of them were invited to the party, though Royal Navy surface warships were.

American submarines sank 214 Japanese naval vessels during the Second World War, along with 1,178 merchant ships, for totals (respectively) of 577,626 tons and 5,053,491 tons.[9] This was about a third of the merchant vessels sunk by U-boats, but the Japanese had far fewer to lose in the first place and once gone could not replace many of them.

Mines sown by American submarines claimed hundreds more Japanese vessels while the IJN lost 127 of its submarines to Allied anti-submarine forces. The USN's submarines also played a key role in scouting out landing sites for amphibious assaults during the campaign in the central Pacific, while supporting General MacArthur's drive through the Philippines and Indies. It was its submarines sinking 66 per cent of Japan's merchant fleet and 16 per cent of the IJN's warships that arguably made the USN's biggest contribution to victory. The submarine force represented only 2 per cent of the navy's strength but achieved an impact out of all proportion to its size.

The formal capitulation of Singapore to the British did not happen until ten days after the surrender signing in Tokyo Bay and the crippled cruiser *Takao* still had a caretaker crew of Japanese sailors.

In late 1945 Lt Fraser and Leading Seaman Magennis stopped off at Singapore while flying back to London to each be awarded the Victoria

Cross by the King. Fraser decided to visit *Takao* and get a close-up look at her. Japanese officers, one of whom had been educated at Oxford and spoke very refined English, gave him a tour of the ship.

The Japanese officer explained to Fraser that *Takao* wasn't blown to bits by the British midget submarine mines because the cruiser's 8-inch shells had been removed. This was common practice for a warship when in port for any length of time, especially if she was to receive repairs or maintenance.

Fraser saw that *Takao* now 'sat on seabed about six feet deeper than when we started the attack'.[10] She had a 60ft long, 30ft wide tear in the bottom of her hull and Fraser asked what had actually caused the flash and explosion. The Japanese officer explained that it was an aircraft crashing on landing at a nearby airfield and blowing up. Even if the attack did not tear *Takao* apart, much of her interior had been wrecked and she was rendered useless as a war vessel.

The final major act by a British submarine in the Second World War demonstrated that even midgets could achieve mighty things despite the effects not being immediately apparent.

How the US Navy's submarines achieved their success was not entirely obvious either. US Pacific Fleet submarine force boss Charles Lockwood would observe two years after the end of the war: 'nothing has been told about the manner in which such outstanding results were achieved by such a relatively small submarine organization'.[11]

According to Lockwood, 'Communication Intelligence' was a vital factor and this came via 'intercept, cryptanalysis and translation of Japanese messages'. Lockwood said it provided the USN's submarine force with 'a continuous flow of information on Japanese naval and merchant shipping, convoy routing and composition, damage sustained from submarine attacks, anti-submarine measures employed or to be employed, effectiveness of our torpedoes, and a wealth of other pertinent intelligence'.

It meant submarines could be deployed 'to the most profitable patrol areas' and also 'specific locations at particular times', with boats already armed with information on convoy composition and the most important targets. Furthermore, said Lockwood, 'enemy course and speed [was] known exactly'. Japanese warships were frequently found in the same fashion – though DF location was rare. As happened in Europe, there were blank spots, during which 'enemy code changes temporarily cut off the supply of Communication Intelligence' according to Lockwood, adding that 'its absence was keenly felt'.

Lockwood explained that during the USN's submarine campaign the number of 'enemy contacts and of consequent sinkings almost exactly paralleled the curve of volume of Communication Intelligence available'. Sometimes every submarine deployed was using Communication Intelligence to hit the enemy where it hurt.

Intercepting and decrypting enemy signals even helped to solve the USN's torpedo problem because the Americans were able to read after-action reports by Japanese ship captains and convoy or task group commanders. This confirmed the contention of angry USN submarine COs that something was badly wrong with their torpedoes. Communication Intelligence also enabled American submarines to evade enemy minefields. Details of enemy vessels sunk, cargo and also how many troops had been killed in a sinking were of enormous assistance in directing the USN's devastating submarine offensive.

The finest tribute to the effectiveness of the American submarines came from a Japanese prisoner who, on being captured at the beginning of 1945, revealed: 'it was a common saying in Singapore that you could walk from that port to Japan on American periscopes'.[12]

PART FOUR

ONLY THE DEAD . . .

1946 to Present Day

'. . . he thought of all they had done together, and all they had gone through both on the field of battle and on the waves of the weary sea.'

Homer, *The Iliad*, Book XXIV[1]

1   The Ashcan of History

Out of 40,900 young men sent to sea in German submarines during the Second World War 28,000 died, a truly horrific casualty rate. A further 5,000 of Hitler's submariners were lucky enough to be taken prisoner. The U-boat force lost 630 of its submarines on patrol, most of them destroyed by British forces.

With the majority of the men he commanded in their graves on the seabed or prisoners of the enemy, the future of the man at the helm of the U-boat campaign remained uncertain in the war's aftermath. Following his brief spell as final Führer and caretaker of the collapsing Reich, Karl Dönitz was taken into custody on 23 May 1945 and transported to a detention centre in Luxembourg. At the requisitioned and heavily fortified Palace Hotel in the small spa town of Mondorf-les-Bains, informally known as Camp Ashcan, he was held alongside some of the other headline acts of Germany's second tilt at military domination, including Hermann Goering, Joachim von Ribbentrop and Field Marshal Gerd von Rundstedt.

Access to Camp Ashcan was very tightly controlled. The only way through the rings of heavily armed troops and barbed wire that surrounded it was, according to one US soldier, 'a pass from God and someone has to verify the signature'. The guards were polite, but found it hard to hide their distaste for the inmates, with one American officer referring to them as 'a bunch of jerks'.[1] The Allies considered summary execution for the German political and military leaders they felt were most responsible for starting the war – and waging it – but it was decided that none of them could be put to death without a trial. They were all to be arraigned before a war crimes tribunal at Nuremberg in Bavaria. This confounded Dönitz, because he regarded himself as a man of honour who had done his best by his country and was no worse than the Allied commanders. Despite strong objections, even from the Royal Navy, Dönitz was charged with waging unrestricted submarine warfare 'contrary to the Naval Protocol of 1936' that Germany had signed up to, along with 'crimes against peace' and 'war crimes'.[2]

Among those who came to see the former Grand Admiral as he brooded on his treatment was a British naval intelligence officer keen to obtain his perspective on why Germany lost.

According to Dönitz, the best chance of success would have been for Germany to possess 1,000 U-boats ready for operations at the beginning of the war.[3]

Even with just 57 in commission in 1939 he did not give up hope of victory, expecting that 'the new type U-boats would radically alter the course of the war', but these were not ready in time. He felt delays in production caused by Allied bombing 'won the war for the Allies' and from winter 1944 more U-boats were 'lost by bombing . . . than were lost at sea'.

Asked if he felt 'to some extent responsible for Germany's loss of the war' the admiral did not give a direct answer. Instead he explained how he worked with designers on new submarine types prior to hostilities and 'from 1938 onwards had pressed for the matter to be taken up as one of urgency'. The army and the Luftwaffe were at the same time 'demanding productive capacity', which delayed the new Type XXI U-boat. On becoming Commander-in-Chief in 1943, Dönitz thought he had finally obtained the authority to ensure submarines were the navy's top priority and to push for a bigger slice of the overall war manufacturing cake. He firmly believed 'an enlightened policy would have struck a proper balance between the demands of the services [for war production] much earlier'.

Dönitz confessed he had never believed that an invasion of England was a realistic proposition. The Kriegsmarine could have managed the job of transporting troops but overall it was 'not a match for the Royal Navy, which would be presumably thrown in to the last man and the last vessel to counter [a] landing'. The Luftwaffe was in his view incapable of defeating the RAF or preventing the Royal Navy from attacking landing forces. Even if the German air force defeated the RAF, Dönitz felt it would still have been 'incapable of keeping the Royal Navy off a seaborne landing force because it had not the necessary weapons'. According to Dönitz, the Kriegsmarine's big surface ships were 'totally inadequate for this task'.

He suggested to his interrogator that his side lost because of a flawed foreign policy 'which committed Germany to a war for which her navy was inadequate' while naval policy 'failed to provide the [necessary] armaments . . .' .

In looking at some of the technological advances made by the Allies that proved fatal for his U-boats, Dönitz claimed to have foreseen radar. Prior to the war he 'pressed for radar development to be taken up as [a] priority by the state instead of being left in the hands of various private individuals who were experimenting with it'. As a relatively junior officer his pleas 'fell on deaf ears'.

In Dönitz's opinion felt the Kriegsmarine's broader inadequacies were a result of the Reich's military being 'designed for continental war, with England either neutral or on the side of Germany'. There was 'a failure of German diplomacy and high planning'. War with Britain should either have been avoided or, said the admiral, 'an adequate fleet [created] to fight a first class maritime power'. Furthermore, Dönitz felt the war at sea evolved into a game of leapfrog that his own side could not win.

'Once Germany was committed to war against the United Kingdom, her whole naval effort was directed against British shipping and sea communications,' according to Dönitz. 'If this campaign failed to achieve decisive results, then Germany's defeat, whatever form it might happen to take, became inevitable.' He thought the anti-shipping effort achieved 'many successes but once Allied anti-submarine measures were fully in operation new tactics had constantly to be thought out, which were then countered by the Allies'.

Dönitz was very angry about his looming trial, the interrogator reporting that he launched 'into a tirade of [sic] the iniquity of his being named as a possible war criminal'.

The Nuremberg hearings started in October 1945 and lasted until 1949, with the principal accused tried in the first year. Dönitz avoided a death sentence but received ten years in jail due to his leading role in running the German war effort. A key reason for this was the testimony of Admiral Chester Nimitz. In a written submission he explained that the German admiral's conduct of the war was similar to the US Navy's own unrestricted campaign in the Pacific, including not rescuing the survivors of torpedoed enemy vessels if it put submarines at risk.[4]

After his release from prison, in 1958 Dönitz published his *Ten Years and Twenty Days*, which presented the story of Germany's submarine wars from his point of view. Dönitz was not aware of the crucial role Huff Duff had played at sea in defeating his submarines, nor of the Enigma codes being compromised, until many years after the war. He did not bother rewriting his memoirs to reflect the latter when the truth emerged in the early 1970s. Dönitz felt it was better for his account to remain a version of events as he had perceived them at the time.[5] Dönitz explained at the end of his book that he had done his duty by Germany and her 'legally appointed Head of State, the man to who I owed obedience' but also confessed to not recognising the 'demoniacal side' of Hitler until 'it was too late'.[6]

2   Best of Enemies

During the Second World War the Allies swept not just enemy submarines from the seas, but also eliminated entire navies. From the inventories of the defeated fleets they cherry-picked a few vessels as war booty – submarines primarily, though taking other ships too, with the Russians even commissioning an ex-Italian battleship into service.

The USA, with almost indecent haste, got rid of 90 per cent of its wartime vessels, for the American public was eager to get sons, brothers and fathers out of uniform while politicians desired a peace dividend. Besides, with no enemies left to fight, there was no need for a large navy. The Russians were not a major naval power and the British were heavily in debt (and would be paying their war loan back to America until 2006). They were unable to sustain their Empire, along with the navy that secured it.

Pax Americana could therefore be established on the cheap, with no need for large, expensive armies or navies. Its most important element appeared to be a new branch of the military, the US Air Force (USAF). As far as most people were concerned it was the B-29 that ended the Second World War, by dropping atom bombs on Hiroshima and Nagasaki, not the submarine. The USAF, which was established in 1947, worked tirelessly to prove that its role in defeating Japan was *the* decisive one.

The air force's bombers were the only means of delivering that devastating weapon – no naval aircraft, surface ship or submarine could yet do it. No other nation had The Bomb either and there was even arrogant confidence in some quarters that the USA could keep the nuclear big stick to itself. A senior air force officer told the other armed services they had better submit to a new reality. The air force was 'going to run the show', warned General Frank A. Armstrong.[1]

It was the same in Britain, where in October 1947 defence minister A.V. Alexander delivered a radical analysis. Even though he had been First Lord of the Admiralty for much of the war he was in awe of The Bomb and the aircraft that carried it. Research into new weapons – and by that Alexander meant Britain's own Bomb – was the top priority, with the RAF and its 'initial striking power' second in importance. 'The third priority is for the maintenance of our sea communications,' said Alexander, 'and, therefore, for the most efficient Navy we can get in the circumstances, and then we will do the best we can for the Army.'[2]

Meanwhile, if the US Navy as a corporate entity had failed to advertise its achievements in the face of the air force's aggressive pursuit of supremacy in national defence, the submarine force was the most silent. During hostilities the USN had been careful to apply strict censorship to the details of submarine movements and missions, also keeping some of their major successes under wraps in order to ensure that the enemy did not change tactics.

A B-29 could drop its bombs and be safely home at its airbase within hours. The boasting about its air raid success could then begin, whereas a submarine that sank a major enemy unit might still be deployed for days if not weeks and at risk from the foe. The use of Japanese Ultra, as Admiral Lockwood had pointed out, required great secrecy, which also helped to paint the submariners out of the picture. In the immediate aftermath of the Second World War there was consequently a perception that the submarine force contribution was less than it actually was.

Even when films and books about the men of the submarine war did appear – both in the UK and the USA – they depicted small, intimate confrontations, claustrophobic contests, rather than grand battles. It was hard to make the connection between a ship being sunk or an escort sinking a U-boat and the strategic defeat of Germany or Japan.

*

There were those in the West who within a few years of the Second World War ending applied themselves to the serious business of how to counter the Russians in any future conflict. At the beginning of 1948 it was decided that the primary role of British submarines was protecting trade from potential attack by Soviet submarines. The following year Vice Admiral Sir Geoffrey Oliver – President of the Royal Naval College, Greenwich, the British fleet's primary centre for intellectual thought on naval matters – produced a paper about the best way to beat them. He proposed placing the Royal Navy's own hunter-killer submarines off Soviet bases in the Kola Peninsula and the White Sea. This would hopefully achieve the destruction of the enemy's boats before they could break out into the Atlantic, where the task of finding and killing them would be so much harder.

That Britain feared the Russian threat may seem quite a turnaround from being allies with the Soviets, but it had been a marriage of convenience. Relations between the British and the Russians in the anti-U-boat campaign were never warm, though some individuals got along well. There was always distrust below the surface, so it was no surprise to British naval intelligence officers that Russia should shape up as a post-war foe.

While the Americans and the British may have seen victory as an opportunity to divest themselves of the bulk of their fleets, Stalin drew a different conclusion and ordered a massive expansion of the Soviet Navy. That it was underway would not become apparent for some years, as firm intelligence was difficult for the West to obtain from inside a totalitarian, centrally controlled police state. Enormous areas of territory were secret zones, just blank spaces on the map.

Based solely on experience in the Second World War, the Soviet Navy might seem poor material to fashion into a major global force, especially its submarine arm. Although massive, it had at best been only competent, despite scoring some notorious sinkings in the Baltic at the end of the war. Inflated accounts of tonnage sunk were delivered to their masters by submarine captains afraid of what might happen if they didn't. The Russian submarine force claimed to have sunk 322 Axis merchant vessels along with 87 enemy warships. The true figure for merchant ships sunk – not including vessels sunk by submarine-laid mines – was 122 (a total of 265,740 tons rather than 938,313 tons).[3]

While Stalin favoured a conventional battle fleet to make Russia a superpower at the top table of world affairs, that plan died with him in 1953. New Soviet leader Nikita Khrushchev favoured investment in civilian infrastructure and industry rather than constructing battleships and heavy cruisers. In 1956 Khrushchev appointed 45-year-old Admiral Sergei Gorshkov head of the Soviet Navy, which he would command until 1985. Hailed as a great leader even by opponents in the West, Gorshkov reputedly displayed a motto on his office wall that summed up his approach to building an effective fighting force: 'Better is the enemy of good enough.'[4]

Gorshkov's vision of the future Soviet Navy placed submarines and anti-submarine vessels at the heart of a worldwide striking force. It was the US Navy's carriers that were feared most of all, as they could sail in international waters close to Russia and launch nuclear-armed bombers, so they were the top targets for Soviet warships and submarines.

By the mid-1950s two armed camps glowered at each other and were ready to repel mass attack. The USA led the North Atlantic Treaty Organisation (NATO) of West European and North American nations – founded in 1949 – while Russia formed the Warsaw Pact with its East European satellites in 1955. Even though their navy was run down the Americans pursued a programme to upgrade existing submarines and build new ones, while the British initiated a programme of reconstructing some veteran war boats. The Soviet Union pursued its own programme of regenerating its submarine forces.

Some USN boats received the major Greater Underwater Propulsive Power, or GUPPY, makeover – including streamlining of the hull and sail, more battery power and a snorkel – while others underwent a more modest refit. What the new or rebuilt submarines of the USA, USSR and UK had in common was captured Nazi submarine technology, which had come too late to save Hitler and the Third Reich but was a gift to the victors. British commando units that raided Germany's Baltic ports ahead of the main Allied force secured some of this technology for the West, not least that which related to the Type XXI. The Russians captured German technicians and shipped them off to the Soviet Union and towed ships and submarines away. The Americans gained some prize people captures, transporting top Nazi scientists across the Atlantic to work on new weapon systems.

In the post-war carve-up of surrendered enemy submarines the USN received two Type XXIs, the RN operated a pair while the French Navy eventually inherited one, which it ran until the late 1960s. The navy of West Germany would operate some of the Second World War-era boats for decades. The Russians took four Type XXIs, which they used as the basis for new Zulu and Whiskey classes of diesel submarines, construction of which began before the end of the 1940s.

A sketch of a Type XXI U-boat, a design that became the template for Cold War submarines on both sides. (*NHHC*)

Devised to project Soviet strike power to the far side of the Atlantic, the Zulus would – if things turned hot – conduct a campaign similar to Operation Drumbeat in the Second World War. By contrast Russia's small Quebec Class submarines were short-range boats with closed-cycle diesel-electric propulsion based on the German war technology used in the Type XVIIB U-boat designed by Hellmuth Walter. They recycled the exhaust gases, mixing them with liquid oxygen, the aim being a submerged speed of around 20 knots. The system proved dangerous, with numerous fires that led to the Quebecs being nicknamed 'Zippos',[5] because they ignited as easily as a cigarette lighter.

Although they experimented with revolutionary closed-cycle propulsion systems, the British found them dangerously unstable, preferring to implement what they had gleaned from the Type XXIs in their radical reconstruction programme for some of the Triton Class submarines. Eight were upgraded as Super-Ts between 1948 and 1956, including war veterans *Taciturn*, *Tabard*, *Tiptoe* and *Trump*. Also modernised were some of the A Class submarines that had been under construction at the end of the conflict.

The Tritons each received a new section that provided a pair of additional electric motors and a fourth battery, giving Super-Ts a submerged maximum speed of 18 knots for short distances. Intelligence-gathering spaces were also part of the remodelling, for it was recognised that a key mission would be spying on what the Russians were up to in their home waters. The casing was cleaned up, with external guns removed to make a sleek boat with a large remodelled fin enclosing the bridge, periscopes and masts.

The Soviet Union's substantial military support for the communist North during the Korean conflict confirmed the prognosis of a Cold War in which the fringes would burn hot, even if the flames did not erupt on the Central Front in Europe itself.

The fight back against North Korea's invasion of South Korea in June 1950 was under the banner of the United Nations (UN) and therefore a multinational effort. The USN deployed an ASW hunter-killer group in case the North Koreans, or their Chinese and Russian sponsors, sent submarines to try to sink American and British aircraft carriers engaged in launching air strikes. In the first five months there were 80 suspected submarine contacts, but during the rest of the war only 16.[6] Task Group 96.7, centred on the carrier USS *Bairoko*, never saw combat, despite newspaper reports of attacks on Russian submarines by American destroyers. These were phantoms and most likely seabed wrecks. The Soviet Pacific Fleet on the outbreak of war had only ten submarines, and commanders ensured they stayed well away from areas where USN warships might be on the hunt. The Russians would, however, transfer two submarines to the Chinese in 1951.[7]

On the outbreak of war the USN immediately sent five submarines forward from the US West Coast to Pearl Harbor, in order to stand by for action. The only boat committed in the early months of the war to reinforce forces already in theatre was USS *Perch*, whose special talents were soon called on.

Unlike the war against Japan there were no long, vulnerable SLOC along which flowed the lifeblood of the enemy campaign. The North Koreans were supported overland by China and Russia. While there was no point of vulnerability at sea, along the north-east coast of Korea there was one where railway lines converged. If these could be destroyed – or at least disrupted – that might check communist forces sweeping down the peninsula, by cutting off their supplies.

One means of severing this supply link was to send ashore raiders from submarines, and *Perch* was tailor-made for just such a mission.[8]

Between January and May 1948 she had been converted into a submarine transport. With the removal of torpedo tubes, a pair of engines and generators, space was created to carry up to 110 commandos and their equipment. *Perch* retained a crew that varied between 35 and 50 men, depending on how many troops had to be squeezed in. As was the case in surface warships, the wardroom was fitted out to act as a medical aid post during combat. Most crucial of all, *Perch* received a snort mast to enable sustained submerged transits into hostile waters, while venting the telltale exhaust into the sea helped preserve stealth. Naval divers could exit the submarine and return to her while she was dived. If she was caught on the surface, *Perch* could submerge in 40 seconds, which was extremely fast for a boat of her size (2,424 tons dived). *Perch* was given a watertight external hangar for equipment, including small boats, while an aerial on the tip of the periscope enabled shore-to-submarine communication by raiding groups so they might inform *Perch* when they were ready to be picked up.

Such attention to detail in converting a vessel once used as a weapon against trade seemed to perfectly reflect a new era in which operations were staged in the shadows, seeking to achieve a decisive effect with minimal footprint ashore, deep behind enemy lines.

In September 1950 *Perch*, under the command of Lt Cdr Robert Quinn, called at a Japanese port to embark 67 British commandos. Their specific objective was to cut or otherwise disrupt railway lines feeding supplies to North Korean forces attacking the Pusan Perimeter.

The troops were from 41 Commando Royal Marines, a dedicated raiding unit under the command of Lt Col Douglas Drysdale, who had seen plenty of action against the Japanese. While operating from *Perch* and also USN surface warships, the Royal Marines wore American uniforms and used US Army weapons, but retained British commando forces green berets.

It took a 14-hour dived passage using the snort mast to reach an offshore position from where the raid would be launched, but the first attempt had to be abandoned. A small, collapsible boat that was to have towed several dinghies full of commandos and their explosives closer to the shore could not be put together in time. A further deterrent were vehicle headlights spotted above the beach; as there was a very bright moon, it was feared somebody had noticed the submarine. *Perch*'s commander chose caution as the better part of valour and so the boat withdrew, using the remaining hours of darkness to charge her batteries before diving.

The following evening, 1 October, the commandos were successfully inserted ashore but were almost immediately engaged in combat with groups of North Korean troops. Holding them off, the Royal Marines managed to place explosive charges in a railway tunnel and culvert.

From the bridge of *Perch*, four miles offshore, Lt Cdr Quinn saw gun flashes and explosions and heard the 'crack of rifles and stutter of machine guns', which he confessed 'wasn't exactly conducive to our peace of mind'.[9] There was a massive flash at 1.15 a.m., followed by the sound and shock wave of an explosion. Quinn knew the objective had been achieved but wondered how many British commandos were still alive. Only one had been killed, with his body being brought back to the submarine when the raiders were successfully retrieved. The next day 18-year-old Royal Marine Peter Jones was buried at sea with full military honours.

Prior to the raid there had been much anxiety in the high command. The Commander-in-Chief of the United Nations Command (UNCOM), General Douglas MacArthur, having previously expressed doubts about the raid's worth versus the risks, only reluctantly gave permission for it to go ahead. Certain aspects of how the raid actually unfolded made senior officers even more twitchy. To extract the raiders *Perch* had stayed on the surface for some hours and this made her potentially vulnerable to attack by North Korean torpedo boats. A decision to send over a destroyer to guard her served only to advertise that something was going on. Subsequent raids by the British commandos were launched from surface vessels.

Between December 1950 and April 1951 submarine patrols off North Korea were put on hold anyway as the severe cold affected efficient operation of the snorkel. During the conflict, which ended in July 1953, USN submarines were deployed to patrol both off the coast of China and the Soviet Union, but in the end *Perch* was the only Western submarine to see combat in the Korean War.[10]

3   Smoking out the Soviets

The starting gun for the contest beneath the seas between East and West was an incident that took place off the Soviet Union on 19 August 1957. It involved USS *Gudgeon*, a Tang Class boat commissioned in late 1952, which between 8 July 1957 and 21 February 1958 achieved fame by circumnavigating the globe, the first ever submarine to do so. It was during this marathon voyage that *Gudgeon*, commanded by Lt Cdr Norman Bessac, took on a somewhat less high-profile spying mission in waters off Vladivostok, which to this day has never received official confirmation.

Bessac had previously managed to take *Gudgeon* under a task group of Russian ships without being caught,[1] so the chances of him getting away undetected again seemed fair. This time Soviet ASW vessels spotted either *Gudgeon*'s snort mast or her fin when she broached just inside Russian territorial waters. *Gudgeon* was relentlessly harassed and kept down for 30 hours. The Russians dropped low power depth charges to try to scare her to the surface until the American boat eventually yielded. As a humbled *Gudgeon* headed out to sea, one of the Soviet vessels sent a light message: 'Thanks for the ASW exercise.'[2] Such a humiliation cried out to be avenged and the US Navy decided to seek payback in seas of its own choosing.

It was a long old haul from their home base at Key West, Florida, but when *Grenadier*, *Atule*, *Grampus* and *Amberjack* set sail in April 1959 their captains and crews were well motivated.

Their official mission was to patrol the Greenland–Iceland–UK (GIUK) gap, the gateway into the North Atlantic for Soviet submarines based in the Kola Peninsula. Mystery craft had been operating off the Eastern Seaboard of the USA and Canada for some time, so they were also to gain firm evidence of 'non-U.S. or known friendly'[3] submarines in the North Atlantic (in other words search for Russians).

Furthermore, stated Admiral Jerauld Wright, the incumbent Commander-in-Chief of the USN's Atlantic Fleet, the first boat to provide this would be rewarded with a case of Jack Daniels Old No.7 black label Tennessee whiskey.

Aboard *Grenadier* 36-year-old Lt Cdr Ted Davis made a broadcast to his men, explaining that to win their tipple would involve a fair amount of risk. Once in the patrol zone, *Grenadier* settled down to wait for a likely submarine contact, which soon transpired. Davis was told by his sonar operators that it 'didn't fit any other pattern we had. No American submarines, no British submarines – this was it.'

The contact faded away but this didn't rattle *Grenadier's* sonarmen. They reckoned the target was heading back home to Russia and if their boat searched in the right direction she'd re-establish contact.

Grenadier had plenty of battery juice to do so, though the air was getting a little foul, not helped by many of the crew puffing on cigarettes.

Davis ordered a course plotted to make a likely interception and that afternoon a sonar operator called out: 'Contact! Close aboard! Port bow!'

The Soviet submarine suddenly turned and came straight for *Grenadier* at top speed, Davis expecting a torpedo any second.

The other boat might even seek to glance off *Grenadier's* screws, or knock her stern hydroplanes or rudder out of shape. Such tactics were a standard part of Russian Navy tactical doctrine. Admiral Gorshkov demanded the utmost aggression from his front line warship captains when engaging with a potential enemy. Apart from *Gudgeon's* rough time there had been another incident in which a Soviet submarine charged an American boat and fired a torpedo with the intention of scaring off the shadower. The sudden turn-and-charge tactic has passed into submarine folklore as 'the Crazy Ivan'.

Grenadier's captain kept a cool head, absorbing the sonar data on the range and bearing of the oncoming Soviet boat. Davis had no idea if the Russian was aware of the American on his tail, or just conducting a precautionary look astern in the sonar blind spot. He decided not to take radical evasive action, or increase his boat's speed, as that risked confirming *Grenadier's* presence by generating more noise. Davis instructed the two officers supervising the passive and active sonars to work together and slowly manoeuvre *Grenadier* using information provided by those sensors.

Grenadier's CO knew that whatever transpired they must not turn away from the Russian submarine, as that would expose his vessel's vulnerable stern. While the junior officers manoeuvred the boat, Davis kept a close eye on them, ready to step in at any moment and take control.

The Russian passed very close down *Grenadier's* port side, the American boat coming around in a smooth turn and assuming the trailing position again. Davis reckoned the Soviet captain 'thought he heard something behind him, but he wasn't sure, so he turned around and did it again. Then we did the same thing and fell right in behind him again.'

Finally confident he wasn't being shadowed, the Russian resumed his boat's voyage home, going at 5 knots. *Grenadier* was 2,000 yards astern of him but the air in the American boat was now depleted it was not possible even to light a cigarette. Lt Cdr Davis decided to surface the boat for some fresh air and to charge the batteries. It didn't mean abandoning the chase, and he sent a radio message to the commander of the Atlantic Fleet submarine force: 'Have contact on Soviet submarine, can track indefinitely.'

This was accompanied by a request for USN anti-submarine aircraft based in Iceland to lend a hand. Keeping *Grenadier* on the surface, with their help Davis reckoned he could still trail the noisy Russian submarine and might even be able to force her up. With batteries charged and air replenished he would be able to dive too, if need be. *Grenadier's* CO recorded in his patrol report: 'We were ready to hold contact for as long as it took to exhaust the adversary.'

A P-2V Neptune maritime patrol aircraft (MPA) arrived just as *Grenadier's* sonar team reported the Russian decreasing depth. Within moments of a periscope emerging the P-2V dropped flares, one of them bouncing off it. Davis laughed at the idea of the Soviet submarine captain being blinded. Having overhead cover was also reassuring. 'I thought that was good,' observed Davis, 'because if he had any ideas about trying to sink us we've got a witness in the air.'

Fed up at being toyed with, the Soviet submarine went deep and silent. Davis ordered *Grenadier* to 'all stop' and broadcast an order for extreme quiet: 'If you're smoking, dump your ashes in your hand . . . don't let your ashes hit the deck.' One of the officers suggested an active sonar ping, but sending out a stab of sound would also pinpoint *Grena-dier*'s location. Instinct told Davis the Russian 'was deep and hovering'.

Things were complicated when a fresh P-2V from Iceland arrived to relieve the first aircraft. It sprinkled too many sonar buoys around, the extra noise making it harder for *Grenadier*'s own sonar to hear where the Soviet submarine might be. 'I needed that like a hole in the head,' said Davis.

With midnight approaching he reckoned the Russian must be near the end of his endurance, thinking 'this guy was out of air; he's out of battery, he's running out of everything . . .' At 12.15 a.m. one of the sonar team called out: 'He's surfacing! He's surfacing!'

The patrol aircraft came in low over the surfacing Russian boat, catching her square in a searchlight. Davis and his crew were delighted, not just with winning the crate of Jack Daniels but also because, as their captain put it: 'we found the first real evidence of a missile-firing Soviet submarine, something our intelligence community was trying hard to get the dope [intelligence] on.'

The Soviet boat remained surfaced for quite some time, with aircraft aloft and *Grenadier* close behind taking photographs and gathering other intelligence, such as sound recordings. Satisfied his boat had gleaned enough, Davis ordered *Grenadier* to break away.

The British also had close encounters with Russian boats and in waters nearer to the Soviet Union. In the late 1950s, Lt Cdr Alfie Roake, a veteran of the Arctic convoy runs during the Second World War, was appointed captain of *Turpin*, a boat engaged in some of the most dangerous work. The level of endurance, stealthy skill and sheer guts showed by British submariners was phenomenal. They risked being depth-charged or striking mines, all while keeping hidden, their crews enduring squalid conditions and often short of water, food and air.

One deployment under Roake's command saw *Turpin*'s hatch shut on Trafalgar Day 1959 and not opened again for another 39 days. The boat spent most of her time carefully husbanding water and air while evading the Soviets in Arctic seas.

Roake likened his contest with the Russians to 'David against Goliath, in my small diminutive "T" boat of some 1,320 tons carrying out a tiny pin prick of an operation against a colossus. We were on our own with the nearest support and succour thousands of miles away.' [4]

On one foray into the Russian Bear's backyard, a Soviet submarine that Roake's boat was recording and photographing from below suddenly dived. *Turpin* dodged out of the way and later the sound of what may have been depth charges was heard, probably the Soviets hunting the intruder in the wrong place. At one point Roake feared that torpedoes had been fired, issuing orders to go deep and turn to avoid them.

On returning home the Royal Navy's diesel submarines got no recognition at all. Anyone going ashore and talking about such intelligence-gathering missions could face a spell in prison, even if they were just telling their loved ones.

The motivation for the risky forays – whether by NATO boats venturing into the Soviet Union's home waters or the Russians sneaking around off Western shores – was simple. Both sides were engaged in nuclear weapons rivalry, with each fearing that the other intended to deliver annihilation. American and British submarines were spying on Soviet weapons tests, many of which were conducted in the bleak, sparsely populated Arctic. They endeavoured to bring back intelligence – photographs, moving pictures, wireless and radar emissions readings – to try and gain the sort of insight that could provide a winning edge should a shooting war erupt. New types of Russian submarine, aircraft and missiles needed to be identified and their respective characteristics recorded. Meanwhile, the Soviet Union's boats sought to do the same by spying on NATO activities.

Also, having fielded the world's first submarine armed with a nuclear-tipped ballistic missile, the Russians tried to place those boats as close as possible to Western shores. They had retrofitted some of their Zulu Class boats to carry two SS-N-4 missiles in the fin (but which could only be launched if the boat surfaced).

By the mid-1950s the Americans had a nuclear-powered attack submarine (a Ship Submersible Nuclear, or SSN) at sea. USS *Nautilus* was the ultimate underwater warship and no longer a submersible. Unlike diesel-electric submarines, SSNs did not need to expose themselves to suck in air and expel fumes. They were completely air independent and could therefore stay hidden for weeks while having enough power to run all the life support systems, weaponry and sensors required to hunt down an enemy.

Completed in early 1954, on 17 January *Nautilus* made history, sending the message: 'Underway on nuclear power.' Commanded by 39-year-old

Cdr William R. Anderson, who had seen plenty of combat action in diesels against the Japanese, in August 1958 *Nautilus* travelled under the North Pole. The SSN's feat showed that no part of the world's oceans was beyond the reach of a nuclear-powered submarine.

If there was one environment that posed extreme difficulties for air-breathing submarines it was under the Arctic ice, which diesel crews could only venture into for short periods and even then at great risk to themselves. They were compelled to search for polynyas – stretches of open water enclosed by ice – through which they must surface from time to time to replenish air.

By making her passage under the North Pole USS *Nautilus* showed how nuclear power in a submarine removed the need for the vessel's crew to be forever occupied in looking for polynyas and fearing a cold, suffocating death if they didn't find one.

A nuclear-powered boat made history again when USS *Triton* carried out the first submerged circumnavigation of the world. Commanded by 42-year-old Second World War veteran Capt. Edward L. Beach, *Triton*'s start line on 24 February 1960 was off Brazil and she took 83 days and ten hours to travel 36,014 miles. Such undertakings had a serious purpose, for the Americans wanted to study how well men coped with a prolonged time under the sea. Psychologists and scientists were part of *Triton*'s complement and they assessed Beach and his 175 men continuously.

This was because the next leap forward in the story of the submarine was to arm a nuclear-powered boat with nuclear weapons. This would make a vessel that at the beginning of the century was viewed as a blundering midget of no worth into the most powerful vessel of war ever sent to sea. The ballistic missile submarine (or Ship Submersible Ballistic Nuclear, SSBN) would be able to launch missiles capable of travelling at thousands of miles an hour and with a very long reach, exiting the earth's atmosphere and then plunging onto the target to distribute death with precision (give or take a few miles).

The launch vessel would remain hidden and constantly moving in the vastness of the ocean. At a stroke the tables were turned on the US Air Force, which had so arrogantly trumpeted the USN's irrelevance little more than a decade earlier. It was now the USAF's turn to be declared obsolete, for no nuclear strike jet could compete with an SSBN.

German scientists played a key role in giving the USA its new dreadnought, though both sides in the Cold War sought to capitalise on Nazi projects for submarine-launched missiles. In 1943 it was even proposed that the new Type XXI U-boats should tow submersible barges containing silos for V2 ballistic missiles to launch points within range of New York.

U-boat captain Friedrich Steinhoff's[5] brother Ernst, who had worked on the V2 ballistic missile and on firing rockets from U-boats, was one of hundreds of German scientists taken to the USA. He joined former V-weapons programme boss Wernher von Braun in the US military's early ballistic missile programme. It is not outlandish to think Steinhoff and other Germans had input to the US Navy's first ballistic missile submarine, with the launch container inserted into the vessel rather than towed. Unlike the V2s, with their conventional explosive warheads, the new ballistic missiles would have nuclear tips capable of killing tens, if not hundreds, of thousands, or even millions.

The Soviets may have been the first to send nuclear-tipped ballistic missiles to sea, but their solution was less than perfect. During the *Grenadier* incident, as the American aircraft circled taking intelligence photographs, Russian submariners had scrambled across the top of that Zulu Class boat's fin. They were trying desperately to hide the caps of her two missile tubes under a tarpaulin. For the Russians, the fate of that boat at the hands of *Grenadier* was an object lesson in the fatal flaws of putting ballistic missiles in diesel-electric submarines. Unlike nuclear-powered boats, they could not remain hidden indefinitely.

The Russian missiles also had comparatively short legs – a 350-mile range – so the Zulus, along with later Hotel and Golf Class boats, had to get to the other side of the Atlantic before they were within range of American cities. The USN had flirted with diesel-electric cruise missile submarines – a pair of Grayback Class boats carrying Regulus, the first submarine-based nuclear weapon – but had decided to back out of that cul-de-sac. They diverted their efforts into creating a fully fledged nuclear-powered ballistic missile submarine.

A George Washington Class SSBN was armed with 16 Polaris A1 missiles (range 1,200 miles),[6] which in terms of combined destructive power exceeded all the bombs dropped in the Second World War.[7]

The boat would dive soon after leaving a home base and remain hidden within thousands of miles of ocean for an entire patrol, using a revolutionary Ship's Inertial Navigation System (SINS) and recirculating air continuously 'scrubbed' to sustain the crew. It theoretically stayed deployed until the food ran out and the crew could psychologically stick no more. In practice the average length of a patrol for a first-generation American SSBN was 60 days. Two crews were allocated to each boat so the vessel could be quickly turned around and spend more time at sea. Their members were carefully selected to be mentally robust and physically fit and were vetted to ensure loyalty to their nation's cause. With their world narrowed down to the confines of a submarine – a claustrophobic space no matter how large – the crews of ballistic missile submarines, whether NATO or Russian, had to live for weeks without sight of the outside world. They were entirely cut off from their families and only had a limited ability to keep fit. They rode with awesome destructive power that, if it was ever used, signalled the end of the world as they had known it. To distract themselves they studied for degrees, watched movies, played board games, made their own entertainments and even built models of warships. An SSBN's officers were continually on the lookout for those who might buckle. They ensured submariners on watch in the lonely, far-flung confines of some compartment were not brooding on their situation. It was best to keep their focus on the day-to-day processes of running sophisticated machinery, though Cold War warriors did not lack confidence in either their cause or the weapon systems.

'It was extremely survivable, assured destruction capability,' said Vice Admiral Joe Williams, who was at one time CO of an American Polaris boat. Williams and his fellow USN deterrent force submariners felt they were 'carrying a great burden for the United States and the free world and that we were running the force that could best ensure the Soviets would not launch a nuclear strike . . . and we were thrilled to be a part of it'.

Among the USN's Polaris submarine captains there would be no hesitation about launching nuclear missiles – if the coded message to do so ever came – though it didn't mean there were no thoughts about the consequences. 'You would hit the targets at the times you were supposed to hit them,' said Williams. 'Did we think about what was back home? Sure we did, but you didn't let that control your actions. It just was not part of the environment that you were in . . . Time to think about that after you'd done your duty.'[8]

Where the Americans led the Russians had to follow and, immediately the USN had its SSBN at sea, work began in the Soviet Union on trying to design and produce the same type of submarine.

For all its technological edge under the sea the West still had great cause to fear the Soviet Navy's submarine force and in the early 1960s it already looked to be a losing battle for NATO.

The Royal Navy's Vice Admiral Richard Smeeton, one of the defence alliance's top officers, gave a rather bleak summary of the situation, explaining that the Russians had the largest submarine force the world had ever seen. It was bigger and more modern than anything in the West, except the USA's, and with a simple mission – to destroy NATO. There was no chance of the Western alliance achieving any kind of victory in a future Battle of the Atlantic without using nuclear weapons to combat Russian predominance. NATO's conventionally armed, non-nuclear forces could only harass the Soviets and would not defeat them.

The British persisted with putting Second World War-era submarines on the front line, still performing the most risky tasks, as they had no nuclear-powered vessels. The new diesel-electric boats the British began to produce in the late 1950s were, however, reckoned among the best in the world.

The first three Porpoise Class diesels were built at Barrow, incorporating all the technological advances of the Type XXI U-boat and adding some British twists (including very effective sonar). Powerfully armed with six bow torpedo tubes, and two in the stern, they could carry up to 30 reloads.

Extremely quiet, they had the same fast dived speed of 17.5 knots as the Super-Ts and by using the snort could potentially conduct an entire patrol of up to six weeks entirely submerged. Should putting the snort above the surface prove too dangerous in hostile waters, they had equipment that created oxygen and removed carbon dioxide and hydrogen from the atmosphere. This enabled them to stay dived without using the snort for up to a week. They could dive to 610ft, although their crush depth was more than 1,000ft, all due to the high quality of the steel used to construct the hull.

It was also possible to distil drinking water from seawater, and the comfort of the 68-strong crew was improved by air conditioning. With a range of 9,000 miles surfaced, both Porpoise and the later Oberon boats would conduct independent operations around the world.

For Lt Cdr Matthew Todd, who had endured gruelling Far East war patrols in the old *Thule* with Alastair Mars, commanding *Narwhal*, the third of the Porpoise boats, in the early 1960s was a delight.

'At last they had built a really good submarine,' he said. 'After years of being in command of elderly scrap iron, I finally had a modern, very capable boat.'[9] Having already taken *Narwhal* out into the Atlantic during a NATO exercise and enjoyed being an elusive, undetected ghost, Todd was required to play the 'enemy' for exercises off Portland, where surface warships were being prepared for deployments.

The incumbent Flag Officer Sea Training (FOST) was Rear Admiral Peter Gretton, the veteran U-boat killer. One day he sent a message to Todd asking for a ride during an exercise, to see what a Porpoise boat could do. The scenario was a convoy attack against two tankers, a pair of stores ships and eight escorts. Todd gave Gretton an opportunity to take a look at the targets through the periscope. *Narwhal*'s captain remarked that he was sure any Soviet submarine commander conducting a similar mission would have read a translation of the British ASW tactical handbook. They would have a good of idea what to do in order to defeat RN countermeasures.

Narwhal made five submerged runs against the surface warships without suffering any attacks by escorts until, said Todd, 'by sheer carelessness I offered fleeting detection to one of the destroyers but shook him off immediately'.

During one incursion *Narwhal* slipped right in among the warships, fired a practice torpedo with an inert warhead set to run under one of them and then cleared the area at 15 knots.

The opposition was totally unprepared for what the fast and stealthy *Narwhal* could do. She was a kind of submarine they had not encountered before – their previous FOST exercise playmates were old Second World War-era 'scrap iron' boats. Todd felt that the RN's Cold War escorts had been denied a chance to do an ASW exercise 'against a decent opponent' for too long. Gretton had his eyes opened, seeing the kind of foe he would have faced 20 years earlier if the Type XXI had ever properly gone to war (though *Narwhal* was even better).

During his time as FOST Gretton received a visit from the CO of a squadron of West German landing vessels that was calling at Portland.

After the usual exchange of greetings, to fill an awkward pause Gretton asked if the other officer was an amphibious warfare expert.

The German replied that he was new to the specialisation, so Gretton asked what he had previously done and got a very interesting response. 'In the former German Navy, I was a U-boat commander,' the visitor revealed.[10] Gretton pointed to a chart of the convoy ONS-5 battle that was displayed on his office wall and enquired: 'Do you know anything about that one?' Looking at the date the visitor said he was very familiar with it and had attacked ONS-5 twice. Impressed, Gretton invited him to his naval base residence for a drink the following day. They discussed the convoy battle in which the Briton had been the defender and the German the attacker.

Not long after this exchange between two former foes a new maritime confrontation suddenly blew up in the Atlantic and Caribbean, during which not just the British Isles but the whole world was potentially at risk of annihilation.

4   By Good Luck & the Grace of God

On 22 October 1962, President John F. Kennedy told the world that Russian nuclear missiles were present on the island of Cuba, just 90 nautical miles from the USA. For a nation that considered itself immune from cities being devastated by armed aggression – at least since the British burned down the original White House and much of Washington DC in the War of 1812 – this was a profound shock.

The 'robot missile scare' of 1945 was all but forgotten, so to have the President go on television and reveal that Russian missiles and nuclear-armed strike jets were in Cuba brought home the peril of the Cold War. How such a situation arose could be traced back to the notorious Bay of Pigs incident of April 1961, when the USA sponsored an invasion by a battalion of Cuban exiles – called Operation Zapata – determined to overthrow communist leader Fidel Castro. In its aftermath Castro turned to Moscow for extra protection. The Russians thought that if

the USA could intervene in the affairs of a foreign state in the Caribbean, then so could they. America had also placed missiles on the Soviet
Union's southern border, in Turkey, while US nuclear weapons were
stationed elsewhere in Europe, too, not forgetting Polaris missile-
armed submarines operating from Holy Loch in Scotland.

The Kremlin saw Cuba as an ideal opportunity to restore the balance
and launched Operation Anadyr in co-operation with Castro, aiming to
sneak land-based missile systems in aboard merchant ships.

The Russian decision to send nuclear forces to the Caribbean triggered a toe-to-toe confrontation between Washington and Moscow in
which each side dared the other to blink first. The world was potentially facing nuclear war and both USAF and US Army senior officers
advised Kennedy to destroy the missile sites before they became fully
operational.

This would require a massive air, land and sea assault on Cuba but
the President realised such a move could trigger a nuclear exchange in
which mankind might be destroyed.

Kennedy believed there had to be another way, a means of exerting pressure on the Russians to withdraw their missiles and strike jets
without combat. This turned out to be a naval quarantine, a cordon of
fighting steel around the island to prevent any more people or weapons
from going in (or coming out). With eight aircraft carriers and 175 other
naval vessels deployed by the USN's Atlantic Fleet into the Caribbean,
Soviet vessels would be told to stop and allow themselves to be searched
or forced to comply. Uppermost in the mind of the Chief of Naval Operations (CNO), Admiral George Anderson, was the undersea threat.
He told senior commanders at sea: 'I cannot emphasize too strongly
how smart we must be to keep our heavy ships, particularly carriers,
from being hit by surprise attack from Soviet submarines. Use all available intelligence, deceptive tactics, and evasion during forthcoming
days. Good luck.'[1]

Even before President Kennedy's announcement to the world the
USN was alert against an upsurge of Soviet submarine operations. A
fortnight before the crisis erupted a Russian boat was spotted on the
surface around 130 miles to the north of the Venezuelan coast. More
alarm bells rang when the Soviet fleet oiler *Terek* appeared in the western Atlantic. On 20 October the Americans sent patrol aircraft to fly
from the Azores to monitor Soviet traffic heading south, which is how

Terek was caught trailing a fuel line over her stern to refuel a Zulu Class boat.

At 11.00 p.m. that night US military forces worldwide – with the exception of Europe, where it might be seen as escalatory – went to Defence Condition 3 (DEFCON 3), requiring an extra level of readiness for action.

As Kennedy told the world about the presence of Soviet missiles on Cuba, a message was flashed to the USN's patrolling Polaris submarines. It ordered them to head for their 'launch stations to supplement silo-launched intercontinental ballistic missiles and Strategic Air Command bombers'.[2] At the same time the American CNO asked Canadian and British allies for help. 'I would greatly appreciate your giving us maximum intelligence support concerning potential undersea troublemakers,' Admiral Anderson wrote to his opposite numbers. 'We have a big job to do and can use all the help we can get.'[3]

Two RN submarines based in Halifax, Nova Scotia, with mixed British and Canadian crews, played their part in trying to detect and trail Russian craft heading for the Caribbean. Other boats set sail from Britain stored for war and ready to trail and destroy Soviet submarines if necessary. A task group spearheaded by the Canadian ASW carrier *Bonaventure*, which included the two Halifax-based RN submarines, covered an area 1,000 miles long and 250 miles broad seeking contacts.

American boats were put on stand-by for a mission to Cuban waters. As a precaution they were to carry out reconnaissance of the beaches across which US forces might seek to invade. This was not a new task – USN submarines previously sent ashore special operations frogmen in April 1962 to carry out beach surveys. Now they might have to check if any landing craft obstacles had since been placed there.

The commander of NATO submarine forces stepped up vigilance in the GIUK and on 24 October the Argentia Sub-Air Barrier was initiated, with US Navy, Canadian and British units establishing a picket line. These forces included ten US Navy submarines and 17 MPAs.[4]

At least three Soviet submarines were thought by then to be at large in the North Atlantic and the Canadians kept a close eye on auxiliary vessels likely to be waiting to replenish them.

On 27 October the Soviet commander in Cuba, General Issa A.

Pliyev, sent a signal to Moscow confirming that 36 of his R-12 nuclear-tipped ballistic missiles were now operational. He said that if ordered he could bombard the USA. Should an invasion be attempted, Frog missiles were ready to nuke landing beaches.

The next day a second Russian submarine was spotted surfacing north-east of the quarantine line but the Soviets had failed to deploy escort vessels with their missile-carrying merchant ships.

They did order four diesel submarines armed with nuclear-tipped torpedoes to the Caribbean, which had permission to fire those weapons if attacked. They were to gather signals intelligence on American intentions as the crisis escalated and to sink vessels trying to land troops on Cuba. USN warships detected these boats and made determined efforts to corner them.

On 31 October one of these Foxtrot Class submarines was forced to the surface after a 35-hour hunt by various American naval units. From inside *B-59* it was hard to tell if the destroyer USS *Cony* was carrying out a full-on attack or if it was just a ploy to force the boat up. Captain Vitaly Savitsky had received advice from naval headquarters in Moscow that only practice depth charges – or 'grenades' – with decreased explosive power would be dropped. Regardless of that message, according to one eyewitness an entire day of depth-charging drove Savitsky to the brink.

Lt Vadim Orlov, a communications intelligence officer assigned to *B-59*, claimed Savitsky ordered the boat's nuclear-tipped torpedo prepared for launch. Savitsky allegedly declared: 'We're going to blast them now! We will die but we will sink them all – we will not disgrace our Navy!' However, it needed three officers to concur before such drastic action took place and during an intense discussion Second Captain Vasili Arkhipov calmed Savitsky down.[5]

With the air growing increasingly foul, the boat's battery power almost exhausted and everybody's nerves on edge, Savitsky instead gave the order to surface. During an exchange of light signals, the Russian captain refused to provide his boat's identity. Claiming to be carrying out 'normal surface running' he declined 'assistance' from the *Cony*. Surrounded by American warships and with MPAs circling, Savitsky's boat was escorted away from the quarantine zone. The following morning *B-59* asked for bread and cigarettes, which the Americans agreed to provide. Closing the distance between herself and the Soviet boat, *Cony*'s bosun used a specially adapted gun to fire a line across in order to carry out the transfer. Thinking they were being shot at, the bridge watch team of *B-59* took cover, feeling foolish when they realised the Americans were only trying to help.

Another tense moment came in the night when a Neptune thundered in low overhead, dropping flares, in order to light up the scene for photographs, making the Russians think they were about to be attacked. *B-59* turned to line up her torpedo tubes on *Cony* and things only calmed down when the American destroyer made a light signal apologising.[6] With batteries recharged, *B-59* dived and continued east, the Americans losing contact as she disappeared into the Atlantic.

During the Cuban Missile Crisis USN units actively pursued 29 suspected submerged submarine contacts, of which half a dozen were confirmed. Between 23 October and 15 November 1962 it is estimated that 136 submarine contacts were also made by the Anglo-Canadian effort. In total, across all patrol zones connected with the crisis, six Soviet boats were found and photographed while three Foxtrots were detected within the quarantine zone. 'So far as can be determined, no Russian submarines committed to the Cuban operation escaped detection and tracking,' reported US Secretary of the Navy Fred Korth.

'By tracking these submarines – and by being capable of destroying them if necessary – the Navy denied their effective use to the U.S.S.R.' Korth added: 'The quarantine operation provided the most demanding test of the Navy's Antisubmarine Warfare (ASW) capabilities since World War II. It was also the first large-scale test of our ASW capability against modern submarines of the U.S.S.R.'[7]

The Americans did not know about the nuclear-tipped torpedoes of the four Foxtrots until the early 1990s. By good luck, the grace of God, the finely balanced judgement of navies and the common sense of both Khrushchev and Kennedy – one agreeing to withdraw weaponry from Cuba and the other from Turkey – the world did not suffer that catastrophe.

5 Their Game of Shadows

In the late 1960s and early 1970s there were collisions between surface ships and close encounters beneath the sea, the Crazy Ivan remaining a favourite tactic of Soviet submarine captains looking to shake off NATO shadowers. Technology devised by the USSR's brilliant scientists and given shape by highly skilled naval architects – combined with advances stolen from the West through espionage – enabled the Kremlin to institute an ambitious naval construction programme during the 1960s.

With Britain no longer the global power that it was, the Royal Navy could not compete in the numbers game with either the Soviets or the Americans. Instead it endeavoured to provide high quality units that could play their part in key operational zones like the Arctic. For that reason it finally managed to enter the undersea nuclear game with the RN's first Fleet Submarine, HMS *Dreadnought*, launched on Trafalgar Day 1960. She was a remarkable product of Anglo-American co-operation, for when Britain hit snags in producing a power plant the USA helped by providing a Westinghouse reactor.

However, a submarine is nothing without a capable crew and is especially flawed if it has not been built in accordance with the highest quality control standards. The sub-surface environment is most unforgiving – errors in handling and construction that are not necessarily fatal in a surface warship can exact the ultimate price. A submarine must be right in all departments at launch, for if it fails catastrophically the boat can be lost along with everybody aboard. Whereas in a surface vessel a defect such as a loss of propulsion would see the crippled craft towed back to port, a submarine could drop like a stone and be crushed. Or worse.

Russian ambitions were undercut by failures in quality control. In 1961 the successful firing of a ballistic missile by *K-19* in the Arctic was followed by a reactor failure on 4 July, off Jan Mayen Island, that threatened to blow up the Soviet vessel. The cause was a meltdown due to a total failure in the nuclear reactor cooling system, which had no back-up.

If it were not for the bravery of the Hotel Class boat's crew – eight of whom sacrificed their lives to create a new cooling system, suffering lethal doses of radiation – millions of people ashore could have been at risk from fall-out. Not for nothing did *K-19* earn the nickname *Hiroshima*.[1]

After the end of the Cold War the Russians would acknowledge seven incidents in which their submarines collided with those of the USN between 1968 and 1987. The Americans have confirmed nine incidents between 1965 and 1975. The British also had a few but they have never officially admitted any. In October 1968 HMS *Warspite* – the third of Britain's SSNs and on her maiden mission in the Arctic – was involved in an incident that even now the UK Ministry of Defence (MoD) claims was an iceberg collision.

At the time two of the Royal Navy's SSNs were equipped for intelligence-gathering, with crews specially trained to operate in the most dangerous Soviet waters. The Valiant Class boat was shadowing a nuclear-powered Soviet Echo II guided-missile submarine when one of the target vessel's two screws was shut down. It was believed the Echo II had turned, so *Warspite* – astern and below to port – tried to follow.

The impact of the collision rolled the British boat dramatically, causing significant damage to her fin and torpedo tubes, with *Warspite* lucky not to have ended up at the bottom of the Barents Sea.

Her XO, Lt Cdr Tim Hale, thought he was about to meet his end.

'This is bloody serious,' he thought, as he waited for *Warspite* to roll back upright. 'The water will come in through the damaged conning tower. I am going to die.'[2]

Warspite managed to right herself and her reactor kept online, despite being designed to cut out when the boat rolled too far. Both submarines made it home, somewhat battered and with their crews subdued by the fright.

The official line from London and Washington DC to this day is that there were no submarines sneaking into Soviet home waters on spying missions. Those boats that came home bearing the scars of that so-called phantom face-off showed that governments were economical with the truth about undersea collisions. Apart from makeshift shrouds draped over damaged submarines on their return to port, a web of lies was spun in the media should anyone happened to get a sniff of the reality – it was an iceberg that did it and definitely not another submarine.

Despite the cover-ups, the evidence was still there in the minds of men who had been deep into the Arctic North. Some of them would never truly recover from the experience; such was the mental trauma they suffered when things went wrong. Submarines could be reconstructed, distracting stories created to hide the reality, but for a few of those who edged into the dark cave of the Barents during the Cold War – battling the dread fear of discovery and death – some part of them never came back. The walking wounded returned in body but not in mind, though the majority of submariners in NATO's intelligence-gathering boats went up there more than once and toughed it out.

There were actual losses of nuclear submarines, too, during the Cold War under the sea, including the American attack boat *Scorpion* in late May 1968. She was destroyed during a death plunge in 10,000ft of water, 400 miles to the south-west of the Azores, along with her entire crew of 99 men. Claims that she was sunk by a Russian submarine persist but are without foundation. *Scorpion* was lost due to one of her own torpedoes exploding in the weapons stowage compartment. The suggestion of a Soviet culprit springs from the Russians supposedly seeking revenge for the Americans allegedly destroying *K-129* in March 1968. The Golf Class boat blew up off Hawaii with the loss of all 100 men. At the time an American submarine was trailing her but in truth she too was the victim of an explosion aboard ship, not a torpedo.

The large SSBN fleets of the Americans and Russians reflected their status as superpowers, but even for them the cost was becoming crippling. By 1969 they were spending in excess of US $50 million a day on creating and operating nuclear weapon systems.[3] The Soviet Union was operating 375 submarines including 60 nuclear-powered boats. At the same time the Americans fielded a force of 156 submarines, a mixture of conventional diesel-electric and nuclear-powered craft. By contrast the Royal Navy had 45 submarines, with just eight of them nuclear-powered, including four SSBNs.

Creating the UK's sea-based deterrent force was still a remarkably efficient project. Taking the Valiant Class SSN design as the starting point, a missile compartment for 16 Polaris missiles was inserted. Not only were the boats built but so was a new base at Faslane on the Clyde and it all took just five years. While American SSBNs were christened in honour of famous leaders – with *Abraham Lincoln* and *Theodore Roosevelt* joining *George Washington* in the first batch – and the Soviets gave their boats numbers, the British vessels had names that could be traced back to the beginnings of England's wealth and naval supremacy – *Resolution, Repulse, Renown* and *Revenge*.

Other nations were also joining the nuclear submarine operators' club. The Chinese began construction of their first SSN in 1968, though it would take them a while actually to commission one at sea. It would be almost two decades before they were able to commission an SSBN into service. The French, meanwhile, prioritised their SSBN programme over building attack boats, with the first of six *Le Redoutable* Class submarines entering service in 1971, three years before serious work began on designing and building an SSN. Both the Chinese (Han Class) and the early French (Rubis Class) SSNs suffered from excessive noise generation, a terrible handicap in combat.

Defence analysts predicted that in any hot war there would be a titanic clash of armoured forces and airpower in and over the Central Front, potentially grinding much of Germany, Poland and Czechoslovakia into dust.

It was anticipated that the whole of Russia's Northern Fleet and Baltic Fleet – along with swarms of maritime strike jets – would come out in a massive do-or-die assault to ensure NATO troops locked in combat on land could not be reinforced or resupplied by sea across the Atlantic. The Russians would also try to prevent NATO forces from breaking into the Norwegian and Barents seas. There were a few variables. *Would the US Navy and other American military forces in the Pacific and Middle East sit back and allow the Russians to focus all their power on the Central Front?* It was unlikely. The Kremlin might gamble on the war being confined to the Central Front due to the West fearing nuclear retaliation if it caused trouble elsewhere.

NATO might find itself unable to cope with much more than defending Atlantic supply lines anyway. Due to the comparative weakness of the Royal Navy and the fleets of other European NATO members the USN would be faced with carrying the main burden, drawing in additional forces from all over the world to bolster its Atlantic effort.

Britain would remain a key player in certain key niche capabilities, a floating aircraft carrier for maritime patrol and strike aircraft and a staging area for troops and supplies heading for the Central Front. Heavily protected air and sea corridors across the Channel and the North Sea would have to be created.

In one nightmare scenario envisaged by NATO planners Soviet tanks would reach the Channel ports within days. Hanging over all this speculation was the dark mushroom cloud of nuclear annihilation, the game changer that made a straight rerun of 1939 or 1940 unlikely. The warped, yet unassailable, logic of Mutually Assured Destruction (MAD) was that neither side could launch a nuclear attack without being wiped out by the other.

MAD was but one part of a carefully graduated system, however.

In any crisis there were meant to be a series of stages, using conventional forces to either deter war in the first place or fight the Soviets to a standstill. Powerful non-nuclear forces were a very important part of the deterrent equation. Yet, for all the resources poured into the military, there were those in the Soviet Union who could see a stark choice laid out before them. The USSR was creaking under the strain of maintaining superpower rivalry with the USA and it had to choose between securing a fair, efficient socialist society and building missiles.

While its leaders grappled with that conundrum, Russia's submariners continued their patrols, taking their missile boats out to try to hide in the Atlantic. Former SSBN captain Admiral Nikolai Ousenko recalled that it was an inherently risky proposition. 'The fact that very tense people were close to nuclear weapons, ready to use those weapons presented a huge danger,' he said, 'and of course we felt uncomfortable but we still had to accomplish our task, like the Americans had to accomplish theirs.' Ousenko reflected that if the day came to launch the missiles then 'it would have had very sad consequences for the world'.[4]

It was a deadly game of shadows in which the stealthiest stood the best chance of survival, of gaining that killer edge. On a Cold War patrol in British SSBNs and SSNs there were various states of 'quiet'. There was 'normal patrol quiet', 'sonar quiet' (to enable the Sound Room to better pick up a contact) and 'ultra quiet' (with some machinery shut down for a brief period, again to help the sonar operators but also to preserve the boat's stealth). As the SSBNs glided through the deep at walking pace, topics of discussion for those off duty could range from the sublime to the chilling – contemplating families who were getting on with their lives far away ashore and what to do if the terrible day ever came.

One topic of discussion aboard HMS *Repulse* during the early 1970s was the possibility of retaining a single missile once others had been fired. *Could it be used as a bargaining chip?* By then, the submarine might be the only element of the British State still functioning, or even in existence.

While the SSBN crews waited for fire orders they hoped would never come, contact with home was maintained by familygrams. These were short, carefully vetted messages transmitted from home base to a submarine for each submariner (if he so wished). Familygrams could convey a range of news so long as it was kept brief, and any disturbing revelations – such as the death of a close relative – were edited out of the message before it was transmitted. Hearing that kind of news while trapped aboard an SSBN for weeks would be unbearable for any submariner – the mission came first not the man, so best not to tell him until his boat returned to base.

With dozens of nuclear-powered submarines prowling the oceans – some trying their best to stay out of each other's way (the SSBNs) and others actively seeking to get into a killer position (just in case The Day came) – it might be thought that conventional submarine warfare was obsolete.

It took a war in the Indian Ocean to prove that wasn't the case.

6 *Hangor*'s Hunt

The Russians were busy offering kindling for brushfire wars between old European powers and those they had previously ruled. The first of the new nations in the Indian Ocean to possess a submarine force was Indonesia (the former Dutch East Indies), which procured a dozen Whiskey Class boats from the Soviet Union. Its first submarine, *Tjakra*, entered service in 1959[1] and Indonesia soon had a large and highly capable flotilla.

As part of a guerrilla war to end European rule its boats were used to insert raiding parties on the shores of West Papua, which was still governed by the Dutch. With the Indonesians gaining control of that territory in 1963, the Australians grew very concerned about the onward march of Russian-backed nationalism so close to their shores, just across the Torres Strait.

The Australians had not operated their own submarines for some decades and since the 1940s had relied on a squadron of Second World War-era British boats operating from Sydney. In 1967, reflecting a sense that it had to do something for its own defence, Australia ordered half a dozen Oberon Class diesel submarines from Britain, which would be run by the RAN.

Meanwhile, British, Malaysian, Australian and New Zealand forces faced down Indonesian expansion between 1963 and 1966, during the so-called Confrontation. This arose because President Sukarno of Indonesia regarded the Federation of Malaysia as illegitimate and a mere fig leaf for Britain seeking to maintain its power and influence in Asia via the naval base at Singapore.

Although it was a jungle contest, due to the archipelagic nature of the territories across which it was staged the Confrontation involved substantial naval forces. These included British submarines that sent ashore Special Boat Service (SBS) teams to carry out missions behind the lines. Indonesia used its submarines to return the favour, deploying commandos to try to infiltrate disputed parts of Malaysia. The British also used their boats to seek a useful edge through intelligence-gathering on Indonesian naval activities, including spying on test firings of missiles by Russian-supplied surface ships.[2]

While the Indonesians were locked in a struggle with the British and their allies, the presence in Pakistan's naval order of battle of the ex-US Navy (Tench Class) diesel submarine *Ghazi* worried the much larger, more modern Indian Navy. In that sense *Ghazi* fulfilled the equaliser role familiar from earlier times, when rising maritime powers could neutralise the superiority of battleship fleets with a few submarines.

With *Ghazi* not long commissioned, on 22 September 1965, during the first Indo-Pakistan War, she had her baptism of fire in the northern Arabian Sea, off Bombay (today Mumbai). *Ghazi* stalked an Indian task group and fired a spread of four contact pistol torpedoes at a frigate, but while two impacts were heard the target was not sunk. Subsequent attempts by Indian warships to sink *Ghazi* with depth bombs from Squid mortars were wide of the mark.

Presented with this alarming demonstration of Pakistan's nascent submarine warfare prowess, the Indians decided they needed to match or even exceed it with similar capabilities. India was also concerned about China sending its submarines into the Indian Ocean, especially as in 1962 the two countries had engaged in a Himalayan border war.

There were negotiations to procure Oberon Class boats from the UK – after all, the majority of warships in India's navy were British in origin – but satisfactory terms couldn't be agreed. The Soviets were only too happy to step in with an alternative, offering submarines and new surface combatants, including Fast Attack Craft (FAC) heavily armed with guided missiles. In December 1967 the first of four Foxtrot Class diesel submarines was commissioned into the Indian Navy, INS *Kalvari*. Faced with this, Pakistan decided to expand its submarine arm and turned to France. Lt Cdr Ahmad Tasnim, former XO of Ghazi, was soon on his way to Brest to receive training in how to operate the first of three Daphné Class diesel boats.

On 26 March 1971 the Bengali nationalist politician Mujibur Rahman claimed independence for East Pakistan, which was to become known as Bangladesh. When Rahman was imprisoned by the authorities there was an uprising, with more than a month of turmoil, causing thousands of deaths and millions of refugees to flee over the border into India. West Pakistan's authority was reasserted but an insurgency broke out, with militants based in India infiltrating East Pakistan.

In a bid to dissuade India from supporting the cause of an independent Bangladesh and providing a sanctuary for the insurgents and military assistance, West Pakistan in early December 1971 unleashed a series of bombing raids on Indian air bases. A ground offensive was launched in Kashmir (a contested territory bordering the West Pakistan–India border). In return the Indians mounted a series of air attacks against Pakistani targets and also sent their army into East Pakistan while blockading its ports.

With the Bengalis emboldened by Indian support the independent state of Bangladesh was declared and fighting in the east ended with 90,000 Pakistani troops and civilians taken prisoner. India did not have it so easy in the west, with several hard-fought land battles raging, while in the air and at sea it sought to exploit superiority in numbers. The Indians staged two seaborne attacks on Pakistan's main port, their larger warships towing the Soviet-origin FAC to within range of Karachi. Subsequent bombardments sank warships and merchant vessels, also damaging the port's infrastructure.

The first of Pakistan's new submarines, *Hangor* (which means Shark in English) was commissioned on 1 December 1969 in France and after work-up both she and a second boat *Shushuk* sailed for Pakistan.

The situation in East Pakistan caused problems even ahead of the Indo-Pakistan hostilities, with 36-year-old Cdr Tasnim receiving advice from senior officers to change some of his crew, just in case of trouble. 'The Bengalis were taken off,' he recalled. 'So *Hangor* now had a mixture of experienced and fresh crew. I surrendered my second in command, Cdr Zafr Mohammed Khan, to go and take command of *Ghazi* as that boat's Commanding Officer had been put ashore.'[3]

Hangor sailed from Karachi on 22 November 1971, in order to be well placed off Bombay before hostilities commenced. While Cdr Tasnim awaited the code word for war operations an Indian Navy task group passed right over his boat, but he held his fire.

It was thought the sea war would be confined to waters off Bangladesh, but *Hangor's* encounter compelled Tasnim to break radio silence and pass on a warning about an Indian task group probably heading for Karachi.

On 4 December *Hangor* received the code word at last, but there was no traffic worthy of an attack in the submarine's patrol box. Tasnim felt this was probably due to the Indians 'being aware that a PN submarine might be there'. Breaking radio silence again, he asked permission for a switch to an adjacent area and received assent. When *Hangor* got there, off Dui Head she immediately detected two enemy anti-submarine warships on patrol. They seemed keen on protecting themselves by sticking to shallow waters where they thought submarines would be unlikely to venture.

Tasnim settled down for 24 hours to see if there were any bad habits of which he could take advantage.

In the for'ard part of the submarine, the Torpedo Officer, 30-year-old Lt Wasim Ahmad, waited for the order to fire, listening to the activity in the control room as *Hangor* stalked the Indian warships. 'At times we were operating so close to the bottom of the sea, there were barely five metres of water below us,' he recalled. 'It was very dicey manoeuvring. I could hear the captain shouting every two or three minutes to the diving officer: "Get me up! Get me up!" We were almost scraping the bottom.'[4]

The targets were *Kirpan* and *Khukri*, both 1,200-ton Type 14 ASW frigates built for the Indians in the UK. On the evening of 8/9 December they were maintaining a speed of around 12 knots, with *Khukri* not zigzagging because, according to Indian accounts, she was testing her sonar equipment and wanted to reduce her own noise generation.[5]

Tasnim knew he couldn't match the speed of the Indian warships while submerged, so he edged his boat to a good firing position that capitalised on the enemy's predictable search pattern. He waited until it brought them close enough for a good shot. In due course, at around 7.00 p.m., about two hours after sunset, they came straight towards where *Hangor* lay.

On the periscope there wouldn't be anything useful to see – especially with the Indian warships keeping their lights doused and with their silhouettes indistinct in the night – so Tasnim put the mast up and used one stab of surface search radar to take the range. It tallied with that produced by the fire control computer from sonar data.

Cdr Tasnim fired the first torpedo against the northerly of the two warships, which was *Kirpan*. A homing weapon, it successfully acquired the target but passed under without exploding.

'There was not enough electromagnetism generated by the ship to explode it,' explained Tasnim. 'This was very demoralising, but this is where your command qualities come into play and so we didn't lose heart but said: "What next?".'

The answer was to fire another torpedo as quickly as possible, before the targets slipped away. The second Indian warship – the more southerly target, *Khukri* – was now very close and the weapon would possibly not have enough distance to arm and run true.

'I couldn't possibly fire a "down the throat" shot,' explained Tasnim, 'so I took a quick decision for what we call an arsehole shot, at the stern. He was passing by quick, so I also increased speed, quickly turned and fired at his stern. The torpedo exploded after about two to three minutes.'

With tons of high explosive packed into an ammunition magazine close to the stern, *Khukri* was ripped apart by the subsequent explosion.

Cdr Ahmad Tasnim, captain of PNS *Hangor* during her historic attack. (*Vice Admiral Ahmad Tasnim collection*)

Displaying Edwardian-style gallantry and calm, the captain of *Khukri*, 45-year-old Capt. Mahendra Nath Mulla, made sure as many of his men as possible got away and when offered a life jacket reportedly responded: 'Go on, save yourselves, do not worry about me.'[6]

Mulla showed incredible calm, sitting in his chair on the bridge as the sea overwhelmed him, nonchalantly 'smoking his last cigarette'.[7]

Aboard *Hangor* 'the explosion was heard loud and clear throughout the ship,' said Lt Ahmad, 'there was a sudden yell of *"Allah ho Akbar!"* from the entire ship's company. There was jubilation all around; everybody patting everyone else's back, shaking hands, congratulating each other.' This was replaced by 'the hissing sounds of air rushing in as the ship sank and cracking of hot pipes as the cold water touched them'.

Cdr Tasnim ordered his boat into a hard turn to starboard to avoid getting under the wreckage.

Hangor's Chief Petty Officer Engine Room Artificer, Mohammad Shafique, was so excited he left his post to convey his congratulations, rushing into the control room and exclaiming: 'Congratulations Captain Sahib!'

A pretty strict disciplinarian, Tasnim responded: 'Thank you, now get back to your bloody duty!'

Having fired two torpedoes, *Hangor* had obviously advertised her

The Pakistan Navy diesel submarine *Hangor*, which sank an Indian frigate in 1971, as she is today preserved at the Pakistan Maritime Museum in Karachi. Deactivated torpedoes are arranged as if being fired from her tubes. (*Usman Ansari*)

presence and the other Indian warship attempted to strike back, detecting the submarine and charging at her location. 'So I fired a third torpedo in self defence,' explained Tasnim. 'On hearing my torpedo, he [*Kirpan*] turned away and increased speed to maximum, but he made a mistake, starting to zigzag and when you're doing the same speed as a torpedo and zigzag, then your speed becomes less.'

Cdr Tasnim was sure the third torpedo had struck the Indian warship, and the submarine's onboard tape recorder picked the sound up, but the frigate got away. There were survivors from the *Khukri* in the water, but Tasnim felt the threat from the enemy was too great to risk surfacing and pick them up. To this day he gives a pretty robust response to anyone who suggests *Hangor* should have done so. 'God damn it [in attacking *Khukri*] I'm not making love. This is a war, with absolutely no question of picking up survivors.'

Eighteen officers and 176 ratings had been killed aboard the Indian frigate, with eight officers and 61 men rescued the following day.[8]

Hangor set course for Karachi, with Tasnim fully expecting Indian retribution because they would be able to estimate his route back to Pakistan's main naval base. He was right and ended up being hunted tenaciously. 'They made life miserable for three days. I could not shake them off. I could not go deeper because the water was only 100m and it was isothermal, with no cold layer which submarines could hide in [and which would deflect sonar].'

Three Indian anti-submarine aircraft and various surface ships carried out a prolonged and intensive search, dropping sonobuoys and depth charges over a wide area. One ship would come from one direction and another from the opposite, the aircraft seeking to drive *Hangor* into their clutches.

The submarine was 'rigged for ultra quiet so that none of the submarine's noise was detected outside', said Ahmad. 'All extra machinery was shut down . . . we talked to each other in whispers. There was pin drop silence all over the boat. I never saw a boat so quiet in my submarining career. Naturally the atmosphere was tense . . . the thought was always there at the back of one's mind that these could be your last few hours, or minutes of life.'

Charging the battery became almost impossible. The snort mast could be spotted while the noise of the diesels might also be a giveaway. Everybody knew that a boat trapped beneath the sea with all battery power gone was eventually doomed to a lingering death along with her crew.

'The morale of the ship was affected,' admitted Tasnim, 'but the nearest the Indians came was a thousand yards. It still shakes you quite a bit, because there are six or four depth charges [dropped] at a layered depth exploding at the same time. During the three days [of the hunt] there was no hot food, there was no water, no air conditioning as we were saving our battery. It was misery. We could not shake them off and when the depth charges were getting nearer and nearer I had two feelings. One was a vacuum in the tummy because death was coming, and the second was a fatalistic, "let's get it over with". Either way I managed not to show it . . . but in my life I've observed there are two types of coolness, one in which you keep cool out of ignorance – sort of *what the hell is happening?* – and then there's the other kind when your mind keeps on ticking. It helps your decision-making. As it was, during our ordeal wisdom dawned on me – in order to shake them off I would have to do something they didn't expect.'

Tasnim is reluctant to say exactly what he did but it seems likely he took *Hangor* back to enemy waters and sat on the bottom until the coast was clear. It was the last place the Indians would look for him. Having taken what her captain admits was 'a long detour course' *Hangor* made it home to Karachi by 18 December, the day after a cease-fire was declared.

On her first war patrol *Hangor* had made history with the first sinking of a warship by a submarine since the end of the Second World War. It was no mean feat for such a young navy against a more powerful neighbour.

Ghazi, on the other hand, was lost with all 82 hands off Visakhapatnam, in the Bay of Bengal on India's east coast, on 3/4 December, officially due to unknown causes. The Indians did claim a depth-charge attack on a contact and a short while later there was an explosion that reportedly rattled window panes in homes overlooking the sea. Various bits of debris and the corpses of some *Ghazi* submariners were found, though Pakistan would not admit the loss of the boat for some weeks.

Until *Hangor* struck, the Indians were absolutely confident they held the upper hand at sea, having suffered no losses. For the other side there had been nothing but grim news of defeat in Bangladesh and heavy fighting in Pakistan. The sinking of both the destroyer PNS *Khyber* and the minesweeper PNS *Muhafiz* by Russian-origin missiles fired by India's attack craft on the night of 4 December were terrible blows, with great loss of life. Fortunately for the embattled Pakistanis, while the Indians deployed three submarines – restricted to attacking only clearly identified enemy warships – they sank nothing. With the sinking of *Khukri* the submarine arm of Pakistan's navy managed to restore some semblance of national honour and pride and even shocked the world. Pakistan was reassured it could rely on its submarines to blunt the Indian Navy, which it could not possibly hope to meet on equal terms with its surface force.

Ahmad Tasnim enjoyed national and international renown for his feat in *Hangor*, followed by a long and successful career that saw him serve as Fleet Commander and retire in the rank of Vice Admiral. Wasim Ahmad was the third CO of *Hangor* and became the first captain of the Agosta-70 Class submarine *Hurmat* in the early 1980s, ultimately attaining the rank of Commodore.

Vice Admiral Tasnim believes the most important effect of *Khukri's* sinking was preventing the Indian Navy from making a third attack on Karachi. Had it managed to do so, he believes 'it would have been absolutely catastrophic'. *Hangor* served on in the front line fleet until 2006. Today she is the star attraction at Pakistan's national maritime museum, with deactivated torpedoes appearing to lunge out of her bow tubes.

7   South Atlantic Shocker

A collection of islands that were a footnote to an imperial past when Britain's navy reigned supreme across the seven seas were the catalyst for a grim milestone in the history of submarine warfare. The Falklands – a one-time coaling station for the Royal Navy in the South Atlantic – lie about 400 miles to the east of Argentina and 7,848 miles from the UK. By the late 1970s, while a military Junta in Buenos Aires obsessed over how to gain sovereignty of the Malvinas – as the islands are known in Argentina – for the majority of Britons they were about as relevant as a crater on the moon. Talks were held about joint sovereignty – despite the opposition of the islands' population – with the UK government seeming to regard the Falklands as an inconvenience.

In late 1977 a small naval task group was sent to the South Atlantic just in case delicate negotiations between Argentina and Britain over the islands' sovereignty broke down.

The frigates *Alacrity* and *Phoebe*, with supporting fleet replenishment vessels, were ordered to stay well away from anywhere the Argentinian Navy might be patrolling, in order not to be provocative. The attack submarine *Dreadnought* was there, too, dived and out of sight but closer to the islands.

A secret submarine deployment might seem to neutralise any deterrent effect – after all, if the Argentinians didn't know *Dreadnought* was there they couldn't be deterred – but she was ready for combat. Sending the large strike carrier HMS *Ark Royal* to the South Atlantic was considered but this was felt too threatening, and would doom the talks to failure.

The Argentinians were actually well aware that SSNs were the UK's ace card and the most serious threat to any invasion fleet should Buenos Aires opt for the military option. Suspecting an SSN was off the Falklands, the head of the Argentinian Navy asked his submarine force boss if his fleet's new German-built Type 209 diesel-electric boats could detect and destroy a British nuclear-powered submarine. He was informed that it was not possible.[1]

Almost five years later, with massive cuts to the Royal Navy proposed by the Thatcher government – including discarding amphibious assault ships, frigates, an aircraft carrier and the ice patrol ship *Endurance* that regularly patrolled the South Atlantic – the Junta decided to chance an invasion.

It believed the British no longer had the will to defend the Falklands and would not have enough forces in the South Atlantic to either stop a landing or evict occupying troops. There was a small force of Royal Marines and some part-time soldiers on the islands and that was it, with *Endurance* due to withdraw.

The old submarine *Santa Fe* – a former US Navy GUPPY boat – was deployed to land commandos near the Falklands capital of Stanley before dawn on 2 April 1982, with the main amphibious force close behind.

News of the invasion hit the UK like a thunderbolt and watching events unfold was veteran submariner Rear Admiral Sandy Woodward. He was likely to be the commander of any carrier battle group the British decided to deploy, something Woodward thought was by no means certain. There were many in the UK and elsewhere who advocated coming to some form of negotiated settlement.

'As far as they were concerned it was "mission impossible",' said Woodward. 'The United States considered the recapture of the Falklands a military impossibility. The Ministry of Defence at Whitehall regarded the whole venture as simply too risky. The British Army considered the operation ill advised because we didn't outnumber the Argentinians by enough on land to guarantee success. The Royal Air Force agreed with everyone else that the operation would fail because the Royal Navy couldn't possibly survive in the face of an Argentine air onslaught. And of course the then Defence Secretary, John Nott, was against the operation because, if it was a success, it would prove that his decision to get rid of our assault ships and carriers in his 1981 Defence Review was wrong.'[2]

After recovering from the shock, Mrs Thatcher was persuaded by the First Sea Lord, Admiral Sir Henry Leach, that a naval task force could recover the Falklands. It would put ashore and support two brigades, one of Royal Marine commandos (with paratroopers attached) and the other composed of Guards and Gurkhas.

The very ships that Mrs Thatcher's government intended discarding were at the heart of the effort, with air cover provided by Sea Harriers flying from the carriers *Invincible* and *Hermes*, but the first British naval vessels to reach Falklands waters were submarines.

Five SSNs – *Spartan, Splendid, Conqueror, Courageous* and *Valiant* – would be committed to action, able to use sustained submerged speed to reach the islands quicker than any surface ship. In addition they could gather intelligence on the situation around, and even on the islands. This would be fed back to the main Fleet Headquarters in a bunker at Northwood, north London. It was then scrutinised by top naval officers and government ministers, with relevant information passed on by satellite communications to the main task force as it sailed south.

Of the submarines, it was *Spartan*, a Swiftsure Class hunter-killer boat – capable of more than 30 knots dived – commanded by 36-year-old Cdr James Taylor that reached Falkland waters first, on 12 April. She was tasked with enforcing a 200-mile Total Exclusion Zone (TEZ), which was to be announced to the world, rather like President Kennedy's quarantine of Cuba 20 years earlier. *Spartan* did not reveal her presence but watched and waited, even though she observed an Argentinian naval vessel laying mines off Port Stanley.

The second submarine to reach waters around the Falklands was *Conqueror*, a 4,900-ton Valiant Class boat. Her captain was 36-year-old Commander Chris Wreford-Brown, a seasoned veteran of patrols against the Soviets and also a former SSBN officer. Wreford-Brown had taken command of *Conqueror* just three weeks earlier and on the long trip to the Falklands pondered how to shape his men psychologically for what might come. 'I took every opportunity to harden my men's minds to the prospect of fighting and to prepare for every eventuality.'[3]

Lt Cdr Tim McClement, *Conqueror*'s second in command, believed there would definitely be war, as neither Mrs Thatcher nor the Junta leader, General Leopoldo Galtieri, would back down.

As it turned out, *Conqueror*'s near future would require a broad range of skills, including intelligence-gathering in coastal waters and landing Special Forces. Just before she had departed her home base of Faslane in Scotland a team of nine Special Boat Service commandos had embarked in *Conqueror*, taking up residence in her torpedo compartment, along with 13 tons of equipment.

Conqueror's first task was to scout along the coastlines of South Georgia and the Sandwich Islands, 960 miles to the east of the Falklands, which were occupied by Argentinians on 3 April. The British wanted to evict them so that South Georgia could become a forward staging post for task force ships should they need it.

Conqueror would act if she detected any vessels carrying supplies or reinforcements to Grytviken harbour, but the sole sonar contact was the sound of the spectacular Fortuna Glacier 'groaning and creaking'.[4] Once the fog dissipated, Wreford-Brown took *Conqueror* in closer, exercising caution as the charts he was using were created for tall ships and steam vessels of the nineteenth century. A periscope look revealed breath-taking glaciers against a backdrop of ragged mountains coated in snow.

As it was winter in the South Atlantic, *Conqueror* would have to watch out for icebergs and there was a setback when rough seas bent her wireless mast. This made it difficult to receive satellite communication messages, though the boat's ability to transmit was not impaired. Using the cover of darkness *Conqueror* twice surfaced so her engineers could try to repair the mast. It was a tricky job in heaving seas, the fin pitching violently, and their efforts were in vain. *Conqueror* would have to rely on trailing her Very Low Frequency (VLF) wire.

On 16 April, three days before *Conqueror* arrived, the *Santa Fe* departed the Falklands carrying naval infantry heading for South Georgia. Experiencing bad weather on the way, and having been warned British surface warships were in the locale, the Argentinian submarine sneaked along close to the coast, hoping to make herself harder to spot against the cliffs.

During the night of 24 April she offloaded the troops and their equipment. It took a long time transferring everything ashore and it wasn't until 5.00 a.m. that *Santa Fe* got under way again, heading out to sea on the surface. *Santa Fe*'s CO, Captain Horacio Bicain, estimated that another five minutes would see the batteries charged but a British helicopter attacked before this could happen.

The day before, *Endurance*, one of several British naval vessels off South Georgia by then, had detected *Santa Fe*'s radar. An exact location fix was not possible but a warning was sent out to other RN units. Fleet HQ in the UK sent a signal to *Conqueror* immediately, asking her to take up position to the west of South Georgia. Unfortunately this message wasn't unscrambled until *Santa Fe* had slipped past, and aboard the destroyer *Antrim* this news provoked consternation. *Antrim*'s best defence against submarines was an embarked Wessex helicopter, but its surface search radar set had earlier been removed to make room for Special Forces troops to be carried ashore on a raid. It was now swiftly put back in and early on the morning of 25 April 'Humphrey', as the helicopter was known, took off from *Antrim* carrying two depth charges.

When the submarine was not sighted, the helicopter's Observer, Lt Chris Parry, decided to use the radar. There would be one sweep only, to prevent the enemy from picking it up and being alerted to Humphrey's presence. Parry had previously marked the various icebergs and other significant pieces of floating ice at the entrance to Cumberland Bay on the radar screen's acetate overlay. He knew instantly that an unfamiliar object revealed by the sweep was worth investigating. Parry fused the depth charges while the pilots, Lt Cdr Ian Stanley (also aircraft commander) and Sub Lt Stewart Cooper, visually confirmed it was an Argentinian submarine.[5]

The Wessex dropped both depth charges – one either side of the boat – the explosions lifting *Santa Fe* out of the water, damaging the submarine's power supply and communications equipment. With the vessel having sustained serious damage, *Santa Fe*'s captain gave up his bid to escape. 'I ordered the boat to be turned back towards the coast,' said Bicain, 'and meanwhile more helicopters were approaching. They started to launch torpedoes, which were fortunately not effective due to the shallow water.'

Only one torpedo was actually dropped, by a Lynx from the frigate *Brilliant*, and according to the British it ran under *Santa Fe*.[6] The Mk46 torpedo was not designed to home in on surfaced submarines.[7] After this, three Wasp helicopters – two from *Endurance* and one from the frigate *Plymouth* – entered the fight and launched missiles.

'Several members of the crew attempted to repel the attack with rifle fire,' said Bicain. 'They prevented the helicopters from flying right over us. Suddenly, one of the helicopters launched an AS-12 missile, which hit and passed through our sail. I was informed one person had been injured, who lost his leg.'[8]

With Argentinian troops ashore firing anti-tank missiles at the pursuing British helicopters to try to put them off their aim, *Santa Fe* limped into Grytviken harbour. As *Santa Fe* settled on the bottom of the harbour – due to punctured ballast tanks – Bicain used the periscope to see if the coast was clear for the majority of her crew to escape ashore. There was a discussion about actually scuttling the boat, but Bicain hesitated as he hoped she might be repaired and get underway later. Once the Argentinians on South Georgia had surrendered – following a bombardment by British warships and an assault by Royal Marines – Bicain was ordered to move *Santa Fe* away from the jetty, as it was feared some of her torpedoes might detonate. A British boarding party was put aboard to make sure he did as ordered.

Bicain and his second in command agreed that once *Santa Fe* was '2,000 metres off the coast, we should sink the ship. We set sail and in the middle of the creek the submarine started to roll. I ordered the rotocompressor turned on, to fill the flooded tanks with air. Suddenly, a British officer appeared [in the submarine's control room] firing his gun and yelling that we were sinking [the vessel]; one of my junior officers was killed. We opened several valves and in flooded water, so that after a couple of hours, the *Santa Fe* hit the bottom, leaving only its sail above the water.'[9]

After the recapture of South Georgia *Conqueror* was released and before departing surfaced in heavy seas to carry out a challenging helicopter transfer of the SBS squad and their equipment to *Plymouth*.

There was a heart-stopping moment when two submariners and a Royal Marine were swept overboard, but they were recovered before succumbing to exposure.

Conqueror headed for a new patrol line to the south of the Falklands, with *Spartan* to the north-east and *Splendid*, commanded by 36-year-old Cdr Roger Lane-Nott, in the north-west. They were covering potential approach routes of the enemy, which had deployed two naval strike groups – one centred on the carrier *25 de Mayo* and the other on the cruiser *General Belgrano*. The nightmare scenario for the British would be a pincer movement, and to prevent that British carrier battle group commander Sandy Woodward strove to ensure his key ships – *Hermes* and *Invincible* – were out of harm's way.

'They accused me of cowardice,' he said, 'and that I placed the carriers and the rest of the battle group so far east of the Falkland Islands I should have been awarded the Burma Star.[10] But a military commander has to shrug such things off. I was the bloke who found himself in charge down there and I thought it wise to avoid disaster no matter what others might say or think. The loss of a ship like *Hermes* or *Invincible* would have been such a blow to British esteem and the morale of the task force I doubt we could have carried on.'[11]

In preparing for his new task of protecting the flank of the carrier battle group Cdr Wreford-Brown studied the UK's TEZ declaration, issued in late April, which said 'any approach on the part of any Argentine warships would be considered a threat to the British, and would encounter an appropriate response'. To Wreford-Brown that was a pretty clear indicator that any Argentinian warships coming close to the TEZ 'could expect trouble'.[12] Yet the Rules of Engagement (ROE) as they stood only permitted an attack if the Argentinians were actually inside the TEZ.

The nuclear submarines were the main enforcers of the TEZ and also the most appropriate, for even a suspicion of their presence could act as a deterrent to the Argentinian task groups. They could also do the job without placing themselves at risk from the formidable enemy air forces that could reach the Falklands from bases on the mainland.

Wreford-Brown had been instructed by Fleet HQ to patrol on the edge of the TEZ, between Burdwood Bank, south of the islands, and the Isla de los Estados. While doing this *Conqueror* was wary of generating noise that might mask the presence of an enemy submarine from her own sonar team while signposting her own position. There was a slim possibility that the enemy's ultra-quiet Type 209 submarines could cause problems and the British did not know where they were, though only one of them was actually available for operations.[13]

It was true that a slow diesel boat would stand no chance of keeping up with an SSN, but British submarines would inevitably have to patrol close to the Falklands and to stand a chance of picking up anything on passive sonar they must reduce speed.

Noise generated by *Conqueror* due to necessary maintenance work by her engineers – or even cooks using the boat's bread maker in the galley – potentially offered the enemy an opportunity to fix her position. Wreford-Brown decided *Conqueror* should use her decisive speed advantage by heading off very fast until the work (or bread-making) was over. She could then go quiet again, giving her sonar operators the silence they needed to listen.

Belgrano was found by *Conqueror* on 1 May, along with escorting destroyers *Hipolito Bouchard* and *Piedro Bueno*. At the same time *Splendid* was keeping an eye on an Argentinian Type 42 destroyer and three A-69 corvettes to the west of the Falklands, but where was *25 de Mayo*? Intelligence sources suggested the carrier was at sea and Cdr Lane-Nott hoped she would join up with the escorts, providing him with a superb set of targets.

Conqueror maintained her trail of *Belgrano* with her own escorts pinging away madly on noisy active sonar, so negating any possibility of detecting a threat. *Belgrano* and her escorts were just beyond the TEZ, so perhaps they felt this made them immune from attack. The enemy warships were at least using the wise tactical ploy of staying close to the shallow waters of the Burdwood Bank, where large nuclear submarines were less likely to venture.

Over the next 30 hours of trailing Cdr Wreford-Brown pondered his potential plan of attack and which weapons to use. His boat's modern wire-guided Tigerfish torpedoes had reliability problems, which made him hesitate to use them.

In addition to Tigerfish glitches, Wreford-Brown also had to take into account that *Belgrano* was a (former US Navy) cruiser and robustly built. Sinking her would need a reliable, big punch and that was offered by the Mk8 – an old but reliable Second World War vintage torpedo for a ship of the same era. Wreford-Brown thought he would only use Tigerfish for a high-speed, precision attack if *Belgrano* dashed for the Burdwood Bank.

As *Conqueror*'s captain considered his attack options, *Belgrano* and her escorts changed course and headed west, away from the TEZ. The Argentinian group's course didn't mean the threat was removed, for at any moment – acting on their own intelligence – the enemy warships could change course and go for the British carrier battle group. *Belgrano*'s 6-inch guns along with the Exocet sea-skimming missiles of the destroyers could do plenty of damage and kill lots of people.

As an ex-submariner, Sandy Woodward knew how to wield SSNs most effectively to destroy a threat. He had even embarked a specialist team of experienced submarine officers aboard *Hermes* to help him co-ordinate SSN operations.

Hermes had the correct communications fit immediately to convey Woodward's orders to the SSNs – the old problems experienced by Roger Keyes in the First World War were long gone – but protocol forbade him from doing so. Thanks to direct satellite communication with front line naval commanders, it was politicians and senior officers thousands of miles away in the UK who were dictating the moves of the submarines that Woodward desperately wanted to unleash.

Northwood continued to run them under North Atlantic-style water space management rules, which were designed for an environment thick with friendly and non-friendly submarines. Against the Soviets NATO submarines were assigned specific boxes and stayed inside them to avoid trailing (or clashing with) friendlies. To avoid blue-on-blue attacks Woodward wanted to bar British SSNs from attacking sub-surface contacts, for he felt Argentinian submarines would pose little, if any, threat.

They would then be freed from having to operate inside strictly controlled water space and be able to go hunting Argentinian surface warships, acting instantly on intelligence and instructions from Wood-ward and his team. Fleet HQ would retain only the right to approve or disapprove attacks but Northwood refused to give up control of the SSNs.

The Commander-in-Chief Fleet and the current FOSM were both senior to Woodward – and also veteran submariners who thought they knew best. Woodward decided to give up arguing but feared it would have a detrimental effect in a situation where swift reaction and freedom of movement could make a life-or-death difference. His mis-givings about Northwood's long-distance control of SSNs and North Atlantic-style water space management were soon borne out.

An opportunity presented itself for one of the SSNs to locate, shadow, and possibly even sink the *25 de Mayo*, which had ten Skyhawk strike jets embarked, primed to attack the British. It was suspected the carrier was in *Splendid*'s allocated box of water, but she had been tasked elsewhere by Northwood, so was not in a position to act before the enemy slipped beyond reach. What made this more frustrating was that *Spartan* was near enough to take action but forced to stay within her box by those infernal North Atlantic rules. Woodward decided he could not tolerate such a situation again so he lodged his own orders on the satellite network for *Conqueror* to 'attack *Belgrano* group' – as soon as he could and regardless of the ROE.[14] This order was soon removed by Northwood to prevent *Conqueror* accessing it when she linked to the communications net. It still served its purpose, galvanising the admirals and politicians back home into issuing new ROE for *Conqueror*, which she picked up on the afternoon of 2 May. Wreford-Brown was now allowed to attack anything he considered a threat, even if it was *outside* the TEZ. Meanwhile, British signals intercepts revealed that it was the Argentinian intention to send *Belgrano* back in to attack the enemy's carriers.[15]

In making his attack run on the *Belgrano* Wreford-Brown was very mindful that 'a nuclear-powered hunter-killer submarine is a big beast and the closest we could get was 1,400 yards – any nearer and we would have been at risk [from being detected] ourselves'.[16]

Conqueror was at right angles to *Belgrano*, on her port beam, with the two destroyers positioned on the cruiser's starboard side. Wreford-Brown intended firing a spread of three Mk8s, which he had worked out with Tim McClement, hoping at least one would hit.

With the torpedoes on their way Wreford-Brown listened intently, counting down the time to impact – 47 seconds. Taking a periscope look he saw the first hit just aft of the bows, 'with a big flash and a bang'. The second torpedo exploded inside an aft machinery compartment. 'When the crew heard the bangs there was certainly a mini cheer throughout the boat,' said Wreford-Brown.[17] The third torpedo missed *Belgrano* but hit *Hipolito Bouchard*, failing to explode but causing shock damage to the destroyer's radar and engines.[18]

As *Belgrano* sank, aboard *Conqueror* they heard the old cruiser breaking up but, contrary to later claims, did not hear the screams of sailors drowning. The Argentinian escorts used active sonar to try to find *Belgrano*'s attacker but their vociferous pinging obliterated whatever chance they had of making a contact. Wreford-Brown gave orders for *Conqueror* to go deep and head east, while well astern of the SSN the Argentinian escorts dropped futile depth charges.

Of the cruiser's 1,093-strong crew, 200 went down with her, many of them killed in the initial explosion and fire storm that spread easily through open hatches and unclipped doors. A further 120 Argentinian sailors died from their wounds and exposure in the rafts. 'We waited to be rescued,' said one of *Belgrano*'s officers. 'We didn't know if we would survive or if it was the end, but we tried to keep our spirits as high as we could, thinking mostly about our families.'[19] It would be 36 hours before they were saved.

Conqueror stayed in the general area for two days, her sonar operators listening to the Argentinian search and rescue ships plying back and forth. Through naval signals and tuning in to radio station news broadcasts, the British submariners learned of the death toll and felt sincere regret. 'They were, after all, fellow sailors just like us,' said Wreford-Brown. 'An attack in a submarine is not like being in an infantry charge with fixed bayonet, where you see the moment of death. The thought processes come later. None of us had a hatred of the Argentinian sailors.'[20] It was, though, a necessary action as far as the Royal Navy was concerned and Tim McClement believed *Conqueror* 'saved a huge number of lives'[21] by preventing an attack on the carrier battle group. Others, many miles away in Britain's Parliament and elsewhere, suggested it was an immoral act, pointing out that *Belgrano* was outside the TEZ and sailing away from it. Such niceties seemed absurd to fighting sailors on both sides, who knew that a warship could easily turn around and that no chances could be taken with a vessel carrying sea-skimming missiles and long-range heavy guns. One of *Belgrano*'s gunners, Ruben Volpe, remarked: '. . . this was a war and the attack was an act of war, not a war crime'. Sinking *Belgrano* beyond the TEZ 'demonstrated the power the British had'.[22]

Belgrano's sinking meant that suddenly the Falklands disagreement was no longer regarded 'as music-hall melodrama'.[23] Now that blood had been shed off the islands Argentinian cinemas stopped showing the British movie *Chariots of Fire* (no matter how popular it was). The Italian government urged a compromise over sovereignty while the leaders of Germany and Portugal issued a joint statement calling on Britain and Argentina to 'put prestige aside and concentrate on a negotiated solution'.[24] On 4 May the Argentinians landed a retaliatory blow on the British with an Exocet missile fired by a French-built Etendard jet. It sank the destroyer *Sheffield*, with 20 of her men killed and 26 injured.

*

Conqueror later achieved a remarkable penetration of the Gulf of San Matías, off Patagonia, sliding through a channel only 150ft deep to gain entry, a very tight squeeze in an SSN. With a periscope depth of 65ft, measured from the bottom of the boat's keel, there was 85ft left for manoeuvre. The topography of the seabed, with pinnacles, made it even tighter.

Once in there the British SSN searched for an Argentinian Type 42 destroyer, taking care to stay just beyond the 12-mile limit. Failing to find her, *Conqueror* withdrew to join other SSNs on radar picket duty off the mainland, watching enemy air bases. Her main role was safeguarding British ships putting troops ashore. This encompassed preventing Argentinian attempts to resupply their own forces on the islands by sea or to send warships to attack the British task force.

Conqueror and other boats provided early warning of incoming Argentinian air raids for the British task force. This was a job that would have been ideal for the *Ark Royal* and her Gannet Airborne Early Warning (AEW) aircraft, but both had been decommissioned in 1978, so the job fell to the submarines. As each enemy strike force took off, *Conqueror* used her periscope and Electronic Support Measures (ESM) to identify the type of aircraft and their number, with the information passed on to Woodward's intelligence cell aboard *Hermes*.

It would give the British defenders 45 minutes of precious warning time and with luck Sea Harriers, with their own air-search radar, could disrupt attacks and save both ships and lives.

While moving to her new operational area *Conqueror's* VLF wire became entangled in her screw. The resulting noise at high speeds potentially offered enemy diesel submarines or surface warships a chance at detecting the SSN. *Conqueror* was forced to choose the lesser of two evils by surfacing, possibly exposing herself to Argentinian eyes (and air attack).

A broadcast was made in the SSN, asking for volunteers to get rid of the wire. It was a dangerous job, for the seas were quite rough. In normal circumstances nobody would have gone out onto the casing, never mind into the water to work on the screw. Eight men volunteered and Petty Officer (Sonar) Graham Libby got the job, with others assisting him from the casing.

Wreford-Brown took Libby to one side and told him that if there was an air attack *Conqueror* would have to dive and this would give him very little time to get back on board'.[25] Libby accepted the risk – and his captain admired his quiet courage. Throughout Libby's 20-minute struggle to remove the wire – in the dark, underwater, wielding a knife, doing it all by feel – aboard the SSN sonar and radar operators studied their displays anxiously while periscope watch-keepers kept their eyes peeled. Fortunately, the task was completed without *Conqueror* being detected, but an officer was washed over the side, though he was safely recovered.

Conqueror's next brush with danger came as she loitered submerged on the radar picket line off Argentina, when enemy strike jets ditched unexpended munitions into the sea before they landed. Tim McClement considered it 'a very rude awakening'[26] and while all the submarines on the picket line experienced 'random bombing' no British SSN came to harm during the Falklands War.

8 Dirty Boat Odyssey

In the nuclear submarine era crews of the diesel-electric submarines that remained in service with the Royal Navy and other fleets took perverse pride in their ability to endure grim conditions at sea.

They revelled in their piratical 'dirty boat' ways and looked on the nuclear submarine force men as pampered pooches – what with their limitless fresh water and electricity, clean uniforms and plenty of room.

For the Royal Navy, the sheer distance between Britain and the theatre of operations – with British-ruled Ascension Island the only staging post – might seem to rule out much of a role for conventional submarines.

Yet also sent to war in the South Atlantic was the diesel-electric boat *Onyx*, which completed a solo journey to the South Atlantic to rival *U-977*'s at the end of the Second World War.

The marathon 116-day patrol took the Oberon Class boat and her

68-strong crew on secret missions in waters around the Falklands under the command of Lt Cdr Andy Johnson. The *Onyx*'s crew endured tough conditions, with even Johnson only managing 'a proper wash' just three times during the entire deployment and otherwise making do with a 'dip in a bucket'.[1]

Roughly 50 per cent of the time away was spent submerged,[2] with every nook and cranny stuffed full of stores, a false deck reducing headroom to a mere four feet in places.

The voyage there and back – a total of 16,000 miles, not including the mileage in the war zone – was agonisingly slow (with a refuelling stop at Ascension). It was not without its mechanical challenges and running repairs. *Onyx* reached San Carlos Water on 31 May and is known to have landed SBS teams on at least one mission. To do so, Lt Cdr Johnson drew on shallow water navigation skills similar to those used by Alastair Mars in the Second World War. *Onyx* also handled early warning duties to spot incoming enemy air attacks and sneaked close to the shore to take periscope photographs of Argentinian positions, scouting out likely landing beaches for inserting both SBS and SAS teams. Big, expensive SSNs could never be risked on such missions – and they were busy elsewhere anyway – but *Onyx* was stealthy and comparatively small. Safely sending Special Forces teams ashore to carry out their tasks was never easy, especially when seas were rough and chucked flimsy dinghies around as they were being launched from the submarine's casing.

A very poignant task given to *Onyx* was sinking the burned-out hulk of the landing ship *Sir Galahad*, which had been attacked by Argentinian jets at Bluff Cove on 8 June. Forty-eight British soldiers and crew lost their lives. To consign them to their last resting place, on 21 June *Onyx* fired two Tigerfish which turned out to be duds, and so resorted to the Mk8.

On the submarine's return to Gosport in August, limping along on one engine, every ship in the harbour sounded sirens and hundreds of sailors cheered *Onyx* home. Nobody knew she had carried back a damaged torpedo stuck in a tube in her damaged bow, the result of grounding on rocks when landing Special Forces. It could have exploded at any moment and had to be very carefully extracted by naval ordnance experts.

*

The actions of *Conqueror* removed the most serious threat to the British task force. 'After the *Belgrano* was sunk the Argentine Navy never dared come out again because it was so scared of our submarines,' said Rear Admiral Woodward.[3] But that did not remove danger at sea entirely.

While *Conqueror*'s sinking of *Belgrano* sent the enemy surface fleet back to port, where it more or less stayed for the remainder of the war, there was one Argentinian naval vessel that attacked the British.

The 1,800-ton Type 209 diesel submarine *San Luis*, commanded by Captain Fernando Azcueta, was active off the Falklands, in waters where the British surface ships operated close to land. This minimised the risk of being found by sonar, due to seabed clutter, and also kept *San Luis* away from deep waters where enemy SSNs were likely to be. The Type 209 was not in great condition, with a leaky snort mast, defective diesel engines and temperamental bilge pumps.[4] Azcueta was new to command of the boat, with many of his crew novice submariners, but the plucky little submarine persevered.

Sandy Woodward had been advised that *San Luis* was at sea and close to the islands, courtesy of an intercepted signal from Argentinian submarine force headquarters, ordering the boat to a specific patrol line.

There were several scares and Captain John Coward, a former submariner but now CO of the new ASW frigate *Brilliant*, judged that on 1 May his ship obtained a sonar contact on an enemy submarine.[5] British helicopters and frigates dropped depth charges and launched anti-submarine torpedoes, but killed nothing other than some unfortunate whales.[6] *San Luis* did launch a torpedo but was relying on hydrophone bearings and not periscope looks. Firing at the extreme range of more than 8,000 yards also made the likelihood of hitting anything slim and the guidance wire broke.

The Type 209 boat bottomed to wait things out, some distance from the enemy's depth-charge attacks. Capt. Azcueta had plenty of time to reflect bitterly on the malfunctioning torpedo, which left him feeling 'a great impotence'.[7] On 8 May Azcueta believed *San Luis* was being trailed by a British submarine and fired a torpedo at the contact, which was probably another whale. The torpedo missed and exploded on hitting the seabed.

On the night of 10/11 May Cdr Chris Craig's frigate *Alacrity* was sent into Falkland Sound ahead of the British amphibious landing ships.

Her scouting mission aimed to test the waters – to see if there were any mines or enemy vessels in there. *Alacrity* would find the mines by the simple expedient of setting them off, a potential sacrifice thought worth it in order to safeguard landing ships packed with troops. Should there be enemy forces entrenched above the proposed British landing beaches their presence would hopefully be betrayed by them firing on *Alacrity*. As Craig's ship steamed in at top speed, sister vessel *Arrow*, commanded by Cdr Paul Bootherstone, waited at the other end to pick up survivors if the worst happened.

Alacrity survived her passage, on the way through using her 4.5-inch gun to destroy an enemy ammunition ship. 'We made a swift exit from the Sound and met *Arrow* for mutual support,' said Craig. 'At this point the *San Luis* fired torpedoes [*sic*] at us . . .'[8]

San Luis first of all spotted *Arrow* and prepared to attack her, but then saw *Alacrity*. With the fire control computer broken, Capt. Azcueta's only option was a wire-guided torpedo manually set. At 4.30 a.m. Azcueta fired, range 5,000 yards, again using a hydrophone bearing. Either the guide wire snapped or the torpedo hit rocks, glanced off a decoy streaming behind *Alacrity* or was detonated by the earth's magnetic field. The British did not spot the attack at the time but they remained convinced *San Luis* was out there somewhere. When ships entered or left San Carlos Water, where British landing vessels sheltered, suitable precautions were taken. Sea King ASW helicopters were available overhead whenever required to check possible threats. On 17 May the SSN *Valiant* was ordered to seek out and destroy *San Luis*. According to intelligence reports the Argentinian boat had moved into deeper waters and was on her way home, but sonar conditions were not favourable and there was no kill.[9]

After the war the humiliated and demoralised Argentinians – who surrendered to the British on 14 June – claimed to have attacked *Invincible*, with one British newspaper reporting *San Luis* firing four torpedoes, which allegedly hit the carrier but failed to go off.

The submarine's fire control problems made it impossible to fire a spread but in the absence of that knowledge at the time these claims were given some credence. While the British task force suffered from periscopitis – a fresh outbreak of that First World War fear of phantom periscopes – *Invincible* was never attacked by Argentinian submarines and nor was *Hermes*. *Conqueror*'s successful attack on *Belgrano* was, on the other hand, the first time since the Second World War that a Royal Navy warship had attacked and sunk an enemy warship. At the time of writing it also remains the only occasion that a nuclear-powered submarine has done so in the history of naval warfare.

After 90 days at sea *Conqueror* returned to Faslane on 3 July 1982 amid much fanfare, with a skull and crossed-torpedoes flag flying. Prominent on it was a ship silhouette to represent the *Belgrano* sinking and a dagger signifying Special Forces tasking. It was rare for any Cold War-era British submarine to receive attention on returning from a mission, but events had rendered overt secrecy redundant. *Conqueror*'s men were shocked at the publicity their boat's activities received. Wreford-Brown recalled: 'While what followed once we reached the area of the Falklands might have created a stir back home – with those famous newspaper headlines like GOTCHA! – we didn't actually know anything about the fuss [in the news media] until much later.'[10]

Reflecting on the war's broader impact, Sandy Woodward believed it 'demonstrated to the Eastern Bloc that the West, if seriously challenged, was not in any way as decadent as they thought. The South Atlantic showed that we would fight fiercely under bloody conditions, take losses of men and equipment, and come back fighting.'[11]

9   Sargasso Sea Chernobyl

By the mid-1980s, thanks to their espionage efforts in the USA, where they cultivated spies who stole key defence secrets, the Soviets were potentially gaining an edge on the West.

They deployed terrifying new ballistic-missile submarines and formidable hunter-killers. The most impressive Russian craft was the gigantic Typhoon Class SSBN, which was as big as an aircraft carrier. Along with Delta IV SSBNs, the Typhoons were now able to strike the West with their ballistic missiles without ever leaving their so-called 'bastions' under the Arctic ice. Russia's latest Submarine-launched

Ballistic Missiles (SLBM) had a range of 5,000 miles. Attack submarines of the Victor III, Alfa and Akula classes protected these bastions, against which NATO deployed highly capable hunter-killer SSNs, such as the UK's Trafalgar Class and the USA's improved Los Angeles Class. Even though the Russians almost attained parity, the West's submariners were on the whole better at gaining their edge and keeping it due to superior training and a slim margin of technological superiority.

By now analysis of what kind of contest might shape up if things turned hot varied. On the one hand it was proposed a new Battle of the Atlantic could be avoided, or at least not made so crucial to the outcome on the Central Front, by pre-positioning most of the equipment and supplies needed for US-based troops assigned to Europe as reinforcements.

When the balloon went up thousands of troops would be flown over the Atlantic in hours, but this was problematic. It would take time to get all the tanks, vehicles and weaponry functioning and the Soviets were not stupid – they would try to eliminate the equipment storage areas and shoot down aircraft with the troops aboard. Sending the troops well before the shooting started could obviate that but it could be an escalatory act at a time of great tension, while NATO airfields were priority targets. Aircraft cannot carry bulky, heavy equipment nor can they transport much by way of supplies, so if pre-positioned materiel was not to be relied on entirely – or had been destroyed – a transatlantic supply line would be essential.

This meant a hot war for control of the North Atlantic and it was estimated 15 million tons of oil and ten million tons of other supplies would be shipped within the first 90 days of any war. This would be for the exclusive use of American forces, never mind what NATO allies needed. That required up to a thousand merchant vessels, with an average of 11 vessels per convoy.[1] It would take a month for the USN to assemble all the escort forces needed for such a job, so the Royal Navy and other NATO fleets would find themselves pulled into a major convoy protection effort.

NATO was predicted to have available between 83 and 146 escorts (even with President Ronald Reagan's 600-ship navy, that reintroduced task groups led by revived and refitted Second World War-era battleships). Russian long-range strike aircraft and surface warships could be expected to prey on convoys and in a far more integrated fashion than anything ever attempted by the Germans in the Second World War.

The RN was at least configured for this by the mid-1980s, having long abandoned any pretence to being a world policeman in favour of a focus on ASW in support of NATO in the Atlantic. It would have to lead the effort to protect convoys for resupplying non-US military forces and indeed sustaining civilians, if the conflict dragged on for more than a few weeks.

The huge Soviet force anticipated to be projected into the Atlantic – from a massive surge through the GIUK – was estimated to include between 60 and 83 submarines for attacking convoys (not including those devoted to protecting their own SSBNs and guided-missile submarines, or SSGNs).

American and British boats would attempt to wipe out Russian vessels as close to their home bases as possible, or try to catch Soviet submarines and surface ships in the GIUK. The Sound Surveillance Underwater System (SOSUS) and MPAs flying from Scotland, Norway and Iceland would assist them. SOSUS was composed of passive seabed hydrophones of great sensitivity linked to land-based listening stations and was used by NATO to detect Soviet submarines and surface warships over great distances.

All the number-crunching and war-gaming was rather academic under the threat of nuclear weapons. It was feared that whichever side appeared to be losing would resort to tactical nukes and this would soon escalate into a world-ending strategic exchange.

In 1983, when NATO staged a large exercise called Able Archer, the Soviets mistakenly feared they were being attacked by nuclear weapons. They only failed to launch a retaliatory strike when a junior officer in the Strategic Rocket Forces relied on gut instinct that told him it was an error in the computerised warning system and switched it off.[2]

Leaders of both East and West realised the Cold War had reached a pivotal moment. Something had to give in order to avoid cataclysm. As if to warn of the dangers, just as US President Ronald Reagan and Soviet leader Mikhail Gorbachev were preparing to meet in Iceland in autumn 1986 the missile compartment of a patrolling Russian submarine caught fire.

The attack boat USS *Augusta* was shadowing the elderly Yankee Class SSBN *K-219* off Bermuda on 6 October, when the incident occurred, but the cause was not a collision between submarines. Structural failure had allowed missile fuel to leak into a launch tube and mix with sea water, triggering a fire. The two warheads mounted on what remained of the RSM-25 missile were ejected over the side, but that did not end the risk. There were still 28 other warheads on board *K-219*.

Captain Second Rank Igor Britanov, on his third SSBN patrol in command, led his crew in a heroic fight to save the boat as she wallowed in the Sargasso Sea. They battled fire and flood and power plant problems but held their nerve despite the very real possibility of nuclear detonation. Two of the crew sacrificed themselves in the effort to fight the fire and shut down the boat's reactor, with four killed in all.

In Moscow an emergency meeting of the Politburo was convened and chaired by General Secretary Gorbachev. Admiral Vladimir Chernavin, the serving USSR Deputy Defence Minister and head of the navy, explained that 'events developed very quickly'.[3]

An attempt had been made by other Russian naval vessels to tow *K-219* but then the situation became hopeless. 'The submarine started to sink,' Chernavin explained. 'We gave permission to nine people who were [still] on the submarine to disembark. A command was given to the captain to disembark as well. He refused. Only when he received an order from the Commander-in-Chief [Chernavin himself] did he get into a dinghy and left [*sic*] the submarine. At 11:03 the submarine has [*sic*] sunk.'

Britanov allegedly scuttled *K-219* to ensure no attempt would be made to tow her home – a risky undertaking for the men ordered to do it and also increasing the danger of some kind of nuclear release. Britanov has denied that he sent his boat on her way, saying he was 'sick of explaining that I did nothing of the sort . . .'.[4] Regardless of that, Britanov was the last man off the stricken SSBN.

When it came to the possibility of subsequent nuclear missile explosions, Admiral Chernavin tried to reassure the Politburo. 'Under certain circumstances, 40 Kg of TNT may go off,' he explained, adding that it 'will not bring about a [nuclear] explosion. The plutonium will disperse and sink. Regarding the charges, they are contained in a metal ball. After it [the submarine] sinks to the bottom, a corrosion process will begin which will lead to the spread of radioactivity. However it will be limited and will not reach the surface. This is a long-term process.'

In stark contrast to the secrecy surrounding the Chernobyl incident in April 1986 – when the Soviets did not initially admit to anything

– rather than cover up what was happening with *K-219*, they kept other governments informed. The US even offered help, while its SSNs and aircraft kept an eye on things. During the Politburo meeting the Russians seemed more concerned about the Americans recovering secret material from *K-219* than the potential for catastrophe. Part of *K-129*, sunk in March 1968 off Hawaii,[5] similarly in very deep water, had been recovered by the USA and that made their fears plausible.

'A question arises,' Gorbachev enquired, 'can they raise our boat to the surface, and if yes, then what kind of information can they obtain?' He was informed there was secret material aboard and, of course, the weaponry. At the Politburo meeting Anatoly Dobrynin – former Russian ambassador to the USA, including during the Cuban Missile Crisis – wondered if 'several ships should be left at the location of the accident so as to deny the Americans an opportunity to try to raise the submarine?'

'And what will happen to the reactor?' Gorbachev asked.

'There will also be corrosion but it happens very slowly, over decades,' said Deputy Chairman of the Council of Ministers Yuri Maslyukov.

Gorbachev concluded the Politburo meeting by explaining he was preparing 'materials for negotiations with Reagan. I will send personally to you the proposals on the main positions for the talks on issues of nuclear disarmament . . .'

Five days later Gorbachev and Reagan discussed getting rid of nuclear weapons at Reykjavik and although they did not on that occasion come to an agreement, it paved the way for subsequent summits that made better progress.

Two years later the Russians ordered a hydrographic survey vessel to the spot where *K-219* sank and deployed deep-diving ROVs. They discovered the wreck upright on the seabed but in two sections, with some of the missile tube lids open and weapons vanished. It was a turn of events eerily similar to some aspects of the plot in the Hollywood movie *The Abyss*, which was released around the same time.[6] Russian fears of secrets being stolen appeared to be well founded, but nobody has ever admitted responsibility. It had to be the USA – no other nation in the world had the capability to carry out the steal and it certainly didn't involve the aliens of *The Abyss* – but its aim was also to make the missiles safe.

*

In the late 1980s, with dozens of submarines from both East and West in the Atlantic, some of them in extremely close proximity to each other, the risk of crashes was ever present.

On 31 October 1986 – less than a month after *K-219* sank – the submarine that shadowed the ill-fated Yankee Class boat was allegedly in collision with another Soviet SSBN, while herself being trailed by a Victor III SSN. The USN has never confirmed the event took place, only admitting *Augusta* was in contact with an 'underwater object'.[7]

An incident involving the British submarine *Splendid* made a big splash in UK newspapers a few months later, provoking heated discussion in Parliament about undue risks being taken. On Christmas Eve 1986, the Swiftsure Class boat encountered a Typhoon in the Barents Sea, momentarily making physical contact. A few years earlier sister vessel *Sceptre* had been in collision with another of those famous 'icebergs' – in reality a Soviet Delta Class SSBN. Fortunately neither boat was lost.

The Cold War seemed to be reaching a new intensity and the Russians were achieving higher force levels and better-quality submarines. By the end of the decade a colossal amount of firepower was at sea – or under the Arctic ice. The US Navy's counter to the Typhoon and Delta IV Class was the equally massive Ohio Class submarine – 18,750 tons submerged displacement and 560ft long. The Ohios were armed with 24 new Trident missiles, which had a range of more than 4,000 miles. This meant the launching submarine could strike the Soviet Union from an even larger arc of ocean.

The British signed up to Trident too, with plans to replace the venerable SSBNs of the Revenge Class with four Vanguard Class submarines almost as big as the Ohios and carrying 16 missiles.

It was a hugely controversial programme due to its immense cost – at least two billion pounds a year – but savings were to be made by leasing the Trident missiles from the USA rather than the UK owning and maintaining them. The warheads would still be made in Britain. The first of the RN's new giants would enter service in the early 1990s, but even by 1986 it was estimated the US Navy's SSBNs alone were able to put 3,000 nuclear warheads at sea and these could 'wipe out the Soviet Union as a nation' by destroying 600 cities.[8] However, first strike by the USA was not likely and the British were never going to mount a unilateral nuclear attack.

In the UK the British were maintaining faith in nuclear-powered ballistic missile submarines as the bedrock of their strategic national defence. Here, HMS *Vanguard* enters her new home base of Faslane on the Clyde for the first time in late 1992 (*Iain Ballantyne*)

There was always the possibility of a miscalculation. Were a mistake to be made in a close encounter between Russian and Western nuclear-powered submarines – either a collision leading to a nuclear accident or an exchange of torpedoes with one or both boats sunk – it might have sparked hot conflict. Nowhere else during the Cold War were combat units of NATO and the Warsaw Pact on a war footing in such close and dangerous proximity. Undersea poker was the name of the game, and thankfully nobody blew it, on either side. Yet by maintaining the pressure at sea, the West forced the Soviet Union's leaders to prioritise their own sea-based nuclear forces ahead of other things, diverting their best people and funds into that effort and away from establishing a sound civilian industrial base.

The Russians in the end had to abandon their side of the arms race, before the USSR collapsed. In that sense the West did rule the waves – or rather it won the poker game under the sea. It is clear – looking across the span of the Cold War – that it was a unique period. The submarine had evolved into the most powerful warship ever created.

The vessels became bigger, faster, more lethal, with the navies of East and West striving to get one jump – or several leaps – ahead of each other. In the end it was the strain of maintaining this effort that did for the Soviet Union. Struggling with poor economic performance, low standards of living, lack of basic human rights and a disastrous war in Afghanistan, the Russians had no choice but to abandon the submarine arms race and accept what followed.

10   Silver Bullet Tomahawk

Russian submarine deployments fell away to virtually nothing between 1991 and 1996 and while a watch was kept in the Arctic, the threat of unemployment hung over NATO's solo hunters of the deep.

They still poked about gathering intelligence in the Barents but found little to report on and for some years the need to find and trail other underwater warships would largely disappear.

To make up for it, a new land attack role kept the foremost submarine operator of the West busy, with the cruise missile added to the weapon inventory of USN boats. The Tomahawk Land Attack Missile (TLAM) leapt to prominence trailing clouds of smoke over the Arabian Gulf as a US-led coalition of nations acted in January 1991 to eject Iraqi invaders from the oil-rich emirate of Kuwait.

Unlike the land-based variant that had provoked protests from anti-nuclear groups outside Greenham Common Airbase in England, the sea-based version was not nuclear-tipped. A tactical weapon, introduced into service in 1986 (three years before the Berlin Wall came down), it was designed for precision strikes at any time of day or night and in all weathers, fired either by a submerged submarine or a surface warship.

With a long, streamlined body, stubby wings, a tail and a rocket motor, the Tomahawk was a descendant of Germany's V1 flying bomb, but with a lot more smarts and a much longer range. Fired from a torpedo tube inside a capsule, once it floated to the surface the Tomahawk burst out, blasted off and sped away, heading towards the coast.

Skimming over land, its computer guidance system would activate, with radar readings compared with a computerised map, a process called Terrain Contour Matching (TERCOM). As a Tomahawk neared the target, it would switch to a camera to track its route, again by comparing it with the map. The precision and power offered by TLAM seemed unreal, especially to the US Army generals in charge of a massive coalition ground force assembled in Saudi Arabia. Ready to unleash hundreds of thousands of troops, thousands of strike jets and also a sizeable array of maritime strike power, they were reluctant to rely on Tomahawk too much.

It was an untested weapon (and so were the US Army's latest tanks but that didn't seem to worry them). The head of the US military at the time, General Colin Powell, told the senior officer in charge of targeting for Operation Desert Storm: 'I don't give a damn if you shoot every TLAM the Navy's got, they're still not worth a shit. Any target you intend to destroy with TLAM, put a fighter on it to make sure the target's destroyed.'[1]

Powell need not have worried, for the cruise missiles fired by two USN submarines and 16 surface warships hit their targets. Allocated to destroy key communications centres and military headquarters the USS *Louisville* was the first SSN to launch Tomahawk in anger, on 19 January 1991.

Cruise missile capability was placing submarines at the heart of establishing what President George H.W. Bush termed 'a new world order, where brutality will go unrewarded and aggression will meet collective resistance'.[2] Tomahawk was to become the silver bullet of choice for politicians eager to hit terrorists or rogue regimes with carefully targeted strikes (especially to avoid civilian casualties).

The Royal Navy did not deploy nuclear-powered submarines into the Arabian Gulf as part of Desert Storm and at that stage neither did the USN. It was regarded as not deep enough for nuclear-powered boats – and so the sub-launched cruise missiles were fired from the Red Sea. British SSNs did not yet have the capability to launch cruise missiles but they did join American boats in patrolling Middle East waters, watching out for air attacks or Scud missile launches by the Iraqis.

The British did still offer a capability the Americans no longer possessed, namely shallow water operations inside the Gulf by diesel-electric boats. They landed intelligence-gathering SBS troops on the shores of Kuwait and even southern Iraq.

The UK MoD has never officially acknowledged the missions of the Oberon Class boats *Otus* and *Opossum*, but some details have crept into the public domain.

For example, in late January 1991 one of these boats allegedly had a close call under an oil tanker in the approaches to an enemy-held port, while retrieving a Special Forces team. A US air strike hit the tanker and the vessel began to sink, forcing the submarine to pull out.

As Iraqi troops in Kuwait recoiled under a massive Allied ground attack in February Saddam issued orders for the skies and seas of Kuwait to be polluted. The destruction of wells, scuttling of tankers and demolition of jetties, storage tanks and derricks released millions of gallons of oil into the Gulf. This precluded further submarine operations as it would have been unsafe.[3] *Opossum* returned home in April and while nothing official was said and she did not fly a Jolly Roger flag, the 27-year-old boat sported pale blue tiger stripes on her matt black hull, a form of shallow water camouflage. Her captain, Lt Cdr Steve Upright, was asked why and gave an inscrutable response: 'All I can say by way of explanation is that we didn't leave Portsmouth with them.'[4]

Otus was not so coy, returning home with the same camouflage but flying a Jolly Roger flag with a dagger on it for Special Forces missions. Further evidence was later provided by the Gulf War campaign medals proudly displayed on the chests of the O-boats' men, who were forbidden from actually explaining how they won them. In recent times some further details have been revealed.

In the shallow, clear waters of the Gulf there was anxiety that an Iraqi aircraft might easily spot *Opossum* when she was at periscope depth, but the most serious threat actually came from mines. The Iraqis created massive minefields off Kuwait and set free drifters to cause chaos in shipping lanes. One almost sank an American frigate in the Gulf during the Tanker War of the late 1980s and in Desert Storm mine strikes inflicted major damage on a USN assault carrier and a guided-missile cruiser.

Opossum's job was to go right among the mines to reach waters off Kuwait and Steve Upright confessed some years later: '. . . the biggest worry was mines. You simply couldn't know if they were there until too late.' The British boat surfaced at night to take in fresh air and charge batteries and doing so in the mine-infested northern Gulf tended to 'concentrate the mind'.

The rigours of life in a diesel-electric submarine remained much the same as they had been in the Second World War or early Cold War. Improved snort ability and better batteries meant a boat like *Opossum* could stay dived with the hatch shut for nearly three months but with 70 people packed into her she 'smelled of diesel, sweat and cabbage waters', according to Upright. But, he said, that didn't bother his men who 'quite happily' endured such conditions. It was the outside world they found revolting: 'the worst smell in the world is when you open the hatch after 85 days . . . Fresh air is absolutely disgusting and made some of the men feel sick.'

During Desert Storm even senior military commanders in theatre were told that submarines could not actually deploy into the Gulf. 'If a submarine's presence is known it becomes vulnerable,' explained Upright. 'That's why so few people know where they are.'[5]

In late March 1999, when NATO wanted to halt Serbia's ethnic cleansing and genocide in its rebellious province of Kosovo, it was the cruise missiles of submarines and surface warships that kicked in the door for conventional strike jets.

It was the first hot campaign waged by NATO in its history.[6] Yet this war to stop war aroused considerable protest, with both China and Russia against it. While even NATO refused to describe Operation Allied Force as a war, distinctly warlike Tomahawks were launched from the Adriatic to destroy key elements of Serbia's air defence systems.

As NATO Supreme Allied Commander Europe (SACEUR) General Wesley Clark ordered the alliance's forces into action he imagined 'spouts of seawater as the submarine-based missiles catapult out of the ocean, fins unfolding and booster igniting'.[7] Radar stations on the coast of Montenegro were the first to be eliminated, with cruise missile strikes and bombers then moving further inland to hit targets in Serbia itself.

The British were by 1999 in the Tomahawk game, the RN Submarine Service becoming the second force in the world to use TLAM in combat, acting alongside the American boats. The aim was to persuade the Serbs to stop their ethnic cleansing campaign and accept an international peacekeeping force in Kosovo.

After trials with the TLAM in the USA the UK had ordered 65 missiles in the Block III configuration, with *Splendid* the first British submarine to launch one in anger. Once the missile was on its way, her CO, 38-year-old Cdr Richard Barker, flashed a signal to the captain of *Turbulent*, another (at the time non-Tomahawk) British SSN closer to the Balkan shore. It consisted of one word: 'Duck!'[8]

For all the formidable NATO firepower arrayed against them the Serbs in Kosovo were very resilient. They used camouflage to hide key military facilities and distracted NATO air strikes away from real tanks and military vehicles with decoys. They also dispersed potential targets and minimised the use of radar to avoid being detected and attacked.[9]

When British PM Tony Blair received a briefing on the first day of the Kosovo operation, 'he learned that the RAF's Harriers had all missed their targets, while a missile fired by a British submarine had nearly sunk a French frigate'.[10]

Up to 1,000 aircraft were involved in the air campaign and both the USN and the RN sent carrier strike groups and other surface warships. The French contributed an aircraft carrier, frigates and also two nuclear-powered attack submarines – *Saphir* and *Améthyste* – while the USN sent two SSNs.[11]

In the war-that-wasn't 329 cruise missiles were fired in total, with *Splendid*, the USN boats and six American surface warships launching 218 of them in 'preplanned and quick-reactions strikes'.[12] The British boat fired 16 TLAMs.[13]

The air bombardment was the beginning and end of war-fighting by NATO forces in Kosovo and Serbia. The sea-launched cruise missiles, while a small proportion of the overall total of munitions expended, tackled some of the more heavily defended targets and vital infrastructure, but 500 civilians were still killed by all kinds of NATO air attack.[14]

Submarine-launched cruise missiles may have played their part in stopping Serbia's slaughter of the Kosovars but Slobodan Milošević – the strong man of Belgrade held responsible for so much bloodshed across the Balkans – still clung on to power. There was an attempt to assassinate him on 7 May but the intelligence used was faulty and instead of hitting his Belgrade villa three cruise missiles slammed into Chinese Embassy buildings.

It caused an almighty diplomatic row between Washington DC and Beijing, but the possibility that next time a Tomahawk might come through his bedroom window must have given Milošević food for thought. During the Serbian elections in 2000, reports that a cruise missile-armed British submarine was in the Adriatic ready to shoot are said to have persuaded him to abide by the ballot box and relinquish power (rather than mount a brutal crackdown).

11   Agents of Decapitation

The roar of sea-launched cruise missile rocket motors was not confined to European skies in the late 1990s. President Bill Clinton pressed the button on strikes in response to attacks by the Al-Qaeda terror group on US embassies in East Africa. He also used them to punish the rogue regime of Saddam Hussein, who remained a thorn in the international community's side despite his defeat in 1991.

Operation Desert Fox was launched in December 1998 as punishment for Saddam not co-operating with UN weapons inspectors, who were seeking to nail down whether or not the Iraqis were still pursuing WMD. More cruise missiles were fired by ships and submarines than during Desert Storm – around 200 TLAMs on the first night alone – in addition to air strikes by B-52 bombers, carrier-based jets and other coalition aircraft. In all, across four days, 415 cruise missiles were launched, including some from the attack submarine USS *Miami*. When asked if killing Saddam Hussein was the aim, a senior US military officer responded: 'We have not been tracking Saddam Hussein and he was not an objective . . .'

Al-Qaeda leader Osama bin Laden was certainly a likely target after an October 2000 suicide boat attack on the American destroyer USS *Cole* in Aden harbour almost sank the ship and killed 17 of her crew while injuring a further 39.

Bin Laden was swiftly identified as the likely mastermind – and a cruise missile strike was planned – but a US inquiry took almost a year to decide that he was definitely responsible.

Before the Americans could act – and nearly 60 years after Otto

Skorzeny proposed using volunteers to guide V1 flying bombs to targets in New York – Al-Qaeda terrorists piloted civilian airliners into the World Trade Center towers. They were demolished and almost three thousand people were killed, bringing fear to a city the Nazis failed to hit.

As retribution for the 9-11 attacks on the USA, American and British submarines launched cruise missiles just over a month later to hit Al-Qaeda targets in Afghanistan. This was a little ironic, for on replacing Bill Clinton as US Commander-in-Chief, President George W. Bush had poured scorn on using them. 'The antiseptic notion of launching a cruise missile into some guy's, you know, tent, really is a joke,' said President Bush. He felt that was something 'impotent America . . . a flaccid, you know, kind of technologically competent but not very tough country' would do. Bush wanted to take action that amounted to more than just 'to launch a cruise missile out of a submarine and that'd be it'.[1]

After the 9-11 attacks Bush did not wait for an inquiry to try to kill bin Laden and wipe out his network of bases in Afghanistan. He unleashed strike jets and heavy bombers, aiming to help the rebel Northern Alliance overthrow the Taliban regime in Kabul for daring to host bin Laden.

The British and American nuclear-powered submarines fired their cruise missiles from the Arabian Sea in the first wave of Anglo-US strikes on 7 October 2001. The SSNs *Trafalgar* and *Triumph* were among the shooters on 13 October too, but by then there was not much left to destroy.

Hugely impressive and powerful technology, designed for use in conventional warfare against a state foe, was again being used to try to kill an individual. While a few flyblown terrorist camps may have been reduced to rubble and ashes and Al-Qaeda foot soldiers killed, bin Laden escaped.

It was now possible thanks to satellite technology to communicate almost instantly with submarines, but the time lag between accurate intelligence being received and cruise missiles being launched was still too long. This would not prevent another attempt to use cruise missiles for an assassination in March 2003. Seeking to conclude the unfinished business of his father's 1991 Gulf War, President Bush authorised strikes against the Dora Farms, a collection of villas on the Tigris where intelligence sources said Saddam was hiding.

Warships and submarines in the Gulf and the Red Sea joined jets in targeting both the Dora Farms and important command and control facilities elsewhere in Baghdad.

The assassination attempt was an on-the-hoof action, as the main attack was not due to start until the following night. Forty cruise missiles were fired just before dawn on 20 March, including from the attack submarines *Montpelier* and *Cheyenne*, but some American officials would later conclude the CIA was deliberately fed false information.[2]

The Iraqis were not stupid, with Saddam especially wily, and nobody in their right minds would stay in a presidential residence with coalition strikes looming.

On 21 March the much-vaunted 'Shock and Awe' offensive was finally launched, aiming to destroy the regime's ability to repress the Iraqi people so they might rise up and overthrow Saddam.

After night fell HMS *Splendid* fired TLAMs along with the American attack submarines *Columbia* and *Providence*, while the USN had a further five SSNs ready to shoot in the Red Sea, the Eastern Mediterranean or waters around Arabia. The submarine strikes were regarded as absolutely vital to the chosen decapitation strategy. By taking out the key elements of the dictatorship's ability to control the Iraqi people and command troops in battle, it was hoped invasion forces would be able to topple the so-called 'Beast of Baghdad' as quickly as possible. Ridding the world of Saddam's alleged WMD was the official aim of the assault, but clearly it was all about regime change.

Many hundreds of precision-guided bombs were dropped and 300 cruise missiles fired, later rationalised as seeking 'specific effects on the enemy that led to a rapid collapse of the enemy's willingness and ability to fight, without having to go through a time-consuming and potentially costly effort to destroy the bulk of the enemy's military forces through a gradual process of attrition'.[3]

Yet it was so precise – causing minimal damage and civilian casualties despite the pyrotechnics – that it did not cause the massive psychological damage needed to create a regime implosion. The ability of Saddam to continue broadcasting propaganda via state television ensured the Iraqi people believed he was enduring and might even win.

A specific target for one British submarine was the main headquarters of the Iraqi intelligence service in Baghdad. According to UK Defence Secretary Geoff Hoon a single Tomahawk strike 'had significant effect on the ability of the Iraqi intelligence service to contribute to the internal repression carried out by Saddam Hussein's regime'.[4]

The time between sensors – spies and Special Forces on the ground, or satellites and reconnaissance aircraft overhead – detecting a target and relaying information to TLAM-armed submarines, surface warships and strike jets – *the shooters* – had been reduced from an average of six hours in 1991 to as little as 45 minutes in 2003.

'The whole situation was very fluid, with changing targeting requirements and time lines,' explained HMS *Turbulent*'s captain, Cdr Andrew McKendrick.[5] 'Exactly where we would end up and what we would be doing was not known.'

With *Turbulent* gliding below the surface of the Gulf – proving that nuclear-powered submarines could operate in there – to keep track of the events in the wider world the submarine's men listened to the BBC World Service. According to the SSN's captain 'the best source of news was via a UK liaison officer in the [USN] 5th Fleet strike cell, who e-mailed us Web pages, including video clips of football matches back home'.

Turbulent's submariners were well aware of 'the massive amount of media coverage of all the opposition to war and preparations in the Gulf', which, felt Cdr McKendrick, 'must have been difficult for our families to deal with. In the submarine, although we knew there was disagreement, we had no idea of the scale of disharmony going on in the international community, but we did worry about the impact on our families. We did get a lot of e-mails from back home, most of which said "good luck . . . you are doing a good job . . . we are proud of you".'

The Gulf was by then packed with Allied shipping, including a Royal Navy amphibious assault force that included the helicopter carriers *Ark Royal* and *Ocean*. They would soon launch the biggest airborne assault by Royal Marines since Suez in 1956. In the meantime *Turbulent* waited, being careful to avoid getting entangled with surface ships.

'Ensuring the crew was busy enough during the waiting period to keep boredom at bay, while not getting them too hyperactive, was a challenge,' admitted McKendrick. 'But, as time wore on, the notice to fire TLAM was being reduced, so we knew something was about to happen.'

Still on station below the waves in the Gulf was *Splendid*, ready once again to launch cruise missiles, and both she and *Turbulent* received a dizzying array of data. 'Everything became more compressed and so, we just had to work faster, ' explain McKendrick. 'The targets and times of firing were continually switching between *Turbulent* and *Splendid*. TLAM is an expensive precision weapon and targets would be assessed all the time, to make sure they were still viable. As the intelligence picture clarified so would the targets and the times.'

A century earlier the submarine was regarded as a vessel barely worthwhile tactically to protect harbours. Now here it was pulling down data bursts from commanders in their war rooms ashore, who saw the submarine as the tip of the spear being thrust into the heart of the Iraqi dictatorship.

Aboard *Turbulent* the moment of truth came down to fingers flying across keyboards in the curiously calm intimacy of the boat's control room.

'There was incredible concentration,' recalled McKendrick. 'It was faces in glowing screens. It's whispered orders, concentration and then that moment when the discharge system actually ejects the missile.'[6]

This was the first time *Turbulent* had participated in a cruise missile strike and those aboard felt 'this great thump and whoosh as the air blasts back into the submarine'. Amid the adrenaline of a successful launch some of the submariners cheered the weapons on their way. As the missile blasted off 'in an absolute blaze of rocket motor' the officer tasked with observing via the periscope issued 'an expletive . . . about how bright it was as it soared away into the night'.[7]

It was a peculiar experience for McKendrick, who reflected that having started his naval career in the Cold War, going on patrols during which he 'never felt it likely we would shoot at anyone', he had now done so.

This new form of warfare for submarines – stitched by the latest communications systems into a multi-layered plan as part of a shooter network – removed them from witnessing the consequences of their actions. It was no longer a case of being a few thousand yards, or less, from the target, with the captain on the periscope as torpedoes slammed into an enemy ship.

'It is funny, you only reflect deeply on what you have been doing some weeks later,' said McKendrick. 'At the time, when you are in the middle of the Gulf, firing at a target hundreds of miles away, you are purely focussed on getting it right. You experience relief when the missiles are away . . . you have achieved what you set out to. Where did the missiles go, what did they land on? I knew the targets, as did some of the strike team. Knowing where the missiles went helped – they were regime targets of a strategic nature. In the rest of the crew there was no great desire to know. They didn't ask.'

Within hours *Turbulent* was informed her services were no longer needed. 'We were told on the evening of 22 March that we could go when we had finished firing the final missile, which was slightly strange. There you were, experiencing the adrenaline of live operations and then they said "you can go now", yet the land war had only just started. But, you simply shifted mindset and changed your focus to thinking of that great day when you would get home.'

Setting course for Devonport was long overdue, for *Turbulent* had completed a deployment lasting more than ten months, the longest ever by a Royal Navy nuclear submarine, in which she had clocked up around 50,000 miles. Although away for 300 days, a process of crew swapping meant only ten of those aboard the SSN were with her for the entire deployment. Pausing at Gibraltar on the way home, in the submarine's messes they tuned in the satellite TVs to catch the latest news and saw a statue of Saddam Hussein being pulled off a plinth in a Baghdad city centre square. The US-led invasion of Iraq had been launched ostensibly to eliminate WMD. This turned out to be a false premise as none were ever found, for Saddam had abandoned his pursuit of WMD in the early 1990s. Tactically the cruise missiles had been extremely effective and the submariners had performed with consummate professionalism, but the war was a strategic blunder. The submarines had contributed to changing a regime and paved the way for a long and painful occupation (and insurgency) in Iraq that arguably destabilised the entire Middle East.

12   Weapon of the Strong . . .

The story of the submarine at war had reached a peculiar juncture.

It appeared to have been transformed from the weapon of the weak

against the strong into a hammer for the strong to wield against comparatively weak rogue regimes or elusive terrorist groups. Torpedoes
were still part of the submarine's armament, as were mines, but it had
all strayed far from Robert Fulton's vision of using plunging boats and
'torpedoes' to liberate global trade – indeed humanity itself – from the
hegemony of the great maritime powers. As the twenty-first century
concluded its first decade, submarines no longer sank ships – only two
warships had been attacked and destroyed by them since 1945 – but
following the end of the Cold War they had fired dozens of missiles
deep inland.[1]

There were those who still saw the submarine as the great leveller in
their struggle with the more powerful. On 26 March 2010, one of the
world's pariah states used a submarine to sink a warship as a demonstration of its potency in the face of a hostile international community.

The 1,200-ton South Korean corvette ROKS *Cheonan* was attacked as
she patrolled a disputed maritime border with North Korea. Forty-six
sailors died but Pyongyang denied being responsible in its usual fiery
fashion.

'. . . the puppet military warmongers, right-wing conservative politicians and the group of other traitors in South Korea are now foolishly
seeking to link the accident with the North at any cost,' stormed the
regime's official mouthpiece.[2]

An investigation by a specially convened Multinational Combined
Intelligence Task Force composed of naval experts from the USA, the
UK, Australia, Canada and Sweden begged to differ. On 20 May it published a report that concluded *Cheonan* was 'split apart and sunk due
to a shockwave and bubble effect produced by an underwater torpedo
explosion . . . The weapon system used is confirmed to be a high explosive torpedo with a net explosive weight of about 250kg, manufactured
by North Korea.'

The real clincher was solid evidence, including a propulsion motor
from a 21-inch CHT-02D torpedo with North Korean markings found
on the seabed amid *Cheonan*'s wreckage. When it came to the means
of attack, the North Koreans had plenty of options for they possessed
20 elderly Romeo Class diesel-electric boats, 40 Sango Class mini submarines and ten midgets of the Yono Class. The investigators were able
to draw on intelligence that revealed 'a few small submarines and a
mother ship supporting them left a North Korean naval base in the West

Sea [Yellow Sea] 2–3 days prior to the attack and returned to port 2–3 days after the attack. Furthermore, we confirmed that all submarines from neighbouring countries were either in or near their respective home bases at the time of the incident.' They dismissed other theories for *Cheonan*'s destruction: 'There is no other plausible explanation.'[3]

Even on the fifth anniversary of the event, South Korean calls for an apology were described by Pyongyang as 'intolerable mockery'.[4] As they continued to deny responsibility for sinking *Cheonan* the North Koreans were busy staging a series of test firings of their first submarine-launched ballistic missile. They had acquired ten ex-Soviet Navy Golf Class submarines in the mid-1990s, allegedly to scrap them. Instead they were used to create a new type called the Sinpo, with one or two missile tubes in its sail like the old 1950s Soviet boats. The 'new' North Korean boat likewise suffered from the problem of being an air breather that would sooner or later be forced to surface (exposing itself for potential attack). It is thought the North Korean aim would be to deploy the Sinpo into the East China Sea at a time of crisis to sit on the seabed, conserving battery power and air while waiting to launch missiles.

The South Koreans were not going to sit back and allow such a development without doing something. In late 2016 the commander of the South's navy reiterated the advisability of reinforcing an already highly capable conventional submarine force with nuclear-powered hunter-killers.

The Americans, who with their Asia-Pacific strategic pivot are devoting the majority of their military forces – including 60 per cent of the USN – to security in that part of the world, have maintained a calm watching brief. 'We have not seen North Korea demonstrate capability to miniaturize a nuclear weapon and . . . put it on a ballistic missile,' said Pentagon spokesman Peter Cook. He added: 'We feel confident that we can respond to that North Korea challenge.'[5]

That pivot to Asia-Pacific was initiated under the Bush administration in 2005, to counter the rising threat of China, which by the end of the first decade of the twenty-first century had created a large and formidable navy. The pivot accelerated after President Barack Obama took office in 2008, dramatically reducing US troop levels in Iraq and Afghanistan.

It also reflected the end of the Cold War and a move by the USA to try to reduce its commitment to NATO. More than a quarter of a century after the fall of the Berlin Wall it still paid 73 per cent of the cost of maintaining NATO's front line operational capabilities.

This was something about which the Americans felt very unhappy, especially with most other alliance nations spending less than NATO's required 2 per cent minimum of GDP on defence. With the Russians no longer perceived as the threat they once were, the Atlantic and the Mediterranean were not considered the most important commitment for the USA, so things had to change strategically anyway.

When the Arab Spring uprisings occurred in 2011, with Libyan dictator Muammar Gaddafi seemingly intent on slaughtering civilians to suppress a revolt in Benghazi, the French and British led the NATO response.

There was still crucial support from the USA, and NATO's actions were authorised under UN Security Council Resolution 1973, initially to enforce a No Fly Zone to prevent bombing by Gaddafi's jets.

American assistance included submarines and aircraft to provide a decisive strike capability and among units committed to the campaign was USS *Florida*, a former ballistic missile submarine converted into an SSGN.

She was the product of a 1994 decision by the Pentagon that four of its 18 Ohio Class SSBNs were surplus to nuclear deterrent requirements. The massive vessels were not laid up for future disposal but converted into a new form of submarine that represents twenty-first century American global conventional power projection at its peak.

The makeover given to *Florida* and her sisters cost around a billion dollars per boat, providing each one with a battery of cruise missiles, a state-of-the-art command centre and two dry-deck shelters for Swimmer-Delivery Vehicles (SDV) to take US Navy SEALS ashore on raids. Missile tubes that used to carry Trident missiles now house Multiple-All-Up-Round Canisters, or MACs (for Tomahawk). Alternately, they can accommodate Unmanned Aerial Vehicles (UAVs) and also Unmanned Undersea Vehicles (UUVs), along with equipment for the 66 Special Operations Force (SOF) operatives whose bunk spaces are in the former Trident missile compartment. Missile tubes can also be used to store food and other supplies, enabling the submarine to stay at sea for extended periods. Two of the missile tubes are now lock-out chambers, to enable Special Forces troops to exit and enter the submarine while she is submerged. Equipped with High-Data-Rate antennas to enable instant communication with the Pentagon (or other headquarters) the Ohio SSGNs can also receive data burst messages. Each of the four SSGNs has the ability to, as the USN puts it, 'serve as a forward-deployed, clandestine Small Combatant Joint Command Centre'.[6]

Run along the same lines as SSBNs, with two crews each to ensure they remain at sea for the maximum time, the US Navy's four SSGNs aim always to be close to any likely crisis zone or wherever the President might require their services.

By the time she returned home on 29 April 2011 following her Libya operations *Florida*, commanded by Capt. Tom Calabrese, had been deployed for 15 months.

Positioned somewhere off the coast of Libya, *Florida* fired 99 of her 154 Tomahawk missiles against Gaddafi regime targets in the opening phase of the campaign, which the Americans called Operation Odyssey Dawn. Apart from *Florida*, the attack boats *Providence* and *Scranton* also launched TLAMs. In Desert Storm, 5 per cent of the Tomahawks fired were launched by submarines, in the Afghan and Iraq wars it was 33 per cent and during the Libya campaign 45 per cent.[7] *Florida* on her own carried more cruise missiles than the Royal Navy possessed in its entire inventory.[8]

Two British SSNs were contributed to Libya operations, including *Turbulent*, which left Devonport in February 2011 on a final ten-month deployment East of Suez before being retired from service.

Commanded by 41-year-old Cdr Ryan Ramsey, she relieved HMS *Triumph* on station in the Gulf of Sirte. *Triumph*, commanded by 48-year-old Cdr Rob Dunn, had fired 12 Tomahawks in the first three days of the operation.[9] Once they were handed the baton, Cdr Ramsey and *Turbulent*'s crew were 'ready to strike without warning and without remorse' and were delighted when asked to go and scout out the Libyan naval base at Al Khums.

Likely targets were sadly lacking. 'The only military activity we detected was an Italian helicopter and a Spanish [war]ship, which randomly transmitted on her active sonar for reasons that none of us understood,' reported Ramsey.[10]

By adopting such a fitful pattern the Spaniard failed to carry out a systematic search and ensured her passive sonar would hear no undersea threats, though Gaddafi lacked operational submarines anyway. While patrolling off Tripoli, *Turbulent* was the closest of any NATO maritime unit to the Libyan coast and Ramsey was notified by higher command of two minefields in the vicinity. He realised his boat had unwittingly already passed through one of them.

While they stayed just outside territorial waters monitoring sea traffic going close to the shore, a suspected gun-running ship was sighted, heading east for Benghazi. Another suspicious vessel was spotted and as it headed out of Libyan territorial waters a report was sent for potential action by other, more appropriate, units. Not long after, 'an incredible explosion from the direction of Tripoli was heard on sonar'.[11]

With no American units by then committed to the action, Ramsey and *Turbulent* waited patiently to be called on for a cruise missile strike. Ramsey found that with each passing day 'there seemed to be even less appetite from HQ to use Tomahawk. The suspicion was that since an RAF man was in charge he had a natural tendency to look after RAF interests first ... which is typical of the politics that always go with war.' Ramsey was pleased that the navy had 'always played the "straight man" in internal politics even though it is sometimes to our disadvantage'.[12]

With no cruise missile strikes to perform Cdr Ramsey contemplated sneaking up on the Spanish warship to see if *Turbulent* was noticed at all. The Spaniard was still blithely blasting away on active sonar and surface search radar. In the meantime Libyan regime gun-running vessels moved up and down the coast without any attempt by NATO at interception or boardings. It was all extremely frustrating.

HMS *Triumph* would be the only British naval unit engaged in offensive, deep-strike operations in Libya. After returning to Devonport in April – flying the skull and crossbones flag, with tomahawk symbols – she replenished her TLAM load and headed back to the Gulf of Sirte to take over from *Turbulent*.

If there was an attempt to assassinate Gaddafi by either submarine or air-launched cruise missiles then it failed. He was eventually found hiding in a drain by rebels and killed by – among other things – a shot to the head from his own gold-plated pistol. With the regime collapsing, the use of cruise missiles had served a humanitarian cause yet again, managing to get rid of a dictator and helping to save civilians from being massacred. Post-war Libya descended into chaos and anarchy, becoming a base for terrorists intent on the West's destruction and indirectly bringing about a resurgence in Russian submarine activity.

13   Much Ado About *Maskirovka*

The dawn of President Vladimir Putin's missile boat diplomacy added a new twist to the post-Cold War deployment of submarines. Following the Gorshkov policy of wielding the Russian Navy as a military-political tool, Putin sent out his submarines and surface warships on increasingly cheeky forays into Western waters and to stake out Moscow's zones of strategic interest.

In addition to the spring 2014 Crimean annexation – to safeguard the Russian Navy's key base at Sevastopol – and interference in eastern Ukraine, Putin's navy has been deployed to test the West's resolve at sea and to boost his image as a strongman for audiences at home and abroad.

Putin took particular exception to the West deposing Gaddafi – a long-standing Russian ally and arms client, plus provider of a useful refuelling stop for its warships – so when the Arab Spring erupted in Syria he was determined not to allow a repeat performance.

The Russians have therefore used their own variant of the Tomahawk – the Kalibr – to help the Assad regime maintain its grip on Syria, though Moscow claims to be fighting terrorism. Four Kalibrs were launched in late 2015 by *Rostov-on-Don* – the second of six new Varshavyanka (Improved Kilo Class) diesel-electric submarines – while she was submerged in the Eastern Mediterranean. The *Rostov-on-Don*'s targets were allegedly in the city of Raqqa, which had been taken over by the Islamic State of Iraq and the Levant (ISIL) terrorist death cult and was the declared capital of a new caliphate. The bombardment was a demonstration of the Russian Navy being back in the power projection business, seeking to guarantee Moscow's forces maintained access to a naval base at Tartus in Syria.

The upswing in the Russian maritime presence has seen attack submarines patrolling close to US Navy bases off the east coast of North America, and possibly even venturing into the Gulf of Mexico. It is likely that Russian mini submarines probed Swedish territorial waters in October 2014, while Finland was similarly provoked in April 2015. Finland's naval vessels dropped low power depth charges as they pursued potential sonar contacts. The Kremlin's conventional submarines have probed the territorial waters of the Baltic States, which have substantial ethnic Russian minority populations and have since 2014 feared they are next for annexation.

At the end of 2015 a Russian submarine, or submarines, tried to detect and trail a Royal Navy SSBN in waters off Scotland as the vessel either departed for or returned from a patrol. The UK was forced to call in anti-submarine aircraft from the USA, Canada and France to help hunt down the alleged Russian trespassers. Following defence cuts in 2010, Britain no longer had the mighty Nimrod or any other purpose-built MPA so it needed help. In addition to at least one Duke Class ASW frigate – and Merlin helicopters – the UK's own response also included a nuclear-powered submarine.

When the new 65,000-tonne strike carrier HMS *Queen Elizabeth* set sail on her maiden voyage in June 2017, there were claims in the media that she would be stalked by Russian submarines keen to gather intelligence on her during sea trials in the North Sea. To counter this the frigates *Iron Duke* and *Sutherland* rode shotgun while Merlins circled overhead. Despite claims of Russian espionage, naval insiders suggested the comparatively shallow North Sea was a poor place for submarines to try to trail the future RN flagship. They would be easily detected and chased away, which didn't stop a senior Russian officer boasting the *Queen Elizabeth* was 'just a convenient, large maritime target'.[1]

Other seas across which *Queen Elizabeth* and her sister ship *Prince of Wales* will sail during their 50-year lifespans will not be quite so benign. Those deeper waters will be packed with submarines some of which may one day seek to repeat the feats of U-boat captains and sink a British carrier. Destroying the biggest warships ever built for the Royal Navy would be the ultimate prize in any hot war. Preventing that eventuality was why in July 2017 steel was cut for construction of the first of eight new City Class ASW frigates, to be named HMS *Glasgow*.

*

After two decades of minimal naval activity the Russians were suddenly at sea in force and test-firing missiles to inspire fear and awe in friend and foe alike. The most spectacular were ballistic missiles with non-nuclear payloads soaring across the top of the world.

Delta IV or new Borei Class SSBNs fired theirs from the White Sea down range to the Kamchatka Peninsula in the Russian Far East, though occasionally the missiles flew the other way, from submarines of the Pacific Fleet. Sometimes these test firings failed shortly after launching, at least one missile exploding in mid-air.

Post-Cold War weapons mishaps have not been restricted to missile launches, with the most notorious occurring in August 2000, when the former Soviet Navy was arguably at its lowest ebb.

The Oscar II Class submarine *Kursk*, a large 18,000-ton guided-missile submarine, was commissioned into service in 1994 and in 1999 made a deployment to the Mediterranean to monitor NATO naval forces shortly after the Kosovo campaign.[2] The purpose was to reassure Slav ally Serbia that Russia still had strategic weight and also to unsettle the West but, compared to the glory days of Soviet maritime power in the 1970s and 1980s, it was a mere gesture.

Less than a year later *Kursk* participated in a rare Northern Fleet combat exercise in the Barents Sea, on 12 August suffering catastrophic damage due to a massive blast, fortunately not involving any of the nuclear-tipped weapons aboard. The explosion was caused by unstable High-test Peroxide (HTP) fuel used in one of her torpedoes, which is believed to have blown up in the tube.

Within two minutes it set off a chain reaction in other weapons, possibly detonating up to four more torpedoes.[3] It has been said that a contributory factor was *Kursk*'s men lacking training in how to handle the weapon safely, having not fired a torpedo since 1998.[4]

The Oscar Class boats are exceptionally robust vessels and designed to withstand direct hits by one or more Western torpedoes, but with such a massive internal eruption *Kursk* stood no chance. The CO, 45-year-old Captain Gennady Lyachin, and most of the crew were probably killed instantly or died within minutes. After trying for a few hopeless moments to surface, *Kursk* slammed into the bottom, a subsequent survey of the wreckage discovering: 'The whole bow part of the submarine had disintegrated.' This left only 'a mass of wreckage and metal debris . . .'[5]

Because the submarine's distress beacon did not instantly deploy – there are claims it was welded into place having proved prone to launching accidentally – it took a while for the Russians to locate the stricken boat.

There were futile attempts to reach any of *Kursk*'s men that might still be alive, using primitive rescue submersibles that even in just 320ft of water were not up to the job. Britain and Norway sent teams to try and rescue survivors, but Russian hesitation to ask the old enemy for help meant that by the time they got to work (on 21 August) it was too late to save any of the 118 men aboard.

Some of *Kursk*'s crew did survive, trapped in aft compartments. They lived for several hours, until a fire consumed their last supplies of air – divers who some weeks later explored the wreck found their burned corpses. A scrawled note discovered in the overalls pocket of Lt Dmitri Kolesnikov, a 27-year-old engineering officer, revealed: 'All personnel from compartments six, seven and eight moved to the ninth. There are 23 of us here. We have made this decision as a result of the accident. None of us can get out.'[6]

After news of *Kursk*'s sinking broke some Russian officials blamed outside actors. On 17 August a defence ministry source claimed it could not have been an internal explosion and *Kursk* must have been in collision with a foreign submarine. When Russian deputy Prime Minister Ilya Klebanov went to meet relatives of *Kursk*'s submariners – after the Russian Navy's antiquated equipment again failed to get the rescue hatches open – he was subjected to a barrage of fury. The distressed mother of one young officer shouted: 'My son is dying in a tin can for 50 dollars!'[7] In front of the world's media the woman was restrained by officials and injected with a sedative to calm her down. The woman later denied she had been forcefully sedated but rather was given prescribed medicine for a heart condition.

Kolesnikov's widow Olga was left to treasure a poem her husband had written for her just before his last voyage, in which he vowed 'when the time comes to die, though I chase such thoughts away, I want to whisper one thing: My darling, I love you'.[8]

Some within Western intelligence circles knew the truth within days, if not hours, of *Kursk*'s demise. They were able to tap into reports from NATO submarines patrolling in the Barents Sea to observe the Northern Fleet exercise. Two events had also registered on seismic recorders in Norway – the first was probably an internal explosion in the vessel and the second the force of *Kursk* hitting the seabed.

Newly elected President Putin felt deep shame at the condition of his nation's navy. Reeling from universal condemnation for not immediately abandoning his holiday to take charge of the response, he openly criticised his country's armed forces, saying their present structure was 'hardly optimal'.[9] He slammed the low level of training and observed that Russian Navy sailors 'hardly ever put to sea'. Putin said he felt bitter when he heard people say Russia's pride had drowned with the *Kursk*'s men, and gave a commitment to reviving the armed forces and the Russian state. He wanted to achieve two things – a reduction in size, and therefore running costs, while defining a new role corresponding to 'the threats Russia faces now and in the future'.

Pravda, the one-time mouthpiece of the Russian state, continues to insist that the British and Americans were responsible for *Kursk*'s destruction. It has explained that the Kremlin only accepted the torpedo explosion theory to 'avoid full-scale nuclear war'.[10]

Alternative theories that persist, without evidence to back them up, are that *Kursk* struck an old mine or a NATO submarine collided with her.

Pravda claimed as recently as August 2016 that the US Navy submarine *Memphis* fired a torpedo at *Kursk*, with the British SSN *Splendid* and USS *Toledo* also somehow involved. Furthermore, suggested the *Pravda* report, *Splendid* was possibly sunk by the *Kursk* explosion. This theory did not tally with cruise missile attacks made by *Splendid* in the Middle East during early 2003 (and her public decommissioning in August the same year). *Pravda* implied these were fabricated to cover up her loss.[11]

When a large section of *Kursk* was raised in October 2001 no evidence was found of collision or torpedo attack – everything pointed to an internal explosion. In February 2002 the Russians decided to cease the use of HTP torpedoes and that June the official inquiry laid the blame squarely on one of those weapons detonating.

There was a brief thawing in relations between Russia and the West in the aftermath of the *Kursk* disaster. Western navies again rushed to assist in the rescue of Russian submariners, this time with Moscow promptly asking for help. A crew of seven were trapped in the midget submarine *AS-28* when the craft was ensnared by cables on the seabed off Kamchatka in 2005. It was the Royal Navy's submarine rescue team that saved the day, using an ROV to cut the cables and enable *AS-28* to surface.

The Russians even joined NATO for naval training, including a submarine rescue exercise in 2011, but the spark of friendship was snuffed out by the annexation of the Crimean Peninsula, which is today being expanded as a submarine base.

With its face once again set against the West, in October 2016 Russia deployed a strike group led by the Severomorsk-based *Admiral Kuznetsov*, a 25-year-old Soviet-era carrier. She pumped out huge amounts of black smoke from her old engines as she progressed around Norway, down through the North Sea, the English Channel and then into the Mediterranean. *Kuznetsov* was heading for waters off the Levant, probably to launch jets on strikes against besieged rebels in Syria's second city of Aleppo. *Kuznetsov* was escorted by the newly refurbished nuclear-powered battlecruiser *Peter the Great*, a pair of Udaloy Class ASW destroyers, *Admiral Kulakov* and *Severomorsk*, and a Sierra II attack submarine (a fast, deep-diving SSN with a titanium hull).

There were howls of protest when it appeared that the Russian battle group was to refuel at a port belonging to NATO alliance member Spain, which, so the protestors claimed, would in essence be replenishing a mission to kill women and children trapped in Aleppo.

The Spanish, whose frigate *Almirante Juan de Borbón* led Standing NATO Maritime Group 1 (SNMG1) as it shadowed the Russian battle group, were severely embarrassed. The Kremlin seemed to recoil in the face of international outrage – refusing to confirm or deny that *Kuznetsov*'s jets would unload their bombs on Syrian targets – and withdrew its request for Spanish fuel. Any thoughts the Kremlin may have entertained about using Malta to replenish warships were sunk by its foreign minister. George Vella tweeted that his island state would 'not be refuelling or bunkering any Russian naval ship in the Mediterranean'.[12]

Amid all this fuss, the reality was that *Kuznetsov* and her consorts were a diversionary muscle show as part of a long-established doctrine of tactical and strategic distraction. During the Great Patriotic War of 1941–45, the Russians perfected a means of military deception they dubbed *Maskirovka* – literally, in English, 'something masked' – in order to deceive their foes into looking one way, while the real work was being done elsewhere by others.

It appeared they had not lost the art, nor the will, to use *Maskirovka*, for as the world railed against the idea of air strikes on Aleppo, it emerged that NATO had detected three submarines allegedly being sent to join the carrier battle group in the Eastern Mediterranean. They were two nuclear-powered Akula II attack boats and another Varshavyanka Class craft, all from Kola Peninsula bases and armed with Kalibr missiles. Along with the newly commissioned frigate *Admiral Grigorovich* from the BSF (also armed with cruise missiles), it was those submarines that could potentially lead the new bombardment on Syria, not the *Kuznetsov*'s strike jets. It was claimed that the latter lacked the power even to take off from her when carrying a full bomb load.

The Varshavyanka Class boat was detected heading south on the surface through the English Channel at about the same time as the Akulas were trailed in the Irish Sea by a Trafalgar Class submarine of the British fleet. 'In the South-West approaches, the Russian submarines made it clear that they wanted us to know they were there,' one British naval source claimed. 'Then, after a period of time, they went deep.'[13]

As the Akulas sped further south the task of shadowing was handed on to other NATO forces, including frigates and destroyers of SNMG1.

The route used by the Akulas was a definite case of 'up yours', for more usually nuclear-powered boats would swing out into the deeper waters of the Atlantic and past the west of Ireland. That wouldn't have taken them within sight of the British ballistic missile submarine base in the Clyde. Putin's submarines were demonstrating that the old days of impotent Russia were over and they could go where they liked and do what they wanted.

That the Royal Navy – now with fewer than half the submarines it possessed at the end of the Cold War – was back in the deadly trade of hunting and trailing Russian submarines had been indicated during the spring of 2015. HMS *Talent* was photographed returning home to Plymouth with substantial damage to her fin but UK defence officials were 'adamant' she had collided with 'floating ice'[14] rather than a Russian submarine. They would not say where or when the incident happened.

Regardless of whether or not *Talent* really did crunch her fin on a

Russian surface vessel (while taking a sneaky underwater look), have a brush with another submarine or collide with ice, there were now so few British submarines that any lack of availability severely affected the UK's ability to defend itself or NATO allies.

More than a year later, as the Russian battle group reached waters off the Levant and the world waited for the latest blitz on Syria, another NATO nation could fill some of the gaps left by the much-reduced British. A Dutch boat shadowing the *Kuznetsov* battle group provoked a complaint from the Russian defence ministry about a 'clumsy and dangerous' manoeuvre,[15] despite the submarine allegedly being 12 miles away and in international waters. According to the Russians, destroyers *Kulakov* and the *Severomorsk* worked with helicopters to detect and corner the diesel boat, forcing it to withdraw.

The Dutch defence ministry would neither confirm nor deny any of this, restricting itself to tweeting: 'In response to recent media reports: We do not comment on submarine operations.'[16] If the Russians wanted to know exactly which boat it was they had chased away they could look on Twitter. Someone helpfully posted a tweet with recent photos of the diesel boat HNLMS *Walrus* as she called at Malta and Crete. The Russians also claimed to have earlier detected one of the new US Navy Virginia Class attack submarines trailing them.[17] A few weeks later NATO warships reportedly tracked Russian nuclear-powered submarines sent to shadow the US Navy's USS *Dwight D. Eisenhower* and the French Navy's FS *Charles de Gaulle* carrier battle groups as they launched air strikes on Islamic State targets in Syria.

In late May 2017 a further Kalibr missile bombardment was unleashed against targets in Syria by the Russian submarine *Krasnodar*, another Varshavyanka Class vessel on her way to join the BSF. The frigate *Admiral Essen* launched missiles at the same time. Joined by the *Admiral Grigorovich*, the same two vessels renewed the Kalibr assault the following month. This was partly in response to a US Navy fighter jet shooting down a Syrian aircraft as it attempted to bomb rebel forces that the USA was supporting.

For some NATO leaders a new struggle for oceanic supremacy was underway even before Russian submarines started bombarding Syria.

Harking back to the famous 1946 'Iron Curtain' speech by Winston Churchill, an American admiral in October 2015 described Russia as constructing 'an arc of steel from the Arctic to the Mediterranean'.[18] Admiral Mark Ferguson, who commanded NATO's Allied Joint Force Command and US Navy forces in Europe and Africa, accurately predicted 'a more aggressive, more capable Russian Navy'.

Syrian operations proved his analysis correct but the Russians hadn't exactly hidden their intentions. In the summer of 2015, during a meeting chaired by Vladimir Putin, senior naval officers and Kremlin officials openly outlined an ambitious new strategy in which Russia would contest supremacy over the Atlantic and the Arctic. Under the major revisions to its maritime doctrine and operational stance, the Russian Navy would also maintain a permanent squadron in the Mediterranean.

President Putin restated that intent in the summer of 2017, issuing a fresh presidential decree explaining that Russia's naval forces would seek to challenge the dominance of the US Navy around the world.

This came just as Chinese warships called at Istanbul before departing for exercises with the Russian Navy in the Eastern Mediterranean. Beijing also ordered its naval vessels into the Baltic for the first time ever. Two Chinese destroyers joined up with units from Russia's Baltic Fleet as a battle group of Northern Fleet vessels headed for the same waters. *Peter the Great* and, most significantly, the Typhoon Class nuclear missile submarine *Dmitriy Donskoy* spearheaded this force.

Ostensibly sent into the Baltic to attend Russian Navy Day celebrations at St Petersburg, *Dmitriy Donskoy* and her consorts were together with the Chinese vessels a powerful demonstration of a global challenge to Western maritime supremacy.

Dmitriy Donskoy – the biggest commissioned submarine in the world – was also the largest ever to sail in the Baltic and so huge that it was doubtful she could even submerge in safety. If a century earlier Britain's submariners found it challenging to slip through the narrow entrance to the Baltic in their tiny E Class boats (of less than 1,000 tons displacement) it was inevitable the 26,000-ton (dived) *Dmitriy Donskoy* would face a tricky passage. It was likely she completed the entire voyage from the Kola to the Gulf of Finland on the surface. Provided she did not run aground the gigantic submarine's presence in the Baltic would have a chilling effect on Western European leaders, representing a bizarre inversion of the stealthy rationale of traditional submarine operations.

Moscow was deploying a type of vessel that had been immortalised in the best-selling novel and hit movie *The Hunt for Red October* as the most fearsome weapon of mass destruction on the planet. The overt sortie of a gargantuan submarine that, despite its size, could still hide in the ocean and let loose a world-ending barrage of 20 Bulava nuclear missiles, showed Russia's neighbours that it was not to be trifled with. Consequently NATO warships closely shadowed the submarine and her battle group.

Britain's failure to maintain effective anti-submarine forces in the inter-war years arguably encouraged Germany to repeat the same strategy of U-boat warfare against shipping. Today NATO is feared and loathed by Russia's leadership and many of its citizens – their feelings whipped up by government propaganda. The deployment of the Typhoon into the Baltic and the firing of cruise missiles into Syria boosted Russian national pride and combated insecurity, a slap in the face for NATO.

Many in Russia see the West as threatening to encircle and suffocate the Motherland, as possibly even planning an invasion from launch points in Ukraine, Poland and the Baltic States. With that mindset it is essential that Russia asserts itself on the high seas to deter any such move by NATO and hence the new struggle for the Atlantic, Baltic, Black Sea and Mediterranean. The main aim of the Russians in the High North is to shut NATO out of the Arctic and claim its rich natural resources. They already operate a deep-diving, scientific submarine – and are building more – that can go under the ice to the Arctic seabed. The Russians have planted their flag and have also gathered rock samples to prove that the Lomonosov Ridge is Russia's and so too is the North Pole.

The Kremlin is also pursuing a reinvigorated bastion strategy by sending SSBNs out to hide under the ice to await orders to fire their doomsday missiles. The effort in the Eastern Mediterranean, meanwhile, safeguards Russia's potentially vulnerable southern flank and ensures it cannot be bottled up in the Black Sea. Hand in hand with its naval effort, the Russian state has also been waging cyber warfare, with an army of hackers creating mischief and seeking to undermine the foundations of democracy and commerce in the West. Its submarines may have a part to play there, too. The USN's Vice Admiral James Foggo warned in early 2016: 'Some analysts believe that even our underwater infrastructure – such as oil rigs and telecommunications cables – may be under threat by these new and advanced [Russian] forces.'[19]

With a world dependent on the Internet to function, fibreoptic cables laid on the seabed might present its Achilles heel. In both the Second World War and the Cold War submarines were used to cut cables, and in the latter case tapped into them to gather intelligence. During the 1960s and 1970s, on missions codenamed Operation Holystone, specially adapted US Navy submarines were sent to clamp themselves onto Russian seabed communications cables and intercept secret transmissions. It is not unfeasible that in any future conflict one side or the other could use submarines to destroy the physical infrastructure of the Internet, aiming to cause global chaos.

The West, due to its open, democratic nature and lack of military muscle – and failure in recent years to invest in ASW capabilities – is the more unprepared for such actions.

Germany's bid to use submarines to defeat its enemies in the West in two world wars only ended in failure because Britain and its allies were able to recover from their lack of preparedness and make a huge effort each time. Today Russia will only gain hegemony over the oceans if the politicians of the West do not wake up and provide the leadership and investment needed on an equally ambitious scale to create the ASW solution. Yet today the majority of Europe's navies only have nominal ASW capability. Their frigate and submarine construction programmes are sluggish at best – and in most cases non-existent – and the Russians know it, which tempts them to try their luck.

Vice Admiral Foggo, who is a former submarine captain, has claimed a fourth Battle of the Atlantic is already underway 'across and underneath the oceans and seas that border Europe.' He adds: 'This is not a kinetic fight. It is a struggle between Russian forces that probe for weakness, and US and NATO ASW forces that protect and deter. Just like in the Cold War, the stakes are high.' Admiral Foggo also observed that the Allies were able to beat U-boats during the world wars 'not by force alone, but by innovation. In the Cold War, the rise of nuclear-powered Soviet submarines required us to develop new acoustic and other technologies. Today, we are once again in a technological arms race with Russia.'[20]

While the Germans may have lost the first and second battles of the

Atlantic, the Russians do not feel they lost the third, but rather with-drew for two decades to gird up their loins for Battle of the Atlantic v3.1.

On the other side of the world Beijing's actions are creating another potential future flashpoint.

As China reaches for true globe-girdling great power status, the new generation ballistic missile submarines of the People's Liberation Army Navy (PLAN) are of great importance. The PLAN wishes to cordon off the South China Sea to create a bastion for hiding these SSBNs. The coral islands and reefs China has in the past few years seized and swiftly turned into naval fortresses – hosts to airstrips and berths for warships – are to project Beijing's ownership over a huge area of ocean. Under a project dubbed the Underwater Great Wall[21] China aims to create a SOSUS cordon, constructing listening posts on the fortress islands and planting seabed hydrophones. It means to ensure that no intruding US Navy or allied submarines can operate in the South China Sea undetected. It will then send Shang Class attack boats along with increasingly powerful and numerous ASW patrol vessels, plus surveillance aircraft, to counter trespassers.

The Chinese are new at the sea-based deterrent game. Their single Xia Class SSBN – which was first commissioned in the 1980s – is reckoned never to have made a patrol, while it is acknowledged that the PLAN's five new Jin Class SSBNs lack stealth compared to those of other navies. The bastion seems to be the solution for keeping them secure, ensuring they need never leave the (hopefully) threat-free South China Sea. Their JL-2 SLBM will still be able to hit the cities of putative foes across Asia, though to reach the USA will require the future Type 096 SSBN, armed with the JL-3.[22]

With the bastion concept fundamental to Beijing's future defence strategy, it did not even matter that an international ruling in July 2016 declared the Chinese annexation of islands and reefs a blatant violation of international law.[23] China's immediate response was to stage a spectacular firepower display by the PLAN in the contested seas in order to stamp its mark on what it regards as *Mare Nostrum*.

14   Nothing Left but Armageddon?

The wheel of history that brought the end of the Cold War has turned again, returning us to a time of political strongmen, land grabs, an age of fear and loathing and a global submarine race. Russia is in a new face-off with the West and China is challenging American naval supremacy in Asia-Pacific, while North Korea is hell-bent on sending nukes to sea to menace the USA.

In April 2017 tensions soared as massive military parades were staged in the North Korean capital of Pyongyang. They featured, among other things, Pukkuksong-1 SLBMs perched on the back of trucks (for the purposes of showing off). Dictator Kim Jong-un boasted he would strike the USA with nuclear weapons, though it was far from clear that North Korea yet had a missile with the range, or even a suitable nuclear warhead. The US Navy marshalled its forces, both overtly and covertly, to potentially spearhead an attempt to defang North Korea's nuclear weapons programme.

As the USS *Carl Vinson* strike carrier group closed with the Korean Peninsula a submarine played a starring role in President Donald Trump's own version of missile boat diplomacy.

The USS *Michigan* pulled in to Busan, having spent some time in waters off Korea, the SSGN's many conventionally-tipped cruise missiles primed for launch and embarked Special Forces standing by for action. What weren't shown, but which the North Koreans also had to reckon with, were at least four American SSNs (similarly packed with cruise missiles) along with South Korean and Japanese submarines prowling the same waters. They were there to establish a Cuban Missile Crisis-style naval cordon off the likely exit points of Kim's submarines, should he order them to swarm out to try to repeat the *Cheonan* feat. Shortly after *Michigan*'s heavily publicised port visit the crisis cooled, probably because everything got a little too frightening for all concerned and China did its best to persuade Kim not to carry out another nuclear test (yet). Within a few weeks he had ordered more missile firings, and in July 2017 tested a land-based missile it was alleged could hit Alaska or Hawaii. In a tweet an exasperated President Trump enquired of Kim: 'Does this guy have something better to do with his life?'[1]

The answer was not long in coming for it soon emerged that North Korea might be carrying out preparations for the first test firing by the Sinpo submarine since August 2016. Both South Korean and American intelligence services in late July 2017 detected a raised level of activity by the North's submarine forces. It was suggested the Sinpo was among boats that had set sail, heading around 100 km into the East China Sea, which was the vessel's longest ever voyage. Furthermore it was suggested the Sinpo is merely a testbed and that North Korea is secretly building a brand new class of ballistic missile submarines (or SSBs).[2]

Beyond events off Korea, submarines today proliferate as never before, reflecting rising tensions and rivalries over access to natural resources and the desire for territorial expansion. A navy without at least a couple of fully functioning submarines risks being a geopolitical irrelevance, at a distinct disadvantage compared to its (potentially hostile) neighbours.

The chief submarine suppliers to the world are Germany, Russia and France (all offering cutting-edge conventional boats). The French and the Germans have in recent times supplied a combined total of 21 countries with modern submarines, while the Russians have sold them to 14 client states.[3] France is even providing the Royal Australian Navy with its future submarine (due to enter service from 2025). Having operated British submarines since the 1960s, then a Swedish design from the late 1990s, Australia has opted for a conventional version of the latest French nuclear-powered attack boat.

China is coming up fast on the outside track as a supplier of comparatively cheap, but good enough, submarines to the world's navies. Bangladesh in late 2016 sought to counter the undersea capabilities of its neighbours through the procurement of two Chinese-built Ming Class submarines, *Nabajatra* and *Joyjatra*. The second-hand, 1990s era diesel-electric boats cost US $203 million,[4] which is pretty cheap, though not an easy stretch for a country as poor as Bangladesh. The investment may be worth it, for Dhaka is eyeing rich mineral resources under the Bay of Bengal and has been competing against India and Myanmar (Burma) to exploit them, the latter having expressed interest in acquiring submarines too.

Beijing was no doubt happy to supply Bangladesh with boats to gain a foothold of influence on the eastern flank of its regional rival India, having already supplied surface warships to Pakistan on the western flank. Beijing is also offering Pakistan eight Air-Independent Propulsion (AIP) submarines, probably based on the Yuan Class design, with deliveries due to begin in 2022.

The introduction of AIP is a game changer in submarine operations, removing the need for conventionally powered boats to surface in order to take in air. Even by the latter stages of the Cold War, the Russians (with their first Kilo Class variant) and the Germans with Type 209s had produced diesel-electric submarines that could, potentially, stay submerged for up to five days (provided they crawled along). AIP was the next step and the world could thank the Nazis yet again. In the 1930s and during the Second World War that brilliant German submarine designer Hellmuth Walter produced experimental boats that used hydrogen peroxide in a closed-cycle propulsion system. This was treated to produce steam and oxygen which combined with diesel in a reaction chamber. While the main players in the Cold War did run trials with captured German AIP boats – and even constructed experimental vessels – apart from the Soviets they opted for nuclear propulsion instead.

Over subsequent decades it was the Swedes, the French and the Germans who most successfully took the idea forward, and modern AIP uses a variety of methods to achieve closed-cycle power generation. It recycles exhaust gases, burns liquid oxygen and diesel or uses 'an electrochemical conversion device' called a fuel cell, which 'combines hydrogen and oxygen to produce water, electricity, and heat'.[5] AIP boats are smaller than nuclear-powered submarines, with more modest patrol endurance (due to small crews and limited food storage capacity) and also have less power for sensors and armament (and more restricted weapons loads).

Nonetheless Germany's latest U-boats – the Type 212 and Type 214 – are very popular in the export market, offering a performance that almost approaches that of an SSN. The Type 212A is quieter than any nuclear-powered submarine, small enough to carry out Special Forces operations in shallow waters more easily, and has powerful submarine-detecting sonar. The Type 212A weapons load is impressive, though it does not currently officially include cruise missiles or Anti-Shipping Missiles (ASM). AIP means a Type 212A can remain submerged (and hidden) for up to three weeks. Such a boat is capable of crossing the Atlantic without once surfacing, or even using its snorkel system (and the Germans allegedly recently deployed one of theirs to patrol the Gulf of Finland and spy on the Russians).

Today, nuclear-powered submarines are more expensive and complex than ever – they are a bigger challenge than the Space Shuttle to manufacture. The Royal Navy's new Astute Class attack boats are costing between £1.178 billion and £1.6 billion each.[6] The conventional wisdom is that naval vessels tend to get cheaper the more you build and the RN has ordered seven Astutes, but delays and the need to revise aspects of the design have led to a price increase.

The fourth, *Audacious*, was launched at Barrow in late April 2017 and with *Anson* well advanced in the massive Devonshire Dock Hall assembly facility. Just over a week earlier BAE Systems was awarded £1.4 billion to deliver Astute Class boat number six, *Agamemnon* (the sixth RN vessel to carry the name, the first being one of Nelson's favourite ships).

The latest comparable Russian vessels, the Yasen Class, cost around a billion pounds each, with up to a dozen likely. The second, named *Kazan*, was launched at the end of March 2017, with the boss of the Russian Navy, Admiral Vladimir Korolyov, expressing pride in his country's submarines being now more active than at any time since the Soviet era. He said they had achieved more than 3,000 days at sea in 2016. This came shortly after claims in the British media that no RN submarines were able to deploy in early 2017 (a situation not helped by one of the Astutes in 2016 receiving damage during a collision with a merchant vessel off Gibraltar). The MoD denied that all British submarines were 'non-operational' due to refits or repairs.[7]

AIP boats remain a good option for states seeking to avoid the crippling costs of creating nuclear-powered submarines and the complex facilities necessary to support and repair them. There is an alternative argument that with fuel costs destined to climb an SSN might in the long term prove more economical when striving for top-end performance.

The RN has since 1994 not operated conventional submarines, selling off its Upholder Class diesels to Canada, which continues to run them. One of these boats, HMCS *Windsor*, was in autumn 2016 sent on a mission to trail Russian targets in the North Atlantic.

In going all-nuclear the British set out to build on infrastructure and industrial skills in which they had already invested billions. It also made tactical sense as only an SSN can effectively protect an SSBN. However, a Type 212A costs 370 million euros (£320 million), which is around a third of the cost of an Astute.

The nuclear submarine league is still topped by the USA, which operates around 50 SSNs and 14 SSBNs, with the British a fairly distant second (seven and four respectively) in terms of sheer capability, quality and combat record. The Russians are coming up fast again (18 SSNs and 13 SSBNs, but many of them are old and of doubtful operational effectiveness).[8]

Perennial members remain France (six SSNs and four SSBNs) and China (five SSNs and five SSBNs), with India now joining the club and even Brazil contemplating the leap. The latter is using French technology and is aiming to send an SSN to sea by the mid-2020s. That boat will be the first nuclear-powered submarine operated by a South Atlantic state, in a part of the world where atomic weapons are banned.

The Indians and their long-standing potential foes the Pakistanis both acquired land-based nuclear weapons in the late 1990s, but only India has so far had the resources to press ahead with an SSBN. Lead boat *Arihant* is already at sea and there have been several missile test firings. To gain experience operating nuclear-powered boats, the Indians in the late 1980s leased a Charlie Class guided-missile submarine from the Soviet Union for three years. Since 2011 the Indian Navy has operated an Akula II Class attack submarine (also leased from Russia) and is likely to commission a second by 2021, probably to replace that earlier boat.

The Indians aim to construct at least three Arihants, which will enable one to be on deterrent patrol at all times. Hidden in the Bay of Bengal or the Arabian Sea, the deployed vessel will carry a dozen K-15 Sagarika missiles, each one with the power to wipe out a city. The problem with India's first-generation SLBM is that it has a range of only 466 miles. That means the launching submarine needs to sail as close to the coast of an enemy – most likely China and/or Pakistan – as the first-generation Soviet ballistic missile boats that were off the USA in the 1950s and 1960s. This reduces the Indian SSBNs' sea room and makes it easier for an enemy to find and destroy them. It also opens up the prospect of an Indian SSBN being forced to slip through the Malacca Strait and the Sunda Strait[9] to access a launch area, making the vessel even more vulnerable to detection and destruction by forward-deployed

Chinese ASW forces. A successor missile called the K-4, with greater reach, is being worked on to avoid such exposure.

Whereas the Indians and Chinese, pursuing their supposed manifest destiny as rising superpowers, have no qualms about constructing new ballistic missile submarines, in the West there is doubt about sea-based nuclear deterrence. This is caused not just by the cost but also by the lack of moral leadership allegedly exhibited by renewing such world-ending capability. The British and Americans are at the time of writing co-operating in designing a common ballistic missile compartment for their respective navies' future SSBNs (which will carry the same SLBMs).

The Americans are also helping the British with creating a new PWR-3 reactor for their boats. This power plant is a US design combined with what has been described as 'next-generation UK reactor technology'.[10]

The new Royal Navy SSBNs will commission sometime in the 2030s. The procurement cost of the UK's four Dreadnought Class (previously known as Trident Successor) submarines is estimated at more than £31bn,[11] including what the UK Government calls 'inflation over the [30-year] lifetime of the programme'. This represents an increase of £7bn over the original estimate for Successor. The Dreadnoughts will be even bigger than the current Vanguard Class SSBNs, having a displacement of 17,900 tons dived (compared to 16,000 tons). The money allocated to the acquisition of the Dreadnoughts is less than three years of UK government overseas aid spending, which in 2016 was £13.3bn. For further comparison, in 2016 the UK government spent £146.4bn on Health, £86.2bn on Education and £47bn on Defence.[12] According to the MoD there is a £10bn 'contingency fund'. The Campaign for Nuclear Disarmament (CND) has, however, predicted that the overall cost across 30 years of the Dreadnoughts could be £205bn.[13]

The USN's future SSBN is known as the Columbia Class, with the lead vessel of a planned 12 costing $8.2bn to procure and subsequent vessels estimated at $6.5bn each.[14] Total acquisition costs are estimated to be $97bn, including $12bn for research and development, with the Columbia Class described by the USN's leadership as its 'top priority'.[15] The US Department of Defense (DoD) has revealed that over the next two decades it will spend $450bn approximately on nuclear forces re-generation (including the SSBNs, which will consume a large slice of that investment pie).[16]

Russia is building Borei Class SSBNs, the first of which, *Yuri Dol-goruky*, was commissioned into the Northern Fleet in 2013. The new SSBN type has been described by President Putin as a 'serious, powerful weapon that will guarantee the security of our country . . .'[17] The first-in-class boat reportedly cost $713m,[18] but even so there are doubts that the Russians – with a GDP less than half that of the UK – can maintain such a heavy investment in both SSBNs and new SSNs while also modernising their older nuclear submarines and building new conventional boats.

Beyond the debate over the sheer cost of such weapons systems – designed never to be used, but operated as if they are ready to fire 365 days a year to deter existential threats – the spectre of nuclear annihilation weighs heavily on humanity's shoulders. The high-powered Nuclear Threat Initiative (NTI) lobby group paints a stark picture of what would happen should submarine or land-based nuclear missiles be launched in anger.

'If a nuclear weapon exploded in a major city, the blast center [*sic*] would be hotter than the surface of the sun,' according to the NTI, 'tornado-strength winds would spread the flames; and a million or more people could die. Survivors would have no electricity, no transportation, no phones – and hospitals would be overwhelmed . . . if they were still standing.' The NTI says countries possess almost 16,000 nuclear weapons, which are 'enough to destroy the planet hundreds of times over'.

According to the NTI, the UK has 215 nuclear weapons, which is 50 fewer than France and 35 fewer than China, while Pakistan has 120, India 110, Israel an estimated 80 and North Korea ten. Russia and the USA possess 93 per cent of the world's nuclear weapons. The Russians have 7,500 nuclear weapons, 300 more than the United States.[19]

Today there is something broken in the mechanism of Mutually Assured Destruction. The Americans have caused great anger in Russia by creating warships that are armed with Anti-Ballistic Missile (ABM) systems and deploying four of them to operate out of Rota naval base in Spain. Meanwhile, the US Navy has constructed shore-based variants of its AEGIS combat system to shield Eastern Europe from missiles. The USA and NATO insist this is to guard against rogue states – Iran and North Korea – but the Russians believe it is set against them and are furious at the old balance of terror being upset. During the Cold War

MAD successfully prevented nuclear exchanges because it was but one part of a carefully graduated system designed to preclude launches. In any crisis you were meant to work your way up through escalating stages, using a show of conventional force to deter war, with politicians coming to their senses before anybody pressed the nuclear button. The best way to prevent world destruction was (and remains) to stop the missiles being launched in the first place, not to wait until they are in the air and then try to shoot them down.

Powerful non-nuclear forces were a very important part of the deterrent equation. Today, while the Americans, Russians, Chinese, Indians, Israelis and North Koreans have large conventional armed forces, in Europe that level of response – and hence deterrent – is missing. None of Europe's small land armies frighten Russia, nor do European air forces, while its navies are not much more robust.

While the British and French do operate SSBNs their conventional deterrent forces have been reduced until the two leading European military powers are in a position where they potentially have a binary choice: Surrender or use the nukes.

Nobody, least of all Vladimir Putin, will believe that a country like the UK that cares so little about its conventional defences would ever destroy whole nations and kill millions, even if attacked with WMD. Capt. Doug Littlejohns, who commanded the British SSN *Sceptre* during the Cold War and later played a key role in overseeing Polaris patrols, wonders: 'Have Putin et al. already discounted our deterrent?' Capt. Littlejohns suggests the UK and NATO have 'signally failed to provide a reasonable and realistic ladder of escalation from skirmish through various levels of warfare before there is nothing left to offer except Armageddon'.

Conspiracy lovers might even suggest successive UK governments since 1991 have hacked away at conventional forces as a means to remove the rationale for Trident, though in 2016 it seemed that Prime Minister Theresa May was determined to press ahead with building the Dreadnoughts.

On the other hand the possible election of a Labour government led by life-long anti-nuclear campaigner Jeremy Corbyn held out the prospect of the UK's Trident submarines being scrapped altogether (despite party policy being to renew the sea-based deterrent).

Regardless of political machinations, as a graduated conventional deterrent response in any crisis is no longer possible for the UK or any other European nation, is Trident Successor actually unsustainable and both intellectually and morally bankrupt? It is a question that most British politicians have shown little sign of even beginning to address.

As if the threat to humanity posed by nuclear-powered submarines armed with atomic weapons is not worrying enough, it is likely that more and more nations will soon have sea-based nuclear missiles in their conventional boats. Even small navies can potentially create nuclear capability using AIP boats to fire suitably adapted cruise missiles. This is a capability the Israelis – operators of advanced, German-built submarines – are thought to already possess. It has been speculated that in any time of heightened crisis – in which they fear being attacked by Iranian ballistic missiles, just as they were by Iraq's during the 1991 Gulf War – the Israelis will deploy their Dolphin Class boats. These vessels will undertake marathon voyages around Africa, as a passage by a Dolphin through the Suez Canal would be highly visible and open to attack (and most likely opposed by Egypt).

Placing submarines in the Eastern Mediterranean to fire nuclear-tipped cruise missiles over land to Iran is not a good idea. It is replete with risk because that kind of relatively slow, low-flying weapon can more easily be shot down during its flight to target than a ballistic missile. It could even accidentally land on a friendly state and detonate.

Once into the Indian Ocean Israeli submarines would patrol off the Iranian shore, ready to fire missiles at Tehran. The Israelis have allegedly already road-tested the idea by firing submarine-launched conventional cruise missiles at terrorist bases in the Horn of Africa.

The advent of nuclear-tipped cruise missiles in submarines also means that even when a boat launches a conventionally-armed one there is a fear of nuclear attack. That could provoke an unfortunate response from the target. The lines between conventional and nuclear weapons are becoming dangerously blurred, with a commensurate risk of terrible consequences.

Extremely bellicose statements by North Korea and Russia in response to what they perceive as provocations by other countries do not help. Russia today does not shrink from threatening nuclear assault if other nations even dare to propose defending themselves from ballistic missile attack.

In the summer of 2014, when asked about his views on the crisis in Ukraine – just days after NATO had presented proof of Russian troops mounting a de facto invasion – Putin's response came straight out of the Soviet playbook. 'Russia is one of the most powerful nuclear states,' he observed, adding with relaxed assurance: 'It's not words, it is the reality . . . we are strengthening our powers of nuclear restraint.'

Putin assured the world that Russia is 'always ready to repel any act of aggression' and then delivered a warning worthy of any Hollywood mafia movie heavy: 'Our partners, regardless of the situation their countries are in or their foreign policy line, have to always realise that it's better not to mess with Russia.'[20]

In the face of such menace European nations felt they had no option but to sign up to NATO's ballistic missile defence shield. In April 2015 the Danes had the temerity to reveal that their new guided-missile frigates would join it. This provoked a dark warning from Mikhail Vanin, Ambassador to Denmark, who told a newspaper: 'If that happens, Danish warships will be targets for Russian nuclear missiles.'[21]

It was not the first time Russia has issued warnings to a NATO nation against fielding warships as part of the BMD shield. Three years earlier it warned Norway not to fit their AEGIS combat system-equipped Fridtjof Nansen Class frigates with Standard missiles capable of shooting down ballistic missiles. It reeked of hypocrisy, the clunking fist being raised against the West while Russia pursued her own shield. In the summer of 2016, as the UK Parliament voted to press ahead with renewing Trident, the Russians were busy upgrading their own formidable (and long established) BMD systems to defend Moscow. The primary aim was to make the new British and American ballistic missile submarines impotent.

Postscript • The Better Angels

We have voyaged across the vast span of submarine warfare history to a point where vessels that men once dreamed of in order to explore the wonders of the deep now carry cargoes of nuclear annihilation. The new rivalry between Russia and the West – including the construction of ballistic missile boats – does seem like a rewind to the bad old days.

China's bid for dominance over the South China Sea to hide its own submarines in a version of the Soviet-era 'bastion' also appears to echo the Cold War. India's entry into the top tier of submarine operators – via its own SSBNs – seems fraught with potential for catastrophic miscalculation as likely opponents arm themselves accordingly.

The fielding of submarines to pursue the latter-day equivalent of MAD is of course not strictly submarine warfare. Ballistic missile boats are political tools – symbols of great power status – and a big stick to wave at people you feel pose an existential threat to your nation or vital interests.

SSBNs arguably prevented a Third World War due to the fear of where a major conventional conflict in Europe might lead. During the Second World War non-nuclear combat killed more than 60 million people[1] while across the course of the Cold War around seven million people died,[2] though this was hardly something to be proud of. What President Abraham Lincoln called 'the better angels of our nature'[3] prevailed through moments such as the Cuban Missile Crisis of 1962 and the Able Archer misunderstanding in 1983.

The paradox of the ballistic missile submarine is that it is not a weapon of war, but rather of peace – designed to prevent major conflict by persuading potential aggressors that there is no point in even thinking of using their own WMD. The danger is that certain political leaders may not understand that. They might see it as a weapon that can be used in combat to gain an advantage politically, economically or militarily. We will live with that possibility until the day nuclear-armed submarines no longer prowl the oceans, young men and women cease their vigil over land-based silos and strategic bombers are grounded permanently.

In the early 1990s it did seem that we had moved beyond all that, with MAD out of fashion and redundant in a world where there was only one superpower, the USA. It was meant to maintain Pax Americana, in which democracy and freedom for all could thrive and tyrants could be tamed or easily deposed. It hasn't happened. For all that, there is a possibility that ballistic missile submarines will continue to be weapons for peace, preventing another world war if not able to stop the conflagrations on the edges of our twenty-first century New World Order.

Away from the prospect of Armageddon, is there still the possibility of conventional submarine warfare? Whether in the hands of rogue states like North Korea or Iran (which also has numerous mini sub-marines at its disposal) or operated by the North American, European, Latin American, African or Asia-Pacific nations, there seems to be a conviction that one day there may be a need to wage war on enemy surface warships and merchant vessels. A large proportion of consumer goods, food, oil and gas – indeed most of everything countries need for work and play – still travels by sea in massive ships. Using submarines to devastate sea trade is an obvious tactic should feuding nations decide to settle their differences through force of arms.

Launching a war of aggression is seldom, if ever, a wise course of action but common sense does not always prevail. It can be overcome by pure hatred for the would-be foe, or fuelled by rampant nationalism or huge resentment and hurt pride.

If the Germans had really thought hard about where events might lead them they would not have embarked on two costly, disastrous wars – including ultimately futile U-boat campaigns – in the space of 25 years. Likewise, any logical assessment of its vulnerability to sub-marine blockade would have suggested to Japan that a war of conquest was not its best course of action to secure the raw materials it needed.

People persuade themselves they can beat the odds and this time it will be different. That faith is why so many young men on both sides went to war in submarines during the global conflicts of the twentieth century, despite their slim chance of surviving.

The undersea warriors of today and tomorrow will, like their fore-bears, reckon they can beat the odds and so will the nations that deploy them on war patrols. To borrow and adapt the Spanish philosopher-poet George Santayana's famous phrase, it is likely only the dead have seen the last of submarine warfare.[4] Humanity will have to put its faith in 'the better angels'. The submarine, for good or ill, seems destined to play a major part in world events, and indeed its activities could yet decide the fate of all humanity.

Appendix: The Price Paid
Unwept, unhonoured, and unsung?

Germany never fielded a balanced navy in the Second World War and in both global conflicts of the twentieth century resorted to the type of vessel it could build plenty of and felt was most useful for its strategy: the U-boat.

Of the 630 U-boats that never returned home from forays in distant waters between September 1939 and May 1945 a total of 521 were destroyed by British and Dominion forces, including 275 by the Royal Navy.* Twenty-one were destroyed by enemy submarines and of these all but one while sailing on the surface.

The majority of Germany's submarine losses occurred between August 1942 and May 1945, with 81 U-boats also sunk in home waters by enemy mines or air attack. A further 257 were lost due to accidents or were scuttled by their own crews at the end of the war.

It made a quite staggering total of 968 U-boats destroyed by all causes, though Germany built 1,162 U-boats during the conflict. Thirty-eight U-boats were decommissioned during the course of the war, with another 11 trapped in neutral ports or boarded and taken over by the enemy.

The Allies received the surrender of 153 U-boats, with many taken to Lisahally, near Londonderry, or kept at Loch Ryan in Scotland while the victors decided how best to divide up the spoils of war.

The Russians were awarded ten U-boats, including four Type XXIs, the French received seven U-boats, the Americans and British each took ten (including two Type XXIs each). Even sunken submarines would be exploited, the Swedes salvaging *U-3503* from the bottom of the Baltic to investigate her cutting-edge technology. The West Germans also raised U-boats for research and even operational use. Second World War-era U-boats served for some years in various navies, including the former *U-2540*. A Type XXI, she was raised by the Bundesmarine in 1957 and rechristened *Wilhelm Bauer* in honour of Germany's first submariner.

Those U-boats not selected for further use by Allied navies in the immediate aftermath of the war were disposed of during Operation Deadlight, which was staged between December 1945 and February 1946. They were despatched by different means, with not all of them eager to go on their last dive. The boats were towed out to sea with no crews aboard, in groups of between six and ten, heading for the 100-fathom line north-west of Ireland. Some sank on the way in terrible weather but having their sea cocks and hatches opened scuttled the majority. A few were torpedoed while others proved very hard to sink, even with gunfire.

But what of those vessels Hitler's submarines sank? The damage done by U-boats in the Atlantic alone was 2,603 merchant vessels sunk (13,500,000 tons in total) along with 175 Allied naval vessels. More than 30,000 Allied merchant mariners were killed in that contest and Allied navies lost 33,000 people.

Such statistics – and it is worth presenting them to make clear the sheer scale of folly and suffering – are an indictment of the futility of war. Only someone totally lacking in imagination could fail to understand from scrutinising them how shocking was the waste in lives and national treasure.

While it was the German submarine force that had suffered the worst casualties, Allied underwater warriors also paid a pretty high price.

The British at their peak during the Second World War had 88 submarines in commission. One naval officer who worked on the staff of FOSM observed that while it was remarkable that it never even reached a hundred that wasn't surprising. The main weapon of the Royal Navy was not the submarine but rather its battleships, cruisers, carriers and destroyers.[1]

The Royal Navy suffered 74 submarines sunk, along with seven X-craft. The last RN submarine lost on patrol in the Second World War was *Porpoise*, a large minelaying boat, probably sunk on 9 January 1945 (by a mine strike off Penang). There were no survivors.

Twenty-five thousand men served in the British submarine arm during the conflict, with 3,142 killed and 359 taken prisoner. The Royal Navy's submarines sank 84 merchant vessels (270,000 tons) in North European waters and 361 merchant vessels (1,157,000 tons) in the Mediterranean. The RN's boats sank six Axis cruisers, 16 destroyers, 35 submarines and 112 other enemy naval vessels. In the Far East British submarines sank 48 Japanese merchant ships (97,000 tons), not including the many minor vessels destroyed, such as sampans.

The Americans suffered 52 boats lost (including two in the Atlantic and two due to accident or mishap) with 3,505 men killed out of the 14,750 who served in the USN submarine force during the Second World War. The Japanese so overestimated their success they claimed to have destroyed 468 American submarines. In reality, 48 boats were destroyed in action against the Japanese.

During the Second World War the Russians lost 101 boats to all causes. France lost 23 submarines, though the majority were flying Vichy colours and so were sunk by the Allies. Holland lost 15 boats – most of them in the Far East, while resisting the invasion of the Dutch East Indies. Poland lost two. Dutch submarines sank two Japanese naval vessels (3,920 tons combined) and ten merchant vessels (42,049 tons) while the Norwegian boat *Ula* destroyed *U-974* in the North Sea in 1944.

On the losing side, the Italians suffered 85 boats sunk by the Allies (between June 1940 and their capitulation in September 1943) while the Japanese lost 127 boats, including 19 sunk by Allied submarines.

In comparison to the deadly harvest reaped by German submarines, the Japanese force scored only 185 merchant vessels sunk (900,000 tons). The IJN's submarines sank two USN fleet carriers and an escort carrier, along with two cruisers and a dozen other smaller naval vessels.

The Italians are reckoned to have sent 129 merchant vessels (668,311 tons) and 13 enemy warships (25,554 tons) to the bottom in all theatres of war. Italy in return lost 2,018,616 tons of merchant vessels.

As Nicholas Monsarrat raged in his memoir of escort warship command, *Three Corvettes*, the Allied merchant mariners sailed for a pittance compared to the black marketeers and others who profited from swindling petrol rations and other supplies. Many of the mariners seeking to deliver petrol for the Allied war effort (and swindlers' cars) died a terrible death in flames on a cruel sea after their ships were torpedoed. This horrible fate made foul profiteering ashore utterly despicable.

> *The wretch, concentred all in self,*
> *Living, shall forfeit fair renown,*
> *And, doubly dying, shall go down*
> *To the vile dust, from whence he sprung,*
> *Unwept, unhonoured, and unsung.*[2]

Nobody could apply those stinging words by Sir Walter Scott to the sailors, marines, soldiers and aviators who sailed in the convoys and protected them. Nothing could be further from the truth of the sacrifice at sea made by merchant and naval mariners, whether they served in ships or submarines. In the case of the Axis submariners their valour was at best misguided and at worst for an evil cause. Regardless of their motivation, those who fought at sea are still honoured and their brave deeds remembered – especially when they extended the hand of mercy to a foe.

Those they left behind weep for them still.

The Deadly Trade is a memorial for them all with the hope that nothing on the same scale ever happens again.

* SOURCES

The statistics for the submarine losses were drawn from a number of published sources, which are as follows:

Bekker, Cajus, *Hitler's Naval War*, Doubleday, 1974

Costello, John and Hughes, Terry, *The Battle of the Atlantic*, HarperCollins, 1977

Greene, Jack, on the Italian Navy in *World War II: The Definitive Encyclopedia and Document Collection*, edited by Spencer C. Tucker, ABC-CLIO, 2016

Hutchinson, Robert, *Jane's Submarines: War Beneath the Waves from 1776 to the Present Day*, HarperCollins, 2001

Kemp, Paul, *The Admiralty Regrets: British Warship Losses of the 20th Century*, Sutton, 1999 and *U-boats Destroyed: German Submarine Losses in the World Wars*, Arms and Armour, 1999

Lipscomb, Commander F.W., *The British Submarine*, Conway Maritime Press, 1975

Polmar, Norman and Carpenter, Dorr B., *Submarines of the Imperial Japanese Navy 1904–1945*, Conway, 1986

Rohwer, Jürgen, *Chronology of the War at Sea 1939–1945: The Naval History of World War Two*, Chatham, 2005

Smith, Gordon, *The War at Sea: Royal & Dominion Navy Actions in World War 2*, Ian Allan, 1989

Stille, Mark E., *The Imperial Japanese Navy in the Pacific War*, Osprey, 2013

Relevant statistics also found on these websites:
HISTORYNET
[http://www.historynet.com]
Naval Historical Society of Australia
[https://www.navyhistory.org.au]
Naval History and Heritage Command
[https://www.history.navy.mil]
USS Bowfin Submarine Museum & Park
[http://www.bowfin.org]

Notes

PART ONE

1: Many Falsehoods, Some Truths
1. *The Iliad*, pp. 364–65, Book 21, lines 17–26.
2. Lt Col. Cyril Field, *The Story of the Submarine*, Chapter 1.
3. Another Archimedes invention.
4. Edwyn Gray, *Disasters of the Deep*, p. 18.
5. Botting, *The U-Boats*, p. 17.
6. Robert Hutchinson, *Jane's Submarines: War Beneath the Waves from 1776 to the Present Day*, p. 8.
7. Richard Compton-Hall, 'For, 'tis Private – the Submarine Pioneers', essay in Edmonds, *100 Years of the Trade*, p. 3.
8. USGS Astrogeology Center, *Gazetteer of Planetary Nomenclature*.

2: Into Perpetual Night
1. Lt Col. Cyril Field, *The Story of the Submarine*, Chapter 3.
2. Wm. Barclay Parsons, *Robert Fulton and the Submarine*, p. 19.
3. As quoted, Lt Col. Cyril Field, *The Story of the Submarine*, Chapter 3.
4. *Western Flying Post*, 4 July 1774.
5. As quoted in Robert Hutchinson, *Jane's Submarines: War Beneath the Waves, from 1776 to the Present Day*, p. 9, and also in *Western Flying Post*, 4 July 1774.
6. *Western Flying Post*, 4 July 1774.
7. Summary of the contents and context, *A Philosophical Dissertation on the Diving Vessel Projected by Mr Day*, Nikolai Detlef Falck, 1775, NMM.
8. Richard Compton-Hall, *The Submarine Pioneers*, p. 34.
9. George Washington writing to Thomas Jefferson. Quoted in a profile of the *Turtle*, US Navy Department Library.

3: 'Humane Torpedoes'
1. Cynthia Owen Philip, *Robert Fulton*, p. 73.
2. Wm. Barclay Parsons, p. 23.
3. Ibid.
4. Fulton's letter to a friend, as quoted by Alice Crary Sutcliffe, in *Robert Fulton*, Chapter 7.
5. Cynthia Owen Philip, p. 99.
6. Compton-Hall, *The Submarine Pioneers*, p. 45.
7. Compton-Hall, essay in *100 Years of the Trade*, p. 6.

8. Cynthia Owen Philip, p. 116.
9. Ibid., p. 154.
10 Barclay Parsons, p. 59.
11. Ibid., p. viii.
12. Barclay Parsons, p. 57.
13. Robert Fulton, *Torpedo War*, p. 8.
14. Ibid.
15. Peter Hore, 'British Submarine Policy from St Vincent to Arthur Wilson', essay in *100 Years of the Trade*, p. 9.
16. Add. MS. 34931, Fulton's letter to Nelson, as featured in an article entitled 'Robert Fulton: A Letter to Lord Nelson', British Library Journal, by R.A.H. Smith.
17. Andrew Lambert, *Nelson*, p. 286.
18. Prior to leaving he made arrangements for his work to be preserved even if he was lost at sea. Fulton wrote to diplomat and businessman Joel Barlow explaining that he had left his drawings inside a metal cylinder deposited with the American Consul in London, General William Lyman. The tin would be forgotten and not opened until the 1920s.
19. Fulton, *Torpedo War*, p. 38.
20. Ibid., p. 41.
21. Cyril Field, Chapter 6.
22. Bushnell's date of birth and year of death vary depending on which source is consulted.
23. Sam Fore, 'David Bushnell (1740–1826)', *New Georgia Encyclopedia*.

4: A Bonnet Full of Secrets

1. Allan Pinkerton, *The Spy of the Rebellion*, p. 401.
2. *Harper's Weekly*, 2 November 1861.
3. Pinkerton, p. 403.
4. Ibid.

5: Troublesome *Alligator*

1. Letter from Brutus de Villeroi to President Lincoln, Navy & Marine Living History Association (NMLHA), *The Hunt for the* Alligator.
2. Ibid.
3. US Census Records, 11 June 1860, via NMLHA.
4. Letter from de Villeroi to Joseph Smith, 29 December 1861, *Letters Relating to* Alligator *Construction & Deployment*, NMLHA.
5. Letter from William Hirst to Joseph Smith, 12 May 1862, NMLHA.
6. Commission Summary to French Navy, 9 June 1863, *Secrets of the* Alligator, National Marine Sanctuaries.
7. Bill Gunston, *Submarines in Colour*, pp. 102–3.

6: The Murdering Machine

1. Information on the *Hunley* obtained by the US Navy from the interrogation

of Confederate deserters, 7 January 1864, US Naval History and Heritage Command NHHC.

2. Quoted in Mark K. Ragan's *Union and Confederate Submarine Warfare in the Civil War*, p. 128.
3. Journal of Operations, Confederate Headquarters, Charleston, SC, 15 October 1863, NHHC.
4. Compton-Hall, *The Submarine Pioneers*, pp. 72–73.

7: First Kill

1. Order of Rear Admiral Dahlgren, US Navy, 7 January 1864, NHHC.
2. Ibid.
3. Lt William H. Alexander, CSA, 'Work of Submarine Boats', a chapter published in *Southern Historical Society Papers*, Volume XXX, 1902, pp. 164–74.
4. Ibid.
5. Ibid.
6. Report of Captain Green, US Navy, commanding USS *Canandaigua*, 18 February 1864, NHHC.
7. Ibid.
8. Report of Lieutenant Higginson, US Navy, Executive Officer USS *Housatonic*, 18 February 1864, NHHC.
9. Quoted in *The H.L. Hunley in Historical Context*, by Rich Wills, NHHC.
10. Report of Lieutenant Higginson, NHHC.
11. *Post & Courier*, Charleston, 28 January 2013.
12. Compton-Hall, *The Submarine Pioneers*, p. 76.
13. Rich Wills.
14. Ibid.
15. Report of Rear Admiral Dahlgren, US Navy, 19 February 1864, NHHC.

8: Captain Nemo's Monster

1. Jules Verne, *Twenty Thousand Leagues Under the Sea*, p. 135.
2. Ibid.
3. Stephen Howarth, *To Shining Sea*, pp. 209–10.
4. Diana Preston, *Lusitania*, p. 42.
5. Roger Branfill-Cook, *Torpedo*, pp. 170–71.

9: I Shall Rise Again

1. *I shall rise again.*
2. William Scanlan Murphy, *Father of the Submarine*, pp. 32–33.
3. Compton-Hall, *The Submarine Pioneers*, p. 86.
4. Ibid.

10: Fenian Ram

1. As quoted in 'John P. Holland, The Liscannor Man who invented the Sub', Clare County Library profile.
2. Quoted in 'John Philip Holland: the Irish inventor who helped take the war underwater', *Irish Times*, 14 August 2014.

3. Profile of John Ericsson, US Office of National Marine Sanctuaries.
4. Quoted in Lincoln Paine, *The Sea and Civilisation*, Kindle edition.
5. At American funfairs in the late 1800s cigars were presented as prizes.

11: Striking the Balance
1. Quoted in a profile of Holland by Edward C. Whitman, *Undersea Warfare*, Summer 2003.
2. Report in the *Daily Express*, 5 July 1901, quoted in Cdr F.W. Lipscomb's *The British Submarine*, p. 3.
3. Hansard, Navy Estimates debate, House of Commons, 17 July 1900.
4. Speech by H.O. Arnold-Forster during a Parliamentary debate on the Navy Estimates 1902, included in a posthumous biography by his wife Mary, p. 177.
5. Lipscomb, p. 5.
6. Compton-Hall, *The First Submarines*, p. 117.
7. Diaries of Lt Arnold-Forster, as quoted by Compton-Hall in *The Submarine Pioneers*, p. 147.
8. Quoted by the author in his book *Hunter Killers*, p. 2.
9. Nicholas A. Lambert, *Sir John Fisher's Revolution*, pp. 80–81.

12: Feelings of Humanity
1. Quoted by Robert K. Massie, *Castles of Steel*, p. 126.
2. Quoted by Diana Preston in *Lusitania*, p. 43.

PART TWO

1: Jump you Devils!
1. Huxley, letter to his father 14 September 1914, *Scotland's War*, HMS Pathfinder.
2. Leake, letter to his mother, 8 September 1914, Hertfordshire Archives (via Herts Memories).
3. Account in *The Great War, the Illustrated History of the First World War*, Vol. I, p. 392.
4. According to Lt Edward Sonnenschein, quoted by Craig Armstrong, *Berwick-on-Tweed in the Great War*, p. 26. Later in the war this officer, though British born, would change his name by deed poll to Stallybrass, to obscure his family's German origins. The change was advertised via a notice in *London Gazette*, 18 January 1918.
5. Leake, letter to his mother.
6. *The Great War*, Vol. I, p. 393.
7. Quoted by James Goldrick, *Before Jutland*, p. 142.
8. Max Hastings, *Catastrophe*, p. 364.
9. Lipscomb, *The British Submarine*, p. 18.
10. Massie, *Castles of Steel*, p. 106.
11. Churchill, *World Crisis*, p. 262.
12. As recorded in *The Fleet Annual and Naval Yearbook 1917*, p. 14. Prize money awarded on 10 July 1916.

2: Slaughter in Narrow Waters

1. Churchill, *The World Crisis*, p. 276.
2. As quoted in *The U-boats*, p. 22.
3. As quoted by Massie, *Castles of Steel*, p. 138.
4. *The Great War*, Vol. II, p. 431.

3: Stealthy, Inhuman Instruments

1. Dr Bernhard Dernburg, Germany's principal propagandist in the USA and former Colonial Secretary, quoted by Massie, *Castles of Steel*, p. 530.
2. *The Submarine Service 1900–1918*, NRS, p. 232, extract from Churchill to Fisher, 1 January 1914.
3. Churchill, *The World Crisis*, p. 477.
4. uboat.net. A comprehensive online database for submarine warfare in both the global conflicts of the twentieth century. For website see Sources.
5. *The Great War*, Vol. II, p. 428.
6. Quoted by John Terraine in *Business in Great Waters*, p. 9.
7. *New York Times*, 1 May 1915.
8. *Gulflight* would sail on for another 28 years, until a U-boat sank her in the next global conflict.
9. Lowell Thomas, *Raiders of the Deep*, p. 93.
10. Ibid.
11. Ibid.
12. Diana Preston, *Lusitania*, p. 348.
13. Lowell Thomas, p. 96.

4: No Surety of Survival

1. William Jameson, *Submariners VC*, p. 13.
2. Quoted in *Submarines in the Dardanelles, 1915*, Australian government account.
3. *The Great War*, Vol. III, p. 390.
4. *The Submarine Service 1900–1918*, p. 300, NRS, Lt Norman Holbrook to Captain Roger Keyes.

5: The Finest Feat

1. *Submarines in the Dardanelles*, Australian government account, quoting Henry Stoker's autobiography, *Straws in the Wind*.
2. Roger Keyes's letter to his wife, as quoted by David Stevens in his book *In all Respects Ready*, p. 119.
3. Stoker Charles Suckling, letter/account of *AE2*'s patrol, Australian War Memorial. As are other quotes from him here.
4. Account by Stoker as quoted in Compton-Hall, *Submarines and the War at Sea 1914–18*, p. 174.
5. Suckling, AWM.
6. Stoker's letter to *The Times*, 11 October 1921.

6: An Embrace of Death

1. Ellis Ashmead-Bartlett, *The Uncensored Dardanelles*, p. 110.
2. Lowell Thomas, p. 65.
3. Ibid.
4. Ashmead-Bartlett, p. 110.
5. Quoted by Nigel Steel and Peter Hart, *Defeat at Gallipoli*, p. 185.
6. Diary of H.V. Reynolds, 25 May 1915, AWM.
7. Post-war Georg von Trapp became a widower but in 1927 married the tutor of his ten children, Maria Kutschera. Following the 1938 Anschluss – the annexation of Austria as part of the Greater German Reich – Georg von Trapp turned down a new commission in the Kriegsmarine. He also declined a request for the von Trapp family singers – made famous in the Hollywood movie starring Julie Andrews as Maria and Christopher Plummer as Georg – to sing at Hitler's birthday. The von Trapps subsequently went on a singing tour of Europe and the USA and decided to settle in Vermont.
8. Georg von Trapp, *To the Last Salute*, p. 14.
9. Ibid., p.15.
10. Ibid., p. 22.
11. Figures from *The Sound of Torpedoes*, June 2000 edition of the *Naval Historical Review* (Australia).
12. uboat.net.
13. Lowell Thomas, p. 125.
14. Quoted by Compton-Hall, *Submarines and the War at Sea, 1914–18*, p. 236.
15. Lowell Thomas, p. 127.
16. Ibid., p. 129.
17. Ibid.
18. Quoted by Compton-Hall, p. 189.
19. Quoted in the *Daily Telegraph*, 21 April 2015.
20. Alan Moorhead, *Gallipoli*, p. 263.
21. Steel and Hart, p. 371.
22. Source for figures, official New Zealand History website, *Gallipoli Casualties by Country*.

7: Baltic Gatecrashers

1. Capt. Ronald William Blacklock, extracts from *Overthorpe and Some Reminiscences*, p. 12.
2. Compton-Hall quoting the control room log of *E9*, *Submarines and the War at Sea 1914–18*, p. 139.
3. Blacklock, p. 18.
4. Michael Wilson, *Baltic Assignment*, p. 55.
5. Blacklock, p. 22.
6. Ibid.
7. Dwight R. Messimer, *Verschollen*, p. 45. A superb reference work for information on U-boats lost during the First World War.
8. The wreck of *U-26* was discovered, largely intact, off Hanko, by Finnish divers

on 20 May 2014. She had sustained severe damage to her stern, indicating a mine strike.

8: The Submarine Officer's Dream

1. Blacklock, p. 37.
2. Ibid.
3. Ibid.
4. Soren Norby, 'Grim Fate of Unlucky Stranded Submarine *E13*', published in *WARSHIPS IFR* magazine, September 2015 and also see Compton-Hall, *Submarines and the War at Sea, 1914–18*, p. 147.
5. Blacklock, p. 35.
6. As related by W.S. Chalmers, *Max Horton and the Western Approaches*, p. 15.
7. Compton-Hall, *Submarines and the War at Sea*, p. 149 and Wilson pp. 121–22.
8. Private Papers of Commander F.H.H. Goodhart, as are all his diary entries for this incident, IWM.
9. Chalmers, *Max Horton and the Western Approaches*, p. 19.

9: Setting the Traps

1. Franz von Rintelen, *The Dark Invader*, p. 57.
2. Churchill, *The World Crisis*, p. 157.
3. Hansard, 18 May 1916.
4. Quoted by John Pollard in *The Unknown Pope: Benedict XV: 1914–1922*, p. 121.
5. Jellicoe advising the Admiralty on how he would conduct a major fleet-versus-fleet battle, quoted by Richard Hough in *The Great War at Sea*, p. 251.
6. Roger Branfill-Cook, *Torpedo*, p. 178.
7. Ibid., p. 181.

10: Turning the Screw

1. Massie, *Castles of Steel*, p. 658.
2. Stuart Legg, *Jutland: An Eye-witness Account of a Great Battle*, p. 138.
3. Admiral Reinhard Scheer, *Germany's High Sea Fleet in the World War*, p. 239.
4. Ibid.
5. Ibid.
6. Stephen Pope and Elizabeth-Anne Wheal, *The Macmillan Dictionary of the First World War*, p. 441 and David Reynolds, *The Long Shadow*, p. 271, p. 365.
7. Lansdowne Letter, quoted in *The New York Times*, 30 November 1917, from original published in the *Daily Telegraph*, London.
8. Massie, *Castles of Steel*, p. 696.
9. Michael L. Hadley and Roger Sarty, *Tin-Pots & Pirate Ships*, p. 149.
10. *NYT*, 8 October 1916.
11. A.A. Hoehling, *The Great War at Sea*, p. 169.
12. Ibid.
13. Ibid., p. 171.
14. John Herd Thompson and Stephen J. Randall, *Canada and the United States: Ambivalent Allies*, p. 95.

15. Justus D. Doenecke, *Nothing Less Than War*, p. 218.
16. Ibid., p. 219.
17. Figures from Lawrence Sondhaus, *World War One: The Global Revolution*, p. 284.
18. *The Great War*, Vol. V, p. 28.

11: An Impossible Task
1. Admiral Jellicoe, *The Grand Fleet 1914–1916*, p. 285.
2. Ibid., p. 286.
3. Richard Hough, *The Great War at Sea 1914 – 1918*, p. 300.
4. *Fear God and Dread Nought, The Correspondence of Admiral of the Fleet Lord Fisher of Kilverstone*, edited by Arthur J. Marder, Vol. III, p. 414.
5. Ibid., p. 416.
6. Claus Bergen account, 'My U-Boat Voyage', in *U-Boat Stories: Narratives of German U-Boat Sailors*, edited by Karl Neureuther and Claus Bergen, p. 49.
7. Ibid., p. 51.
8. Ibid., p. 90.
9. *The Great War*, Vol. 9, p. 29.
10. Recounted by Churchill in *The World Crisis*, Vol. II, pp. 730–31.
11. F.W. Lipscomb, p. 32.
12. Massie, p. 718.
13. Lipscomb, p. 32.
14. Zimmerman Note, document held in The National Archives, UK.
15. Von Rintelen, p. 195.
16. This voyage was cancelled. It was feared hostilities might maroon the unarmed vessel overseas or lead to her sinking.
17. *NYT*, 5 February 1917.
18. *Chicago Tribune*, 28 February 1917.

12: Struggle by Hunger
1. Jason Tomes, *Balfour and Foreign Policy*, p. 173.
2. *The Life and Letters of Walter H. Page*, pp. 273–74.
3. Von Rintelen, p. 227.
4. Compton-Hall, *Submarines and the War at Sea 1914–18*, p. 264 and Stevenson, *1914–1918*, p. 321.
5. Compton-Hall, *Submarines and the War at Sea 1914–18*, p. 264.
6. Stevenson, *1914–1918*, p. 321.
7. Page, pp. 254–55.
8. Ibid., p. 269.
9. Ibid., p. 272.
10. Rear Admiral W.S. Sims, *The Victory at Sea*, p. 20.
11. Ibid.
12. Ibid.
13. Ibid.
14. Figures from Inverclyde Shipbuilding & Engineering, *The First World War*.
15. Sims, p. 28.

16. Ibid., p. 30.
17. Ibid.
18. Ibid.

13: Demands Upon the World

1. *British Naval Documents 2014–1960, Considerations on a defensive war against Algiers, 1681*, p. 200.
2. Sims, p. 33.
3. Ibid.
4. Julian Thompson, *The War at Sea*, p. 328.
5. Richard Hough, *The Great War at Sea*, p. 308.
6. David Lloyd George, *War Memoirs 1916–1917*, p. 89.
7. Ibid.
8. Ibid.
9. Ibid.
10. Thompson, p. 328.
11. Herbert Richmond, *National Policy and Naval Strength and Other Essays*, p. 99.
12. D.K. Brown, *The Grand Fleet*, p. 125.
13. Ibid., p. 131.
14. Ibid., p. 129.
15. Cdre S.S. Hall, report on Submarine Service work 1 July–31 December 1918, *British Naval Documents 1204–1960*, p. 832.
16. Compton-Hall, *Submarines and the War at Sea*, p. 303.
17. Ibid.

14: Paradise for U-boats

1. Henry Newbolt, *Naval Operations*, Vol. IV, p. 175.
2. Ibid.
3. Terraine, *Business in Great Waters*, p. 99.
4. Introduction by Ettore Cozzani to *The Feast of Saint Gorizia*, Vittorio Locchi.
5. Ibid.
6. Michael Wilson and Paul Kemp, *Mediterranean Submarines*, p. 170.

15: Out Like a Lion

1. Lieutenant L. H. Ashmore of *E18*, as quoted by Compton-Hall, *Submarines and the War at Sea*, p. 249.
2. As quoted by Michael Wilson, *Baltic Assignment*, p. 202, from a letter to the commander of the Submarine Service (Cdre Hall) by Cromie, 19 February 1918, relating to a discussion involving Vice Admiral Hopman and a Russian admiral.
3. King George V did present Cromie's widow with the Order of the Bath.

16: A Damned Good Twist

1. Naval War College Newport Papers, Jan S. Breemer, *Defeating the U-boat*, p. 2.
2. As quoted by Nathan Miller, *The US Navy*, p. 189. Also Josephus Daniels, *Our Navy at War*, p. 144.

3. Sims, p. 316.
4. Ibid., p. 319.
5. Hough, p. 314.
6. Marder, *Fear God and Dread Nought*, p. 532, letter to press written by Fisher on 25 April 1918, but not sent.
7. Ibid., p. 461, Fisher letter to Sir William Watson, 24 June 1917.
8. Stevenson, *With Our Backs to the Wall*, p. 312.
9. H.E. Adams, IWM document. All the quotes from him in this account of the Zeebrugge raid are from the same source.
10. Haig exhortation, quoted by Peter Hart in *1918*, Kindle edition, p. 236.
11. Paul von Hindenburg, *Out of My Life*, e-book edition, p. 337.
12. Ibid., p. 308.
13. Exchange of signals recounted by Philip Warner, *Zeebrugge Raid*, p. 105.

17: Glorified Trench Raid

1. Adams, IWM, as are all quotes from him in this chapter.
2. Carpenter, as reported in the *Ashburton Guardian*, 14 May 1919.
3. Churchill, *World Crisis*, Vol. II, p. 1242.
4. Marder, *Fear God and Dread Naught*, p. 532, letter to George Lambert, 3 May 1918.
5. Lloyd George, *War Memoirs, 1918*, p. 346.
6. Scheer, p. 414.
7. Stevenson, p. 312.
8. Minutes of the War Cabinet, 24 May 1918.
9. Scheer, p. 415.

18: Until Exhaustion

1. Stevenson, *With Our Backs to the Wall*, p. 312.
2. According to uboat.net the largest vessel sunk by a submarine in the conflict was the hospital ship *Britannic*, of 46,758 tons. Claimed on 21 November 1916 in the Aegean, her killer was a mine laid by *U-73*.
3. According to *The U-Boats*, p. 69.
4. Karl Dönitz, *Ten Years and Twenty Days*, Kindle edition.
5. Ibid.
6. Ibid.
7. According to the account of this episode in the papers of Sub Lt Charles Murray, NMM.
8. Quoted by Alexander Watson, *Ring of Steel*, p. 551.
9. Quoted by Holger H. Herwig, *The Luxury Fleet*, p. 247.
10. *The U-Boats*, p. 71.
11. War Cabinet meeting, 4 November 1918.
12. Lowell Thomas, p. 302.

19: Immunity Lost

1. Lowell Thomas, p. 305.
2. Von Trapp, p. 188.

3. *Ludendorff's Own Story*, Vol. II, e-book, p. 328.
4. B.H. Liddell Hart, *A History of the First World War*, p. 549.
5. Ibid., p. 550.
6. BBC TV, *The Great War*, Episode 26, broadcast 22 November 1964.
7. Holger Herwig, *The Luxury Fleet*, p. 247.
8. Clay Blair, Prologue to *Hitler's U-boat War: The Hunters 1939–1942*, Vol. 1, p. 19.
9. Ibid.
10. Reflecting the late entry of the USN into the war and limited deployment, plus scarce targets anyway.
11. As quoted by Blair, *Hitler's U-boat War*, Vol. I, p. 22.
12. Stevenson, *With Our Backs to the Wall*, p. 313.
13. Lowell Thomas, p. 295.
14. D.K. Brown, *The Grand Fleet*, p. 135.
15 As quoted by Henry Kissinger, *Diplomacy*, p. 250.

PART THREE

1: Secret Seedcorn

1. Quoted by Charles Seymour in *Woodrow Wilson and the World War*, p. 42.
2. Quoted by Chalmers, *Max Horton and the Western Approaches*, p. 16.
3. Chatfield, *The Navy and Defence*, p. 193.
4. Ibid.
5. Former captain of both diesel and nuclear-powered submarines Cdr Rob Forsyth to the author.
6. Chatfield, *The Navy and Defence*, p. 196.
7. The Avalon Project, Yale Law School, Lillian Goldman Law Library (online resource). Versailles Treaty, Articles 181, 188, 189, 191 and 209 set out the relevant restrictions and also the disposal of the existing German submarine force.
8. Finland operated five submarines by 1939, all of German design. It fought the Russians in the so-called Winter War, which ended in March 1940 with Finland ceding territory. When the Germans invaded the Soviet Union the Finns resumed their conflict with the Russians and also declared war on Britain (in retaliation for the British declaring war on them). By March 1945 Finland had switched sides, this time to fight with the Allies against Germany. Finland's submarines were minelayers and caused plenty of trouble that way, but torpedo problems frustrated numerous attacks. They did manage to sink three Red Navy submarines in late 1942. All five of Finland's submarines survived hostilities. Only the 300-ton (dived) *Vesikko* avoided being sent to the breakers under the terms of the 1947 Paris Peace Treaty. It banned Finland from building and operating submarines. *Vesikko* is preserved as a museum at Suomenlinna. For more information: http://sotamuseo.fi/en/submarine-vesikko There is a good history of Finland's submarines at http://kotisivut.fonet.fi/%7Earomaa/Navygallery/Submarines/submarines.htm.
9. Zara Steiner, *The Lights That Failed*, p. 591, *Jane's Fighting Ships*, 1931 edition.
10. *Gettysburg Times* report, 14 October 1933.
11. uboat.net biography.

2: It Shall be Attacked

1. Winston Churchill, *The Second World War*, Vol. I, p. 109.
2. Chatfield, *It Might Happen Again*, p. 74.
3. A commentary quoted by William Shirer in *The Rise and Fall of the Third Reich*, p. 287.
4. Ibid., p. 289.
5. Chatfield, *It Might Happen Again*, p. 75.
6. Syd Goodman, *WARSHIPS* IFR magazine Battle of the Atlantic supplement, June 2003 edition.
7. Deutsches U-Boot Museum, *Kriegsmarine U-Boats and the Spanish Civil War*.
8. Tom Buchanan, *Britain and the Spanish Civil War*, p. 59.
9. Quoted in Mike Farquharson-Roberts and John A. G. Roberts, *Royal Naval Officers from War to War*, p. 185.
10. Ibid.
11. *Examiner*, Launceston, Australia, 2 February 1938.
12. Statement read out to MPs in the House of Commons on 7 February 1938, Hansard.

3: Battle Stations Immediate

1. Alastair Mars, *British Submarines at War*, p. 27.
2. *Northern Times*, Carnarvon, W.A., 9 October 1937.
3. As reported by *Sydney Morning Herald*, 11 October 1937.
4. Rear Admiral J.R. Hill, *Anti-Submarine Warfare*, p. 109.
5. Shirer, p. 622.
6. Private Papers of Vice Admiral Sir Ian McGeoch, IWM. McGeoch saw much action in the Second World War and in the 1960s was the RN's Flag Officer Submarines (FOSM).
7. Dönitz, *Memoirs*.
8. Hansard, 15 November 1937.
9. Dönitz, *Memoirs*.
10. Lemp biographical details via uboat.net and also C.B. 4051 (23), *U-110 Interrogation of Survivors, May 1941*, by the Naval Intelligence Division. This official British document was accessed via the excellent online U-boat Archive. For website address, see Sources.
11. Signal quoted in Lawrence Paterson's *First U-Boat Flotilla*, p. 14.
12. Marc Milner, in *Battle of the Atlantic*, mentions the torpedo circling and threatening to hit *U-30* (p. 18) while in *Hitler's U-boat War*, Vol. I, Clay Blair says after holing *Athenia* and surfacing Lemp tried to fire a third torpedo into the ship, but it 'malfunctioned or missed' (p. 67).
13. *NYT*, 5 September 1939.
14. Ibid., 6 September 1939.
15. Signal quoted in Cajus Bekker's *Hitler's Naval War*, p. 20.
16. *NYT*, 6 September 1939.
17. Shirer, p. 637.
18. *NYT*, 6 September 1939.

19. Ibid.

4: Slow off the Mark

1. IWM recorded interview with John Henry Eaden, as are all quotes from him in this chapter.
2. To the Board of Inquiry. As recounted by Peter Smith for the Naval Historical Society of Australia, 'The Loss of HMS Oxley 1939'. Article on NHSA website but originally published by the Submarines Association of Australia.
3. 'Account of the sinking of the S.S. *Fanad Head*', IWM documents. By an anonymous passenger travelling from Montreal to Belfast aboard the merchant vessel.
4. Ibid.
5. Ibid.
6. Ibid.
7. William Jameson, *Ark Royal*, p. 26.
8. A.D. Divine, *Destroyer's War*, p. 7.
9. Ibid., p. 10.

5: Like Hungry Gulls

1. IWM *Fanad Head* passenger account.
2. Ibid.
3. David Owen, *Anti-Submarine Warfare*, p. 75.
4. According to Peter C. Smith in *Skua*, p. 70.
5. *Fanad Head* passenger account, IWM.
6. Recorded interview with Guy Griffiths, IWM.
7. *Fanad Head* passenger account, IWM.
8. Some accounts say an officer was also present but Griffiths only mentions two German submariners.
9. *Fanad Head* passenger account, IWM.
10. Ibid.
11. Griffiths, IWM.
12. Ibid.
13. Ibid.
14. Ibid.
15. Ibid.
16. Peter C. Smith, *Skua*, Kindle edition.
17. After a failed bid to escape Griffiths was sent to Stalag Luft III, which would gain fame as *The Great Escape* PoW camp. A talented artist, Griffiths helped fake German documents for various would-be escapers.
18. Vice Admiral Lionel Wells, Vice Admiral Aircraft Carriers; his report on *Ark Royal*'s actions during this period. Via Naval-History.Net, another fantastic online resource. See Sources.
19. U-boat Force War Log, 27 September 1939, via U-boat Archive.
20. Hansard, 26 September 1939.
21. Ibid.

22. Eaden, IWM recording, as are all the quotes from him.
23. There is analysis of this situation by Donald McLachlan in *Room 39*, and also by Mallmann Showell in *German Naval Code Breakers*.

6: Boldest of Bold Enterprises

1. Dönitz, *Memoirs*.
2. Ibid.
3. Ibid.
4. Quoted by Wolfgang Frank, *Enemy Submarine*, p. 34.
5. Ibid.
6. Ibid, p. 37.
7. Prien's log, *U-47 Second War Patrol*, via U-boat Archive.
8. Ibid.
9. Ibid. A fourth torpedo did not leave its tube.
10. Ibid.
11. Ibid.
12. Report, 'Sinking of *Royal Oak*', British Admiralty translation, via U-boat Archive.
13. In March 2016, a torpedo possibly fired by *U-47* that missed *Royal Oak* was found on the seabed at Scapa by a Remotely operated Vehicle (ROV). Vessels were advised to avoid dropping their anchors in its vicinity. Royal Navy divers subsequently disposed of the torpedo with controlled explosions.
14. Churchill, *The Second World War*, Vol. I, p. 385.
15. Quoted by Franz Kurowski in *U-48*, p. 54.
16. During an interview with the author, June 2014.
17. '*U-110* Interrogation of Survivors' report, via U-boat Archive.
18. Ibid.

7: Cheated of Certain Success

1. Papers of Vice Admiral A.H. Talbot, IWM. Other quotes from him in this chapter are from the same source.
2. This is also from the Talbot papers, IWM.
3. Ibid.
4. Dönitz, U-Boat War Log, 29 November 1939, via U-boat Archive.
5. Papers of Admiral John Godfrey, NMM.
6. Ibid.
7. Terraine, p. 237.
8. Interview with the author, August 1999.
9. uboat.net.
10. Blair, *Hitler's U-boat War*, Vol. I, p. 119.
11. Talbot, IWM.
12. Patrick Beesly, *Very Special Admiral*, p. 130.
13. Dönitz summing up the U-boat force torpedo problems in the War Log, 18 April 1940, via U-boat Archive.

8: Magnificent Days

1. Lipscomb, p. 55.
2. Chalmers, *Max Horton and the Western Approaches*, p. 70.
3. Mars, *British Submarines*, p. 32.
4. Chalmers, *Max Horton and the Western Approaches*, p. 70.
5. Bryant in *Submarine Commander*, quoted by Timothy P. Mulligan in *Neither Sharks Nor Wolves*, p. 154.
6. Issued late November/early December 1939. Dönitz would explain at his Nuremberg war crimes trial that it applied to boats operating during winter weather in waters close to enemy land and not to Atlantic U-boats. They were still expected to rescue people, he claimed, if it did not endanger the U-boats. By November 1940, so Dönitz claimed during the trial, he had rescinded the order. The cross examination of Dönitz is contained in Nuremberg Trial Proceedings Vol. 13, accessed via the Yale Law School, The Avalon Project (online resource). There are minor variations of the text, depending on translation.

9: Last Stand of the *Shark*

1. Eric Eaton, IWM recording, as are all other quotes from him in this chapter.
2. The majority of *Shark*'s men were PoWs until the end of the war. Determined not to remain behind the wire, Engine Room Artificer (ERA) Frederick Hammond teamed up with fellow ERA Donald Lister, another submariner PoW, from *Seal*. The two managed to tunnel out of a camp at Sandbostel, near Hamburg and after being recaptured were both sent to Colditz, which was meant to be a camp for officers who were hardened escapers. Complaining about this (but secretly obtaining expertly forged documents from the talented escapers held in Colditz) the submariners were sent to a less heavily guarded PoW camp. They soon escaped again. After many adventures Hammond and Lister made it across the border into neutral Switzerland and eventually back to Britain, the only captured Royal Navy submariner PoWs ever to make a successful home run.
3. German officer's encounter with *Shark* survivors recounted by Eaton, IWM recording.
4. As quoted by Mulligan, p. 58.
5. Between 27 May and 4 June 338,226 British and Allied troops were evacuated from Dunkirk and the surrounding beaches, largely by the ships of the Royal Navy.
6. Talbot, IWM.
7. Ibid.
8. Ibid.
9. *The Merchant Navy: Britain's Lifeline*, Merseyside Museum.
10. Figures from a report in the *Advocate*, Tasmania, 30 May 1939.
11. David Edgerton, *Britain's War Machine*, p. 14.
12. According to *The Battle of the Atlantic* (three part documentary series, written and produced by Andrew Williams), part one, *The Grey Wolves* (first broadcast

July 2002). Probably the finest ever production of its kind on the struggle in the Atlantic during the Second World War, by virtue of its skilful presentation, but most of all because it featured the testimony to camera of warriors from both sides and merchant sailors and civilians embroiled in it. Another valuable source of analysis on this is Richard James Hammond's *Food and Agriculture in Britain, 1939–45, Aspects of Wartime Control.* A more contemporary concise source is Martin Brayley's *The British Home Front 1939–45.*

13. Article published by the *Kerryman*, 10 January 1999.
14. Ibid.

10: Wolves Unleashed

1. Donald Macintyre, *The Battle of the Atlantic*, p. 37.
2. Dreyer quotes come from the Talbot papers, IWM, which include a submission by the admiral to the committee investigating ASW called *Memorandum A.*
3. Talbot papers, IWM.
4. Private papers of Vice Admiral Sir Roderick Macdonald, IWM, as are all quotes from him in this chapter.
5. Volkmar König, during on-camera interview for *The Battle of the Atlantic*, BBC TV documentary.
6. 'U-99 Interrogation of Survivors', via U-boat Archive.
7. Ibid.

11: The Quiet Fury of Silent Otto

1. *NYT*, 23 September 1940.
2. Quoted in IWM online account of the sinking.
3. *NYT*, 24 September 1940.
4. Ibid., 23 September 1940.
5. Hansard, House of Commons debate 9 April 1941.
6. Capt. Gilbert Roberts during an on-camera interview for *The World at War*, Thames Television documentary series, episode entitled *Wolf Pack.*
7. Michael Irwin, recorded interview, IWM, as are other quotes from him.
8. Papers of Lt Cdr Ronald Keymer, Merseyside Maritime Museum, as are other quotes from him.
9. The Night of the Long Knives was a massacre in June 1934 of political and paramilitary leaders and members who Hitler believed posed a threat.
10. As detailed Blair, *Hitler's U-boat War*, Vol. I, pp. 199–200.
11. U-boat force War Log, 20 October 1940, via U-boat Archive.

12: Prime Minister's Peril

1. Churchill, *The Second World War*, Vol. II, pp. 529–30.
2. Report of Proceedings HG-53, National Museum of the Royal Navy (NMRN).
3. U-boat force War Log entry, 9 February 1941, via U-Boat Archive.
4. William Pollock, recorded interview IWM, as are all quotes.
5. Gretton, *Convoy Escort Commander*, p. 110.
6. For more details, see 'Liverpool and the Battle of the Atlantic', online fact sheet, Merseyside Maritime Museum.

7. Ibid.
8. Noble took over from Admiral Sir Martin Dunbar-Nasmith, as he was then known. Dunbar-Nasmith, the former captain of *E11* and winner of the VC, held various positions between the wars including Rear Admiral in command of the Submarine Service. Made a full admiral in 1936, he was appointed Commander-in-Chief Plymouth and Western Approaches in 1938, tackling the U-boat menace in a very difficult period. The enemy's forces were growing and becoming more deadly with the escort force struggling to cope with a lack of numbers and poor quality in vessels, along with faulty tactics.

13: This Horrible Foe

1. Figures from Redford, *A History of the Royal Navy, World War II*, p. 46.
2. Churchill, *The Second World War*, Vol. III, p. 101.
3. Ibid., p. 100.
4. Ibid., p. 106.
5. Ibid.
6. Churchill, *The Second World War*, Vol. II, p. 529.
7. Admiralty official, *The Report by the Captain of the Destroyer HMS* Wolverine, *Lieutenant-Commander J.M. Rowland, on the attack on* U47 [as reproduced in *Enemy Submarine* by Wolfgang Frank, pp. 11–16]. Same source for Rowland quotes in the rest of chapter.
8. U-Boat force War Log 1–15 March 1941, via U-boat Archive.
9. Frank, p. 151.

14: Phantom of Destruction

1. The blackened hulk burned until morning and would stay afloat and be brought under tow. *Erodona* was later reconstructed and brought back into service.
2. Donald Macintyre, *U-Boat Killer*, p. 33.
3. '*U-99* Interrogation of Survivors', via U-Boat Archive.
4. Macintyre, p. 35.
5. '*U-99* Interrogation of Survivors', Admiralty summary of the action contained therein.
6. Terence Robertson, *The Golden Horseshoe*, p. 145.
7. Ibid., p. 148.
8. Ibid., p. 147. The signal from *U-99* was recorded in the relevant 'Interrogation of Survivors' report as: 'Depth charges – captured – Heil Hitler – Kretschmer'.
9. V&W Destroyers Association website profile of HMS *Walker*.
10. Kretschmer testimony, *The World at War*, collection of transcripts from participants in the TV series, p. 177.
11. Churchill, *The Second World War*, Vol. III, p. 110.

15: The Enigma of Fritz-Julius Lemp

1. Quoted by Hugh Sebag-Montefiore, *Enigma*, p. 138.
2. '*U-110* Interrogation of Survivors' report, via U-Boat Archive.
3. Ibid.

4. Ibid.
5. Ibid.
6. Related by Sebag-Montefiore, p. 138.
7. Stephen Roskill, *The Secret Capture*, p. 135.
8. '*U-110* Interrogation of Survivors'.
9. Roskill, *The Secret Capture*, p. 238.
10. Ibid., p. 140.
11. The U-boat's Quartermaster, as reproduced in '*U-110* Interrogation of Survivors' report.
12. Sebag-Montefiore, p. 140.
13. Roskill, p. 140.
14. '*U-110* Interrogation of Survivors'.
15. Ibid.
16. Andrew Williams, *Battle of the Atlantic*, p. 132.
17. Ibid.
18. As recounted by Ecke in the BBC TV series *The Battle of the Atlantic*, Episode two of three, *Keeping Secrets*.
19. Wilde interviewed in the same episode of the above TV series.
20. Roskill, p. 142.
21. Ibid., p. 143.
22. Pollock, IWM.
23. David Balme, IWM, recorded interview.
24. Paul Kemp, *U-boats Destroyed*, p. 70.
25. Sebag-Montefiore, p. 143.
26. Pollock, IWM.

16: Look at this, Sir

1. Balme, IWM.
2. Pollock, IWM.
3. Ibid.
4. Ibid.
5. Ibid.
6. Balme, IWM.
7. The officers-only settings were just that – for signals sent for the attention of a U-boat's officers only. Such messages were actually encoded twice – first using the current officer settings and then again using the standard (extant) settings distributed to boats for their non-commissioned communications specialists to use (as explained by Sebag-Montefiore, *Enigma*, p. 150). Sebag-Montefiore also points out that the materials seized from *U-110* were not as immediately useful as those from the weather ship *München*. This vessel was intercepted and seized in Arctic waters by a boarding party from HMS *Somali* on 7 May 1941. Officer settings taken from *U-110* were still crucial to code-breaking later in the war. Another earlier capture, from the armed trawler *Krebs*, came during a commando raid on the Lofoten Islands on 4 March 1941. *Somali* was again responsible, encountering *Krebs* coming out of harbour to see what all the fuss

was off the islands. The guns of the British destroyer disabled the German vessel but did not sink her, enabling a boarding party to seize Engima materials (as recounted in the author's account of the Lofoten raid in his book *HMS Rodney*, p. 119).

17: The Suspicions of Admiral Dönitz

1. U-Boat force War Log, 18 April 1941, via U-boat Archive. As the war progressed the anxiety surfaced again, with U-boats operating in coastal waters in 1944, for example, identified as particularly vulnerable. An incident in which the Russians salvaged *U-250* – sunk in the Gulf of Finland on 30 July 1944 – and retrieved Enigma material (along with new homing torpedoes) led to the U-boat command issuing a warning to its submarine captains. 'Loss of U-boats in shallow waters gives the enemy the possibility of diving for cipher material and data.' U-boat captains were in December 1944 ordered to ensure that 'cipher data are so kept that water can actually come into contact with the red [soluble] print.' This would ensure that the settings dissolved. Furthermore U-boat captains were instructed that when the cipher machine was not being used it should be disconnected, with the crucial rotors removed and 'disarranged'. The U-boat command also ordered: 'Keep everything concealed in separate places' while the 'keyword orders' were to be known by no more than three officers. Failure to take such measures could lead to 'unforeseeable results for the U-boat war'. The threat of boarding by the enemy was also much on the U-boat command's mind. In January 1945 it would advise captains: 'So great is the enemy's interest in new devices – ENIGMA cipher machines and cipher aids of U-boats – that he attempts in every possible way to board U-boats . . .' Despite these fears and instructions, the US intelligence services believed that even on surrender, when the Germans handed over their 'cipher keys' to the Allies, the U-boat force still did not realise there had been 'a cryptanalytic compromise'. The above is detailed (along with text of instructions to U-boat captains) in *German Naval Communication Intelligence, Battle of the Atlantic Volume III*, accessed via the NHHC online archive. The *U-250* salvage operation was completed by the Soviets even while they were under fire from the enemy's shore batteries and marauding torpedo boats. Once pumped out at Kronstadt, the Type VIIC submarine's interior was plundered, the Russians not sharing any of the craft's secrets with the Allies. For more on *U-250's* demise and recovery see Kemp's *U-Boats Destroyed*, pp. 206–7 or uboat.net account.
2. This meeting was detailed by Robertson in *The Golden Horseshoe*, pp. 159–60.
3. Patrick Beesly, *Very Special Intelligence*. Introduction by W.J.R. Gardner, 2000 edition, p. xix.
4. Peter Gretton transcript, *The World at War* oral history book, p. 175.
5. *U-570* went on to become HMS *Graph*, making war patrols under Royal Navy colours, also providing many useful insights into the handling characteristics of German submarines. These were fed to the commanders of escort groups so they could anticipate how their foe might manoeuvre under attack. *Graph* came close to sinking *U-333* in late 1942, but her torpedoes missed or detonated prematurely.

6. Anthony Martienssen, *Hitler and His Admirals*, p. 125.
7. uboat.net biography.
8. U-boat force War Log, 16–30 November 1941, via U-boat Archive.
9. *NYT*, 5 September 1941.
10. Ibid.

18: Prisoner of War No. 1.

1. Quoted in Oliver North and Musser's *Heroism in the Pacific*, p. 28.
2. Sakamaki's obituary, *NYT*, 21 Dec 1999.
3. Quoted in *Dec 7, 1941* by Gordon W. Prange, with Donald Goldstein and Katherine V. Dillon, p. 92.
4. It would be decades before the wreck of the Japanese submarine was found, on the seabed at a depth of 1,200ft.
5. Prange et al., p. 93.
6. Ibid., p. 235.
7. The craft attacked by *Monaghan* was raised a few weeks later and its wreckage incorporated in the foundations of a new naval base pier. Sakamaki's boat was restored and sent on a war bonds tour of the USA, bringing in more than enough money to cover the cost of raising Pacific Fleet battleships from the bottom of Pearl Harbor (and also of restoring them to front line service). Another midget submarine would be recovered from waters outside Pearl Harbor in the early 1960s and presented to the Japan Maritime Self-Defense Force (JMSDF) for display as a memorial vessel. No signs of where, or how, the other two midget submarines met their end have ever been found.
8. Roosevelt speech, FDR Presidential Library & Museum.
9. Roskill, *The Navy at War 1939–1945*, p. 193.

19: Deadly Drumbeat

1. Roskill, *The Navy at War*, p. 194.
2. War Cabinet Weekly resume, July 30 to August 6 1942.
3. Roskill, p. 196.
4. From transcript of Capt. Roberts as published in *The World at War* oral history book, p. 17.
5. Walker's pet name for his wife.
6. The novelist Nicholas Monsarrat was a WATU student and must have listened intently to his lectures, gaining inspiration for the title of a famous novel he wrote after the war. He heard Roberts describe the Battle of the Atlantic as 'the war of the little ships and the lonely aircraft; long, patient and unpublicised, against our two great enemies the U-boat and the cruel sea'. Monsarrat filed that description away, producing an unyielding account of the battle against the U-boats called *The Cruel Sea*, published in 1952.

20: Serve Some Tea

1. As quoted by John Frayn Turner, *VCs of the Royal Navy*, p. 79.
2. Such was the high regard in which Wanklyn was held among his brother

officers they commissioned renowned artist Harry Morley to create a portrait. Unveiled at the summer 1943 show of the Royal Academy in London, it depicts Wanklyn, binoculars in hand, on the bridge of *Upholder*, eyes fixed firmly on the far horizon. It is currently on show at the Royal Navy Submarine Museum in Gosport, Hampshire.

3. Quotes taken from Raikes's unpublished, unabridged memoir, a copy of which was given to the author when he and the submarine captain met for an interview in 1996. Raikes's reflections on his war, including those garnered during the interview, were subsequently published in the *Western Morning News*, 25 November 1996. Another copy of Raikes's memoirs was provided to the author by the RNSM.
4. Raikes to author and also in his memoir.
5. War Cabinet, Weekly Resume, July 2 to July 9 1942.

21: Of Monstrosity and Mercy
1. Clay Blair, *Hitler's U-Boat War*, Vol. I, p. 508.
2. Gaylord Kelshall, *The U-boat War in the Caribbean*, p. 56.
3. *Jornal Pequeno*, 18 August 1942.
4. Account of the action, *Daily Express*, 6 February 2015 and official Italian Navy profile of Primo Longobardo.
5. U-210 *Sunk by HMCS* Assiniboine *7-6-42, Post Mortems on Enemy Submarines*, Division of Naval Intelligence, via NHHC. Elements of the story of *U-210* in this chapter, as told from the U-boat's perspective, sourced in the remarkable information yielded from the interrogation of survivors contained within this document.
6. Personal diaries of Commander Arthur Layard, NMRN. All quotes from Layard in this chapter from this source.
7. *Interrogation of survivors from U-379*, as are other quotes referenced in this episode from the perspective of the U-boat and also the actions of escorts. Via U-boat Archive.
8. Roskill, *The Navy at War*, p. 223.

22: Tipping Point
1. As Mars recounts, when he first brought his boat out to Malta, a flotilla staff officer told him: 'Don't chase the war, young Mars. The war will catch you up.' *Unbroken*, p. 102. Now war had finally caught up . . .
2. According to the historian James Holland in the TV documentary *The Battle* for Malta.
3. Stephen Budiansky, *Battle of Wits*, p. 271.

23: With all Battle Flags Flying
1. *Battle of Midway: Preliminaries*, NHHC.
2. Many of Japan's I Class boats were rechristened from May 1942, with, for example, *I-68* becoming *I-168*, though others still carried the old form of name, such as *I-58*. There were wartime name changes in the Royal Navy too.

According to Antony Preston in *The Royal Navy Submarine Service* (p. 123) in the mid-1920s, while First Sea Lord, Admiral Beatty decreed new submarines should not just have letters and numbers, denoting class and order of build plus for use in signals, but should also be named, as that was more inspirational. However, in the early days of the Second World War this practice was modified for new-build RN submarines, which again used solely their pennant numbers. Instigated at the behest of Max Horton on becoming FOST, it was supposedly to make it harder for enemy intelligence to assess how many boats, and of which type, the British had in commission. All new submarines, of whatever class, received the letter P, followed by a number (an unpopular move among the vast majority of submariners). Winston Churchill also thought this unimpressive and ordered that names should be used again. The change took time to introduce across the Submarine Service and Preston relates that sometimes the numbered British boats were actually sunk before it could happen. Alastair Mars was told in late 1941 that he would assume command of *P42* but she soon officially became *Unbroken*. Paul Akermann's *Encyclopedia of British Submarines 1901–1955* is excellent on the names issue, plus much else about the RN Submarine Service.

3. Yahachi Tanabe with Joseph D. Harrington, 'I Sank the *Yorktown* at Midway', *Proceedings* magazine, Volume 89, Issue 5, 1963.
4. Ibid.
5. Ibid.
6. Ibid.
7. *USS* Hammann *(DD-412) Action Report*, NHHC.
8. Ibid.
9. *USS* Yorktown *Action Report*, NHHC.
10. Ibid.
11. Peter C. Smith, *Midway*, p. 91.
12. Clay Blair, *Silent Victory*, p. 253 / USS *Nautilus* ship biog., NHHC.
13. As detailed in Fujita's obituary, *New York Times*, 3 October 1997.

24: Gaining the Edge

1. U-boat force War Log, 21 August 1942, U-boat Archive.
2. All material on Op Haggis from Capt. Frederic Walker's papers, NMRN.
3. IWM, recorded interview with Stanley Reynolds.
4. Ibid.
5. *Report on the Interrogation of Survivors from U-595 sunk on November 14, 1942*, US Office of Naval Intelligence, via NHHC.
6. Ibid.
7. Dönitz observations in U-boat force War Log 16–30 November 1942, U-boat Archive.
8. Ibid.
9. U-boat force War Log, 25 November 1942.
10. Roskill, *The Navy at War 1939–1945*, p. 227.
11. Ibid., p. 226.

12. Vice Admiral Sir Roderick Macdonald, related during after dinner speech, Naval Club, Hill Street, May 1991, IWM document.
13. Atkinson, recorded interview, IWM, as are all quotes by this officer.
14. Macintyre, *The Battle of the Atlantic*, p. 168.
15. Ibid.
16. Jak P. Mallmann Showell, *Hitler's Navy*, p. 198.

25: Black March
1. Details of this incident from RAN *Anti-Submarine Report October 1943*, based on the Admiralty's official (and at the time secret) 'Interrogation of Survivors from *U-432*'.
2. Figures from War Cabinet, *Forecast of Monthly Loss Rates of Dry Cargo Ships*, 13 July 1943.
3. Gretton, *Convoy Escort Commander*, p. 118.
4. Macintyre, *The Battle of the Atlantic*, p. 182.
5. Mallmann Showell, *Dönitz, U-Boats, Convoys*, p. 180.
6. Macintyre, *The Battle of the Atlantic*, p. 171.
7. Kenneth Poolman, *The Sea Hunters*, p. 8.

26: The Fulcrum
1. U-boat force War Log 16 April 1943, U-boat Archive.
2. Atkinson, IWM sound recording, as are all quotes from this officer. The Admiralty plainly thought more U-boats were arrayed against the convoy HX-231 than actually were – but it was better to overestimate than underplay the threat.
3. Gretton, *Convoy Escort Commander*, p. 130.
4. Gretton, *Crisis Convoy*, p. 86.
5. Kemp, *U-Boats Destroyed*, p. 109.
6. Gretton, *Convoy Escort Commander*, p. 126.
7. U-boat force War Log, 7 April, U-boat Archive.
8. As quoted by Williams, *Battle of the Atlantic*, p. 247.
9. As quoted in *War at Sea: A Naval History of World War II*, by Nathan Miller, p. 346.
10. Dönitz, *Memoirs*.
11. Martienssen, *Hitler and His Admirals*, e-book edition, p. 243.
12. Dönitz, *Memoirs*.
13. Ibid.
14. Exchange recounted in Martienssen, *Hitler and His Admirals*, p. 245.
15. Macdonald, IWM.
16. Interview for *The World at War*, episode *Wolf Pack*.

27: The Führer is Watching
1. U-boat force War Log, 7 May, U-boat Archive.
2. Interview in *The World at War*, *Wolf Pack* episode.
3. Macintyre, *U-boat Killer*, p. 100.

4. Beesly, *Very Special Intelligence*, p. 195.

5. Blair, *Hitler's U-boat War*, Vol. 2, p. 421.

6. Williams, *Battle of the Atlantic*, p. 275.

7. Chalmers, *Max Horton and the Western Approaches*, pp. 206–7.

8. *Escort Group Commander, Cdr M.J. Evans, commander of the B3 Group in HMS Keppel*, report of proceedings, as are other quotes from him in this chapter.

9. The previous HMS *Itchen* was a destroyer, also sunk by a U-boat while on convoy escort duty (in June 1917) with eight of her 70-strong crew killed. Lt Cdr Bridgman was not among the three survivors picked up following the demise of the Second World War *Itchen*.

10. U-boat command War Log 16–30 September, U-boat Archive, Blair, Vol. II, p. 425.

11. Blair, *Hitler's U-Boat War*, Vol. 11, p. 425.

12. *Battle of the Atlantic, Technical Intelligence From Allied Communications Intelligence* (Vol. IV), NHHC.

13. Branfill-Cook, *Torpedo*, p. 62, who writes that altogether 640 were fired.

28: To Slay the Beast

1. Admiralty Battle Summary No. 29, *The Attack on the Tirpitz by Midget Submarines (Operation 'Source') 22 September 1943*, as reproduced in FOSM official account *Hunting Tirpitz*.

2. Ibid.

3. Interviewed in *Tirpitz: The Lost Heroes*, broadcast BBC2 TV, 2004.

4. Ibid. Same source for previous quote, 'full of apprehension'.

5. *Hunting Tirpitz*.

6. Ibid.

7. There were 100 German casualties due to the wild firing of troops and shore batteries at non-existent attackers.

8. Quote from Place's obituary, *Daily Telegraph*, published 27 December 1994.

9. *Hunting Tirpitz*, p. 111.

10. *Hunting Tirpitz*, p. 122.

29: Shooting Blind

1. Capt. Edward L. Beach, interviewed in *The Submarines of World War II*, History channel series.

2. Ibid.

3. According to Clay Blair in his book *Silent Victory*, p. 67. Blair was a Second World War veteran submarine officer as well as producing the most comprehensive histories of submarine warfare in the global conflicts of the twentieth century.

4. F.G. Hoffman, *The American Wolf Packs – A Case Study in Wartime Adaptation*, published by the National Defense University Press.

5. Cdr Daniel E. Benere in his paper, 'A Critical Examination of the US Navy's Use of Unrestricted Submarine Warfare in the Pacific Theater During WWII'.

6. Beach, quoted in the History channel series.

7. Figures from *Why Japan Really Lost the War*, analysis on the combinedfleet.com website.

30: Uncle Sam's Wolf Packs

1. Benere, 'A Critical Examination of the US Navy's Use of Unrestricted Submarine Warfare in the Pacific Theater During WWII'.
2. Legion of Merit citation, NHHC biography of Charles Bowers Momsen.
3. Interrogation of Capt. Abe Tokuma, *Escort of Shipping*, 29 November 1945, *United States Strategic Bombing Survey [Pacific]*, via NHHC.
4. Interrogation of Lt Cdr Noriteru Yatsui, *Attacks on Japanese Shipping*, same source as above.
5. Admiral Lockwood COMSUBFORPAC, Tactical Bulletin, 22 November 1943, quoted by Hoffman in *The American Wolf Packs*.
6. Brayton Harris, *The Navy Times Book of Submarines*, p. 319.

31: A Ruinous Obsession

1. Interrogation of Vice Admiral Paul H. Wenneker, 11 November 1945, *United States Strategic Bombing Survey [Pacific]*, via NHHC. Other quotes in this chapter from Wenneker are from the same source.
2. William B. Hopkins, *The Pacific War*, p. 207.
3. As Brayton Harris points out in *The Navy Times Book of Submarines*, p. 314, this was in waters off Australia and also the wider Indian Ocean where Allied escort forces were weaker.
4. RAN *South-West Pacific Anti-Submarine Report*, September 1943.
5. Commander Destroyers Pacific, *Briefs of Narratives of Co-ordinated Anti-Submarine Action Including USS* England, *USS* George, *USS* Raby, *USS* Spangler *and USS* Hazelwood *of 19–31 May 1944*. Accessed via USS *England* and also published on Destroyer Escort Sailors Association websites. See Sources.
6. Ibid.
7. Rear Admiral J.L. Kauffman, Commander Destroyers, Pacific Fleet, 29 August 1944, observations on USS *England*'s attacks, via Destroyer Escort Sailors Association.
8. Orita, *I-Boat Captain*, p. 214. In December 1941 this remarkable officer took his submarine to within a few miles of the Golden Gate Bridge in San Francisco. He sent a wireless message to his commanders explaining he was about to shell the brightly illuminated structure. They banned him from doing so as it was the Christmas holidays and they feared such an act against a famous US landmark might enrage the Christian sensibilities of Axis allies Germany and Italy. Episode recounted by Denis Warner, who met Orita after the war, in an article for the *New York Times*, A Curious War Beneath the Waves, published 3 March 1995.
9. RAN *South-West Pacific Anti-Submarine Report*, September 1943.
10. Hopkins, p. 208.
11. Interrogation of Cdr Chikataka Nakajima, 21 October 1945, *Gilberts-Marshalls Operation, Naval Strategic Planning*, contained within *Interrogations of Japanese Officials – Vols I & II*, part of *United States Strategic Bombing Survey [Pacific]*, via NHHC.
12. Wenneker interrogation, via NHHC.
13. Hopkins, p. 207. This was Mochitsura Hashimoto, then a Lt Cdr who

commanded *I-58* and attacked the cruiser USS *Indianapolis* in 1945. See Chapter 42.

14. Wenneker interrogation, via NHHC.
15. *NYT*, 18 July 1995.
16. Blair, *Hitler's U-Boat War*, Vol. 2, p. 567.
17. DANFS, USS *Archerfish*.

32: Captains Charismatic

1. DANFS, USS *Wahoo*.
2. Chief Yeoman Forrest Sterling, quoted in USN COMSUBPAC press release/bio on Morton and *Wahoo*'s final patrol, by Darrell D. Ames.
3. Quoted in *Newsweek*, 3 May 1943, as cited in *United States Submarine Losses in World War II*, p. 66.
4. DANFS, USS *Wahoo*.
5. Ibid.
6. Ibid.
7. Blair, *Silent Victory*, p. 470.
8. Ned Beach, *Submarine*, p. 64.
9. DANFS, USS *Wahoo*.
10. *Time* magazine, 18 October 1943, as cited in *United States Submarine Losses in World War II*, p. 65.
11. As quoted in History channel documentary series *The Submarines of World War II*.
12. As related by one of his officers, George Grider, who saw what happened and recorded it in his book *War Fish*, p. 73.
13. Ibid.
14. *The War Below: The Story of Three Submarines That Battled Japan* by James Scott, p. 132.
15. There was a similarly controversial episode in the Mediterranean, involving future VC winner Anthony Miers, who was sent into the Aegean in the summer of 1941 following the German ejection of British and Commonwealth forces from Crete. His job in command of HMS *Torbay*, using intelligence furnished by Bletchley Park – which had cracked Italian naval codes – was to intercept and destroy transport vessels, including those carrying troops. During the course of this it seems *Torbay* used her machine guns to kill enemy troops who survived an initial attack. *Torbay* was, as Tim Clayton observed in *Sea Wolves* (p. 230), not well placed to invite enemy troops aboard as prisoners. Post-war some have claimed Miers committed a war crime, but at the time senior officers approved of *Torbay*'s 'offensive spirit' (Clayton, p. 231). According to Brian Izzard in his biography of Miers (*Gamp VC*, p. 57) the British submarine went alongside a damaged caique with German troops still aboard, one of whom made to hurl a grenade while another lifted his rifle to shoot at submariners on *Torbay*'s casing. Both men were shot while Germans who abandoned ship into a rubber raft were also later killed, according to Miers, 'to prevent them regaining their ship' (Izzard, p. 57). Max Horton, the incumbent head of the Submarine Service

was disturbed by Miers's actions and worried about the other side seeking retribution. In September 1941 Horton pointed out to the Admiralty Board that the enemy had, as far as he was aware, not committed such acts, even against military personnel (Izzard, p. 246). The logic for Miers was the same as that exhibited by Morton – to eliminate enemy soldiers who could make it ashore and later kill British troops.

16. Quoted in COMSUBPAC biog. of Morton, by Darrell D. Ames.
17. Forrest Stirling quoted in the above.

33: Hit 'em Harder

1. Edward C. Whitman, 'Submarine Hero – Samuel David Dealey', article on website of USS *Nautilus*.
2. DANFS, USS *Harder*.
3. USS *Harder*, report of Fifth War Report, via NHHC.
4. Ibid.
5. Ibid.
6. Ibid.
7. DANFS, USS *Harder*.
8. As quoted by Blair, *Silent Victory*, p. 72.
9. This was the so-called Momsen Lung. Invented by 'Swede' Momsen prior to the war, he applied his experience and technical skill to designing an escape breathing apparatus. Momsen led by example, embarking on escapes from trials submarine S-4 at a depth of 206ft to test out the new equipment.
10. DANFS, USS *Tang*.
11. O'Kane would be presented with his Medal of Honor by President Harry S. Truman after release from captivity. The citation saluted his final patrol in *Tang* as 'one of the greatest submarine cruises of all time, led by her illustrious, gallant and courageous commanding officer, and his crew of daring officers and men'.
12. DANFS, USS *Darter*.
13. As quoted in *The US Navy* by Nathan Miller, p. 237. This episode also features in Clay Blair, *Silent Victory*, p. 776.

34: Ebb and Flow

1. Ships and displacements, uboat.net, plus also some details contained within an account of Indian Ocean operations, papers of Cdr Anthony Goord, NMM.
2. Mars, *HMS Thule Intercepts*, p. 46.
3. Ibid.
4. Riverdale Electronic Books [TM], *Interview with Arthur Baudzus*, U-859 survivor, published online.
5. Mars, *HMS Thule Intercepts*, p. 48.

35: No Lazy Sunday

1. Quoted in Roskill, *The Navy at War*, p. 352.
2. The British also called this counter-measure the Submarine Bubble Target (SBT)

and, as if that wasn't enough, it was also dubbed BOLD by the Allies (in tribute to its ability to cause mischief, like the Kobold spirit of German folklore).

3. As interviewed in the BBC TV documentary series *The Battle of the Atlantic*, in the 3rd episode, *The Hunted*.

4. Monsarrat in his Foreword to Heinz Schaeffer's *U-Boat 977*, p. 8.

5. Walker's nickname for his warships, which he was due to meet again at the Plymouth dockyard and naval base, where he also started his naval career in 1914 as a midshipman aboard the new battleship HMS *Ajax*.

6. Alan Burn, *The Fighting Captain*, p. 181.

7. Account by Jim Booth, as published in *WARSHIPS* IFR magazine, special section entitled *Destination D-Day*, August 2004 edition. The author also interviewed Jim Booth on Sword Beach, Normandy, 6 June 2004, the 60th anniversary of *X23*'s exploits off that very spot.

8. The unfortunate pilot of this boat was Joachim Langsdorff, whose father was Captain Hans Langsdorff, CO of the pocket battleship *Admiral Graf Spee*, which was pursued and damaged by British cruisers in December 1939. *Graf Spee* was subsequently scuttled on the River Plate, off Montevideo. Capt. Langsdorff shot himself while, according to an IWM account of the *Biber* recovery, his son made the error of failing to ensure the engine exhaust system vented its fumes outside the boat.

36: Target New York

1. Exchange reported by Charles Foley in *Commando Extraordinary*, p. 123.

2. Preanatt and Stille, *Axis Midget Submarines*, p. 14.

3. Paul Kemp, *U-boats Destroyed*, p. 250.

4. Adam Siegel, *Wartime Diversion of US Navy Forces in Response to Public Demands for Augmented Coastal Defense*, Center for Naval Analysis, via NHHC.

5. Kemp, p. 250.

6. *Brooklyn Daily Eagle*, 8 January 1945.

7. Quoted by Siegel.

8. *Brooklyn Daily Eagle*, 8 January 1945.

9. Quoted by Siegel.

10. *Brooklyn Daily Eagle*, 8 January 1945.

37: Total Underwater Warfare

1. 'Review of Anti-U-Boat Warfare for the Year 1944', as contained in the Royal Australian Navy's *Monthly Naval Warfare Review*, published March 1945.

2. Blair, *Hitler's U-Boat War*, Vol. 2, p. 552.

3. According to Gallery in his book *Twenty Million Tons Under the Sea*, p. 307, this involved 3,000 of his men not uttering a word about their amazing achievement until after war's end, which was no mean feat in itself.

4. *Iron Coffins* is the title of U-boat captain Herbert Werner's powerful memoir of his time in German submarines during the Second World War. It is partly a bleak account of what the U-boats became for their crews in the heavily patrolled waters around the British Isles – the 'wrecking yard'.

5. *Technical Intelligence from Allied Comms Intelligence, Vol. IV*, accessed via NHHC.
6. Ibid.
7. Ibid.
8. Papers of Lt Cdr R.W. Keymer, Merseyside Maritime Museum.
9. 'Review of Anti-U-Boat Warfare for the Year 1944', RAN *Monthly Naval Warfare Review*, March 1945.
10. Ibid.
11. Ibid.
12. Arthur Hezlet, *British and Allied Submarine Operations in World War II*, Vol. I. Hezlet pointed out, on p. 314, that had the war gone on longer British submarines would have been called back from the Far East, to reinforce efforts to follow *Venturer* and *Tapir's* example in detecting and killing schnorchelling U-boats 'while on passage'. He also felt that if the Type XXI and Type XXIII U-boats 'proved a serious menace' British submarines would have applied themselves to the task of countering them 'with some success'.
13. State of the Union Address to Congress, 6 January 1945, accessed via *The American Presidency Project* [TM].
14. Horton speech in Germany, post-surrender, as related in Chalmers, *Max Horton and the Western Approaches*, p. 228.
15. Malcolm Llewellyn-Jones, *The Royal Navy and Anti-Submarine Warfare*, p. 70.
16. Chalmers, p. 228.
17. Blair gives a pretty devastating critique of the Type XXI's flaws in *Hitler's U-Boat War*, Vol. 2, pp. 709–10. Chester Wilmot also outlines problems in Type XXI design and production in *The Struggle for Europe*, p. 343.
18. Werner, p. 284.
19. Günter Grass, *Crabwalk*, p. 155.
20. uboat.net and account of *Wilhelm Gustloff* sinking on the website called 'M.S. *Wilhelm Gustloff*'.
21. The story of Marinesko's life can be found on the WW2 Gravestone web site.

38: Endgame Europa

1. Wilmot, p. 737.
2. Deutsches U-Boot Museum, on *U-864* and Operation Caesar, also The History Learning Site.
3. Ibid.
4. BBC TV Timewatch, *The Hunt for U-864*, broadcast 2008.
5. Ibid. and Paul Kemp, *Submarine Action*, p. 66.
6. Kemp, *Submarine Action*, p. 66 and also detailed by Hezlet in his superlative chronicle of British and Allied submarine operations in the Second World War, pp. 313–14.
7. *Tapir* war patrol report, TNA.
8. Adam Siegel, *Wartime Diversion of US Navy Forces in Response to Public Demands for Augmented Coastal Defense*, Center for Naval Analysis, NHHC.
9. Kemp, p. 253.
10. Kemp, p. 260.

11. Kemp, p. 232 and David Miller, *U-Boats*, p. 102.

12. Skorzeny was soon involved in a plan to insert German troops disguised as American soldiers behind the lines during the Ardennes offensive of December 1944, the last big push by the German armies in the West. It also failed but led to war crimes accusations.

13. In August 1986 a Danish diver discovered a U-boat wreck on the seabed, a dozen miles off Anholt Island. It was *U-534*. Despite German government opposition, a scheme to raise *U-534* was formulated. It was perfectly permissible as the submarine was not a war grave. Funded by Danish publisher Karsten Ree, the project saw a Dutch salvage company lift the boat from the depths in August 1993. Eight of her former crew and even two of the RAF airmen who sank her witnessed the salvage operation. Filled with silt and containing ammunition in a potentially dangerous state, the delicate process of investigating the U-boat began. It was discovered that 450 rounds of anti-aircraft ammunition remained. The ammo was carefully disposed of while the Royal Danish Navy took three acoustic homing torpedoes found in the U-boat into their custody. No gold or jewels were found aboard, nor the skeleton of Martin Bormann or even Adolf Hitler. The submarine was, though, a treasure trove of Kriegsmarine artefacts and these are today on display as part of the superb U-boat Story visitor attraction, also featuring the constituent parts of the boat – arrayed like a gigantic model kit – at the Woodside Ferry Terminal in Birkenhead.

14. Monsarrat, *The Cruel Sea*, p. 441.

39: U-977 & the Stowaway Führer

1. Schaeffer, *U-977*, p. 152.
2. Ibid.
3. Ibid., p. 172.
4. *Report on the Interrogation of Prisoners from U-977 Surrendered at Mar del Plata*, 17 August 1945, USN document, via U-Boat Archive.
5. Schaeffer interview transcript in the above.
6. Brian Dunning, Skeptoid podcast, *No, Hitler Did Not Escape*, 23 February 2016.
7. Schaeffer, p. 201.
8. Ibid., p. 205

40: Fires on a Darkening Shore

1. In an interview with the author, 3 December 2014, as are all quotes from Todd here.
2. Mars, *HMS Thule Intercepts*, pp. 148–49.
3. Ibid., p. 154.
4. Ibid., p. 182.
5. Views of captured German submarine officers under interrogation, as reported in RAN *Monthly Naval Warfare Review*, March 1945.
6. Mars, *HMS Thule Intercepts*, p. 187.
7. Vice Admiral Sir Arthur Hezlet, *HMS Trenchant at War*, p. 146.
8. Ibid., p. 149.

41: Sink the *Takao*

1. Ian Fraser, IWM Sound Archive interview. All quotes from Fraser in this chapter are from the same source.
2. T.J. Waldron and James Gleeson, *The Frogmen*, p. 143, which also quotes extracts from the official report by Capt. Fell on the mission.
3. An amphetamine taken by British submariners and also escort vessel captains (as revealed by Nicholas Monsarrat in *The Cruel Sea*, p. 391) when they needed to stay hyper alert and physically fit for long periods. The operators of Germany's Biber and Seehund midget submarines and V3 manned torpedo took an adulterated methamphetamine called D IX, which included cocaine in its mix, as detailed by Norman Ohler in *Blitzed*. It was not a success and after a brief high debilitated them physically and mentally.
4. Fraser, IWM Sound Archive.
5. Obituary of Max Shean by Timothy Brown, published in *The Australian*, 26 June 2009.
6. Australia's War 1939–1945 (Australian Government website), article entitled 'Cutting Cables'.
7. Waldron and Gleeson, p. 132.

42: The Road to Tokyo Bay

1. Testimony of Commander Mochitsura Hashimoto at Court Martial of Captain *Charles B. McVay, 13 December 1945*, NHHC.
2. Ibid.
3. Doug Stanton, *In Harm's Way*, p. 130.
4. Ibid., p. 69.
5. Quote from *Jaws*.
6. *All Hands*, official magazine of the US Navy, 20 Aug 2015 article, 'Survivors of the Sinking of the USS *Indianapolis*', by Mass Communication Specialist 2nd Class Jason Kofonow.
7. Hashimoto testimony to McVay court martial.
8. M. Hill Goodspeed, *US Navy, A Complete History*, p. 526.
9. Cdr Daniel E. Benere, 'A Critical Examination of the US Navy's Use of Unrestricted Submarine Warfare in the Pacific Theatre During WWII', US Naval War College paper, May 1992.
10. Fraser, IWM Sound Archive.
11. Lockwood quotes, from *COMINT [Communications Intelligence] Contributions [to] Submarine Warfare in WWII* SRH [Special Research History] 235, 17 June 1947 VADM C.A. Lockwood USN COMSUBPAC, via NHHC.
12. As recounted by Lockwood in the above.

PART FOUR

1: The Ashcan of History

1. John Kenneth Galbraith, 'The "Cure" at Mondorf Spa', a *Life* magazine report, 22 October 1945.
2. *Trial of the Major War Criminals*, p. 311.

3. Interrogation record for Admiral Dönitz, 6 September 1945, IWM.
4. A major piece of evidence offered against Dönitz at Nuremberg was his so-called Laconia Order, an instruction to U-boat captains not to pick up passengers from torpedoed ships if it endangered their own vessels. This was prompted by *U-156*, commanded by Korvettenkapitän Werner Hartenstein, torpedoing the British troop ship *Laconia* off West Africa on the night of 12 September 1942, then surfacing to take aboard survivors after cries for help in Italian were heard. *Laconia*, 19,695 tons, was armed with eight guns for self-protection with soldiers and naval personnel to operate them, and even depth charges (according to Dönitz in his *Memoirs*). She was still no match for a U-boat and at the time was without any escort. Heading for the UK, she was carrying 2,741 people (German U-boat Museum figures, see Sources) including 1,809 Italian PoWs (hence the Italian voices in the night) and 80 civilians. Hartenstein took aboard dozens of people, and towed four lifeboats containing many more, staying on the surface as he made broadcasts in clear language to other submarines for assistance and asking Allied, neutral and Axis surface vessels to assist. He promised the former would not be attacked. Hartenstein also advised Dönitz of his predicament. The admiral ordered U-boats to the scene, warning them to be wary of Allied attack. Kapitänleutnant Harro Schacht, the guilty party in the earlier sinkings off Brazil that killed hundreds of troops and civilians, was ordered to take *U-507* to the scene. *U-506*, commanded by Kapitänleutnant Erich Wuerdemann was similarly ordered to intervene. Both submarines had been hunting off Freetown on their way home. These U-boats, according to Dönitz, picked up 800 of the 811 British aboard *Laconia* and saved 450 Italian PoWs. An American VLR Liberator attacked *U-156* on 16 September, despite Red Cross flags being clearly displayed on the casing of the boat, which was damaged. Hartenstein had to put off the majority of survivors, release the tow for four lifeboats and dive. Official British naval historian Stephen Roskill said of the incident that he felt all the U-boat captains involved 'behaved with marked humanity towards the survivors' and judged the ordering of a Liberator to mount an attack 'a serious blunder' (see *The Navy at War 1939–1945*, pp. 224–25). Afterwards Dönitz issued what was to become known as the Laconia Order. It instructed that 'all attempts to rescue crews of sunken ships will cease forthwith'. Combined with his Standing Order 154 of 1939 (see Part Three, Chapter 8) this was interpreted by the Nuremberg tribunal as indicating U-boat captains should take measures to leave no survivors. The Dönitz defence was assisted by Admiral Nimitz pointing out in his written evidence to the tribunal that US Navy submarines did not rescue survivors if such a gesture endangered them. At Nuremberg it was pointed out that commanders had to place the safety of their submarines and men first, and that the likely arrival of enemy aircraft made it extremely risky to carry out rescues. Dönitz, while criticised for violating the pre-war Submarine Protocol, was not judged to have 'ordered the killing of shipwrecked survivors' (See *Trial of the Major War Criminals*, p. 313).
5. Jürgen Rohwer in the Introduction to Dönitz's *Memoirs*.
6. Dönitz, *Memoirs*.

2: Best of Enemies

1. Quoted by Nathan Miller, *The US Navy*, p. 248.
2. As related by Richard Humble, *Fraser of North Cape*, p. 311.
3. Norman Polmar and Jurrien Noot, *Submarines of the Russian and Soviet Navies 1718–1990*, p. 134.
4. Gorshkov's variant of a saying by Voltaire or Clausewitz (take your pick).
5. Polmar and Noot, p. 150.
6. *History of US Naval Operations: Korea*, Chapter 10, NHHC.
7. Igor Kozyr, 'Dispelled Myths of Soviet Subs', published by RusNavy website.
8. The second American boat to carry the name. Her predecessor was lost in March 1942 during a battle with the Japanese in the Java Sea. *Perch* II was commissioned in January 1944, completing six war patrols.
9. *US Navy Special Operations in the Korean War*, NHHC.
10. USS *Perch* went on to see service during the Vietnam War. In the mid-1960s, among other things, she landed naval reconnaissance and raiding groups on the Vietnamese coast. During one mission she was fired on by the Viet Cong and responded with cannon and machine gun fire. Norman Polmar and K.J. Moore give details of the submarine's post-Korean War activities in *Cold War Submarines*.

3: Smoking out the Soviets

1. Sherry Sontag, Christopher Drew, Annette Lawrence Drew, *Blind Man's Bluff*, p. 27.
2. Ibid., p. 38.
3. *Diesel Sub Commander Recalls Historic Soviet Sub Chase*, US Navy account by Dean Lohmeyer, details publicly released 29 May 2009. All quotes in this account taken from that USN source.
4. Lt Cdr Alfie Roake, essay on his submarine's missions into Arctic waters, in the collection of the Royal Navy Submarine Museum.
5. As related elsewhere in the book, Kapitänleutnant Friedrich Steinhoff deployed from Kristiansand on 1 April 1945 in command of *U-873*, initially leading the Seewolf group. The boat then headed for the Caribbean using the *Schnorchel* during the day and only surfacing at night. Although ordered back to base, *U-873* sailed on and was instructed to surrender on 10 May (having been told on 4 May not to attack US or British shipping). As a consequence *U-873* still had a full war load of torpedoes, though the Enigma machine and other secret materials were destroyed. Kapitänleutnant Steinhoff was kept in a Boston prison and subjected to special interrogation by the Federal Bureau of Investigation (FBI). He killed himself on 19 May, by making what the death certificate described as an 'incised wound right wrist'. To do this he used a piece of broken glass from sunglasses and wire taken from his cap. A US Navy inquiry concluded that prisoners from *U-873* had been ill-treated and senior officers were censured for not ensuring that prisoners were handled within the Geneva Convention. Interrogators who said Steinhoff was arrogant and, on the contrary, had threatened them, denied the allegations of ill-treatment. The U-boat Archive offers some original USN and other documents relating to this officer's demise.

6. Norman Polmar, *The Polaris: A Revolutionary Missiles System and Concept*, NHHC.

7. Chuck Lawliss, *The Submarine Book*, p. 98. This way of terming the awesome destruction that could be inflicted by a single Polaris submarine is widely used in various books, but is nonetheless a horribly simple and effective way of explaining what just one of these boats could do to the planet. By the end of 1963 the US Navy would have five Washington Class, ten Ethan Allen and five Lafayette Class SSBNs in service, carrying a total of 320 Polaris missiles. A further 26 Lafayettes would be constructed by 1973, with the even more powerful Poseidon missile introduced.

8. Quotes taken from interview with Vice Admiral Joe Williams, transcript, National Security Council and also as broadcast in *Cold War*, 24-part series for CNN broadcast in 1998, episode 'M.A.D.'

9. Author's interview with Matthew Todd, 3 December 2014, as are all quotes and details of this episode.

10. Accounts of this encounter in the papers of Vice Admiral Sir Peter Gretton held by the National Maritime Museum in the UK. This former U-boat captain was Hartwig Looks, who had survived the sinking of his boat, *U-264*, at the hands of Walker's group in the summer of 1944 (see Part Three, Chapter 35). During the ONS5 battle in April/May 1943, Kapitänleutnant Looks managed to evade the escorts and put torpedoes into two merchant vessels, which sank. After surviving a depth-charging *U-264* attacked a third ship, but failed to sink her. The escorts struck back with both depth charges and an attempted ramming, but *U-264* made it home on that occasion.

4: By Good Luck & the Grace of God

1. *The Naval Quarantine of Cuba, 1962*, NHHC.

2. *Cuban Missile Crisis, United States Naval Aviation Operations*, USN.

3. *The Naval Quarantine of Cuba, 1962*, NHHC.

4. Jeffrey G. Barlow, *Some Aspects of the U.S. Navy's Participation in the Cuban Missile Crisis*, NHHC.

5. *Recollections of Vadim Orlov*, accessed via The National Security Archive. Three officers needed to concur with firing for it to happen. *B-59*'s captain did give orders for the nuclear-tipped torpedo to be assembled but that was as far as it got.

6. Tense encounter detailed by Peter A. Huchthausen, *October Fury*, pp. 168–71, and also by Gary E. Weir and Walter J. Boyne in *Rising Tide*, pp. 102–3.

7. *Annual Report of the Secretary of the Navy: July 1, 1962, to June 30, 1963, extract. Navy and Marine Corps Operations: Cuba*, NHHC.

5: Their Game of Shadows

1. *K-19* fully earned the nickname after a second accident in which 28 men died. She was also known as the Widowmaker.

2. As told to the author in an interview for the book *Hunter Killers*.

3. As revealed in *Cold War*, CNN documentary series, episode entitled *M.A.D.* Broadcast in 1998 on BBC2 in the UK.

4. Ibid., Ousenko interviewed on camera.

6: *Hangor*'s Hunt

1. Rear Admiral Agung Pramono, Indonesian Navy, 'The History of the Indonesian Submarine Squadron', Spring 2013 edition, *Undersea Warfare*.
2. Peter Hennessy and James Jinks, *The Silent Deep*, p. 286.
3. All quotes taken from interviews with Vice Admiral Ahmad Tasnim and Commodore Wasim Ahmad conducted in Pakistan specially for this book by Usman Ansari.
4. Metric depth-keeping used in French-built boat.
5. Commodore (Retd) Ranjit B. Rai with Joseph P. Chacko, *Warrng Navies*.
6. *Times of India* report, as quoted in *Warrng Navies*, p. 162.
7. *Warring Navies*, p. 58.
8. Ibid., p. 165.

7: South Atlantic Shocker

1. Sir Lawrence Freedman, *The Official History of the Falklands Campaign*, Vol. I, pp. 85–86.
2. Sandy Woodward interviewed by the author, 1992, for a Falklands War tenth anniversary special published by the *Evening Herald*, Plymouth.
3. As revealed by Wreford-Brown in his account published in *The Submariners*, edited by John Winton, p. 281.
4. Ibid., p. 282.
5. Chris Parry, *Down South*, pp. 95–98.
6. Freedman, *The Official History*, Vol. II, p. 246.
7. Parry, p. 97.
8. Quotes from Bicain taken from an article by Juan Carlos Cicalesi and Santiago Rivas, published in the May 2007 edition of *WARSHIPS IFR* magazine.
9. In 1985 the wreck of the *Sante Fe* was towed out to sea and scuttled about 12 miles off South Georgia.
10. Woodward, interview with author, 1992. The Burma Star was the campaign medal awarded to services personnel who served in the British-led battle for parts of the Far East during the Second World War.
11. Woodward interview, 1992.
12. Wreford-Brown, *The Submariners*, p. 289.
13. Chris Craig, *Call for Fire*, p. 82.
14. Sandy Woodward, *One Hundred Days*, p. 154.
15. This is according to a *Daily Telegraph* report published 13 April 2012, citing a revelation by retired military intelligence officer David Thorp in his book *The Silent Listener*. Thorp wrote that intercepted Argentinian signals revealed 'the *General Belgrano* had been instructed to alter course and head in the direction of the RV [possible rendezvous point with other warships] inside the exclusion zone'. In other words, the Argentinian junta lied when they said the cruiser was heading back to port.
16. Wreford-Brown, interviewed by the author, 1992.

17. Ibid.
18. Freedman, *The Official History*, Vol. II, p. 296.
19. Quote taken from an article by Juan Carlos Cicalesi and Santiago Rivas, 'The Sinking of the Cruiser ARA *General Belgrano*', The Survivor's Story, published in the June 2007 edition of *WARSHIPS IFR* magazine.
20. Wreford-Brown interview with the author, 1992.
21. Video interview with British Forces News, May 2012.
22. Interviewed in a report published by the *Daily Telegraph*, 28 April 2012.
23. *The Falklands War*, A Day-by-Day Account, p. 58.
24. As quoted, *The Falklands War*, p. 59.
25. Wreford-Brown, *The Submariners*, p. 291.
26. McClement's account of *Conqueror*'s Falklands War deployment, published in *Global Force 2007*, an official RN publication.

8: Dirty Boat Odyssey

1. Johnson's account of his '116-Day War Patrol', *The Submariners*, p. 96.
2. Account of the HMS *Onyx* war patrol, as published on the Barrow Submariners Association website.
3. Interview with the author, 1992.
4. Account given by Azcueta for a chapter entitled *Almost Successful, ARA* San Luis *War Patrol*, by Mariano Sciaroni with Matthew J. Gillis, published in *2008 Submarine Almanac*, compiled and edited by Neal Stevens.
5. Woodward, *One Hundred Days*, p. 123.
6. As related by Chris Craig in *Call for Fire*, p. 61.
7. *2008 Submarine Almanac*.
8. Craig writing in *WARSHIPS IFR*, August/September 2002 edition.
9. Hennessy and Jinks, *Silent Deep*, pp. 434–35.
10. Interview with the author, 1992.
11. Interview with the author, 1992.

9: Sargasso Sea Chernobyl

1. Scenario as outlined by James Cable in *Britain's Naval Future*.
2. According to the Channel 4 documentary *Able Archer 1983, The Brink of Apocalypse*, broadcast 2008.
3. *Session of the Politburo of the CC CPSU, 6 October 1986*, transcript via National Security Archive. As are all quotes from the Politburo meeting.
4. As quoted in the *Independent* newspaper report dated 31 August 2004.
5. *K 129* sank in 16,000ft of water.
6. As related by Peter Huchthausen, Igor Kurdin and R. Alan White in their book *Hostile Waters*, p. 333. In the 1989 movie *The Abyss*, written and directed by James Cameron, a US Navy SSBN, USS *Montana*, chases a mystery contact going at incredible speed into an undersea canyon, hitting the side at around 2,000ft and sliding to her doom. US Navy SEALS with special diving skills are sent to work with civilian divers to recover the warheads of the SSBN's missiles. In the process one of the Navy SEALS goes mad and threatens to detonate a warhead,

but it is defused. The incredible aspect of the fictional story is not necessarily the aliens, however. In the movie the SSBN sits in *only* 2,000ft of water (on a shelf) whereas *K-129* hit bottom around 16,000ft down and someone, somehow still managed to spirit away a pair of missiles.

7. *Chicago Tribune*, 23 July 1997.
8. Moore and Compton-Hall, *Submarine Warfare*, p. 253.

10: Silver Bullet Tomahawk

1. Rick Atkinson, *Crusade*, p 15.
2. State of the Union Speech 29 January 1991.
3. Norman Friedman, *Desert Victory*, p. 317.
4. Steve Upright interview with the author, May 1991.
5. Interview given to *The Press*, York, 5 October 2011.
6. Adam Roberts, 'NATO's "Humanitarian War" over Kosovo', IISS.
7. Wesley Clark, *Waging Modern War*, p.196.
8. John Roberts, *Safeguarding the Nation*, p. 259.
9. Bruce R. Nardulli et al., *Disjointed War*, RAND report for US Army.
10. Tom Bower, *Broken Vows*, p. 130.
11. Anthony H. Cordesman, *The Lessons and Non-lessons of the Air and Missile Campaign in Kosovo*, CSIS study of Kosovo operations.
12. *Report to Congress – Kosovo Operation Allied Force After-Action Report*, 31 January 2000.
13. BBC News online report, *HMS Splendid arrives home*, 9 July 1999.
14. Nardulli et al., *Disjointed War*.

11: Agents of Decapitation

1. Bob Woodward, *Bush at War*, Part 1, p. 38.
2. Thomas E. Ricks, *Fiasco*, p. 117.
3. Report for US Congress, *Iraq War: Defense Program Implications*, published 4 June 2003.
4. Televised news briefing on 22 March 2003, by UK Defence Secretary Geoff Hoon.
5. Interviewed by the author aboard HMS *Turbulent* in Devonport, 2004. All quotes from McKendrick taken from this source, except where otherwise noted.
6. Interview by Rebecca Ricks with McKendrick for an Iraq War tenth anniversary series published in *The Herald*, Plymouth, 23 March 2013.
7. Ibid.

12: Weapon of the Strong . . .

1. Dan van der Vat came to the same conclusion at the end of his book *Stealth at Sea* (p. 346), similarly drawing on Arnold-Forster's contention that submarines could not just be 'the weapon of the weaker power' (see Part One, Chapter 11). Admiral Fisher had labelled the submarine as looming large 'as the weapons of the strong' as far back as 1903. See p. 77. Writing in 1994, just five years after the fall of the Berlin Wall, van der Vat forecast that nuclear-powered submarines

would go the way of the dinosaurs. They were simply too expensive to operate. While it is true that they continue to place a huge strain on a nation's economy – van der Vat's 'financial millstone' – there is, actually, no loss of appetite for building nuclear submarines, as this chapter demonstrates.

2. Korean Central News Agency, quoted in the *Los Angeles Times*, 18 April 2010.
3. Quotes from *Investigation Result on the Sinking of ROKS 'Cheonan'*, official report into the incident.
4. BBC News online report, 'North Korea: "No apology" for S Korea *Cheonan* sinking', 24 March 2015.
5. As reported in May 2016 edition of *WARSHIPS IFR*.
6. US Navy briefing on SSGNs, accessed via USN website.
7. Official USN unit citation for USS *Florida*'s part in Operation Odyssey Dawn
8. Nick Childs points out in *Britain's Future Navy*, p. 98, that, in fact, the 99 missiles that USS *Florida* launched during Libya operations were 'more than the Royal Navy's entire stock'.
9. Figure given in the Congressional Research Service report, *Odyssey Dawn. (Libya): Background Issues for Congress*, by Jeremiah Gertler, published 30 March 2011.
10. Ryan Ramsey, CO of *Turbulent* in 2011, gives his insider's perspective on the boat's Libya mission in the book *SSN14*, pp. 86–88.
11. Ibid.
12. Ibid.

13: Much Ado About *Maskirovka*

1. BBC News online report, Russia says new UK aircraft carrier 'a convenient target', 29 June 2017.
2. Peter Truscott, *Kursk: Russia's Lost Pride*, p. 122.
3. Weir and Boyne, *Rising Tide*, p. 227 and p. 251.
4. Ibid., p. 252.
5. *The Kursk Accident*, Norwegian Radiation Protection Authority report, published 2001, pp. 11–12.
6. *NYT*, 27 October 2000.
7. *Daily Telegraph*, 25 August 2000. In a later report on 27 August, in the same newspaper, the woman denied she had been silenced via injection.
8. *NYT*, 27 October 2000.
9. As reported in *WARSHIPS IFR* magazine, September 2000.
10. *Pravda*, analysis article, published 12 August 2016.
11. Ibid.
12. Twitter, 27 October 2016. Vella also told his parliament Russian warships would not refuel in Malta. However, in late 2015 NATO member Spain had permitted the Russian Varshavyanka Class submarine *Novorossiysk* to take on diesel in its North African enclave of Ceuta. The boat's submariners reportedly enjoyed a run ashore, much needed as their voyage from St Petersburg to the Black Sea was quite a stretch even for a modern diesel boat. What caused most upset in the West was the thought that the *Novorossiysk* would be based in Crimea, annexed by Russia in March 2014.

13. Quoted in *Daily Mail* report, 30 October 2016.
14. Quoted in *Daily Mail* report, 4 April 2015.
15. BBC News website report, 9 November 2016.
16. Twitter, 9 November 2016.
17. *Guardian*, 9 November 2016.
18. Churchill issued his own warning, vividly describing the division of Europe and the start of the Cold War, in March 1946, by famously telling an audience at Fulton in the USA: 'From Stettin in the Baltic to Trieste in the Adriatic, an iron curtain has descended across the Continent.' Admiral Ferguson made his speech to the Atlantic Council summit, Washington DC, on 6 October 2015.
19. Vice Admiral James Foggo and Alarik Fritz, 'The Fourth Battle of the Atlantic', *Proceedings* Magazine, June 2016.
20. Ibid.
21. *IHS Janes' Defence Weekly*, 17 May 2016.
22. Brendan Thomas-Noone and Rory Medcalf, *Nuclear-armed submarines in Indo-Pacific Asia: Stabiliser or menace?*, Lowy Institute for International Policy report, published September 2015.
23. *The South China Sea Arbitration (The Republic of the Philippines v. The People's Republic of China)*, PCA Award 12 July 2016.

14: Nothing Left but Armageddon

1. Tweet quoted in the *Daily Telegraph*, 4 July 2017.
2. 38 North website report, 20 July 2017.
3. Figures from Nuclear Threat Initiative (NTI) report on global submarine proliferation.
4. Zee News report, *Bangladesh takes delivery of two submarines from China*, 14 November 2016.
5. Edward C. Whitman, 'Air Independent Propulsion: AIP Technology Creates a New Undersea Threat', published in *Undersea Warfare* magazine, accessed via Web.
6. UK National Audit Office, *Ministry of Defence Major Projects Report 2015 and the Equipment Plan 2015 to 2025*, published 22 October 2015.
7. *Defense News*, 31 March 2017 on the *Kazan*'s launch, the *Sun*, 10 February 2017 and the *Daily Telegraph*, 10 February 2017 on British submarine problems.
8. Russian figures from RussianShipsinfo.
9. Brendan Thomas-Noone and Rory Medcalf, Lowy Institute for International Policy report.
10. Congressional Research Service, *Navy Columbia Class (Ohio Replacement) Ballistic Missile Submarines (SSBN[X]) Program: Background Issues for Congress*, report by Ronald O'Rourke, published 22 March 2017.
11. UK Govt *Dreadnought submarine programme: factsheet*, updated 20 January 2016.
12. Figures from http://www.ukpublicspending.co.uk and the overseas aid figure from http://www.bbc.co.uk/news/uk-politics-39658907.
13. Kate Hudson's blog on CND website, '£205 billion?! How the cost of Trident replacement doubled', posted 12 May 2016.

14. CRS, *Navy Columbia Class* report.
15. Admiral Greenert quoted in the above.
16. *National Defense Magazine*, 22 March 2017.
17. Quoted in the author's book, *Hunter Killers*, p. 438.
18. Figure from *The Diplomat*, 4 March 2015.
19. *The Nuclear Threat*, NTI report.
20. As reported in *WARSHIPS IFR* magazine, October 2014 edition.
21. The Local, Danish English language news website, 21 March 2015, quoting Russian ambassador's commentary in the *Jyllands-Posten*.

Postscript • The Better Angels

1. Max Hastings, *All Hell Let Loose*, pp. 669–70.
2. Joshua Goldstein, 'Think Again: War', article published by *Foreign Policy* Web news site, 15 August 2011.
3. President Abraham Lincoln's first inaugural address, 4 March 1861, accessed via Bartleby website.
4. *'Only the dead have seen the end of war'*. Sometimes attributed to Plato via General Douglas MacArthur, but actually coined by George Santayana (*Soliloquies in England and Later Soliloquies*, p. 102) in response to President Woodrow Wilson's famous 'war to end all wars' statement. Santayana also coined the aphorism: 'Those who cannot remember the past are condemned to repeat it' (*Reason in Common Sense*, p. 271, Samizad ed. Vols I–V).

Appendix: The Price Paid

1. Cdr F.W. Lipscomb in his book *The British Submarine*, p. 139.
2. Taken from *The Lay of the Last Minstrel*, a narrative poem by Sir Walter Scott, first published in 1805.

Bibliography and Sources

BIBLIOGRAPHY
Factual

Akermann, Paul, *Encyclopedia of British Submarines 1901–1955*, Periscope, 2002

Allfrey, Anthony, *Man of Arms: The Life and Legend of Sir Basil Zaharoff*, Thistle, 2013

Anderson, Commander William and Clay Blair, *Nautilus 90 North*, Hodder, 1961

Armstrong, Craig, *Berwick-on-Tweed in the Great War*, Pen & Sword, 2015

Ashmead-Bartlett, Ellis, *The Uncensored Dardanelles*, Hutchinson, 1920

Atkinson, Rick, *Crusade: The Untold Story of the Persian Gulf War*, HarperCollins, 1994

Bagnasco, Erminio, *Submarines of World War Two*, Arms and Armour, 1977

Bainton, Roy, *Honoured by Strangers: The Life of Captain Francis Cromie CB DSO RN*, Airlife, 2002

Ballantyne, Iain, *Hunter Killers: The Dramatic Untold Story of the Royal Navy's Most Secret Service*, Orion, 2013

— *Strike from the Sea: The Royal Navy and United States Navy at War in the Middle East 1949–2003*, US Naval Institute Press, 2004

— *H.M.S. London: Warships of the Royal Navy*, Pen & Sword, 2003

— *H.M.S. Rodney: Warships of the Royal Navy*, Pen & Sword, 2008

Beach, Cdr Edward L., *Submarine!*, Bluejacket, 2003

Beesly, Patrick, *Very Special Intelligence: The Story of the Admiralty's Operational Intelligence Centre 1939–1945*, Seaforth, 2015

— *Very Special Admiral: The Life of Admiral J.H. Godfrey C.B.*, Hamish Hamilton, 1980

Bekker, Cajus, *Hitler's Naval War*, Doubleday, 1974

Blackman, Raymond V.B., *The World's Warships*, Macdonald, 1969

Blair, Clay, *Silent Victory: The U.S. Submarine War Against Japan*, Bluejacket, 2001

— *Hitler's U-boat War, The Hunters 1939–1942* (Vol. 1), Orion, 2000

— *Hitler's U-boat War, The Hunted 1942–1945* (Vol. 2), Orion, 2000

Botting, Douglas and the Editors of Time-Life Books, *The U-Boats*, Time-Life Books, 1979

Bower, Tom, *Broken Vows: Tony Blair, The Tragedy of Power*, Faber & Faber, 2016

Bowers, Paul, *The Garrett Enigma and the Early Submarine Pioneers*, Airlife, 1999

Boyd, Carl and Akihiko Yoshida, *The Japanese Submarine Force and World War II*, Bluejacket, 2002

Branfill-Cook, Roger, *Torpedo: The Complete History of the World's Most Revolutionary Weapon*, Seaforth, 2014

Brayley, Martin, *The British Home Front 1939–45*, Osprey, 2005

Breemer, Jan, *Soviet Submarines: Design, Development and Tactics*, Jane's Information Group, 1989

Brown, D.K., *The Grand Fleet: Warship Design and Development 1906–1922*, Seaforth, 2010

Brown, D.K. and George Moore, *Rebuilding the Royal Navy: Warship Design Since 1945*, Seaforth, 2012

Buchanan, Tom, *Britain and the Spanish Civil War*, Cambridge University Press, 2008

Budiansky, Stephen, *Blackett's War: The Men Who Defeated the Nazi U-Boats and Brought Science to the Art of War*, Alfred A. Knopf, 2013

— *Battle of Wits: The Complete Story of Codebreaking in World War II*, Simon & Schuster, 2002

Burn, Alan, *The Fighting Captain: The Story of Frederic John Walker RN, CB, DSO and the Battle of the Atlantic*, Pen & Sword, 1997

Cable, James, *Britain's Naval Future*, Palgrave Macmillan, 1983

Campbell, John, *Jutland, An Analysis of the Fighting*, Conway, 1998

Chalmers, Rear Admiral W.S., *Max Horton and the Western Approaches*, Hodder and Stoughton, 1954

Chatfield, Admiral of the Fleet, Lord, *It Might Happen Again: The Autobiography of Admiral of the Fleet Lord Chatfield, P.C., G.C.B., O.M. Etc.*, Vol. II, Heinemann, 1947

— *The Navy and Defence: The Autobiography of Admiral of the Fleet Lord Chatfield, P.C., G.C.B., O.M. Etc.*, Windmill, 1942

Childs, Nick, *Britain's Future Navy*, Pen & Sword, 2012

Churchill, Winston S., *The Second World War*, Vol. I, Vol. II & Vol. III, Cassell, 1948, 1949 & 1950

— *The World Crisis*, Vol. I. & Vol. II, Odhams, 1938

Clark, General Wesley K., *Waging Modern War: Bosnia, Kosovo and the Future of Combat*, PublicAffairs, 2001

Clayton, Tim, *Sea Wolves: The Extraordinary Story of Britain's WW2 Submarines*, Abacus, 2012

Compton-Hall, Commander Richard, *The First Submarines*, Periscope, 2004

— *The Submarine Pioneers*, Sutton, 1999

— *Submarines and the War at Sea, 1914–18*, Macmillan, 1991

Conway's All the World's Fighting Ships 1947–1982, Part I: The Western Powers, Conway Maritime Press, 1984

Craig, Capt. Chris, *Call for Fire: Sea Combat in the Falklands and the Gulf War*, John Murray, 1995

Cunningham of Hyndhope, Admiral of the Fleet, Viscount, *A Sailor's Odyssey: The Autobiography of Admiral of the Fleet Viscount Cunningham of Hyndhope, K.T., G.C.B., O.M., D.S.O.*, Hutchinson, 1951

Daniels, Josephus, *Our Navy at War*, War College Series, 2015

Davies, Roy, *Nautilus: The Story of Man Under the Sea*, BBC Books, 1995

Divine, A.D., *Destroyer's War: A Million Miles by the Eighth Flotilla*, John Murray, 1942

Doenecke, Justus D., *Nothing Less Than War: A New History of America's Entry into World War I*, University Press of Kentucky, 2014

Dönitz, Karl, *Memoirs: Ten Years and Twenty Days*, Frontline, 2012

Drummond, John D., *H.M. U-Boat*, British Book Centre, 1958

Edgerton, David, *Britain's War Machine: Weapons, Resources and Experts in the Second World War*, Allen Lane, 2011

Edmonds, Martin *et al.*, *100 Years of the Trade: Royal Navy Submarines Past, Present and Future*, CDISS, 2001

Edwards, Bernard, *Dönitz and the Wolf Packs: The U-boats at War*, Cassell, 2002

Edwards, Kenneth, *Men of Action*, Collins, 1943

Elliott, Peter, *The Cross and the Ensign: A Naval History of Malta 1798–1979*, Grafton, 1989

Everitt, Don, *The K Boats: The Amazing Story of Britain's Steam Submarines*, NEL, 1972

The Falklands War: A Day-by-Day Account from Invasion to Victory, Marshall Cavendish Editions, 2007

Farquharson-Roberts, Mike, *A History of the Royal Navy, World War I*, I.B. Tauris, 2014

Field, Lt Col. Cyril, *The Story of the Submarine: From the Earliest Ages to the Present Day*, J.B. Lippincott, 1908

Fisher, Admiral, Lord, *Memories*, Hodder & Stoughton, 1919

— *Records*, Hodder & Stoughton, 1919

The Fleet Annual and Naval Yearbook 1917, Forgotten Books, 2013

Foley, Charles, *Commando Extraordinary: The Spectacular Exploits of Otto Skorzeny*, Pan, 1954

Frank, Wolfgang, *Enemy Submarine: The Story of Günther Prien, Captain of U47*, NEL, 1977

Freedman, Sir Lawrence, *The Official History of the Falklands Campaign, Volume I: The Origins of the Falklands War* and *Volume II: War and Diplomacy*, Routledge, 2006

Friedman, Norman, *Desert Victory: The War for Kuwait*, NIP, 1991

Fulton, Robert, *Torpedo War and Submarine Explosions*, William Elliot, 1810

Gaddis, John Lewis, *The Cold War: A New History*, Penguin, 2007

Gallery, Rear Admiral Daniel V., *Twenty Million Tons Under the Sea: The Daring Capture of the U-505*, Bluejacket, 2001

Gibbons, Floyd, *And They Thought We Wouldn't Fight*, Otbebookpublishing, 2015

Goldrick, James, *Before Jutland: The Naval War in Northern European Waters, August 1914–February 1915*, NIP, 2015

Goodspeed, D.J., *The Armed Forces of Canada 1867–1967: A Century of Achievement*, Canadian Forces Directorate of History, 1967

Goodspeed, M. Hill, *US Navy, A Complete History*, Hugh Lauter Associates, 2003

Gray, Edwyn, *Disasters of the Deep: A Comprehensive Survey of Submarine Accidents & Disasters*, Pen & Sword, 2003

— *British Submarines in the Great War*, Pen & Sword, 2001

The Great War: The Illustrated History of the First World War, Vols I, II, III & IV (reprint of 13-volume set, published 1914–1918), Trident Press International, 1999

Gretton, Vice Admiral Sir Peter, *Crisis Convoy: The Story of HX231*, Peter Davies, 1974

— *Convoy Escort Commander*, Corgi, 1971

Grider, George, as told to Lydel Sims, *War Fish*, Pyramid, 1966

Gunston, Bill, *Submarines in Colour*, Blandford Press, 1976

Hadley, Michael L. and Roger Sarty, *Tin-Pots & Pirate Ships: Canadian Naval Forces &*

German Sea Raiders 1880–1918, McGill-Queen's University Press, 1991

Ham, Paul, *Hiroshima Nagasaki: The Real Story of the Atomic Bombings and Their Aftermath*, Doubleday, 2012

Hammond, Richard James, *Food and Agriculture in Britain, 1939–45: Aspects of Wartime Control*, Stanford Press, 1954

Harris, Brayton, *The Navy Times Book of Submarines: A Political, Social, and Military History*, Berkley, 2001

Hart, Peter, *1918*, Phoenix, 2009

Haslop, Dennis, *Britain, Germany and the Battle of the Atlantic: A Comparative Study*, Bloomsbury, 2015

Hastings, Max, *Catastrophe: Europe Goes to War 1914*, Collins, 2013

— *All Hell Let Loose: The World at War 1939–1945*, HarperPress, 2011

— *Armageddon: The Battle for Germany 1944–45*, Macmillan, 2004

Hastings, Max and Simon Jenkins, *The Battle for the Falklands*, Pan, 1983

Hendrick, Burton J., *The Life and Letters of Walter H. Page*, Vol. II, Doubleday, 1923

Hennessy, Peter and James Jinks, *The Silent Deep: The Royal Navy Submarine Service Since 1945*, Allen Lane, 2015

Herwig, Holger H., *The Luxury Fleet: The Imperial German Navy 1888–1918*, Prometheus, 1987

Hezlet, Vice Admiral Sir Arthur, *British and Allied Submarine Operations in World War II*, Vol. I, Royal Navy Submarine Museum, 2001

— *HMS Trenchant at War: From Chatham to the Banka Strait*, Pen & Sword, 2001

Hill, Rear Admiral J.R., *Anti-Submarine Warfare*, Ian Allan, 1984

Hindenburg, Paul von, *Out of My Life*, Cassell, 1920

Hoehling, A.A., *The Great War at Sea: The Dramatic Story of Naval Warfare 1914–1918*, Corgi, 1967

Holmes, Richard, ed , *The World at War: The Landmark Oral History from the Classic TV Series*, Ebury Press, 2011

Homer (translated by Martin Hammond), *The Iliad*, Penguin, 1988

Hool, Jack and Keith Nutter, *Damned Un-English Machines: A History of Barrow-Built Submarines*, The History Press, 2003

Hopkins, William B., *The Pacific War: The Strategy, Politics, and Players that Won the War*, Zenith, 2009

Hough, Richard, *The Great War at Sea 1914–1918*, Oxford University Press, 1986

How to Pilot a Submarine, A Fascinating Insight into the Life of a Submariner, Amberley Publishing 2014 (reprint of US Navy publication called *The Fleet Type Submarine*, published 1946)

Howarth, Stephen, *To Shining Sea: A History of the United States Navy 1775–1991*, Weidenfeld & Nicolson, 1991

Huchthausen, Peter A., *K19, The Widowmaker: The Secret Story of the Soviet Nuclear Submarine*, National Geographic, 2002

— *October Fury*, John Wiley, 2002

Huchthausen, Peter, Igor Kurdin and R. Alan White, *Hostile Waters*, Arrow, 1998

Humble, Richard, *Fraser of North Cape: The Life of Admiral of the Fleet Lord Fraser [1888–1981]*, Routledge and Kegan Paul, 1983

Hutchinson, Robert, *Jane's Submarines: War Beneath the Waves from 1776 to the Present Day*, HarperCollins, 2001

Isaacs, Jeremy and Taylor Downing, *Cold War*, Abacus, 2008

Izzard, Brian, *Gamp VC: The Wartime Story of Maverick Submarine Commander Anthony Miers*, Haynes, 2009

Jameson, William, *Submariners VC: Fourteen men of the Royal Navy's Silent Service who received the highest award for bravery*, Periscope, 2004

— *Ark Royal: The Life of an Aircraft Carrier at War 1939–41*, Periscope, 2004

Jellicoe, Admiral Viscount, *The Grand Fleet 1914–1916: Its Creation, Development and Work*, Ad Hoc, 2006

Jordan, John, *Soviet Warships 1945 to the Present*, Arms and Armour, 1992

— *Soviet Submarines, 1945 to the Present*, Arms and Armour, 1989

Keele, Kenneth, *Leonardo Da Vinci's Elements of the Science of Man*, Academic Press, 1983

Kelshall, Gaylord, *The U-boat War in the Caribbean*, NIP, 1994

Kemp, Paul, *The Admiralty Regrets: British Warship Losses of the 20th Century*, Sutton, 1999

— *Submarine Action*, Sutton, 1999

— *U-boats Destroyed: German Submarine Losses in the World Wars*, Arms and Armour, 1999

Kennedy, Paul, *Engineers of Victory: The Problem Solvers who Turned the Tide in the Second World War*, Allen Lane, 2013

Kissinger, Henry, *Diplomacy*, Pocket Books, 1994

König, Paul (translated by Vivien Ellis), *The Voyage of the Deutschland*, Project Gutenberg, 2014

Kurowski, Franz, *U-48: The Most Successful U-boat of the Second World War*, Frontline, 2011

Lake, Simon, *The Submarine in War and Peace, Its Developments and Its Possibilities*, J.B. Lippincott, 1918

Lambert, Andrew, *Nelson: Britannia's God of War*, Faber & Faber, 2004

Lambert, Nicholas A., *Sir John Fisher's Revolution*, University of South Carolina Press, 2002

Lawliss, Chuck, *The Submarine Book: A Portrait of Nuclear Submarines and the Men Who Sail Them*, Thames and Hudson, 1991

Legg, Stuart (compiler and editor), *Jutland: An Eyewitness Account of a Great Battle*, Rupert Hart-Davis, 1966

Liddell Hart, B.H., *A History of the First World War*, Pan, 2014

Lipscomb, Commander F.W., *The British Submarine*, Conway Maritime Press, 1975

Llewellyn-Jones, Malcolm, *The Royal Navy and Anti-Submarine Warfare*, Routledge, 2005

Lloyd George, David, *War Memoirs, 1916–1917*, Odhams, 1938

— *War Memoirs, 1918*, Odhams, 1938

Ludendorff, Erich von, *Ludendorff's Own Story, August 1914–November 1918: The Great War from the Siege of Liège to the Signing of the Armistice as viewed from the Grand Headquarters of the German Army*, Vol. I and Vol. II, Pickle Partners, 2013

Macintyre, Donald, *U-Boat Killer: Fighting the U-boats in the Battle of the Atlantic*, Cassell, 1999
— *The Naval War Against Hitler*, Batsford, 1971
— *Fighting Under the Sea*, Evans Brothers, 1965
— *The Battle of the Atlantic*, Batsford, 1961
— *Fighting Admiral: The Life and Battles of Admiral of the Fleet Sir James Somerville, G.C.B., C.B.E., D.S.O.*, Evans Brothers, 1961
— *Narvik*, Evans Brothers, 1959
McKee, Alexander, *Black Saturday: The Tragedy of the Royal Oak*, Hamlyn, 1978
McLachlan, Donald, *Room 39: Naval Intelligence in Action 1939–45*, Weidenfeld & Nicolson, 1968
Mair, Michael and Joy Waldron, *Kaiten: Japan's Secret Manned Suicide Submarine and the First American Ship it Sank in WWII*, Berkley Caliber, 2014
Marder, Arthur J., ed., *Fear God and Dread Nought, The Correspondence of Admiral of the Fleet Lord Fisher of Kilverstone*, Vol. III, Jonathan Cape, 1959
Mars, Alastair, *Unbroken: The Story of a Submarine*, Pen & Sword, 2011
— *British Submarines at War 1939–1945*, William Kimber, 1971
— *HMS Thule Intercepts*, Pan, 1958
Martienssen, Anthony, *Hitler and His Admirals*, Pickle Partners, 2016
Massie, Robert K., *Castles of Steel: Britain, Germany and the Winning of the Great War at Sea*, Jonathan Cape, 2004
Maurer, John H. and Christopher M. Bell, *At the Crossroads Between Peace and War: The London Naval Conference of 1930*, NIP, 2014
Messimer, Dwight R., *The Baltimore Sabotage Cell: German Agents, American Traitors, and the U-boat Deutschland During World War I*, NIP, 2015
— *Verschollen: World War I U-boat Losses*, NIP, 2002
Miller, David, *The Illustrated Directory of Submarines of the World*, Greenwich Editions, 2004
— *U-Boats: History, Development and Equipment 1914–1945*, Conway, 2000
Miller, Nathan, *The US Navy: A History*, Naval Institute Press, 1997
— *War at Sea: A Naval History of World War II*, Simon & Schuster, 1996
Milner, Marc, *Battle of the Atlantic*, Tempus, 2003
Monsarrat, Nicholas, *Three Corvettes*, Cassell, 2003
Moore, Captain J.E., *The Soviet Navy Today*, PBS, 1975
Moore, Captain J.E. with Commander Richard Compton-Hall, *Submarine Warfare Today and Tomorrow*, Michael Joseph, 1986
Moore, Robert, *A Time to Die: The Kursk Disaster*, Doubleday, 2002
Moorhead, Alan, *Gallipoli*, Ballantine, 1993
Mulligan, Timothy P., *Neither Sharks Nor Wolves: The Men of Nazi Germany's U-boat Arm, 1939–1945*, NIP, 1999
Murphy, William Scanlan, *Father of the Submarine: The Life of the Reverend George Garrett Pasha*, William Kimber, 1987
The Navy List for December, 1918, HMSO/J.J. Keliher, 1918
Neureuther, Karl and Claus Bergen, eds, *U-boat Stories: Narratives of German U-Boat Sailors*, Naval and Military Press, 2009

Newbolt, Henry, *Official History of the War: Naval Operations*, Vol. IV, Longmans, 1928

— *A Note on the History of Submarine War*, Longmans, Green, 1918

North, Oliver L. with Joe Musser, *War Stories II: Heroism in the Pacific*, Regnery, 2004

O'Brien, Philips Payson, ed., *Technology and Naval Combat in the Twentieth Century and Beyond*, Frank Cass, 2001

Ohler, Norman, *Blitzed: Drugs in Nazi Germany*, translated by Shaun Whiteside, Penguin, 2017

Orita, Zenji with Joseph D. Harrington, *I-Boat Captain: How Japan's Submarines Almost Defeated the U.S. Navy in the Pacific!*, Major Books, 1976

Owen, David, *Anti-Submarine Warfare: An Illustrated History*, Seaforth, 2007

Padfield, Peter, *War Beneath the Sea: Submarine Conflict 1939–1945*, Thistle, 2013

Paine, Lincoln, *The Sea and Civilisation: A Maritime History of the World*, Atlantic Books, 2014

Parkes, Oscar, ed., *Jane's Fighting Ships 1931*, David & Charles

Parry, Chris, *Down South: A Falklands War Diary*, Viking, 2012

Parsons, Wm. Barclay, *Robert Fulton and the Submarine*, Columbia University Press, 1922

Paterson, Lawrence, *First U-Boat Flotilla*, Pen & Sword, 2001

Paterson, Michael, *Voices of the Code Breakers, Personal Accounts of the Secret Heroes of World War II*, David & Charles, 2007

Philip, Cynthia Owen, *Robert Fulton: A Biography*, Watts, 1985

Pinkerton, Allan, *The Spy of the Rebellion; Being a True History of the Spy Systems of the United States Army During the Late Rebellion. Revealing Many Secrets of the War not Made Public*, G.W. Carleton, 1883

Pollard, John, *The Unknown Pope: Benedict XV: 1914–1922 and the Pursuit of Peace*, Cassell, 2000

Polmar, Norman, ed., *The Modern Soviet Navy: An Assessment of the USSR's Current Warships, Naval Capabilities and Development*, Arms and Armour, 1979

Polmar, Norman and K.J. Moore, *Cold War Submarines: The Design and Construction of U.S. and Soviet Submarines, 1945–2001*, Potomac, 2003

Polmar, Norman and Jurrien Noot, *Submarines of the Russian and Soviet Navies 1718–1990*, NIP, 1991

Poolman, Kenneth, *The Sea Hunters: Escort Carriers v. U-Boats, 1941–1945*, Arms and Armour, 1982

Pope, Stephen and Elizabeth-Anne Wheal, *The Macmillan Dictionary of the First World War*, Macmillan, 1997

— *The Macmillan Dictionary of the Second World War*, Macmillan, 1995

Prange, Gordon W. with Donald Goldstein and Katherine V. Dillon, *December 7, 1941: The Day the Japanese Attacked Pearl Harbor*, Harrap, 1988

Preanatt, Jamie and Mark Stille, *Axis Midget Submarines 1939–45*, Osprey, 2014

Preston, Antony, *The Royal Navy Submarine Service: A Centennial History*, Conway, 2001

Preston, Diana, *Lusitania: An Epic Tragedy*, Berkley, 2002

Prince, Stephen, *The Blocking of Zeebrugge: Operation Z-O*, Osprey, 2010

Ragan, Mark K., *Union and Confederate Submarine Warfare in the Civil War*, Savas Woodbury, 1999

Rai, Commodore (retd.) Ranjit with Joseph P. Chacko, *Warring Navies, India & Pakistan: The Story of the Wars, and Operations of the Navies, and Tales of Heroism on Both Sides of the Border*, India Publications Company, 2014

Ramsey, Ryan, *SSN14*, Xlibris, 2016

Redford, Duncan, *A History of the Royal Navy: World War II*, I.B. Tauris, 2014

— *The Submarine: A Cultural History from the Great War to Nuclear Combat*, I.B. Tauris, 2015

Reynolds, David, *The Long Shadow: The Great War and the Twentieth Century*, Simon & Schuster, 2013

Richmond, Vice Admiral Sir Herbert, *National Policy and Naval Strength and Other Essays*, Longmans, 1928

Ricks, Thomas E., *Fiasco: The American Military Adventure in Iraq*, Allen Lane, 2006

Rintelen, Capt. Franz von, *The Dark Invader*, Penguin, 1936

Roberts, John, *Safeguarding the Nation: The Story of the Modern Royal Navy*, Seaforth, 2009

Robertson, Terence, *The Golden Horseshoe: The Wartime Career of Otto Kretschmer, U-Boat Ace*, Frontline, 2011

— *Walker R.N.*, Pan, 1969

Roskill, Stephen, *The Secret Capture: U-110 and the Enigma Story*, Seaforth, 2011

— *The Navy at War 1939–1945*, Wordsworth, 1998

Ruge, Friedrich, *The Soviets as Naval Opponents 1941–45*, NIP, 1979

Ryan, Cornelius, *The Longest Day*, Corgi, 1974

Santayana, George, *Soliloquies in England and Later Soliloquies*, HardPress, 2013

— *Reason in Common Sense*, Dover, 1980

Schaeffer, Heinz, *U-Boat 977*, William Kimber, 1953

Scheer, Admiral Reinhard, *Germany's High Sea Fleet in the World War*, Shilka, 2013

Scott, James, *The War Below: The Story of Three Submarines That Battled Japan*, Simon & Schuster, 2013

Scott, Admiral Sir Percy, *Fifty Years in the Royal Navy*, Endeavour Press, 2015

Sebag-Montefiore, Hugh, *Enigma: The Battle for the Code*, Folio Society, 2005

Seth, Ronald, *The Fiercest Battle: The Story of Convoy O.N.S.5*, Hutchinson, 1961

Seymour, Charles, *Woodrow Wilson and the World War: A Chronicle of Our Times*, Ulan Press, 2012

Shirer, William, *The Rise and Fall of the Third Reich: A History of Nazi Germany*, Book Club Associates, 1973

Showell, Jak P. Mallmann, *Dönitz, U-Boats, Convoys: The British Version of his Memoirs from the Admiralty's Secret Anti-Submarine Reports*, Frontline, 2013

— *Hitler's Navy: A Reference Guide to the Kriegsmarine 1935–1945*, NIP, 2009

— *German Naval Code Breakers*, Ian Allan, 2003

Sims, Rear Admiral W.S., *The Victory at Sea*, John Murray, 1920

Skinner, Michael, *USN*, Arms and Armour, 1986

Smith, Gordon, *The War at Sea: Royal & Dominion Navy Actions in World War 2*, Ian Allan, 1989

Smith, Peter C., *Midway, Dauntless Victory: Fresh Perspectives on America's Seminal Naval Victory of World War II*, Pen & Sword, 2007

— *Skua! The Royal Navy's Dive-Bomber*, Pen & Sword, 2006

Sondhaus, Lawrence, *World War One: The Global Revolution*, Cambridge University Press, 2011

Sontag, Sherry, Christopher Drew and Annette Lawrence Drew, *Blind Man's Bluff: The Untold Story of Cold War Submarine Espionage*, Arrow, 2000

Southern Historical Society Papers, Volume XXX, The Southern Historical Society, 1902

Stanton, Charles D., *Medieval Maritime Warfare*, Pen & Sword, 2015

Stanton, Doug, *In Harm's Way*, Bantam, 2001

Steel, Nigel and Peter Hart, *Defeat at Gallipoli*, Papermac, 1995

Steiner, Zara, *The Lights That Failed: European International History 1919–1933*, Oxford University Press, 2005

Stevens, David, *In All Respects Ready: Australia's Navy in World War One*, Oxford University Press, 2014

Stevens, Neal (compiler and ed.), *2008 Submarine Almanac: Naval Stories, Submarines History, and Game Development From Experts and Enthusiasts*, Deep Domain

Stevenson, *With Our Backs to the Wall: Victory and Defeat in 1918*, Allen Lane, 2011

— *1914–1918: The History of the First World War*, Penguin, 2005

Stille, Mark E., *The Imperial Japanese Navy in the Pacific War*, Osprey, 2013

Story-Maskelyne, Mary, *Hugh Oakeley Arnold-Forster: A Memoir*, Edward Arnold, 1910

Sutcliffe, Alice Crary, *Robert Fulton*, Macmillan, 1915

Tarrant, V.E., *Jutland, the German Perspective*, Arms and Armour, 1997

Terraine, John, *Business in Great Waters: The U-Boat Wars 1916–1945*, Pen & Sword, 2009

Thomas, Lowell, *Raiders of the Deep: The Whole Spine-Tingling Story of the German U-Boats in World War I*, Award Books, 1964

Thompson, John Herd and Stephen J. Randall, *Canada and the United States: Ambivalent Allies*, University of Georgia Press, 2008

Thompson, Julian, *The War at Sea 1914–1918: The Face of Battle Revealed in the Words of the Men Who Fought*, Sidgwick & Jackson, 2005

— *The Royal Marines: From Sea Soldiers to a Special Force*, Pan, 2001

Thorp, David, *The Silent Listener*, The History Press, 2011

Tomes, Jason, *Balfour and Foreign Policy: The International Thought of a Conservative Statesman*, Cambridge University Press, 1997

Trapp, Georg von (translated by Elizabeth M. Campbell), *To the Last Salute: Memories of an Austrian U-boat Commander*, University of Nebraska Press, 2007

Trial of the Major War Criminals Before the International Military Tribunals, Nuremberg 14 November 1945–1 October 1946, published 1947, under Allied Control Authority for Germany

Truscott, Peter, *Kursk: Russia's Lost Pride*, Simon & Schuster, 2002

Tuohy, William, *The Bravest Man: Richard O'Kane and the Amazing Submarine Adventures of the USS Tang*, Ballantine, 2001

Turner, Barry, *Karl Doenitz and the Last Days of the Third Reich*, Icon, 2015

Turner, John Frayn, *VCs of the Royal Navy*, Harrap, 1956

United States Submarine Losses in World War Two, Originally printed by Commander Submarine Force, Pacific Fleet, 1946, reprinted by Periscope Film LLC, 2008

Van der Vat, Dan, *Stealth at Sea: The History of the Submarine*, Weidenfeld & Nicolson, 1994

Vause, Jordan, *Wolf: U-Boat Commanders in World War II*, Airlife, 1997

Waldron, T.J. and James Gleeson, *The Frogmen: The Story of the Wartime Underwater Operators*, Pan, 1954

Warner, Philip, *Zeebrugge Raid*, Pen & Sword, 2008

Warren, C.E.T. and James Benson, *Above Us the Waves: The Story of Midget Submarines and Human Torpedoes*, Pen & Sword, 2006

Watkins, Paul, *Midget Submarine Commander: The Life of Godfrey Place VC*, Pen & Sword, 2012

Watson, Alexander, *Ring of Steel: Germany and Austria-Hungary at War, 1914–1918*, Allen Lane, 2014

Weir, Gary E. and Walter J. Boyne, *Rising Tide: The Untold Story of the Russian Submarines That Fought the Cold War*, Basic, 2003

Werner, Herbert, *Iron Coffins: A Personal Account of the German U-boat Battles of World War II*, Da Capo Press, 2002

Whinney, Bob, *The U-Boat Peril: A Fight for Survival*, Cassell, 2000

White, John F., *U Boat Tankers 1941–45: Submarine Suppliers to Atlantic Wolf Packs*, Airlife, 1998

White, Michael, *Australian Submarines: A History*, Vol. II (second edition), Australian Teachers of Media, 2015

White, Rowland, *Vulcan 607: The Epic Story of the Most Remarkable British Air Attack Since the Second World War*, Corgi, 2007

Whitestone, Cdr Nicholas, *The Submarine: The Ultimate Weapon*, Davis-Poynter, 1973

Whitley, M.J., *Cruisers of World War Two: An International Encyclopedia*, Arms and Armour Press, 2001

Williams, Andrew, *The Battle of the Atlantic*, BBC Books, 2003

Williams, Mark, *Captain Gilbert Roberts R.N. and the Anti-U-Boat School*, Cassell, 1979

Williamson, Gordon, *U-Boat Crews 1914–45*, Osprey, 1995

Wilmot, Chester, *The Struggle for Europe*, The Reprint Society, 1954

Wilson, Michael, *Baltic Assignment: British Submariners in Russia 1914–1919*, Leo Cooper/Secker & Warburg, 1985

Wilson, Michael and Paul Kemp, *Mediterranean Submarines: Submarine Warfare in World War One*, Crecy, 1997

Winton, John, *The Submariners: Life in British Submarines 1901–1999*, Constable, 2001

Woodman, Richard, *The Real Cruel Sea: The Merchant Navy in the Battle of the Atlantic 1939–1943*, Pen & Sword, 2013

Woodward, Bob, *Bush at War*, Part 1, Simon & Schuster, 2003

Woodward, David, *The Russians at Sea: A History of the Russian Navy*, William Kimber, 1965

Woodward, Admiral Sandy, *One Hundred Days: The Memoirs of the Falklands Battle Group Commander*, HarperCollins, 1992

Young, Edward, *One of Our Submarines*, Rupert Hart-Davies, 1952

Fictional

Beach, Edward L., *Run Silent, Run Deep*, Phoenix, 2003

Bucheim, Lothar-Günther, *Das Boot*, Cassell, 2013

Conan Doyle, Arthur, *Danger! and Other Stories*, Project Gutenberg, 2007

Grass, Günter, *Crabwalk*, Faber & Faber, 2003

Hackett, General Sir John, and others, *The Third World War: August 1985, a Future History*, Sphere, 1979

Locchi, Vittorio (translated by Lorna de' Lucchi), *The Feast of Saint Gorizia*, L'Eroica, 1919

Monsarrat, Nicholas, *The Cruel Sea*, Penguin, 2009

(I have classified Monsarrat's *Three Corvettes* as factual, as the majority of it is in fact just so, though it does contain some short works of fiction)

Verne, Jules, *Twenty Thousand Leagues Under the Sea*, Wordsworth, 1992

COLLECTIONS OF OFFICIAL DOCUMENTS

Hunting Tirpitz, Royal Navy Operations Against Bismarck's Sister Ship, University of Plymouth Press, 2012. Published in association with Britannia Museum, Britannia Royal Naval College, Dartmouth (which supplied the content). Foreword by Admiral Sir Mark Stanhope and Introduction by Dr G.H. Bennett, it was part of a Britannia Naval Histories of World War II series, seeking to publish documents previously kept away from the public due to being 'classified' or 'restricted'. The Admiralty's *Battle Summary No.29, 'The Attack on the Tirpitz by Midget Submarines (Operation "Source") 22 September 1943'* contained in this volume was pivotal in constructing the chapter (Part Three, Chapter 28) on the X-craft attack against *Tirpitz*.

The Submarine Service 1900–1918, edited by Nicholas Lambert, Navy Records Society, 2001. A collection of the texts of original documents relating to the history of the Submarine Service in its early days, drawing on various archives. Those quoted for this book are as follows:

Fisher Papers, FISR 1/14 – *Extract from Churchill to Fisher.*

Keyes Papers, Mss 4/36 – *Lieutenant Norman Holbrook VC to Captain Roger Keyes on receipt of the Victoria Cross for sinking Turkish battleship.*

Also consulted was *British Naval Documents 1204–1960, British Naval Documents 2014–1960, Navy Records*, edited by John B. Hattendorf, R.J.B. Knight, A.W.H. Pearsall, N.A.M. Rodger and Geoffrey Till, Navy Records Society, 1993. Quoted The National Archives, ADM 2/1750 – *Considerations on a defensive war against Algiers, 1681.*

Some books consulted were accessed either as PDF scans of the originals or in full text variants (which is why in Notes sometimes chapter locations have been mentioned – for example Chapter 3 rather than a page number). The full book titles, authors and publisher are included above. The majority of these books were accessed via Internet Archive [https://archive.org], a huge undertaking that makes out of copyright books accessible, in this case from the libraries of: Robarts-University of Toronto; New York Public Library; University of California; University of Florida; University of North Carolina; Erindale College; University of California Los Angeles; University of North Carolina Greensboro. Other digital, copyright-free books were accessed via Project Gutenberg [http://www.gutenberg.org/ebooks].

NEWSPAPERS
(including those accessed online)

Advertiser, 10 November 1915, Adelaide, 'German Cruiser [*Undine*] Sunk, Torpedoed in the Baltic' [http://trove.nla.gov.au/newspaper/article/8653715]

Advocate, Tasmania, 30 May 1939, 'Great Britain's Immense Imports' [http://trove.nla.gov.au/newspaper/article/68560471/6692955]

Ashburton Guardian, New Zealand, 14 May 1919, 'Zeebrugge Raid, Canadians Welcome Leader' [https://paperspast.natlib.govt.nz/newspapers/AG19190514.2.36?query=Zeebrugge%20raid]

Brisbane Courier, 23 August 1915, 'Submarine *E13*, Attacked by German Destroyers While Aground' [http://trove.nla.gov.au/newspaper/article/20051888?searchTerm=Submarine%20E13%2C%20Attacked%20by%20German&searchLimits=]

Brooklyn Daily Eagle, 8 January 1945, 'V-Bomb Attack Here Probable, Says Navy' [https://www.newspapers.com/newspage/53702671/]

Chicago Tribune, 28 February 1917, 'How *Laconia* Sank', by Floyd P. Gibbons [http://archives.chicagotribune.com/1917/02/28/page/1/article/how-laconia-sank]

Chicago Tribune, 23 July 1997, 'For Nuclear Subs and Their Crews, The Cold War is Far From Over', by Michael Kilian [http://articles.chicagotribune.com/1997-07-23/features/9707230242_1_submarine-russian-navy-nuclear]

Cornell Daily Sun, Ithaca, New York, 19 March 1917, 'Sinking of Three American Ships Virtually Causes a State of War, Unarmed Merchantmen Attacked Resulting in Probable Loss of Life', Associated Press report. PDF of the edition as published, accessed via http://cdsun.library.cornell.edu/cgi-bin/cornell?a=d&d=CDS19170319.2.2

Daily Express, 6 February 2015, 'World War Two hero who destroyed seven enemy U-boats in the Battle of the Atlantic', by Mark Reynolds [http://www.express.co.uk/news/history/556541/REVEALED-World-War-Two-hero-who-destroyed-seven-enemy-U-boats-in-Battle-of-the-Atlantic]

Daily Mail, 4 April 2015, 'Bang goes the no claims! Royal Navy nuclear submarine suffers £500,000 damage after "hitting floating ice" while tracking Russian vessels', by Mark Nicol for the *Mail on Sunday* [http://www.dailymail.co.uk/news/article-3025839/Royal-Navy-nuclear-submarine-suffers-500-000-damage-hitting-floating-ice-tracking-Russian-vessels.html]

Daily Mail, 30 August 2015, 'Spain accused of "provocation" after letting Russian submarine refuel 19 miles off the coast of Gibraltar', by Kate Pickles for Mailonline [http://www.dailymail.co.uk/news/article-3215434/Spain-accused-provocation-letting-Russian-submarine-refuel-19-miles-coast-Gibraltar.html]

Daily Mail, 30 October 2016, 'Russian submarines are spotted in the IRISH Sea as three of the stealth craft navigate through UK waters in latest provocation by Putin's navy', by James Dunn for Mailonline [http://www.dailymail.co.uk/

news/article-3887706/Russian-submarines-spotted-IRISH-Sea-three-stealth-craft-navigate-UK-waters-latest-provocation-Putin-s-navy.html]

Daily Telegraph, 25 August 2000, 'Widow's outburst stopped with syringe', by Marcus Warren [http://www.telegraph.co.uk/news/worldnews/europe/1367631/Widows-outburst-stopped-with-syringe.html]

Daily Telegraph, 27 August 2000, 'I was not silenced, says *Kursk* mother', by Guy Chazan and Philip Sherwell [http://www.telegraph.co.uk/news/worldnews/europe/russia/1367868/I-was-not-silenced-says-Kursk-mother.html]

Daily Telegraph, 10 February 2008, 'Henry Stoker: sailor, sportsman, actor, hero', by Jasper Copping [http://www.telegraph.co.uk/news/uknews/1578218/Henry-Stoker-sailor-sportsman-actor-hero.html]

Daily Telegraph, 18 April 2012, 'Thirty Years on, Argentine survivors of the *Belgrano* sinking recall the moment Falklands war erupted around them', by Philip Sherwell [http://www.telegraph.co.uk/news/worldnews/southamerica/argentina/9233976/Thirty-years-on-Argentine-survivors-of-the-Belgrano-sinking-recall-the-moment-Falklands-war-erupted-around-them.html]

Daily Telegraph, 22 April 2015, 'Gallipoli campaign: The man who sank 97 ships', by Tom Rowley [http://www.telegraph.co.uk/news/worldnews/europe/turkey/11552801/Gallipoli-campaign-The-man-who-sank-97-ships.html]

Daily Telegraph, 10 February 2017, 'Ministry of Defence denies Britain's entire fleet of attack submarines are "out of action"', by Laura Hughes [http://www.telegraph.co.uk/news/2017/02/10/britains-entire-fleet-attack-submarines-action/]

Dominion, 1 May 1915, New Zealand, 'The Sinking of the *Léon Gambetta*, Story of the Submarine Attack' [https://paperspast.natlib.govt.nz/newspapers/DOM19150501.2.38]

Examiner, Launceston (Australia), 2 February 1938, 'British Ship Torpedoed Off Spain, Sunk by Spanish Rebel Submarine' [http://trove.nla.gov.au/newspaper/article/52189972]

Gettysburg Times, 14 October 1933, 'Germany Quits Disarmament Conference; Leaves League', AP report [https://www.newspapers.com/newspage/45731184/]

Guardian, 25 May 2000, 'Enigma variations', by Hugh Sebag-Montefiore [https://www.theguardian.com/film/2000/may/25/1]

Guardian, 9 November 2016, 'Russian warships drive away Dutch submarine tailing fleet on the Mediterranean' [https://www.theguardian.com/world/2016/nov/09/russian-warships-drive-away-dutch-submarine-shadowing-fleet-in-mediterranean]

Harper's Weekly, 2 November 1861, 'A Rebel Infernal Machine', facsimile of original news magazine, accessed via the Civil War website [http://www.sonofthesouth.net/leefoundation/civil-war/1861/november/submarine.htm]

Herald, Plymouth (UK), 23 March 2013, '"Absolute focus" as we launched missiles at Iraq', by Rebecca Ricks [http://www.plymouthherald.co.uk/absolute-focus-launched-missiles-iraq/story-18541288-detail/story.html]

Independent, 31 August 2004, 'Soviet submarine captain wins Hollywood payout', by Andrew Osborn [http://www.independent.co.uk/news/world/europe/

soviet-submarine-captain-wins-hollywood-payout-558453.html]

Irish Times, 14 August 2014, 'John Philip Holland: the Irish inventor who helped take the war underwater', by Mary Mulvihill [http://www.irishtimes.com/news/science/john-philip-holland-the-irish-inventor-who-helped-take-the-war-underwater-1.1891563]

Jornal Pequeno, Recife, Brazil, 18 August 1942, quoted on the website Sixtant, War II in the South Atlantic [http://www.sixtant.net]

Kerryman, Ireland, 10 January 1999, '"Submarines in the bog holes": West Kerry's experience of World War II', by T. Ryle Dwyer [accessed via http://www.u-35.com/sources/Kerryman1999.htm]

Liverpool Echo, 13 October 2007, 'Danger! Mines in the Bay', by Dawn Collinson [http://www.liverpoolecho.co.uk/news/liverpool-news/danger-mines-in-the-bay-3501347]

Liverpool Echo, 11 May 2013, 'Battle of the Atlantic: Remembering Johnnie Walker, Britain's Number One U-boat Killer', by Peter Elson [http://www.liverpoolecho.co.uk/news/nostalgia/battle-atlantic-remembering-johnnie-walker-3571561]

Local, Denmark, 21 March 2015, 'Russia delivers nuclear threat to Denmark' [https://www.thelocal.dk/20150321/russia-threatens-denmark-with-nuclear-attack]

Los Angeles Times, 18 April 2010, 'North Korea denies role in South Korean naval disaster', by John M. Glionna [http://articles.latimes.com/2010/apr/18/world/la-fg-north-korea-ship18-2010apr18]

The New York Times (NYT): 1 May 1915, 'German Embassy Issues Warning, Advertises Notice of Danger to Travelers in War Zone'; 26 October 1915, 'Nearly All Perished on *Prinz Adalbert*, Berlin Confirms the Sinking of the Cruiser in the Baltic'; 29 July 1916, 'Germans Execute British Skipper'; 8 October 1916, 'Sea Visitor Unheralded, Giant *U-53* Meets U.S. Submarine Outside and is Piloted into Port'; 5 February 1917, 'U-Boat Captain Gave *Housatonic* An Hour's Warning Before Sinking'; 19 March 1917. Patrol Picks up Survivors, *City of Memphis* Crew is Abandoned at Sea in Five Open Boats, *Vigilancia* Saw No U-boat, 30 November 1917, 'Lansdowne Urges Stating War Aims; Balfour Declares Britain Menaced When French Block Cuts in Submarines', by Edwin L. James.

All of the above were accessed via *The New York Times* online archive and downloaded as PDFs of the original newspaper stories as set in print. To search for NYT stories in this archive visit https://www.nytimes.com.

The following *New York Times* stories were accessed via a DVD-ROM carrying the indexed news coverage of the newspaper during the Second World War: 5 Sept 1939, '*Athenia* Lifeboat Capsized As It Neared Rescue Ship', United Press (UP) report; 6 Sept 1939, 'Reich Denies Attacking Ship' (UP); 28 December 1939, 'Crew Tries to Save Half Torpedoed Tanker [*San Alberto*]'; 23 September 1940, 'Father Loses 5 on Liner'; 24 September 1940, 'Hull Calls Sinking "A Dastardly Act"'; 5 September 1941, 'Torpedoes Go Wild'. The DVD-ROM was provided with *The New York Times Complete World War II 1939–1945: The Coverage from the Battlefields to the Home Front*, edited by Richard Overy with a foreword by Tom Brokaw, published by Black Dog & Leventhal, 2013. The DVD-ROM itself contains more than 90,000 articles. Highlights are published in the book.

These *NYT* articles were accessed via the Web:

7 January 1981, 'War Veterans Come to Bury, And to Praise Doenitz', by John Vincour, Special to the *New York Times* [http://www.nytimes.com/1981/01/07/world/war-veterans-come-to-bury-and-to-praise-doenitz.html] 3 March 1995, 'A Curious War Beneath the Waves', by Denis Warner [http://www.nytimes.com/1995/03/03/opinion/03iht-edwarn.html] 18 July 1995, 'Lost Japanese Sub With 2 Tons of Axis Gold Found on Floor of Atlantic', by William J. Broad [http://www.nytimes.com/1995/07/18/science/lost-japanese-sub-with-2-tons-of-axis-gold-found-on-floor-of-atlantic.html?pagewanted=all] 27 October 2000, '"None of Us Can Get Out" *Kursk* Sailor Wrote', by Michael Wines [http://www.nytimes.com/2000/10/27/world/none-of-us-can-get-out-kursk-sailor-wrote.html] 4 July 2001, 'Captain, Once a Scapegoat, Is Absolved', by David Stout [http://www.nytimes.com/2001/07/14/us/captain-once-a-scapegoat-is-absolved.html?_r=0]

Northern Times, Carnarvon, Western Australia, 9 October 1937, 'Submarine Attack, The *Basilisk* Incident, Submarine Believed Sunk by Depth Charge' [http://trove.nla.gov.au/newspaper/article/75122751/7359712]

Oamaru Mail, 5 July 1901, news-in-brief, Paris, 4 July, 'During the French manoeuvres, the submarine boat *Gustave Zédé* starting from Toulon fired a dummy torpedo at the battleship *Jauregenberry* [sic]'. Scan of original report, accessed via the Web.

Oamaru Mail, 23 September 1918, 'Sinking of the *Justicia*' [http://paperspast.natlib.govt.nz/newspapers/OAM19180923.2.21]

Otago Daily Times, New Zealand, 22 November 1918, 'U-Boats Sunk, One Hundred and Fifty Commanders Names Given' [http://paperspast.natlib.govt.nz/newspapers/ODT19181122.2.56]

Post & Courier, Charleston, SC, USA, 28 January 2013, 'Dixon's watch offers no clues', by Brian Hicks [http://www.postandcourier.com/news/dixon-s-watch-offers-no-clues/article_dff33a18-82e1-5173-86bd-5042fd3f3ecc.html]

Pravda, 12 August 2016, 'It was US and UK that sank Russia's *Kursk* submarine', by Anatoly Miranovsky [http://www.pravdareport.com/society/stories/12-08-2016/121163-kursk_submarine-0/]

The Press, York (UK), 5 October 2011, 'Former submarine commander Captain Stephen Upright is running York's Merchant Adventurer's Hall', by Matt Clark [http://www.yorkpress.co.uk/features/features/9287822.Submariner_rises_to_a__new_challenge/]

San Diego Union-Tribune, 28 May 2015, 'Finnish navy: Underwater intruder possible foreign submarine', AP report [http://www.sandiegouniontribune.com/sdut-finnish-navy-underwater-intruder-possible-foreign-2015may28-story.html]

Sun, 10 February 2017, 'Subs: Zero, The Royal Navy's ENTIRE fleet of attack submarines is out of action – and Theresa May doesn't know because "chiefs fear reaction"', by David Willetts [https://www.thesun.co.uk/news/2829355/uks-entire-fleet-of-attack-submarines-is-out-of-action-and-theresa-may-doesnt-know/]

Sydney Morning Herald, 11 October 1937, 'The *Basilisk* Incident, Counter-attack,

But No Attack, German Criticism' [http://trove.nla.gov.au/newspaper/article/17418216]

The Times, 11 October 1921, 'Turkish Crimes, Treatment of British Prisoners', letter to the Editor of the newspaper, as scanned from original and reproduced on the official Bram Stoker website [http://www.bramstokerestate.com/Henry-Hew-Gordon-Dacre-Stoker-submariner.html]

Western Flying Post, 4 July 1774, 'Extract of a Letter from Plymouth, June 24'

Western Morning News, 27 April 2015, 'Attack off Scilly', by Clive Mumford [http://www.westernmorningnews.co.uk/WEST-Attack-Scilly/story-26395015-detail/story.html]

MAGAZINES & PERIODICALS
(including those accessed online)

Defense News, 8 December 2015, 'Russian Submarine Hits Targets in Syria', by Christopher P. Cavas [http://www.defensenews.com/story/breaking-news/2015/12/08/submarine-russia-kalibr-caliber-cruise-missile-syria-kilo/76995346/]

Defense News, 31 March 2017, 'Russia adds "Kazan" to its nuclear attack submarine fleet', by Matthew Bodner [http://www.defensenews.com/articles/russia-adds-kazan-to-its-nuclear-attack-submarine fleet]

The Diplomat, 4 March 2015, 'Putin's "Red October": Russia's Deadliest New Submarine', by Franz-Stefan Gady [http://thediplomat.com/2015/03/putins-red-october-russias-deadliest-new-submarine/]

Foreign Policy, 15 August 2011, 'Think Again: War', by Joshua S. Goldstein [http://foreignpolicy.com/2011/08/15/think-again-war/]

IHS Jane's Defence Weekly, 17 May 2016, 'China proposes "Underwater Great Wall" that could erode US, Russian submarine advantages', by Richard D. Fisher [http://www.janes.com/article/60388/china-proposes-underwater-great-wall-that-could-erode-us-russian-submarine-advantages]

Life, 29 January 1940, 'Hero of British Submarine 65 Finishes a Great Trip' [profile of Bickford and his submarine *Salmon*]

Life, 22 October 1945, pp. 17–18, p. 20, pp. 23–24, '*Life* Reports: The "Cure" at Mondorf Spa, How Nazi War criminals lived in Luxembourg jail', by John Kenneth Galbraith [https://books.google.co.uk/books?id=pksEAAAAMBAJ&pg=PA29&lpg=PA29&dq=Life,+22+October+1945+the+cure+at+Mondorf+spa&source=bl&ots=shsDsjUTQQ&sig=11g1-unJx41vMbNmNHT6GB2_6Mc&hl=en&sa=X&ved=0ahUKEwibpqW6u-XTAhXhLMAKHeniC1gQ6AEIJTAB#v=onepage&q=Mondorf&f=false]

National Defense Magazine, 22 March 2017, 'Cost of New Submarine Could Threaten Navy Fleet Expansion', by Jon Harper [http://www.nationaldefensemagazine.org/articles/2017/3/22/cost-of-new-submarine-could-threaten-navy-fleet-expansion]

Newsweek, 3 May 1943 and *Time*, 18 October 1943, quotes about the career of USS *Wahoo* and her captain Dudley Morton. Taken from the book *United States Submarine Losses in World War Two* (see Bibliography and Notes 3 and

10, Part Three, Chapter 32). 'Russian Military Uses New War Weapon to Fight ISIS in Syria', by Tom O' Connor, 5 July 2017 [http://www.newsweek.com/russia-military-new-war-weapon-fight-isis-syria-632082] 'Russia's Naval Plan Calls for Defense Against the U.S. "Across the World Ocean"' 21 July 2017 [http://www.msn.com/en-gb/news/world/russia's-new-military-plan-calls-for-defense-against-the-us-across-the-'world-ocean'/ar-AAovXZq?ocid=News]

Proceedings, May 1963, 'I Sank the Yorktown at Midway', by Yahachi Tanabe, formerly Lieutenant Commander, Imperial Japanese Navy, with Joseph D. Harrington, 1963 [https://www.usni.org/magazines/proceedings/1963-05]

Proceedings, June 2016, 'The Fourth Battle of the Atlantic', by Vice Admiral James Foggo III, US Navy, and Alarik Fritz [https://www.usni.org/magazines/proceedings/2016-06/fourth-battle-atlantic]

Smithsonian, 30 June 2014, 'The Amazing (If True) Story of the Submarine Mechanic Who Blew Himself Up Then Surfaced as a Secret Agent for Queen Victoria', by Mike Dash [http://www.smithsonianmag.com]

Survival, Vol. 41, No. 3, Autumn 1999, 'NATO's "Humanitarian War" over Kosovo', by Adam Roberts, IISS

WARSHIPS *International Fleet Review* articles and news reports: September 2000 (reproduced in January 2009 edition), 'Death of the *Kursk*', by Peter Hore and Iain Ballantyne; August/September 2002, 'The Lessons of War, an account of HMS *Alacrity*'s part in the Falklands War', by Captain Chris Craig; June 2003, Battle of the Atlantic 60th Anniversary Supplement, 'A Fight to the Finish', by Syd Goodman; August 2004, 'Destination D-Day' [special section to mark 60th anniversary of the Normandy landings], 'During the day we came to periscope depth . . .', by Jim Booth; May 2007, 'The *Santa Fe* Submarine During the Malvinas [Falklands] War', by Juan Carlos Cicalesi and Santiago Rivas; June 2007, 'The Sinking of the Cruiser ARA *General Belgrano*, The Survivor's Story', by Juan Carlos Cicalesi and Santiago Rivas [both articles published as part of Falklands War 25th anniversary special sections]; October 2014, 'Putin Brandishes Russia's Nuclear Big Stick'; June 2015, 'The Whole World Looks With Horror', by Peter Hore [article to commemorate 100th anniversary of *Lusitania* sinking]; September 2015, 'Kremlin Launches New Battle for the Atlantic (and the Arctic & Mediterranean)', by Iain Ballantyne; May 2016, 'North Korea Loses Submarine, Threatens Nuclear War', by Usman Ansari.

OBITUARIES

Martin Dunbar-Nasmith, Scotland's War website, The University of Edinburgh [http://www.edinburghs-war.ed.ac.uk/Moray/People-Morays-VCs/Admiral-Sir-Martin-Eric-Dunbar-Nasmith-VC-KCB-KCMG]

Eugene Fluckey, *The Times*, London, 20 July 2007 (clipping) Discusses his tonnage total in relation to other Allied submarine captains including Malcolm Wanklyn, who it suggests was the highest (133,940 tons), though Fluckey's own research suggested he got more: 145,000 tons.

Ian Fraser, *Daily Telegraph*, 2 September 2008 [http://www.telegraph.co.uk/news/obituaries/2670609/Ian-Fraser-VC.html]

Nobuo Fujita, *The New York Times*, 3 October 1997 [http://www.nytimes.
    com/1997/10/03/world/nobuo-fujita-85-is-dead-only-foeto-bomb-america.html]
Otto Kretschmer, *Independent*, 24 August 1998 [http://www.independent.co.uk/arts-
    entertainment/obituary-admiral-otto-kretschmer-1173919.html]
Godfrey Place, *Daily Telegraph*, 27 December 1994 [http://www.telegraph.co.uk/
    news/obituaries/military-obituaries/naval-obituaries/8328587/Rear-Admiral-
    Godfrey-Place-VC.html]
John Scott Russell, Institution of Civil Engineers, 1887 [http://www.gracesguide.
    co.uk/John_Scott_Russell:_Obituaries]
Kazuo Sakamaki, *The New York Times*, 21 December 1999 [http://www.nytimes.
    com/1999/12/21/world/kazuo-sakamaki-81-pacific-pow-no-1.html]
Max Shean, *Australian*, 26 June 2009 [available as a PDF download via http://www.
    submarineinstitute.com/ Obituary-LCDR-Max-Shean-DSO-and-bar-RANVR-
    Rtd.html?fp=58]

INTERVIEWS

My submarine warfare education for this book goes back a long way. An extraordinary submarine captain I was privileged to interview was the late **Richard Raikes**, whom I went to meet at his Somerset home in 1996. As a memento of his time as a submarine captain, Raikes used the head of a U-boat periscope as a doorstop in the kitchen. He drew it to my attention so that I wouldn't stub my toe on it. We went for a whisky and to continue our chat in a nearby pub, discussing the good, the bad and the ugly of his career at sea in submarines, not least his adventures when captain of *Seawolf*.

Another Second World War veteran I interviewed, in August 1999, for my book *Warspite*, was the late **Frederick 'Ben' Rice**, the Swordfish pilot who sank a U-boat in a Norwegian fjord, the first submarine destroyed by an aircraft in the Second World War.

In June 2004, on Sword Beach in Normandy, during the 60th anniversary of the D-Day landings, I met **Jim Booth**, the X-craft submarine officer who, during an impromptu interview, told me about his role in ensuring the invasion troops got safely ashore on 6 June 1944.

It was amazing to talk with him not far from where he hid beneath the waves to perform that vital function. He later wrote a piece especially for my magazine, *WARSHIPS IFR*.

Anniversaries of conflicts are useful excuses for meeting people who had a decisive part in shaping famous events. While working as a newspaper reporter in 1992, I sat next to the late **Sandy Woodward** during a lunch to mark the tenth anniversary of the Falklands War. I interviewed him about his experiences in command of the British naval battle group and he was surprisingly frank, a quality I also came to appreciate when he wrote some pieces for *WARSHIPS IFR*. The same year I met **Chris Wreford-Brown**, captain of *Conqueror*, for a coffee in a hotel on Plymouth Hoe, while he was commanding the Second Submarine Squadron at Devonport. A decade later I met his XO in the SSN, **Tim McClement**, in London, while he was Assistant Chief of the Naval Staff. Both of these interviews provided rare insights into the sinking of the *Belgrano*.

My encounter with **Steve Upright**, in the reception area of the old *Western Morning News* building in Plymouth city centre in May 1991, was a rather odd affair. He clearly had things he wanted to tell me about his submarine's recent deployment during the period of the 1990–91 Gulf War, but couldn't give much, if anything, away. He had to let me fill in the gaps on what his boat might have been doing. More details have since emerged and I met Steve again in 2014 when he introduced me for a talk on my book *Hunter Killers* at York University. Afterwards we had a pint in a charming pub in the city centre.

In pursuit of material for news features over the years, I have visited a few submarines alongside in their home bases, not least the SSBN HMS *Vengeance*, at HM Naval Base Clyde. It was rather humbling to meet the men charged with taking that awesome, and terrifying, deterrent capability to sea. Passing between the huge boat's Trident missile tubes offered a few moments to contemplate the world-ending power they represented.

I have also been to sea twice in the same nuclear-powered attack submarine, HMS *Triumph* – once during weapon and sonar systems tests off the west coast of Scotland (1991) and then for a three-day voyage from Plymouth to the mouth of the Clyde (1997). Submerged for part of the trip through the Irish Sea, at night I slept on a rack in the torpedo room, cuddling up to a live torpedo and a Harpoon Anti-Shipping Missile. I especially enjoyed a chicken tikka dinner in the boat's wardroom (at a depth of 300ft) and was later in the voyage offered a brief look through the periscope to track frigates under mock torpedo attack during an exercise. Dropped off by an auxiliary transfer craft at Largs, the jetty was right next to an arcade where as a young boy (on holiday, visiting relatives in Scotland) I used to play a U-boat versus convoy game. Actually, I had last been to Largs a few years earlier to catch a ride in a Duke Class anti-submarine frigate, going south to Plymouth. The last anti-submarine frigate I visited in a high threat zone was HMS *Chatham*, in 2008. Due to defence cuts she was patrolling the Arabian Gulf without a fully operational anti-submarine warfare suite, nor did she have a full-time team of sonar specialists embarked. This showed me how much a latter-day UK government was prepared to gamble on defence, by not equipping front line warships with the life-or-death capabilities they needed to have on call at all times.

Among the numerous vessels I have visited in Devonport was HMS *Turbulent*, sister to *Triumph*, in 2003. It was for an interview (subsequently published in the *Guide to the Royal Navy 2004*, of which I was editor) with **Andrew McKendrick** about his experiences as CO of the SSN during cruise missile strikes on Iraq a few months earlier.

Those whom I interviewed at length in 2010–12, during the process of researching and writing *Hunter Killers*, provided many submarine tutorials. Former Cold War submarine captains **Tim Hale**, **Rob Forsyth** and **Doug Littlejohns** are all quoted in this account too. Both Rob and Doug were captains of the same attack submarine, HMS *Sceptre*, which in 2010 I joined in Plymouth Sound for the final few nautical miles of her last-ever homecoming at the end of a 32-year front line career. See *Hunter Killers* for more on that veteran SSN. The few hours I spent aboard *Sceptre* enabled me to talk to a wide range of submariners about their lives under the sea, from the Cold War of the 1980s to operations in the modern era, for an article in *WARSHIPS IFR*.

These days Second World War veterans are rarely encountered, as most have crossed the bar, but in 2014 I was fortunate to arrange interviews with two of them. That June I travelled to Newcastle to meet **Yves Dias**, who had survived an attack by the notorious *U-48*. In the December I went to Hampshire to have a long fireside chat with the redoubtable **Matthew Todd**, who navigated HMS *Thule* on her marathon voyages in the Far East under the command of the legendary Alastair Mars. Matthew also told me about his Cold War adventures off the Dorset coast in command of the diesel boat *Narwhal*.

Finally, two remarkable interviews that have provided exciting material for this account were not carried out by me, but rather by my very good friend Usman Ansari, in Pakistan. He furnished me with the transcripts of his in-depth Q&A sessions with **Ahmad Tasnim** and **Wasim Ahmad**. These have enabled me to bring to life the remarkable 1970s episode in which the Pakistan Navy submarine *Hangor* torpedoed an Indian frigate.

MUSEUMS

Documents, sound recordings and other material, accessed both on site and via the Web
Research was carried out at several locations between June 2014 and June 2016, with more than one visit in each case to the archives of the **Imperial War Museum** (IWM) at Lambeth, the **National Maritime Museum** (NMM) Greenwich, the **National Museum of the Royal Navy** (NMRN), Portsmouth, and the **Merseyside Maritime Museum** in Liverpool.

There was also a research trip to the **Royal Navy Submarine Museum** (RNSM) at Gosport, with work in the archives and a tour of the preserved submarine HMS *Alliance*. During one research trip I gained entry to the underground bunker complex from which the British fought their side of the Battle of the Atlantic (nowadays known as **Liverpool War Museum: Western Approaches**). Across the Mersey at Birkenhead I received an insight into the other side of the contest during a visit to the preserved *U-534* and associated exhibit. In the same location I also encountered a full-size facsimile of Garrett's *Resurgam*, made by engineering apprentices in the late 1990s, a lovingly crafted salute to the Reverend's ill-fated genius. Back across the Mersey is a statue of Capt. Frederic 'Johnny' Walker, in typical U-boat hunting pose and seagoing garb, his eyes seemingly fixed on *U-534* as his next kill.

A further reminder of the grim business of *The Deadly Trade* is available not far from where I live, for on the Naval War Memorial on Plymouth Hoe are the names of hundreds of sailors and marines who lost their lives to submarine attack (and who themselves hunted U-boats).

Among those named on the Plymouth memorial is Harry Stretch, a 36-year-old English submariner serving in the Australian boat *AE1*, lost in mysterious circumstances off the Bismarck Archipelago less than a fortnight after the First World War began.* The remains of *AE1* and her crew have never been found, despite several searches. The deeds and thoughts of submariners in various conflicts, and in the inter-war periods – along with some of those who fell foul of their actions or fought against them – live on in the archives of the museums that hold their papers. They are also alive in the sound recordings of their testimony, some of which were consulted for this book and are listed below.

* As recorded in *Australian Submarines: A History*, Vol. II, p. 712. See bibliography.

IWM
Documents:
Account of the sinking of the SS *Fanad Head*, September 1939
Cat No: Documents.5300
Intelligence Reports on the German Navy, Second World War
Cat No: Documents.7968
[Includes record of Admiral Dönitz interrogation on 6 September 1945 by British
   naval intelligence officer]

Exhibit:
Submersible, Midget Submarine Biber (90), German, History note
[http://www.iwm.org.uk/collections/item/object/30004028]
Cat No: MAR 558
Oral history interview (accessed during research at the IWM)
Guy Beresford Kerr Griffiths
Cat No: 16641

Oral history interviews (accessed via www.iwm.org.uk)
Robert Atkinson
Cat No: 25182
David Edward Balme
Cat No: 12023
John Henry Eaden
Cat No: 9864
Eric Eaton
Cat No: 14140
Ian Fraser
Cat No: 9822
Hugh Michael Irwin
Cat No: 9956
William Stewart Pollock
Cat No: 11948
Stanley Reynolds
Cat No: 21587

Articles:
'Leading Seaman James Magennis VC' [short account of his life and exploits]
   Edited by Gemma Lawrence [http://www.iwm.org.uk/history/
   leading-seaman-james-magennis-vc]

'The Story of Child Evacuee Beryl Myatt and the Sinking of the SS *City of Benares*' by Ian Kikuchi, website article [http://www.iwm.org.uk/history/the-story-of-child-evacuee-beryl-myatt-and-the-sinking-of-the-ss-city-of-benares]

Private Papers of:
H.E.E. Adams
Cat No: Documents.16116
Commander F.H.H. Goodhart
Cat No: Documents.2175
Vice Admiral Sir Roderick Macdonald
Cat No: Documents.1670
Vice Admiral Sir Ian McGeoch
Cat No: Documents.11143
Vice Admiral A.G. Talbot
Cat No: Documents.22714

NMM
Papers of:
Admiral John Henry Godfrey:
GOD/92 – bound typescript volume, entitled 'Top Secret. N.I.D. Vol 9b', containing post-war analysis of NID intelligence including of the Battle of the Atlantic
Cdr A.B. Goord:
RIN/15/1 – 'The Longest Chase', an account of the pursuit of a U-Boat, August 1944
Vice Admiral Sir Peter Gretton:
GTN/8/3 – an account of a post-war encounter with Commander Looks, Captain of *U-264*
Gretton, Peter William, concise biography on website [http://collections.rmg.co.uk/collections.html#!csearch]
Sub Lt Charles Wadsworth Murray:
MUR/8 – notebook on German submarine warfare in the First World War

Publication:
A *Philosophical Dissertation on the Diving Vessel Projected by Mr Day*, Nikolai Detlef Falck, 1775 [http://www.rmg.co.uk/discover/behind-the-scenes/blog/philosophical-dissertation-diving-vessel-projected-mr-day-and-sunk]

NMRN
NMRN 1990.271 – Diaries of Commander Arthur Layard
RNM 2003/59/3 – Precis of the Proceedings, convoy HG-53
RNM LI/2015 Walker – Capt. Frederic Walker's papers (including Operation Haggis)

RNSM

RNSM A1982/005 – *Overthorpe and some Reminiscences* by R.W. Blacklock (originally published 1958, but excerpt published by IMES Ltd in 2001 to mark 100 years of the RN Submarine Service, by kind permission of Lt Col. Michael David Blacklock)

RNSM/A207/302 – 'Some Light-heart Memories', unpublished memoir of Lt Cdr Dick Raikes

RNSM A1994/163 – Account of his deployments into the Barents 1959/60 by Lt Cdr Alfie Roake

MERSEYSIDE MARITIME MUSEUM

D/KEY – Papers of Lt Cdr R.W. Keymer
'The German threat', website article
[http://www.liverpoolmuseums.org.uk/maritime/collections/boa/history/german-threat.aspx]
'Liverpool and the Battle of the Atlantic', website article
[http://www.liverpoolmuseums.org.uk/maritime/collections/boa/history/liverpool.aspx]
'The Merchant Navy: Britain's Lifeline', website article [http://www.liverpoolmuseums.org.uk/maritime/collections/boa/history/merchant-navy.aspx]

LIVERPOOL WAR MUSEUM: WESTERN APPROACHES MUSEUM

History of Derby House, an account of the Western Approaches Command nerve centre's creation and role in the Second World War, 2015 version (the updated account, 2017, is much shorter and lacking some of the details found when the relevant site page was accessed on 30 June 2015). [http://www.liverpoolwarmuseum.co.uk]

HANSARD

(all House of Commons sittings)
Navy Estimates debate, 17 July 1900
[HC Deb 17 July 1900 vol. 86 cc241–340]
Peace and Submarine Warfare (Vatican Action), 18 May 1916
[HC Deb 18 May 1916 vol. 82 c1634]
Air-Raid Precautions Bill, 15 November 1937*
[HC Deb 15 November 1937 vol. 329 cc41–165]
[HC Deb 07 February 1938 vol. 331 cc655–61]
U-Boat Warfare, 26 September 1939
[HC Deb 26 September 1939 vol. 351 cc1239–46]
Ways and Means, 9 April 1941
[HC Deb 09 April 1941 vol. 370 cc1606–63]
All accessed via http://hansard.millbanksystems.com
* Sir Samuel Hoare began the second reading for the Bill – itself a response to the new fear of 'air terror' from massed bomber formations – by reminding the

House that in 1917 it was feared the submarine would 'shake the empire to its foundations'. He went on: 'Scientific research, the experience of the naval staff, the courage of the Navy, and British common sense faced the problem, and to-day we are justified in saying that, although we regard the submarine as an extravagant nuisance that ought to be abolished, the submarine is no longer a danger to the security of the British Empire. We have got to make the aeroplane as little dangerous to the British Empire as we have made the submarine.'
Statement read out to MPs in the House of Commons, on 7 February 1938, by Anthony Eden, then Secretary of State for Foreign Affairs

THE NATIONAL ARCHIVES (TNA) UK
War Cabinet Conclusions 1916 to 1918:
CAB/23/6 – Minutes of War Cabinet meeting, 24 May 1918
CAB/23/8 – Minutes of War Cabinet meeting, 4 November 1918
[http://www.nationalarchives.gov.uk/cabinetpapers/cabinet-gov/cab23-first-world-war-conclusions.htm#Imperial%20War%20Cabinet%20Minutes]

Cabinet Memoranda 1929 to 1945:
CAB/66/26/18 – War Cabinet, Weekly Resume, 2 July to 9 July 1942
CAB/66/27/23 – War Cabinet Weekly Resume, 30 July to 6 August 1942
CAB/66/39/7 – War Cabinet, *Forecast of Monthly Loss Rates of Dry Cargo Ships*, 13 July 1943
(Also accessed via TNA, though scans of original documents made available to download do vary depending on when accessed.)
HW 3/18/7 – Zimmerman Note (also known as the Zimmerman Telegram). This variant is a scan of a handwritten transcript (accessed via http://germannavalwarfare.info/02subm/07/hw78.html but of a document held by the TNA). There is a scan of a typed transcript of a page from the Note available [https://history.blog.gov.uk/2017/01/16/the-zimmermann-telegram-and-room-40/] with an article by Foreign Office historian Tara Finn, with a slightly different translation. This scanned document is TNA (HW 3/187).
ADM 199/1845 – HMS *Tapir* – Report of First War Patrol
File of photocopies of records from the Public Record Office relating to the ramming of a U-boat by HMS *Wolverine* on 12 August 1942

BRITISH LIBRARY
Add. MS. 34931, Fulton's letter to Nelson, as featured in an article entitled 'Robert Fulton: A Letter to Lord Nelson', by R.A.H. Smith, published in the *British Library Journal* [https://www.bl.uk/eblj/1999articles/pdf/article13.pdf]

ARCHIVES OUTSIDE THE UK
(including some items from official naval sources)

Australian War Memorial (AWM)
Diary of H.V. Reynolds, 25 May 1915

[https://www.awm.gov.au/blog/category/diary-anzac/]
Indonesian Confrontation, 1963–66
  [https://www.awm.gov.au/atwar/indonesian-confrontation/]
Memoir of Charles Suckling (scans of his handwritten account of his time on *AE2*,
in this case those pages relevant to the submarine's sinking)
  [https://www.awm.gov.au/collection/RCDIG0001112/]

Royal Australian Navy (RAN)

ACB 0233/44(3) & ACB 0254/45 (4)
  South-West Pacific Anti-Submarine Warfare Reports (WWII) and Monthly
Naval Warfare Reviews for the period June 1943–May 1945 [http://www.navy.gov.
au/media-room/publications/acb-0233443-south-west-pacific-anti-submarine-
warfare-reports-wwii & http://www.navy.gov.au/media-room/publications/
acb-0254454-royal-australian-navy-monthly-naval-warfare-review-wwii]
  These downloadable scans of original documents contain a wealth of detail not
only about the war against Japanese and German submarines in the Pacific but also
elsewhere, including the Indian Ocean and the Atlantic.
  For example, the story of *U-432*'s demise was contained within the *South-West
Pacific Anti-Submarine Report* dated October 1943 (under the title 'U-Boat's Comedy
of Errors'). The 'Review of Anti U-Boat Warfare for the Year 1944' was in the March
1945 report, including a forecast of a 'Second Battle of the Atlantic' to come before
war's end. Also included in such reports was useful information such as particulars
of new Allied ASW weapons (Squid is detailed in the October 1943 and November
1944 reports, the latter featuring *Loch Killin*'s kill of *U-736*) and on US Navy 'Wolf
Pack Success' (November 1944).
  Lieutenant Commander Henry Hugh Gordon Dacre Stoker (official biography)
[http://www.navy.gov.au/biography/lieutenant-commander-henry-hugh-gordon-
dacre-stoker]
  'The RAN in "Konfrontasi" [Indonesian Confrontation] – 50 Years On',
Semaphore, Sea Power Centre – Australia, Issue 03, 2016

US Navy (USN)

All Hands, official magazine of the USN, 20 August 2015, 'Survivors of the Sinking
  of the USS *Indianapolis*', by Mass Communication Specialist 2nd Class Jason
  Kofonow [http://www.navy.mil/ah_online/ftrStory.asp?issue=3&id=90695]
Cuban Missile Crisis, United States Naval Aviation Operations, USN official chronology
  in PDF format (accessed via US Department of Defense Defence Technical
  Information Center) [http://www.dtic.mil/dtic/tr/fulltext/u2/a227065.pdf]
Florida *Awarded Navy Unit Commendation*, official USN unit citation for USS *Florida*'s
  part in Operation Odyssey Dawn in 2011 [http://www.navy.mil/submit/display.
  asp?story_id=72132]
Official USN press release, 29 May 2009, 'Diesel Sub Commander Recalls Historic
  Soviet Sub Chase', by Dean Lohmeyer [http://www.navy.mil/submit/display.
  asp?story_id=45746]
United States Navy Fact File: Guided Missile Submarines – SSGN [http://www.navy.mil/
  navydata/fact_display.asp?cid=4100&tid=300&ct=]

USN COMSUBPAC press release, 'Attack! The USS *Wahoo*'s Final Patrol', by Darrell
D. Ames (quotes Chief Yeoman Forrest Sterling), accessed September 2016
[http://ussmortondd948.org/About_Cdr_Morton.html]

NAVAL HISTORY AND HERITAGE COMMAND (NHHC)
All the documents below were accessed via the website of the USA's Naval History
and Heritage Command (NHHC), which offers a vast amount of digitised material,
including analysis of major actions and operations, combat reports, intelligence
reports, profiles of notable people and also ship histories. The documents below
were accessed via the NHHC's Online Reading Room [https://www.history.navy.
mil/research/library/online-reading-room.html]. I have listed them under the
relevant conflicts.

American Revolutionary War
The Submarine *Turtle*: Naval Documents of the Revolutionary War

American Civil War:
The Sinking of the USS *Housatonic* by the Submarine CSS *H.L. Hunley*, off
    Charleston, South Carolina, 17 February 1864
Specifically, within the above section:
Extract from Journal of Operations, kept at Confederate headquarters, Charleston, S.C.,
    regarding the accident to the submarine torpedo boat. 15 October 1863
Information on the Hunley *obtained by the U.S. Navy from the interrogation of Confederate*
    deserters, 7 January 1864
Order of Rear-Admiral Dahlgren, U.S. Navy, commanding South Atlantic Blockading
    Squadron, ordering defensive measures against Confederate torpedo boats. Flag-Steamer
    Philadelphia, Off Morris Island, South Carolina, 7 January 1864
Report of Captain Green, U.S. Navy, commanding USS Canandaigua, *on the sinking of the*
    Housatonic. U.S.S. *Canandaigua,* Off Charleston, S.C., 18 February 1864
Report of Lieutenant Higginson, U.S. Navy, executive officer of the USS Housatonic.
    U.S.S. *Canandaigua,* Off Charleston, S.C., 18 February 1864
Report of Rear-Admiral Dahlgren, U.S. Navy, commanding the South Atlantic Blockading
    Squadron [No. 69]. Flag-steamer *Philadelphia,* Port Royal Harbor, S.C., 19
    February 1864
The H.L. Hunley *in Historical Context,* by Rich Wills, former Assistant Underwater
    Archaeologist, Naval Historical Center, originally published online 25 May 2001

First World War:
American Naval Participation in the Great War (With Special Reference to the European
    Theater of Operations), by Captain Dudley W. Knox
German Submarine Activities on the Atlantic Coast of the United States and Canada.
    Publication No. 1, Historical Section, Navy Department
German Submarines, In Question and Answer, Navy Department Office of Naval
    Intelligence, June 1918

Second World War:

The Aleutians Campaign Combat Narratives

Allied Ships Present in Tokyo Bay During the Surrender Ceremony, 2 September 1945

Battle of the Atlantic, German Naval Communication Intelligence Vol. III [SRH-024]

Battle of the Atlantic, Vol. IV, Technical Intelligence From Allied Communications Intelligence

Battle of Midway: Preliminaries – U.S. Navy Carrier Operations, 7 December 1941–10 March 1942

Blockade-Running Between Europe and the Far East by Submarines, 1942–44 [SRH-019], 1 December 1944

Interrogations of Japanese Officials – Vols I & II, United States Strategic Bombing Survey [Pacific]: Cdr Chikataka Nakajima, quizzed on the *Gilberts-Marshalls Operation, Naval Strategic Planning,* 21 October 1945; Capt. Abe Tokuma, quizzed on *Escort of Shipping,* 29 November 1945; Vice Admiral Paul H. Wenneker, *Observations on the Course of the War,* 11 November 1945

COMINT [Communications Intelligence] Contributions [to] Submarine Warfare in WWII: SRH [Special Research History] 235, 17 June 1947 VADM C.A. Lockwood USN COMSUBPAC

Final Report on the Interrogation of Survivors from U-210 sunk by H.M.C.S. Assiniboine, 6 August 1942

German U-Boat Casualties in World War Two

Japanese Naval and Merchant Shipping Losses During World War II by All Causes. The Joint Army–Navy Assessment Committee, February 1947

Japanese Submarine Casualties in World War Two (I and RO Boats)

Radio Intelligence Appreciations Concerning German U-Boat Activity in the Far East. (January–April 1945), declassified 2 March 1983

Record Group 457, Records of the National Security Agency

Report on the Interrogation of Survivors from U-595 Grounded and Scuttled off Cape Khamis, Algeria, 14 November 1942

Submarine Report: Depth Charge, Bomb, Mine, Torpedo and Gunfire Damage, Including Losses in Action, 7 December 1941 to 15 August 1945, Vol. 1

Testimony of Commander Mochitsura Hashimoto at Court Martial of Captain Charles B. McVay, 13 December 1945

U-210 *Sunk By HMCS* Assiniboine 7-6-42, Post Mortems On Enemy Submarines – Division of Naval Intelligence – Serial No. 4

U-571, *World War II German Submarine: Background on Events Involving German Submarines Boarded by the U.S. and Britain During World War II* A corrective to the story of the Hollywood movie *U-571*, released in 2000, which stirred up great controversy by allegedly appropriating the British capture of Enigma materials and making out the Americans did it. The introduction to this piece points out: 'The Movie *U-571* is not based on the actual circumstances of the naval career of the German Submarine named *U-571*. Rather, it is a fictional narrative, loosely based on events involving several different German submarines during World War II, including *U-110, U-570, U-559,* and *U-505*.' (All but the last boat were Enigma 'pinches' by the British.)

U-595 *Scuttled and Sunk Off Cape Khamis, Algeria 11-14-42. Post Mortems On Enemy Submarines* – Division of Naval Intelligence – Serial No. 7

Ultra and the Campaign Against the U-Boats In World War II, by Commander Jerry C. Russell, United States Navy – Studies in Cryptology, NSA, Document SRH-142

ULTRA Extracts Regarding Japanese Submarine Movements, I-58 Attack, and Lessons Learned

United States Naval Administration in World War II History of Convoy and Routing, Headquarters of the Commander in Chief, United States Fleet, And Commander, Tenth Fleet (up to VE Day, 8 May 1945)

United States Submarine Losses World War II, Reissued with an Appendix of Axis Submarine Losses, by Naval History Division Office of the Chief of Naval Operations Washington: 1963

Wartime Diversion of US Navy Forces in Response to Public Demands for Augmented Coastal Defense, by Adam Siegel, Center for Naval Analysis

Korean War:

History of US Naval Operations: Korea (Chapter 10: The Second Six Months)

US Navy Special Operations in the Korean War

Cold War:

Annual Report of the Secretary of the Navy: July 1, 1962, to June 30, 1963, extract. *Navy and Marine Corps Operations: Cuba*

Cuban Missile Crisis: The Naval Quarantine of Cuba, 1962

Some Aspects of the U.S. Navy's Participation in the Cuban Missile Crisis, by Jeffrey G. Barlow. Part of *A New Look at the Cuban Missile Crisis Colloquium on Contemporary History*, 18 June 1992, No. 7

Part of *'More Bang for the Buck': U.S. Nuclear Strategy and Missile Development 1945–1965, Colloquium on Contemporary History*, 12 January 1994, No. 9

The Polaris: A Revolutionary Missiles System and Concept, by Norman Polmar

Action/War Patrol Reports:

Commanding Officer, USS Hammann *(DD-412), Serial 2 of 16 June 1942*

Commanding Officer, USS Yorktown, *of 18 June 1942*

USS Harder (SS 257) – *report of Fifth War Patrol*, by Sam Dealey

Biographies:

Charles Bowers Momsen, 21 June 1896–25 May 1967 (includes Legion of Merit citation)

Commander Samuel D. Dealey, USN (1906–1944)

Dictionary of American Naval Fighting Ships (DANFS)

Entries for the following submarines and surface warships:

Archerfish (SS 311), *Darter* (SS 227), *England* (DE 635), *Harder I* (SS 257), *Indianapolis* (CA-35), *Nautilus* (SS 168), *Perch* (SS 313), *Sculpin* (SS 1919), *Sealion* (SS 315), *Tang* (SS 306) and *Wahoo* (SS 238)

U-boat Archive

This remarkable venture by former US Navy sailor Jerry Mason and his wife Charla, an engineer with an interest in U-boats (and a family history of involvement in U-boat design) makes available a vast amount of digitised records and other material. Those consulted and quoted in this book are listed below, including the War Diary of the U-boat force. Standing Orders (*Kriegstagebücher* [KTB] & *Stehender Kriegsbefehl*) are made available on the site thanks to the provision of translations of originals by the NHHC in Washington DC [the KTBs] while the Standing Orders, the British naval intelligence reports on the interrogation of U-boat survivors and other materials were provided to the U-boat Archive by two very hard-working UK-based researchers, Tony Cooper and Roger Griffiths. Cryptology historian and researcher Ralph Erskine provided the archive with material related to Japanese submarine *I-52*'s interception and destruction. To explore further visit www. uboatarchive.net

U-boat force War Log entries for the following dates/periods were studied and some were quoted: 27 September 1939, 29 November 1939, 18 April 1940, 20 October 1940, 9 February 1941, 1–15 March 1941, 18 April 1941, 16–30 November 1941, 21 August 1942, 16–30 November 1942, 7 April 1943, 16 April 1943, 7 May 1943, 16–30 September 1943, 1–15 August 1944, 1–15 January 1945.

British Admiralty (Naval Intelligence Division) Interrogation of Survivors reports relating to the following U-boats, which I accessed via the U-boat Archive:

U-99 [C.B. 04051 (20)]

U-100 [C.B. 04051 (19)]

U-110 [C.B. 4051 (23)]

U-379 [C.B. 04051 (47)]

U-570 [C.B. 4051 (31)]

Also U-977 *Report on the Interrogation of Prisoners from U-977 surrendered at Mar del Plata, 17 August 1945, US Navy.*

Other documents accessed via U-boat Archive:

U-47 *Second War Patrol*, Günther Prien's log (translation by Jerry Mason with the help of Ken Dunn)

I-52 *Sunk by VC-69 aircraft from USS* Bogue, *June 24 1944* – Excerpt from *Report of Operations, Task Group 22.2, for the period 4 May 1944 to 3 July 1944*, plus Ultra intercepts concerning *I-52*

Report on 'U-570' (HMS Graph*)* [C.B. 4318]

Scans of Steinhoff death certificate and other documents related to his demise, original US official records.

Sinking of Royal Oak, British Admiralty translation of German account [N.I.D. 24/T. 16/45]

Translation of a Diary written by the Chief Quartermaster of 'U-110' after his capture, as reproduced in the Admiralty's U-110 *Interrogation of Survivors* report [C.B. 4051 (23)]

National Security Archive

Accessed via this online source:

Interview with Vice Admiral Joe Williams, transcript of his interview for the *Cold War* documentary series (see below) [http://nsarchive.gwu.edu/coldwar/interviews/episode-12/williams1.html]

Recollections of Vadim Orlov (USSR Submarine B-59), *We Will Sink Them All, But We Will Not Disgrace Our Navy* [http://nsarchive.gwu.edu/nsa/cuba_mis_cri/020000%20Recollections%20of%20Vadim%20Orlov.pdf]

Session of the Politburo of the CC CPSU, 6 October 1986 transcript [http://nsarchive.gwu.edu/NSAEBB/NSAEBB562-Soviet-nuclear-submarine-sinks-off-U.S.-coast/]

Navy & Marine Living History Association (NMLHA)

A website set up by the US-based NMLHA, in co-operation with the National Oceanic & Atmosphere Administration (NOAA) and the Office of Naval Research (ONR) [http://www.navyandmarine.org/alligator/].

Under the banner *The Hunt for the Alligator* it offers a treasure trove of material, including transcripts of official documents from the 1860s, all the result of what it describes as '*collaborative research on the part of a number of individuals, including (in alphabetical order): Dan Cashin, Jim Christley, Jeffrey Malone, Michiko Martin, Catherine Marzin, David Merriman, Richard Poole, Mark Ragan, Tim Smalley, Alice Smith, and Chuck Veit*'.

To tell the story of the US Navy's first operational (if unsuccessful) submarine I have quoted from the following transcriptions made available by this website:

Letter from Brutus de Villeroi to President Lincoln, 8 March 1861

Letter from de Villeroi to Joseph Smith, 29 December 1861

Letter from William Hirst to Joseph Smith, 12 May 1862

U.S. Census Records for Brutus de Villeroi, 7th Ward, 1325 Pine Street, Philadelphia, PA11 June 1860

I also consulted the site's profiles of:

Sam Eakins, Brutus de Villeroi, the *Alligator*'s crews, along with pages on *Alligator*'s *Missions, Newspaper Reports on de Villeroi's Submarine* and *J. Winchester, Acting master of the* Sumpter, *to Gideon Welles* [US Navy Secretary], *9 April 1863* (the last a letter on how the *Alligator* met her end).

NOAA

Among other documents consulted was a press release from the NOAA, 'Navy Continue Hunt for Lost Civil War Submarine *Alligator*, 47-foot-long sub was the Navy's first' (issued 6 September 2005).

The NOAA also gives an account of de Villeroi's attempts to interest the French in a submarine of his devising (after he had fallen out with the Americans). *Secrets of the Alligator, De Villeroi* also includes downloads of scans of the original handwritten letters from de Villeroi to Emperor Napoleon III and the Commission Report (and summary) that outlined why France rejected his proposals [http://sanctuaries.noaa.gov/alligator/history/villdoc.html].

Also useful in telling *Alligator*'s story was the US Navy's account of the submarine's life, called *Alligator: The Forgotten Torchbearer of the U.S. Submarine Force* (available via navy.mil).

Papers & Reports

Disjointed War, Military Operations in Kosovo, 1999, RAND report for US Army, by Bruce R. Nardulli, Walter L. Perry, Bruce Pirnie, John Gordon IV, John G. McGinn, 2002 [http://www.rand.org/pubs/monograph_reports/MR1406.html]

Investigation Result on the Sinking of ROKS 'Cheonan', investigated and written by an international Joint Civilian–Military Investigation Group for the South Korean defence ministry, published 20 May 2010 [http://www.cfr.org/north-korea/investigation-result-sinking-roks-cheonan-may-2010/p22180]

The Kursk *Accident*, by Ingar Amundsen, Bjørn Lind, Ole Reistad, Knut Gussgaard, Mikhail Iosjpe, Morten Sickel, Norwegian Radiation Protection Authority, 2001 [http://www.nrpa.no/publikasjon/straalevernrapport-2001-5-the-kursk-accident.pdf]

The Lessons and Non-lessons of the Air and Missile Campaign in Kosovo, Center for Strategic & International Studies (CSIS), by Anthony H. Cordesman, revised August 2000 [https://www.csis.org/analysis/lessons-and-non-lessons-air-and-missile-campaign-kosovo]

Navy Columbia Class (Ohio Replacement) Ballistic Missile Submarines (SSBN[X]) Program: Background Issues for Congress, CRS, by Ronald O'Rourke, 22 March 2017 [https://fas.org/sgp/crs/weapons/R41129.pdf]

Nuclear-armed submarines in Indo-Pacific Asia: Stabiliser or menace? by Brendan Thomas-Noone and Rory Medcalf, Lowy Institute for International Policy report, September 2015 [https://www.lowyinstitute.org/publications/nuclear-armed-submarines-indo-pacific-asia-stabiliser-or-menace]

Odyssey Dawn (Libya): Background Issues for Congress, Congressional Research Service (CRS/Library of Congress) by Jeremiah Gertler, 30 March 2011 [https://archive.org/details/161350OperationOdysseyDawnLibyaBackgroundandIssuesforCongress-crs]

Report to Congress – Kosovo Operation Allied Force After-Action Report, 31 January 2000 [https://archive.org/stream/ReporttoCongressKosovoOperationAlliedForceAfterActionReport/Report%20to%20Congress-Kosovo%20Operation%20Allied%20Force%20After-Action%20Report_djvu.txt]

Report for US Congress, Iraq War: Defense Program Implications, published 4 June 2003. Contributors: Richard A. Best Jr, Christopher Bolkcom, Steve Bowman, Edward F. Bruner, Robert L. Goldich, Steve A. Hildreth, Ronald O'Rourke [http://www.au.af.mil/au/awc/awcgate/crs/rl31946.pdf]

Submarine Proliferation Resource Collection, Nuclear Threat Initiative (NTI), 2016 [http://www.nti.org/analysis/reports/submarine-proliferation-overview/] According to the NTI this report is 'produced independently for NTI by the James Martin Center for Nonproliferation Studies at the Middlebury Institute of International Studies'.

UK National Audit Office, *Ministry of Defence Major Projects Report 2015 and the Equipment Plan 2015 to 2025*, published 22 October 2015 [https://www.nao.org.uk/

wp-content/uploads/2015/10/Major-Projects-Report-2015-and-the-Equipment-Plan-2015-2025.pdf]

UK Government *Dreadnought submarine programme: factsheet*, updated 20 January 2016 [https://www.gov.uk/government/publications/successor-submarine-programme-factsheet/successor-submarine-programme-factsheet]

Academic Papers Made Available Online

A Critical Examination of the US Navy's Use of Unrestricted Submarine Warfare in the Pacific Theater During WWII, by Cdr Daniel E. Benere, Naval War College Newport, 18 May 1992 [http://www.dtic.mil/dtic/tr/fulltext/u2/a253241.pdf]

Beyond the Water's Edge: United States National Security & the Ocean Environment, A Thesis Presented to the Faculty of The Fletcher School of Law and Diplomacy, by John Mark Di Mento, December 2006 [http://www.dtic.mil/dtic/tr/fulltext/u2/a468078.pdf]

Defeating the U-boat. Inventing Antisubmarine Warfare, by Jan S. Breemer, Naval War College Newport Papers 36, August 2010 [https://www.usnwc.edu/getattachment/e1387487-5948-47de-a649-ca71869fd4f6/36-2.pdf]

MISCELLANEOUS
38 NORTH

'Sinpo South Shipyard: Preparations for a New SLBM Test?', by Joseph S. Bermudez, 20 July 2017 [http://www.38north.org/2017/07/sinpo072017/]

BBC News

'HMS *Splendid* arrives home', 9 July 1999 [http://news.bbc.co.uk/1/hi/uk/389954.stm]

'US gives Russia report on *Kursk*', 7 September 2000 [http://news.bbc.co.uk/1/hi/world/europe/914330.stm]

Televised news briefing on Iraq War progress, 22 March 2003, by UK Defence Secretary Geoff Hoon, transcribed at the time by author

'Russians remember *Kursk* submarine disaster, 10 years on', 12 August 2010 [http://www.bbc.co.uk/news/world-europe-10950701]

BBC Local news report, 'Southampton's Capt Charles Fryatt remembered at IWM', 18 October 2010 [http://news.bbc.co.uk/local/hampshire/hi/people_and_places/history/newsid_9095000/9095420.stm]

'North Korea: "No apology" for S Korea *Cheonan* sinking', 24 March 2015 [http://www.bbc.co.uk/news/world-asia-32013750]

'Russian ships "chase away" Dutch submarine in Mediterranean', 9 November 2016 [http://www.bbc.co.uk/news/world-europe-37928222]

'Russian says new UK aircraft carrier "a convenient target"', 29 June 2017 [http://www.bbc.co.uk/news/world-europe-40442058]

CNN

'Russian Warships Fire Missiles at ISIS in Syria', 23 June 2017 [http://edition.cnn.com/2017/06/23/asia/russian-warships-fire-missiles-at-isis-targets-in-syria/index.html]

Naval Historical Society of Australia (NHSA)
(including *Naval Historical Review*)
'The Loss of HMS *Oxley* 1939', as recounted by Peter Smith [https://www.navyhistory.org.au/the-loss-of-hms-oxley-1939/]
British and German submarine statistics of World War II, comparative stats [https://www.navyhistory.org.au/british-and-german-submarine-statistics-of-world-war-ii/]
'A Submarine Episode during the Indian-Pakistan War of 1971', by Capitaine A. Corau, FN, March 1979 edition NHR [https://www.navyhistory.org.au/a-submarine-episode-during-the-indian-pakistan-war-of-1971/]
'The Sound of Torpedoes', June 2000 edition NHR [https://www.navyhistory.org.au/the-sound-of-torpedoes/]
'*U-859* – From Germany to Japan', March 2007 edition NHR [https://www.navyhistory.org.au/u-859-from-germany-to-penang/]

The Independent Barents Observer
'Now we set course for the Baltic Sea, says Northern Fleet', report by Atle Staalesen, 18 July 2017 [https://thebarentsobserver.com/en/security/2017/07/now-we-set-course-baltic-sea-says-northern-fleet]

US President - Speeches
President Abraham Lincoln First Inaugural Address, 4 March 1861 [http://www.bartleby.com/124/pres31.html]
Franklin D. Roosevelt, 'Day of Infamy' speech to Congress, 8 December 1941, via FDR Presidential Library & Museum [https://fdrlibrary.org/document-december]
State of the Union Address to Congress, 6 January 1945, accessed via The American Presidency Project [TM] [http://www.presidency.ucsb.edu/ws/?pid=16595]
George H.W. Bush, *Address Before a Joint Session of the Congress on the State of the Union*, 29 January 1991 [http://www.presidency.ucsb.edu/ws/?pid=19253]

Undersea Warfare
(Official magazine of the US Submarine Force)
'Air Independent Propulsion: AIP Technology Creates a New Undersea Threat', by Edward C. Whitman (no date) [http://www.public.navy.mil/subfor/underseawarfaremagazine/Issues/Archives/issue_13/propulsion.htm]
'The History of the Indonesian Submarine Squadron', by Rear Admiral Agung Pramono, Indonesian Navy, Spring 2013 edition [http://www.public.navy.mil/subfor/underseawarfaremagazine/Issues/PDF/USW_Spring_2013.pdf]
'John Holland, Father of the Modern Submarine', by Edward C. Whitman, Senior Editor, Summer 2003 [http://www.public.navy.mil/subfor/underseawarfaremagazine/Issues/Archives/issue_19/holland.htm]
'The Submarine Force of the Royal Australian Navy', by Cdr David M. Hendricks, USN, Summer 1999 [http://www.public.navy.mil/subfor/underseawarfaremagazine/Issues/Archives/issue_04/submarine_royalaustralian.html]

'The Submarine Heritage of Simon Lake', by Edward C. Whitman, Fall 2002 edition
   [http://www.public.navy.mil/subfor/underseawarfaremagazine/Issues/PDF/
   USW_Fall_2002.pdf]

Deutsches U-boat Museum

(leading German archive of U-boat history)
U-864 – 'Operation Caesar' [http://dubm.de/en/u-864-operation-caesar/]
Kriegsmarine U-Boats and the Spanish Civil War [http://dubm.de/en/
   the-spanish-civil-war/]

Historic Naval Ships Association (HNSA)

(US-based)
History of Early Torpedoes (1800–1870) [http://www.hnsa.org]
German U-505, online guide [http://www.hnsa.org/hnsa-ships/german-u-505/]

US Department of State

Lend-Lease and Military Aid to the Allies in the Early Years of World War II, Office
   of the Historian, concise explanation of how it worked, including old
   destroyers transferred from the USN to RN [https://history.state.gov/
   milestones/1937-1945/lend-lease]
The Neutrality Acts, 1930s [https://history.state.gov/milestones/1921-1936/
   neutrality-acts]

Naval-History NET

(UK-based naval research site)
Vice Admiral Lionel Wells, Vice Admiral Aircraft Carriers: his report on *Ark Royal*'s
   actions during autumn 1939, transcribed, appears within the site's *Service Histories
   of Royal Navy Warships in World War 2*, by Lt Cdr Geoffrey B. Mason RN (Rtd),
   HMS Ark Royal – Fleet Aircraft Carrier, including Convoy Escort Movements. Editing &
   additional material by Mike Simmonds.
'World War 1 at Sea: French Navy, Part 1 of 2 – Battleships, Cruisers, Seaplane
   Carriers', article by Gordon Smith [http://www.worldwar1atsea.net/
   WW1NavyFrench.htm]

uboat.net

This impressive archive of data, articles, logs and more not only covers U-boats
in the two world wars, but also includes their opponents in the escorts and Allied
submariners.
   It is owned and maintained by Gudmundur Helgason, who also carries out
research, Web design, editing and programming. The uboat.net site was an
invaluable asset in swiftly double-checking facts and figures and details of people
who fought at sea. Gudmundur has an indefatigable team assisting him: http://
uboat.net/about/crew.htm
   In addition to the data, the following were of use:
Allied Warship commanders, Benjamin Bryant DSO, DSC, RN – uboat.net profile [http://
   www.uboat.net/allies/commanders/387.html]

U-Boat Commanders, Hans-Diedrich Freiherr von Tiesenhausen [http://uboat.net/men/tiesenhausen.htm]

WWII U-boat Commanders, Werner Fürbringer [http://uboat.net/wwi/men/commanders/81.html]

VARIOUS
Biographies

'Louis Brennan (1852–1932) – The Wizard of Oz', biography by Turtle Bunbury on his website in the Heroes and Villains section [http://www.turtlebunbury.com/history/history_heroes/hist_hero_louis_brennan.html]

'David Bushnell (1740–1826)', biography by Sam Fore in *New Georgia Encyclopedia* [http://www.georgiaencyclopedia.org/articles/history-archaeology/david-bushnell-1740-1826]

'Submarine Hero – Samuel David Dealey', article by Edward C. Whitman on the website of USS *Nautilus* [http://www.ussnautilus.org/medalofhonor/dealey.shtml]

'Rudolf Christian Karl Diesel – Biography, Facts and Pictures' on the Famous Scientists website [http://www.famousscientists.org/rudolf-christian-karl-diesel/]

'Rudolf Diesel, Inventor of the Diesel Engine', website article by Mary Bellis, 20 April 2017 [https://www.thoughtco.com/rudolf-diesel-diesel-engine-1991648]

Profile of John Ericsson, accessed via the website of the US Office of National Marine Sanctuaries, celebrating the 150th anniversary of the USS *Monitor* [http://monitor.noaa.gov/150th/ericsson.html]

James Fife, Jr. (1897–1975) & Charles Andrew Lockwood, Jr. (1890–1967), biographies, *The Pacific War Online Encyclopedia*

'John P. Holland (1841–1914), The Liscannor Man who invented the Sub', biog. from the Clare People section of Clare County Library website [http://www.clarelibrary.ie/eolas/coclare/people/people.htm#h]

Marina Militare official biography and citation for Capt. Primo Longobardo's Gold Medal for Valour award [http://www.marina.difesa.it/storiacultura/storia/medaglie/Pagine/LongobardoPrimo.aspx]

'Ernst August Wilhelm Steinhoff', biography on *Encyclopedia Astronautica* [http://www.astronautix.com/s/steinhoffernst.html]

'An Unsung RAN Hero – Lieutenant Commander Henry (Dacre) Stoker DSO, RN, Commanding Officer HMAS *AE2*', article by Rear Admiral Peter Briggs

'Robert Whitehead', short biography [http://spartacus-educational.com/FWWwhitehead.htm]

'Sir Basil Zaharoff', *Encyclopaedia Britannica* biography [https://www.britannica.com/biography/Basil-Zaharoff]

Documents & Records

Escort Group Commander, Cdr M.J. Evans, commander of the B3 Group in HMS *Keppel*. Action report, accessed via Warsailors.com, which offers transcribed official records under *Convoy ONS 18 / ON 202 Reports* [http://www.warsailors.com/convoys/on202report.html]

Aldous Huxley, letter to his father 14 September 1914, taken from *Scotland's War, HMS* Pathfinder [http://www.edinburghs-war.ed.ac.uk/WestLothian/Home-Front/HMS-Pathfinder]

Capt. Francis Martin Leake, letter to his mother, 8 September 1914, Hertfordshire Archives (via Herts Memories website, which has in the past attributed them erroneously to Lt Martin Leake) [http://www.hertsmemories.org.uk/content/herts-history/diaries-and-letters/hertfordshire-voices/the_letters_of_lieutenant_martin_leake/torpedo_hits_the_hms_pathfinder_on_8_sept_1914]. This officer is sometimes referred to as Francis Martin-Leake, but in the official *Navy List for December 1918* he is Francis M. Leake.

Commander Destroyers Pacific Fleet, Brief Narratives of Co-ordinated Anti-Submarine Actions Including USS *England*, USS *George*, USS *Raby*, USS *Spangler* and USS *Hazelwood* in the period 19–31 May 1944.

Rear Admiral J.L. Kauffman, Commander Destroyers, Pacific Fleet, 29 August 1944, observations on USS *England's* attacks: *(A) Summation of A/S contacts made 19–31 May 1944; (B) Brief Narratives of A/S Actions 19–31 May 1944; (C) Brief of Tactics used in A/S Actions.* (Accessed via the Destroyer Escort Sailors Association and USS *England* websites [http://www.desausa.org/uss_england.htm & http://de635.ussengland.org])

MISCELLANEOUS OTHER

Action between *E35* and *U-154*, 11 May 1918, background notes for auction of medals belonging to Cdr A.M. Coleman by DNW auctions [https://www.dnw.co.uk]

'Admiral Isoroku Yamamoto Quotes', by Bruce Danforth, 11 October 2015, Pearl Harbor website [https://pearlharboroahu.com]

'A hundred year old World War I mystery solved – SM *U-26* has been found', press release from Badewanne diving group Finland, 2 June 2014, revealing their discovery [http://badewanne.fi/a-hundred-year-old-world-war-i-mystery-solved-sm-u-26-has-been-found/]

'Always Ready Always There: December 7 1941 – Today in Guard History', Short account on US National Guard website of the capture of Ensign Kazuo Sakamaki [http://www.nationalguard.mil/AbouttheGuard/TodayinGuard History/December.aspx]

'ASW Weapons of the United Kingdom/Britain', information on usages, types and stats, NavWeaps website [http://www.navweaps.com/Weapons/WAMBR_ASW.php]

Australia's War 1939–1945 (Australian Government website), article entitled 'Cutting Cables' [http://www.ww2australia.gov.au/farflung/cuttingcables.html]

The Avalon Project, Yale Law School, Lillian Goldman Law Library (online resource). Versailles Treaty, Articles 181, 188, 189, 191 and 209 [http://avalon.law.yale.edu/imt/partv.asp]

'The Battle of Lemnos, The 5th of January 1913', by Lt Junior Grade of the Hellenic Navy, Panagiotis Gerontas, History Service of Hellenic Navy, published 6 January 2014

'Brazil and World War II: The Forgotten Ally. What did you do in the war, Zé

Carioca?' Article by Frank D. McCann of the University of New Hampshire [http://eial.tau.ac.il/index.php/eial/article/view/1193/1221]

Brian Dunning, Skeptoid Podcast 507, 'No, Hitler Did Not Escape, There is no truth to the popular myth that Hitler escaped Berlin and went to Argentina', transcript, 23 February 2016 [http://skeptoid.com/episodes/4507]

'Century Passes Since First Royal Navy Ship Was Sunk by U-boat', account published 5 September 2014, RN website [http://www.royalnavy.mod.uk/news-and-latest-activity/news/2014/september/05/140905-hms-pathfinder]

'Dutch Submarines: The Ingenieurskantoor voor Scheepsbouw submarine design bureau', article on the Dutch Submarines website [http://www.dutchsubmarines.com]

Gallipoli Casualties by Country (official New Zealand History website) [https://nzhistory.govt.nz/media/interactive/gallipoli-casualties-country]

History of Diving: Chronology, World Confederation of Underwater Activities (CMAS) [http://history.cmas.org/chronology-120217122507]

'The History of the Russian Navy, The Great War, The Black Sea', website account [http://www.neva.ru/EXPO96/book/chap11-3.html]

'Hitler's Antarctic base: the myth and the reality', by Colin Summerhayes, Scott Polar Research Institute, University of Cambridge, and Peter Beeching, of Toronto, Canada, published in *Polar Record* 43 (224): 1–21 (2007)

F.G. Hoffman in 'The American Wolf Packs', case study published by National Defense University Press [http://ndupress.ndu.edu/Media/News/Article/643229/the-american-wolf-packs-a-case-study-in-wartime-adaptation/]

HMS *Onyx* war patrol, as published on the Barrow Submariners Association website [http://rnsubs.co.uk/boats/subs/oberon-class2/onyx2.html]

Igor Kozyr, 'Dispelled Myths of Soviet Subs', published by RusNavy website [http://rusnavy.com/history/branches/sub/mythsaboutsovietsubs.htm]

'Interview with Arthur Baudzus, U-859 survivor' published online (link defunct) by Riverdale Electronic Books [TM]

Inverclyde Shipbuilding & Engineering, The First World War (website) [http://www.inverclydeshipbuilding.co.uk/home/general-history/wwi]

'The Kaiser Sows Destruction: Protecting the Homeland the First Time Around' [about Germany's sabotage campaign in the USA during the First World War] by Michael Warner, published on the Central Intelligence Agency (CIA) website, 27 June 2008

Kate Hudson's blog on the CND website, '£205 billion?! How the cost of Trident replacement doubled', posted 12 May 2016 [http://www.cnduk.org/cnd-media/item/2450-£205-billion?-how-the-cost-of-trident-replacement-doubled]

'Lt Cdr Henry Stoker – an Historic Journey. The *AE2* and the Gallipoli Campaign', article published by the ANZAC Day Commemoration Committee, on their website [https://anzacday.org.au/ww1-lt-cdr-henry-stoker]

Note on the sinking of HMS *Bombola*, Islington Remembrance Project [http://bookofremembrance.islington.gov.uk/BookOfRemembrance/EventFolder.aspx?id=9121]

'Operation Caesar', The History Learning Site, by C. N. Trueman, 16 August 2016

[http://www.historylearningsite.co.uk/world-war-two/world-war-two-and-eastern-europe/operation-caesar/]

'Operation "Pedestal", Convoy to Malta, 11–15 August 1942: with particular reference to the strategic value of Malta in the Mediterranean during the Second World War', Dr Malcolm Llewellyn-Jones, Historian, Naval Historical Branch [UK], Naval Historical Branch Information Brief [http://www.royalnavy.mod.uk/~/media/Files/Navy-PDFs/News-and-Events/Special%20Events/20120801%20%20Operation%20Pedestal%20Aug%2042.pdf]

'Punching the Convoys Through: "Hunter-Killers" in the Atlantic, 1943–1945', account on the website of *The Mariners Museum and Park*, Newport News VA, on the close working relationship between Cdr Kenneth A. Knowles USN and Cdr Rodger Winn RNVR [https://www.marinersmuseum.org/sites/micro/battle_of_the_atlantic/gg01.htm]

'The Saga of the Submarine: Early Years to the Beginning of Nuclear Power', article originally published in the *All Hands* magazine (official USN) September 1967, but revised and updated using historical records. Accessed via www.pigboats.com

'The Sinking of the M.S. *Wilhelm Gustloff*', article on www.wilhelmgustloff.com

The South China Sea Arbitration (The Republic of the Philippines v. The People's Republic of China), Permanent Court of Arbitration (PCA) Award 12 July 2016 [https://pca-cpa.org/en/news/pca-press-release-the-south-china-sea-arbitration-the-republic-of-the-philippines-v-the-peoples-republic-of-china/]

'Submarines in the Dardanelles, 1915: Lieutenant Norman Holbrook VC and the HMS Submarine *B11*' and 'Lieutenant Commander Henry Stoker and HMAS Submarine *AE2*', articles on the official Australian Government Department of Veterans' Affairs website to commemorate the Gallipoli campaign [http://www.gallipoli.gov.au/submarines-in-the-dardanelles/holbrook-hms-sub-b-11.php] and [http://www.gallipoli.gov.au/submarines-in-the-dardanelles/henry-stoker-and-the-ae2.php]

Tyler Rogoway, 'Chinese Naval Group To Sail The Baltic Sea At The Same Time As Russian Armada', report published on The Drive web site 19 July 2017[http://www.thedrive.com/the-war-zone/12656/chinese-naval-group-in-baltic-sea-at-same-time-as-russias-biggest-sub-and-cruiser]

USGS Astrogeology Center, *Gazetteer of Planetary Nomenclature* [https://planetary names.wr.usgs.gov]

V&W Destroyers Association profile of HMS *Walker* [http://vandwdestroyer association.org.uk/HMS_Walker/index.html]

The Wartime Memories Project – HMS *Britannia* during the Great War [http://www.wartimememoriesproject.com/greatwar/ships/view.php?pid=1451]

'Why Japan Really Lost the War', analysis on the combinedfleet.com website [https://pearlharboroahu.com]

Zee News report, 'Bangladesh takes delivery of two submarines from China', 14 November 2016 [http://zeenews.india.com/news/world/bangladesh-takes-delivery-of-two-submarines-from-china_1949705.html]

SOME WEBSITES

Convoy and convoy battles in the Second World War
  http://www.warsailors.com/convoys/hg73.html
Cornelius Drebbel information
  https://sites.google.com/site/ukdrebbel/
Database of Allied and Axis unit histories and officer biogs
  http://www.unithistories.com
For everything on HMAS *AE2*
  http://ae2.org.au
Hansard, for Commons and Lords debates etc.
  www.parliament.uk
Information on the Soviet Navy and Russian Navy
  http://russianships.info/eng/
US Naval History and Heritage Command
  https://www.history.navy.mil
RN Subs
  http://rnsubs.co.uk
U-boat Archive
  http://www.uboatarchive.net
uboat.net
  http://uboat.net
Website on the fighting life of Captain Johnny Walker RN
  http://www.captainwalker.uk
For biographical details of Russian submarine captain Alexander Marinesko
  https://ww2gravestone.com

TELEVISION
Documentary

The Battle of the Atlantic (three part documentary series, written and produced by Andrew Williams) first broadcast July 2002. Viewed on DVD/BBC *World War II Collection*.

BBC TV, *The Great War*, Episode 26, broadcast 22 November 1964. Viewed on DVD/DD Home Entertainment.

Captain Fryatt, British Pathé footage (no sound): *Captain Fryatt's body at Dover, Kent* [repatriation post-war] and *Captain Fryatt at St. Paul's, London* [funeral]. Viewed via: http://www.britishpathe.com

Captain Gilbert Roberts during on-camera interview, for *The World at War*, Thames Television documentary series, episode entitled *Wolf Pack* (originally broadcast on ITV, 1973). Viewed on VHS.

Cold War, 24-part series for CNN broadcast in 1998, featuring the inside story from key participants who were on both sides of the East–West confrontation. Viewed on VHS/DD Home Entertainment.

The Submarines of World War II, History channel series, three disk DVD set: 1 – *Attack Plans of World War II, Submarine Captains of World War II, Deterrence from the Deep*; 2 – *Submarine Special Ops, Torpedoes of World War II*; 3 – *Submarines of the*

Atlantic, Wolfpack: U-Boats of World War II. Set released 2014.

Vice Admiral Tim McClement, video interview with British Forces News, May 2012, about his time as XO of HMS *Conqueror* during the Falklands War. Viewed via Internet.

Also viewed: *The Battle for Malta,* broadcast 14 August 2013, BBC Two; *Tirpitz: The Lost Heroes, Timewatch,* broadcast 2004, BBC Two; *The Hunt for U-864, BBC TV, Timewatch,* broadcast 2008, BBC Two; *Able Archer 1983, The Brink of Apocalypse,* broadcast Channel 4, 2008.

Drama

The Sinking of the Laconia, three parts, written by Alan Bleasdale, broadcast on BBC Two, January 2011. Viewed on iTunes.

Movies (DVD)

The submarine drama is an established genre – claustrophobic, drenched in tension and packed full of life-or-death moments. Some classic accounts have been produced and among the best are *Das Boot, The Hunt for Red October, Above Us the Waves* and *Run Silent, Run Deep.* They cover the full gamut of submarine warfare from the point of view of both sides – during the Second World War and the Cold War – and from the Pacific to the North Atlantic and the Norwegian fjords. Some movies featured submarines as part of the story rather than as the main focus (*The Abyss,* for instance) but were still worth watching in the context of writing and researching this book. The Enigma code-breaking efforts at Bletchley have prompted several dramas on the big and small screen, with *Enigma* not a bad effort. The American production *U-571* is not the worst movie ever made about submarine warfare, though it did upset a lot of people for appearing to suggest that the Americans made the key Enigma capture. For this author's money the two top movies made about the Battle of the Atlantic in the Second World War are *Das Boot* and *The Cruel Sea* (probably because the authors of the novels on which they are based both saw war service). Likewise, *Run Silent, Run Deep* is based on a novel of the same name by Edward L. Beach, who acquired plenty of combat experience in the Pacific against the Japanese.

The movies that informed the author's process were:

Above Us the Waves (Carlton, 1999*)

The Abyss (20th Century Fox, 2001)

The Cruel Sea (Studio Canal, 2007)

Das Boot – The Director's Cut (Columbia Tristar, 1998)

The Enemy Below (20th Century Fox, 2012)

Enigma (Buena Vista, 2002)

The Hunt for Red October (Paramount, 2003)

Jaws (Universal Pictures UK, 2004)

K-19 – The Widowmaker (Paramount, 2003)

Run Silent Run Deep (MGM, 2004)

U-571 (Universal, 2001)

We Dive at Dawn (Carlton, 1999)

* The years listed relate to the specific DVD edition viewed.

Imperial War Museum: The Official Collection

Also viewed were three DVDs of (Second World War) Admiralty wartime instructional films and what might today be termed drama-documentaries from the museum archives.

Close Quarters (DD, 2005), features a war patrol by the fictional HMS *Tyrant*, off the Norwegian coast.

Protect the Convoy (DD, 2005) offers five short films – *Night Attack on a Convoy, Food Convoy, Escort Teams at Work, Merchant Seamen* and *Operational Height*. Though the acting style is somewhat stilted by today's standards, in many cases the participants are real merchant mariners, RN sailors and submariners. All these films give a thoroughly authentic insight into how the British fought their war under the sea and against the U-boat menace. *Close Quarters* and *Western Approaches* are particularly well shot, the latter with cinematography by the renowned Jack Cardiff.

Western Approaches (DD, 2004) tells the tale of a torpedoed merchant ship's survivors supported by *A Seaman's Story* (interview with a Newfoundlander who has been torpedoed four times).

Glossary

AA: Anti-aircraft.

ABM: Anti-Ballistic Missile.

Ace: Top scoring submarine captains of all nations could be described as 'aces' (their ranking defined by the amount of tonnage sunk) but it was the U-boat force that formalised the designation, explained by Germany's determined pursuit of a tonnage war in both global conflicts of the twentieth century. To become an 'ace' in the U-boat force in the Second World War required a captain to reach 100,000 tons sunk, which also won him the Knight's Cross (*see below*).

ACNS: Assistant Chief of the Naval Staff. A role first established in the Royal Navy in 1917, at the height of the anti-U-boat war. During the Cold War this was the senior officer who acted as the First Sea Lord's troubleshooter in matters of naval policy.

AEGIS: In the context of this book an all-seeing combat system fitted to modern-day US Navy major warships, and so named after the all-protecting shield of the Greek god Zeus. While commonly capitalised it isn't actually an acronym.

AGNA: Anglo-German Naval Agreement.

AIP: Air-Independent Propulsion.

AMC: Armed Merchant Cruiser.

Asdic: Named after the Allied Submarine Detection Investigation Committee, the body that devised the British version of sonar. *See below.*

ASW: Anti-Submarine Warfare.

Axis: Germany, Italy and Japan were collectively known as the Axis during the Second World War, due to their various military co-operation agreements. The other side (the democratic nations fighting against them) were known as 'the Allies'.

Ballast tanks: Tanks in a submarine that are filled with air on the surface to provide positive buoyancy. They are vented on diving and filled with water to achieve negative buoyancy.

Battery: When a conventional submarine is dived, it cannot use diesel engines to drive generators that supply power to electrical propulsion motors. It must therefore switch to massive storage batteries (which themselves will have been charged by the diesel engines).

Battlecruiser: A capital ship-sized cruiser, with the large guns of a battleship but with lighter armour to enable great speed.

BCF: Battle Cruiser Fleet, a major fighting formation of the Royal Navy during the First World War.

B-Dienst: Short for Beobachtungsdienst (in English, 'Observation Service'). A division of German naval intelligence tasked with intercepting and analysing enemy wireless communications.

Bearing: Direction of a contact, whether detected by Asdic/sonar or other means (such as the human eye).

BEF: British Expeditionary Force.

BMD: Ballistic Missile Defence.

Boat: A submarine, no matter how large, is a boat, not a ship. There are various reasons for this proposed. One suggests that a vessel unable to carry a boat is therefore not a ship – but submarines can carry boats (witness USS *Perch* during the Korean War and today's Special Forces-capable craft, such as the Ohio Class conversions and the Astute Class). Another suggestion down the years has been that a submarine is always a boat because it just has one deck. This may have been true before the Cold War, but from the 1950s onwards the big nuclear-powered submarines have boasted more than one deck. Of course, in the early days of submarines the admirals in their big ships derided submersibles as underhand and ineffectual, so referred to them as boats out of fear and contempt. Whatever the reason, the label 'boat' has stuck (even though the largest submarines today are a lot bigger than many ships).

BSF: Black Sea Fleet, one of four major Russian Navy formations, the others being the Northern Fleet (based mainly in the Kola Peninsula), the Baltic Fleet and the Pacific Fleet. Russia additionally maintains a flotilla in the Caspian.

Bulkhead: A steel 'wall' in a ship, forming a subdivision within the vessel.

CAG: Co-ordinated Attack Group, the American version of the German wolf pack. *See below.*

Casing: Free flooding superstructure on a submarine, providing a walkway for use when on the surface and a streamlined outer skin around fixtures and fittings.

CO: Commanding Officer, or captain, of a submarine or other kind of warship.

Conning tower: The elevated part of the superstructure of a submarine – a tower – from which the craft is navigated on the surface. Referred to in the Royal Navy as the fin and in the US Navy as the sail. In some (diesel) submarines it also contained the compartment from which the captain used the periscope to help control the submarine during an attack. *For more see Fin, below.*

Contact: Term used to describe anything detected using visual or electronic means.

Control Room: The nerve centre of the submarine, from which the vessel is usually operated and commanded.

Corvette: Maid-of-all-work anti-submarine vessel, bigger than an armed trawler (enabling more endurance at sea and bigger armament) but not as complex, large, fast or heavily armed as a destroyer. Corvettes are easier to construct quickly and in large numbers.

Crash dive: Emergency submergence of a submarine to avoid detection and/or attack from a surface vessel or aircraft.

CVE: Escort carriers, known as Carrier Vessel Escorts. A simple and easy-to-construct vessel with a minimal air group dedicated to anti-submarine patrols while in company with convoys.

Deck gun: The medium-calibre gun fitted to submarines from the First World War until the 1970s to enable them to shell merchant vessels, other warships or targets ashore.

Destroyer: The most lethal form of anti-submarine vessel (*see Corvette*), although the Germans described any anti-submarine vessel as a 'destroyer' (*Zerstörer*).

Diesel: In common submariner parlance it can be used to refer to a non-nuclear powered (also known as 'conventional') submarine, with diesel–electric propulsion. Such a design requires access to air, in order to operate diesel generators and recharge batteries (used for submerged running) and also to ventilate. The name springs from the fuel used.

Drop collars: As with launch frames and cradles, these were a means to carry externally mounted torpedoes, with a release mechanism that would set the weapons free to run against a target once their motors were started.

Echo sounder: Downward-pointing sonar used to measure depth beneath the keel. An upward-pointing one is used in under-ice operations.

Eel: German colloquialism for a torpedo.

Enigma: Often used as a catch-all to describe the codes used by the German military during the Second World War, in fact Enigma was the machine that encrypted wireless messages.

FAT: *Federapparattorpedo*, a type of U-boat torpedo that could be set to carry out violent manoeuvres when fired into a convoy, increasing the chances of hitting something.

Fido: A US-origin air-dropped homing torpedo.

Fin: The vertical structure on the hull of a submarine enclosing the masts (periscopes, radar, Electronic Counter-Measure, Snort, etc.), with a conning (ship control) position (also known as 'the bridge') at the top for navigation on the surface. Connected to the inside of the boat via the conning tower, which is sealed by top and bottom hatches.

Fish: Allied colloquial name for a torpedo.

FOSM: Flag Officer Submarines, the uniformed head of the Submarine Service of the Royal Navy (until 2015, when the title was changed to Rear Admiral Submarines).

Foxer: Noise-making device trailed behind an Allied warship, designed to distract an enemy homing torpedo.

Frigate: Long-established warship type, used for all manner of missions from escort work and reconnaissance to fleet protection and shore bombardment, though not as swift or heavily armed as a destroyer.

Galley: A ship's kitchen.

GIUK: Greenland-Iceland-United Kingdom Gap. The principal avenue of entry into the North Atlantic used by Russian submarines and surface warships deploying from their Arctic bases. Likely to be a NATO-enforced chokepoint in any hot war.

GNAT: German Naval Acoustic Torpedo (as known to the Allies) but in the Kriegsmarine known as G7ES *Zaunkönig*, or 'wren'.

GUPPY: Greater Underwater Propulsion Programme conversion boats.

H.E.: High Explosive.

Heads: The toilets aboard a warship, including submarines, so-called because in the days of the sailing navies the ratings did their business through holes over the bow.

Hedgehog: Forward-throwing anti-submarine mortar/projector.

HF/DF, or Huff Duff: High-frequency direction-finding device used to fix the location of an enemy by detecting radio transmissions.

HTP: Hydrogen Test Peroxide. Highly volatile liquid propellant used in some torpedoes and missiles.

Hunter-killer: Nuclear-powered submarine designed to hunt and kill enemy submarines and surface ships using torpedoes. Today it can also launch cruise missiles against land targets. In the First World War the British constructed the world's first ever fully-fledged hunter-killer submarine (the R Class boat, *see main text*). During the Second World War the British and American navies formed hunter-killer groups centred on aircraft carriers to destroy enemy submarines.

Hydrophone: A microphone immersed in water and fitted to a warship or submarine to listen for the distinctive sound of other submarines or surface craft. It enables detection of a potential target (or threat) over long distances. Sound interference such as rain hitting the surface of the ocean, sea creatures calling out, the noise generated by the host vessel's own machinery, or water rushing over its hull and/or propellers can obscure the noise of potential targets/threats. Operators have to develop an ability – almost a sixth sense – to tell the difference between all the various sounds.

Hydroplanes: Horizontal control surfaces mounted on the bows or fin of a submarine, and also at the stern, to control the attitude, and therefore depth, of the vessel under the water. Also known as 'planes'.

Igewit: Ingenieurbüro für Wirtschaft und Technik.

IJN: Imperial Japanese Navy.

IvS: Ingenieurskantoor voor Scheepsbouw.

Knight's Cross: Top medal for valour in the face of the enemy bestowed by the German military in the Second World War.

Knots: Speed of a ship or aircraft expressed at a rate of nautical miles per hour. One knot is equivalent to 1.15 nm.

Kriegsmarine: The German Navy in the Second World War (literally, 'the war navy').

Lewis gun: Light machine gun mounted on British submarines and other war vessels.

MAD: Mutually Assured Destruction. The balance of terror between the two sides in the Cold War. As opposed to Magnetic Anomaly Detector, the system used to detect dived submarines.

Medal of Honor: The highest award for valour that can be given to those serving in the US armed forces.

Milch Cow: Tanker U-boat used to provide oil, ammunition and other supplies to friendly submarines deployed mid-ocean.

NATO: North Atlantic Treaty Organisation.

NID: Naval Intelligence Division of the Royal Navy.

OIC: Operational Intelligence Centre of the Admiralty in the Second World War.

Periscopeitis: Paranoia about enemy submarines manifested in false sightings of periscopes.

Pre-dreadnought: Steel battleship with a variety of guns constructed before the advent in 1906 of the all-big gun HMS *Dreadnought*, which set the pattern for such ships thereafter.

Pressure hull: Tough inner hull that can withstand pressure at great depth to protect the machinery and equipment of the boat and the lives of the crew.

Q-ship: Armed naval vessel disguised as a harmless merchant vessel.

Radar: Radio Detection and Ranging. A means of emitting radio waves, which, when they hit an object in the air, on land or the surface of the sea, are reflected back and enable distance and range to be calculated.

Rating: Non-commissioned sailor, whether junior or senior, including Petty Officers and Chief Petty Officers.

RCN: Royal Canadian Navy.

RN: Royal Navy.

ROE: Rules of Engagement.

Scuttling: The process of denying the use of a vessel to the enemy by opening sea cocks, setting off charges or shelling or torpedoing by one's own side.

SEALS: Sea, Air and Land Forces, as in US Navy SEALS Special Forces.

SLBM: Submarine-Launched Ballistic Missile.

SLOC: Sea Lines of Communication.

Sloop: A term used to describe escort vessels of different sizes and types.

Snort/Snorkel (aka *Schnorchel*): The means by which a submerged diesel-engine submarine draws fresh air for running the engine (to recharge batteries) into the submarine (down the induction mast) and exhausts engine fumes (via the exhaust mast).

Sonar: Sound Navigation and Ranging. A technology employing underwater sound propagation to detect objects on or under the surface of the water. *Passive* sonar listens for the sound made by vessels. *Active* sonar emits pulses of sound and listens for echoes. The sounds are detected on *hydrophones*, which are nowadays analysed electronically using computers.

Sonobuoy: A small air-dropped floating sonar emitter that transmits whatever it picks up to friendly aircraft for them to mount attacks or to guide in naval vessels.

SOSUS: Sound Surveillance Underwater System. Passive seabed hydrophones of immense sensitivity linked to land-based listening stations. Used by NATO during the Cold War to detect Soviet submarines and surface warships over vast distances. Similar systems are still in use today.

Sound Room: The compartment in a submarine hosting the sonar sets and also the operators.

Squid: Forward-throwing anti-submarine mortar programmed by computer rather than by hand and with bombs that exploded even if they did not hit an enemy submarine.

SSBN: Nuclear-powered submarine carrying nuclear-tipped ballistic missiles.

SSGN: Nuclear-powered submarine armed with cruise missiles. In some SSGNs, depending on national offensive naval warfare doctrine, such weapons may be nuclear-tipped.

SSK: Diesel–electric patrol submarine.

SSN: Nuclear-powered attack submarine.

SSS: Wireless code for 'submarine sighted and/or I am under attack by submarine' as sent by British merchant vessels in the Second World War.

Stripe: The method by which U-boats arranged themselves across the path of a convoy after being directed by their headquarters to attack it.

Submersible: Until the dawn of the nuclear age all submarines were submersibles – fighting boats that dived only to achieve stealth in the moment of attack or for self-preservation. In common usage all such craft are simply submarines.

Super-T: Second World War-built T-Class submarine converted post-war for operations against the Soviets.

TEZ: Total Exclusion Zone.

Tinfish: Slang term for a torpedo, as used by Allied forces in the Second World War.

TLAM: Tomahawk Land Attack Missile, the naval version of the USA's groundbreaking cruise missile.

Trim: Achieving a state of neutral buoyancy whereby the submarine requires minimal use of hydroplanes to maintain depth.

Type VII: Standard type of submarine used by Germany during the Second World War, along with the bigger and longer-ranged Type IX. The Type XIV, or 'Milch Cow', was used to replenish other submarines at sea while the Type XXI and Type XXIII were advanced boats commissioned in small numbers at the end of the war.

U-boat: *Unterseeboot,* in literal English an undersea boat.

USAF: United States Air Force.

USN: United States Navy.

USSR: Union of Soviet Socialist Republics.

Victoria Cross: Highest award for valour in the face of the enemy that can be awarded to those serving in the British and Commonwealth armed forces.

VLR: Very Long Range, a colloquialism for the B-24 Liberator long-range maritime attack aircraft operated by the American, British and Canadian air forces during the Battle of the Atlantic in the Second World War.

WAC: Western Approaches Command, the umbrella organisation running Britain's part in the Battle of the Atlantic (located at Plymouth 1939–early 1941 and from then until war's end in Liverpool).

War Log: The official record of a military organisation's activities (and related topics) during a conflict.

Warsaw Pact: Defence alliance formed by the Soviet Union in 1955 with satellite nations, devised as a counter to NATO. Dissolved in July 1991.

WATU: Western Approaches Tactical Unit.

WMD: Weapon of Mass Destruction.

Wolf pack: U-boats deployed as a group and ordered to assemble in 'stripes' across routes of Allied convoys and then to attack as and when opportunities permitted.

W/T: Wireless Telegraphy.

XO: Executive Officer. In a British submarine the most senior officer of the Seaman specialisation. He (or she) is also known as 'The XO' and 'First Lieutenant' and is second in command. In nuclear-powered boats an XO is fully qualified for command. Similar systems of command are run in all navies.

Acknowledgements

Credit should be given where credit is due and it is Alan Samson, Publisher Non-fiction at Weidenfeld & Nicolson, who should be saluted above all, for suggesting that my next book should be a history of submarine warfare. We had kicked around a few ideas but this one was hiding in plain sight as the logical sequel to *Hunter Killers*, which told the story of the Royal Navy's submarines and the select band of brothers who took them out on patrol during the Cold War.

The first thing I did in rising to the challenge, aside from brushing up on my general submarine warfare knowledge, was to create a gallery of the people who had played decisive roles in the development of submarines through the ages and had also taken them to war. For, while technology was important, it was the people who mattered most. As I researched and wrote what was soon christened *The Deadly Trade* I crossed off each one's portrait on reaching their part in the epic story.

In terms of personal motivation – other than an enduring fascination with naval history and providing a new perspective – I can't claim any forebears who were distinguished submariners as inspiration.

My late father had in the past mentioned a relative who had served in submarines. So, when I was carrying out research in the archives of the Royal Navy Submarine Museum, out of curiosity I asked the RNSM's indefatigable archivist George Malcolmson if it was possible to track down the service record. Peter Cloughley was the husband of my father's first cousin and it turned out that he served as a 20-year-old fourth lieutenant in HMS *Unsparing* shortly before the end of the war in Europe. By June 1945 he was in *U-2529*, a surrendered Type XXI boat later renamed *N27* in British service. Further research indicated Peter helped to sail her from Norway to internment at Lisahally in Northern Ireland. His service record shows that he saw out the rest of the war at Lisahally, in the pool of Royal Navy submariners taking care of surrendered U-boats until their disposal. *N27* was ultimately handed over to the Soviets as part of their war booty and commissioned into the Baltic Fleet as *B-27*. It was very rewarding to turn up that link, no matter how modest and indirect, to the Submarine Service. It showed how the records of the RNSM can flesh out long-told family history tales.

I do vividly recall being impressed with the honours board at Portsmouth Grammar School, which as a teenager I passed every day on the way to assembly, upon which were displayed the names of three VC winners. They included Lt Norman Holbrook, the first British submariner to win that award, for his exploits as captain of *B11* (as recounted in this book).

That recollection rekindled an awareness of submariners' extreme valour, which I became determined to reflect in the narrative. Also helping to enthuse me were some great friends I made in creating *Hunter Killers* – all of them veterans of many adventures beneath the waves in the face-off with the Soviets. They were on hand for *The Deadly Trade* to help with technical proofreading, giving me notes to correct some inaccuracies and providing additional insight into The Trade where and when necessary.

Those submarine captain stalwarts were Cdr Rob Forsyth, Cdr Tim Hale and Commodore Doug Littlejohns. Warrant Officer Michael Pitkeathly entertained and educated me yet again – providing some handy little 'dits' (true life tales) of his own time on patrol in Cold War submarines.

Usman Ansari made an incredible effort on my behalf by interviewing Vice Admiral Ahmad Tasnim and Commodore Wasim Ahmad in Pakistan specially for this book. I'd like to extend thanks to him and those two distinguished warriors for agreeing to talk to him.

It was through Caroline Edser, who is married to my school friend Richard Clapperton, that I got to meet and interview Matthew Todd. I am extremely grateful to her for providing the introduction and to Matthew for agreeing to talk to me about his experiences during the Second World War and in command of a 1960s submarine.

Thanks are also due to the Trustees of the Imperial War Museum, London, for allowing access to the IWM's collections. Also deserving of my gratitude are: the staffs of the Imperial War Museum; the National Maritime Museum, Greenwich, London; Western Approaches Museum; National Museums Liverpool (Merseyside Maritime Museum, Maritime Archives); the Naval History and Heritage Command in the USA and both the National Museum of the Royal Navy and the Royal Navy Submarine Museum (in Portsmouth and Gosport respectively).

I'd especially like to thank Heather Johnson, Curator (Archives) at the NMRN and Matthew Sheldon, Executive Director of Heritage at the NMRN, for their assistance, along with submarine specialist archivist George Malcolmson (who has helped out with both this book and its predecessor). Lorna Hyland at the Merseyside Maritime Museum also helped smooth my path, so deserves a mention too.

My sometime naval guru Peter Hore deserves a nod for over the years sharing with me occasional insights and reflections on the Royal Navy's attitude past and present to submarine warfare. He also conveyed my request to Sue Balme for permission to use photographs of *U-110*'s capture and of her late husband David as a young officer, for which I am deeply appreciative. Thanks are also due to Captain Patrick Walker, grandson of the legendary U-boat hunter Captain Frederic (Johnny) Walker, for pointing me in the direction of some extra details of Op Haggis (see pp. 385–6).

Signals of appreciation are sent to Dennis Andrews and Paul Slidel for creating the maps, John O'Brien for supplying me with research material relating to John Day (the first recorded submarine casualty) and Jonathan Eastland for providing a sympathetic ear.

Others who have helped are name-checked in the Sources and my sincere apologies to anyone I have forgotten.

Throughout this project Tandy Media, the publisher of *WARSHIPS International Fleet Review*, the global naval news monthly of which I am Editor, have been most understanding and their support was highly valued.

The calm professionalism and flexibility of the team at Orion Books has been key to enabling me to produce what I hope is a good effort. It has benefited greatly from the steady hand of Lucinda McNeile, Editorial Director at Orion, on the tiller and Alan Samson on the admiral's bridge in overall command. The excellent endeavours of Tony Hirst in the engine room of copy-editing must not be overlooked. He spotted defects that needed rectification, occasional inaccuracies and tested the logic and sense of various elements. Any residual errors are in the end entirely my own fault. Also keeping the ship on course was Tim Bates, Senior Agent at Peters, Fraser & Dunlop (PFD) Literary Agents. Tim was once again the cool-headed navigator.

Finally, gold medals for patience and understanding must go to my family – my wife Lindsey and sons Robert and James – who were heroically unfazed by their dad's enthusiasm and delight at discovering a Seehund midget U-boat during a summer 2017 holiday in Brittany. This was despite suffering my submarine warfare obsession for several years already.

Index

Picture Credits

Section 1
1. (top and below) NHHC
2. (top and below) NHHC
3. (top and below) NHHC
4. NHHC
5. (top) NHHC; AJAX Vintage Picture Library
6. (top) NHHC; (middle) NHHC; (below) NHHC
7. (top) NHHC; (below) NHHC
8. NHHC

Section 2
9. (top) NHHC; (below) NHHC
10. (top) NHHC; (below) NHHC
11. (top) IWM; (below) Strathdee Collection
12. (top) NHHC; (below) NHHC
13. (top and middle) NHHC; (below) NHHC
14. (top) NHHC; (middle) IWM; (below) NHHC
15. (top) Strathdee Collection; (middle) NHHC; (below) Iain Ballantyne
16. US National Archives / NHHC

Section 3
17. (top) NHHC; (middle and below) Paul G. Allen
18. (top) USMC; (middle) NHHC; (below) US Navy
19. (top) US Navy; (below) NHHC
20. (top) NHHC; (middle) David Billinge; (below) US DoD
21. (top) Iain Ballantyne; (below left) Dennis Andrews; (below right) Nigel Andrews
22. (top left and right) Nigel Andrews; Cem Devrim Yaylali
23. (top and below) US Navy
24. (top and below) Michael Nitz, Naval Press Service